Sketch of General Washington,
Stolen at Mount Vernon while
he was looking to discover
a distant Vessel on the Potowmac, in which he expected some of his friends from
Alexandria.

George Washington's Eye

Landscape, Architecture, and Design at Mount Vernon

Joseph Manca

THE JOHNS HOPKINS UNIVERSITY PRESS   BALTIMORE

© 2012 The Johns Hopkins University Press
All rights reserved. Published 2012
Printed in the United States of America on acid-free paper
9 8 7 6 5 4 3 2 1

The Johns Hopkins University Press
2715 North Charles Street
Baltimore, Maryland 21218-4363
www.press.jhu.edu

Library of Congress Cataloging-in-Publication Data

Manca, Joseph, 1956–
    George Washington's eye : landscape, architecture, and design at
Mount Vernon / Joseph Manca.
        p. cm.
    Includes bibliographical references and index.
    ISBN 978-1-4214-0432-5 (hdbk. : alk. paper)—ISBN 978-1-4214-
0561-2 (electronic)—ISBN 1-4214-0432-X (hdbk. : alk. paper)—ISBN
1-4214-0561-X (electronic)
    1. Washington, George, 1732–1799—Aesthetics.   2. Mount Vernon
(Va. : Estate)   I. Washington, George, 1732–1799.   II. Title.
III. Title: Landscape, architecture, and design at Mount Vernon.
    NA737.W37M36 2012
    711′.409755291—dc23   2011044973

A catalog record for this book is available from the British Library.

Frontispiece: Benjamin Henry Latrobe, *Sketch of General Washington Stolen at Mount Vernon while he was looking to discover a distant Vessel in the Potowmac, in which he expected some of his friends from Alexandria,* 1796, pen and ink on paper. Courtesy of The Maryland Historical Society (MS 523).

Special discounts are available for bulk purchases of this book. For more information, please contact Special Sales at 410-516-6936 or specialsales @press.jhu.edu.

The Johns Hopkins University Press uses environmentally friendly book materials, including recycled text paper that is composed of at least 30 percent post-consumer waste, whenever possible.

CONTENTS

Color plates follow pages 92 and 180.

This is a book about George Washington's eye for art and how he shaped the aesthetic world around him at Mount Vernon. He designed the expansions of his mansion house, provided plans for other buildings on his estate, and laid out and beautified elaborate gardens. He and Martha Washington filled their house at Mount Vernon with fine and decorative art. George Washington was keenly aware of the social and symbolic importance of his visual and material world, and although we are not concerned here in detail with Washington as military leader, legislator, agriculturalist, or president of the United States, his aesthetic activity occurred within the context of his life and historical era. Artistic issues for Washington were inextricably linked with moral and social concerns. The Mount Vernon estate was Washington's public face, and his artistic decisions there must be seen against the backdrop of his personality, moral beliefs, and unique place in eighteenth-century American society.

George Washington was deeply interested in art, architecture, and landscape gardening, and I hope that this book shows the breadth and depth of Washington's artistic creations and interests. He was a leading landscape gardener of his time and was the author of a fairly extensive architectural oeuvre. Washington stood in the forefront among American collectors of landscape art, and along the way he developed a good eye for style in paintings and prints. We need to reassess his place in early American intellectual life; the chapters that follow offer a glimpse into one part of his contributions to early American culture.

A study of George Washington is rewarding, as his life and art are well documented, and his aesthetic endeavors are in large part preserved and presented at Mount Vernon today. Washington's actions were broadly consistent with those of other men of the social elite in eighteenth-century America, and at one level he serves as an example of an upper-class American patron: he built a large, stylish home, taking a leading role in determining its size and appearance; collected and displayed fine and decorative arts; developed beautiful gardens around his mansion house; and did it all with an awareness of his social position and how he would be perceived by others. But while there were other elite Americans and other wealthy Tidewater planters, there was only one George Washington, and his situation stands as a special case. He lived a large life and garnered an extraordinary amount of public attention, and he made a special effort to have his estate proclaim his own virtues and those of the new nation he helped to establish.

Washington's artistic interests were varied, but one is struck by his extraordinary understanding of landscape, in the broadest sense. He apologized for his lack of knowledge of architecture, he was modest about his art collection, he feigned reluctance to sit for portraitists, he claimed no knowledge of poetry or music, and in his orders for furniture and other decorative arts he tended to rely on current or accepted taste. In the sphere of landscape gardening, though, he was lord and master. He worked for years at his designs, and he had the will, the knowledge, the land, the financial means, and the hired and enforced laborers to achieve what few others in America could accomplish. Lucky enough to have inherited an ideal site high on a broad river, he used this good fortune to advantage. The view of lawns, trees, and water that he created from the portico of his house is one of the great American works of art, a living canvas of space, color, and light. In the sphere of shaping nature he was unsurpassed in eighteenth-century America, and the theme of landscape runs throughout his life. He measured nature as a young surveyor and later shaped and adorned it, creating beautiful farms, setting his house to take perfect advantage of the prospects of forests and water, and carving vistas through the woods. He collected and displayed two-dimensional landscape art, had his house ornamented with stucco work of farm implements and flora, and wrote to others about the natural setting of his estate and his happy place in it. Like the theme of moral action and reputation, issues of landscape form a leitmotif throughout this book.

There is a large bibliography on Washington, much of it dealing with issues concerning the architecture of Mount Vernon and its gardens and collection, and I am deeply indebted to this previous scholarship. Robert Dalzell Jr. and Lee Baldwin Dalzell's *George Washington's Mount Vernon* and Allan Greenberg's *George Washington, Architect* provide in-depth information about Washington's architectural designs. There have been several useful studies of the gardens, including Mac Griswold's *Washington's Gardens at Mount Vernon*. Carol Borchert Cadou's excellent recent volume, *The George Washington Collection,* discusses many fine examples of the art collection in Washington's home, and Susan Detweiler's *George Washington's Chinaware* throws light on his acquisition and display of porcelain. A number of books and exhibitions, including works by Wendy Wick (*George Washington, American Icon,* with an introduction by Lillian Miller) and Hugh Howard (*The Painter's Chair*), have explored the portraits of Washington and the vital role of his imagery in the context of Revolutionary and early national America. My task would have been difficult without one of the great scholarly projects of our time, namely, the ongoing publication of the George Washington Papers by the University of Virginia, a project that has online and searchable texts. Any scholar who works on George Washington stands on the shoulders of others and shares the company of many who have explored a complex person and his rich historical context.

Many people and institutions aided this project. I am grateful to the Mount Vernon Ladies' Association for their continued efforts to present Mount Vernon to the public and for providing fine research facilities that are so useful for scholars of early American history. I am especially indebted to the work of Mount Vernon's curators, archaeologists, archivists, and librarians, past and present, who have gathered and disseminated information on George Washington's life and activities. Of these, I have received assistance from Jill Dewitt, John Gibbs, Justin Gunther, Shandel Johnson, Christina Keyser, Jennifer Kittlaus, Dean Norton, Jordan Poole, and Emily Shapiro. I especially want to thank Mount Vernon's Dawn Bonner, who was instrumental in gathering and sending me images and information needed for captions. Joan Stahl frequently helped me find research material in Mount Vernon's library. Esther White and Dennis Pogue discussed with me discoveries related to the buildings and gardens at Mount Vernon. Historian Mary Thompson shared ideas related to the history and context of the Mount Vernon estate. Curators Carol Borchert Cadou and Laura Simo discussed with me the collections at Mount Vernon and made object files accessible.

Others who have provided information or help useful for this project include Steve Bashore of Stratford Hall; Nicole Bouché of the University of Virginia; Cary Carson of the Colonial Williamsburg Foundation; Abbott Lowell Cummings, emeritus of Yale University and the SPNEA; Susan Drinan of the Philadelphia History Museum; Lorelei Eurto of the Munson-Williams-Proctor Arts Institute; Katherine Gardner of Washington and Lee University; Ana Guimaraes and Laura Linke of the Cornell University Library; Paul Johnson of the National Archives (UK); Annika Keller of Art Resource; Bruce Kirby of the Library of Congress; Carl Lounsbury of the Colonial Williamsburg Foundation and the College of William and Mary; Christine Waller Manca of the Museum of Fine Arts, Houston; Marianne Martin of the Colonial Williamsburg Foundation; Margaret McKee of the Museum of Fine Arts, Houston; Del Moore of the Rockefeller Library; Kathleen Mylen-Coulombe of the Yale University Art Gallery; Marilyn Palmeri of the Morgan Library and Museum; Dana Puga and Christopher Kolbe of the Library of Virginia; Albert Small, Washington, DC, and Barbara De Santi Pappas for help in providing the image of the drawing from Mr. Small's collection; Jennifer Stertzer of the Maryland Historical Society; Olga Tsapina of the Huntington Library; and Lael White of the Colonial Williamsburg Foundation.

Jet Prendeville of the Brown Fine Arts Library at Rice University was always helpful. Andrew Taylor and Kelley Vernon of the Visual Resources Center of the Department of Art History at Rice University helped produce or edit a number of the illustrations in this book. I received research assistance from several Rice students who held fellowships from Rice University's Humanities Research Center; these included Mary Draper, Kay Fukui, Sandra Marcatili, and Claire O'Connor. I am grateful to Rice University's Humanities Research Center for providing an individual faculty fellowship in the fall of 2009, and I appreciate the support from the center's director, Caroline Levander.

I am especially grateful to Robert J. Brugger of the Johns Hopkins University Press for his support of my project and for seeing the editorial process through from beginning to end. I benefited from his advice and suggestions, as I also gained from the anonymous readings of my manuscript. I also wish to thank Kara Reiter, Julie McCarthy, and Courtney Bond at the Press for their help, and I am grateful to Julia Smith for her skillful copyediting of the manuscript.

CHAPTER ONE

George Washington

Morality and the Crafting of Self

The virtuous simplicity which distinguishes the private life of General Washington, though less known than the dazzling splendour of his military atcheivments, is not less edifying in example & ought not to be less interesting to his countrymen.

DAVID HUMPHREYS, "Life of General Washington," c. 1788–1789

GEORGE WASHINGTON liked to shape his own circumstances. Over the years he carefully crafted both his inner self and his public persona, as well as many aspects of his aesthetic world. Washington's life formed a unity, and his morality formed part of the backdrop to his designs at Mount Vernon. His house, gardens, and art collection—and his own writings about them—were a major part of the public face of his virtue.

Washington usually acted with conscious moral purpose. "Moral" is meant here in the broadest possible sense, including such ethical matters as maintaining a public reputation, using one's time wisely, fulfilling one's duties to society, and living without luxuries. In the eighteenth century, the conception of morality also included the achievement of individual perfection, such as living a rational, tranquil, and harmonious life. Washington was obsessed, perhaps even more keenly than his contemporaries, with matters of honor, appearance, dignity, and duty to society. As a schoolboy, Washington copied down the maxim that "every action one takes should be in consideration of all of those present," and indeed his lifelong actions as architect, collector, and landscape gardener were done in consideration of the public's valuation of his moral worth.[1]

Until about 1774, Washington's actions took place in the context of his stature as a wealthy Tidewater planter. He had a widespread reputation across the colonies because of his earlier military exploits, but he was not yet truly a national leader. He built the mansion at Mount

Vernon before his rise to national fame, and the architecture and gardens can be seen in that light. Washington's consciousness of public perception increased along with his social standing and fame, and his aesthetic taste and ethical/moral presentation of self were intertwined during those years. After the Revolutionary War, Washington was an international figure, and the eyes of the world were upon him. He was the new Cincinnatus, the retiring hero-soldier going back to his farm and leaving the scepter of power behind. Finally, during the presidency and the brief years of retirement afterward, the weight of scrutiny was even greater, as he symbolized the new nation and was expected, implicitly and explicitly, to express a level of taste and culture appropriate to his status and the ideal image of the new republic. It was widely believed that a democratic republic was best sustained by a virtuous populace, and Washington—in his evolving role as national leader—was determined to set a good example.

Washington stated that he lived by his family motto (*Exitus acta probat*) when he wrote to estate manager James Anderson that he aspired "to let my designs appear from my works, than by my expressions." He lived up to the motto, roughly translatable as "The outcome demonstrates [the value of] the deeds," and we can judge his artistic interests by the results he left behind. Washington, by all accounts, exemplified the type of person devoted to the *vita activa* rather than the *vita contemplativa*. But, fortunately, beyond Washington's actions, he also used words to establish and make known his moral self and how it related to the material, aesthetic world that he created around him.[2] He ended up establishing a great house, collection, and gardens, even without the benefit of a vast education, notable training in the arts, travel abroad, or having inherited an art collection or great library of books. In the aesthetic realm, he was largely self-made. Indeed, in all aspects of his life, he crafted himself, and he sought both to be and to seem perfect, presenting himself as he would have history see him.

Despite whatever qualities and talents he possessed, Wash-ington was not without intellectual limitations and faults. He was no cultural virtuoso like Thomas Jefferson. He was well read for an American of his time but was hardly erudite; Jefferson and John Adams called attention to Washington's lack of book learning, while a foreign visitor, Gijsbert Karel van Hogendorp, complained that Washington's mind "is not adorned with learning, he has no vivacity."[3] Washington could play no musical instrument, nor sing well. He could be an engaging conversationalist but was not reputed to be a brilliant one, and he sometimes fell into taciturnity or self-absorption. In languages, he knew only English and begged off from learning French. Except for a brief trip to Barbados as a teenager, he never traveled abroad. He enjoyed the theater, but to an Englishman, John Bernard, Washington said of the arts of poetry and drama that he was "too old and too far removed to seek for or require this pleasure myself."[4] In other matters, as well, one can find fault with him. No one today can be happy that he owned slaves, whose forced labor carried out much of the construction, gardening, and farming at Mount Vernon. Some might dislike that Washington produced and sold whiskey and grew opium (even if the latter was for medicinal purposes). Many at the time criticized his military caution during war and his political indecisiveness as president.

Washington was hardly perfect, yet he also possessed an extraordinary set of virtues and talents. He was said, by various people, to be the best farmer in Virginia, or even in America, and by Thomas Jefferson to be the best horseman of his age. He was broadly acclaimed to possess, if not a brilliant, at least a tenacious and effective military mind; Jefferson praised his remarkably sound judgment. Numerous witnesses mentioned his naturally noble bearing, and he was known to be an ideal host at his estate, to evince a good sense of humor, and to be genteel. (Frenchman François Marbois had "never seen anyone who was more naturally and spontaneously polite.")[5] Washington was little schooled in his youth, yet he was sensible of what kind of education a gentleman needed, and he set out to endow a college in the new nation's capital. He possessed many virtues and skills held dear by his contemporaries. It is also apparent, as we will see in later chapters, that, among his other virtues and achievements, he was among the best gardeners of his age, he was an eighteenth-century American architect who, especially through the design of his great portico, left a lasting legacy on later building in the United States, and he was a highly knowing collector of art.

There has been a healthy trend in the recent literature on George Washington to uncover the great man's human side, and to note that he laughed, became angry, and harbored tender feelings like regular mortals. This present study, in its own way, might assist in this revision of Washington. Still, we must also acknowledge that many contemporaries found him personally to be inexpressive, silent, and stiff, and his portraitists represented a man who was less than fully approachable. He felt and expressed a kind of natural superiority, and he was often cool with others. One side of this reticence and reserve, however, was that he was remarkably steadfast, calm, and persistent. Among the highest of Washington's virtues was what we might call today his "emotional quotient," or mental balance. His letters show few signs of bitterness, hurt feelings, or jealousy. When it was appropriate, he did reveal a softer side. The loss of nearly every letter to Martha Washington deprives us of an opportunity to see the more intimate and domestic sentiments he felt over time, but we have other evidence that he enjoyed life in a variety of ways. In looking at his architectural production, art collecting, and gardening, we can see a steady hand, firm purpose, and a fervent, personal engagement. In a famous incident, during the battle for Manhattan in 1776, Washington, facing the defeat of his forces and the doom of the American cause, sat down and wrote a letter to his estate manager, addressing, of all things, details of decoration of his new dining room. General Washington wrote, "The chimney in the new room [Large Dining Room] should be exactly in the middle of it—the doors and every thing else to be exactly answerable and uniform—in short I would have

the whole executed in a masterly manner."[6] For Washington, the visual and material world at Mount Vernon was a haven from travails and a place for him to exercise control.

Part of Washington's self-creation occurred in his prolific letter writing. When Louis-Philippe, future king of France, visited George Washington in 1797 at Mount Vernon, he noticed that Washington had only managed to get a few hours of sleep, yet was vigorously carrying out his morning rounds on his farms. When asked about this, Washington told Louis-Philippe that "I always sleep well, because I have never written a letter nor even a single word that could not be published."[7] Washington lived and acted forcibly, but he also employed writings to shape perceptions of himself, just as he used the arts to do so. We will see, especially in chapter 8, that he wrote a series of letters to Europeans in which he attempted to establish a name for himself as a good writer and to seem to be an ideal *exemplum virtutis,* a living example of virtue itself. This Plutarchan description of his own virtues was most effective through a good literary style, and Washington could write remarkably well.

Sobriety, Simplicity, and Order

Sobriety and moderation stood at the core of Washington's moral self and informed the presentation of his house, gardens, art collection, and even the food at Mount Vernon, all of which were calculated to demonstrate Washington's sense of restraint and order, virtues highly touted among eighteenth-century Tidewater elites. One had to display one's wealth but do so with restraint and moderation. This was already true in 1773, when he was a planter, and more salient later because of his unique historical position. Washington was keenly conscious of moral issues and the broader social import of his words, actions, and material surroundings, and he expressed his own virtue but also set precedents for the presidency and indeed for the young nation as a whole. Moderation, the most central of Aristotelian virtues, was widely touted at the time. Washington had long embraced a moderate, sober sense of order and restraint, and modera-

FIGURE 1.1. West front of the mansion house, Mount Vernon. Photo: Author.

tion continued to be a hallmark of his moral projection during the years of the young Republic. He used the words "sober" and "order" or "orderly" often in his writings; these words described virtues that he looked for in other people and embodied the characteristics that he sought for the material and aesthetic world that he created around him.

The mansion house at Mount Vernon, conceived before Washington achieved national and international fame, conveyed the character of its builder and resident (see Figure 1.1; Plates 1–3). With arguments rooted in ideas of classical antiquity, a long tradition of English writers held that an aristocratic house was a mark of the owner himself and should express his values. Eighteenth-century mansion houses in America sometimes comprised ornate elements, but Washington's home was in line with those colonial Tidewater plantation houses, including Berkeley, Stratford Hall, and Carter's Grove, that were imposingly plain and restrained. The interior at Mount Vernon was more adorned than the exterior, as was true in the Anglo-American tradition. The sense behind having solid and unadorned exteriors had been stated long before by seventeenth-century designer Inigo Jones, in one of the great moral quotes in the great age of British architecture: while interiors might well be ornate and fanciful, "in architecture ye outward ornaments oft to be sollid, proporsionabl according to the rules, masculine and unaffected."[8] Not every British architect between the time of Jones and the age of George Washington had the reserve that Jones had, and some taste for ornateness of exterior set in by the end of the seventeenth century and the early eighteenth century in the work of Christopher Wren, John Vanbrugh, and James Gibbs. The possibility of exterior architectural ornamentation was not unknown in the colonies, and some buildings, such as Mount Pleasant in Philadelphia and the Colony House in Newport, tended to decorativeness. Still, there was a tendency to keep a distinction between outside and in, and by the time of the eighteenth-century Palladians in England, it was customary to have a split between the interior and the elevations, as shown by the difference between the simple exterior of Chiswick House and its ornate interiors by William Kent. Inigo Jones stressed the moral aspects of articulating a domestic architectural exterior: great men were sober on the outside, and this should be reflected in their domestic architecture. Washington's mansion house presented to the world a manly and simple front.

A significant aspect of the simplicity and sobriety of the mansion house was Washington's use of the Tuscan order. A less ornamented version of the already spare Doric of Greek tradition (the Tuscan lacks triglyphs, for example), the Tuscan order is also close to the simple Roman Doric.[9] The exterior of Washington's mansion house utilizes variants of the Tuscan order on the portico, the colonnaded arms connecting the house to the dependencies, the Venetian window lighting the Large Dining Room, and the surround of the west door. The order is articulated at Mount Vernon in an especially spare way, and the square columns on the exterior could have surmounted high pedestals, but as it is they have the most minimal possible base. We should not take for granted Washington's choice of the Tuscan order for the portico or see its adoption as owing to reasons of convenience and budget, although it is true that the Tuscan and Doric orders are the simplest and least expensive orders to make, especially in the capitals. To be sure, neither the Tuscan nor Doric was inevitable for Washington. Landon Carter's Sabine Hall was in the Corinthian order, as was Whitehall in Maryland, while Lansdowne in Philadelphia (house of John Penn) was in two superimposed orders. For the interior of his house, Washington commissioned a number of ornately designed ceilings, moldings, and reliefs, and Ionic

capitals do appear there. The use of the Tuscan order on the exterior was a consistent and conscious choice, and this opens up the question of the history of the order in Anglo-American building. Relying on Italian Renaissance and European Baroque traditions, which themselves filtered the attitudes of classical antiquity, the Tuscan order, like the Doric, was the most masculine of orders and had long been associated with a heroic, manly, and even martial sensibility, as well as simplicity, economy, and restraint. A fitting choice for Washington, its basic character corresponded well to the rubbly rustication connoted by the shaped pine boards and uniform white paint of the exterior.

A remarkably restrained aspect of the mansion house at Mount Vernon is the doorway surround of the west facade, which faced those entering the grounds from the west (land) side (see Figure 1.1). Inigo Jones conveyed his sense that architecture marked the moral sense of a man. Writing at a similar time to Jones, Henry Peacham observed that the frontispiece of a grand house was used as a yardstick of the character of the owner: "There is no one thing that setteth a fairer stampe upon Nobility then evennesse of Carriage, and care of our Reputation, without which our most gracefull gifts are dead and dull, as the Diamond without his foile: for hereupon as on the frontispice of a magnificent Pallace, are fixed the eyes of all passengers, and hereby the height of our Iudgements (even our selves) is taken."[10] Anyone seeing the "frontispice" of Mount Vernon would have been struck by the moderation and restraint of the design, and the viewer would indeed make a "Iudgement" about the owner of Mount Vernon. Indeed, the west facade has, quite remarkably for a house of its quality and size, almost no door surround, quite different from the portals of such residences as William Byrd's Westover or Matthias Hammond's home in Annapolis. Indeed, the whole west front of Mount Vernon is remarkably blunt; the front itself was astylar and lacked color or a projecting pavilion. It comes across as practical and restrained.

The architecture of the mansion house at Mount Vernon

conveys the sense of sobriety that Jones suggests. In 1773, for a man with a military past, for a planter trying to show his trustworthiness (Washington was only recently out of heavy debt to Robert Cary and Co. of London when he designed the house and portico), and for one who held public office and trust, the simple Tuscan order conveyed a desirable message of sobriety and economy. The good faith of contracts, his partnerships with land and river development companies, his ability to borrow money, and his numerous relations with other leading families were all of great importance for Washington. His house conveyed a message of prudence, orderliness, and moderation. Within the larger design of the mansion house, the portico—presented without a pediment, without an extravagant staircase, and in the spare Tuscan order—was striking to contemporaries like Benjamin Henry Latrobe, who, perhaps to our surprise, thought the house modest in scale and effect. Washington built the house as a wealthy planter and retired colonel, and when he returned to it in late 1783 as a national hero, the sobriety of the house still worked well for his reputation.

Thomas Jefferson generally shared the view expressed in material terms by Washington. Jefferson spoke of "chaste" architecture as an ideal and made a particularly apt remark about ornamentation: "The genius of architecture seems to have shed its maledictions over this land. Buildings are often erected, by individuals, of considerable expence. To give these symmetry and taste would not increase their cost. It would only change the arrangement of the materials, the form and combination of the members. This would often cost less than the burthen of barbarous ornaments with which these buildings are sometimes charged."[11] This was the kind of rhetoric that Washington might have heard in conversation with members of the Virginia elite, including the morally freighted aversion to "charging" a building with a burthen of barbarous ornament. A gentleman with taste needed to offer restraint and good proportion, and avoid extravagance.

A number of visitors conflated restrained architectural style and virtuous lifestyle when talking about Mount Vernon and Washington. As early as 1777, English traveler Nicholas Cresswell noted that the newly famous general was known for his honesty and for being a "just man," and that while Washington offered the "genteelest" entertainments, his lifestyle was not marked by the "foolish, giddy and expensive frolics natural to a Virginian."[12] Frenchman Pierre-Étienne Du Ponceau wrote that when he visited Mount Vernon in 1780 he found the mansion house in line with his idea of where Cincinnatus ought to live, and the two rooms (West Parlor and Small Dining Room) respectably but not luxuriantly furnished. Linking the general's morals with his simple way of living, Baron Ludwig von Closen, who visited Mount Vernon in 1782 during Washington's absence, stated that there was no luxury anywhere and that "indeed, any ostentatious pomp would not have agreed with the simple manner of the owner."[13] North Carolinian William Blount agreed that "the house presents no appearance of luxury—the simple, honest character of Washington is alone conspicuous." In 1784, Charles Varlo, an English businessman, reported that "the General's house is rather warm, snug, convenient, and useful, than ornamental. The size is what ought to suit a man of about two or three thousand [pounds] a year in England. The out-offices are good, and seem to be not long built; and he was making more offices at each wing to the front of the house, which added more ornament than real use. The situation is high, and commands a beautiful prospect."[14] In the same year, Chevalier de la Luzerne visited and noted that Washington dressed in a gray coat "like a Virginia farmer" and showed no trace of his great role in the world. One European visitor in 1788 wrote that at Mount Vernon "simplicity, order, unadorned grandeur, and dignity had taken their abode."[15]

Other early comments indicate that Washington succeeded in impressing visitors to Mount Vernon with his restraint and dignity, embodied in what he called his "easy, plain style of living." The Rev. Thomas Coke, who found the president at his "very elegant" home in Virginia in 1793, said it similarly in stating that Washington "is quite the plain, Country Gentleman."[16] In 1788, Frenchman Brissot de Warville characterized the house as being "of an elegant and majestic simplicity." Another visitor was struck by the modesty of the house, remarking that it looked like a house in England of someone with an income of 500 or 600 pounds a year.[17] David Humphreys wrote in his unpublished biography of Washington of the "elegance united with simplicity in his dress, furniture & equipage."[18] This characterization continued and multiplied after Washington's death. Gen. Andrew Jackson visited in November 1815 and pronounced the style of the mansion house "plain and simple," like the great George Washington himself.[19]

Washington certainly played a role in verbally shaping his public image as the dignified Cincinnatus farming on and dwelling in his simple abode. The fine and decorative arts and rusticated "stone" mansion at Mount Vernon suggest to us today that this was no humble farmhouse, but Washington was happy to present it more modestly, especially to Europeans who were unlikely to visit. As early as 1779, and in preparation for life after the war, Washington invited the Marquis and Marquise de Lafayette to Mount Vernon, referring to his house as a "rural Cottage, where homely fare and a cordial reception shall be substituted for delicacies and costly living." To Irishman Edward Newenham, Washington wrote soon after the war's end in June 1784: "[I] shall be happy in every opportunity of giving you proofs of its rectitude; but none will be more pleasing to me than the opportunity of welcoming you, or any of your family, to this land of liberty—and to *this* my retreat from the cares of public life; where in homespun & with rural fare, we will invite you to our bed & board." This was a leitmotif of his presentation of the house and estate: that here the rectitude of the house echoes the owner, and the modest home and lifestyle ("homespun and rural fare") were just right for the American republic, "this land of liberty."[20] His virtues were of national importance. Even the unsympathetic visitor, Dutchman Gijsbert Karel van Hogendorp, noted that

"the virtues of Washington are simplicity, gentleness of character, generosity and composure . . . He needed no exceptional measure of common sense to manage his country's affairs, but he did need his inborn firmness, [and] his indifference to intrigues and to the ambitions whence they spring."[21]

Washington himself expressed the idea that America should avoid the sort of decadence widespread in Europe, remarking in 1785 that the virtues of America countered the European lust for luxury and material goods. Doubtless, conversations with the Marquis de Lafayette encouraged an international language of liberty as well as a recognition of the moral gulf thought to divide the New World from the Old, a trope that preceded Washington and would continue long after him. Tying simplicity to virile action and virtue, Washington wrote to James Duane in 1785 that "The Nations of Europe are ripe for Slavery—a thirst after riches—a promptitude to luxury—and a sinking into venality with their concomitants, untune them for Manly exertions & virtuous Sacrifices." Several years later, in another letter, he elaborated on this idea: "A good general government, without good morals and good habits, will not make us a happy People; and we shall deceive our selves if we think it will. A good government will, unquestionably, tend to foster and confirm those qualities, on which public happiness must be engrafted. Is it not shameful that we should be the sport of European whims and caprices? Should we not blush to discourage our own industry & ingenuity by purchasing foreign superfluities & adopting fantastic fashions, which are, at best, ill suited to our stage of Society?"[22] Washington felt obliged to keep his style of life at Mount Vernon—clothing, wine coolers, plain and neat furniture, table fare, and so forth—away from the caprice of European whims and any "fantastic" style. He arranged his gardens, too, without luxuries such as marble statues, stone bridges, and fine metal gates, and he created sensible gardens compatible with the "good habits" of his American context.

Washington's clothing reflected this scheme, carried out

most publicly when he wore plain, brown homespun wool clothing to his inauguration in 1789. Awareness of the need for sartorial restraint long preceded that inauguration. When his stepdaughter Patsy died in 1773, Washington ordered a suit as follows: "This Letter is intended to desire you to make me a genteel Suit of Second Mourning, such as is worn by Gentlemen of taste, not those who are running into the extreame of every fashion. Make these Cloaths of Broad Cloth, but at the same time send me a proper kind of Waist-coat & Breeches to wear with the Coat when the Weather is warm."[23] Washington advised his young nephew Bushrod in 1783 that "plain genteel dress is more admired and obtains more credit than lace and embroidery in the Eyes of the judicious and sensible."[24] A telling, and also mirthful, expression of his fostering restraint in clothing came in advising the choice of uniforms for veterans of the War in Alexandria. Washington told James McHenry that he should let the uniforms be "handsome, but not more expensive than becomes Republicans (not Bachite Republicans) is reqd. If you think a Motto would be proper, the choice of one 'chaste & unassuming'—is left to your own judgment."[25] Even the veterans' motto should be modest and "chaste." As we will see, he questioned Jefferson whether the French sculptor Jean-Antoine Houdon should represent him (Washington) in classical or modern dress. About a portrait miniature of Martha to be set on a ring, Washington wrote in 1779: "The dress is not less pleasing for being a copy of antiquity, it would be happy for us, if in these days of depravity the imitation of our ancestors were extensively adopted; their virtues wd. not hurt us."[26] John Fitzpatrick noted that Nicholas Rogers's letter of 6 April 1779 indicated that the miniature "showed Mrs. Washington in an Elizabethan ruff and hood," and "the common view was that that was a period of manliness, action, and female virtue."[27] Washington's words and actions indicate that he keenly sensed the connection between garments and morality.

After the war and later, especially during the presidency, Washington had only to build on the appearance of restraint and sobriety that he had inculcated earlier as a member of the Tidewater elite class. He was most keenly aware of appearances during the presidency. When ordering mirrors from England in 1789, he asked for "mirrors for a table, with neat & fashionable but not expensive ornaments for them; such as will do credit to your taste."[28] Gouverneur Morris acquired for the president a number of table pieces and ornaments while in London and Paris. Morris, understanding Washington's needs, even recommended a design for some coolers: "I have ordered at a capital manufacturers the plated Coolers which you desired. Nothing of this Sort has ever yet been executed here except in a coarse and clumsy manner in lacquered Ware. As far as I can judge from the Design which has been drawn consequent upon my Directions they will be very elegant, and cheaper than in a Form less beautiful."[29] He recognized Washington's need for elegance, but he also intuited that extravagance would accord poorly with the collection of a republican president. Morris wrote:

> I think it of very great Importance to fix the Taste of our Country properly, and I think your Example will go very far in that Respect. It is therefore my Wish that every Thing about you should be substantially good and majestically plain; made to endure. Nothing is so extravagant in the Event as those Buildings and Carriages and Furnitures and Dresses and Ornaments which want continual Renovation. Where a Taste of this kind prevails, each Generation has to provide for itself whereas in the other there is a vast Accumulation of real Wealth in the Space of half a Century. Something too much of this perhaps, therefore I will call a new Cause.[30]

Sharing these values, and this strategy, every action that Washington took as president was done with great consciousness concerning its reception and its perceived moral value as it reflected on him and on the new republican nation. He wrote to Morris in 1789: "One idea however I must impress you with and that is in whole or part to avoid extravagance. For extravagance would not comport with my own inclination, nor with the example which ought to be set."[31]

One of Washington's most quoted statements about art

as his own expression of political and moral sensibility occurs in a letter he wrote about Samuel Vaughan's gift in 1785 of an elaborate marble mantelpiece (Plate 32). Many regard as a joke his remark to Vaughan that the work might be too extravagant for his republican living, but he was probably serious to some extent, and his joke at least contained the truth that he had to think about the public perception of his collection and his tastes. Washington was judging the mantelpiece from the number of boxes in which it was shipped and had not yet seen the work itself, but it is by some American standards objectionable, and Samuel Powel of Philadelphia complained about the Siena colored column. It is perhaps surprising that no contemporary complained of the subject matter, which includes a bare-breasted woman in the central panel, a urinating boy on the left, and on the right two frisky rabbits, whose reputation for eager procreation was already widely acknowledged by that time. Washington did keep the marble and made it the centerpiece of his finest room, adorning it with a garniture set that Vaughan also sent and with the painting *Moonlight on Rocky Coast*.[32]

There was from the beginning a consistent taste on Washington's part for moderation and the "plain and neat," and he sought to raise his stepchildren Jacky and Patsy in that manner. Washington's consciousness of luxury and ornament changed over time and with circumstances. In 1770, Washington praised a young man who was "modest of deportment," noting that the youth could "never fail to command esteem that will improve upon acquaintance." This view was all part of his world and his mindset.[33] Still, it should be acknowledged that in his earlier years, the ornate Rococo taste was prevalent in America in the decorative arts, and he himself indulged in purchases without the worry of having to be the virtuous head of a democratic, republican nation. After his marriage to Martha, the young couple ordered every kind of fancy good possible from England, seemingly without regard to economy or chasteness, from silver buckles to fanciful silver table pieces, and Martha acquired a fine wardrobe. The bills mounted, and the purchases put them into some debt to agent and creditor Robert Cary in London. But Washington's earlier desires for ornate and fine objects were eroded by his appearance on the great world's stage, and he often made a public show of his moderation. During the confederation period and beyond into the presidency, Washington set a new tone. He was ever careful to guard his reputation as a sober, chaste executive without royal pretensions or any trappings of Old World aristocracy. Tobias Lear, hoping to please the president, wrote that a repaired and newly decorated coach for Washington's use would look, "when finished, very rich and elegant, and much more conformable to the present style of Carriages than I ever thought any workman could have made it." Washington chastised him, saying, "I had rather have heard that my repaired Coach was plain and elegant than 'rich and elegant.'"[34] Washington had to be ever on guard against charges of extravagance but was pleased when an item was "conformable to the present style."

We might look here at the maxims concerning public civility and behavior that, at the age of fourteen, he copied in his own hand as a school assignment. These are open to overinterpretation, since they were not his original ideas but borrowed from advice found in an English translation of French Jesuit rules of the late sixteenth century, and he never directly quoted the rules again in adulthood. Still, some of the precepts are worth keeping in mind, as their major thrust has to do with self-control and projecting an image of appropriateness and sobriety, and they indicate the kind of education that he received. Rules 8 and 24 admonished one not to speak or laugh too loudly in public, so as not to stand out too forcibly and rudely. Rule 19 was to keep one's countenance pleasant, but in serious matters grave; the exterior of the mansion house bears a pleasant but grave appearance, and this precept was certainly borne out in Washington's demeanor when sitting for portraits. Related, and perhaps most closely linked to our discussion of Washington's moral sentiments and material culture, is Rule 87: "Let thy carriage be such as becomes a man: grave, settled, and attentive to that which is spoken," recalling the sober and settled style of his mansion house. Another speaks of modesty and appropriateness of dress: "In your apparel be modest and endeavor to accommodate nature," and Rule 54 admonishes one to "play not the peacock, looking everywhere about you to see if you are well decked." This precept is echoed in a remark the adult Washington made to young Bushrod Washington in 1783, recommending "plain genteel dress" and advising him not to "conceive that fine Clothes make the fine Men, any more than fine feathers make fine Birds."[35] These are the rules that George Washington had imbibed at an early age and that, reinforced by other social pressures, informed his life and public presentation of self.

Many of the *Rules of Civility* have to do with social class and deference. These rules were written for the young and admonished them to defer to their betters by not contradicting them, not standing too close to them, and standing on the proper side when one walked. Mount Vernon, for its gravity, is also a socially prominent place, and deference is owed it by others. Washington and his social peers were aware of the Aristotelian notion of "magnanimity," in which a great-souled person recognizes his own greatness and acts accordingly. A person of Washington's social class and moral standing deserved to have a substantial house, covered ways, and a colonnade in the colossal order, with a vast estate surrounding it. He had been weaned on this idea, and the rules of civil behavior were only one minor part of this lesson, which he read in school but knew more forcibly from life experience with the Fairfaxes, Byrds, and Carters of Virginia. As Henry Peacham notes in *The Compleat Gentleman* of 1634: "For as in a garment, whatsoever the stuffe be, the owner (for the most part) affecteth a costly and extraordinary facing; and in the house of a countrey Gentleman, the porch, of a Citizen, the carved gate and painted postes carry away the Glory from the rest."[36] Peacham was writing about a porch in the fashion of the tower porch, but the point is that the country landholder was expected to show his prominence and taste by putting a good "facing" on his house.

People of the time noticed if a house was too pretentious, too much of a "folly," while they also expected a great man to have a magnificent home. A number of domestic residences of colonial and early America were denounced or at least chided for their ostentation of style and size, or materials, and the owners were faulted for their extravagance, which carried moral implications (excess and pride) as well as suggestions of extravagance. All builders had a fine line to walk between magnificence and extravagance as they tried to create structures that were dignified but not associated with a middling social class.

It would be wrong to exclude Martha Washington from this discussion of sense and sobriety, as her self-presentation was part of the larger scheme of living at Mount Vernon and of sharing in the virtuous public persona of her husband. She shared George Washington's vision and was noticeably sober and simple in her daily life. Martha may even have had a greater inclination than he did for modest living. When she had a chance to decorate her and her husband's bedroom in 1775, she asked Lund Washington for it to be "done quite plain, no ornaments upon the Cielg the Sides [walls] plain Stucco" (Figure 1.2). Witnesses noted her moderation in dress; Claude Blanchard recorded in 1777 that Mrs. Washington dressed plainly and simply.[37] How Mr. and Mrs. Washington arrived at the confluence of interests so completely is not difficult to guess: they shared ideas and occupied the same social class, place, and generation. In addition to any kind of natural proclivities toward the same, undoubtedly they planned their public self at every level, as was customary for a time when issues of etiquette, social rank, hospitality, were widely discussed in books and elsewhere. At any rate, Martha struck most visitors as avoiding the superfluities of life, as having little interest in finery, in setting a sober table and running an orderly house, and in speaking in a frank and friendly way. Like her husband, she sought Mount Vernon as a refuge from the world's affairs and some of her thoughts on this subject were actually written down by George Washington, thus indicating how their ideas may on a daily basis have

FIGURE 1.2. Martha and George Washington's bedroom, second floor of the mansion house, Mount Vernon. During the construction of the room during the Revolutionary War, Martha insisted that the room be made plain and simple, without fancy stuccowork. Courtesy of the Mount Vernon Ladies' Association.

come to shape each other. She described being the First Lady in New York as like being in prison, and she shared George Washington's antipathy to some aspects of public life. Their similarity of interest is clear from a letter that the president wrote on 9 January 1790 to Catharine Sawbridge Macaulay Graham, speaking of himself and Martha: "I think that our plans of living will now be deemed reasonable by the considerate part of our species. Her wishes coincide with my own as to simplicity of dress, and every thing which can tend to support propriety of character without partaking of the follies of luxury and ostentation."[38] They presented a united moral front and set an example of good republican living.

Washington's self-presentation of sobriety perdured to the end of his life, and beyond. Washington's will stipulated a quiet burial, without pomp or oration but, as it turned out, the Masonic lodge, with the consent of Martha Washington, staged an elaborate funeral service. Washington was not alone among Tidewater elite in wanting a simple burial. The ever-informative tutor, Philip Vickers Fithian, remarked that Robert Carter III of Nomini Hall wanted a simple tomb where he could rest in peace.[39] Washington did ask in his will for a new tomb to be constructed, only because the old one was in a dilapidated state. In the end, the grand funeral, against his wishes, took place in theatrical fashion on the estate, the ceremony unfolding at the dreary mansion of the tomb, the vine and fig trees of the Mansion House Farm, the shady orchards and paths, and the stream flowing nearby, as he described in his retirement letters. Washington's body was set out in state in the Large Dining Room, the main room for entertaining in the house. The body was then placed on the portico and a great parade went by, formed of Masons and others. The river was employed, too, with ships firing cannons. Since the new tomb was not to be commenced until after his demise, Washington knew that he would at first be buried in the old tomb, and he surely knew that the instructions for a burial without pomp or oration would project a humble image of himself, like that of a saint or one of the primitive early Christians. Not surprisingly, however, larger forces came into play, and the funeral ended up being a theatrical event, more like a state funeral, using the very stage—house, portico, lawns, and prospect—that Washington had created to impress visitors.

Hospitality, Magnificence, and Public Stature

The great country estates of England and America were machines for hospitality. Mount Vernon was particularly well appointed for this purpose, as the estate accommodated not only family and friends but also statesmen as well as anonymous passersby. In 1794, Washington proclaimed to a manager that he had no objections to "any sober and orderly person's gratifying their curiosity in viewing the buildings, Gardens &ca. about Mount Vernon." The virtue that is sometimes called Southern hospitality (Washington once referred to it as "Virginia Hospitality") often found expression in the gardens, portico, and even the dinner table at Mount Vernon, and Washington complained to his mother that the mansion house was not unlike a well-resorted tavern.[40] This was no mere custom but was a moral issue. Like many other colonial American virtues, hospitality was a continuation of long-standing practice in Britain, where in the great country houses the offering of food to passersby or to the local poor was a well-established tradition, a duty of noblesse oblige. Hospitality was especially important for someone of Washington's social status and position as great landholder. Giving was an attribute of moderation and showed a nonacquisitive side. A great man was supposed to be magnanimous, and there was an unwritten rule that generosity to strangers and passersby was necessary and a kind of duty. There is ample evidence that visitors were welcome at Mount Vernon, as was true at the time of most great estates in the region. Poorer visitors could walk about and received some food, but they could expect to get no further than the utilitarian outbuildings near the mansion house, while those with introductions gained access to the family spaces. Jonathan Trumbull Jr. called attention to the abundance there even during the war: "At Mount Vernon General Chastilux arrives with his aids. A numerous family now present. All accommodated. An elegant seat and situation, great appearance of oppulence and real exhibitions of hospitality & princely entertainment."[41] Those who received lodging sometimes reported that Washington himself escorted them to their rooms with a candle or brought tea to their sleeping chambers. At any rate, Washington and his peers were not merely stoical in daily life: they aimed at happiness and at pleasant living within their framework of duty, honor, and other higher ideals. Hospitality also occurred within a framework of sharing and social welcoming. If there was pleasure in the gardens and food on the table, it

was a gift and was provided for others. Thus, hospitality could be conceived as helping others and for the common weal, and even the fine art collection and the exotica in the gardens were maintained as a kind of public good.

We have emphasized the restrained aspects of the house and its inhabitants' lifestyle, but the magnificence at Mount Vernon needs to be considered, as well. A great man needed a great home, and the Aristotelian notion that one should embrace one's own status and importance was a hallmark of Anglo-American aristocratic society. The large-souled quality of Washington—his elevated economic status, leading place in society, and moral worth—all found embodiment in his mansion house, the covered ways, the lofty portico, and spacious grounds. The other Aristotelian virtue of the golden mean, expressed in the temperance of a great man, worked in tandem with his right to magnificence and with the propriety of expressing his elevated social position.

Washington's residence was perhaps influenced by vernacular traditions, but ultimately Mount Vernon is as high style as he could reasonably make it. The estate comprises a Palladian villa with arms and dependencies, details of which are drawn from eighteenth-century pattern books by Abraham Swan and Batty Langley. The size of the house is substantial; the formal gardens are carefully worked in the modern landscape gardening mode. The house was filled with luxury items in furniture, silver, and ceramics, and Washington made an effort to get original oil paintings, prints, and other artwork in the best style. When he asked Lund Washington in 1776 to make everything in the new Large Dining Room masterful and symmetrical, he was expressing his sense that the house was to be one of control and power.

Early on, from the *Rules of Civility* and elsewhere, Washington learned, along with others of his generation and social class, that one should achieve a social distinction but keep a moderate appearance in public and not make a show of oneself in an ostentatious way. The concept of *dignitas* has its roots in antiquity, and a man's house had to express his worth and values, his worthiness in the most encompassing sense of the word. The idea passed along via Andrea Palladio (*Four Books on Architecture*) and Leon Battista Alberti (*Ten Books on Architecture*) to English writers and builders, who knew to scale buildings and calculate ornament based on the intended self-presentation of the owners. The moderate classicism of Mount Vernon fulfilled the ideal of Washington as the classical country gentleman who dwelled in a villa that was grand and commodious but sober and manly in style.

The magnificence of the mansion house at Mount Vernon, including its portico, cupola, substantial size, lofty setting, and apparent stone material all adumbrate the public character and participation of the owner, even though it is a private dwelling. The cupola, stone appearance, and the house's long, low shape—similar to so many public buildings, whether statehouse, hospitals, schools—as well as the dominating site all bespeak public architecture. One of the most significant moral aspects of eighteenth-century life among the elite was the duty to be a public figure and to take part in public affairs. Washington acted as a surveyor to the colony of Virginia, served as a member of the House of Burgesses, fought in the provisional forces, served as Justice of the Peace in Fairfax County, and was ready at any time to take on leadership roles, which, of course, he did. All of this activity was in seeming contradiction to the desire for retirement and withdrawal from the world's affairs; however, withdrawal to an estate with house and gardens allowed development of one's self and one's virtues, and it could also give way, through the virtue of the owner, to a sense of duty to the needs of a broader public. Without the second ideal

in place, the first would degenerate into a selfish desire for isolated pleasures, and that was far from the ideal held by English or American landed aristocrats. Washington's favorite model would not have an Epicurus or Zeno, a philosopher engaged in contemplation, but rather a leader such as Cato, the sacrificial statesman whose pursuit of public duty and unselfish interest in justice was a mirror of Washington's own ideal. Not surprisingly, Washington suggested that Joseph Addison's drama *Cato* was his favorite play. The semipublic character of the mansion house establishes its role in the greater political community. For Washington, Mount Vernon embodied both private enjoyment and public duty.[42] Still, the house was a place of pleasant everyday life, and Robert and Lee Dalzell have rightly noted the "pleasure and power, freedom and restraint" of the mansion house, its form striking a delicate balance between the need to create a public face through architecture and foster pleasurable living for the household and guests.[43]

Although Washington was hospitable and offered punch and other pleasure to individual visitors or small groups, he did not hold substantial parties or dances on the estate. Even for political events, he held off on using his grounds, which were the center of a working farm. The painter Charles Willson Peale, who had good social interactions with the family, mentioned dancing at Mount Vernon, but it was for the purpose of giving exercise to Martha ("Patsy") Parke Custis, who had been ill, and the dancing group was small.[44] In general, Mount Vernon remained dedicated to its role as a farm and center of family life, not a place for extravagant social activities like large dancing and musical parties.

CHAPTER TWO

The Mansion House at Mount Vernon and Other Architectural Designs

The Mansion House itself, though much embellished by yet not perfectly satisfactory to the chaste taste of the present Possessor, appears venerable & convenient. The superb banquetting room has been finished since he returned home from the army.

DAVID HUMPHREYS, "Life of General Washington," c. 1788–1789

GEORGE WASHINGTON did not build his famous home from scratch. Lawrence Washington, George's older half-brother, inherited the estate at Little Hunting Creek from their father, Augustine, and named it Mount Vernon in honor of Adm. Edward Vernon, with whom Lawrence had served in 1741–1742. When Lawrence died in 1752, his will stipulated that George would receive Mount Vernon after the death of Lawrence's wife, Ann Fairfax, and daughter, Sarah. Ann offered a long-term lease of Mount Vernon to George on 17 December 1754, near the time of young Sarah's death; actual ownership came to him after Ann passed away in 1761. The estate comprised over 2,100 acres and included a one-and-a-half-story residence, with a central passage and chimneys at either end (Figure 2.1).[1] Beginning in 1757, Washington altered the respectable but modest house into a larger, two-and-a-half-story structure (Figure 2.2). The changes, underway before his courtship of Martha Dandridge Custis, were ready in time for his marriage to her in 1759. That expanded building retained the earlier house's layout of a central passage and four ground-level rooms. Washington added such features as new upstairs bedrooms, paneling and a grander staircase in the central passage, and, on the exterior, beveled wooden boards covered in pigment and sand to resemble stone blocks. In its ample size and updated style, Washington's residence expressed the achievements of a successful Virginia planter.

In 1773, Washington decided to expand that already substantial house into a much larger

FIGURE 2.1. Reconstruction drawing of Lawrence Washington's mansion house at Mount Vernon. George Washington's half-brother Lawrence built a residence by 1743 that still forms the core of the present house. Their father, Augustine Washington, had earlier constructed a modest house on the estate. Drawing: Kay Fukui and Claire O'Connor.

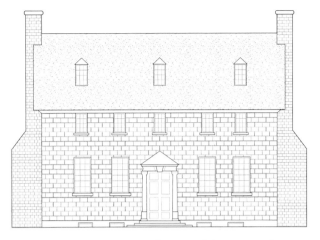

FIGURE 2.2. Reconstruction drawing of the mansion house at Mount Vernon built by George Washington in 1757–1759. The young colonel, anticipating his retirement from the military, planned the expansion of the mansion house in 1757; much of the work was done in 1758. Washington himself provided a "Plan" for the expansion, which was carried out by workmen in his absence. Drawing: Kay Fukui and Claire O'Connor.

mansion that would have striking, even idiosyncratic, features. This new mansion house had a five-part plan, with a large central domestic block and arcaded wings that connect it to substantial dependencies, the whole forming a symmetrical and expansive villa format (Figure 2.3; Plates 1–3). It embodied the high social and economic status that Washington had achieved by the early 1770s. At the age of sixteen, George had been a fatherless boy working as a surveyor of frontier lands. Since that time, he had enjoyed a meteoric rise in his social fortunes.[2] Enlisting in the military at nineteen, he became a wartime celebrity throughout the colonies because of his heroic actions in the French and Indian War and his military leadership in Virginia. He was elected to Virginia's House of Burgesses in 1758. The wealthy widow Martha Custis brought to the marriage in 1759 a fortune of over £23,000 pounds, including hundreds of slaves and real estate holdings. After he inherited Mount Vernon in 1761, George added steadily to his local and frontier land ownership and to the number of slaves. He divided the Mount Vernon estate into variously named farms, which came to be designated as Mansion House (or Home House), Dogue Run, Muddy Hole, Union, and River farms, together finally

totaling over 8,000 acres. By 1773, Washington's agricultural business was diversified and flourishing. And when Martha's daughter, Patsy, died in June of 1773, George inherited £8,000 that had remained hers as a patrimony from Daniel Parke Custis. Washington paid his debts to Robert Cary, his buying agent and creditor in London, and was eager to improve his surroundings. George Washington had yet to attain the level of wealth of the richest families in Virginia, such as the Carters and Byrds, but he was now closer to their economic rank, and his public service as a soldier gave him a social advantage over many other Tidewater elites. When completed, the final mansion house at Mount Vernon stood more than ninety feet across and was two-and-a-half stories tall, with a cupola, dormers, twin dependencies, and elegant, colonnaded wings connecting the dependencies to the mansion house. Until 1773, the most substantial house in the area was at Belvoir, built between 1736 and 1741 by William Fairfax.[3] The mansion at Mount Vernon now surpassed the size of Belvoir's, which George had ad-

FIGURE 2.3. Mansion house at Mount Vernon as redesigned by George Washington, c. 1773. The east facade, impressive portico, and lawn became a favorite of visitors and American artists. Photo: Author.

mired when growing up and which he continued to visit through early adulthood. The mansion house at Belvoir comprised four rooms on the ground floor and a central passage, and five rooms and a passage on the second story, while the expanded mansion of Mount Vernon would have six main rooms on the ground floor, one of which, the Large Dining Room (New Room), surpassed in size anything at Belvoir.[4] Washington would spend the rest of his life improving the gardens and outfitting his house with fine and decorative arts.

Washington as Architect and Patron

Several writers, including Walter Macomber, Scott Owen, John Waite, Robert and Lee Dalzell, and Allan Greenberg, have documented the personal interest that Washington took in the construction of his house, and they have very ably traced many of the sources of the design details.[5] Despite the substantial surviving record of letters and payments for supplies and workmen, we lack certain documentation

of Washington's own role. Was George Washington the architect of his residence at Mount Vernon?

Washington twice enlarged and improved the house, and he was most likely responsible for the overall design, such as the footprint, proportions, and general appearance of the exterior. It is more difficult to know whether he designed or even guided the choices for moldings, capital types, the style of the mantelpieces, particulars of the stucco work, and other such matters. The evidence shows that while craftsmen perhaps received suggestions from Washington, he could not provide designs for many of the particulars and was absent during much of the construction. The final architectural details resulted from an interplay of his guidance and the professional knowledge of those working at the site. Although some twentieth-century writers underestimated Washington's role as architect of his house, we should not go the other way and overestimate his role in shaping the particulars of his residence. He was both an architect and a patron of the mansion house, contributing his ideas only so far as his talents and availability allowed. Like a number of elite Tidewater builders of the eighteenth century, Washington took it upon himself to design and undertake the building of his mansion house and outbuildings, providing plans and instructions but also depending on craftsmen for their expertise, especially in putting on the finishing touches.[6]

We have many fewer documents concerning the building from 1757 to 1759 than we do for the 1770s expansion, and no useful remarks by early observers concerning the authorship of the building's design. While Washington was away from the estate, neighbor and friend George William Fairfax looked into the progress of the expansion. Fairfax talked to the builder, John Patterson, and offered "to assist Mr Patterson with my advice if wanted."[7] On 5 August 1758, Fairfax wrote to Washington:

> I have scarcely time to acquaint you, That I was Yesterday at Mount Vernon to Visit Mr Patterson, who consulted me about taking up the upper Floors, as you gave him no orders about them, whereupon I had them clean'd in order to View them the better, and found most of them very uneaven and several defective planks, upon which I made Patterson calculate the difference of Expence between New laying them & intire new, which you'l see is too trifling to hesitate a moment provided you choose either. Undoubtedly they may do with a little plaining, but that cant bring them even, or make them of a piece with the rest of the House. If you prefer a new Floor, there must be new Doors also, So that we beg you'l consider this matter and lett us have your directions—This word reminds me of breaking one of yours, which we hope youl pardon, But it was upon seeing full imploy for the joiners, and that it would take too much of their time That I took the liberty to hire a hand to paint the House, which is suffering for want of it—I think the Chimneys above are to much contracted, and would be better were they inlarged. For if you remember they are taken in, but whether to prevent Smoaking or for a Stove you perhaps can best tell, and the only one that can direct us.[8]

A little over a week later, Patterson wrote to Washington, referring to the "Plan" the colonel had devised but also noting that he made a decision about the placement of the stairs to the garret.[9] We can deduce from these documents that Washington designed the additions himself but that some lesser decisions were made by those on the spot (John Patterson, William George Fairfax). Washington left the "directions" and a "Plan" and was the "only one" who could decide large matters.

We have even more certain indications of Washington's design of the 1770s expansion. Washington's voluminous correspondence about the house includes mention of carpenters, stucco workers, and painters, yet there is no letter, record of payment, or other notice of any outside architect. In one of the few letters by him on this topic, he stated to Cary on 6 October 1773 that he was "under a necessity of making some Repairs to, and alteration in my House." Similarly, he told Bryan Fairfax on 4 July 1774, "I am very much engaged in raising one of the additions to my house, which I think (perhaps it is fancy) goes on better whilst I am present, than in my absence from the workmen." Much later, in May 1798, Washington wrote to Sally Fairfax, who had left Belvoir and the Virginia colony for England in 1774, that "I made considerable additions to my dwelling house, & alterations in my Offices, & Gardens." While these statements seem to support the attribution of the design to him, they are hardly conclusive. Still, a number of observers during and after Washington's lifetime suggested or clearly proclaimed his authorship of the expanded mansion.[10]

Martha's grandson George Washington Parke Custis (b. 1781) spent his childhood at Mount Vernon, where George and Martha raised him. Custis wrote of George Washington that "all the embellishments of the house and grounds are owing to his creative hand," and noted his responsibility for the "elegant and tasteful arrangement of his house and grounds." The great man, Custis claimed, served as "his own architect and builder, laying off everything himself—the buildings, gardens, and grounds all arose to ornament and usefulness under his fostering hand."[11] When English merchant Robert Hunter Jr. visited the estate on 17 November 1785, he noted:

He has about 4000 acres, well cultivated and superintends the whole himself. Indeed, his greatest pride now is to be thought the first farmer in America. He is quite a Cincinnatus, and often works with his men himself: strips off his coat and labors like a common man. The General has a great turn for mechanics. It's astonishing with what niceness he directs everything in the building way, condescending even to measure the things himself, that all may be perfectly uniform. The style of the house is very elegant, something like the Prince de Conde's at Chantille near Paris, only not quite so large. But it's a pity he did not build a new one at once, as it has cost him nearly as much repairing his old one. His improvements, I'm told, are very great within the last year.[12]

Thomas Lee Shippen, visiting from Philadelphia in 1790, wrote to relatives, calling attention to the "taste and industry of our Washington," relating George's aesthetic contribution and his "industry" in bringing the house to completion. More direct was the opinion of Baron Friedrich von Steuben, who passed by Mount Vernon in 1780. The baron spent a good deal of time conversing with Washington and understood him to be the architect. Commenting on the "external appearance" of the mansion house, the baron said that if "Washington were not a better general than he was an architect the affairs of American would be in a very bad condition." Pierre-Étienne Du Ponceau, the baron's aide-de-camp, heard the remark and recorded it in 1837.[13]

After Washington's death, some visitors expressed an awareness of his authorship of Mount Vernon. Thomas P. Cope, a Philadelphia merchant who wrote a lengthy diary of his travels and activities, visited Mount Vernon in 1802: "The building & style of finishing is quite plain. There are few architectural ornaments about it. Considering that it is the produce of patchwork, it preserves more uniformity than is common in like cases. It was an old family residence, & the General has from time to time made such additions & improvements as occasion required. Yet on the whole it is a slight building, neither is the furniture uncommonly rich or elegant. It has rather a comfortable, substantial appearance, not void of fashion or taste." Similarly, artist William Birch,

who visited Mount Vernon in 1803, wrote in his *Country Seats of the United States* (1808): "The additions of a piazza to the water front, and of a drawing room, are proofs of the legitimacy of the General's taste."[14] Gen. Andrew Jackson attributed the design to Washington, writing in November 1815 that at Mount Vernon "stands the venerable dwelling of the patriarch of our Liberties, corresponding in its style, with the plain and simple taste of him who planned it." Scottish visitor John Duncan (*Travels* [1823]) noted that "some partial alterations were made on the house by the General, but report says that he subsequently regretted that he did not entirely rebuild it."[15] Even more helpful is the description in 1822 by tourist Charles Ruggles. In a letter to his sister, he criticized the design and suggested that the architecture could be ascribed to Washington himself:

Mount Vernon is by nature a most beautiful place. The house is of wood—old, plain, and has rather a gothic appearance. It was built by Laurence Washington. The General added to it a piazza of more modern fashion than the original building, and two wings which have nothing to distinguish them from farmhouse architecture. A stranger is struck with the plainness, and I may add, the stiffness of appearance by which the whole is characterized. It would perhaps be unfair to judge of General Washingtons taste by what we now see, because he did not originally build the house; and because its appearance may be changed since his death. The changes which have taken place are, however, chiefly produced by decay—few from purposed alterations: and on the whole one would be led to think that the General paid no great regard to ornament and that in whatever he attempted in that way he was unsuccessful.[16]

Finally, the last major pre–Civil War piece of writing on Mount Vernon, Benson Lossing's *Mount Vernon and its Associations* (1859), published later as *The Home of Washington* (1870), claimed that "Washington was his own architect, and drew every plan and specification for the workmen with his own hand."[17]

In eighteenth-century continental Europe, and even in Scotland, elite owner-architects were rare, but there was a flourishing tradition of them in England and her colonies.[18]

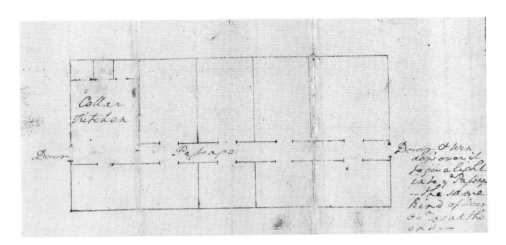

FIGURE 2.4. George Washington, drawing for the basement level of the mansion house at Mount Vernon, c. 1773, pen and ink on paper, 6.5″ × 8.15″. Washington carefully drafted a floor plan for the basement level, including barrel-vaulted storerooms, three of which were built. Courtesy of the Mount Vernon Ladies' Association (W-1369a verso).

Gentlemen generally possessed enough knowledge of architecture to be able to enjoy it during travels, discuss it intelligently, and design the overall lines of a fine residence. The need for designing one's own house was rather pressing in the colonies, where trained architects were difficult to find; it commonly occurred that owners drew up plans for their residences and called on competent craftsmen to build them. Barbara Mooney has called attention to the leading role that colonial Tidewater plantation owners took in planning and designing their residences, and serving, effectively, as contractors who coordinated the erection of their mansion houses.[19] A result of this practice was that, without the weight of academic training, these amateur architects created some especially original buildings. Despite its untraditional or unorthodox aspects, or perhaps because of them, George Washington's impressive mansion house indicates his thoughtful participation in an ongoing architectural tradition. The unacademic, even vernacular, aspects of Mount Vernon, including the asymmetries of the fenestration, further support attributing the design to Washington and argue against the authorship of a trained, professional architect, such as those who designed the Tayloes' Mount Airy, Matthias Hammond's house in Annapolis, and Mount Pleasant in Philadelphia.

Gentlemen-architects sometimes made their own drawings or models. Two drawings in Washington's hand survive, made in preparation for the renovation of the mansion house that began in 1773 (Figures 2.4 and 2.5). Washington later noted that it would be as impossible to manage a farm without a regular system as it would "for an Architect to erect an Edifice without a Plan," and he carefully planned the expansion of his residence.[20] We see here, as in his other designs for buildings, that Washington's skill in architectural draftsmanship was limited. Despite his background as a surveyor, he never developed a fine hand for plans or elevations; he was certainly no Thomas Jefferson in his talents at architectural drawing.

The inconsistencies between the drawings and the actual mansion suggest that they are early and fundamental designs for the expansion of the house, not later studies for adjusting the position of windows or for some other minor purpose.[21] The plan of the basement (see Figure 2.4) includes an inscription (also in Washington's hand) calling for doors with windows on top at each end to allow lighting to the lower level ("Door, and window over it to give a light into ye Passage—the same kind of Door etc. as at the end"). The sheet includes provision for five vaulted spaces under the portico (the five rooms on the bottom of the drawing); that only three were built confirms this drawing to be an early study. The east facade wall of the building is marked by the line between the basement passage and these vaulted rooms,

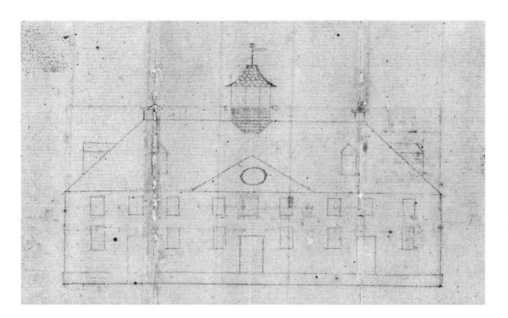

FIGURE 2.5. George Washington, drawing for the west elevation of mansion house at Mount Vernon, c. 1773, pen and ink on paper, 6.5″ × 8.15″. Washington set out several ideas for the proportions and architectural elements of his about-to-be expanded mansion house. Courtesy of the Mount Vernon Ladies' Association (W-1369a recto).

and shows Washington planning the 3:1 ratio of length to width of the building as it would (and does now) appear above ground (Figures 2.6 and 2.7).

For its part, the sketch for the facade (see Figure 2.5) shows proportions that differ from the final result (cf. Figure 1.1 and Plate 1) and indicate that this is also an early study. For example, the height of the pediment here is one-third the total height of the rectangular body of the house plus the pediment, whereas the ratio is 1:4 in the final building as we have it. The drawn pediment itself is 1:3 in its ratio of height to width, which does not hold for the pediment as built. The dormers in the sketch are one-fourth the height of the pediment, again differing from the final building. In the drawing, the chimneys are as high as the base of the cupola, whereas no such alignment appears now. One of the more complex proportions, appearing in the pen drawing only, is the 2:5 ratio of the width of the facade to the height of the building measured from the base of the facade to the roofline. The sketch also shows a sharper angle of roofline than appears in the final house. The sketch, in short, shows Washington working out the proportions and appearance of the mansion, and many fundamental aspects changed in the ul-

timate elevation and plan. Many other proportions as built are present in the sketch, though, including the 5:1 ratio of width to height of the facade, the equality of the height of the facade up to the entablature with the height from the entablature to the top of the chimneys, as well as the 3:1 ratio of the width of the facade to the width of the pediment. In both the sketch and the actual building (judging from the weathervane added later), the height to the top of the pediment from the base of the facade is about the same as from that upper point to the top of the weathervane.

From a Palladian point of view, the proportionality of the built house's fenestration is an improvement over the sketch, as the large windows in the actual structure are the same height as the door openings. The symmetry of the windows in the sketch, however, was never achieved in the house as built, as Washington left the imbalances that were present in the design of 1757–1759. If Washington wanted to have the cupola placed directly in the center of the house, as shown in the sketch, this did not quite happen during construction, as the cupola is fourteen inches to the right of the central axis, an asymmetry easily seen from the west side. At any rate, the two sketches show Washington thoughtfully work-

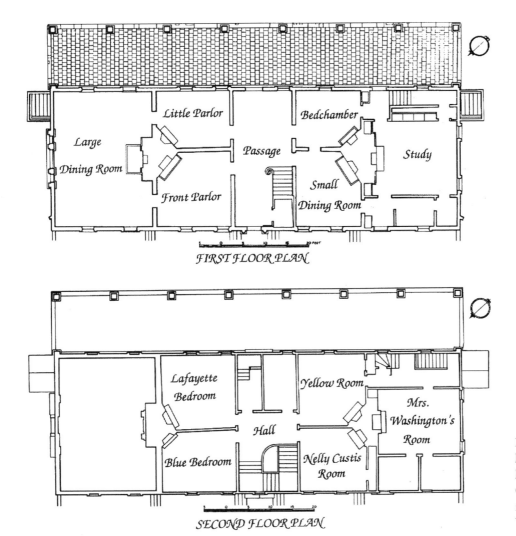

Large Dining Room

Little Parlor

Front Parlor

Passage

Bedchamber

Small Dining Room

Study

FIRST FLOOR PLAN

Lafayette Bedroom

Yellow Room

Hall

Blue Bedroom

Nelly Custis Room

Mrs. Washington's Room

SECOND FLOOR PLAN

FIGURE 2.6. Morley Williams, 1937, plan of mansion house, Mount Vernon. *Top,* Ground floor. *Bottom,* Second floor. Courtesy of the Mount Vernon Ladies' Association.

ing out basic design elements, window and door placements, and proportional relationships for the expanded residence. Enough differences exist between the drawings and the final building, though, to indicate that the builders did not use the sketches on site; the drawings are likely a late draft for the project. All in all, these two drawings, along with the verbal evidence, affirm Washington's vital, creative role in the final expansion of the mansion house.

Washington designed the overall footprint, elevations, and floor plans for new rooms, but he played a limited role in selecting the ornamental details, serving as patron rather than as designer. For the moldings, doorway and fireplace surrounds, stucco ornaments, details of the capitals, and so forth, the written records indicate that he allowed the professional workmen to choose the forms and to determine whether these details represented the widespread or current taste, particularly in England, a standard he also adhered to in such aesthetic matters as the decorative arts and sartorial fashion. Washington's inexperience with decorative details was hardly unusual. In looking at colonial Tidewater patterns of building, Barbara Mooney underscores the "definite limits to the extent of an architectural patron's expertise"

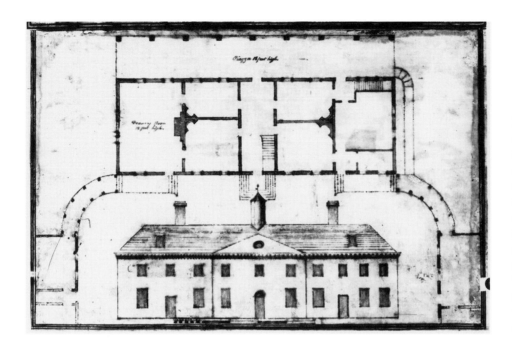

FIGURE 2.7. Samuel Vaughan, detail of his plan of the central part of the Mount Vernon estate, 1787, ink and watercolor on paper, 32″ × 16.26″ (size of whole sheet). As part of his larger plan of the estate (cf. Figure 4.4), Vaughan recorded the layout of the rooms at the ground level of Washington's mansion house. Courtesy of the Mount Vernon Ladies' Association (W-1434).

and points to the owner's reliance on the knowledge of craftsmen. Similarly, Kevin Sweeney has concluded that for many eighteenth-century mansions the inspiration came not from pattern books but "were shaped primarily by the experiences and aspirations of patrons and the skills and ideas of the builders."[22] A few owners in colonial America hired professional architects to undertake the construction of their residences, but many elite patrons did what Washington did, designing the house's overall scheme and turning over the details to trained craftsmen, whose work, nonetheless, still had to conform to the owner's essential desires.

We find well-documented evidence of this process in the decoration of the Large Dining Room, what Washington usually called the "New Room," the adornment of which was finished in the 1780s after Washington had had years to act as a builder and to acquaint himself with architecture and architectural drawings (Plates 4 and 32). Even at this late date he was somewhat passive and, at times, befuddled about some of the particulars of the room's design. During its construction in 1776, Washington instructed manager Lund Washington (a distant cousin) to make sure that the

fireplace opening was in the center of the room and that doors were placed symmetrically on either side of it. ("The chimney in the new room should be exactly in the middle of it—the doors and every thing else to be exactly answerable and uniform.")[23] When the general returned to Mount Vernon after the war, he undertook to complete the details of the room. Rather than create or commission a fireplace surround that would fully harmonize with a new arrangement of design details, he installed the gift of a marble work sent to him cold by London merchant and American sympathizer Samuel Vaughan (Plate 32). Washington wanted a major scheme of stucco decoration and fine carved moldings, and he asked for a plain and neat style, but beyond that he left the design to knowledgeable professionals.

Washington first described his desires for the New Room on 29 August 1785 in a letter to craftsman John Rawlins, an Englishman who had worked in Annapolis and Baltimore and who died soon after his labors at Mount Vernon:

I have a room 32 by 24 feet, & 16 feet pitch, which I want to finish in stucco: it is my intention to do it in a plain neat style; which, independantly of its being the present taste, (as I am inform'd) is my choice. The Chimney is in the centre of the longest side, for which I have a very elegant marble piece; directly opposite thereto is a Venetian window, of equal breadth & pitch of the room; on each side of the Chimney is a door, leading into other rooms; & on each of the short sides is a door & window.

I mention these things that you may be apprized of the sort of work; the time it may take you to execute it, and that you may inform me upon what terms; and also, if you are inclined to undertake it, that you may have leisure to think of a design.[24]

On 30 November 1785, with a price estimate and Rawlins's designs in hand, Washington wrote:

Your Letter & plan came safe; tho' I do not pretend to be a competent judge of this kind of work, yet from the little experience I have had in it, & from a certain knowledge that most of the mouldings & decorations are with great ease & expedition cast, of a material too which is by no means expensive, I do not scruple to declare that your Estimate exceeded my expectation.

This, & not understanding the plan fully from an unaccustomedness to drawings, together with the indifinite charge of travelling expences, which may be great or little [etc.] . . . If an Agreement takes place, I wish to know precisely, & as soon as may be, what will be previously necessary for my Joiners & Carpenters to do, or to prepare that there may be no delay after you arrive.[25]

It is noteworthy that Washington was unaccustomed to drawings for a decorative scheme and that this hampered his ability to understand the design in question. On the same day, Washington wrote to the intermediary acting on his behalf, former aide-de-camp Tench Tilghman, beginning with a mirthful turn of phrase concerning the cost: "The plan is plain, as I requested—but the estimate, I think, is large; however as I pretend not to be a competent judge of work, and know that we are always in the power of workmen, I will not decide absolutely upon the moderation he pretends to have observed; especially as I confess that I do not clearly understand the plan."[26] When Tilghman, writing from Baltimore, sent Washington a drawing to be used by carpenters to prepare the room for Rawlins's work, he did not take for granted that Washington would understand it. He explained, "Inclosed you have a plan or pattern in paper of the Joiner's Work necessary to be done about the Cornice previous to beginning upon the Stucco Work—This, Rawlins says, your Carpenters will understand—He also desires that the *Grounds* round the Windows—Doors and SurBase may be put up previous to his going down in the Spring."[27]

Work on the decorative aspects of the New Room stretched into 1787 and eventually resulted in the spectacular array of stucco work found on the ceiling as well as over the doors and around the Venetian window (Plate 4). Rawlins's style was clearly influenced by the archaeological neoclassicism of Robert Adam, and included anthemia, acanthus, and swags, all set out with great linear clarity.[28] The result is even more readable and vivid than the style of Adam himself, perhaps reflecting Washington's desire for neat and plain. The introduction of farm implements in the ceiling panels likely resulted from a suggestion by Washington himself for agricultural iconography, although it could be that Rawlins developed that conceit. If Washington discussed stylistic options with Vaughan or Rawlins, we have no record of it, and the correspondence indicates only that Washington left the design to Rawlins's invention and that it was carried out by Rawlins and assistants, including craftsman Richard Thorpe.[29] The New Room would be adorned with stucco and be in the "present taste in England," as Washington proudly noted early on (14 January 1784) to Vaughan, anticipating the application of the up-to-date stucco medium and the likelihood that Rawlins and Thorpe would create a fashionable and "plain, neat" decoration.[30]

Washington's admission that "we are always in the power of workmen," that he had an "unaccustomedness to drawings" and did not "clearly understand the plan," is a stark and modest acknowledgment of his limits in the creation of architectural detailing. Still, he did make some decisions for the completion of the New Room. Washington wanted to apply "plain blew or green Paper" that would give the room a "rich & handsome look," the gilded borders made, as he had seen elsewhere, "of Papier Mache fastned on with Brads or Cement round the Doors & window Casings, surbase &ca." He also determined in 1787 that the number of window lights in the New Room would be forty-eight instead of thirty-six.[31] Here, as was usually the case, he chose the color and other decorative particulars, as he could trust his own taste and base his decisions on what he had seen in other fine houses. Not surprisingly, he tended to choose paint colors that were in current fashion. The colors in place at the mansion house reflect those present at the time of Washington's death, and the hues in the New Room (two shades of a bluish-green), the Small Dining (strong verdigris green), the West Parlor (deep Prussian blue), central passage (grain painted mahogany), and elsewhere in the house are found in other elite Tidewater homes of the eighteenth century. The colors in the New Room, like the stucco work and furnishing, represented "present taste," and Washington would have based his choices on his own experience and tastes, the advice of workers and other owners, and the availability of paint.

Washington was present at Mount Vernon during the completion of the Large Dining Room. A similar commission, for the ornament of the Small Dining Room during the Revolutionary War, indicates how the process went in his absence (Plate 5). With Going (or Gowen) Lamphire, William Bernard Sears, and an unidentified stucco worker engaged in the decoration, manager Lund Washington coordinated their work and reported back to George Washington on 12 November 1775 that the room was advancing well: "The Dineg Room will I expect be finishd this week now come in—it is I think very Pretty[.] the Stucco man agrees the Cielg is a Handsomeer one than any of Colo. Lewises, altho not half the worck in it[.] it was a plan recommen'd by Sears." Following the suggestion ("plan") by Sears to use an English, printed source for the ceiling, the anonymous stucco man adapted plate 62 from William Pain's *The Practical Builder* (1774). George Washington accepted the contributions of these skilled workmen, who supplied the up-

to-date and fine design, and he turned to other elite builders for help, in this case in borrowing the stucco specialist from brother-in-law Fielding Lewis of Fredericksburg, Virginia. The final result at Mount Vernon is similar to that of Lewis's home, but even the nameless stucco man himself, as Lund noted in November, remarked that it was "hansomer" than Lewis's, though less intricate ("not half the work in it").[32] Thomas Jefferson lamented in his *Notes on the State of Virginia* that Virginia architecture lacked elegance, and that "a workman could scarcely be found here capable of drawing an [architectural] order."[33] Washington struggled with this limitation and did his best to find craftsmen who could provide good design details.

Local craftsmen carved two of the three main fireplace surrounds at Mount Vernon. The first was installed in the West Parlor in the later 1750s (Plate 6), the second in the Small Dining Room in 1775 (Plate 5). In the West Parlor, the design is adapted from Abraham Swan's *British Architect* (1745, and later editions), a widely imitated source on both sides of the Atlantic (Figure 2.8).[34] Washington's (unknown) craftsman turned to this trendy Rococo source, though he greatly flattened the design and reduced the florid, naturalistic elements. There is no evidence that Washington possessed Swan's book either then or later, so perhaps the craftsman himself owned or borrowed it. In 1775, a second skilled worker, William Bernard Sears, produced a much finer imitation of Swan's model (Plate 5). Lund Washington oversaw this commission, and it is far from certain whether the general, absent from the estate and utterly occupied with his military duties, had any role in choosing or even approving the particular design. He likely knew little of the appearance of the room until 1781, when he returned to Mount Vernon for the first time since leaving home after taking up military command.

Washington contemplated replacing both of these fireplace surrounds during the renovations after the war but decided against it, writing to nephew Bushrod in early 1784: "When I came to examine the Chimney pieces in this House,

FIGURE 2.8. Abraham Swan, fireplace surround. Washington's craftsmen relied on Swan's designs as models for the fireplace surrounds in the West Parlor and Small Dining Room. Craftsmen working in elite residences in the American colonies frequently turned to Swan. *The British Architect: or, The Builder's Treasury of Stair-Cases* (London, 1745). Photo: Andrew Taylor.

I found them so interwoven with the other parts of the Work and so good of their kind, as to induce me to lay aside all thoughts of taking any of them down—for the only room which remains unfinished [the Large Dining Room] I am not yet fixed in my own mind but believe I shall place a Marble one there, at any rate I shall suspend the purchase of any of those mentioned in your letter." Washington made no mention of the difference of quality between the fireplace surrounds in the West Parlor and Small Dining Room, noting only that they are both "good of their kind."[35]

Washington indeed got a marble chimneypiece for the Large Dining Room, a gift from Samuel Vaughan (Plate 32). In materials and style, the work is something of an aberra-

tion in the house. Probably made about 1745, it has been attributed, plausibly, to Englishman Henry Cheere, who may have been assisted in making the figurated panels by pupil and collaborator William Collins. Vaughan seems to have acquired it in 1770 and installed it in the library of his home, Wanstead House, in Essex. He later gave the work to Washington, who commented upon receiving it that it was "by the number of Cases (ten) too elegant & costly by far I fear for my own room, & republican stile of living."[36] As it turns out, the figural manner is soft and almost Rococo in flavor, not incompatible with the derivations from Abraham Swan in Washington's house, and the idyllic subject matter is appropriate for a country residence. Visitors in the next two decades often praised the work, although one American critic, Samuel Powel, did not like the colored, Siena marble columns, which differed from the "plain and neat" sensibility of the surroundings. Benjamin Henry Latrobe perspicaciously called the chimneypiece "of the taste of Sir Wm. Chambers," referring to the rich style of the English architect, whose stolid and heavily ornamented classicism was in favor in the generation before the mantelpiece was installed at Mount Vernon.[37] Washington—if we are to believe his stated hesitation—installed it somewhat passively and against his better judgment. Still, the elegant marble piece, representing agricultural and other rustic scenes, made a notable and appropriate addition to his home, even if it was in a style that by 1785 was falling out of fashion in England.

Washington owned only one English pattern book capable of serving as a model for his craftsmen, Francis Price's *British Carpentry* (1765). Yet Price's designs and advice for the making doorways, columns, and so forth are not reflected in the architecture at Mount Vernon. To cite one example of many, Price calls for a Tuscan order with columns seven times as high as their diameter; the elongated square columns of Mount Vernon's portico do not correspond to this recommendation.[38] The books reflected in the architectural ornament of the mansion house were Batty Langley's *City and Country Builder's and Workman's Treasury of De-*

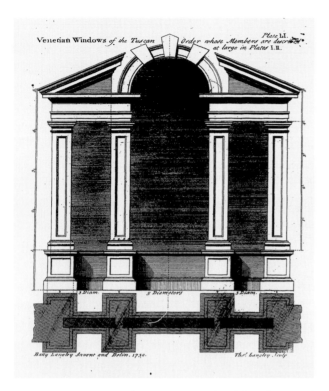

FIGURE 2.9. Batty Langley, Venetian window. This plate served as a model for the exterior frame of the Palladian window on the north facade of Washington's mansion house. Langley designed his window decades before Washington's craftsmen adapted it. *City and Country Builder's and Workman's Treasury of Designs* (London, 1745), plate 51. Photo: Andrew Taylor.

signs, Langley's *Builder's Director* or his *Builder's Jewel,* and Thomas and Batty Langley, *Ancient Masonry*; however, none of these publications were in Washington's library later, and at the time of the adaptations were presumably borrowed or owned by the craftsmen who served him. Langley's books certainly served as a model for important parts of the ornament of the house, including the exterior articulation of the Venetian window in the New Room (Figures 2.9 and 2.10), the square columns of the portico, the east central exterior door, the front door surround on the west elevation (see Figure 1.1), the rusticated elliptical window on the pediment of the west facade (Plate 2), the Ionic door frames in the West Parlor (Plate 6), the interior doorway in the central passage

leading to the portico, and a few other details.[39] But we know of no instructions by Washington to his workmen to use these sources. He likely reviewed the decorative plans or design sources for approval, and, once a room or exterior was complete, he either dictated or offered suggestions for paint color, wallpaper, and borders, those being matters within his sphere of knowledge.

There is little doubt that Washington's modesty about his acquaintance with architectural terms, details, and theory was justified. In a letter to architects James Hoban and Stephen Hallet concerning the plans for the Capitol, Washington confessed his own "small knowledge in Architecture."[40] Despite his modesty and his real limitations, however, he was hardly hesitant to take a leading role as overall architectural designer. Washington, a born leader, brimmed with confidence in life and had a natural bent toward independence. Again and again, he designed his own buildings, shaping his surroundings "in the building way."

Other Architectural Projects

Along with the surviving documentation about Mount Vernon, we have written and visual documentation for several other architectural projects by Washington. These buildings are of interest for their own sake but also suggest how he came up with ideas for the architecture of his house. The development of these projects followed a similar pattern. Washington gathered ideas, learning about existing buildings either from correspondence with others or (although this is less well documented) from looking at structures in existence. He probably consulted books for ideas, but in no known case did he simply imitate ideas gained from bookplates or printed descriptions of buildings. After getting background knowledge, he produced some useful if rudimentary drawings for a building's overall appearance and floor plan; he left the details to the skilled craftsmen in his employ and advised about particulars only when he felt capable of doing so. This design process, used for the mansion house at Mount Vernon, unfolded for other structures, in-

FIGURE 2.10. Venetian window, north elevation of the mansion house, Mount Vernon. The room was framed in the mid-1770s but not finished until after the Revolutionary War. Washington's craftsmen adapted and simplified Langley's design (see Figure 2.9). Photo: Author.

cluding Washington's Greenhouse at Mount Vernon; an icehouse (1784) on the edge of the east lawn; the townhouses that he designed in the District of Columbia in the 1790s; frontier forts designed by the young colonel during the French-Indian War; the stable near the mansion house at Mount Vernon; a manager's house to be built near his Dogue Run gristmill; a sixteen-sided barn, also at Dogue Run Farm; brick barns at his Union and River farms; a modest house that he constructed between 1769 and 1771 in Alexandria; and a small house he planned to build in Bath, Virginia (1784).

The Greenhouse, which stood on the north flank of the upper garden (Figures 2.11 and 2.12; Plate 13), was destroyed by fire in 1835, but its approximate appearance is known from documents, archaeology, and some sketchy, early images made of what was by then nephew Bushrod Washington's estate (Figures 2.13 and 2.14). The Greenhouse was rebuilt in 1950–1952 in its approximate original form, although details are necessarily conjectural.[41] The reconstructed

Greenhouse sports wooden pilasters set on plinths, although the evidence that the original Greenhouse had pilasters is ambiguous. While pilasters seem to be present in an insurance company view made in 1805 (see Figure 2.14), they are not present in an earlier and more crisply drawn insurance view from 1803 (see Figure 2.13). No visitors described pilasters, nor is there physical evidence for them. The payment records to workers on the building are incomplete, but it is noteworthy that the documents for the labors of T. Mahoney, T. Brannagan, Matthew Baldridge, and T. Green make no mention of pilasters, half-columns, or capitals, while records of their labor from January to April 1787 do note their work on the cornices, pediment, sashes, and other architectural elements.[42] It could well be that the Greenhouse's pediment originally lacked the support of columns or pilasters, an arrangement often found elsewhere in Washington's architecture (mansion house, icehouse, townhouses for the nation's capital, and the Mount Vernon stable). The Green-

FIGURE 2.11. Greenhouse, upper garden, Mount Vernon (reconstructed 1950–1952). Washington designed the Greenhouse, which became the architectural centerpiece for the upper garden. Photo: Author.

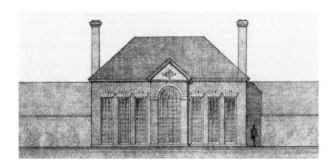

FIGURE 2.12. Walter Macomber, proposal to reconstruct the Greenhouse, upper garden, Mount Vernon, mid-twentieth century. The Greenhouse, which burned in 1835, was considered by early Americans to be an impressive garden building, and it sheltered tropical plants and trees from the winter weather. Macomber's suggested design reconstructs the Greenhouse with piers, not pilasters or half-columns, supporting the pediment. Courtesy of the Mount Vernon Ladies' Association.

house was reconstructed with a hipped roof, present in the early insurance views. The oval window in the pediment, which echoes the one in the mansion house itself and reflects the shape of the elliptical turnaround there, appears in the early views; Washington referred to it with the vernacular designation "Ox eye window." The keystone over the central arch is original and was found during excavations.[43]

By 1784, George Washington had produced the basic design for the scale, placement, and proportions of the Greenhouse, but he needed help in some technical matters appropriate for the building's function, and workmen took care of the details of architectural ornament. The footprint for the structure had been established and the walls were already being raised when Washington wrote to Tench Tilghman in Annapolis on 11 August 1784, asking his former military aide to get information on the recently built greenhouse of a

FIGURE 2.13. Lewis M. Rivalain (signed), drawing of the principal buildings at Mount Vernon, 1803, pen and ink, 13.5″ × 11.25″ (top section) and 11.25″ × 18.25″ (bottom section). This insurance view of the property and one from 1805 (see Figure 2.14), made during Bushrod Washington's early years as owner, are valuable records of the appearance of some of the principal aspects of the Greenhouse, mansion house, and other structures. Declarations and Revaluations, 1796–1966 (acc. no. 30177), vol. 26, Mutual Assurance Society of Virginia, Business Records Collection, Library of Virginia, Richmond.

leading citizen there, Mrs. Charles Carroll, whose estate at Mount Clare was outside of Baltimore. There were few substantial greenhouses in America at the time. One of the earliest was the 1747 structure at Drayton Hall near Charleston, and Edward Lloyd built a stone greenhouse on his estate at Wye Plantation in Maryland at about the time Washington was planning his own. With few precedents for Washington to study, he sent Tilghman, who was Mrs. Carroll's brother-in-law, a list of specific questions:

> I shall essay the finishing of my Green Ho. this fall; but find that neither my own knowledge, or that of any person abt me, is competent to the business.

Shall I, for this reason, ask the favor of you to give me a short detail of the internal construction of the Green House at Mrs Carrolls?

I am perswaded *now*, that I planned mine upon too contracted a Scale—My House is (of Brick) 40 feet by 24 in the outer dimensions—& half the width is disposed of for two rooms back of the part designed for the Green House; leaving not more than about 37 by 10 in the clear for the latter. As there is no cover on the walls yet, I can raise them to any height.

> The information I wish to receive is on the following points.
> The dimensions of Mrs Carrolls Green House?
> What kind of a floor is to it?

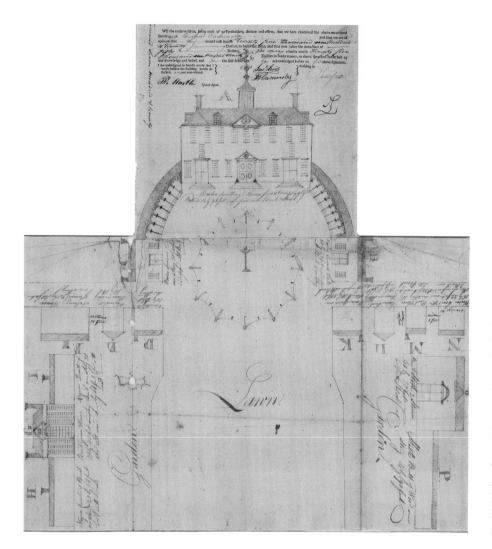

FIGURE 2.14. Samuel Lewis and F. Hamersley (signed), drawing of the principal buildings at Mount Vernon, 1805, pen and ink, 12.5″ × 7.5″ (top section) and 9.25″ × 14.75″ (bottom section). Declarations and Revaluations, 1796–1966 (acc. no. 30177), vol. 35, policy no. 18, Mutual Assurance Society of Virginia, Business Records Collection, Library of Virginia, Richmond.

How high from *that* floor to the bottom of the Window frame?

What height the Windows are from bottom to top?

How high from the top to the Cieling?

Whether the Cieling is flat? or of what kind?

Whether the heat is conveyed by flues and a grate?

Whether the grate is on the out, or inside?

Whether the Flues run all round the House?

The size of them without, and in the hollow?

Whether they join the Wall, or are seperate from it?

If the latter, how far are they apart?

With any other suggestions which you may conceive it necessary to give.

I should be glad to hear from you on this subject soon, as I shall leave home on or before the first of Next Month on a journey to the Westward, and wish to give particular directions to the workmen before I go.[44]

Tilghman wrote a substantial response and provided detailed answers concerning the "internal construction," including advice that Margaret Carroll offered. He noted that "your Floor being 40 feet long, Mrs Carrol recommends two Flues to run up the Back Wall, because you may then increase the number of Flues which run under the Floor, and which she looks upon as essential."[45] She made further suggestions concerning windows and practical matters that would sway the choice for the height of doors ("The Door of the House to be as large as you can conveniently make it—otherwise when the Trees come to any size, the limbs are broken and the Fruit torn off in moving in and out"), character of the plaster ("smooth stucco she thinks preferable to common Plaister because dryer"), and the height of the windows. Tilghman included with his message to Washington a pen-and-ink sketch for the width and height and placement of flues (Figure 2.15). His drawing was not a design for a whole greenhouse but was intended to give Washington the kind of particular technical help he needed for the construction and placement of flues.[46] Tilghman accepted Washington's proportions as a fait accompli, and his (and Margaret Carroll's) advice concerned flues, doors, and windows, and also implementation, such as putting planting boxes directly on the heated floor, rather than setting "the Boxes upon Benches."[47]

Washington wrote a memorandum illustrated by two drawings for this project (Figure 2.16), and another drawing (undated, like the memorandum) includes two related ideas for the floor plan (Figure 2.17). The memorandum reads:

> Notes, if the Buildings intended for the Quarters is 16 feet wide which I think enough, the half of that added to the 4 feet projection will give sufficient width to the Green house; and the three Chimneys as p[e]r plan will, I conceive, convey sufficient heat; otherwise instead of one centre Chimney there must be two at n.o 1 and 2; but I think one will do, especially if instead of making them angle Chimneys, as above, they were made with the backs directly to the Green House, and the Fireplaces a little further apart, but drawn together as the Chimney rises.—There must in the front part of the Green House be, if I mistake not, two tier of windows—and the windows in each very near together.—
>
> The Chimneys in the Quarter part of the above building should be equi-distant—one Chimney will afford two fire places—one in each room.—and if you think it as well, the back part (rather the Front of the Quarters) might be wood with brick underpi[n]ning and fitting—the Center (or Green House part) must, I should conceive be all brick to the Eves.— The Rafters should have the same range or angle in order to keep their parallel distance (as below) to make the building look well.—The Pitch of the Green House need be no more

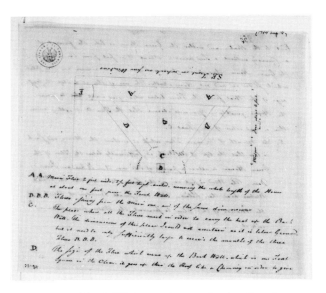

FIGURE 2.15. Tench Tilghman, drawing for the Greenhouse at Mount Vernon, pen and ink on paper. Tilghman, former aide-de-camp to Washington, sketched some ideas for Washington based on information he received from the Carrolls of Maryland. Tench Tilghman to George Washington, 18 August 1784, George Washington Papers, 1741–1799, Series 4: General Correspondence, 1697–1799, Library of Congress.

above that of the Quarters than to allow the two tier of Windows, with very little space between the Tiers (and I believe no Brick work.) And the lower windows not high from the paved floor of the House.—the Reason why I think there generally is, and ought to be two tier of Windows, is, that as much Sun, and heat, may be conveyed through the glass as possible, to the Plants within.—[48]

Although this memorandum is undated, it apparently precedes the planning that led to the final design. Between when this memorandum was written and when the Greenhouse was built, for example, the fenestration changed from two rows of smaller windows to a single row of tall ones. At any rate, the memorandum is revealing, and it is useful that Washington supplied, in his own hand, pen drawings for the floor plan and for the side elevation.[49] His notes to Tilghman, his memorandum, and the drawings clearly show him in confident command of the most important design issues, and they offer a glimpse into how Washington designed buildings. He initially set out the footprint for the Green-

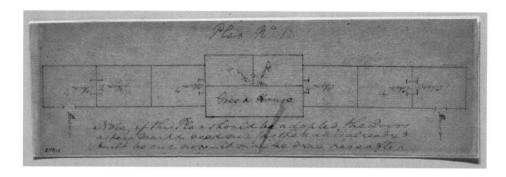

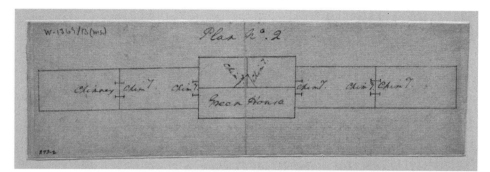

FIGURE 2.16. George Washington, drawings for Greenhouse, two plans, undated, pen and ink on paper, 2.5″ × 9″. *Top,* Recto. *Bottom,* Verso. Washington thought through the basic issues of size, style, and functionality of his Greenhouse and later altered the plan he had sketched out in this early draft. Courtesy of the Mount Vernon Ladies' Association (1369b).

house as twenty-four by forty feet, a harmonious 3:5 ratio, which is close to the Golden Mean. Later, he determined the width of the appended quarters for slaves and the depth of the projection of the Greenhouse from the plane of the long walls of the quarters, giving a 4:1 ratio (16:4 feet) of the quarters' width to the Greenhouse's projection. He was interested in establishing other aesthetic details such as choosing materials (brick) or making the rooflines similar so that they would run parallel and "look well" together (cf. Figure 2.17). He conveyed his intentions with simple sketch drawings, which would have been useful enough for the workmen involved.

Following the 1784 correspondence, no work was done on the Greenhouse until January 1787, and it was finished in the middle of that year; work on the appended slave quarters dragged on until 1794. Following his early start and the subsequent consideration of the Carroll greenhouse, Washington considered his options and eventually enlarged the footprint from what he had feared was "too contracted a scale" (he built a greenhouse not twenty-four by forty feet

but twenty-eight by forty-three feet) and worked out the practical aspects of fenestration and heating.[50] According to the undated memorandum, Washington had planned to have the Greenhouse walls on the north and south (facing the garden and facing away) extend four feet from that of the slave quarters, but he changed his mind, and the Greenhouse is flush with the quarters on the north and projects eight feet on the south into the garden. Washington determined the color of the moldings (white) but not the color of the roof tiles, for which manager George Augustine Washington suggested the muddy reddish hue of Spanish brown.[51] Washington did not truly duplicate proportions and solutions from the Carroll greenhouse, but he did use some of its general ideas for such elements as floor tiles, windows, and door placements. Although he owned a copy of Englishman Philip Miller's *Gardener's Dictionary,* which included a detailed illustration of a greenhouse, Washington designed the main lines of his own building, which did not resemble Miller's plate. For his greenhouse's functional particulars,

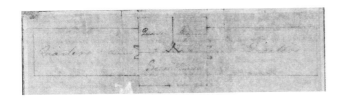

FIGURE 2.17. George Washington, designs for the Greenhouse at Mount Vernon, undated, pen and ink on paper, 6.5″ × 7.75″. *Top,* Plan. *Bottom,* Side elevation and slave quarters. Washington designed his Greenhouse based on his observations of other structures and advice he received from others. This drawing shows an early idea for the structure. Washington wanted the rooflines of the Greenhouse and adjoining slave quarters to look well together. Courtesy of the Mount Vernon Ladies' Association (W-799).

he turned to an American "competent to the business," namely, a member of the Carroll family.[52] In the final result, the steep roofline of the Mount Vernon Greenhouse, its tall chimneys, the oval window in the pediment, and the steep pitch of the pediment itself were features of the already designed mansion house and dependencies. Whatever fine details of dentils or moldings were present (the early insurance sketches allow only an approximate idea) may have been approved by Washington, but they would have been created by skilled craftsmen with expertise in making moldings and other details.

Another example of Washington's design is a small icehouse, which he built in 1785 on the edge of the east lawn before the declivity of the hill, strategically placed between the house and the source of ice (the Potomac River). The icehouse's principal purpose was to keep meat cool in the warmer months. Even in the relatively warm Virginia climate, the icehouse was moderately successful and was uti-

lized regularly for its intended purpose. Records indicate that ice was kept there in 1788, 1789, and 1792 (and may have been in other years as well), and Washington gave instructions from afar in 1794, 1795, and 1796 to store ice there, if possible.[53] As with the Greenhouse, when faced with a question about how to proceed, Washington asked about a similar structure built by someone of his social class, Robert Morris of Philadelphia. (Morris's icehouse, which at the time was a new kind of structure in America, has been unearthed, and its foundations lie within the present Liberty Bell Center.) Washington asked Morris about "the size—manner of building, & mode of management" of his icehouse. Morris responded in great detail, giving no particular stylistic ideas for the exterior but conveying information about materials (stone, mortar, and wood), size, depth in the ground and height above the ground, drainage, best position of the door, and how to pack in the ice and use straw for insulation.[54]

Washington built an icehouse with a somewhat complex form, despite its small size; it is described in period documents as having a vaulted interior (formed of wood) and a pediment over the door. He did not follow the model set out by Morris, who described a stone structure, ten feet high from the ground, and thatched in the roof. Washington's was brick (good stone was easier to acquire in Pennsylvania), lower in height from the ground, and differed in other ways, although the drainage system and the placement on a hill relied on Morris's advice. Washington's structure was not greatly visible to visitors, as the part above ground was obscured by the angle of viewing from the house and most of the east lawn, and later Washington used ivy to adorn what little bit was visible to strollers in the pleasure grounds. The only known stylistic flourish on the little structure was the pediment over the door. This and other details are not extant, as the icehouse was reduced at the time Bushrod's summerhouse was built, and it later fell into further ruin.[55]

We can gain further insight into Washington's building process from the autograph drawing and letters related to

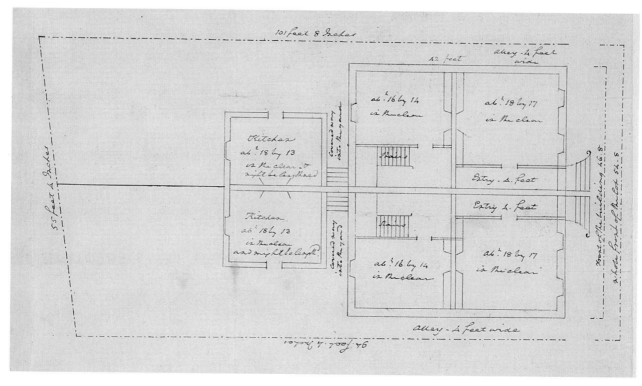

FIGURE 2.18. George Washington, floor plan for townhouses in Federal City, 1798, pen and ink on paper, 11″ × 6.75″. Washington designed paired townhouses for the new capital city; he also received some suggestions from architect William Thornton. The building, on the north side of the Capitol, is no longer extant. The Albert H. Small / George Washington University Collection, Washington, DC. Photo: Courtesy of Mr. Albert Small, Washington.

his design of paired townhouses in the new District of Columbia on the north side of Capitol Hill; he built them to produce rental income and to help develop the fledgling city. Washington provided his ideas to William Thornton, who suggested some changes and remained as the builder of Washington's designs. A fire gutted the townhouses in 1814; they were rebuilt in altered form and then destroyed in 1913. Although there is some discrepancy in the various contracts and letters, and some doubt about what was actually built, the appearance that Washington intended can be summarized based on the written documents and Washington's surviving drawing for the floor plan (Figure 2.18).[56]

The two-unit structure stood three stories high, with windows of equal height on the first two stories and smaller windows on the third floor. Each of the two principal floors was a generous twelve feet in height. There were "Rub'd and gaug'd arches over Windows," stone window sills, and a stone "Strings cource [sic] facia." Washington planned that there would be a single, broad pediment, again unsupported by columns or pilasters, uniting the two residences. There were six dormers on the front, two skylights, and a parapet. The double doorway surround in the middle was carved in stone and fine in style, with fanlights over the doors and four columns supporting a flat entablature. The front and back facades were "faced with good common Bricks," made with "the best stock Brick," while the sides were made of "good mortar and stone." Washington contracted that elements of the exterior would be covered with paint that, when wet, was coated with pulverized rock ("the softest free stone"); he did this with "all my Houses" to give them a sandy stone look. This method of creating the appearance of stone may well have been applied to the plastered side walls, and it was used on the wooden elements such as the building's cornice, which was "painted, sanded, and Painted to match the stone String course." The floor plan indicates a side passage for each house, an eighteen by fourteen foot parlor in the front, dining rooms behind (16 × 14 feet), and kitchens safely isolated in the rear. The moldings of the exterior and interior, such as the chair moldings, cornices, and arches over doors, are difficult to reconstruct in the imagination, but the contract mentions such features as "neat arches," "plain handsome plaster Cornice[s] in lower rooms and passages," and "Plain Pillasters," all indicating a restrained and legible ornament characteristic of the neoclassical period style.[57] None of the ornament was likely of Washington's own design, but it was all consistent with economy and his plain and neat taste.

The building of the townhouses provides more evidence of Washington's hand as architectural draftsman (see Figure 2.18), and he exchanged letters with District of Columbia commissioner Alexander White and architect William Thornton on the subject of architectural style. Washington asked Thornton, who acted as the builder, for his advice and opinions, but Washington produced the basic floor plan and ideas for the exterior. Thornton contributed his expertise and must have helped determine many decorative details, designing what Washington himself called a "handsomer appearance to the Windows."[58]

The letters from Washington indicate that he brought a mixture of humility and boldness to his role as architect. He told Alexander White on 12 September 1798 that

> I am not skilled in Architecture, and perhaps know as little of planning, but as the houses I mean to build will be plain, and (if placed on lot 16 in sqr. 634) will be adapted to the front of the lot, leaving allies [alleys], or entries to the back buildings, I enclose a sketch, to convey my ideas of the size of the houses, rooms, & manner of building them; to enable you to enter into

the Contract . . . My plan when it comes to be examined, may be radically wrong; if so, I persuade myself that Doctr Thornton (who understands these matters well) will have the goodness to suggest alterations.[59]

Although he claimed to lack skill, he clearly had no hesitation in providing his own sketch for what would be a very visible building near the Capitol building in the new city. Washington boasted, "I never require much time to execute any measure after I have resolved upon it," and promised to finish the buildings by the following summer.

Thornton questioned the unorthodox use of a single pediment to unite the pair of townhouses. Washington had suggested the pediment verbally and possibly via a now-lost drawing. On 20 December 1798, responding to the notion that such a pediment was undesirable, Washington wrote with obvious satisfaction to Thornton that he had found a pair of townhouses in Philadelphia that included the kind of design he had already proposed for his land in the federal city: "two houses united, Doors in the centre—a pediment in the roof and dormar window on each side of it in front—skylights in the rear," adding that "if this is not incongruous with rules of architecture, I should be glad to have my two houses executed in this style."[60] He was not certain about the design, however, writing to Thornton on 30 December:

> I shall, if no disavantage will attend the delay, suspend my determination until I can visit the City, & receive some further explanations respecting the consequent alterations which will be occasioned by this Pediment—not at present well understood by me; owing to my entire ignorance of the technical terms in which they are expressed. At which time also, I will make arrangements for giving him further pecuniary aids . . . These ideas, as you will readily perceive, proceed from a person who avows his ignorance of Architectural principles, and who has no other guide but his eye, to direct his choice.[61]

Again, despite his modesty, Washington forged ahead with his plans. He had provided the drawings and verbal articulation of his ideas, determined the building materials, and approved paying extra money to have the frontispieces

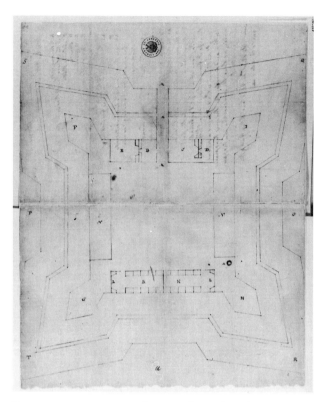

FIGURE 2.19. George Washington, design for a fort, 1756, pen and ink drawing. Washington accompanied such drawings with verbal instructions, including proportions for storerooms and barracks, such as appear in this drawing. George Washington Papers, 1741–1799, Series 4: General Correspondence, 1697–1799, Diagrams of Frontier Forts, 1756, Library of Congress.

around the doors made of stone and not wood.[62] Although he seemed to suspend judgment about whether to add the grand pediment or not, he was delaying this decision not because of Thornton's judgment but because of practical considerations that he would discuss with Mr. Blagdin, who prepared a cost estimate for him. The record indicates that the building received "A Pediment, and Parapet." Noting the vogue for concealing the roof completely, Thornton had suggested a balustrade, which would have concealed any dormers. Washington, defiant if somewhat defensive, replied that dormers are appealing in that they visually break up the roof surface (a point that must have motivated him at

Mount Vernon). Despite Thornton's leading role in the U.S. Capitol project at the time, Washington set out the main lines of the townhouses himself and took advice from Thornton only reluctantly. With the contributions of the various skilled craftsmen and ideas from Thornton, the result was consistent with the Federal style of the time and thus more "modern" than the house at Mount Vernon; still, the townhouses exhibited many of the hallmarks of Washington's architecture as seen in the expanded mansion house, including a floating pediment, false stone elements, simple but dignified doorway surrounds, dormers, and an overall plain and neat appearance.

Like Washington's high-style or brick architecture, his wooden and more vernacular projects followed similar patterns of design and execution. In designing practical military buildings, Washington was, at the age of twenty-four, already an architect while serving as a colonel in the French and Indian War. Young Washington provided drawings and some verbal instructions for officers to build substantial forts in scattered frontier locations. The drawings for "Fort Laudon near Winchester and Fort Cumberland" at Wills Creek are crisp and eminently useful for the purpose, although they are hardly concise, and they share the amateurish quality of all of Washington's architectural drawings (Figures 2.19 and 2.20).[63] Washington provided details of fortified walls and indicated private rooms ("apartments") for officers. The young colonel's crisp hand gives expression to the essential geometry of the designs. His efforts were linked to his training as a surveyor and resulted in a holistic understanding of geometry, axiality, and the practical incorporation of sight lines vital for the projects. Washington also adumbrated his later interest in simple ratios of room size: an apartment fifteen by twenty feet, a prison ten by twenty, barracks for soldiers in a 3:1 ratio (60 × 20 feet), and square spaces for storing food (20 × 20 feet) and for the use of officers (also 20 × 20 feet). We see the confidence with which the young colonel provided such sketches, his fluency with overall architectural design, his abilities in creating spatial

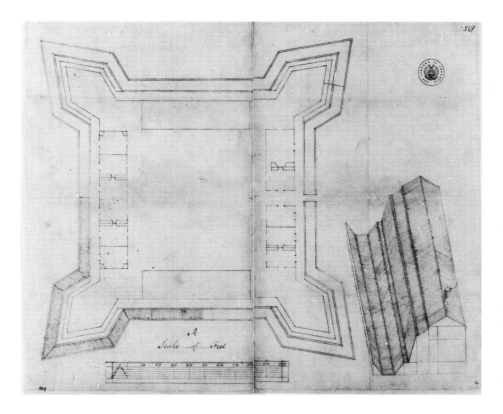

FIGURE 2.20. George Washington, design for a fort, 1756, pen and ink drawing. The young colonel was charged with designing forts along the frontier during the French and Indian War. This example includes an impressive rendering on the right of a wall elevation and roofline. George Washington Papers, 1741–1799, Series 4: General Correspondence, 1697–1799, Diagrams of Frontier Forts, 1756, Library of Congress.

ratios and geometric structuring of large-scale building forms, and his general ease and mastery of working in "the measuring way." Washington sent two fort plans to neighbor William Fairfax for his opinion and suggestions, and Fairfax responded that he found "either of Them well design'd." He defended Washington from the "invidious" criticism of Governor Innes, who considered the footprints to be too large, like that of a "Citadel."[64]

Washington thought highly of his drawings for forts. In one note intended for the on-site builders, he wrote: "If due attention is given to this plan, it will be impossible to err. tho. you otherwise may be unacquainted with the Rules of Fortification." He recommended that "if you can get a Compass and Chain to lay of[f] the Foundn it will be highly expedt to do it," adding that if "you cannot, it may be done with[ou]t but not so exactly."[65] He told officer Thomas Waggener on 21 July 1756 that he was sending plans "which if you observe, you can not possibly err . . . with such plain

and easy directions for constructing these Buildings . . . you cannot mistake the design." Similarly, he wrote to another officer, Robert Stewart, on 22 July 1756, "I enclose you two plans of the kind of forts that are intended to be built—one of the ground-work, the other of the House and all conveniences; with such directions, that I think it impossible for you to err—if you will attend thereto."[66] William Fairfax sympathized with Washington's efforts and thought that Washington should get extra recompense for the great "Thought and Fatigue" that went into the drafting of the sheets.[67] This whole process prefigured how Washington would proceed when he built other buildings: getting the opinions of others, confidently going forward on his own, making useful overall drawings, and letting the builders or "undertakers" come up with approximate translations of his overall ideas and provide the details.

For the stable at Mount Vernon, built in 1782–1783 to replace the one burnt in 1781, Washington—away at war—

FIGURE 2.21. Stable, Mount Vernon, north facade, c. 1782. George Washington sent a drawing to manager Lund Washington to use to build the stable, which replaced the structure that burned in 1781. Washington insisted on symmetry in the construction of the central pediment and dormers on either side. Photo: Author.

sent a plan to Lund Washington (Figure 2.21; Plate 11). The drawing is no longer extant, but the general referred to it in a letter, and his verbal instructions survive. Lund, who had encouraged Washington to build a new stable, served as estate manager and builder, and he had the help of others, including a workman called Evans. George wrote to Lund that "the Coach House should be in the middle [of the Stable] and a pediment over it, with a door in the pediment for the purpose of receiving hay &ca." He asked Lund for information, noting that "I can then form some plan, and make a disposition of the doors and Windows, and transmit it to you; you may also, at the time of furnishing me with these materials to work upon, give me your Ideas of a proper plan; and may consult Evans if he is a man capable of design upon the subject." He also gave Lund the option of using his judgment and extending the size of the stalls.[68]

Following Washington's instructions, Lund constructed a stable with a central pediment, an opening for hay, and windows that accorded with the general's ideas. George Washington insisted on an equidistant placing of dormers from

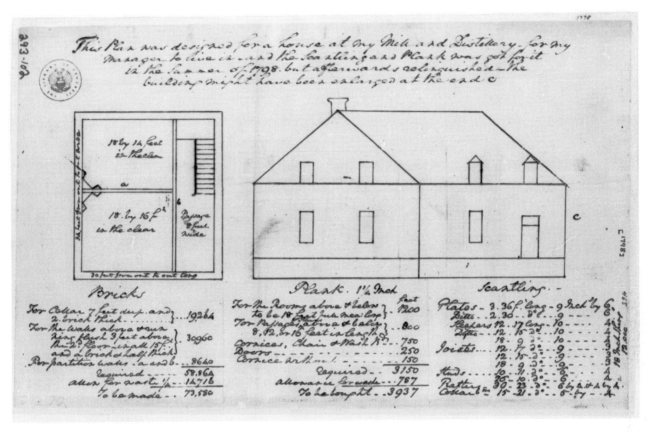

FIGURE 2.22. George Washington, drawing for an overseer's house at Dogue Run Farm, pen and ink on paper. Despite the careful list of building materials, Washington's inscription on the sheet indicates that this drawing was not used to construct a house. George Washington Papers, 1741–1799, Series 4: General Correspondence, 1697–1799, House for Miller: Plan and Specifications, Library of Congress.

the central axis of the building, underscoring his interest in symmetry. During his presidency, Washington wrote to managers Howell Lewis (August 1793) and William Pearce (July 1795), instructing that two dormers be added on the rear, or the side with the open stalls, thus creating symmetry from back to front as well.[69] The stable's pediment is consistent with Washington's penchant for building them without supporting pilasters or brackets or a protruding central pavilion.[70] The brickwork at Mount Vernon's stable is English bond, as are other outbuildings on the Mansion House Farm; the consistent use of this somewhat old-fashioned bond type, which features alternating rows of stretchers and headers, unified the buildings on the estate and must have been prescribed by George Washington. The stable's final form is

owing to the main lines he established, although Lund and the carpenters on site also contributed ideas for execution and articulation of details. In building the kitchen and wash house near the mansion in late 1775, Lund Washington pleaded to depart from George's intentions and make the buildings "look well" together by constructing each with the same number and position of doors on the front. We can assume that Washington, for the stable of 1782 and for other outbuildings, chose the main elements of the design and site but that managers like Lund played some role in determining the final appearance, with George Washington inviting them to offer him their "Ideas of a proper Plan."[71]

Washington's other building designs include an autograph drawing (Figure 2.22) and instructions for materials

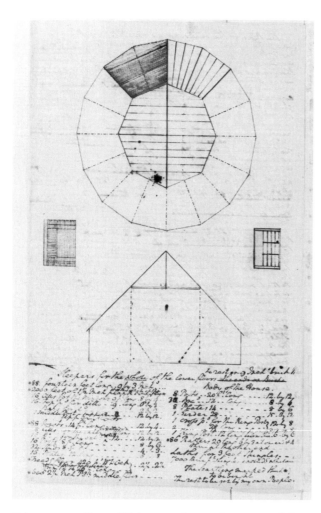

FIGURE 2.23. George Washington, drawing for sixteen-side barn to be built for the Dogue Run Farm, pen and ink on paper. Washington took time during his presidency to send his builders at home detailed drawings and lists of building materials needed to construct the threshing barn. George Washington Papers, 1741–1799, Series 4: General Correspondence, 1697–1799, 28 October 1792, Plan for a Barn, Library of Congress.

for a manager's house he intended to build near his gristmill and distillery, now reconstructed on their original foundations on the edge of the Dogue Run farm. Washington's inscription on the undated sheet indicates that the project was "relinquished" and this particular design thus never utilized. The rudimentary sketch is accompanied by an impressively

detailed list of building materials. The list of items—with precise instructions given for the size, number, and purpose of wood—is exact, while the drawing for the floor plan and front and side elevation, and list of specific bricks and wood needed is carefully considered and would have been eminently usable by a master builder.[72] The highly simplified elevation evinces difficulties in the perspective and an amateurish placement of dormers but was useful enough for a building of no architectural pretense.

Similar to the Mount Vernon stable and Dogue Run house project are the drawings and instructions for the innovative, sixteen-sided barn (Figure 2.23).[73] Based on early photographs and Washington's instructions, the barn has been convincingly rebuilt near the Potomac on what was part of the Mansion House Farm rather than at the original site at Dogue Run Farm (Figure 2.24). Washington again produced practical drawings to be used in the construction, and he drew up a remarkably detailed list of materials and instructions for building, all the more noteworthy in that he was in Philadelphia at the time and occupied with the duties of the presidency. Lacking a pediment or any other ornament, this barn has a certain beauty in its form's geometric clarity. The centralized plan is reminiscent of Washington's early compass drawings (cf. Figure 7.2), even in the number of divisions and subdivisions. Washington reveals his knowledge of framing construction techniques, and the elaborate list of elements (posts, studs, plates, girders, "cills," and feet of plank) shows his mastery of the building process. There is a cathedral-like beauty and complexity to the interior, aesthetically pleasing but also necessary. The framing system sustains a structure of this size and creates the space that allows the running of horses to thresh wheat with their hooves, with the grain falling below through gaps in the floorboards. The barn itself was set in a sensible and symmetrical arrangement with adjoining yards, lanes, dung repositories, and fences.[74]

In Alexandria, George Washington built a small house between 1769 and 1771; it served for short stays, and in some

FIGURE 2.24. Sixteen-side barn, exterior (reconstructed), Mount Vernon. Demolished in the nineteenth century, the Dogue Run Farm barn and the wooden buildings that Washington designed around it have been reconstructed on what was part of the Mansion House Farm. Photo: Author.

years he rented it or let family members use it. The house, recorded in an early view, was demolished but has been reconstructed in approximate form and is a private home (508 Cameron Street; Figure 2.25). From Washington's diaries, letters, and payment accounts, we know that several workers, including joiner Edward Rigdon, Matthew Lawson, William Bushby, James Connell, and Richard Lake received payments for construction of the house, their work including joinery, cabinet work, and painting.[75] There is no record that any of them had a larger design role, and, as Wash-

ington had to convey to them the kind of house he wanted, there is no reason to think that he did not sketch out the main floor plan and elevation for this modest house. He did not oversee very closely the actual construction of the house, although a diary entry of 28 September 1769 notes, "I rid to Alexandria to see how my House went on. Returnd to Dinr." Again on 4 October, he "Rid to Alexandria to see how my carpenters went on with my Ho[use]. Returnd to Din[ne]r."[76] While undertaking alterations to the house in April 1794, Washington showed some frustration with read-

FIGURE 2.25. Attributed to George Washington, house in Alexandria, Virginia, 1769–1771. Based on an early artwork recording the structure, the house was reconstructed c. 1960 in Alexandria (near the corner of Pitt and Cameron Street). Although his authorship is not well documented, we can attribute to Washington the design of the small house, which over the years he used for short stays, rental, or a place for family members to live. Photo: Author.

ing a plan sent to him, reminiscent of his work with Rawlins on the Large Dining Room. He wrote to manager William Pearce: "Thomas Green's account of the dimensions of the Rooms in my house in Alexandria, is so confused & perplexed, that I can make neither head nor tail of it. The length, breadth & height of each, with the distance from the washboard to the Chairboard, & the number of doors & windows in each room, was all I wanted; instead of these he has attempted to draw a plan which no one can understand, and has given an explanation of it that is still more incomprehensible."[77] Washington was most comfortable with the kinds of basic drawings that he himself made and apparently had some difficulty in reading drawings created by craftsmen.

The house in Alexandria was quite simple in form. It had dormers, to let in light and perhaps to break up the insipidity of the plain roof, as Washington would say later about his townhouses, and there is a symmetry of the door and windows. In the height of the basement level and the raising of the little door above the street, he perhaps anticipated the need for accommodating bulk storage, an apt purpose in a port town. The early view of the house seems to show the basement level as stuccoed over in the front (presumably stucco over fieldstone), with clapboard on the main level. George allowed Martha's niece, Frances (Fanny) Bassett Washington, recently a widow, to occupy the house rent-free for a while beginning in 1794. When preparing it for her, the president sent orders from Philadelphia, giving the workers specifications for painting (a "stone colour" for the body of the house and a red roof), plastering the walls, fencing, and paving the basement with bricks. Before moving in, when Fanny asked him to add another story, he replied that this would put too great a stress on the existing structure, although he could not remember the details about the framing of the house and even whether it had more than one plane on any exterior.[78] He seems to have paid little attention to the house, at least during the later time of his ownership.

In 1784, Washington designed a "dwelling House" in Bath, Virginia.[79] The house, never built, had two levels of galleries and rooms of harmonious dimensions: the overall footprint was planned to be in a 3:2 ratio, individual rooms in ratios of 4:3 and 6:5, and a cellar "half the size" of the house as a whole. Washington specified:

> The dwelling House is to be 36 feet by 24, with a gallery of 7 feet on each side of the House, the whole fronts. Under the House is to be a Cellar half the size of it, walled with Stone, and the whole underpined. On the first floor are to be 3 rooms; one of them 24 by 20 feet, with a chimney at the end (middle thereof)—the other two to be 12 by 16 feet with corner chimneys. On the upper Floor there are to be two rooms of equal sizes, with fire places; the Stair case to go up in the Gallery—galleries above also. The Kitchen and Stable are to be of the same size—18 by 22; the first with a stone Chimney and good floor above.[80]

Even in this meager record, we can see consistent application of Washington's architectural practice, including the embracing of galleries, insistence on symmetry (chimneys in the "middle thereof"), and spatial regularity.

The kinds of ratios planned at Bath, and earlier in the colonel's specifications for rooms in frontier forts in 1756, appeared at Mount Vernon in secondary buildings, standing as examples of the "good order of the master's mind."[81] We have to assume that Washington had a role in determining aspects of various practical structures on the estate, although we generally do not know who designed the various outhouses, servants' residences, smokehouse, and so forth, or even large buildings such as the distillery and gristmill at Dogue Run. There is evidence that Washington sometimes handed over the design of outbuildings to others. For example, although he offered suggestions and probably chose the location and size for the gardener's house of 1775 (see view in Figure 4.9), Lund Washington designed and built it in the owner's absence. Later, George Washington made his intentions known in 1793 when partitions in the small building were added for quarters.[82] Lund was apparently working from ideas set forth by George for the new kitchen and servants' hall (which Lund called the "Wash House") in September 1775, but Lund wrote to George questioning whether the buildings should follow the plan and differ in their number of doors.[83] To be sure, the record is incomplete. Without better evidence, as with the Greenhouse, we often cannot confirm who designed the practical structures of Mount Vernon. Even when absent, though, George Washington might have provided verbal instructions or architectural plans, and he at least likely determined the site, approximate sizes, and the consistent off-white coloring of the exteriors of the outbuildings.

Washington as Architectural Theorist and Critic

Washington expressed few thoughts concerning architectural theory or criticism, but what little he did say about these matters throws light on his ideas and his own work as architect. In the realm of theory, his most extensive expression is found in correspondence (30 December 1798) with William Thornton concerning Washington's townhouses in the new capital city of the United States. Washington wrote:

> Rules of Architecture are calculated, I presume, to give symmetry, and just proportion to all the Orders, & parts of buildings, in order to please the eye. Small departures from *strict* rules are discoverable only by skilful Architects, or by the eye of criticism; while ninety nine in a hundred—deficient of their knowledge—might be pleased with things not quite orthodox. This, more than probable, would be the case relative to a Pediment in the roof over the *doors* of my houses in the City.
>
> That a Parapet in addition (for the reasons you have assigned) would have a pleasing & useful effect, cannot be doubted. When the roof of a building is to be seen, and when it is designed for Chambers it must be seen, something to relieve the view of a plain and dead Surface, is indispensable: for this reason it was, I thought, and still do think, that Dormars are to be prefered to Sky lights in the front; on the other hand, if the roof is so flat as not to be seen at all, or so low as, in a manner to be hid by a Parapet, I should give a decided preference to Sky lights.
>
> These ideas, as you will readily perceive, proceed from a person who avows his ignorance of Architectural principles, and who has no other guide but his eye, to direct his choice. I never, for a moment, contemplated *two* Pediments, one over the door of each house: my great object, was to give the two the appearance of one. But as I have observed in the former part of this letter, I will suspend coming to any decision until the consequences of the proposed alterations are better understood by me.[84]

Washington expressed his belief that architecture is essentially meant to please the eye. Whether or not symmetry and proportion correspond to some larger structure of the universe, he concluded that they are intended for visual pleasure. Departures from rules could be effective, and nearly everyone "might be pleased" with things not quite orthodox in architecture. He thus indicated some disdain for an academic approach to architectural design and preferred a kind of utilitarian and democratic solution characteristic of American pragmatism: if ninety-nine viewers out of one hundred gained pleasure from an architectural design, he would ignore the desires of the bookish architects and critics who would object. His statements here clearly correspond to his work as a builder: he relied greatly on his own visual sense, and it was his creativity and judgment that led to solutions "not quite orthodox," such as the innovative portico and the unusual nature of the unsupported pediment on the west front. Someone like neighbor Bryan Fairfax could also find pleasure in inventive architecture that broke with accepted norms of architectural design: "I was Yesterday at Mt Vernon, where I hope it will please God to return You in Time, & like the House because it is uncommon for there has always appeared too great a Sameness in our Buildings."[85]

For economy and ease, Washington did not attempt to make the windows symmetrical at the mansion house, and the cupola is, probably inadvertently, fourteen inches to the right of the central axis. The north elevation also contains asymmetries, with the cellar door not balanced by a similar opening on the other side. Still, the letter to Thornton indicates Washington's awareness of the importance of symmetry. He wrote on 30 September 1776 to Lund Washington, as we have seen, demanding that the "chimney in the new room should be exactly in the middle of it—the doors and every thing else to be exactly answerable and uniform." For the mansion house, he told Lund that "you ought surely to have a window in the gable end of the new cellar (either under the Venitian window, or one on each side of it)," again a call for symmetry, as he would require later at the stable (1782–1783) in the equidistant placing of the dormers from a central axis. Washington preferred symmetry and was willing to forgo it only when circumstances or issues of convenience arose, as with the fenestration of the mansion house.[86]

In his letters, diaries, and comments recorded by others, we find few instances of Washington expressing his ideas about existing architecture, including his own mansion house. As president, he traveled widely and took notes on what he saw, but he tended to record information about buildings that was economic; that is, he described their form, materials, quality, and state of repair. Even as we understand the narrow intention of his diary entries, it is still remarkable

that although he went through towns, cities, and countryside from New England to the southern states, he wrote down few critical remarks about architecture. He did note when houses seemed poorly constructed, or modest in size, or were made of wood, or were fine or substantial. Typical is his diary entry for 21 October 1789, about houses in Connecticut: "great similatude in their buildings—the general fashion of which is a Chimney (always of Stone or Brick) and door in the middle, with a stair case fronting the latter, running up by the side of the latter [former]—two flush Stories with a very good shew of Sash & glass Windows. The size generally is from 30 to 50 feet in length and from 20 to 30 in width exclusive of a back shed which seems to be added as the family encreases."[87] He was largely unimpressed with the homes in Portsmouth, New Hampshire ("in general they are indifferent"), and he disapproved that they were "almost entirely of wood." In April 1791, he praised the houses of Wilmington, Delaware, for being "compactly built."[88] On his tour of the southern states, he again focused on materials and general appearance: "Excepting the Towns, (and some Gentlemens Seats along the Road from Charleston to Savanna) there is not, within view of the whole road I travelled from Petersburgh to this place, a single house which has anythg. of an elegant appearance. They are altogether of Wood & chiefly of logs—some indd. have brick chimneys but generally the chimneys are of Split sticks filled with dirt between them."[89]

Washington did not comment as substantively on James Hoban's work on the president's house (White House), but he did offer noteworthy statements about Thornton's designs for the U.S. Capitol. Washington praised the "Grandeur, Simplicity and Beauty of the exterior" and the "Grandeur, Simplicity and Convenience" and approved moving forward with the project, giving Thornton the commission and pushing aside Stephen Hallet.[90] His praise of "Simplicity" corresponds to Thomas Jefferson's contemporary preference for "chaste" architecture and is in harmony with characteristic taste of the 1790s in the Anglo-American world. The emphasis on "Grandeur" echoes a typical idea in neoclassical thought, the term evoking the greatness of antiquity and the moral quality of the classical style.[91]

Washington's correspondence about the Capitol project reveals his most florid use of language to describe high-style buildings. While he used the word "elegant" to express approval of a style, whether for architecture or, as we will see, the decorative or fine arts, it was among the few critical adjectives that he used, at least in writing. He noted that Jacky (John Parke Custis) had "elegant buildings" on land he inherited from his father, and he told one correspondent just some months before his death that his townhouses in the District of Columbia "are not costly, but elegantly plain." In a similar spirit, he wrote in a cost estimate of the townhouses that "plainness and simplicity will run through [the] work."[92] Washington hardly possessed a vast vocabulary for architectural criticism, and his thoughts on the topic are rarely evident. His strength was in designing and overseeing the construction of buildings, not in talking or writing about them.

The Mansion House at Mount Vernon: Style and Sources

Washington's library contained little that touched on architecture in any way, and he most likely gained his information by studying actual buildings, from conversation, and perhaps from consulting books owned by others.[93] We should not underestimate, however, Washington's access to architectural practice and ideas. Although he never visited Europe, he traveled broadly within the colonies and knew a great number of leading men in the Tidewater region and urban taste centers further north; many of these men possessed books on architecture or were themselves conversant with major trends of the time in England and the American colonies. He knew well the country mansion houses in Tidewater Virginia and Maryland, and just before the death of Martha's daughter, Patsy, in July 1773, and thus immediately before he came into the ample inheritance that encour-

aged his expansion of the mansion house, he went to New York, passed through Philadelphia, and stayed at Lord Stirling's estate in Basking Ridge, New Jersey. Stirling's place is known to have had a deer park, gardens, and house, "in imitation of a large British estate." Washington had already made repeated trips to Annapolis in the spring of 1772 and 1773, and he was at Mount Airy, the Maryland estate of the Calverts, in July 1773. His diary was full of visits to men of taste and means, including William Hamilton, John Penn, and John Cadwalader of Philadelphia, and William Paca, Edward Lloyd, and Richard Sprigg of Annapolis.[94]

The architecture of the mansion house at Mount Vernon, both as designed by Washington and as fleshed out with ideas provided by his skilled craftsmen, is, in some ways, idiosyncratic and provincial, but it is also steeped in English or English-influenced practice and shows relationships to classicism, late Baroque stylization, Palladianism, and other architectural trends of the eighteenth century in Britain and her colonies.

George Washington's first expansion of the house—planned in 1757, with most of the construction done in 1758–1759, stood for only about fifteen years. Its appearance is somewhat conjectural, but we can surmise its overall appearance (see Figure 2.2).[95] It was rather standard for the time and place in being two-and-a-half stories in height, with central passage (already present), four main rooms on the ground level, and chambers upstairs more or less corresponding to the rooms below. Washington was constrained in many ways by the existing plan of Lawrence's house, especially in the establishment of the ground floor, and we have only limited ability to judge his "eye" at this point. He chose not to realign the windows with an absolute "Georgian symmetry," and he had the exterior covered with rusticated, beveled, white boards that imitate stone. Inside, he added a large staircase embellished with mahogany in the central passage, paneling and coloring to the central passage (Lawrence had only plastered walls, with no paneling), and moldings and carvings to other chambers. The small bedroom downstairs is perhaps the only room to retain Lawrence's moldings.

In his redesign, Washington considerably expanded the house's size and the feeling of sheer monumentality. The earlier version was impressive enough, but the final design featured key elements associated with the grand classical tradition, including a pediment (on the west facade); a lofty portico; the curved colonnades of the arms connecting the mansion to the dependencies, which created a five-part plan; a cupola; and a dominating Venetian window in the Large Dining Room.

The changes in the mansion house were only part of the architectural additions and alterations to the estate. Near the main residence, the store house and wash house on the north side of the drive, in existence from 1752 or so, were removed in 1775, as were the similarly dated kitchen and dairy buildings on the south side. Washington replaced these with the dependency buildings that exist now—kitchen and storehouse–clerk's quarters on the south, servants' hall and gardener's house on the north—and over time added other practical buildings (smokehouse, wash house, spinning house, salt house, blacksmith shop) on the north and south lanes.[96] The gathering of buildings on the west side changed from a V-shaped arrangement with the mansion house in the center to the present arrangement of buildings and oval drive, with further definition created by the locking in at the sundial of the alignment of the north and south lanes, which stand at right angles to the axis moving from the west from the house. The kitchen and servants' hall, as well as the gardener's house and storehouse, were rusticated on the front, in harmony with the mansion house, and the effect of quoins is present on the corners where the rustication ends on the side walls, an effect Washington desired. The roofs of these two dependency buildings are particularly steep and somewhat out of character with the mansion house. Whether or not Washington designed such roofs, he at least chose not to alter them after the Revolutionary War, and the sharply angled roofline effect is something that Washington must have accepted and perhaps even favored.

The new mansion house at Mount Vernon had both conservative and forward-looking aspects. Many elements of the new mansion house's exterior could, in the English context, have been designed one hundred years earlier. With the work of Roger Pratt (1620–1684) and others of his and the next generation, the facade with a central pediment, quoins, fine stonework, cupolas, dormers, rusticated oval windows, tall end chimneys, and rectangular sash windows were all well-established features by the second half of the seventeenth century and later. A number of British houses could be cited in comparison; some of the plates in Colen Campbell's *Vitruvius Britannicus* (1715–1725), such as Horseheath Hall, Cambridgeshire, designed by Roger Pratt (1663; Figure 2.26) or William Samwell's Eaton Hall, Cheshire (1675) already contain the essential elements of Washington's mansion house, built a century later.[97] A house like Bourne Park in Kent (c. 1700, architect unknown) also indicates the widespread British style shared by Washington's later mansion house.

One feature that sets the final mansion house at Mount Vernon apart from those of the seventeenth- and early eighteenth centuries is the plan. Over the course of the eighteenth century, a circuit plan was coming into vogue in England and America, allowing residents and visitors to move in a circle through the various rooms.[98] The 1750s floor plan at Mount Vernon, a legacy from Lawrence, comprised an older arrangement where the rooms radiated from the central passage but did not form a circuit. After the expansion of 1773, on the south side of the house a circuit existed, with movement possible from the hallway and study to the small bedroom and Small Dining Room, although in practice the circuit was hindered by the private nature of the study, which was rarely part of any visit and usually off limits (see Figures 2.6 and 2.7). North of the passage on the ground floor, with Washington's addition of the Large Dining Room, one could move in a circle through the public rooms, from the entrance door, central passage, West Parlor, Large Dining Room, Little Parlor (a bedroom before 1797) on the east

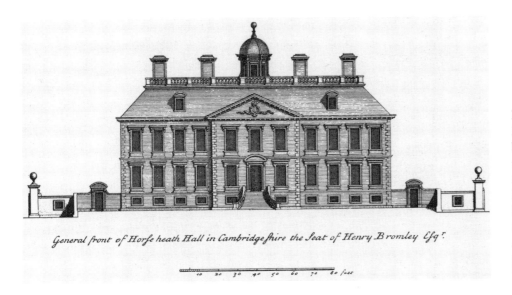

General front of Horse heath Hall in Cambridgeshire the Seat of Henry Bromley Esq.

FIGURE 2.26. Roger Pratt's Horseheath House, Cambridgeshire, 1663. The essential elements of Washington's mansion house were established in English architecture by the seventeenth century. Colen Campbell, *Vitruvius Britannicus* (1715–1725), C. 3, plates 91–92. Photo: Andrew Taylor.

side of the house, and back to the central passage. This modern plan was consistent with English practice by the middle and later eighteenth century, and in variant forms appears in such American homes as William Hamilton's Woodlands in Philadelphia and Jefferson's Monticello (although neither was influenced by Mount Vernon). Such a plan was consonant with later eighteenth-century architectural and garden design, which evolved from compartmentalization to more open and sweeping layouts.

If many of the aspects of the facades are based on long-standing English tradition, the five-part plan flourished more recently. A villa plan with mansion, arms, and connected twin dependencies was quite in vogue in England after 1748, following the expansion of building following the peace treaty and the consequent construction boom.[99] Building in a scale that was modest by English standards but impressive by earlier colonial American customs, a number of Tidewater builders turned to the five-part villa plan, often associated today with Andrea Palladio. These include several mansions in Annapolis, such as the house for Matthias Hammond, the Tayloes' Mount Airy in Virginia, Blandfield (Essex County), and Tazewell Hall (Williamsburg). Washington was in the first generation of Americans who used the Palladian villa plan with five-part layout, but he was hardly in the forefront.[100]

The villa plan, portico, proportions, and other ideas at Mount Vernon are roughly consonant with Palladio's architecture as well as with many later attempts to apply or reinterpret his style. Still, the architecture at Mount Vernon should not be confused with spare Palladianism as it was understood in England by Lord Burlington and his circle.[101] The mansion house at Mount Vernon also embodies a late Baroque classicism, as shown by such elements as the heavy rustication around some of the windows, the large keystone that bursts through the entablature of the front door, the tall chimneys, and the breadth of the facade, all of which are consonant with the later Baroque style as practiced by Christopher Wren, James Gibbs, John Vanbrugh, and John Pratt in England. Washington's mansion is rich in texture, and the apparent stonework gives the building a subtle surface shadow. He arranged through manager Lund Washington to have the visually enriching effect of quoins adorn two of the dependency buildings, to be modeled after those on the Pohick Church.[102] The use of dormers at Mount Vernon, where they are somewhat underscaled in comparison with better English usage, helps to create a jumpy effect on the roofline and is more typical of British style of the seventeenth century or early eighteenth century. By Washington's time, and under neoclassical influence, newer British mansions usually had lower rooflines and cleaner roof surfaces, and dormers were increasingly out of fashion. In all, Washington's mansion house had more in common with the rich classical Baroque than with the more restrained versions of British Palladianism.

To get a sense of Washington's style in the transatlantic context, it is useful to compare the final composition of Mount Vernon with a British structure that more fully embodied Palladian proportionality: the dependency of Robert Walpole's Houghton Hall in Norfolk, designed by Colen Campbell in 1723. Washington may well have known of this dependency structure as illustrated in Campbell's *Vitruvius Britannicus,* published in 1715–1725 (Figure 2.27).[103] That building, compared to Washington's, evinces less of a vertical thrust via the cupola and chimneys, is stabilized through the presence of the belt course between the stories, is anchored on the ends by the quoins, and sports a central pavilion, which breaks up the amorphous expansion of the facade, again with quoins defining and anchoring the ends of the pavilion. Campbell's second floor windows rest on a belt course and are squarish, as opposed to the more vertically rectangular ones at Mount Vernon. Washington's dormers appear small and fussy in comparison, and the chimneys at Mount Vernon are less in harmony with the cupola than at Houghton Hall. It is certainly inexact to compare a mansion house with the dependency of one, but the comparison is useful. Washington's overall design is not only conservative (not far from an English design made half a century before) but even less progressive than that of its predecessor because it possesses unstable qualities associated with late Baroque design in Britain.

The mansion house at Mount Vernon and its dependencies display a calming white coloring that distinguishes the place from some exuberant eighteenth-century residences. Washington clearly rejected the kind of coloristic tradition that marked English Baroque classicism and that is seen in a number of American mansions endowed with variously colored stucco or wooden elements, brick quoins, string courses, and so forth. Contrast of colors and textures plays almost no role at Mount Vernon, beyond the wooden roof shingles, painted deep red on the mansion house, arms, and dependencies by the 1790s, and the green planks in the spandrels of the dependency arms, the verdant color harmonizing with the honeysuckle leaves that climbed up the columns and were trained onto the spandrels.[104] The whiteness of the mansion house and other buildings on the estate likely owes to several factors: an outgrowth of vernacular whitewashing widespread in the American colonies; an expression of Washington's plain and neat sense, characteristic of much Tidewater domestic architecture; and the period sense of coloristic purity or unity. The result is calculated to trick the eye by giving the appearance of fine stone, but the effect is also of restraint and dignity, a country cousin of English Palladian houses with subdued coloration.

One aspect of Mount Vernon's style that demands attention is the pediment on the west facade, which shows Washington's independence and the idiosyncracy of his design. It was the custom in Continental European and English architecture to place a pediment over either a portico or a projecting pavilion. Washington could have built up a slightly protruding pavilion or installed pilasters beneath the ends of the pediment, yet he chose not to do so, instead having the pediment project only a foot or so from the edge of the roofline. The uncanonical design of the west facade is exacerbated by the off-center placement of the windows and the cupola itself. Allan Greenberg argued that Washington made this choice deliberately for aesthetic reasons, but when he built from scratch he did not develop such asymmetries, and we have seen that he sometimes insisted that his builders create axial symmetry.[105] The architectural asymmetries that appear at Mount Vernon were the result of inertia and economy, but they did lend the building a rustic charm that became useful when Washington became the humble "Cincinnatus" of America after the Revolution. At any rate, the

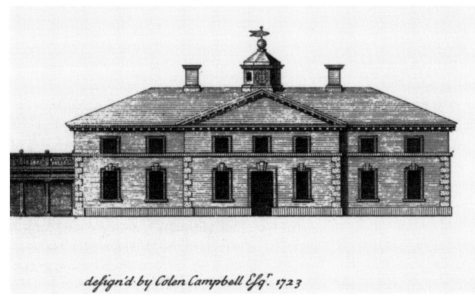

defign'd by Colen Campbell Efq.ᵣ 1723

FIGURE 2.27. *Left,* The mansion house at Mount Vernon. *Right,* Dependency of Robert Walpole's Houghton Hall in Norfolk, designed by Colen Campbell, 1723. George Washington may well have known this plate from the *Vitruvius Britannicus,* as suggested by a comparison with the west front of his mansion house. Engraving from Colen Campbell, *Vitruvius Britannicus* (1715–1725), C. 3, plates 29–30. Photo: Author (mansion house, Mount Vernon) and Andrew Taylor (*Vitruvius Britannicus*).

vernacular nature of the west elevation is reinforced by other unprofessional aspects of the design, from the pressing of the second-floor windows into the entablature of the facade, the under-scaling of the dormers, and the odd grouping of windows that would exist even if the asymmetries were corrected. These irregularities all point to Washington's amateur status as a designer and his struggles with twice expanding a preexisting building.

Going from the exterior to the interior, one sees—as was conventional in architectural traditions of the Renaissance and later—a vastly more ornate style. The architectural ornament installed by Washington's craftsmen followed, with varying time lags, vogues in British practice. The bookplate designs of Batty Langley carried a flavor of the late Baroque; these are echoed in the exterior of the Venetian window, the door surround in the West Parlor, and the door surround and rusticated oval window on the west facade. The plates in Abraham Swan's *British Architect* (1745) provided Rococo-inflected design models for the mantelpieces in the West Parlor (1750s) and Small Dining Room (1770s).[106] Similarly, the stucco work in the ceiling of the Small Dining Room is Rococo in flavor, while a neoclassical and Adamesque style appears in the stucco adornment in the Large Dining Room and the West Parlor ceiling. Washington was not a stylistic ideologue and, as was widespread among patrons in colonial America, accepted various interior styles over time as they became fashionable. He generally preferred a plain and neat style, but within certain parameters he accepted what was current in taste.

The mansion house incorporated many aspects of English and American style as it flourished in the earlier and later eighteenth century, including proportionality, a strong feature of English architecture from Inigo Jones through later eighteenth-century designers. In looking at Washington's drawings for the house (see Figures 2.4 and 2.5) and comparing them to the final result, we see that the elevations and plan are full of proportionalities, such as the 1:5 ratio of height to width of the east and west facades and the 1:3 proportion of width of the pediment to width of facade itself. As for the overall footprint, the house is about three times as broad as it is deep.[107] In designing the porch, Washington gauged its depth so that the measure from the outside of the base of the square columns to the wall of the mansion house is about the same as the width of the central passage (which is 12 feet, 9.5 inches across).[108] Clearly, Washington wanted to unify the interior and exterior measurements, and one experiences a spatial continuity when walking from the central passage to the paved portico.

Washington paid great attention to the design of proportions for exterior elements, but he had less leeway for the interior floor plans, as these were largely determined during earlier construction periods. Still, he infused harmonious relationships in several places in the final plan. Washington himself called attention to the 2:3:4 proportion of the Large Dining Room, noting for craftsman Rawlins that the room was thirty-two feet long, twenty-four wide, and sixteen high.[109] These numbers also imply two spaces each sixteen feet high, sixteen wide, and twenty-four long, each thus with a 2:3 ratio of the floor measurements. Such proportions were the staple of seventeenth- and eighteenth-century architecture in England and appear in prominent works like the cube room and double cube room at Wilton House by Inigo Jones (by 1652), and the Great Room at Marble Hill House by Roger Morris (1724–1729). In the American context, Thomas Nevell infused Mount Pleasant (outside Philadelphia, 1760s) with spatial ordering, for a double cube of space is present in the main parlor. Other rooms of Washington's house contain regular kinds of measurement, the study being close to the intended ideal of a 4:5 ratio (20 × 16 feet; actually built as 19′ ½″ × 16′ ⅞″), and the Lafayette Bedroom upstairs is about seventeen feet square.

Among the features of the mansion house, several aspects are noteworthy in the history of American architecture and deserve particular attention: the rusticated exterior, the cupola, the arcading of the arms (what he called, using the widespread period term, "covered ways"), and the monumental porch on the east side. The rusticated wooden exterior is somewhat unexpected for the time and place, as the practice was rare in American building, especially south of New England. In expanding the smaller house that Lawrence had built, George could have made a house of brick or clapboard exterior, but he wanted the fancier and more substantial look of stone. Washington decided on a labor-intensive solution that was less expensive than using actual fine stone: pine boards beveled and coated with paint and sand or pulverized stone.

Washington mentioned in letters of 1792 and 1793 having brought beach sand to Mount Vernon for this purpose from Point Comfort, Virginia, but in a later document (1 October 1799) he said it was hard to find "Sand perfectly white, & clean," and he claimed to Thornton to have turned to crushed stone and "Sanded" "all" of his houses "with the softest free stone, pounded and sifted." In a 1796 letter, he advised his manager to experiment with sand versus pulverized stone to see which worked better:

> To ascertain the difference with certainty between the sand and pounded Stone take two pieces of Plank (plained, a foot square each will be sufficient) and paint them in the usual manner with whi[t]e lead gr[oun]d. In oil and after the first coat is dry give them a second (the paint a little thicker) and while it is fresh throw (the board standing perpendicular on one edge) sand against one, and pounded stone against the other, as long as they will stick, and till every part of the paint is well covered. You will then, when they are dry, be able to decide which will look best and most resemble stone.[110]

This letter demonstrates the subtlety of Washington's eye and the care he took in achieving a visual effect. Whether he used sand or pounded stone at Mount Vernon, the rustication was indeed intended to have the appearance of stone, in large part because the sand or pounded and sifted stone would have adhered to the surface of the paint, rather than being mixed in and therefore covered by the white paint. This delicate technique is difficult to maintain over time, but only the casting of sand or powdered stone on the surface of the paint would embody Washington's intentions and effectively mimic the visual appearance of stonework.

Washington later commented approvingly on the process of rustication, noting that the paint and sand help to preserve the wood itself from the elements. In not building a residence of bricks or real stone, Washington might have been motivated by the widespread belief that wooden houses were best for one's health. In his *Notes on the State of Virginia,* Jefferson pointed out the belief of his contemporaries in Virginia that wood buildings, being drier inside than stone or brick, were healthier for the inhabitants. Stone is, of course, more prestigious than wood or brick, and Washington himself made the decision to have a real stone "frontispiece" installed on his townhouses on Capitol Hill, in addition to the paint and sand applied to parts of the exterior of

FIGURE 2.28. Redwood Library, Newport, Rhode Island, c. 1748. The library, later expanded in the rear, was designed by merchant and architect Peter Harrison, based on Palladian English inspiration. The library's surface of wood, paint, and sand was meant to imitate fine stone, and Washington likely saw this building just before he applied such a surface to the expansion of his mansion in 1757–1759. Photo: Author.

those townhouses. Washington criticized wooden houses during his presidential travels, and Jefferson famously decried the wooden houses of Williamsburg.[111] In short, the rusticated wooden panels at Mount Vernon were an economical way to achieve a grand effect, preserve health, and protect the disguised wood itself.

Investigation of the structure has revealed that Washington turned to rustication in the expansion of 1757.[112] Paint and sand surfaces were hardly widespread in American architecture at that time but were far from unknown. Not long before adding the rustication, Washington had traveled to Newport and Boston and surely saw the treatment on the Redwood Library (Figure 2.28), and if he visited the home of Governor William Shirley in Roxbury he would have seen the idea applied there. The Isaac Royall House in Medford had a second primary facade made of rusticated boards. Much closer to home, there was a modest, rusticated house twenty miles away in Dumfries, Virginia—the Merchent House, now destroyed.[113] Unfortunately, there is no record of the sources for Washington's idea, and we have lost too much wooden architecture from the eighteenth century to confirm what may or may not have influenced him.

The use of false stone had been well known in European architecture since the Italian Renaissance, the effect achieved with textured stucco or via painted representation in fresco. There was little qualm in colonial America about falsifying interior and exterior surfaces, including painting faux grain on cheaper woods and marbleizing woodwork. Mount Pleasant in Philadelphia was covered in stucco scored to look like fine stone, and Robert Carter's Nomini Hall was made of brick covered with a stony white mortar.[114] Many houses of the time in the colonies, including wooden buildings, were painted "stone" colors, including off-whites, light greys, bluish-gray, and light greens. Part of the visual ambiance that Washington would have known was the painting of soft stone, especially sandstone, to preserve it and give it a color of one's choice, as was later done to the president's house (White House) in the District of Columbia. In 1771, the soft stone elements of the exterior of the Pohick Church, where Washington worshiped and served as a vestryman, were "painted with white Lead and Oyle" to help preserve it.[115] The rusticated effect at Mount Vernon impressed and sometime even deceived viewers. Even the sophisticated Samuel Powel thought that the mansion was made to look stone and "may easily be mistaken for it." John Singleton Copley Jr., son of the noted artist, visited Mount Vernon and wrote in 1795 of "the house . . . built of stone," while English visitor Joshua Brookes wrote in 1799 that "the house is of stone." Latrobe called the house "sanded," and Pennsylvanian Alexander Graydon, writing to his sister Rachel Graydon of Harrisburg in 1814, observed that "the house is wood though very much resembles stone being washed with a kind of white sand and lime."[116]

With a rusticated mansion house, Washington had to decide whether to use exterior shutters to protect his windows. Shutters appeared often on wooden houses but were somewhat less customary for stone. For decades, Washington avoided installing exterior shutters, and he only added them in the 1790s to protect the interiors from moisture and light. He did so gradually, adding shutters on the second story of the west front in 1796 after they proved useful on the ground floor of that facade.[117] Shutters are restored to the house today, as the goal is presently to make the house appear as it did in 1799, but they were a late and probably reluctant addition by Washington, who at first felt them to be vernacular and not ideally suited for what he hoped would be perceived to be a stone house.

The grandeur and pretense of the exterior is echoed by another effective feature of the mansion house at Mount Vernon: the octagonal cupola/lantern that caps the central part of the house (Plates 1 and 25). This was not an innovation on Washington's part, as it appears more frequently in American architecture than, say, rustication, and he could have seen a number of examples in the public and private realm. Still, it was special enough that it caught the attention of visitors. A cupola is redolent of public rather than domestic architecture, and Graydon pointed out its institutional character, saying that "on the top of the house is a Cupola not unlike the one on our Courthouse [in Pennsylvania], though not quite so large."[118] The cupola had the effect of elevating the mansion house at Mount Vernon above many other domestic residences in the region, and its placement on the hill overlooking the Potomac reinforced the quasi-public monumentality of the effect. Comparing Mount Vernon to a structure like the Public Hospital in Williamsburg (Figure 2.29) indicates the overall public qualities of the mansion at Mount Vernon and in turn underscores how institutional architecture of the time often resembled fine domestic architecture writ large.

After the rusticated boards and the cupola, both striking but neither unknown before, a novelty of the design at Mount Vernon was the open arcading of the arms of the covered ways. Arms, or hyphens, were not new in America in 1773. Arms connecting dependencies were planned but never built at Mann Page I's Rosewell (begun 1725), on the east bank of the York River near Williamsburg.[119] As in the

FIGURE 2.29. Public Hospital (reconstructed), Williamsburg, Virginia, 1771–1773, designed by Robert Smith. The basic lines and elements, when compared to Washington's house, indicate how the distinctions between elite domestic architecture and public, institutional building blurred during this era. Photo: Author.

models by Palladio himself, and following British practice, arms of the colonial American five-part plan were often interior spaces, as was the case with the hyphens of the typical Chesapeake or Maryland five-part plan, or there was a wall behind and an open arcade in the front. In an example of the latter formula, Landon Carter's Sabine Hall (by 1764) had, connecting the mansion house to the dependencies, long arms that were open on one side, forming long colonnaded "piazzas." Similar wings, with back walls and columns in front, also connected the mansion house to the dependencies at Drayton Hall (begun 1738) near Charleston, South Carolina.[120] At Mount Vernon in the 1750s, there were walls or fences, "running Walls for the Pallisades [fences]," standing between the house and dependencies on what is now the east lawn.[121] In the scheme developed in the 1770s, Washington installed the impressive "covered ways" that lacked the customary wall or walls.[122] This important innovation served to open up views toward the river and toward the groves seen between the square columns, and it has a strong effect on the visitor's experience of the place. Washington took the initiative to break with architectural tradition, thereby achieving a result that is ideal for the site and for his intentions. Although the colonnades are solidly architectural, the flat, unrusticated boards in the spandrels and the scantling in the ceiling added something of a vernacular touch, and he originally paved the ways in brick rather than stone. In addition—overlooking any discrepancies caused by later rebuilding and reconstruction of the colonnades—the length of the arches varied depending on their position, an unacademic touch similar to Washington's other "not quite orthodox" uses of the classical tradition.

A fourth major novelty of the mansion, and the most important for the history of American architecture, is the lofty colonnade overlooking the river view. This portico merits its own extended consideration; chapter 3 treats the style, sources, and uses of this important contribution to American architecture, and later chapters show how the portico functioned with relationship to the gardens and prospect of the Potomac.

Critical Fortunes

George Washington's house, as architecture, produced a mixed impression over time. The site, view, and gardens were widely admired, but the style and appearance of the mansion house were not always well received. Bryan Fairfax liked it because of its novelty, but not all contemporaries found it appealing, and its critical fortunes declined in the early nineteenth century.

Visitors' opinions even during Washington's lifetime were mixed. Agricultural reformer Richard Parkinson, fresh from England, noted at the end of the century that "the house is a very decent mansion: not large, and something like a gentleman's house in England, with gardens and plantations; and is very prettily situated on the banks of the Potowmac, with extensive prospects."[123] No less an authority on architecture than Benjamin Henry Latrobe, who had studied with John Soane and who visited Mount Vernon in 1796, stated that the "8 square pillars" were of "good proportions and effect."[124] There was, however, dissatisfaction with the house.

William Blount, an official from North Carolina, said in 1790, "The house is not elegant having originally been begun on too small a scale, but it is now very roomy and commodious and the dining room is very large and elegant." Baron von Steuben said that if "Washington were not a better general than he was an architect the affairs of America would be in a very bad condition."[125] When Revolutionary War general Nathanael Greene visited 13 September 1782, he noted that "house has more dignity than convenience in it," probably a reference to the floor plan that on the ground floor isolates rooms on the north and south additions. Abigail Adams reported that the house was not as grand as she anticipated and thought her own in Massachusetts to have a "handsomer front," larger rooms, and better furnishing. Charles Varlo, an Englishman visiting in October of 1784, was vaguely disappointed, saying that the house "is rather warm, snug, convenient, and useful, than ornamental. The size is what ought to suit a man of about two or three thousand [pounds] a year in England."[126]

David Humphreys, who was what we would call Washington's official biographer, and who knew Mount Vernon and the owner well, suggested that Washington himself was not happy with the architectural result of the mansion house. Humphreys noted that "the Mansion House itself, though much embellished by yet not perfectly satisfactory to the chaste taste of the present Possessor, appears venerable & convenient."[127] The application of the word "chaste" here perhaps implies that by 1789, when Humphreys was writing, Washington no longer accepted the more ornate styles of the earlier periods, including the Baroque and Rococo ornament of the early fireplace surrounds, or some of the earlier stucco work in the mansion. Thomas Jefferson referred to the "barbarous ornaments" of some of the public buildings in Williamsburg, referring to the kind of ornament widespread in the classical Baroque style of English architecture, and he, too, preferred a "chaste taste." Humphrey's remark suggests that Washington had come to share this sentiment. Washington himself made a comment along these lines when

he noted that, when considering replacing the mantelpieces in the West Parlor and Small Dining Room, he found them "so interwoven with the other parts of the Work and so good of their kind," that he let them stand. The phrase "so good of their kind" seems laudatory but implies that he thought them good examples of the outdated style, worth keeping because of the expense of replacement and because they were interwoven with the decoration of the rooms as a whole. As for the entirety of the house, its rooms felt, and still feel, somewhat cramped, and we can well believe Isaac Weld, who noted that Washington said that, rather than expanding, he should have torn the whole house down and started over. John Duncan echoed this sentiment in 1818—writing independently or having read Weld's account—when he stated that "report says" that Washington "subsequently regretted that he did not entirely rebuild it" rather than making partial alterations.[128] Other observers picked up on the old-fashioned proportions of the early rooms (several of the main ones dating to Lawrence's time) and seemed relieved by the spacious and up-to-date Large Dining Room, which was widely admired. Had he started from scratch, Washington would have avoided the asymmetry of the fenestration that came about during the two renovations of Lawrence's original structure.

Despite Washington's godlike reputation, it was inevitable that the reputation of the house as architecture would fall during the nineteenth century, when tastes changed. In 1810, Vermont native Elijah Fletcher, having moved to Virginia, passed through the Mount Vernon estate and wrote, "I did not find it so magnificent and extraordinary as I expected. It is truly a very pleasant place and commands a butiful [sic] prospect of the river and there are some very fine improvements about it. The house is in quite an old fashioned style but quite large."[129] Bostonian Sally Foster Otis, who herself lived in a residence built by the avant-garde architect Charles Bulfinch, praised the siting and romantic appearance of the mansion house in 1801. The house was "antique like the inhabitants" but also "capacious and substantial." She declared that the "wings are more modern," perceptively suggesting that the open arcading was a progressive aspect of the building. Mrs. Otis complained that the "chamber where he died" and his study and dressing room have "nothing to distinguish them from the chambers of any other house." For Manasseh Cutler in 1802, the house and gardens "were not in so high a style as I expected to have found them." Clearly, some visitors wanted to believe that the hero Washington dwelled in more spacious or stylish surroundings than they found at his country seat.[130] Englishman Sir Augustus John Foster declared that the mansion house was the only one in the area "that I had yet seen which resembles a Chateau," but there was "only one good Room in the House," presumably the Large Dining Room. Scotsman John Duncan called the house "old fashioned," and "perhaps not a very comfortable residence," but "sacred" because of its former owner.[131] Pierre-Étienne Du Ponceau, writing in 1837 of his visit of 1780, opined that "the house at that time might be considered handsome and perhaps elegant but at present the most that can be said of it is that it is a modest habitation, quite in keeping with the idea that we have of Cincinnatus and of those of the other great commanders of the Roman Republic."[132]

Observers in subsequent generations, including recent architectural historians, have generally held a favorable impression of the house, its siting, and its importance in the history of American architecture. Like the adjacent gardens, it was much visited and admired. Its image has been often captured in the visual arts, and the architecture echoed in numerous copies and variant copies, particularly during the Colonial Revival period in the twentieth century. The portico was perhaps the aspect most admired and copied over time; in the next chapter we look at the history of the porch in America and explore Washington's grand colonnade.

CHAPTER THREE

George Washington's Portico

The mansion house [has] . . . a capacious open Piazza towards the water, supported by a proper number of pillars, very lofty and majestic columns.

WINTHROP SARGENT, 13 October 1793

THE MONUMENTAL PORTICO on the east side of the house at Mount Vernon is Washington's greatest contribution to American architecture (Figure 3.1; Plates 3 and 15). In any consideration of his aesthetic interests, it holds a chief place because of its originality, fame, and key role as mediator of house and landscape. The magnificent portico stood out for visitors as the most striking and impressive aspect of the expanded design. Viewers of the time called this porch a "portico" or "piazza," and Washington himself also described it as a "colonnade" or "gallery."[1] The octastyle portico is in the colossal, Tuscan order. The square columns are slender, in about a 13:1 ratio of height to width, rather than the Renaissance ratio of 7:1 more commonly used for this order. Had Washington borrowed from any book on architecture that illustrated ancient Roman, Italian Renaissance, or English porticoes, or had he looked at the few American examples of the large domestic portico, he might have arrived at a more academic and mainstream design: a portico capped by a pediment covering only the central part of the building rather than the full width, perhaps with four or six columns across, the whole structure standing on a raised platform approached by stairs. But with its combination of the colossal order and the full extent across the facade, there was no other porch like it in America.

We have no early drawing for the east front and no letters from Washington to his managers about the portico before its construction. As evidence that a portico was planned early on, Washington's draft for the basement level (see Figure 2.4) shows five rooms (three of them

FIGURE 3.1. View of the riverfront of Mount Vernon. The view of the east facade, portico, and lawn later became a favorite of American artists. Photo: Author.

were built, with vaulting) beneath what would be the porch flooring, and the basement needed a portico overhead to help keep off rainwater. Instructions or permission for using the Tuscan order must have come from Washington, but as he was absent from the estate during the war, a craftsman or manager Lund Washington must have chosen the design source. Although Washington initially paved the colonnade with some local hard stone, he sought an even finer material and spent great effort acquiring fancy paving stones from England. He wanted them at least one foot square, but he told agent John Rumney Jr. in 1785 that the final size should depend on Rumney's sense of the "taste of the times" in England.[2] The previous year, Washington had asked wealthy Philadelphian William Hamilton for advice about cementing binder but indicated that he wanted stone or whatever "will stand the weather." Hamilton told Washington about his own floor of variegated (probably alternating) colors,

and for a while Washington sought a black and white checkered pattern, but economy and availability of stone led him to settle for one off-white color, close to the paving today (which is entirely replaced).[3] When he finally got his "Flaggs" (flagstones) from England, he was unhappy that they were not as polished as the sample he had received: "The Flags came very reasonably and will answer my purposes very well though the workman did not keep to the sample in two or three respects—particularly on the thickness, and dressing of the Stones—some not being more than ¾ of an inch thick (scarcely that on one side) and none with the same polish of the pattern—enough however may be picked out of the whole to floor my Gallery which is all I wanted." Washington was interested in having the portico's details right, and in general he was aware of measurements and proportions, so either it was a rare case of forgetting or he wanted to impress Hamilton when he exaggerated the length by at least several feet and reported that the porch was one hundred feet long and "ten or twelve" feet wide.[4]

The structural stability of the porch and its paving was also important to the basement level underneath. The paving lies atop three subterranean rooms, each with a brick barrel vault, the vaults running lengthwise parallel to the house.[5] The basement of the mansion house is composed of brick and soft stone that dates from the earlier versions of the house, and George Washington seems to have moved or otherwise repurposed some of the stone that Lawrence Washington had placed there. The poor qualities of the Aquia Creek sandstone elsewhere in parts of the basement must have argued against its further use in the foundation, and in building the three vaults Washington chose to use brick. Similar vaulting appears elsewhere in Tidewater building; at Shirley Plantation in Virginia, archaeology shows that a barrel vault was used under the original narrower porch there. The impressive series of barrel vaulted chambers at Mount Vernon make an almost classical Roman series of spaces and are useful for storage, the vaults being accessed through the long corridor that runs through the basement. Washington covered the vaults with a layer of mortar, forming the base for the paving stones of the portico.[6]

Sources in Europe and America

George Washington's portico was innovative in the Anglo-American tradition in being a full-length, domestic porch in the colossal order. Many modern writers assume that porches were highly unusual in colonial America and that Washington knew only a limited range of them, including, for example, porticoes on houses that he might have seen during his brief trip to Barbados when he was nineteen, bookplates representing English or Italian Renaissance buildings, or some Tidewater houses thought to have had one-story porches.[7] The consensus opinion of scholars is that "porches were just beginning to be used in America at the time, but Washington could have seen nothing conceived on this scale, or at any rate diligent research has failed to uncover any even

vaguely similar examples."[8] While there is no portico exactly like Washington's in American architecture, there was a rich and varied tradition of porches already by his time, and, despite its relative novelty, Mount Vernon's portico had various precedents. These models fall into several categories: pre-Georgian loggias, galleries, and porches in England, Virginia, and Maryland; vernacular and high-style domestic porches in Georgian architecture in England and colonial America; ethnic, non-Anglo domestic porches in America; public and commercial buildings in the colonies, including such structures as courthouses and taverns; and Asian porches as they appear in chinaware and are interpreted in Anglo-American wallpaper, japanned furniture, and other decorative arts.

In the pre-Georgian tradition, open loggias, often with a garden orientation, were used in sixteenth- and seventeenth-century English and colonial American architecture. The medieval cloister, with its stone walkways and arcaded galleries facing a central garden or yard, ultimately stands at the origins of this tradition, which was updated in Britain in the sixteenth century and later by a conscious desire to imitate the one-sided, outward-facing porticoes of antiquity and Renaissance Europe. Rather than constructing only enclosed arcades, as were characteristic of the medieval period, English Renaissance builders often utilized the portico for viewing a more distant prospect. Porticoes came to form impressive aspects of mansion facades and were visible from a distance. According to architectural historian Paula Henderson, covered but open galleries "were incorporated into most early Tudor royal houses as means of communication between buildings or as sheltered walks extending into gardens;" by the seventeenth century, in addition to the term "loggia," "the words 'cloister,' 'gallery' or 'open gallery,' and 'terrace' or 'open terrace' were used," and the practice expanded.[9]

The earliest known English loggia built along these lines was at Horton Court (Gloucestershire) and dates to about 1530 (Figure 3.2). This structure, commissioned by owner

William Knight in his garden's estate, was always a free-standing outbuilding.[10] Knight had studied and traveled in Italy and would have known classical garden *loggie* from his visit there. The Italian tradition of the garden loggia was long established by 1530, and its use was already recommended in the fifteenth century by theorist and architect Leon Battista Alberti, who noted in Book 9 of his *De re aedificatoria* (1485) that in a villa "there should be gardens full of delightful plants, and a garden portico, where you can enjoy both sun and shade."[11] Ultimately, the portico at Mount Vernon forms part of this long-standing European building practice, which passed to Britain and then her colonies.

The loggia at Horton Court is an early example of the English tradition of the classicizing garden arcade, later versions of which were usually not freestanding but were built as part of larger architectural complexes. In high-style, domestic projects in Tudor and Jacobean England, extensive loggias (also called galleries and terraces, although the former term also referred to long, interior rooms) appeared with frequency. Hardwick Hall (built 1590–1597) is graced with an octastyle loggia on the entrance front and paving stones set near ground level, the porch being about fifteen feet in depth (Figure 3.3). Not unlike the portico at Mount Vernon, such a loggia was quite long, had paved floors set at just above ground level, and served as garden fronts and offered natural vistas. The Holland House in London, designed by John Thorpe for Sir Walter Cope in the early seventeenth century, sported an open, three-sided porch on the ground floor and an open viewing platform above. The nearby Camden House, also designed by Thorpe, had a long seven-bay porch, called in the architect's drawing of the second scheme a "terrazo," which faced the rear toward the gardens. Cranborne Manor, designed by William Arnold c. 1609, had a rear "tarris" (terrace) supported by twelve freestanding piers.[12] Many of these porches were set between wings or projecting pavilions, but at Cranborne Manor—like Mount Vernon later—the portico protruded from the mansion house itself.

FIGURE 3.2. Ambulatory, Horton Court, Gloucestershire, England, c. 1530. Built for William Knight, this is the earliest known English example of the Renaissance garden loggia, a precursor to the portico at Mount Vernon. Photo: J. Petty.

In addition to garden fronts, some of these loggias adorned entrance facades. A few mansions had both kinds of loggias, as did Old Hall of Nether Hambleton (built c. 1600–1610). Similarly, there are multiple loggias at Houghton House (c. 1615), one of which is on a garden facade and is built with a fine Tuscan order.[13] Thus, even by the 1620s, when Inigo Jones constructed the inset, second-story portico at the Queen's House in Greenwich, there was a venerable tradition of the loggia in England, and these often had the

FIGURE 3.3. Hardwick Hall, Derbyshire, England, 1590–1597, designed by Robert Smythson, built for Bess of Hardwick. Open galleries facing gardens or other views were widespread in Britain as early as the late sixteenth and seventeenth centuries. Photo: Kevin Sinclair.

purpose of offering easy access to an adjacent garden and providing prospects of the landscape. Such loggias began to go out of fashion during the seventeenth century, but in the eighteenth century, under the influence of Palladianism, other kinds of more purely Renaissance porticoes arose, continuing and reinvigorating the tradition of the open gallery. No porch in the colossal order was constructed in pre-Georgian England, but colossal pilasters did appear during that time in domestic architecture as facade ornament. The Georgian porch in the colossal order would become rather widespread, setting an immediate precedent for Mount Vernon. The giant order appeared as early as the sixteenth century in Kirby Hall (Northamptonshire), which was begun in 1570. Even beyond application of the colossal order in pre-Georgian England, a number of English mansions of the pre-eighteenth-century period had superimposed orders, which was another way of expressing *magnificentia*. At Hatfield House, home of Robert Cecil, chief minister to James I (1607–1612), the superimposed orders, open loggia, and broad extent (eight bays) exemplified for contemporaries a noble house front.[14]

Such garden loggias might seem far removed from the world of George Washington, who never traveled to England. Accounts by a host of witnesses indicate, however, that Washington was curious and liked to question visitors from afar for detailed information about weather, geography, crops, and many other subjects. There is every reason to think that he would have known about the significant traditions of formal English architecture, including that loggias and galleries were not uncommon in fine mansions in Britain and provided prospects of gardens and waterways. From the Fairfaxes, his half-brother Lawrence, or many others who had traveled or lived abroad, Washington could easily have learned that great men in England built long loggias on their front or garden facades, using impressive architectural design and details.

The facade with open gallery had found expression in Virginia near Jamestown in a prominent building well known by George Washington. Green Spring, built as the home of Virginia governor William Berkeley (d. 1677), was graced with a garden loggia in the English taste, the style and place-

FIGURE 3.4. Benjamin Latrobe, *View of Greenspring House,* July 1796, pencil, pen and ink, and watercolor on paper, 7″ × 10.25″. Latrobe recorded the altered mansion house that Washington would have known from his visits. Courtesy of The Maryland Historical Society (1960.108.1.2.33).

ment reminiscent of the porches of prodigy houses and other British country mansions of the late sixteenth and early seventeenth centuries. The structure, of which only foundational traces remain today, consisted of an original house datable to 1643–1645, and an extensive addition, built by the 1670s.[15] On this addition was an open gallery formed of thick piers and round arches; above it there was likely a wooden platform that served as either a long open deck or an actual covered portico. The loggia appears in a view of the house from 1683 by county surveyor John Soane which seems to show a balustrade or crenellated low wall above the long ground-level loggia. No roof or wooden porch above appears in that schematic view of 1683, but these are seen in a watercolor by Benjamin Henry Latrobe from 1796 (Figure 3.4). Whether this roof was original to the seventeenth-century structure or was a later refinement (as is more likely), Latrobe shows the whole complex in a dilapidated state in the last years of the eighteenth century, and there is little reason to think that it was not present during George Washington's visits. He saw the house as early as 1754 when he attended a meeting there concerning his military commis-

sion; he may well have also visited later.[16] For Washington, the sight of a full-length loggia in such a genteel setting must have made a strong impression.

Green Spring was no ordinary house. In 1679, Berkeley's widow boasted that it was "the finest seat in America and the only tollerable place for a Governour." Cary Carson has described it as "the country's first fully developed English country house set in an expansive park-like landscape."[17] Despite the grand and—what seems to our eyes—somewhat forbidding appearance, the mansion was originally sited well in elegant surroundings, and visitors and residents had easy access to the arcuated brick loggia from the grounds of the estate, following English tradition. This whole garden facade was calculated to impress, to offer access to rooms on two levels, and to provide a second-story porch or platform deck for viewing the garden. Carson described the loggia in a way reminiscent of the form and function of the portico at Mount Vernon:

The loggia, arcaded below and no doubt balustraded above, ran the full length of the new structure. At its center a handsome divided staircase rose from the garden to the platform that roofed the loggia. From the top of the stairs the entrance led through a two-story, open-sided brick porch . . . [Berkeley's loggia] overlooked the garden. When he and his guests tired of strolling along the paths, they climbed the staircase and stepped out on the gallery-like loggia to gaze down on the garden from above. In effect, it was a roofless belvedere affording fine perspective view of the parterres below and probably Berkeley's famous deer park in the distance.[18]

The portico at Mount Vernon shared a purpose and even a rough appearance with Green Spring, as it did with British, pre-Georgian garden loggias.

In considering other pre-Georgian houses from the Tidewater region, we are missing out on the fuller picture of the precedents for Mount Vernon if we ignore the presence of some smaller tower-porches that were open to the air. These did not look like the portico at Mount Vernon, but their usage suggests the complexity of the early evolution and development of the portico in Virginia. In American documents of the seventeenth and early eighteenth centuries, "porch" usually signified an enclosed towerlike protrusion from the plane of the facade. In New England and New York, the porch typically projected from the central chimney bay, while in Virginia and Maryland (with the chimneys often located at the ends), the porch was often an extension of a larger space or passageway in the center part of the house. Given the warmer weather in the South, and the essential spatial continuity of the porch with the rest of the house, there was some inducement to open up the porch tower to the elements, at least at the lower level. This did not happen often. The porches at such places as Arthur Allen's mansion, later dubbed Bacon's Castle (1665; Surry County, Virginia), remained enclosed, as did many others that are now lost but whose appearances are known from photographs or early drawn and painted views. These porches often sheltered a staircase or else typically contained an entrance space below and a chamber ("porch chamber") above, all protected by a door and walled in from the elements.

At least a small number of Chesapeake area porches were open to the exterior to some extent on the ground level, ef-fectively creating what we would call a porch in the modern sense of a covered, open-to-the-air space abutting a house. For a semi-open wooden porch in which the apertures were apparently permanent, we have the evidence of Bond Castle in Calvert County, Maryland. Early photographic record shows the lower level somewhat exposed to the air; apertures through the grillwork of turned spindles on three walls make this a semi-open porch. This is a small-scale and, by English standards, vernacular expression of the open tower porch, which was quite widespread in Britain, and which also appeared in America in public buildings, including the Maryland State House in St. Mary's City (1676), the late seventeenth-century State House in Annapolis (destroyed 1704), and the second State House there, built c. 1707. A brick house with a similar porch space opened partially to the elements was Malvern Hill in Henrico County, Virginia. Based on the evidence of its ruins and on early photography, the porch was open at the ground level with three arches and offered an elevated area for seating on either side (Figure 3.5).[19]

In a description that recalls the porches of Bond Castle and Malvern Hill, William Fairfax apparently mentions such partially open porches in a 1735 letter to his cousin Robert Fairfax back home in England: "Dear Cosen . . . a Plan for your House will be very acceptable in which I shall beg your Assistance. They build their Houses here very low, their best bedchambers being below Stairs over head is little better than Garrets. They have a large Porch before the Door & generally another behind the House, in one of which or Hall & passage they always sit & frequently dine & sup. but the Musquetoes there are very troublesome."[20] Unless he was merely alluding to the practice of leaving the doors of a tower-porch open, the letter implies that some porches were open to the air. Other early documents suggest the opening up of a tower-porch at the ground level. In 1742, a house in Prince George County was built to have two porches "six feet square closed on each side," implying that the front was left open.[21] Unlike Green Spring's extended loggia, these small, open or perforated porches did not form a compelling

FIGURE 3.5. Malvern Hill (reconstruction based on early photos), Henrico County, Virginia, c. 1690–1697, built for Thomas Cocke. Seventeenth-century domestic architecture in the Chesapeake included some open porches such as this one. From Henry Forman, *Architecture of the Old South* (Cambridge, Mass., 1948), 84, fig. 110.

visual model for Washington's Mount Vernon and its extensive, classicizing colonnade. Still, the act of sitting on a porch—even in the pre-1740 sense of a tower-porch—and experiencing the breeze, weather, and (less pleasantly) mosquitoes was accommodated even by the earlier architecture of Washington's Virginia, and these porches deserve mention here.

Among other earlier traditions, enclosed galleries also preceded the form and function of the open gallery / portico at Mount Vernon. The long indoor gallery was a widespread feature of elite architecture in Britain in the sixteenth through the eighteenth centuries, used for the display of paintings, entertainment, and other purposes. These were not common in the colonies, but William Byrd II of Westover (1674–1744) sometimes recorded that in cold weather he walked not in the garden or on the grounds of his plantation but in his "gallery."[22] (He was referring to an earlier house

at Westover that was gone by the mid-eighteenth century; how it looked is unknown.) He likely meant a long interior room, which in itself would have been a rarity in the colonies. On 9 February 1740, Byrd noted: "I walked in the gallery and had the pleasure to see it [the snow] thaw." That he used the room for walking during severely cold weather indicates that it was most likely a protected, inside space.[23] George Washington, who sometimes called his portico a "gallery," likely had never seen this particular room on William Byrd II's estate, but Byrd's writings make it clear that long galleries were known in Virginia well before Washington, useful for walking and entertaining, as well as conveying prestige.

The loggias of Tudor and Jacobean England, Green Spring's impressive portico, semi-open tower porches in the Tidewater area, and long interior galleries all influenced Washington's invention at Mount Vernon. But the most immediate and determinative influence was the Anglo-American portico of the Georgian period. This type of porch includes the long vernacular "piazza" as well as the high-style, Palladian temple-front porticoes constructed in the years before Washington's expansion of his home in the 1770s. In the fifteen years before the 1773 additions to Mount Vernon, as well as afterward, a number of substantial houses in America were built incorporating impressive porticoes. The belief had apparently become widespread in America, as it certainly had been in England, that an important man's building would gain prominence by having a large portico, and there was vigorous competition among gentlemen to build substantial and fine porches.

As the English were keenly aware, there was a tradition in Roman antiquity of villas with long porticoes facing the prospects of sea and landscape, as described by Pliny the Younger in the first century A.D. and as confirmed by archaeology and by images in wall paintings discovered at Pompeii and Herculaneum. The increasing knowledge of such a classical tradition, which itself was imitated during the Italian Renaissance, left its mark in Britain.[24] It cannot be ruled out that Washington knew of the ancient practice of the grand villa colonnade, and his portico at Mount Vernon may well have been a conscious reflection of this kind of ancient Roman *porticus.* At any rate, with the tradition rooted in antiquity, the extensive portico appears often in Renaissance building and is illustrated in sixteenth-century printed books, notably Andrea Palladio's *Quattro libri dell'architettura* (*Four Books of Architecture*). In considering domestic models, Allan Greenberg has suggested that Washington possibly knew the Villa Serego at Santa Sofia, Plate 49 from Book 2 of Palladio's text, which has a two-story, colossal octastyle portico.[25] Even if Washington did not know this particular plate, the popularity of Palladio's book in the Anglo-American world meant that word-of-mouth information about building in antiquity and Renaissance Italy was widespread.

The long colonnade appeared on some fine homes in the classical manner in seventeenth and eighteenth-century England, continuing and updating the pre-Georgian loggia/gallery tradition. As early as 1610, before Inigo Jones practiced his Renaissance style in England, John Osborne planned his Salisbury House Porticus, an unbuilt colossal portico that showed an immediate application of ideas from antiquity. Still, one would have to wait until the eighteenth century for actual construction of more studied and classicizing forms of the portico/colonnade. Some of these were colonnaded wings on such a large scale that they gave a more monumental effect than the smaller and lower covered ways with columns found in America. John Vanbrugh's monumental Blenheim Palace (finished by 1722) for the first Duke of Marlborough has, in addition to front and back temple-front porticoes in the colossal order, two lengthy, large-scale porticoes that face the entrance courtyard. At Canons (or Cannons), built by James Brydges, first Duke of Chandos in Middlesex, the colossal order, rusticated facade, and longitudinal emphasis (including six columns placed near the facade) were in the spirit of Roman antiquity.[26] Even closer to the time of Mount Vernon are the porticoes at Stowe, expanded by Earl Temple in 1771–1779 and given lengthy north colonnaded arms around 1772.[27] Just as he knew that a gentleman's rural house should be built of stone (or at least appear to be of stone), sport a cupola, have wings and dependencies, and be surrounded by a significant garden, Washington was likely aware of some recent English examples of the long, classicizing colonnade on country mansions.

In addition to these long, high-style porticoes in England, there were in America more modestly styled and scaled long porches. The climate that fostered the veranda in the West Indies in the eighteenth century also encouraged the development of the piazza and balcony in Georgia, the Carolinas, and Virginia.[28] Even for earlier in the century, there is fairly substantial evidence in the southern colonies for the presence of extensive one-story porches, which were often sited with a garden or river view. Long porches, two-story porches, and balconies were found in the Carolinas in domestic residences, usually on the sides of the houses but also on the backs and fronts. These were being built as early as 1700, when a law was passed in Charleston, South Carolina, that piazzas had to be restricted in depth. In the 1730s, two open porches of uncertain width are documented on South Carolina parsonage houses. George Milligen Johnston, an English physician, noted in the 1760s that of the 1,100 dwelling houses in Charleston, "many of them have a genteel Appearance, though generally incumbered with Balconies or Piazzas." As for structures known to have long porticoes, a house was put up for sale in 1748 in Charleston with "a piazza 12 feet wide [deep] and 48 long paved with good square stone."[29]

By 1765, naturalist John Bartram noted in his diary that "ye inhabitants of both Carolinas & Georgia generaly buildes piazas on [written "or"] one or more sides of thair houses, which is very commodious in these hot climates[.] thay screen of[f] ye violent scorching sunshine & draws ye breese finely & it must be extream hot indeed if one cant sit or walk very comfortably in these when out of employ[.] & much conversation both sitting & walking is held in these." Similarly, John's son, William, noted in April of 1774 that in Sunbury, Georgia, "there are about one hundred houses in the Town neatly built of wood framed, having pleasant Piasas round them. the inhabitants are genteel & wealthy, either Merchants, or Planters from the Country who resort here in the Summer & Autum[n]."[30] Washington, although he had not traveled there himself, might have learned from conversations with others about such Carolina and Georgia porches and heard about their considerable length, square stone paving, and commodious character.

Closer to home for Washington than the Carolinas were extensive porches in the Chesapeake area. One house with such a portico was advertised for sale in the *Virginia Gazette* (August 1766):

> To be sold to the highest bidder, on Monday the 10th of November next (if fair, otherwise next fair day) at the house of Capt. Fox, in Port Royal, A beautiful tract of Land, situated on Rappahannock river, about half a mile below Port Royal, con-

taining 700 acres, on which is a very good brick house one story high, 4 rooms and 3 closets on the lower floor, and 2 above, a good cellar under it, a portico 52 feet long and 8 wide facing the river, a 12 foot porch on the front side, a good kitchen and laundry with a brick chimney, a garden 200 feet square paled in with sawed pales, poplar rails, and cedar posts, a good strong barn 40 by 20 floored and cieled with plank, with two 8 feet sheds, and all other convenient out-houses; also the best shad and herring fishery on the river, with a good fish house on the shore . . . —Lawrance Taliaferro.[31]

The seller must have assumed that buyers knew the nature and usefulness of the "portico," as this element is featured in the description. On the other side from the portico was a "porch"; this was perhaps a tower-porch in the older sense of the word, but it could also have been an open, one-story porch, since no porch chamber above is mentioned in the advertisement.

That the Taliaferro portico was not unusual in Virginia is suggested by a reference to a domestic, early eighteenth-century porch in Mason Locke Weems's life of George Washington. Weems, the parson whose early bestseller spawned a number of the great Washington legends, is notably untrustworthy, and one cannot rely on the veracity of the details of any of his accounts. Still, it is clear that Weems assumed his readers in 1800 understood that a piazza was a characteristic architectural form for a Virginia house in the 1730s. In a fanciful anecdote, Weems describes a porch at Washington's boyhood home:

> "I dreamt," said the Mother of Washington, "that I was sitting in the piazza of a large new house, into which we had but lately moved. George, at that time about five years old, was in the garden with his cornstalk plough, busily running little furrows in the sand, in imitation of Negro Dick, a fine black boy, with whose ploughing George was so delighted that it was sometimes difficult to get him to his dinner. And so as I was sitting in the piazza at my work, I suddenly heard in my dream a kind of roaring noise on the eastern side of the house."[32]

Traveler Isaac Weld confirmed that, by the time Weems was writing, Tidewater houses often sported porches, and

FIGURE 3.6. *View of Holly Hill,* overmantel painting, oil on panel, by 1733, probably c. 1723–1729, signed "AS," Holly Hill, Friendship, Maryland (mansion house first built in 1698, and enlarged in 1713 and again by 1733), built for Samuel Harrison. This early painting shows a Tidewater mansion with a garden porch; real or imaginary, the view indicates the aspirations of the time for a classical portico. Courtesy of the Colonial Williamsburg Foundation and the Clagett Family.

Weems implied that the portico in the area long predated the Revolution.[33] Of course, he was describing a dream house, not a real one, but it is significant that Weems expected his readers to share the belief that a piazza was a normal part of a house built in Virginia more than sixty years before. In this tradition of vernacular building, George Washington designed two modest houses in Bath, Virginia, in 1784, the structures intended to include full-length porches seven feet deep on two levels: "The dwelling House is to be 36 feet by 24, with a gallery of 7 feet on each side of the House, the whole fronts . . . galleries above also." These projected houses formed part of a building practice that went back much further in Tidewater tradition.[34]

Tidewater houses with full-length porticoes were hardly widespread before the Revolution. In addition to the Taliaferro house, however, the presence of a long portico in the Chesapeake region is indicated in a painting that must predate 1733, and perhaps dates to the 1720s, of Holly Hill, built

by Samuel Harrison in Anne Arundel County, Maryland.[35] Holly Hill's early appearance is recorded in an extant overmantel painting now in situ there (Figure 3.6). The house, which still stands in altered form, is shown in the picture as brick, a story and half high, and with the Georgian features of dormers and sash windows with rectangular panes. The porch, resting on paving stones, turns the corner, and two darker columns frame the entrance door to the wing on the right added in the 1720s. There is no existing porch like this on the house, and because the portico supports were apparently not integral to the framing, it is difficult to establish the painting's veracity. Even if it were a product of the artist's fantasy, the painting indicates aspirations of the Tidewater elite and records the transmission of ideas from England, where extended, ground-level loggias and porches had long been widespread in fine architecture, as we have seen. The Holly Hill painting is linked, as was Mount Vernon's porch, to the English upper-class tradition of the long country portico.

Another long "piazza" in a fine style is recorded from the colonial period, but it is no longer extant. In 1765, Landon Carter gave his mansion house, Sabine Hall (Richmond County, Virginia), two piazzas graced with fine capitals carved of stone. Carter noted in his diary that he had borrowed the carver who had worked for Col. John Tayloe at nearby Mount Airy: "Colo. Tayloe's stone cutter Ralph finis[hed] 16 Capitols for my Piazzas and went away home at night." One of Carter's piazzas connected the mansion house to a secondary kitchen building, while the other one, more interesting for our purposes, "extended the 60-foot length of the main core of Sabine Hall."[36] This single-story portico faced the adjacent river and must have given a classical air to the Georgian mansion house, which still stands, although the only remaining portico there was constructed in the 1820s.

The lengthy covered loggia/gallery/piazza also appeared in the British colonies before Washington's time in the form of inset loggias. This type again has deep roots in early English building practice, and a characteristic example is the long inset loggia at Godolphin in Cornwall, built in the 1630s. In an American manifestation of this form, Tudor Hall (St. Mary's County, Maryland) was originally (c. 1760) endowed with an inset loggia (now altered) of seven bays.[37] A similar house was the home of botanist and naturalist John Bartram, built between 1731 and 1770 outside Philadelphia, with an inset porch and a colossal order of vernacular stone columns. Such inset loggias were stylistic cousins of Mount Vernon's east colonnade.

George Washington's eye and his competitive spirit were shaped not only by awareness of lengthy loggias but also by narrower porticoes. To be sure, such porticoes, whether one story or two, did not bear strong visual resemblance to Washington's porch, as these porticoes were restricted in width compared to Washington's and usually sported a pediment, but the scale and fine effect were—like his—imposing and were similarly linked to the expansion of classical architectural forms in the Anglo-American world. Washington's lofty colonnade at Mount Vernon was a calculated response

to this expansion of the high-style portico in fine colonial American homes in the two decades before the Revolution. Such fine porticoes included that of Charles Carroll at Mount Clare in Baltimore County, Maryland.[38] Nomini Hall, home of the great landholder Robert Carter III, had two impressive, colossal porches.[39] Near this time (1770), Thomas Jefferson designed his two-story, Palladian portico for Monticello, some columns for which remain on the present east portico that he redesigned in the later 1780s after his stay in France. Richard Sprigg's Strawberry Hill in Annapolis had a large portico, and Horatio Sharpe's nearby Whitehall was among the few residences in colonial America to be built with a freestanding, colossal temple-front portico. Shirley, the James River plantation house of Charles Carter, had a portico, as indicated by archaeological study (but a smaller porch than is present today), and the Harrison family's Brandon (c. 1765) also had a one-story portico that graced the center block of the sprawling Palladian villa.[40]

Mount Airy is another impressive Palladian villa design, with a main stone mansion house, two curved arms, and dependencies on either side. There are two porches of sorts, formed of insets at the ground level on each main facade.[41] Pediments and pilasters on the central pavilions on each side suggest classical temple fronts. A lofty porch facing a river stands in the Roger Morris House in Manhattan (designed 1765); even if the present porch was rebuilt in the Federal period, it is likely that there was some sort of porch as part of the giant order from the beginning. A recent structural analysis provides good evidence that The Woodlands in Philadelphia, which was restored and expanded by William Hamilton in the 1780s, already had a porch around 1770; the still-surviving riverfront portico is in the Renaissance tradition of the colossal, central, raised temple-front porch (Figure 3.7). Washington visited Philadelphia in 1773, just before designing his own porch, and could have seen this impressive, tetrastyle portico on a visit or from a boat trip on the Schuylkill River.[42] Some of these Georgian porticoes were rather extensive in length, as much as half the width of

FIGURE 3.7. The Woodlands, Philadelphia, Pennsylvania, earlier house expanded by builder William Hamilton, c. 1770 and later. Hamilton built a colossal portico facing the Schuylkill River. The residence was well known to Washington before the second expansion of his mansion house at Mount Vernon. Photo: Author.

a facade. Before designing his own portico, Washington could not have seen Drayton Hall (for John Drayton, 1738–1742) outside Charleston, South Carolina, but he perhaps knew the plans for the now destroyed Lansdowne (Philadelphia), which had an extensive two-story porch.[43] That there was a rush to build porticoes in the years before the Revolution indicates the increasing formality of style and heightened competition among elite builders in late colonial America.

Of special interest in this discussion is George Mason's Gunston Hall, seven miles distant from Mount Vernon. Mason was in close contact with Washington, and each knew the other's estate well. Gunston Hall is more modest in scale than Washington's home after 1773, but a number of connections remain between the estates. Mason maintained a deer park, a garden embellishment later adopted for a time by Washington, and his mansion house offered a fine prospect of the land and Potomac beyond his formal garden and deer park. Mason's house, the main body of which dates to c. 1755–1759, was embellished by William Buckland and William Bernard Sears, who crafted woodwork for the dining room and other formal rooms. Sears later worked for Washington at Mount Vernon. Buckland designed for Mason

a garden porch facing the Potomac (Figure 3.8). Built in the latest, fashionable, Chippendale-Gothic taste, this little porch was hardly a stylistic model for Washington's portico, but the fine form, the advantage the portico takes of the river view, and its engagement with the garden would not have escaped the notice of Mason's neighbor.[44]

An aspect of the portico at Mount Vernon that gives it its special character is the colossal order. The colossal (or giant) order, in which the columns or pilasters extend for more than one story, never appeared in pure form in antiquity. Unknown to the Greeks, it was occasionally adumbrated by the Imperial Romans (e.g., the Temple of Bacchus at Baalbek). Leon Battista Alberti employed the colossal order in hybrid form on the facade of Sant'Andrea in Mantua in 1470, but it was not fully embraced in Renaissance architecture until Michelangelo Buonarroti used it in the 1530s (Campidoglio, Rome). When influential architects such as Andrea Palladio and Sebastiano Serlio utilized the colossal order and illustrated it in their published books, the form became widely diffused in Continental and, later, British building.

George Washington would have known the colossal order as a new and prestigious form in American domestic architecture. Perhaps he never saw the Charles Pinckney House in Charleston, South Carolina, graced with colossal pilasters (1746; now destroyed), but other houses in the giant order would have been well known by him. Some of the other Georgian houses mentioned above used the giant order in their porticoes, including Whitehall, near Annapolis; and The Woodlands in Philadelphia. When Washington went in 1758 to visit Governor Shirley in Massachusetts to protest British military interference with his exercise of authority in the Virginia Regiment, he perhaps went to the governor's home in Roxbury, a mansion with colossal engaged pilasters (Figure 3.9).[45] He might have seen, or heard about, the colossal order of Ionic pilasters on the Isaac Royall House in Medford, Massachusetts. Nearly contemporary with the 1770s expansion of Mount Vernon was the John Vassall House (later Vassall-Longfellow House) in Cambridge, a mansion Wash-

FIGURE 3.8. Gunston Hall, Lorton, Virginia, 1750s, built for George Mason; garden portico designed by William Buckland. Washington's neighbor George Mason built two porticoes on the mansion house, including this Gothic-style porch on the garden front. Photo: Author.

FIGURE 3.9. Shirley Mansion, ascribed to Peter Harrison, Roxbury, Massachusetts, c. 1747–1751, built for William Shirley. By midcentury it was becoming increasingly wide-spread in the colonies for elite residences to have columns or pilasters in the giant order, part of the stylistic back-ground to Washington's colossal porch at Mount Vernon. Photo: Tim Sackton.

FIGURE 3.10. Mount Vernon, paving of the portico (rebuilt), original from the 1780s. The paving has been replaced more than once since Washington's day, but the present Whitehaven tiles correspond to the color, size, and source of the original flagstones. Photo: Author.

ington commandeered as his headquarters in 1775 and which is graced with giant, engaged pilasters on the exterior. It was becoming clear to any builder in the 1770s that a great man would do well to have a substantial portico and a house in the colossal order to make a prestigious display, and George Washington incorporated both ideas in his mansion house.

Like the rusticated boards on the adjacent facade that are shaped and colored to look like fine stone, one of the aspects of his lofty colonnade closely linked to contemporary Georgian practice was the fancy stone paving (Figure 3.10). Washington wanted his paving to be in fine, contemporary taste and not merely vernacular in form and materials. Landon Carter put in fancy paving in his piazza at Sabine Hall, and, although he was not usually prone to offer aesthetic appreciation, he noted on 21 July 1772, "Laying my Piazza Pavement. It is very pretty with marble dots." For Mount Clare in Baltimore County, Maryland, Charles Carroll ordered 150 gray flagstones "thick and strong for an outside piazza." In interior and exterior flooring, going back to medieval and early modern times, it had been the height of taste in England and America to install checkered black and light squares, and initially Washington sought such an effect for his portico. Certainly, hearing that a man of taste such as

William Hamilton of Philadelphia enjoyed alternating colors of paving in his gallery at Bush Hill would have induced Washington to put down a checkered pattern. Frustrated in his attempt to get dark, blackish "Flaggs[tones]" from his English source, he contented himself with the single color of off-white paving. We should imagine the paving with the more varied and livelier checkered effect that he first sought (Figure 3.11) rather than the blander result of uniform gray. At any rate, Washington went to great lengths to get the fine Whitehaven stone that he installed, and it is no surprise that later, in 1793, he expressed his intention to pave the platforms on the west side of the house with marble imported from Italy and available for sale in Philadelphia.[46]

We have looked so far at seventeenth- and eighteenth-century Anglo-American traditions and in particular at Tidewater domestic architectural precedents for various aspects of the portico at Mount Vernon. The houses with long porches noted above, from Green Spring, to Holly Hill, to the house of Lawrance Taliaferro advertised in 1766, served as precedents, but there were other kinds of porches in America that Washington could have known, and some of these belonged to the building traditions introduced by non-Anglo ethnic groups in the colonies.

FIGURE 3.11. George Darley, drawing of checkerboard pattern for the flagstones at Mount Vernon, pen and ink on paper. Washington's English agent drew a sample of what Washington's portico would look like in an alternating black and white pattern in the pavement. For reasons of economy, Washington ordered stone tiles in one color only. George Washington Papers, 1741–1799, Series 4: General Correspondence, 1697–1799, Darley to Washington, 2 November 1784, Mount Vernon Flagstones, Library of Congress.

Chief among the porticoes derived from Continental European traditions were those of the Hudson Valley Dutch. George Washington went to Boston in 1756 to meet with Gov. William Shirley to protest the hierarchy of command between British officers and provincial officers as it was being interpreted in Virginia at the time; they also discussed a territorial dispute between Maryland and Virginia. Washington traveled through New Jersey and then stayed in Brooklyn for two days; he also—in a modern-sounding excursion—visited Manhattan to accompany a young lady to a light entertainment. He continued on his journey to New England, then returned home by a similar route, passing again through New York and northern New Jersey before returning to Virginia. Thus, Washington visited areas to which the Dutch and related northern European ethnic groups (French Huguenots and German Palatines) had brought the tradition of the porch. In May of 1773, just before Washington redesigned Mount Vernon, he took his step-son Jacky to King's College (now Columbia University), then located in lower Manhattan Island.[47] He must have seen a number of Dutch houses during his documented passage through or to Trenton, Princeton, Basking Ridge, Morristown, Newark, Perth Amboy, and other towns.

From an early period, and certainly by George Washington's time, the Dutch had well established the practice of building long porches for their homes.[48] Dr. James Thacher,

a surgeon with the American revolutionary forces, described open porticoes held up by posts in Dutch towns in northern New Jersey: "These towns are inhabited chiefly by Dutch people; their churches and dwelling houses are built of rough stone, one story high. There is a peculiar neatness in the appearance of their dwellings, having an airy piazza, supported by pillars in front, and their kitchens connected at the ends in the form of wings. The land is remarkably level, and the soil fertile, and being generally advantageously cultivated, the people appear to enjoy ease and happy competency."[49] This description does not specify the length of these porches, but use of the word "piazza" suggests not smaller porches around doors but long, probably full-length, porches. Some surviving examples of Dutch porches in the Hudson Valley show that the form was pervasive even well before Washington's time and certainly was widespread from the 1750s and later. Because of the path of economic development, and since the porch was most useful in farm settings, surviving structures tend to be in more rural areas in the Hudson Valley. On Staten Island, the Guyon-Lake-Tysen house has a full-length porch that probably dates to the 1760s (Figure 3.12). Further north, in Gardiner, New York, the reconstructed portico in the Evert Terwilliger house contains elements of the original porch dating to the 1730s. In Newburgh, New York, the Jonathan Hasbrouck House, which became Washington's headquarters toward the end of the Revolutionary War, has a porch on the riverfront, the portico dating to no later than 1750. These are just a few examples of the sort of Dutch porches that Washington saw when he traversed the area in the 1750s and early 1770s.[50]

Dutch-American porticoes were on substantial and fine homes as well as more vernacular dwellings. Anne MacVicar Grant, a British girl who learned Dutch and visited widely in the upper Hudson Valley where her father was on military duty, described a genteel form of portico used for leisure and enjoyment of nature, as Mount Vernon's was. Referring to her time in the New York colony from 1758 until 1763, she wrote of the Schuyler residence north of Albany:

FIGURE 3.12. Guyon-Lake-Tysen House, Historic Richmond Town, Staten Island, New York City, c. 1760, with later additions, built for Joseph Guyon. In Dutch-American houses in New York and northern New Jersey, undoubtedly known to Washington from his travels, there was a long tradition of building light, airy piazzas. Photo: Author.

This house had also two appendages common to all those belonging to persons in easy circumstances there. One was a large portico at the door, with a few steps leading up to it, and floored like a room; it was open at the sides, and had seats all round. Above was either a slight wooden roof, painted like an awning, or a covering of lattice-work, over which a transplanted vine spread its luxuriant leaves and numerous clusters . . . What gave an air of liberty and safety to these rustic porticoes, which always produced in my mind a sensation of pleasure that I know not how to define, was the number of little birds domesticated there . . . While breakfasting or drinking tea in the airy portico, which was often the scene of these meals, birds were constantly gliding over the table with a butterfly, grasshopper, or cicada in their bills, to feed their young, who were chirping above.[51]

Perhaps the most spectacular of aristocratic porches for a Dutch-American family of the Hudson Valley is the wrap-around portico at Van Cortlandt Manor in Croton-on-Hudson, which survives and occupies three sides of the mansion house (Figure 3.13). The porch probably dates to c. 1749, when Pierre Van Cortlandt became the first year-round resident-owner.[52] It was built for a family of Dutch descent that had assimilated into the Anglo society of colonial New York, and it is related to both the more vernacular Hudson Valley Dutch tradition of the porch and to the European portico of classical influence. Washington may well have heard of the Van Cortlandt porch from conversations with others, although he did not visit there until after the design of his own portico.

The Dutch seemed to have helped inspire the building of "piazzas" by other groups in the area. At various times, those of English stock around New York took up the extended porch, which again would have supplied examples for Washington to see and consider for adaptation. As early as 1739, we have a reference to the porch of the New Windsor home of an English resident in the Hudson Valley:

To be sold the Farm belonging to Mr. John Haskell at the Highlands in the County of Ulster, containing two-thousand Acres joining on the Land of Mr. Ellis, Mr. Alsop, and Will. Chambers Esq; at the distance of one Mile from Hudson's River . . . there is a good House 55 foot long and 24 wide two stories high with sash Windows and a Cellar the whole length of the House, in the Front is an open Gallery 25 foot long, from whence (and all the Front Windows) there is a pleasant Prospect of the River and Hills, and Settlements dispers'd thro the neighboring Woods . . . It will be sold very Cheap, the Owner designing to return soon to *England*, inquire of *James Allexander*, Esq: at *New-York*, or the said *Haskell* at the *Highlands*.[53]

This offer of sale is reminiscent of Lawrance Taliaferro's advertisement from the *Virginia Gazette* of 1766 and is a further reminder that the long portico and its usefulness for work and for providing views were hardly rare in America. An often-cited exchange between John Singleton Copley and his half-brother in Boston, Henry Pelham, indicates that the porch was a widely found form in New York by 1771, a fact that Pelham did not know, for the character of the "piazza" had to be explained to him.[54] As Washington was traveling in the 1750s and 1770s, the piazza was becoming even more widespread in the northeast and was well on its way to becoming an identifiably American form.

Beyond the Dutch, other ethnic groups in the New

FIGURE 3.13. Van Cortlandt Manor, Croton-on-Hudson, New York, early eighteenth century; second story and porch added c. 1748–1749 by Pierre van Cortlandt. This remarkable, three-sided porch combined the Dutch porch tradition with the classical, high style of Anglo groups in America. Photo: Author.

World that had a tradition of the domestic porch, including long galleries, were the Spanish and French. Washington might have heard of the "spanish fashion" of house, such as that described by John Bartram in the autumn of 1765 during his visit to St. Augustine, Florida: "A row of pillars or arches generaly supports A roof continuing from ye common roof of ye body of ye house." French settlements were widespread in North America, and examples of the kinds of galleries the French built in the New World range from the noted "Cahokia Courthouse" in Illinois, constructed c. 1740 as a domestic residence, to the late eighteenth-century New Orleans house (extant) known as Madame John's Legacy. Washington had some contact with French military settlements during the years of the French and Indian War. None of the early descriptions of forts by Washington or others mention galleries or porches, but perhaps these escaped the written records, which were focused on fortification (height, thickness of walls, and so forth) rather than embellishment.[55]

Beyond the forts in these frontier locations, other French cultural groups were closer at hand, including in the Hudson Valley region, where they blended and perhaps ex-

changed ideas with the Dutch and other groups. A substantial French emigrant population lived in pockets along the east coast, such as in New Rochelle in New York. In New Paltz, New York, the Bevier-Elting house of the early eighteenth century had a porch along the side; this was a French Huguenot home built in a larger region dominated by Dutch cultural influence.[56] A pre-Revolutionary mention of the domestic, rural piazza in the Hudson Valley appears in the writings of J. Hector St. John de Crèvecoeur, a native of Caen, France, who had lived and traveled in England and Canada before settling down in Orange County, New York, along the banks of the Hudson by 1769. In his essay "On the Situation of an American Farmer," Crèvecoeur painted a picture of the leisure use of his own porch: "Some time ago, as I sat smoking a contemplative pipe in my piazza, I saw, with amazement, a remarkable instance of selfishness displayed in a very small bird, which I hitherto respected for its inoffensiveness. Three nests were placed almost contiguous to each other in my piazza."[57] Crèvecoeur left the area—and eventually the country—during local upheavals in 1776. Some of these New York area porches were more genteel in style than others, but even when not overwhelmed with the aesthetics and the prestige of vernacular porches, Washington must have noted their usefulness for sitting and dining and how they allowed access to various rooms and served as an outside hallway, as the portico would do at Mount Vernon.

George Washington was, of course, not designing a public building at Mount Vernon. Still, there was in colonial elite architecture a fluidity between the public and private; borrowing from prestigious public buildings conferred status on the private dwelling and reflected the public responsibilities of the owners. Although he held no national office in 1773, Washington already had a public image and held political posts as justice of the peace and member of the House of Burgesses. In looking for inspiration for creating a useful, attractive, and prestigious porch on the river side of his house, he would have been willing to consider imitating prestigious public buildings. The sheer breadth of Mount Vernon, its monumental siting on the hill, the impressive turnaround oval with thirty-two posts at the entrance drive, the cupola, and the arcading on the arms served to blur the difference between public and private, a blending that was achieved in many upper-class house designs in the colonial period.

The noble colonnade had long been associated with the dignity of public buildings, even more than with private homes. Washington likely saw the porch at Peter Harrison's Redwood Library in Newport (see Figure 2.28), significant for us in that it had a rusticated facade of beveled and painted wood such as Washington had incorporated into Mount Vernon in the late 1750s. The fine portico was becoming widespread in ecclesiastical architecture, including at Saint Michael's (1752–1761) in Charleston, South Carolina, and (with a portico on a much smaller scale) the First Baptist Meetinghouse in Providence, Rhode Island (1774–1775). Closer to home, various kinds of porches existed at courthouses in Virginia, the Capitol in Williamsburg, and many other public buildings.

Williamsburg provides several examples of porches as part of public architecture. The Wren Building of the College of William and Mary had a piazza on the rear facade. The 1705 version of the Capitol in Williamsburg had a "piazza" (loggia) with arcuated piers connecting the paired wings of the structure, as well as rounded porches on each side supported by wooden columns. After the fire of 1747, the Capitol was rebuilt in 1751 as the building Washington would have known; the two-tiered portico facing the Duke of Gloucester Street had engaged columns against the wall and free-standing columns in front, with a pediment above.[58] The courthouse at Williamsburg was, oddly, without columns, but elsewhere in Virginia there were porticoes on courthouses fronted with free-standing piers or columns. The King William County Courthouse, c. 1725–1740, was well known to George Washington and was built with a ground-level portico sustained by wide, brick piers and arched openings. A similar portico, also with five bays, appeared on the Hanover County Courthouse (c. 1740).[59] These early courthouse porticoes served the practical function of sheltering the public, and they conveyed a sense of importance, expressed also in such details as fine moldings, rubbed brick, and cupolas.

It is worth noting the wording that Washington used to describe his portico at Mount Vernon. He often referred to the porch as a "piazza," especially when communicating with Lund Washington about its construction, but when describing it to his social equals, he sometimes called it a "gallery" or even a "colonnade." Both of these are fancy words, "gallery" going back to the English Tudor garden tradition and "colonnade" suggesting a public building or the rows of columns in large, high-style homes.[60] Washington apparently thought of his colonnade as equal to that of a public building or the best mansion houses.

Beyond the public portico, the essential idea of the porch was deeply rooted in other nondomestic buildings, from high-style public architecture to vernacular utilitarian or commercial structures. Washington experienced the grand porticoes of libraries and courthouses but also the most humble and utilitarian "porches," such as the "open shed" in which his tobacco was stored and was suffering as a result (January 1760). Manager Lund Washington asked the general in January 1776 whether the "Negroe houses" on the estate should be built with sheds. Open sheds were common in work and agricultural contexts, and they served the same purpose later served by porches, as in a passage from 1682: "Hogs increase in Carolina abundantly, and in a manner without any charge or trouble to the Planter, only to make them Sheds, wherein they may be protected from the Sun and Rain."[61] Even his horse and mule stalls at Mount Vernon can be said to be porches, with their free-standing columns and long, portico-like appearance (Plate 11). One contemporary, Scottish visitor Robert Hunter Jr., described Washington's horses as living a life of leisure in their stables, and he used the kind of language one might have employed to imagine the general himself relaxing in his portico from his years of work for the nation: "The General makes no manner of use of them [his old horses] now; he keeps them in a nice stable, where they feed away at their ease for their past services."[62] In cities, commercial structures with overhangs stood in market places in Philadelphia, Boston, and New York. There was no lack of precedent for porches or porch-like, open-air coverings in colonial America.

Among commercial structures, tavern porches were rather common at this period. These were semipublic buildings and had to accommodate customers sitting and, at country taverns, waiting for arrivals and departures. Porches on taverns and inns were common in Continental Europe in the seventeenth century and were certainly widespread in America by the 1780s and earlier, as George Grieve, the English translator of the Marquis de Chastellux's travels in America, noted in 1787. Indeed, there is evidence of porches in front of English taverns in the seventeenth century, and as early as 1744, one source mentions what was apparently an open portico at the Black Horse Tavern in New York "fronting the street." In Philadelphia, the City Tavern had a canvas

FIGURE 3.14. Charlton's Coffeehouse (reconstruction on original site by the Colonial Williamsburg Foundation), Williamsburg, Virginia, by 1767, built for Richard Charlton. This porch is typical of the kind of commercial piazza often seen on taverns and inns; these were widespread during Washington's time. Courtesy of the Colonial Williamsburg Foundation.

overhang, just one example of the many canvas overhangs in the colonial period used over windows, doors, and sometimes across facades, forming vernacular and ephemeral porches.[63]

Washington availed himself of the tavern porches in Williamsburg. He frequented Christiana Campbell's from 1771 to 1774, when the owner established her business at the present location; archaeology has discovered that it had long front and rear porches, and its present reconstructed state gives an approximate idea of the tavern's original appearance. Wetherburn's Tavern also had a long porch along the back. The Raleigh Tavern had, as early as 1733, a porch with an open side, and during Washington's visits in the 1770s, it is known to have sported a long front porch with "pillars" (not presently reconstructed). The nearby Richard Charlton's Coffeehouse of 1765 also had a porch, which has been recently reconstructed on its site on the Duke of Gloucester Street (Figure 3.14). Elsewhere in Virginia, structural investigation has revealed that the Rising Sun Tavern in Fredericksburg in the 1770s had twenty-five-foot-long porches in the front and the rear; English visitor John Davis described

FIGURE 3.15. Teapot and lid, China, c. 1755, porcelain, 6.4″ (height). Eighteenth-century chinaware often included representations of open porches, which could have encouraged the development and expansion of the portico in early America. Washington acquired this teapot in the 1750s. Courtesy of the Mount Vernon Ladies' Association (W-131/A).

its "piazzo," raised on steps. The inn at the King William County Courthouse, visited by Washington in November 1768, had a portico running its entire length of seventy-two feet.[64] The practicality and commodiousness of these commercial porches would have been well known to Washington, and the number of meals and teas that he took on his own veranda show some similarity of use.

Washington needed, however, to distinguish his portico from these ubiquitous tavern porches, agricultural sheds, canvas awnings, marketplace coverings, and so forth. The slow development of the porch in early America, particularly in New England, indicates a reluctance to endow one's home with such a structure. It is likely that the association with tavern porches, stables, tobacco and hog sheds, and market stalls reduced the apparent gentility of a piazza. To separate their porticoes from commercial piazzas or overhangs, Washington and others of his social class needed to design porches with proper paving, a classical architectural

order, proportional spacing, and so forth. By building in the colossal order and with fine details, Washington set his portico apart from vernacular long porches in Virginia, New York, and elsewhere.

We might consider one final source for the porch in colonial America: the porches that appeared in "japanned" furniture, Asian-inspired wallpaper, chinaware, and other Asian or Asian-influenced sources, which have rarely been mentioned in considerations of the development of the porch in America. In Anglo-American, eighteenth-century society, there was considerable admiration for a broad range of Asian imports, from tea tables and services, to ball-and-claw feet to Marlborough legs to irregular garden design to japanning itself. Chinese fretwork was widespread in the colonies, and Asian influence is apparent in a small Chinese-style footbridge at the William Paca garden in Annapolis. The prominent architect William Chambers wrote two works—an essay, "Of the Art of Laying Out Gardens Among the

Chinese," (1757) and a book, *Dissertation on Oriental Gardening* (1773)—in which he called on the English to imitate Chinese gardens.[65] Chambers designed for royal Kew gardens a tall, Chinese-style pagoda (1762) that has an open portico all around. Wallpaper and plateware from China was exported to England and admired by British designers, who imitated the gracious summerhouses, porches, and open gazebos they depicted. Chinese buildings and scenes appear in the surviving original wallpaper in the passage and stairway of the Jeremiah Lee Mansion in Marblehead, Massachusetts. George Washington owned by 1757 a tea service (pot, cups, and saucers) imported from China, the porcelain pieces including scenes of figures near several structures with porches and open, columned facades (Figure 3.15). Washington also later owned a garniture set that featured views of Chinese buildings set in picturesque landscapes.[66] Chinese paintings in enamel on silvered glass were popular in the eighteenth century; we do not know if Washington himself saw any of these, but porches, including extensive ones, appear in them.[67]

In the realm of furniture, "japanning" was a period term referring to the design in England and America of Asian scenes on furniture and mirror frames. Japanned images imitated the enameling, gilding, and lacquering techniques of the East and represented characteristic Asian scenes, including strolling figures, bridges, gardens, dragons, and so forth. These vignettes often show scenes of leisure, with garden views, streams, and little buildings with overhangs or porticoes and slender columns. The scenes are loosely based on Asian models but interpreted through Western eyes. A high chest made in Boston around 1730 shows a porch sustained by two square columns (Figure 3.16).[68]

The porches in Asian and Asian-influenced scenes are usually not raised up but are near the ground level and are easy and approachable, like the portico at Mount Vernon. These Asian-styled porches are part of Anglo-American visual culture of the late seventeenth and eighteenth century, and these images flourished before the widespread use of

FIGURE 3.16. Japanned high chest (detail), made in Boston, c. 1730, 87″ (height). Japanned furniture and Asian or Asian-influenced art such as wallpaper design often showed open and airy garden porches. Courtesy of the Museum of Fine Arts, Houston; Bayou Bend Collection, gift of Miss Ima Hogg (B.69.348).

the porch in non-Anglo society in the American colonies. Without a broad range of visual imagery passing before them, colonial Americans would have been struck by these Asian porches and garden. The images themselves suggest the form's usefulness and gentility. Indeed, what is most striking about Asian or Asian-inspired designs is how the artists contrived to depict the social setting as corresponding with an eighteenth-century Western ideal, with a harmony of house and garden and an emphasis on views, strolling, and aristocratic ease.

The porch at Mount Vernon is the result of Washington's desire for innovation within the larger sphere of classical revival, and it is the product of his admiration, not imitation, of antiquity. Going beyond classical models, though, the possible sources for his porch were numerous, as we have seen, from vernacular and tavern porches to magnificent colonnades in fine public and private architecture. The portico at Mount Vernon was inventive, but it was neither unexpected nor audacious for Washington's contemporaries; none of them are recorded as commenting on its originality.

Functions of the Porch

Mount Vernon's portico was designed to produce prestige for the owner and aesthetic pleasure for the viewers, but its appearance cannot be considered without regarding its function for Washington, his family, and visitors. Its purposes included providing a refuge from heat and rain, allowing work and play activities, offering access to interior rooms, sheltering exercise walks, and facilitating dining and the taking of refreshments.

Despite any resistance that may have existed, over time porches flourished in the colonies. In America, the winters are colder, the summers hotter, and the thunderstorms more frequent and intense than in Europe. In Virginia, the summer heat and humidity made porches a welcome addition to houses. Its protective function was crucial to the development of the American porch from the eighteenth to the mid-twentieth century (when air-conditioning, the advent of the television, and other factors brought about a retreat inside into sealed spaces).

In a travel account that predates Mount Vernon, Edward Kimber says of the orphan house in Savannah, "It is a square Building, of very large Dimensions, the Foundation of which is of Brick, with Chimneys of the same, the rest of the Superstructure of Wood; the Whole laid out in a neat and elegant Manner. A Kind of Piazza-Work surrounds it, which is a very pleasing Retreat in the Summer."[69] A 1732 description of the courthouse in Savannah, seen by William Stephens (President of the Province of Georgia), makes a similar point: "The Body of the house is one entire Building, formed in the inside Commodiously, with Benches of different Sorts . . . This was built in the year 1736, and soon after there was added to it a Cloister or Colonade, encompassing the front and both ends of the house, which was not only Ornamental, but very, usefull likewise, in breaking off the Violence of the Weather; more Especially the heats."[70]

In his letter to his half-brother Pelham, Copley praises the beauty of the piazza and its use against inclement weather in summer and winter:

> You say you dont know what I mean by a Peaza. I will tell you than. it is exactly such a thing as the cover over the pump in your Yard, suppose no enclosure for Poultry their, and 3 or 4 posts aded to support the front of the Roof, a good floor at bottum, and from post to post a Chinese enclosure of about three feet high . . . some have Collums but very few, and the top is generally Plasterd; but I think if the top was sealed with neat plained Boards I should like it as well. these Peazas are so cool in Sumer and in Winter break off the storms so much that I think I should not be able to like an house without.

Copley noted that piazzas make a house appear taller, so aesthetic considerations were important to him in addition to the practical advantages.[71] For his part, Benjamin Henry Latrobe, who visited Mount Vernon, later offered an observation on the useful function of the overhanging roof in sunny and rainy New Orleans: "In the Summer the walls are perfectly shaded from the Sun, and the house kept cool, while the passengers are also shaded from the Sun, and protected from the rain."[72] Had George Washington designed a typical Palladian three-bay, four columned portico, it would not have shielded this part of the house from the sun as well or provided much space for sitting in the heat of summer. He designed a porch suitable to the American climate rather than using the more standard temple-front portico seen widely in England and in eighteenth-century America.

George Washington's natural place was out of doors, and the portico facilitated this. He wanted not only shelter from the weather but access to it as well. In his youth, he wanted to go to sea, and during his military career and his years surveying and farming, he was constantly and, it seems, happily, out of doors. He carefully tracked the weather in his diaries, and his frequent rounds of his farms happily exposed him to fresh air and the elements. He built an airy, uncompressed, and "lofty and majestic" space that covered him and his guests from the sun and light rain and allowed the passage of fresh, cooling air. Visitors appreciated the cooling nature of the portico at Mount Vernon and described Washington's use of it for that purpose. Lt. John Enys of England visited in 1788 and noted the value of the porch at Mount Vernon: "As the Dinner was not quite ready we took a walk out into his grownds on the other side of the house. This front is placed towards the south in front of which is a Portico supported with Pillars near thirty feet high and Paved with flagg stones which must form a Charming shade in warm weather. From hence is one of the most delightfull Prospects I ever beheld." In 1805, Augustus John Foster noted the unpleasant experience of visiting Mount Vernon when the thermometer read 93.5 degrees in the shade, and "the bedrooms were miserably small and of course dreadfully hot, tho' the portico being to the south east, sitting under it was pleasant of an evening."[73] Over the years, Washington acquired more than two dozen green Windsor chairs for the portico, which were supplemented by the indoor chairs and tables brought there on occasion.

Mount Vernon's porch in a moderate drizzle, let alone a thunderstorm, is not as effective a shelter as a one-story porch, and Mount Vernon visitor Samuel Powel mentioned that the portico "renders the [second floor] chambers dark." The loss of shelter and light might have kept others before Washington from building their porches on that colossal scale. A two-tier portico, such as at Sabine Hall and Lansdowne, was the choice for other elite builders of Washington's generation in America, and their choice was more practical as shelter from rain. In building the portico at Mount Vernon, Washington seems to have been more concerned with creating a fine form, exhibiting elegance and grandeur, as well as providing ample sitting space provided, but there was still, of course, some shelter from rain, wind, and dew.

It is impossible to separate the function of the porch from that of the central passage, connected as they were by spatial continuity and function. As the Polish visitor Julian Niemcewicz put it, "one enters into a hall which divides the house into two and leads to the *piazza*;" he thus sensed that the piazza was the natural culmination of the path through the great central passage.[74] The physical aspect of the porch as a continuation of the passage meant that it could serve as an extension of it. The porch is linked to the culture of the central passage, one of the hallmarks of Georgian design. Even before midcentury, many houses in the South, designed with chimneys at the ends, had a central door that opened to a parlor or, in some cases, to a hall or passageway. After 1750 or so, the central passage became a mark of colonial American design. There was a confluence of aesthetics and use in the Georgian central passage: it was useful for creating at least a general bilateral balance, for permitting grand entrances from above, for offering a route at times discouraged for servants (who could use a smaller, back staircase), for offering a view through the house, for flaunting a sense of conspicuous consumption of space and materials, and for providing a breezeway ideal for dining, dancing, or other leisure activities. In this space, the second story landing made an ideal location for musicians during a party, and the long rectangular shape of the passage worked well with the line dancing or contra dancing popular at the time. There was a continuity of space from the passage to the porch at Mount Vernon, facilitating the movement of people for celebrations, meals, and other gatherings. The porch surface, measured from the east mansion wall to the inside of the square columns, is about as wide as the central passage. The approximate match of width of passage and porch surface gives guests a sense of spatial and practical harmony.

The portico and flagstone surface not only are useful as an extension, spatially and proportionally, of the central passage but also serve as a kind of exterior hallway. In some houses in the French Mississippi Valley, the exterior gallery was the only way to gain access to various rooms. Mount Vernon's porch made the rooms of the house particularly penetrable from the outside. Even today, the established tourist route from the Large Dining Room to the porch and back in to the central passage indicates the usefulness of the portico as a means of access from one interior space to an-

FIGURE 3.17. Thomas Prichard Rossiter and Louis Rémy Mignot, *Washington and Lafayette at Mount Vernon, 1784,* 1859, oil on canvas, 87″ × 146.5″. Although painted decades after the event shown, the picture gives an evocative impression of the site and usage of the portico at Mount Vernon, with Washington talking to the Marquis de Lafayette and family members enjoying leisure activities. The Metropolitan Museum of Art, New York (05.35). Image copyright © The Metropolitan Museum of Art / Art Resource, NY.

other. Such accessibility was useful for Washington and his family, as well as for visitors and for servants, who could discretely enter and leave from the outside without going through a suite of rooms in the house. Washington himself addressed explicitly the question of the function of his "piazza" in the layout of the mansion house: "Whilst the weather is warm, the Common Hall and piazza will do very well, as a substitute for the Drawing room or Parlour; but when the weather becomes cool, we must retire to a fireside."[75]

Apart from providing shelter from the elements, the portico served a number of specific practical purposes, as did many Tidewater porches. Reflecting on his early life at Gunston Hall, John Mason, son of Founding Father George Mason, recalled that his father washed his head on the porch of their modest but otherwise high-style mansion house: "His habit was to bathe his head in cold water winter & summer in an open porch every morning immediately after rising—a practice I have heard him say he had followed all his life and which he kept up to the time of his death."[76] The porch was often a place of conversation. The portico at Mount Vernon was also a site of political work for Washington himself, and he carried out a number of formal and informal discussions while on the portico.[77] On a light note, Boston merchant Thomas Handasyd Perkins, described an exchange with the general in the summer of 1796: "On one occasion, when sitting there [on the piazza] with the family a toad passed near to where I sat conversing with Gen.

Washington; which led him to ask me if I had ever observed this reptile swallow a fire-fly. Upon my answering in the negative, he told me that he had; and that, from the thinness of the skin of the toad, he had seen the light of the fire-fly after it had been swallowed. This was a new, and to me a surprising, fact in natural history." In this versatile space, where the children played with (and damaged) a model of the Bastille prison, Martha Washington kept bird cages, re-calling the passages by Anne Grant and Crèvecoeur about the enjoying of the songs of birds on their porticoes.[78] We can easily imagine Martha engaged in needlework while seated near her birds.

Apart from relaxed conversational exchanges, the portico also formed a kind of stateroom where Washington met with dignitaries on a number of occasions. Thomas Prichard Rossiter's and Louis Rémy Mignot's evocative painting of 1859 captures this dual function of work and leisure, depict-ing a fanciful but ultimately plausible meeting of Wash-ington and the Marquis de Lafayette taking place on the portico (Figure 3.17). John Marshall, later to be chief justice of the Supreme Court, reported that he sat for hours with Washington on the porch discussing political and legal mat-ters.[79] Washington also read newspapers for long periods there, another kind of political activity. His ideal that Mount Vernon would be a retreat from the cares of the larger world was not always realized, and the porch occasionally func-tioned as an out-of-doors office.

We have seen that walking in long interior galleries was widespread in England, and William Byrd walked in his gallery at Westover, probably a covered interior space. The benefits of walking were appreciated in the eighteenth cen-tury, as was, more generally, lengthy exposure to open, fresh air. The long portico at Mount Vernon was ideally suited for this. Tutor Edward Hooker was presumably quoting Judge Bushrod Washington when he wrote in his diary in 1808 that during his tour of Mount Vernon he "came to the 'long and lofty portico where oft the hero walked in all his glory.'" The imported Whitestone paving was good for more than

FIGURE 3.18. Benjamin Henry Latrobe, *Sketch of a groupe for a drawing of Mount Vernon,* after July 1796, pencil, pen and ink, and watercolor on paper, 7″ × 10.25″. In this idealizing image, Wash-ington family members use the porch at Mount Vernon for taking light refreshments. Courtesy of The Maryland Historical Society (1960.108.1.2.21).

beauty, as the hard surface countered the damp ground and frost of the rainy season and winter. Washington's grandson, George Washington Parke Custis, reminisced that in the winter the elder George "was in the habit of walking for an hour in the eastern portico of the mansion, before retiring to rest." Martha also walked the long colonnade in inclement weather, using the flagstoned piazza on rainy, cold, or damp days as a substitute for a walk in the gardens. In 1801, Sally Foster Otis noted that the "grown'd was damp and we per-ceived Mrs. W. [Washington] walking in the Piazza."[80]

Food and drink were often served on the piazza in good weather. Inventories and accounts of the time indicate that the portico at Mount Vernon sheltered at least two dozen Windsor chairs, coated in green paint, that residents and visitors used for sitting, dining, and taking in the views and fresh air. A good verbal account of the use of the portico for refreshments appears in the reminiscences of Julian Niem-cewicz, while the best visual record is found in Benjamin Henry Latrobe's drawings and watercolors of 1796, illustrat-ing the use of fine tables and chairs, carried there by servants (Figure 3.18). Latrobe's pictures, though idealized, correspond to the verbal evidence for the use of the porch; they show Washington and his immediate family taking tea and enjoying the distant view.[81]

The taking of meals in outdoor loggias occurred even in the late Middle Ages and early modern period, as is shown in Northern Renaissance prints. In the English tradition, banqueting houses, garden loggias, covered wall seats, and viewing platforms were widespread in elite architecture in the sixteenth and seventeenth centuries and later.[82] Medieval and Renaissance towers and independent garden structures were the precursors to Mount Vernon's porch, which stands in a long line of such leisure spaces in Anglo-American architectural history.

In addition to comparing it to the appearance and function of late medieval and early modern banqueting houses and garden loggias, the portico at Mount Vernon has to be seen in light of the more recent phenomenon of the summerhouse and the gazebo in Anglo-American culture. Roofed but otherwise open structures for viewing and seating in good weather, gazebos were widespread in England. Summerhouses were small pleasure buildings, often with an internal second story; the prospect was improved by one's sitting in this upper story. Of fine style and sited to advantage in the gardens and along waterways, summerhouses were at the height of popularity in the eighteenth century. John Crowley has traced the summerhouse and portico culture in America to English ideas about outdoor sitting, leisure, and health.[83] Washington—notably—did not have a summerhouse anywhere on his grounds, and his portico essentially served the purpose that one would have filled: offering

cooling breezes and leisure space to residents and visitors to the estate and its gardens. A summerhouse was built by Bushrod Washington in the early nineteenth century atop the site of the little-used ice house at the edge of the east lawn. It appears in the painting by Rossiter and Mignot (see Figure 3.17), which highlights the portico, indicating how Washington's open and inviting porch and the summerhouse served a similar purpose.

The portico's success can be judged by the splendid critical reception that it enjoyed in Washington's time and soon thereafter. Winthrop Sargent praised it in Washington's lifetime. David Humphreys wrote in 1789 that it had "a pleasing effect when viewed from the water," and Latrobe admired it in 1796: "Along the other [east] front is a portico supported by 8 square pillars, of good proportions and effect."[84] Usually ignoring the inventiveness of the portico, early writers were content to note its grandeur, loftiness, and length. Of course, the view caught everyone's attention. Artist Charles Willson Peale, William Loughton Smith of South Carolina, and John Enys of England were not alone in noting that as they stepped onto the portico, they were immediately struck by the broad view of the Potomac.[85] This aspect of Washington's portico—its role as mediator of inside and outside, and as a platform for viewing the gardens and distant landscape, was among its chief functions and is an important tool in helping us understand George Washington's eye. In the next chapters, we look at the genesis of Washington's gardens and his creation of a landscape, of which the porch offered a superb view.

CHAPTER FOUR

Washington as Gardener

Creating the Landscape

[Mount Vernon has] good gardens, and if I am a judge[,] fine and elegant ones. Delightful walks, straight, circular and serpentine handsomely and tastily shaded with the best chosen trees. Among them the Lombardy poplar, or the poplar of the Po of which Ovid sang many hundred years ago is found and much admired.

WILLIAM BLOUNT, 1790

GEORGE WASHINGTON was passionate about natural beauty, and he personally oversaw the aesthetic development of the gardens at Mount Vernon. (We use the word "gardens" broadly here to describe, as early viewers did, both the extensive improved landscape and the smaller walled gardens at the estate.) It is striking how intensely he attended to the most minute details of the gardens at Mount Vernon. The day before he died, perhaps causing or exacerbating the fatal infection of his epiglottis, he went out in the cold and snow of December to mark trees that were to be cut down in order to improve the view.[1] Mount Vernon's landscape and walled gardens, along with the famous house itself, formed George Washington's great work of art. He aesthetically linked the estate grounds, beautiful in themselves, to the mansion house and its site, and carefully calculated the views from the house and portico. Washington enjoyed a range of artistic interests in his life, but none of them were as sustained over time or as personal in character as his improvement of the land around his mansion house.

Evidence is scanty concerning what gardens might have existed before Washington took up residence at Mount Vernon in 1754, leasing it from his half-brother Lawrence's widow. Archaeology has determined that early on, perhaps in Augustine and Lawrence's time, the road leading to the front (west) door was straight and direct, probably bordered by a symmetrical planting of trees.[2] Lawrence's family was at Mount Vernon from 1743 to 1754, and they certainly maintained some kind of vegetable and herb garden near the house. Lawrence likely planted a fruit orchard and perhaps kept some kind of small flower gardens in regular arrangement, following the taste of the time in the colonies. From what little we know or can surmise, there is no evidence that any elaborate or important gardens existed at Mount Vernon before George Washington's time.

Over the years, Washington expanded the mansion house, added outbuildings, and altered the agricultural lands at Mount Vernon. Along with these changes, his gardening schemes at Mount Vernon—all (as far as we know) concentrated at the Mansion House Farm—became ever more elaborate. In giving form to the layout that existed at the time of his death, the greatest campaigns occurred in the early and mid-1770s during a large-scale renovation and expansion of the mansion house, from about 1784 to 1789 between the war and the presidency, and from 1797 to 1799 during his final retirement.[3] By far the most important period of the gardens' development was from 1784 to 1789, when Washington came up with a new master plan and turned much of the estate into a rambling, natural garden, with curving, graveled walks and abundant, varied plantings. He was present at Mount Vernon during much of that time, so he was able to implement his ideas vigorously and firsthand. Even when he resided away from Mount Vernon while carrying out his military and political duties, Washington played a guiding role through letters of instruction to those in charge of the grounds. In the brief post-presidency period, Washington added significantly to the gardens, building on his scheme of the 1780s. By 1798, he had decided to grow no more substantial crops at the Mansion House Farm but continued to do so at his other four farms. On the land not far from the mansion, however, he kept some sheep, mules, poultry, and other animals, continued the production of corn and grasses, and grew herbs, flowers, fruit, and vegetables, largely for use at the estate. By 1799, Mount Vernon

contained a complex arrangement of walled gardens, shaded gravel walks, open grassy parkland, woods, farmlands, and orchards. As Washington developed the beauty of the gardens, they increasingly served as a major attraction for visitors to the famous estate.

We would do well to preface our modern account of Mount Vernon and its gardens with a concise and elegant description by military officer, aide de camp, foreign minister, historian, and poet David Humphreys, who knew the estate well from visits in July 1786 and later. His description, written about 1788–1789, was intended for his never-completed, authorized biography of Washington:

Mount Vernon, the celebrated seat of General Washington, is pleasantly situated on the Virginian bank of the river Potowmac, where it is nearly 2 miles wide & about 280 miles from the sea. Mount Vernon is 9 miles below the flourishing Town of Alexandria & 4 above the beautiful Situation of the late Honorable Colonel George Fairfax, called Bellevoir. The area of the Mount, is 200 feet above the surface of the water, and after furnishing a lawn of 5 acres in front & about the same in rear of the buildings, falls off rather abruptly on those two quarters. On the north-end it subsides gradually into extensive pasture grounds; while on the south it slopes more steeply in a shorter distance, and terminates with the coach-house, stables, vineyard & nurseries. On either wing is a dense & opaque grove of different flowering forest trees. Parellel [*sic*] with them, on the land-side, are two spacious gardens, into which one is led by the two serpentine gravel-walks, planted with weeping willows & umbrageous shrubs. The Mansion House itself, though much embellished by yet not perfectly satisfactory to the chaste taste of the present Possessor, appears venerable & convenient. The superb banquetting room has been finished since he returned home from the army. A lofty Portico, 96 feet in length, supported by eight pillars, has a pleasing effect when viewed from the water; and the *tout ensemble,* of the green-house, school-house, offices & servants-hall, when seen from the country-side, bears a resemblance to a rural village: especially as the lands in that site are laid out somewhat according to the form of English gardens, in meadows & grass-grounds, ornamented with little copses, circular clumps & single trees. [O]n the opposite side of a little creek to the Northward, an extensive plain, exhibiting cornfields & cattle grazing, affords in summer a luxurus landscape to the eye; While the cultivation declivities, intermingle with woodlands on the Maryland shore concludes the prospect; While to blended verdure of woodlands & cultivated declivities on the Maryland shore variegates the prospect on another side in a charming manner. A small Park on the margin of the river, where the English fallow-deer & the American wild-deer are seen through the thickets, alternately with the vessels as they are sailing along, adds a romantic & picturesque appearance to the whole scenery. Such are the philosophic shades, to which the late Commander in Chief of the American armies has retired, from the tumultuous scenes of a busy world.[4]

Humphreys' vivid passage calls attention to the house and landscape gardening, which comprised parkland, vistas, walled gardens, pastures, outbuildings, and a romantic and picturesque setting of the house and grounds.

Like Humphreys, we offer here a brief tour of the grounds, seeing them as they appeared to a visitor in the late 1790s. In chapter 5, we look at the sources behind Washington's gardening ideas.

First Vista and Approach to the Mansion House

Nearly all guests went overland to reach Mount Vernon, and most came from the north. The distance from Alexandria to the Mansion House Farm was eight miles as the crow flies, but the land route was a winding, eleven-mile journey on what travelers characterized as a rocky, tedious, and poorly maintained road that stood inland from the river and only at times offered a good view of it. John Singleton Copley Jr. described the trek from Alexandria as being through "open fields, not remarkable for any particular beauty, the soil is barren, the roads rough and hilly." Along the way, visitors traveled through a piece of Washington's Muddy Hole Farm, and his River Farm was further off to the east, or left, along the Potomac, both part of his set of five extensive farms (Figure 4.1). While approaching the Mansion House Farm, one passed through what Polish visitor Julian Niemcewicz called "a road newly cut through a forest of oaks."[5] In her account

of 1801, Bostonian Sally Foster Otis described this forest as "a thick wood" that extended for four miles.[6] Along this sylvan road, perhaps about two miles from Washington's residence, one passed through the first of several gates, but the residence remained out of sight. Then, about two-thirds of a mile from the house, travelers came to their first glimpse of Mount Vernon's mansion (Figure 4.2). Visitors arriving from the south rather than from Alexandria, or those crossing the river from Maryland, could have climbed the hill and also reached this spot.

This area, near the present west gates, stood at one end of a magnificent vista. From this spot, Washington made sure to present a clear, sudden, and picturesque view of the mansion house, which is seen across fields and lawns and through the openings left by the curving lines of trees. This memorable vista, which existed by 1787 and was improved and cleared further in 1792, was highly calculated. Washington took exception when Englishman Samuel Vaughan drew a plan of the grounds incorrectly showing trees across the west end of the bowling green, where they would cut off the vista, and he pointed out the error to Vaughan (Figures 4.3 and 4.4).[7] The garden curators at Mount Vernon maintain this view across the fields and bowling green, retaining the kind of vista that Washington so carefully crafted. The whole area from the beginning of the vista to the bowling green is presently off-limits to visitors to Mount Vernon, although this first vista point is next to a public road outside the estate and, of course, is seen in reverse in the view from the mansion house.

There is no archaeological trace of gates in the area of the initial vista of the house, nor are there early views showing gates there in Washington's time. No eighteenth-century visitor specifically mentions gates here, but Philadelphian Samuel Powel did say that here he arrived at the "Entrance" from the road. Rev. Manasseh Cutler mentioned in 1802 a "gate" where the first full view of the house was, and it is likely that George Washington placed gates there, namely, the "White Gates" that are frequently referred

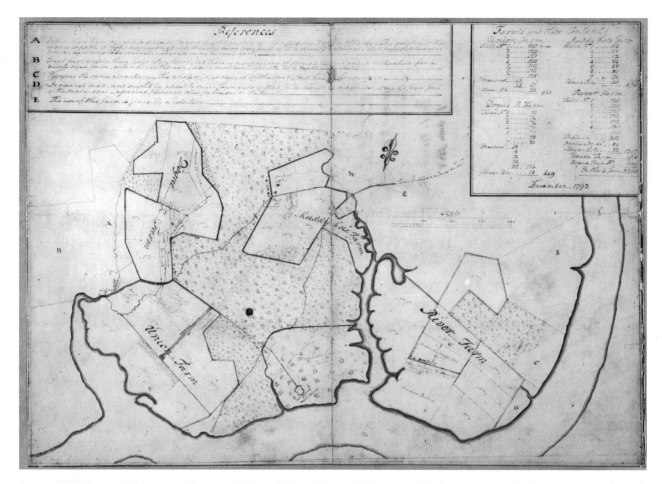

FIGURE 4.1. George Washington, "Survey and Plan of Mount Vernon" ("Five-Farm Map"), 1793, pen and ink on paper, 14.75″ × 21″. Washington prepared this map to provide knowledge of his five farms, four of which he hoped to rent to English farmers. Reproduced by permission of The Huntington Library, San Marino, California (HM 5995).

to in early documents. George's nephew Bushrod Washington put gates and gatehouses on the present spots; Edward Hooker, returning from Columbia, South Carolina, in 1808 noted that "about 1/4 mile from the mansion you enter a gate, pass through a pleasant grove of small, neat, well-trimmed oaks, follow the path in some parts straight in others winding among hills, at length ascend a tolerably steep hill and are present at the house."[8] The present wooden gates are modern replicas of the kind used in the late eighteenth century. The brick gatehouses are also reconstructions of the pressed and dried clay structures first built there

by Bushrod sometime between September 1810 and March 1812.[9] These white gatehouses are fairly visible from the mansion and work against the impression of woodland that George Washington carefully calculated from the mansion house. There was originally a greener endpoint to the vista, and any gates—even if painted white—would have been barely detectable from the house. In a letter to Samuel Vaughan in 1787, Washington described the vista west from the mansion as giving "an open and full view of the distant woods."[10]

An eighteenth-century traveler, arriving at the vista spot

FIGURE 4.2. Early visitors enjoyed a first, distant sight of the mansion house, which they encountered in sudden fashion on the route from Alexandria. Photo: Author.

from the road and getting the initial sight of the mansion, formed a sense of the scale, character, and style of the gardens and estate. Beginning at this point and facing a simple farming field, one could see that this was a substantial estate in the American context, even if modest by Old World standards. The fields in front of the gate and continuing to the bowling green were planted with various crops but were described in 1802 by Philadelphia merchant Thomas P. Cope as "little better than a barren heath."[11] The fields immediately suggested to visitors that this was a working farm, a

villa (a word Washington himself sometimes used) in the Italian sense, and not a mere mansion and pleasure gardens. The agricultural holdings were an integral part of the visual experience of Washington's estate.

From this first vista point, one began the next leg of the journey to the house. An earlier tradition called for an allée of trees leading from the entrance up to a mansion house, as was the case, for example, at George Mason's nearby Gunston Hall, and as had been the arrangement of the final stretch up to the residence until the mid-1780s. In contrast,

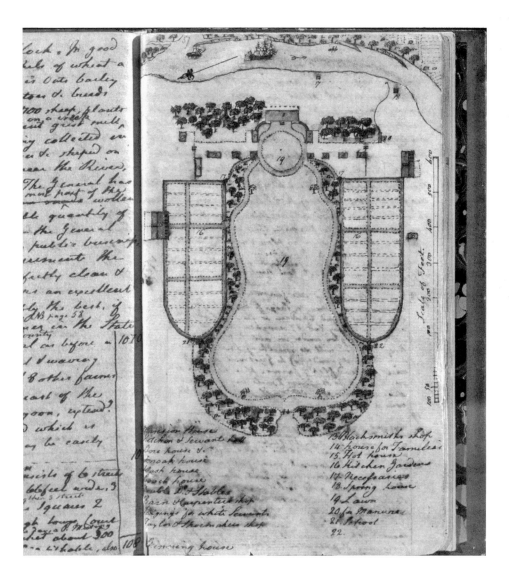

FIGURE 4.3. Samuel Vaughan, plan of the central part of the Mount Vernon estate, ink and watercolor on paper, 7.6″ × 5″ from his personal journal, June–September 1787. Englishman Vaughan visited Mount Vernon and sketched out this plan of the mansion, pleasure gardens, and environs. This plan served as a model for the plan he sent to Washington (cf. Figure 4.4). Courtesy of the Mount Vernon Ladies' Association (MS-4996).

the long route Washington finally designed was curving and indirect (Figure 4.5).[12] From the beginning of the approach, the road toward the house at Mount Vernon veered to the left. Arriving guests lost the fine vista of the house for a few hundred yards as they traveled a picturesque road. The curving route was encouraged by the presence of two broad ravines between the entrance and the hill upon which the mansion house stood. The two declivities were deep enough that the view of the mansion house would have been lost anyway along this route, and trees stood along the first part of the road so that one traveled as if through rather dense and irregular woods. That Washington carefully planned this sylvan effect is indicated by Powel's 1787 report that "the Grounds on each Side of the Road are cleared of the under wood & the Saplings neatly trimmed so as to promise to form a handsome Wood in future. Passing thro' this young Wood the road lies thro' a bottom till you approach the House." Fourteen years after Powel's visit, the trees on this route, no longer mere saplings, had matured, and Benjamin Henry Latrobe noted that "the house [first] becomes visible

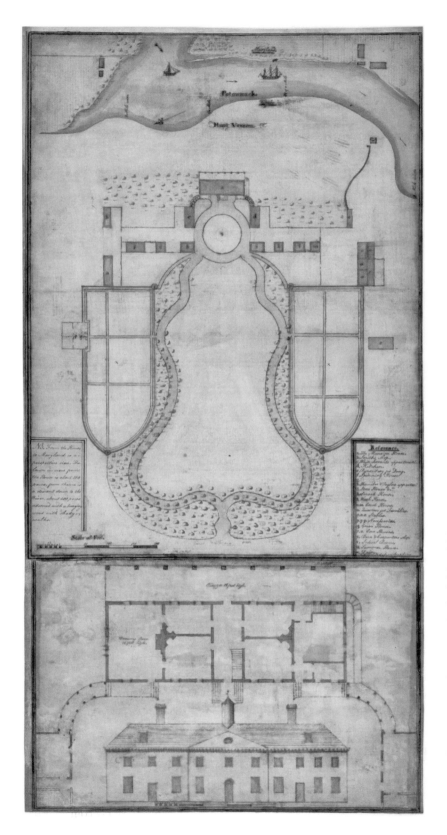

FIGURE 4.4. Samuel Vaughan, plan of the central part of the Mount Vernon estate, 1787, ink and water-color on paper, 32″ × 16.25″. Based on his memory and on the more rapid sketch he made of the estate (see Figure 4.3), English merchant Vaughan produced this plan after his return to England, and he sent it as a gift to George Washington. The plan is an invaluable guide to the early appearance of the buildings and grounds. Courtesy of the Mount Vernon Ladies' Association (W-1434).

FIGURE 4.5. Visitors from the first vista point two-thirds of a mile west of the mansion house probably traveled a curving route similar to that sketched here. Drawing: Kay Fukui.

between two Groves of trees at about a miles distance," his account also confirming the presence of a similar grove on the other (right) side of the open field.[13] This section of the road on the long slope from the first vista point, presently not accessible to visitors, today offers some sense of the trip for an eighteenth-century visitor, although we need to imagine the trees trimmed and the ground less obscured by undergrowth. The success of Washington's planning of the entrance and approach comes across in early praise, as in a visitor's account of 1801: "The approach is very handsome and variegated by hill and vale and plain fields highly improved, the forest trees left standing[,] trimmed[,] and cleared of underwood."[14]

A few hundred yards from the present entrance gates, at the bottom of a hill on the way to the mansion, visitors on horseback or in carriages began a dramatic rise up the hill toward the bowling green and house. As Allan Greenberg and Dennis Pogue have pointed out, the original path of the road in this small stretch going up the hill is uncertain. Powel stated that before the hill the road lay "thro' a bottom," and the terrain indeed encourages a route to the left before the field that stands in front of the bowling green. The road then must have turned back to the right and to-

ward the axis perpendicular from the house, close to the country lane that still crosses a field toward the bowling green gates (Figure 4.6).[15] That one veered from the left back to the center of the field is supported by a view penned by Latrobe (Figure 4.7). He inscribed the drawing, "sketch from memory, showing the effect of Mount Vernon on approaching this place from the West on the road from Colchester."[16] The drawing is generalized and cannot be trusted for details, showing, as Latrobe wrote, only the "effect" of the approach. At any rate, Latrobe places the viewer near the center point of the axis and seems to show the bowling green trees at some distance forward, implying that he is in the approaching field. Latrobe gives us here an impressionistic but telling record of the approach to the bowling green gates somewhat to the north of the central axis from the house.

While ascending the "eminence" and approaching the bowling green, one gained a good view of the mansion house. That Mount Vernon was a productive place became increasingly apparent during this stretch of the journey, as one traveled through or near a field planted (depending on the season or year) with orchard grass, buckwheat, timothy, or corn, and the fruit orchards and other fields came into view further in the distance on the right.[17] The riders then came to a serpentine brick ha-ha wall (sunken wall) punctuated by a gate at the end of the bowling green, all built after the Revolutionary War and planned along with the vista to and from the woods in the west. Here the mansion house was in fairly full view, again framed on either side by the serpentine line of trees and shrubberies that surrounded the lawn (Figure 4.8). The road outside the gate was slightly lower than the bowling green itself, and the lawn and house still seemed higher up and yet to be attained.

Washington, gifted with the eye of a surveyor and known for his attention to measurements, must have been conscious of the placement of the bowling green gates off-center from the door of the mansion. Unless forced by site constraints, it should have been easy to put the gates on a direct line running perpendicular from the central front door of

FIGURE 4.6. Approach to the bowling green across an agricultural field, Mount Vernon. Photo: Author.

the west facade, but the bowling green gates, built in 1785, are slightly off to the right when viewed from the house (Plate 10).[18] Other asymmetries, some desired and planned, some encouraged or forced by circumstances, appear throughout the design of the mansion house and grounds. Where this practice was desired or at least allowed by Washington, it breaks with the traditional symmetry of earlier Georgian design and corresponds to avant-garde tastes of the later eighteenth century.

In considering the route from the bowling green gates to the house, some modern writers believe that the usual way was through the gate itself and toward the house by the serpentine roads or paths on either side of the lawn, which were established in 1784–1785. Powel apparently traveled that route in November 1787, passing through the "large Court yard" between the brick walls of the upper and lower gardens that comprised the bowling green: "After ascending the Eminence on which the Mansion is placed you enter a very large Court Yard, with a pavilion on each Side & proceed thro' a circular Road covered with rough Gravel till you come to the Offices, from which the Road is paved to the House."[19] Frenchman Jacques-Pierre Brissot de Warville is

FIGURE 4.7. Benjamin Henry Latrobe, *Sketch from memory, showing the effect of Mount Vernon on approaching this place from the West on the road from Colchester,* pencil, pen and ink on paper, 7″ × 10.25″. Latrobe visited Mount Vernon in July 1796. Here, he showed the approach to the mansion house. Further forward is the bowling green, mansion house, and other buildings. Courtesy of The Maryland Historical Society (1960.108.1.2.12).

more ambiguous but could have followed Powel's route during his visit of 1788. From the first vista point, he wrote, one rides, and "after having passed over two hills, you discover a country house of an elegant and majestic simplicity. It is preceded by grass plats; on one side are the stables, on the other a green-house, and houses for a number of negro mechanics." Brissot may have approached the house directly the way Powel did, but his account is inconclusive.[20]

Other evidence suggests that the normal path for most travelers on horse or in a carriage who wanted to get from the bowling green gate to the house was to lose sight of the house again and turn down toward the right. They might continue on the road between the lower garden and paddock and the fields further down the hill (called the Vineyard Enclosure), and then, turning left at the stable (cf. Plate 11), ascend the hill to the house (Figure 4.9). Powel visited soon after the bowling green area had been laid out, and perhaps Washington had not yet determined the roundabout route and was still using the area for carriage entrance. It could be that Powel went that way because it was November and wet ground made this upper route necessary. Or perhaps Powel's elite social position as a wealthy, former mayor

of Philadelphia and friend of Mount Vernon's owner merited a direct path. In 1794, Washington had manager William Pearce offer the best wines only to "some of the *most* respectable foreigners" and "persons of some distinction" who might visit the estate.[21] Powel was one of the rare visitors to enter Washington's private study in the mansion house, and it would not be surprising if, on the occasion of his visit, Washington encouraged him to approach the house along the bowling green.

Powel is the only early visitor to clearly report his access to the house via the bowling green paths. Latrobe complained in 1796 that "the approach is not very well managed but [instead] leads you into the area between the Stables;" his journey went to the right of the lower garden and toward the stable rather than through the bowling green gate and along the west lawn.[22] A description by young English merchant Joshua Brookes in 1799 throws further light on how one approached the mansion house. Brookes wrote:

The house is situated on a hill, a gravel road leads up it, which divides when in sight of the house, the north or left hand going to the negro huts, the south or right hand to the farm yard. Before the house is a circular grass plot, surrounded by a post and

PLATE 1. Mansion house, Mount Vernon, west front. After enlarging a smaller house on the site fifteen years before, Washington greatly expanded the size of the residence in 1773 and later. The house as restored and maintained today reflects its appearance at the time of Washington's death in 1799. Photo: Scott Gilchrist / Archivision.com.

PLATE 2. Central pediment and weathervane, mansion house, Mount Vernon. The house is sheathed in pine boards that were beveled, painted white, and coated in sand to resemble fine stone. Photo: Author.

PLATE 3. Mansion house, Mount Vernon, east front, seen from the northeast. The monumental porch—which Washington called at various times a piazza, colonnade, portico, or gallery—garnered praise at the time and was among the most inventive aspects of the mansion house. On the right, in the north grove, Washington intended as early as 1776 that there be planted irregularly clustered locust trees, and later he supplemented the grove with other trees and shrubs. Photo: Author.

PLATE 4. View of Large Dining Room (also called the New Room), mansion house, Mount Vernon. This large room, framed before the war but not finished until 1788, was the architectural and fine arts showcase of the home. Courtesy of the Mount Vernon Ladies' Association.

PLATE 5. Small Dining Room, mansion house, Mount Vernon. William Bernard Sears and other craftsmen created a rich interior while Washington was away at war. The highlights include the fireplace surround and the Rococo ceiling stucco. In later years, Washington had the room painted a strong verdigris color. Courtesy of the Mount Vernon Ladies' Association.

PLATE 6. West Parlor, mansion house, Mount Vernon. The chimneypiece, from the 1750s, is more abstract in style than the later one in the Small Dining Room, although both derived from published designs by Englishman Abraham Swan. Washington hung many family portraits in this room. Courtesy of the Mount Vernon Ladies' Association.

PLATE 7. Central passage, mansion house, Mount Vernon. Washington inherited this space from his half-brother Lawrence but added the staircase, paneling, and grain painting of the walls. Courtesy of the Mount Vernon Ladies' Association.

PLATE 8. Washington's study, mansion house, Mount Vernon. The walls were grain painted to mimic fine wood, and Washington maintained a masculine iconography here with a hunting scene, a painting of his half-brother Lawrence, and busts of notable men. Courtesy of the Mount Vernon Ladies' Association.

PLATE 9. View of the lower garden (kitchen garden), Mount Vernon. Tours of the grounds by early guests included visits to the practical lower garden, generally devoted to items grown for the table. The garden was reconstructed in the 1930s; its format of walks and well is characteristic of Colonial Revival gardens, but the planting of fruit trees and vegetables is consistent with the original function of this plot of land. Photo: Author.

PLATE 10. View from mansion house, Mount Vernon, toward the west. Washington calculated that this vista would be toward "distant woods," framed by willow trees placed sixty yards apart at the end of the bowling green. Photo: Author.

PLATE 11. Part of an entrance route to the mansion house, Mount Vernon. On the right was the Vineyard Enclosure, and on the left is the horse and mule paddock. Architect Benjamin Henry Latrobe traveled this roundabout route to the mansion house, complaining that the approach was "not well managed." Photo: Author.

PLATE 12. Serpentine walk along the bowling green, Mount Vernon. The curving walk was graveled and bordered by artfully mixed plantings of trees and shrubs. Photo: Author.

PLATE 13. Upper garden, Mount Vernon, with a view of the Greenhouse. The upper garden, in addition to more mundane vegetables and fruit trees typical of Virginia, harbored exotica, including orange, coffee, and palm trees, which were sheltered in the winter in the Greenhouse. For variety, Washington also planted a formal, old-fashioned arrangement in front of the Greenhouse, perhaps similar to the shaped boxwood plantings shown here. Photo: Author.

PLATE 14. Attributed to Edward Savage, *The West Front of Mount Vernon*, c. 1791, oil on canvas, 21.75" (height) × 35.5". Savage left a vivid record of the house and gardens of the time. Courtesy of the Mount Vernon Ladies' Association; bequest of Helen W. Thompson, 1964 (H-2445-A).

PLATE 15. Attributed to Edward Savage, *The East Front of Mount Vernon,* c. 1791, oil on canvas, 21.75″ × 35.5″. The artist represented the north ha-ha wall, deer park, Greenhouse, and slave quarters, as well as the mansion house and grove of trees on the north end. Courtesy of the Mount Vernon Ladies' Association; bequest of Helen W. Thompson, 1964 (H-2445-B).

PLATE 16. Lawn, south grove, and mansion house, Mount Vernon. Washington planned a grove here more mixed in character than the north grove, with an abundance of trees and shrubs. The present reconstruction, dominated by magnolias, reflects Washington's original desire to have "clever," flowering trees in the groves. Photo: Author.

FIGURE 4.8. View of the mansion house from the bowling green gate. Visitors usually went around and approached the house from the left or right of the walled gardens, leaving the bowling green, serpentine paths, and adjoining shrubberies and wildernesses as a pedestrian zone. Photo: Author.

chain [fence], a handle like a bell handle in the middle of each, round this is a paved carriage way. East of it is the house and west of it a lawn defended by posts and rope from cattle entering. At the end of the house and wings etc. are planted evergreens which hide the huts and farm yard, the house etc. These and [the] lawn form a semicircle.[23]

This important passage confirms that from outside the bowling green gate ("in sight of the house") he proceeded not through the gate and into the large courtyard but either left or right on the roads around the walled gardens. Latrobe took the right, which was likely the preferred way, and it was perhaps enforced by gates, temporary barriers, or verbal suggestion. Indeed, it is difficult to imagine that Washington preferred that visitors arrive in the direction of what Brookes said was the way of the "negro huts" and brick slave quarters, a crowded area that made manifest the presence of slavery on the farm. The coach house and stable, ready to receive horses, stood on the southerly route to the right. This path

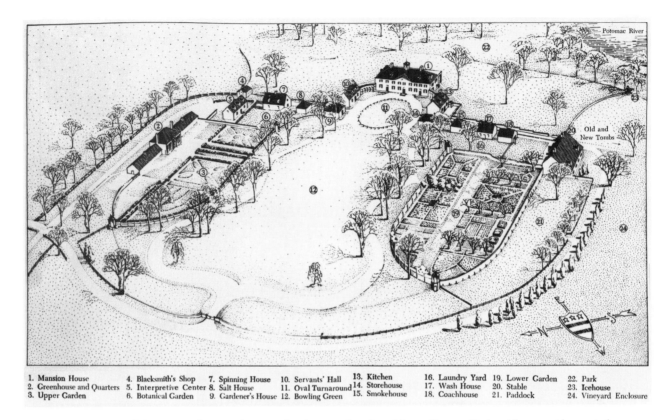

1. **Mansion House**	4. **Blacksmith's Shop**	7. **Spinning House**	10. **Servants' Hall**	13. **Kitchen**	16. **Laundry Yard**	19. **Lower Garden**	22. **Park**
2. **Greenhouse and Quarters**	5. **Interpretive Center**	8. **Salt House**	11. **Oval Turnaround**	14. **Storehouse**	17. **Wash House**	20. **Stable**	23. **Icehouse**
3. **Upper Garden**	6. **Botanical Garden**	9. **Gardener's House**	12. **Bowling Green**	15. **Smokehouse**	18. **Coachhouse**	21. **Paddock**	24. **Vineyard Enclosure**

FIGURE 4.9. Layout of the mansion house and surrounding lawns and gardens, Mount Vernon. Updated from a mid-twentieth-century guidebook image, this perspective view shows the present configuration and designations of the mansion house and nearby outbuildings and grounds at Mount Vernon. Original image courtesy of the Mount Vernon Ladies' Association; adapted by Sandra Marcatili, 2011.

was most likely the one encouraged by Washington, as we know it was for Latrobe. This arrangement and the route have suggestive implications for the nature of the visit and the impression one received from the estate. Going that way, visitors passed by orchards and open green areas, reinforcing a sense of the estate's agricultural and productive character.

A notable oil painting attributed to Edward Savage (Plate 14) shows the route to the house roundabout the courtyard (bowling green area), going from the south of the bowling green and lower garden, past the stable, and up the south lane. The bowling green is enjoyed by Mr. and Mrs. Washington, Martha's grandchildren, Nelly Parke Custis and George Washington Parke Custis, and an adult male figure (perhaps Pierre L'Enfant). In that picture of c. 1791, a car-

riage is seen approaching from down the hill and up into the grand entrance oval.[24] Assuming that it is moving and not stationary, the carriage's angle implies that it is entering from the south service lane, not from the paths around the bowling green. The whole painting, while idealized, does reflect the known arrangement of buildings and gardens, and shows the bowling green area as a place for walking and leisure.

Adding complexity to the history of the approach to the house is a letter that Washington wrote to estate manager William Pearce on 5 June 1796 as his presidency was winding down and he was planning his return home:

In the few days after *we* get there, we shall be visited, I expect, by characters of distinction; I could wish therefore that the Gardens, Lawns, and every thing else, in, and about the Houses, may be got in clean and nice order . . . And as the front gate of the Lawn (by the Ivies) is racked, and scarcely to be opened, I wish you would order a new one (like the old one) to be immediately made, and that, with the new ones you have just got made, and all the boarding of every kind that was white before to be painted white again. If Neal and my own people cannot make the front gate, above mentioned, get some one from Alexandria to do it, provided he will set about and finish it immediately. This must be the way up to the House.[25]

First, by needing to write that going through "the front gate of the Lawn," that is, the bowling green gate, "must be the way to the House," Washington implied that this approach was unusual or a change from the previous arrangement, which was surely the case if the gate was indeed "racked" and inoperable. Secondly, he had decided that the prestige of future visitors would make the bowling green route recommended for visitors of a new, higher level. This leaves open some questions: Why did Latrobe and Brookes not go this way even though they visited after 1796, the time of Washington's request to have the bowling green gate repaired? Why did no other visitor after Powel in 1787 mention going through the bowling green? We do not know if Washington actually followed through on his decision of 1796 to make the bowling green route the "way to the house," and perhaps the large number of visitors or experience with the new route finally discouraged such a plan. We can conclude that a few visitors, such as Samuel Powel in 1787, and possibly other "characters of distinction" after 1797, were encouraged or permitted to go this way, but the majority were directed to go around, right or left, and not use the serpentine paths, so that the bowling green and surrounding gardens served as a pedestrian area for family and guests. We have no record of how Washington managed the route for visitors of different social classes, but every other visit to Mount Vernon was marked by such distinctions: who took guests on a tour of the gardens, where they sat at the dinner table, where one slept, and how much time and attention one received from Washington himself all differed from visitor to visitor.

The area including the slave quarters that were attached to the Greenhouse, the huts across the road, and the brick Family House formed part of the visual experience of the estate and was adjacent to the gardens; it would have been seen by anyone approaching the house or walking on the road to the left (north) side of the bowling green and upper walled garden. Washington prided himself on his treatment of his slaves, whom Nelly Custis said "feared & loved" the general, and Washington Irving reported that Washington treated his slaves with kindness.[26] Washington, harboring misgivings toward the institution and not unaware of good publicity, arranged in his final will to free his slaves upon Martha's death. Still, his ownership of slaves remained a mark against him, particularly outside of the southern states, and it would not be surprising to know that Washington hoped that travelers would avoid the area with "negro huts" (Brookes) as they journeyed to the house. Nor did he want the slave residences to be seen from the house itself. Washington took steps in June 1791 to remove the brick Family House (or Old Quarters) for slaves that was close to the mansion house.[27] The structure was adjacent to the brick Greenhouse and slave quarters, located between them and the mansion house (visible on the right in Plate 15). In his account of the estate in 1791, William Loughton Smith reported that Washington owned "300 slaves, about 150 or 160 workers; no negro houses are seen near the mansion; they are all at a distance and not visible from the house."[28] In addition to the removal of the Family House in 1791, Washington forbade the slave children from playing in the grass near the house itself or in the walled gardens.[29] As household servants and to some extent as garden workers, slaves could not be kept away from visitors entirely, but by the 1790s the presence of slaves on the estate was a point of shame in Washington's national and international reputation, and he took steps to shield visitors from seeing them.

One part of the landscape at Mount Vernon that is little described by early visitors is the land along the road leading to the stable, that is, on the road south of the lower garden and running parallel to it (Figure 4.9 and Plate 11). On the left there was a paddock largely used for mules and horses. Also on the left, a carpenter's shop, which shows prominently on Samuel Vaughan's plan of 1787 ("S"; see Figure 4.4), burnt down in 1792 and was not replaced, leaving the area more open and green. The slaves who worked and lived there were removed from that roundabout entrance route to the house. On the right of this section of the paddock lane, there was an orchard and fields down the little hill from the road. Washington called that section the Vineyard Enclosure; it held a variety of kitchen plants and an orchard and is presently restored as such (see Figure 4.9). Manasseh Cutler (1802) described the orchard as consisting principally of "large cherry and peach trees."[30] Between the Vineyard Enclosure and the road was a strip of soil planted as Gen. James Taylor described in 1805: "parallel with the avenue on that side, is a complete wilderness of evergreens, cedars, pines, etc. resembling nature."[31] Although some five years had passed since Washington's death, it is likely that Taylor's account described the effect arranged by Washington, who had artfully mimicked Nature with this intermingling of varied trees. This plan had the effect of creating a forest-like view from any glimpse from the bowling green level, lower garden, or the adjacent road itself and reinforced the idea that the house, pleasure gardens, and agricultural aspects were deeply embedded in wooded countryside, similar to the impression that Washington created when he arranged for the prospect from the west door to face toward "distant woods."

Upon approaching the house, one rode or walked around the elliptical, cobblestoned entrance drive to reach the front door (Plates 1 and 10). This oval (in nonmathematical speech, the elliptical form is and was freely called an oval, and vice versa) was the only basic geometric shape on the grounds outside of the walled gardens. The posts were thirty-two in number, evenly spaced, and are documented as placed there under Washington's own direction in 1785, certainly evidence of Washington's own personal design work.[32]

Each post had a chain of metal dangling like a swag with "a handle like a bell handle in the middle of each" serving for decoration, the chain and posts intended to help keep traffic away from the flat, grassy lawn in the middle. The chains and "bell handles" appear in an insurance drawing of the house in 1805 (see Figure 2.14).[33] In the center of the oval, Washington placed a small sundial of English manufacture, a rare example at Mount Vernon of a crafted, nonarchitectural object of beauty on the garden grounds. The sundial was spare in style and noticeably underscaled for its site but formed an appealing accent point in the middle of the oval lawn. The metal was mounted on a modest wooden support, known from early views; the support, undoubtedly made locally, is presently reproduced at Mount Vernon, along with a copy of the sundial. (The original is preserved in Mount Vernon's museum.)[34]

The elliptical shape of the turnaround often appeared to visitors to be a circle, and indeed ellipses can appear circular when seen obliquely. Washington sometimes referred to it as a "circle," and a drawing by Samuel Powel also records this as a circle, as does the plan of Samuel Vaughan. The insurance company drawings of 1803 and 1805, however, map it out as an oval (see Figures 2.13 and 2.14). Washington called it an "oval" in his diary entry of 10 March 1785 and noted that the posts were turned by "Mr. Ellis [William Allison]" at "the Snuff Mill on Pohick [Creek]," but in 1795 he ordered "Locust Posts for the circle before the door." Elsewhere, Washington in 1793 represented the turnaround on a map, and though he drew it as an oval, he set it the long way across the facade.[35] He drew measurements of his grounds and confirmed the oval shape, information that is echoed by the reference in 1805 by visitor James Taylor to "an oval of say 40 by 60 feet." Archaeological work has confirmed the original elliptical form, the cobblestone surface, and location a foot or so below grade of the present reconstructed ellipse.[36]

The choice of the oval shows Washington's sensitive eye; it helps to fill the space defined by the house, colonnaded arms, dependencies, and two outbuildings. It also echoes the oval window over the central pediment of the mansion (and the window of the Greenhouse), and works well with the serpentine paths on either side of the bowling green and the curving brick walls of the upper and lower gardens. The elliptical turnaround and lawn form a visually satisfying conclusion to the serpentine shape of the bowling green. The sundial is in line with the center of the north and south lanes, further locking the ellipse in place within the context of the estate. Washington, always aware of measurements and proportions, must have planned that the distance from the center of the oval (the sundial) to the center of the mansion house would equal the length of the oval itself, and that, thus, from the end of the ellipse near the house, it is the same distance both to the sundial and to the center of the house.

Robert Adam and others in England embraced the ellipse as a more "natural" form than the circle or square, and it found a wide application in American Federal architecture and decorative arts.[37] Before concluding that Washington was in the avant-garde in this regard, however, it should be recalled that public and private oval entrance drives were widespread in England and America well before the generation of Adam and his followers. George Washington's choice of the ellipse was influenced largely by that tradition and was further encouraged by the space in front of his house created by the dependencies and colonnaded arms and by the oval in the pediment.

Bowling Green and Walled Gardens

The oval drive, as well as being a practical turnaround, forms a visual link to the serpentine paths and bowling green on the west side of the mansion. Washington referred to this vast green as a "lawn" and a "platt," and the whole area between the brick garden walls as a "courtyard," but no document survives indicating that he himself called this a bowling green, although it is labeled "Bolling Green" on the insurance view of 1803.[38] Nor is there evidence that Washington or anyone else actually played bowls or any similar game on

the west lawn during his lifetime. The term "bowling green" in the eighteenth century was customary for an open, grassy spot, whatever its actual purpose. We can use the phrase for convenience, as was done as early as 1785 by Mount Vernon visitor Robert Hunter Jr., and by the Marquis de Chastellux, who called the lawn a "bowlingreen."[39]

Washington developed the serpentine walks surrounding the lawn after careful planning. When finished, the paths occupied varying widths, up to nineteen feet or so, wider than the present range of nine to fifteen feet, which is necessary because of the mature trees that line the walkways (Figures 4.10 and 4.11; Plate 12). The gravel, gathered locally, was irregular in shape, mixed in color, about one-half to three-quarter inches in width, and was set on a reddish soil; the walkways stood about a foot below the present grade, as indicated by recent archaeological work.[40] Washington wrote to Henry Knox in Boston in February 1785 to get information about the kind of gravel used for walks in New England, hoping to find a mixture good for walking and horse and carriage traffic:

> In the course of your literary disputes at Boston . . . I perceive, & was most interested by something which was said respecting the composition for a public walk; which also appeared to be one of the exceptionable things. Now, as I am engaged in works of this kind, I would thank you, if there is any art in the preparation, to communicate it to me—whether designed for Carriages, or walking. My Gardens have gravel walks (as you possibly may recollect) in the usual Style, but if a better composition has been discovered for these, I should gladly adopt it. the matter however which I wish principally to be informed in, is, whether your walks are designed for Carriages, and if so, how they are prepared, to resist the impression of the wheels. I am making a Serpentine road to my door, & have doubts (which it may be in your power to remove) whether any thing short of solid pavement will answer.[41]

Knox answered rather inconclusively on 24 March 1785, writing that gravel is put down in Boston without cement, and he conveyed no solution for Washington's desire to lay down a support suitable for both walking and carriage traf-

FIGURE 4.10. George Parkyns, *View of the West Front of Mount Vernon,* 1795, aquatint and etching, 10″ × 13.3″. Parkyns, with some artistic liberties, captured the general appearance of the gravel walks and bowling green and the mansion house in the distance. Courtesy of the Mount Vernon Ladies' Association (M-1657).

fic.[42] Apparently, there was a question from the beginning of how these paths might be used.

While they were under construction or development, Washington called the serpentine paths both "walks" and "roads," expressing the potential different usages.[43] Samuel Vaughan, who visited the same year as Samuel Powel (1787), called them "walks 19 feet wide, with trees on each side." John Searson, the poet, visited in May 1799 and took note of "the walks well-gravell'd, smooth'd and very neat" on the estate in general. Amariah Frost of Milford, Massachusetts, visiting the estate on business, noted that between "two gardens is the great green and circular walk."[44] For his part, James Taylor in 1805 made a distinction between the "carriage way" around the oval and the "avenues" that emanated from the house and ran along the long bowling green, implying that carriages stayed at the oval, and that the avenues had a different purpose; that is, they were for pedestrian traffic.[45] It is clear from the exchange with Knox that early on Wash-

ington wanted horses and carriages to be able to pass through the bowling green "roads," but the fact that Washington never found an ideal stone for pavement serves as another reason why the courtyard did not end up as the regular carriage route to the house and remained best suited for pedestrians.

Washington took an intense and longstanding interest in the development of the lawn and the pleasure garden surrounding it. He shaped the bowling green (Plate 10) to be almost perfectly flat, instructing his laborers to work hard to put what he called "an even face" to this lawn, and they used rollers to smooth the surface and help in "compressing the Ground."[46] No less a visitor than royal exile Louis-Philippe d'Orléans was impressed and described "a kind of courtyard with a green carpet" in front of Washington's home. Niemcewicz called the grass "a green carpet of the most beautiful velvet."[47] Washington experimented with different kinds of grasses over the years. At the beginning of the project (No-

FIGURE 4.11. Serpentine walk and plantings along the bowling green. Washington called the plantings on the outsides of the paths either shrubberies or wildernesses, the latter being farther from the mansion house. Contemporary viewers reported a remarkable variety of growth, with an abundance of flowering trees and shrubs. Photo: Author.

vember 1784), he described what he wanted: "The grass I mean has different names . . . By some it is called English Grass, by others Goose Grass, By others spear grass, but the kind I want is that which affords the best turf for walks and lawns, and is the purpose for which I want it."[48] Richard Parkinson, English farmer and agricultural author, noted that at Mount Vernon, "I saw no green grass there, except in the garden: and this was some English grass, appearing to me a sort of couch-grass; it was in drills."[49] Following the method

of the time, the lawn was cut with scythes, so the grass was kept less sharply clipped than it would be today. (The lawn-mower as we know it was invented c. 1830.) A vivid water-color from c. 1825 of Monticello, which admittedly was in decline because of Jefferson's financial duress, shows a more unkempt lawn than we might expect, resulting from the use of scythes, the difficulty of acquiring seed, and the labor costs of maintaining lawns. Early views of Mount Vernon show a healthier lawn than that, but there were, undoubtedly, spotty patches and rough borders, and Washington's workers had difficulty in times of drought getting water to the hilltop site.

Washington saw to it that the area adjacent to the lawn and along the walkways was planted with a well-chosen and varied mixture of plants, shrubs, and trees. The plantings constituted Washington's most finely worked piece of open landscape art. He called the strips of land on the far (west) side of the bowling green "wildernesses," following the usage of the word in England. In addition to adorning the paths for pedestrians there, these wildernesses, along with the willow mounds, framed the prospect from the west door of the house toward the forest land near the present west gates. These wildernesses were denser, less distinctly planted, and more varied in size of growth than the plantings along the walks on either side closer to the house, which he called "shrubberies," again using a word common in English gardening.

Visitors described, and Washington's papers recorded, the trees in some detail. Near the dependencies ("near each angle of the house and in advance of the store houses, and between them and the entrances of the avenue"), stood on either side a magnolia tree and a Spanish chestnut tree. The chestnuts were much admired by visitors over time, and several, including John Duncan, marveled that these had "sprung from nuts planted by the General's own hand."[50] At the far end of the bowling green (Figure 4.12), Washington set two romantic weeping willow trees into mounds of earth on the lawn itself. ("I set the people to raising and forming the mounds of Earth by the gate in order to plant weeping willow thereon.") He noted in a 1787 letter that these mounds, made the year before, were sixty yards apart, and they defined the width of the vista at that point from the mansion house and bowling green to the distant woods. It was difficult to maintain willow trees on the mounds, as they needed a wetter soil, and by 1804, General James Taylor noted that a single cedar tree "not more than 10 or 12 feet" capped each artificial mound.[51] Other trees around the ser-

pentine walks of the bowling green included tulip poplars, which lined each side of the north and south paths. Two magnificent tulip poplars, one on either side of the lawn, and one eastern hemlock (near the upper garden gate) survive from Washington's time, still shading visitors along the serpentine paths. Other trees that appear on Washington's planting lists could have found a place along the paths, including pecans, live oaks, cayenne pepper, pistachio, Lombardy poplar, and spruce, and the shrubberies included ash, aspen, dogwood, hawthorn, holly, lilac, magnolia, mock orange, pawpaw, redbud, sassafras, and swamp red berry trees. Fruit trees intermingled with the others, like the apricot and peach trees that Washington noted had been planted "in the borders of the grass plats." Polish nobleman Niemcewicz singled out the tulip poplars, magnolias, catalpa, spruce, and willows.[52]

Washington established special areas that he called his "Pine labyrinths" on both sides of the bowling green garden. He noted in his diary on 18 March 1785 that he "planted 20 Pine trees in the lines of Trees by the sides of the Serpentine roads to the House" and went to the Dogue Run farm to oversee the taking up of pine trees "for my two wildernesses," that is, the areas around the far ends of the serpentine path near the bowling green gate. Sally Foster Otis, who rose early "to regale myself in these enchanting walks," responded well to the densely clustered pine trees that Washington planted in March 1785, noting that "the walks are irregular & serpentine[,] cover'd by trees of various kinds but what most pleased me was a labyrinth of ever greens where the sun cannot even now penetrate[;] this must be a little Paradise in summer."[53]

The exact appearance of the shrubberies and wildernesses is difficult to reconstruct, as the early views are generalized or idealized. Verbal descriptions and documents are useful but not enough to help us create a thorough idea of the appearance. In his letters, Washington implied that the plantings in the shrubberies were not to be overly dense and must be calculated to appear spontaneous but should be kept

FIGURE 4.12. Mound with a willow tree, visible in the center of the photograph. Washington placed one mound on either side of the far end of the bowling green, sixty yards apart. They framed the prospect from the mansion house to the distant woods on the west. Photo: Author.

discrete and cleanly divided from each other. For example, when absent at the Constitutional Convention in July 1787, he sent instructions to keeper George Augustine Washington to treat the shrubberies with care and make sure that the ground between plantings is clear ("P. S. Keep the Shrubberies clean.").[54] Rather than imitating Nature, this was an improvement of it, a cleaner version. There was great variety of color and form. Washington's letters indicate the number of species and his careful ordering of their arrangement. Niemcewicz stressed the incredible variety, marveling that "the path which runs all around the bowling green is planted with a thousand kinds of trees, plants and bushes."[55] Faced with having to accommodate tourist traffic, the present garden curators would find it inconvenient to attempt to reproduce the infinite variety and delicate arrangement of plantings, and any attempt to recreate the original wildernesses, shrubberies, and pine labyrinths would necessarily be conjectural.

The presence of flowers in the bowling green area is not well documented, but Washington did plant many flowering trees and bushes there. In March 1785, he "planted the Scarlet or French honey suckle (as my Gardner calls it, & which he says blows all the Summer) at each Column of my

covered ways—as also against the circular walls between the Store house &ca. and the two new necessaries. Also planted the Gilder rose & Persian Jessamine opposite thereto on the Walks leading up to these necessaries—4 of the first and Six of the latter on each walk." Niemcewicz is particularly helpful in confirming the presence in the shrubberies and wildernesses of "a thousand other bushes, for the most part species of laurel and thorn, all covered with flowers of different colors, all planted in a manner to produce the most beautiful hues."[56]

Another opportunity for planting flowers, shrubs, and small trees was in the six oval beds (two larger and four smaller) that Washington added to the bowling green area in the last decade of his life. These beds must have formed a picturesque and striking part of the bowling green garden, adding variety and more curving shapes to the area. We do not know where these beds were located, and they are little discussed in the literature. They were probably located along the edges of the bowling green, and Washington's predilection for symmetry in larger shapes, as with the paths themselves, suggests that the ovals were placed on one side as on the other. Washington highly prized the vista from the front door to the west, and it is unlikely that he would have blocked it with the trees from the ovals, which were thus probably planted along the paths, running east and west themselves and echoing the shape of the serpentine walks. Overall, the beds added a touch of curvilinearity and variety to the lawn, and Thomas Jefferson established ovals on his lawn at Monticello, adopting the device of the elliptical beds as found widely in England.

Washington exercised masterly control and scrupulous care as gardener, even when absent. On 15 April 1792, George Augustine Washington reported that he had planted three hundred shrubs in the ovals. Washington saw the results, however, and he wrote to gardener John (Johann) Christian Ehlers in November with directions to achieve both symmetry and unkempt variety within the beds. He wanted "in the Centre of every Oval" to have "one of the lofty growing trees planted." At the two large ovals, two lofty trees should also be planted on the ends, while in the four smaller ovals Ehlers should plant "trees of lesser size." He wanted "no regularity" to be observed in other plantings of the ovals and was disappointed when he visited and saw that this had not been done before. The directive included a list of items for the ovals purchased from Bartram's nursery near Philadelphia, including "Philadelphus coronarius, as sweet flowering shrub (called mock Orange)," "Pinus Strobus . . . (White Pine)," "Prunus Divaricata," "Hydrangia arborescens," and "Laurus nobilis" (bay laurel).[57] Although he offered detailed instructions, Washington's exchange of letters with manager William Pearce about these six ovals also indicates the role that those on site had in determining details of the gardening scheme. Pearce made the oval beds larger than Washington had wanted and told the president that he would be pleased with the results when he came home and saw the beds.[58] Washington's managers and gardeners took a role in shaping the gardens, much as managers and craftsmen had played a part in developing the architecture of the mansion house, filling out the particulars within parameters laid out by Washington. He took firmer control when present at the estate, but the creative contributions of the managers and gardeners were necessarily greater during the owner's long absences from Mount Vernon. At any rate, Washington did what he could from afar to get the ovals to his satisfaction. We can only regret that we have little in the way of visual record or visitor response to these six ovals, which must have been an extraordinary and rich feature of the gardens.

The bowling green area itself was a microcosm of the gardens as a whole, embracing both order and disorder. The serpentine paths themselves "curved in a kind of festoon to relieve the monotony of direct lines." Yet, trees planted here formed something of a symmetrical balance across the lawn, to judge from the Vaughan plans and from comments by visitors, such as New Englander Amariah Frost, who wrote in 1797 that "there are . . . rows of trees exactly corrisponding with each other, between which and the two gardens is the great green and circular walk fronting northerly from the house seen at a great distance." In general, large trees kept a kind of order, while the smaller plantings added variety and a sense of spontaneity. This was true of the ovals, too, where a tree in the center of the smaller ones and trees at both ends of the larger ovals provided axiality and symmetry to areas of otherwise mixed plantings. In addition to the orderly directives to his gardeners, Washington insisted that they make the trees in the shrubberies and wildernesses grow straight, adding a sense of order to Nature.[59] As part of this balance of planting in this area, the serpentine paths were, unlike the asymmetrical garden paths at Monticello, symmetrical from side to side. Latrobe referred to the "extremely formal serpentine walk," the symmetry differing from the taste for more irregular walks that had developed in the England. In taking in the whole scene, North Carolinian William Blount picked up on the variety of the presentation but also the order of the straight lines: "Delightful walks, straight, circular and serpentine."[60] The whole effect was a kind of hybrid of a formal courtyard and rambling nature. Washington had devised gardens that balanced order and disorder, and he created conscious and obvious Art rather than an imitation of a random occurrence of Nature.

The success of the bowling green garden and some idea of its appearance are revealed in comments by Niemcewicz and others. Winthrop Sargent visited in 1793 and described his experience of the serpentine walks: "on either side are continued to the Road deep embowering Shades of Myrtle, Cypress Cedar and a variety of aromatic 'ever Greens'—Into one of those Recesses I entered—the feather Songsters and turtle Doves had been invited by the Beauties of the Scene— the various Avenues are as artfully continued as in a very limited Area to afford the most delightful promenades— impervious almost even to the Solar Ray but small Interstices of Admission purposely disposed upon the Margin— Whilst admiring the [hand?] of Art and Nature in the Miniature Labyrinth, the great Bell summoned me to Breakfast."[61] The painting, attributed to Edward Savage, that illustrates the Washington family enjoying the bowling green (Plate 14) is a thoughtful record of the garden and house;[62] without putting too much stock in the details, it captures the character of the bowling green and its function, and depicts the beginning of the "Shrubbery" on the north side of the bowling green. Apart from the Vaughan plans and other rough or generic drawings and prints, Savage's painting is the only visual representation of the bowling green made during Washington's lifetime that has any overall sense of veracity of appearance and usage. The whole area—comprising walks, wildernesses, shrubberies, pine labyrinths, lawns, oval beds, and mounds with trees—consisted by 1799 of plantings that were rich and greatly varied, one's visual experience, in season, dominated by flowering trees and shrubs, and everything kept sharply delineated and separated despite the variety. The gardens there indeed formed a shaded and fragrant "little paradise" for visitors.

On either side of the bowling green were two walled gardens. The upper garden, on the north, did yield some herbs, fruit, and vegetables for everyday consumption but also served as the main site at Mount Vernon for propagating and displaying luxury plants. The lower garden, to the south, served largely as the kitchen garden (Plate 9). Lund Washington built rectangular walls for each while George was away in 1775; the original right-angled format undoubtedly reflected the general's intentions of the general. After he returned, however, Washington altered the walls (1785) to their present form, recorded in Vaughan's plans (see Figures 4.3 and 4.4). These two gardens are often described as bullet shaped; we might rather look at them as Gothic shapes, vertical with skewed, pointed arches. The pointed arch form corresponds well with the garden greenery and serpentine shape of the bowling green walks. Gothic shapes were well known to those of Washington's generation working in furniture design, and they were associated with the natural in Rococo artistry, as in Thomas Chippendale's bookplates, which combine Gothic and flowing natural forms. Washington himself bought a metal, hanging oil lamp in 1761 with ogival shapes, and he used it in the central passage, where it remains.[63] The overall form and arches of the garden are not unlike the lancet shapes found in Gothic windows or eighteenth-century furniture. The Gothic was associated with Nature, and the lancet shapes here were appropriate for the garden setting. Gothic follies, towers, and other garden buildings were widespread in England in the eighteenth century, and even the arch-classicist Thomas Jefferson planned Gothic style buildings for the gardens of Monticello, although he never built them.

The presence of walled gardens, so different in their enclosed character from the rest of the parkland and practical buildings and roads at Mount Vernon, raises questions. But the two walled gardens were first established—in rectangular form (Figure 4.13)—in the 1770s, not during the more "natural" and advanced gardening schemes of the 1780s and 1790s. It is possible that, had Washington built them after the Revolution, he might not have made them as large and as prominent, nor perhaps so close to the house. After 1785, he did take the trouble to shield the walls from the bowling green by trees and shrubberies, and he artfully changed the shape of the footprints.[64] In the end, as a practical and economical man, he retained, in expanded and altered form, the

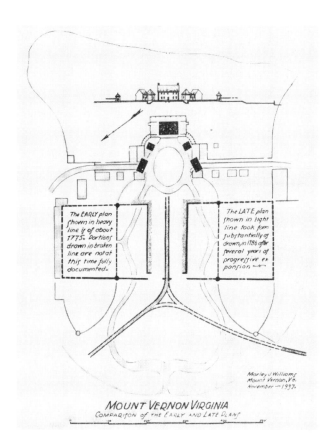

The EARLY plan
shown in heavy
line is of about
1775. Portions
drawn in broken
line are not at
this time fully
documented.

The LATE plan
shown in light
line took form
substantially of
drawn, in 1786 after
several years of
progressive ex
pansion →

MOUNT VERNON VIRGINIA
COMPARISON OF THE EARLY AND LATE PLANS

Morley J Williams
Mount Vernon, Va.
November — 1937

FIGURE 4.13. Morley Williams, layout at Mount Vernon, c. 1775, reconstruction (dated 1937). Washington's master plan after the Revolutionary War would greatly alter the layout of the estate. This earlier scheme had a straight entrance drive, rectangular walled gardens, and a V-shaped arrangement of main buildings. Courtesy of the Mount Vernon Ladies' Association.

walled gardens. They served a good function, while the curving shapes complemented the serpentine paths built near them in the 1780s. As with the expansions of the original house in 1757 and 1773, Washington altered and adapted an earlier work in purpose and style. In practice, walled gardens were commonly found even on the most natural and "advanced" of English gardens, sometimes standing as holdovers from earlier gardens.[65] Walled gardens managed to coexist in the Anglo-American world even with the advent of open landscape gardening.

The paths, at right angles—as confirmed by archaeology

and by Vaughan's plans—differed only slightly from those of the lower garden, which had less of an acentrality of axis of the long path running east-west. Recent restoration work (completed in 2011) has removed the curving pathways in the upper garden familiar to visitors in the last generation and has returned the gardens to their probable early layout, with larger beds and wider paths.[66] The gravel paths in the walled gardens, like those along the bowling green, followed the most fashionable trend in natural gardening in England and America. Washington generally avoided the more old-fashioned path coverings of oyster shells, tamped sand, or brick, although he perhaps used this last material for some walkways in the lower garden. Two diminutive outbuildings in each garden, similar in design to each other, graced different points along the walls; these served as necessaries and as garden sheds, and one at the west end of the upper garden served for a time as a tiny schoolhouse (Figure 4.14). These formed part of the ensemble of structures around the walled gardens, as do the slave quarters on the north side.

Standing to the south, below the level of the bowling green by some feet (and therefore moister than the upper garden), was the lower garden, serving as the principal kitchen garden where vegetables, fruit, and herbs were grown (Plate 9). The garden is situated so as to offer a mid-range prospect toward the Vineyard Enclosure, which to some extent supplemented the function of the kitchen garden. Although George Washington likely directed a large part of the choice of the plants and their cultivation, it was usual that such vegetable or kitchen gardens were the province of the lady of the house, and Martha would have helped choose plants, too, and given instructions for their harvesting and use. Martha proclaimed that the "vegetable is the best part of our living in the country," and she asked for them to be available for the table after a return from Philadelphia to Mount Vernon. Taking on greater responsibilities on the estate, Martha's granddaughter Nelly Parke Custis took up "gardening" in 1797, saying that she hoped "to make some proficiency in it," learning about the growth and cultivation of plants

FIGURE 4.14. Outbuilding, c. 1785, west end of the upper garden. This little building was for a time pressed into service as a schoolhouse for the children on the estate. Photo: Author.

and their use for cooking.[67] As for the day-to-day maintenance and direction, Niemcewicz, who saw growing there "*Corrents, Rasberys, Strawberys, Gusberys,* [and] quantities of peaches and cherries," reported in 1797 that the gardener in charge was an "Englishman," likely referring to Scotsman William Spence.[68]

The lower garden lacked the many fine or exotic specimens grown in the upper garden, and early observers mentioned it less often in their writings. Still, for those interested in following the progress of the growth of vegetables and fruit, it was a place to tour and enjoy. Diaries of contemporaries, such as that of tutor Philip Vickers Fithian at Nomini Hall, indicate that eighteenth-century strollers studied and enjoyed seeing the progress even of practical, everyday plants. Washington himself gained great pleasure from this garden and wrote a moralizing letter to English agricultural

innovator Arthur Young about the joy of farming: "The more I am acquainted with agricultural affairs the better I am pleased with them. Insomuch that I can no where find so great satisfaction, as in those innocent & useful pursuits. In indulging these feelings, I am led to reflect how much more delightful to an undebauched mind is the task of making improvements on the earth; than all the vain glory which can be acquired from ravaging it, by the most uninterrupted career of conquests."[69] Sally Foster Otis called the kitchen gardens at Mount Vernon "beautifully cultivated" and was one of many to include it in her tour of the gardens and grounds in general, calling attention to the "spinach & young Cabages growing in the open air." Washington and his contemporaries carefully noted details of growth and the beauty of plants of all kinds. In his diary, he wrote (16 April 1785) that "the Service tree was showing its leaf and the Maple had been full in bloom ten days or a fortnight. Of this tree I observed great difference in the colour of the blossoms; some being of a deep scarlet, bordering upon Crimson—others of a pale red, approaching yellow."[70] When he received a list of plants being sent from Bartram's nursery in Philadelphia in March 1792, the list was accompanied by some aesthetically sensitive descriptions. For example, Bartram wrote to Washington of *Crategus aria,* "foliage beautiful; silvered with white cottony down, underside"; of *Aesculus pavia varietas,* he said that "their light & airy foliage, crimson & variegated flowers, present a gay & mirthful appearance." The list added that "the Colutia arborescens exhibits a good appearance, foliage pinnated, of a soft pleasant green, colour, interspersed with the large yellow papillionacious flowers, in succession."[71] These remarks echo other period accounts: eighteenth-century garden visitors and owners paid attention to horticultural details with the eyes of connoisseurs, and they found beauty in all kinds of growth, from trees to flowers to the kinds of common vegetables that grew in the lower garden at Mount Vernon.

The present placement of the pathways and the well in the lower garden are not based on archaeology or other evidence and are more characteristic of the Colonial Revival period when they were set out. As for the plantings, documents and reports from visitors indicate espaliered fruit trees along the walls at Mansion House Farm. Staple vegetables such as spinach, onions, beets, peas, asparagus, carrots, and turnips grew on the farm, as well as sage, rhubarb, rutabaga, lima beans, kale, basil, artichokes, horseradish, and lavender.[72] The widespread planting of fruit and nut trees, vegetables, and herbs—in the lower garden, upper garden, and the Vineyard Enclosure down the hill—gives some credence to the assessment of Anglo-Irish visitor Isaac Weld, who said that Mount Vernon appeared more like a nursery than a pleasure garden. In the corner of the lower garden closest to the house stands the base of a small outbuilding, with beveled wood siding and a pepper pot roof. At least one early visitor was mildly surprised to learn that this was a

necessary; the contents collected overnight were used as fertilizer in the nearby beds.[73]

To the north of the bowling green was the upper garden (see Figures 4.9 and 4.14; Plate 13). Beyond the natural items, the most striking sight there was the Greenhouse, built from 1784 to 1787 (Figure 2.11). Heated by the sun and by wood fires in winter, it allowed the protection of beautiful and useful warm-weather exotics, such as lemon and orange trees. The Greenhouse, like the whole upper garden, was a place of luxury and enabled the manipulation of nature and the flourishing of potted trees and non-native varieties. In 1796, Latrobe, with a British eye accustomed to even larger and more luxurious structures, called it a "plain Greenhouse." The building seems modest in size today, but most eighteenth-century visitors, unacquainted with the large glass and metal greenhouses of the nineteenth century, thought it sizable and elegant. Samuel Vaughan called it in his *Journal* "a stately hot house," and as late as 1805, Gen. James Taylor described it as "exorbitant," indicating that this was especially large and high in style for an American garden of the time.[74]

The upper garden was laid out in rectangular beds; visitor Taylor called them "bordered with dwarf box-wood interspersed with handsome flowering shrubs with ornamental trees around the exterior of the inclosure."[75] The beds, until recently standing in smaller units than those Washington built, have recently been restored to their original size and contained a great variety of plants for beauty and food. Characteristic of Anglo-American practice, the arrangement in the boxes would likely have been "theatrical": tall plants planted toward the middle and shorter ones closer to the edges. That this was the normal and widespread form of planting in boxes is indicated by English gardener Batty Langley's text: "I shall not, under a Pretence of Discovery, offer any Directions, that Flowers of the highest Growth, ought to possess the Middle of a Border; while those of the lowest Rank, the extream Parts; and them of a mean Growth, a Medium Place between the two Extreams:

Because that every Gardiner is perfectly acquainted there-with." Washington himself called for a graded planting in the west lawn in the oval planting beds.[76] While Colonial Revival garden reconstructions were typically dense, the plantings in Washington's time would have been separated for readability. Washington was unhappy with the appearance of John and William Bartram's botanical garden near Philadelphia, and he must have felt that the arrangement was unartistic and meant for practical rather than aesthetic purposes. Abundance and variety in a garden were not enough for Washington; he was always careful to instruct his gardeners to keep a clean separation between items planted and to scrupulously remove weeds, all for visual purposes and for the health of the vegetation. Latrobe noted that the upper garden was "boxed with great precission," and we should imagine an horticultural version of the "plain and neat style" that Washington preferred in the decorative arts.[77]

Washington filled his gardens with flowering trees, bushes, and flowers, although the flowers are not well documented in the records or early descriptions. In addition to what must have been many other varieties, flowers recorded as having been planted at Mount Vernon included bachelors buttons, cardinal flowers, crown imperials, flower fences, geraniums, larkspurs, and Lady peas. Large, Chinese porcelain flower-pots occupied various spots in the public rooms on the first floor of the mansion house. Washington visited William Prince's gardens in Flushing, Long Island, in October 1789 and complained that "the shrubs were trifling and the flowers not numerous," again suggesting that flowers must have been plentiful at Mount Vernon.[78] Archaeology and the accounts of period visitors indicate both the lush variety and complexity of color and forms—including flowers—in the upper garden.

In front of the Greenhouse was a formal garden in the old-fashioned style (Plate 13). Writing in the late 1790s, Latrobe complained about this peculiar relic of past gardening techniques, characterized by a sparse planting of shaped foliage and the order and geometry preferred by an earlier

generation: "Along the North Wall of this Garden is a plain Greenhouse. The Plants were arranged in front, and contained nothing very rare, nor were they numerous. For the first time again since I left Germany, I saw here a parterre, chipped and trimmed with infinite care into the form of a richly flourished Fleur de Lis: The expiring groans I hope of our Grandfather's pedantry."[79] It is possible that Washington retained this formal garden for the sake of Continental European visitors who would feel comfortable here. The exact early appearance is undocumented, but there seem to have some "flower knots" in the upper garden, perhaps in the beds near the Greenhouse. Lund Washington mentioned "Flour knots" in the Mount Vernon gardens as early as December 1775, so those of the 1790s may well have been a continuation of an earlier practice.[80] Today, the restored state of part of the upper garden near the Greenhouse gives an idea of a formal, geometricized garden by using shaped boxwoods. It is possible that the design, even if approved by Washington, was owing to the advice or design of a "Dutch" (German) gardener several visitors mentioned meeting, presumably John (Johann) Christian Ehlers, who worked at Mount Vernon from 1788 to 1797.[81]

It is unlikely that Washington built an entire garden section only to please the few foreign visitors who came to his estate annually. There was already a certain order to the upper garden, and its domination by a brick Greenhouse made it a laboratory rather than an open imitation of raw Nature. The regularity of the whole place was not unappreciated at the time. John Latta, of Bucks County, Pennsylvania, described the upper garden as follows: "The garden is very handsomely laid out in squares and flower knots, and contains a great variety of tree, flowers, and plants of foreign growth collected from almost every part of the world."[82] The old-fashioned aspects in the upper garden were not necessarily objectionable to Americans, nor was the regularity of the "square" scheme. Latrobe, steeped in the more recent English garden tradition, objected to this geometric form of natural art, but there were other reasons to keep a garden of this type: to offer variety, to steep the whole estate in tradition, to show knowledge of the potentiality of gardening, and indeed perhaps to entertain foreigners. However this geometric and rigid garden design came about, it shows the complexity of Mount Vernon and Washington's openness to try different ideas and raise points of conversation. A geometric garden served an overall aesthetic purpose at Mount Vernon, countering his less regimented gardening scheme. Eighteenth-century British garden theorist Horace Walpole recommended that owners should retain "a warm and even . . . old-fashioned garden" out of the way of the main sweep of the park-like garden.[83] In this bit of traditionalism, Washington cleverly provided the variety in gardening that several theorists in Britain had openly encouraged.

The upper garden was Mount Vernon's showcase for fine plants and trees; it was a visual treat, and many of its products graced the Washingtons' table. Even in 1782, during the war, the garden was well stocked with fine fruit trees; Baron von Closen wrote "there is an immense, extremely well-cultivated garden behind the right Wing. The choicest fruits in the country are to be found there." By 1799, the variety and luxuriousness of the plantings had grown considerably. In that year, poet John Searson called attention to the exotic contents of the Greenhouse itself: "A hot-house here a stranger soon will find: / Hundreds of flow'rs and herbs you here may see, / That in a common garden cannot be."[84] Latrobe, who had seen ornate gardens and hothouses in England, thought the horticultural display rather modest, noting that "nothing was very rare," but American visitors were more impressed. The upper garden was used as a staging area for pruning, grafting, and other such experiments that interested Washington. James Taylor noted in 1805 that "the first elder tree or shrub I ever saw [was] in this garden,—it was said to be upwards of 100 years old . . . There were a number of large orange and lemon trees of large size full of fruit of great beauty."[85] Among Washington's fanciest specimens, a coffee tree and a celebrated lemon tree survived well into the nineteenth century. Benson Lossing described

and illustrated the lemon tree, and in 1839 visitor L. Osgood "procured a lemon as a token of him that planted the tree." Amariah Frost admired "the gardens and walks, which are very elegant, abounding with many curiosities, Fig trees, raisins, limes, oranges, etc., large English mulberries, artichokes, etc."[86] A sago palm, mentioned by a number of early visitors, perdured after Andrew Jackson removed it from Mount Vernon to the grounds of the White House. Sadly, the fire of 1835 that destroyed the Greenhouse also killed many exotic trees present during that cold winter night.

The upper garden retained its character through the time of Bushrod, who added to its plantings. Elijah Fletcher wrote in 1810, "The garden was the greatest curiosity I found. It is very handsomely tended by a Dutchman who told me he had been in it 23 years. It contains most every vegetable and plant that grow in any climate. Lemon and orange trees were hanging full of their fruit, and pine apples, coffee, and tea plants were growing."[87] Alexander Graydon wrote in 1814 of "the gardens which are very spacious and elegant—the hot houses are very curious—they contain orange and lemon trees loaded with fruit—pineapples growing on a stock very similar to a cabbage stock—coffee trees loaded with fruit very much like cherries, figs and almons [sic] growing in abundance. As I am nothing of a Botanist I cannot inform you of the hundredth part of what I seen in the gardens—the gardener told me it took him and 4 negroes the whole year round to attend to the gardens alone." Early keepers sometimes referred to a section of the upper garden as the "West Indies."[88] Use of this term likely postdated George Washington's time, but it is possible that it was a designation that started in the president's day. The orange and lemon trees grown in the Greenhouse were meant to supply the needs that Washington had filled for years by trade with the West Indies, to which he shipped herring and shad from the Potomac in exchange for citrus fruit and other items. Seeds for exotic plants recorded as available to Washington in 1799 included those for loquat, mango, lichee, betel nuts, crape myrtle, marjoram, spirea, cactus, and coffee.[89]

Powell's Books CHICAGO

amazon.com

SHIPMENT TRACKING ID: 9241 9901 4082 4219 5915 36

ORDER NUMBER:

SHIPPING **STANDARD**

DATE 11/20/2022

COL Paul Trotti
2085 WYETH WALK
MARIETTA, GA 30062-6031

Sku	Title
P006682	George Washington's Eye: Landscape, Architecture, & Design at Mount

The Greenhouse and the fancy trees and plants growing within or before it (depending on the season) were often the first destination of visitors, especially in Washington's last years and after Martha became a widow. It was like a picture or sculpture gallery, containing fine plants instead of fine arts. Or, to make another analogy, it was a cornucopia, a horn of plenty of American fruitfulness and production. It is true that there were elements that were hardly natural, republican, or local about the garden, which contained trees, plants, and flowers from afar, and the citrus trees were artificially kept alive in the winter in the innovative greenhouse, in which the heat radiated underneath the floor. These were live growths, however, unlike the artful ornaments of high-style European gardens, and many common vegetables grew in the upper garden. Still, visitors did tend to recall the strange and colorful imports more than they did the everyday plants.

While some visitors were left to wander on their own through the landscape of Mount Vernon, this particular garden was often shown on "guided tour" and immediately after arrival, with a family member or head gardener acting as guide. John Latta noted in 1799, in one of the last known visitor accounts before George's death, that Martha lamented that "there [was] none of the family to go with me" to the garden. "She, however, shows me the way to them." Martha had never met him before or heard of him, but in a show of "Virginia Hospitality" was still anxious to show him the way. George appeared later, heard for the first time of Latta's background, and ordered some punch to be served.[90] Amariah Frost, visiting in June 1797, noted that Mr. Law, George Washington's son-in-law, apologized for being ill and excused himself from showing him around before directing Frost to the garden.[91] Other visitors spoke to the head gardener, who discussed with them individual specimens and plantings. On the whole, the walled upper garden served as a kind of fine "private collection" of natural growth.

Washington ordered or requested exotic plants from off-site, and he received plants and trees as gifts. For architectural details he often relied on craftsmen to produce fashionable designs, but gardening, including landscape gardening, was in Washington's sphere of knowledge. We see in letters his confident direction in determining what to purchase or otherwise obtain, where to plant, and how to sustain what was growing. Beyond book learning or what he learned from conversation or correspondence, part of Washington's pragmatic knowledge of botany stemmed from his careful study and experimentation with plants. Near the upper garden, behind the spinning house, was what Washington called his "botanical garden" or "little garden," a walled and fenced-in experimental place established in 1785. This area is currently presented in a way to suggest its original purpose and appearance (Figure 4.15). The mundane "little garden" was aesthetically the least important garden area but was located close to the mansion house because of the shelter and so Washington could most easily monitor the progress of his seedlings and little plants.

Returning to the west facade of the mansion, we continue our look at the estate grounds. From either side of the oval drive, one had a view of the service roads, which Washington called "lanes," leading north and south, each lined, mostly on the west side, with buildings of the most practical kind: overseer's quarters, kitchens, smokehouse, spinning house, and so forth (see Figure 4.16). With the practical buildings on the straight roads, the view down the lanes was like a glimpse at a scenic, orderly, country village. Through the arrangement of buildings, Washington made it clear that the Mount Vernon estate was no seat of a pleasure palace but was a productive, practical place. Many of these buildings were screened or obscured from view from the mansion house (except when the deciduous trees had lost their leaves), but they were, of course, highly visible on the approach. Visitors could sense that this was the center of a great agricultural enterprise including multiple farms, with cattle fields and the River Farm visible on the north. Washington had created a farming village, anchored in the middle by the man-

FIGURE 4.15. Between the mansion house and the upper garden, Washington maintained a small plot he called the "botanical garden," in which he experimented with seeds and tended new or delicate plants. Photo: Author.

sion house and outbuildings, and the gardens and his more distant farms were visually integrated into a larger picture.

East Lawn and Parklands

The viewer standing between the bowling green and the oval drive got a first glimpse of the river view and trees through the arched openings of the two arcades, a view Washington had carefully arranged by eliminating the traditional back wall (cf. Figure 4.17; Plate 1 and 17). This effect, which we discussed under Washington's architecture in chapter 2, was as much about the landscape as about architecture itself. From the west side of the house, the view to the right through the south colonnade was more open and revealed the river, while the view through the north colonnade was, especially in the warmer seasons, largely blocked by a grove of irregularly planted locust trees and other greenery. These trees on the north most likely pressed close to the house, as a number of early views show them approaching quite near the window of the Large Dining Room (Figure 4.18). The more open view to the right of the house and through the south colonnade, while still blocked by some trees, was calculated by Washington to offer a generous and

FIGURE 4.16. The south lane at Mount Vernon, with a view toward the entrance oval. Practical farm buildings, including a stable (*left*) and dung repository (*right*), lined the north and south lanes as one approached the west facade of the house. Photo: Author.

dramatic glimpse of the Potomac. The approximate arrangement of the trees there is seen in the Samuel Vaughan plans of 1787, and the effect can be seen in the painting from about 1791 ascribed to Edward Savage (Plate 15), and in various early views (cf. Figure 4.18). The pairing of a more open view with one more closed and leafy—each seen through a different colonnade—indicates Washington's good sense for creating variety and delightful asymmetry in the landscape.

The view through the colonnades is seen, from either the oval drive or the bowling green, through the square columns of the rounded "covered ways." For each of these, Washington instructed that a single honeysuckle tendril be planted below and allowed to climb and spread out over the boards above the arches, as is still maintained (see Figure 4.17; Plate

17). On 31 March 1785, he noted in his diaries, "Planted the Scarlet or French honey suckle (as my Gardner calls it, & which he says blows all the Summer) at each Column of my covered ways—as also against the circular walls between the Store house &ca. and the two new necessaries." Washington instructed that the boards be painted green, harmonizing with the honeysuckle vines spreading over them: "I want them [honeysuckles] to run up, and Spread over the parts which are painted green."[92] Robert Beverley notes in his *History of Virginia* (1705) the honeysuckles on William Byrd's summerhouse and describes the number of birds who "delight exceedingly" in that flower. Washington owned Beverley's book but also likely knew of the use of honeysuckle on gardens and houses of his time.[93] Going beyond the use of

FIGURE 4.17. Arcade between the mansion house and servants' hall. Washington created curved, open colonnades, his "covered ways," that permitted a view of the river and parkland to the east. Photo: Author.

honeysuckles on fences, walls, and pleasure buildings, Washington brought the clinging, irregular vines onto the structural architecture of classical twin colonnades.

Moving from the west side of the building to the east, visitors who passed through the central hall to the portico reached a place where people of the time marveled at what they saw as an ideal view (Plates 18 and 19). Chapters 5 and 6 treat in more detail the views and other pictorial aspects of the estate, especially on this east side, but here we can state that this was a dramatic prospect, where Nature both tamed and unkempt came together. The view from the portico and

east lawn formed a climax of the garden experience at Mount Vernon. One saw a broad lawn, and the views left, right, and center were all kept continuously green through the use of ha-ha walls (sunken walls), which created the illusion of continuous grassy lawns and wooded areas (Figure 4.19; see Figure 6.4). The river is seen from here as broad and curving. The trees below on the hill were either too young to obstruct the prospect or were kept clipped on top, generally not rising high enough to interrupt the view. Below the lawn, the ground sloping to the river was lightly wooded, and for some years (c. 1786–1792) Washington kept a deer park there;

FIGURE 4.18. William Russell Birch, *Potomac Front of Mount Vernon*, c. 1801–1803, watercolor and graphite on paper, 7.4″ × 10″. This early view shows the locust grove on the north side of the house, which formed a kind of green screen for anyone looking out the window of the Large Dining Room. Birch, altering some of the figures and minor details, later published an engraved version of this view, "Mount Vernon, Virginia, the Seat of the late Gen.l G. Washington," in his *Country Seats of the United States of North America* (1808), plate 7. Courtesy of the Mount Vernon Ladies' Association (Print-6193).

later, he cut a vista opening the view from the house to the river. He built the ha-ha walls on the right and left (north and south) in the 1780s, but the undulating ha-ha wall on the lower end of the east lawn only dates to 1798. Before that time, a wooden paling fence, some sixty feet closer to the river than the present ha-ha wall, kept the deer enclosed. The icehouse (right side of Figure 4.19) existed for some years against the edge of the ha-ha wall. Later, Bushrod Washington put a summerhouse on this spot (cf. Figure 8.5).[94]

The terrain on the east lawn was not as flat as on the bowling green, and it undulated slightly and descended the hill rather steeply near the east ha-ha wall (Figure 4.20). By the end of Washington's days, the view from the portico was largely natural landscape of farm and woodlands. Washington kept several trees planted closer to the top of the hill, and these served to push back the space for a viewer near the house, increase the sense of distancing between house and river, and contribute to the varied appearance of the scene. In all, this was the climactic view for those touring the grounds of the estate, and many visitors described the details

FIGURE 4.19. View across the south lawn showing the (reconstructed) ha-ha wall, which preserved the continuously green view for viewers at the house and portico. Photo: Author.

of the prospect and recorded their feelings. Visitor after visitor was struck by the dramatic view of the broad river and the landscape with lawns, deer park, woods, and meadows.

On the north side of the house was a thickly planted grove of locust trees, which grow quickly and were ideal for forming a green mass outside of the New Room window and screening some of the service buildings from view from the mansion (Plate 15; cf. Figure 4.18). Washington ordered that these ought to look as if they had grown there by chance, "Planted without any order or regularity (but pretty thick, as they can at any time be thin'd) and to consist that at the North end, of locusts altogether."[95] Later on, the grove was more varied. For example, in April 1786, Washington planted some magnolia and live oak trees: "Transplanted as many of the large magnolio into the Grove at the No[rth] End of the Ho[use], as made the number there [ ] [.] Also transplanted from the same box, 9 of the live Oak—vis., 4 in

the bends of the lawn before the House and five on the East of the grove (within the yard) at the No. end of the House."[96]

As for the south grove, Washington wanted to see a variety planted there (Figure 6.5 and Plate 16). On 19 August 1776, at a dangerous and critical time in the war, George took the trouble to write Lund: "at the South [grove], of all the clever kind of Trees (especially flowering ones) that can be got, such as Crab apple, Poplar, Dogwood, Sasafras, Lawrel, Willow (especially yellow & Weeping Willow, twigs of which may be got from Philadelphia) and many others which I do not recollect at present—these to be interspersed here and there with ever greens such as Holly, Pine, and Cedar, also Ivy—to these may be added the Wild flowering Shrubs of the larger kind, such as the fringe Tree & several other kinds that might be mentioned." Both groves—like the rest of the gardens—were always works in progress, and he planted Honey locusts in his south grove and two in the

FIGURE 4.20. View across the east lawn, Mount Vernon. Washington built a serpentine ha-ha wall and gate separating the lawn from the wooded hillside below. Photo: Author.

north grove in March 1785. This south grove is presently planted with a several magnolia trees, reflecting his planting of a large number of them after the war.[97] Before the war ended, George asked Lund to plant shrubs and ornamental and "curious" trees north and south of the house, and upon his return, which by then he foresaw with some confidence, he would decide which clustering would be a more unified grove and which a varied "wilderness." He would achieve this by taking away some of the new plantings, noting that it is easier to pull trees and shrubs down than plant them.[98] One tree that did not form part of the scheme is the venerable pecan tree next to the house on the southeast corner; today it looms over the house, but it is not original to George Washington's period.

In addition to the views discussed—the main prospect from the entrance, the views through the colonnades from the bowling green, and the view from the portico—other vistas included some through pine groves down the hill southwest of the house, as is discussed in chapter 5. About half of the Mount Vernon estate was woodland, framing those vistas and serving as a backdrop to them. The woods along the Potomac and its estates were long admired. As early as 1715, visiting Irishman John Fontaine wrote that "We entered the mouth of the Potomac River, which is made by Virginia on the west side, and Maryland on the east side. Those are the finest rivers that ever I was in, and all the borders of the rivers covered with noble trees."[99] Washington labored to keep this beautiful sylvan impression. Apart from aesthetics, there were practical reasons for keeping woods, whether for fuel, hunting, or fighting erosion. Washington stated that at least a quarter of the properties he was renting had to be kept in woodlands, and he maintained an even greater ratio at Mount Vernon, which shows on his own map of the estate in 1793 (see Figure 4.1). Some land is kept forested today, and visitors can experience the woodland effect.

Beyond considering what a visitor in 1799 would have seen in the walled gardens and the aesthetically developed parks and woods around the mansion house, we should note Washington's final but unfulfilled intentions as a gardener involving the land between the mansion house and river. In the post-presidency period, he greatly improved the east lawn area by putting in the ha-ha wall and gate in 1798. The east ha-ha wall, first contemplated as early as 1780, is reconstructed on the old lines (the original brick in the lowest courses is presently not visible), while the brick steps to the ha-ha wall gate are original and the gate reconstructed.[100] Washington also removed the necessary/outhouse still present on the "brow of the hill" in 1796. He apparently added a gravel walk on the lawn near the house, according to Brookes, the path probably going somewhere near the mansion and south orchard toward the icehouse.[101] By December 1799, Washington was planning even further improvements in the east area. At the time of his death, he had formulated what would have been a kind of capstone to his landscaping, transforming his gardens into an even more open, natural, and varied experience. The centerpiece was the transformation of the deer park, defunct since 1792, from an enclosed space to an accessible sylvan park, and the development of the river and its integration into the broader parkland. An unnamed Philadelphia gentleman wrote on 20 January 1800 that Washington had intended to put in a graveled walk by the side of the river and a fishpond nearby: "The General, a little time before his death, had begun several improvements on his farm. Attending to some of these, he probably caught his death. He had in contemplation a gravel walk on the banks of the Potomac (see Figure 4.21); between the walk and the river there was to be a fish-pond. Some trees were to be cut down, and others preferred. On Friday, the day before he died, he spent some time by the side of the river, marking the former."[102] Another early account corroborates that Washington planned some major changes east of the house toward the river, adding that he wanted to create a broad prospect from the house to the river in the direction of the family tomb (which was to be removed) and beyond to the water. James Paulding, in his *Life of Washington,* reported information gained from a nephew of Washington, probably Howell Lewis: "During this [the nephew said], my last visit to the General, we walked together about

the grounds, and talked about various improvements he had in contemplation. The lawn was to be extended down to the river in the direction of the old vault, which was to be removed on account of the inroads made by the roots of the trees."[103]

This dramatic extension of the lawn to the water, along with the development of paths on the hill where the deer park stood, would have helped to remove the isolation of the house from the water, which is still felt today. Vaughan wrote in 1787 that there were shady walks on the hill toward the river, but Washington wanted to improve the area further to facilitate walking. That this became an area of foot traffic was also noted in 1802 by Manasseh Cutler, who saw that "between the tomb and the bank a narrow footpath, much trodden and shaded with trees, passes round it. Here Mrs. Washington, in gloomy solitude, often takes her melancholy walks."[104] Differing greatly from the enclosed deer park that existed from 1786 to 1792, the layout planned at the time of Washington's death would have created a free park more in the style of later eighteenth-century English design. Descending the hill, one would have come to a wilder part of the estate, a steepish bank, or declivity, that one observer described in 1805 as being "rough and undulating and shaded by small cedars and other shrubbery."

The inclusion of water in the larger experience of the visitor was an important change at Mount Vernon. Washington had discussed with manager Anthony Whitting the possibility of diverting the spring that was undermining the area near the Old Tomb, sending it across the hill where a small pond might be formed somewhere between the east ha-ha wall and the river's edge.[105] This scheme never came to fruition, and Washington turned to incorporating the most obvious watery element, the Potomac. Even now, the edge of the river, normally inaccessible to visitors, makes a charming walkway (see Figure 4.21). Washington was determined to develop the whole of the old deer park from the mansion to the water's edge and thus give his garden easy access to water. Aside from the Potomac and the somewhat distant Little

FIGURE 4.21. Banks of the Potomac at foot of the hill before the mansion house, Mount Vernon. At the time of his death, Washington was apparently planning to develop the area by the river with a fishpond and a gravel walk along the banks. Photo: Author.

Hunting Creek, there is at Mount Vernon no stream, lake, or waterfall to provide variety and interest. It was with some effort that Jefferson put in a fishpond to the side of his lawn and serpentine walk, and Washington did not go to such lengths to create a hilltop fishpond. The Potomac was a ready resource for leisurely pedestrian traffic and a potential source of water for a small pond that could be both useful and picturesque.

Another part of Washington's final plans was the shaping of the lawn between the portico and the east ha-ha wall. Latta wrote in July 1799 that "between the home and the descent of the bank is a very beautiful and extensive green, and to enhance its beauty still more the General, whilst I was there, was engaged in the new modeling of its form, that to the beauty of nature he might add the embellishments of art in such a manner that the improvements would still appear natural." James Taylor also noted that the "declevity of the bank" had "been graded in waves along the summit of the bank," in other words, the area of the lawn near the ha-ha wall and the hill just below it had been consciously graded in a wavy fashion.[106] That Washington directed this grading is attested by a memorandum to manager James Anderson of 1 November 1798: "Davis, with those who are now with him, may continue sloping the hill—above the New Wall, in the manner I have directed him."[107] This shaping seems to have been a moderate, stepped terracing of the lawn as it descended from the flatter part near the porch toward the east ha-ha wall. This naturalistic terrace seems to have been about the width of the house and piazza.[108] Unfortunately, the exact nature of this shaping is not captured with clarity in any early view, and erosion and conscious alteration of the land over time has obscured the exact intentions. We can conclude, however, that Washington planned a series of alternating little hills and plateaus to help one descend the hill toward the gate at the ha-ha wall and leading further down to the (planned) gravel walk, riverbank, and fishpond.

(It is likely that the present depression [see Figure 4.20] that forms a broad and deep kind of gully down the hill is not according to Washington's intention.) All of this would have capped off the aesthetic development of the gardens. Washington's plans for developing gravel walk, paths, and fishpond were not fully completed, but the gate in the ha-ha wall still attests to his intention to invite strollers to the shady paths of the hill and the scenic banks of the Potomac.

Critical Fortunes of Mount Vernon's Gardens

Enough viewers in Washington's lifetime saw the gardens and recorded their impressions to give us a sense of how they were received by his public. Heir Bushrod maintained and added to his uncle's scheme after Washington's death, and visitors continued to comment, passing critical judgment on his achievements. The gardens received praise, but—as with the estate's architecture—there were some qualms about their quality and appearance. There was a great outpouring of praise for the view of the river, for the exoticism and variety of the upper garden, and the sweep of the natural parklands. But the godlike reputation of Washington led some to expect finer gardens on the estate. Young John Singleton Copley Jr. thought in 1796 that the "gardens even of the presidential residence display neither culture nor beauty."[109] Abigail Adams, visiting in the cold month of December in 1800, recorded that "the grounds are disposed in some taste, but they currently show that the owner was seldom an inhabitant of them, and tho possessing judgment, he lacked guineys instead of acres, it required the ready money of large funds to beautify and cultivate the grounds so as to make them highly ornamental—it is now going to decay."[110] This interpretation overlooks Washington's naturalistic intentions; she perhaps wanted to see a finely worked ornamental garden.

Other visitors noticed the gardens' decay after Washington's death. In 1802 Manasseh Cutler stated that Martha Washington offered "any of the shrubbery or young trees" as gifts. She apparently regarded these as dispensable and as making good souvenirs.[111] No wonder the gardens quickly declined. Still, there was continued recognition that the gardens were well laid out. Roger Griswold said that "the gardens, out houses (which are very numerous) and pleasure ground are laid out with great tast[e], and I do not recollect ever to have seen a situation more pleasing." William Blount praised them in 1790 and was inspired to make a classical reference to the trees of classical antiquity.[112]

Foreigners were somewhat less dazzled than Americans. Niemcewicz compared them to the "most beautiful" gardens in England, his praise mildly diminishing Washington's achievements by emphasizing reliance on an established style.[113] Latrobe, trained and raised in England, noted that the gardens were trim and well maintained, but his assessment is a bit flat: "On one side of this lawn [bowling green] is a plain Kitchen garden, on the other a neat flower garden laid out in squares, and boxed with great precission. Along the North Wall of this Garden is a plain Greenhouse. The Plants were arranged in front, and contained nothing very rare, nor were they numerous."[114] Isaac Weld showed some surprise that the grounds overall looked more like a nursery than a pleasure garden; indeed, considering the character of the lower garden, the Vineyard Enclosure, the botanical garden, and the boxes and pots of the upper garden, we can see his point, especially if comparing it to an English or Continental European garden. Another Englishman, Joseph Hadfield, also making a distinction between the productive and the pleasure parts of the estate, noted that Washington's "gardens and pleasure grounds on the banks of the Potomac were very extensive, productive and beautiful, and the views from Mount Vernon are amongst the finest in America."[115]

George Washington's gardens were creative, flexible, and combined art and practical necessity. We will see in chapter 5 how his gardening ideas intersected, or not, with British garden theory and practice and how he worked with the "genius of the place" to develop his ideas.

CHAPTER FIVE

Mount Vernon and British Gardening

In the course of Eight miles riding we got one or two other tollerable prospects, when we got a sight of the Generals House, and soon after entered by a new Road he is making. He seems to be laying out his grownds with great tast[e] in the English fashion. [Lancelot "Capability"] Brown was he alive and here would certainly say this spot had great Capabilities but he could never call it good soil.

LT. JOHN ENYS

FROM THE EIGHTEENTH CENTURY to today, visitors to Mount Vernon have pointed out the English influence on Washington's gardens. As with other features of colonial and early national culture in America, from architectural style to political thought to tastes in music and literature, the English shaped American taste in gardening. Washington's gardens were not slavishly beholden to English theory or practice, though, and he shaped his landscape into a consciously personal form that expressed his unique place in American society.

From what little we know about Washington's gardening schemes before the end of the Revolutionary period, we can conclude that they derived from the most conservative models of European gardening, following practices current in the American colonies but characteristic of British gardening of two generations before or earlier. There are no visitors' descriptions of them, and much of the work was altered during his later efforts. Before the war, he had a straight entrance drive; square, walled gardens; view-blocking fences connecting the mansion house to dependencies; and conservative, geometric arrangements of trees, planting beds, and walks. Washington referred in March 1775 to the rows and gravel walk near the "head of the Octagon" in the gardens near the house.[1] A "Cherry Walk" stood north and east of the house, and he planted some holly trees on the "Circular Banks."[2]

Washington revised this older scheme in the 1780s and 1790s in well-documented efforts that came to embody his mature ideas. It is useful to consider Washington's designs in an international context by looking at Mount Vernon within the history of the several forms of English gardening. Tastes and attitudes from England passed to America just as easily after the Revolution as before, and it is hardly surprising, as Julian Niemcewicz recognized that Washington had come close to the English style: "In a word the garden, the plantations, the house, the whole upkeep, proves that a man born with natural taste can divine the beautiful without having seen the model. The G[eneral] has never left America. After seeing his house and his gardens one would say that he had seen the most beautiful examples in England of this style." Similarly, David Humphreys wrote that at Mount Vernon, "lands . . . are laid out somewhat in the form of English gardens, in meadows & grass-grounds, ornamented with little copses, circular clumps, & single trees." In another passage, Humphreys noted that Washington learned much from conversations with others, especially foreigners: "Nor are his conversations with well-informed men, less conducive to bring him acquainted with the various events which happen, in different countries of the globe. Every foreigner, of distinction, who visits America, makes it a point to see him."[3] Washington was well aware of trends abroad. Still, it is equally striking how Washington departed from English practices. He responded to his American context, to his own place in history, and to the extraordinary natural site of his estate. Nevertheless, his language and resulting gardens were shaped by English thought, and one needs to look at their theory and practice.

Beginning in the early eighteenth century, English gardeners began to turn away from the geometric, formal gardening style of the Continental European schools (Italian, French, and Dutch) and to produce something closer to Nature itself or to a landscape painting. Certain avant-garde authors,

such as William Temple, Joseph Addison, and Stephen Switzer, expressed this idea in writing even before any broad application of the ideas in practice. Richard Steele, along with Addison, spoke out early against the clipped hedges and other constructions of the formal Continental styles.[4] In a movement that became known in the eighteenth century with designations such as "modern gardening" and "landscape gardening," the English began to embrace the ideal of the natural garden, which would oppose the artificial, geometric garden characterized by topiaries, square beds and parterres, and straight allées of trees. There arose a variety of styles within the overall British practice, which English writer and gardener Horace Walpole described as turning a garden into a park. The less formed, open lawns and meadows, terrain for deer, pretty little winding streams, and rambling paths through fields took over more and more of the estate.

During the eighteenth century, the English reached a height of enthusiasm and national pride over this topic; they felt that they were producing the finest gardens the world had ever seen. Walpole exclaimed:

> How rich, how gay, how picturesque the face of the country! . . . If no relapse to barbarism, formality, and seclusion, is made, what landscapes will dignify every quarter of our island, when the daily plantations that [we] are making have attained venerable maturity! . . . Enough has been done to establish such a school of landscape as cannot be found on the rest of the globe. If we have the seeds of a Claud or a Gaspar amongst us, he must come forth. If wood, water, groves, valleys, glades, can inspire poet or painter, this is the country, or this is the age to produce them.[5]

Acknowledging interest in landscape gardening in Roman antiquity, Walpole called attention to the elements of rural gardens and variety as described by Pliny the Younger. At his villa, Pliny noted that "beyond the wall lies a meadow that owes as many beauties to nature, as all I have been describing within does to art; at the end of which are several other meadows and fields interspersed with thickets." In a more

FIGURE 5.1. Parklands at Blenheim, Oxfordshire, c. 1765. Lancelot "Capability" Brown moved English gardening even further in the direction of the natural and spontaneous. In this landscape, one of his masterworks, Brown turned a stream into a serpentine lake and adorned it with a crafted waterfall. Late in his life, Washington planned to create a graveled path along the Potomac and shady walk leading to the river's edge. Photo: Author.

regular area, "here and there little obelisks rise intermixed alternately with fruit-trees: when on a sudden in the midst of this elegant regularity, you are surprised with an imitation of the negligent beauties of rural nature."[6] Given the belief that the irregular, rural garden was rooted in antiquity, and with the contemporary French practice as a counterexample, natural landscape gardening spread quickly in eighteenth-century England. This approach was encouraged also by the scientific study of nature, which was greatly expanding in Enlightenment Britain; the natural garden was in some ways an outgrowth of the increased study of and respect for natural law itself.

The notion of the picturesque was a key concept in British gardening and aesthetics of the time. Later in the eighteenth century, for writers William Gilpin and Richard Payne Knight, the word "picturesque" connoted irregularity and varied landscape. Earlier, the notion had conveyed a more general meaning that gardens or happenstance landscape were best when they contained those devices that made landscape painting a success: unity in concept, variety in detail, attention to perspective, and the evocation of emotional response in the viewer.[7] As Alexander Pope (d. 1744) proclaimed, "All gardening is landscape-painting. Just like a landscape hung up."[8] Horace Walpole noted that as one travels throughout English gardens, "every journey is made through a succession of pictures ... The flocks, the herds, that now are admitted into, now graze on the borders of our cultivated plains, are ready before the painter's eyes, and groupe [*sic*] themselves to animate this picture." For his part, gardener Lancelot "Capability" Brown was markedly against using such devices openly, and he claimed to bring out the best in Nature by directly choosing her finest features, without the intermediary of painting models (Figure 5.1). Still, his work came to be compared to the soft, flowing landscape style of Claude Lorrain, just as the public likened other gardens to the work of painters. For enthusiasts of the new style, the improvements to England's country estates were turning the countryside into a glorious picture. Here was a chance, moreover, for English gardeners to surpass the Continental countries, where the primacy of painting as an art form held sway. English landscape painters competed, with perhaps mixed success, with Continental artists, but it was in landscape gardening that Britain stood in the avant-garde. The English provided the real thing in their landscape gardens, where they shaped Nature itself through Art and improved the landscape through the efforts of the human mind.

FIGURE 5.2. View of the gardens at Stourhead, after 1741, near Mere, Wiltshire. Owner Henry Hoare II laid out his gardens as an embodiment of ideal landscape painting, including some well-placed and very visible buildings, several designed by Henry Flitcroft. Photo: Author.

English gardeners drew inspiration from what we could call the classical or ideal landscapes of the seventeenth and eighteenth century, but they rarely borrowed directly from two-dimensional works. For example, owner Henry Hoare and architect Henry Flitcroft, in composing the lake, buildings, and greenery at Stourhead, were inspired by the paintings of Claude Lorrain, Gaspard Dughet, and others (Figure 5.2), but they did not rely on any specific paintings for composing the landscape and architectural design.[9] English writers or owners of the time who compared a certain garden to a landscape view by Claude, Nicolas Poussin, Salvator Rosa, and Dughet were showing off their connoisseurial skills without implying a true match between garden and pictures. British viewers arrived in gardens with knowledge of landscape art, Some intensified the experience by using a "Claude" glass—a convex, tinted mirror—and created their own pictorial compositions in the mirrored surface as they strolled or sat. Visitors expected that a fine garden landscape would be like a good picture, and the English consciously borrowed pictorial devices, such as coloristic and formal variety, *repoussoir* devices and distancing, chiaroscuro, framing with trees, the creation of distant prospects, and the use of water to visual advantage. The natural elements in gardens—groves, lawns, wildernesses, and lakes—worked with man-made objects, especially little classicizing buildings and bridges, to create an evocative and pictorial equivalent.

When Tobias Smollett wrote his *Travels through France and Italy* in 1766, he offered a concise description of what the English hoped to find in a good garden:

In a fine extensive garden or park, an Englishman expects to see a number of groves and glades intermixed with an agreeable negligence, which seems to be the effect of nature and accident. He looks for shady walks encrusted with gravel; for open lawns covered with verdure as smooth as velvet, but much more lively and agreeable; for ponds, canals, basins, cascades, and running streams of water; for clumps of trees, wood, and wildernesses, cut into delightful alleys, perfumed with honey-suckle and sweet-briar, and resounding with the mingled melody of all the singing birds of heaven: he looks for plats of flowers in different

FIGURE 5.3. Gunston Hall, Lorton, Virginia, garden, laid out c. 1755–1760. George Mason's garden, seven miles from Mount Vernon, had much in common with Washington's, including a deer park, garden mounds, and vistas to the river, but Mason's layout was more traditional and geometric. Photo: Author.

parts to refresh the sense, and please the fancy; for arbours, grottos, hermitages, temples, and alcoves, to shelter him from the sun, and afford him means of contemplation and repose; and he expects to find the hedges, groves, and walks, and lawns kept with the utmost order and propriety.[10]

Smollett's passage underscored that there was indeed a shared culture in eighteenth-century England and that the regimented, measured gardens of the French and Italian traditions gave way to a new kind. English designers in the field and at the drafting table set aside rule and level and built up the gardens based on curving lines and apparently natural forms. Despite any seeming unity, however, a number of competing ideas were at work over the course of the century. If Washington's gardens approach the beauty and form of those in England, as Humphreys and Niemcewicz suggest, what kinds of gardens had influenced him? Indeed, one can see that some of what Smollett mentions is lacking at Mount Vernon. As he did with farming, geography, and architec-

ture, Washington learned about gardening from speaking to others. He must have compared notes with others of means; his "conversations with well-informed men" made him acquainted with "different countries of the globe."[11] He also had some access to British ideas through books in his own library and perhaps through borrowing publications. As we will see, his letters and the known results indicate a thorough knowledge of English eighteenth-century gardening trends.

Peter Martin's survey indicates that by the 1780s most gardens in Virginia were traditional in the British sense, with terraces, mounds, and a good deal of geometry: Sabine Hall, Carter's Grove, Nomini Hall, Gunston Hall (Figure 5.3), Mount Airy, and the Governor's Palace in Williamsburg (Figure 5.4), for example, were fraught with tradition and shared but little of the avant-garde ideas of mid-eighteenth-century England. The same was true of gardens such as Lady Skipwith's Prestwould Plantation, the Lees' Virginia home Stratford Hall, and William Paca's garden in Annapo-

FIGURE 5.4. Governor's Palace, Colonial Williamsburg, Virginia. This reconstructed garden, offering an early-eighteenth-century appearance, is characteristic of the kind of highly geometric arrangement that would have been present there during George Washington's time. Photo: Scott Gilchrist.

lis, to cite a smaller in-town garden.[12] The notable estate at Belvoir, the main paragon for Washington in his neighborhood, had a small, flat, formal garden immediately behind the house and terracing toward the Potomac, a formal arrangement out of style in England at the time the Fairfax family abandoned Belvoir in 1774.[13]

As for a true landscape garden in Virginia, Monticello's was being developed near to the time of Mount Vernon, but Jefferson was abroad in France at the moment of Washington's greatest expansion and radical thinking, and we cannot credit Monticello as a model for Mount Vernon's gardens. The Woodlands in Philadelphia, a house and gardens brought to fine form along English lines in the 1780s, was developed only after William Hamilton's return from England after the war and so was most likely not an influence on Washington. Similarly, gardens in New England, as elsewhere in America, retained to the end of the eighteenth century "an emphasis upon formality in landscape design and the layout of gardens" (Abbott Lowell Cummings).[14] It is clear that Washington turned most forcibly to ideas emanating from En-

gland, and a review of English trends is necessary to throw light on Washington's gardening efforts at Mount Vernon.

Backdrop to Mount Vernon's Gardens: British Schools of Thought

One can divide the English movements from the early eighteenth century to the 1780s into six broad groups: natural landscape gardening, adorned with a certain amount of decorative and fine art or architecture; the even more radically natural style of Lancelot "Capability" Brown; gardens and garden structures in the manner of the Chinese; the ornamental farm; the jagged, curiously picturesque style championed by William Gilpin, Uvedale Price, and others; and the continuation of earlier regular or geometric styles. We can see where George Washington's ideas stood in relation to each of these movements.

The first style we can identify is the early natural movement that incorporated a number of architectural and other decorative objects into the scene. The natural gardening style associated with the great age of landscape gardening of the eighteenth century was embodied by the work of William Kent, designer during the 1720s and later of the gardens of Richard Boyle's (Lord Burlington's) Chiswick House (Figure 5.5), Rousham, and elsewhere. Kent threw out his measuring tools, embraced the cursive line and swelling hill, made clever use of water, and allowed Nature, albeit shaped and planned, to take primary place. As his contemporary Horace Walpole said in a glorifying account: "He [Kent] leaped the fence, and saw that all nature was a garden. He felt the delicious contrast of hill and valley changing imperceptibly into each other, tasted the beauty of the gentle swell, or concave scoop, and remarked how loose groves crowned an easy eminence with happy ornament, and, while they called in the distant view between their graceful stems, removed and extended the perspective by delusive comparison."[15] Despite his embrace of an apparently spontaneous Nature, however, Kent included many created structures and

FIGURE 5.5. Garden at Chiswick House, outside London, c. 1726. William Kent was among the first to challenge the more ordered, Continental style of gardening, although he was early in the landscape gardening movement and his contributions at Chiswick House for Lord Burlington relied in part on contrived, straight lines and a substantial presence of stone buildings and sculpture. Photo: Author.

objects in his gardens. While visiting Chiswick House in 1786, Thomas Jefferson complained that the temples, bridges, obelisks, and marble urns intruded on the natural effects.[16]

Kent's approach was widely followed by other theorists and practitioners in the eighteenth century. Perhaps the most famous English garden of the time was at Stourhead. Banker Henry Hoare II at his country estate created a lake and surrounding landscape garden, with the help of architect Henry Flitcroft, who over the course of time added classical buildings about the grounds. These man-made objects sometimes detracted from the overall natural approach, but they contributed to pictorial ideals by harkening back to Renaissance and Baroque pictures. The taste for classicism, the sense of conspicuous consumption, and the desire to evoke classically influenced paintings made the building of such adornments irresistible. The "Palladian" bridges at Wilton and Stowe dominate their settings and preside over rolling landscapes and gentle streams. Structures, hermit caves, slabs for inscriptions carrying moral or otherwise thought-provoking messages, fountains, metalwork clairvoyées, and so forth

were scattered across the vast estates. Some of these specimens of "art" were minor and incidental, while others, such as the medieval-style Alfred's Tower at Stourhead, formed major focal points.[17] In addition to unmanned hermit grottoes, one garden had a hapless actor living there playing the role of a hermit; Walpole mocked this practice, calling it extravagant to give a quarter of one's garden over to the theme of melancholy.[18] Throughout the eighteenth century, the building of fake ruins and the incorporation of real ruins on estate grounds remained in vogue in England.

In English gardens the man-made objects catch the eye as they jump out from the background of leafy or grassy landscapes. The contemplation of such objects provokes not just the question of crafted objects versus Nature, for the practice is rooted in a deeper question asked by English theorists, namely, whether a garden existed to provide visual beauty per se or the emotional associations it raised. The placement of inscriptions, hermits, temples, statues, and grottoes were all meant to evoke feelings, associations, and thoughts of other realms. Some contemporaries complained about the staggering scale and number of eighteenth-century structures at Stowe, which, even with parts designed by Kent and Brown, is still replete with its monument to British Worthies (Figure 5.6), Temple of Virtue, Palladian bridge, faux ruins, and other objects. One strolls through Stowe and encounters a range of historical, sentimental, and inspirational sights fashioned in stone. This mixture of fine art and natural gardening derived from a long-standing Renaissance ideal of improving Nature as well as the eighteenth century focus on feelings and pleasure by association, and it helped make the gardens something better than and not subservient to Dame Nature.

This mixture of Nature and Art was successful and popular. Even the relatively strict Thomas Whately, who lived later than Kent and was even more of an ideologue in favor of the natural, thought it appropriate to surround a house with statues, urns, and termini, and even to place such objects as isolated vases in the garden. Whately acknowledged

FIGURE 5.6. William Kent, "British Worthies" monument, Stowe, Buckinghamshire, 1734. Stowe gardens, developed over many decades, were replete with sculptures, temples, bridges, and monuments. Photo: Author.

the emotive effects of ruins, and thought it appropriate for one to construct artificial ruins for the purpose of exciting the imagination with the passage of time. He wrote favorably of the erection of buildings for adornment in gardens "from the Grecian down to the Chinese" in style.[19] By the end of the century, a number of English designers, perhaps most notably Humphrey Repton, continued this form and reintroduced such ideas as the terrace around the house.

By the time Washington was working as garden designer in the 1780s, the prevalent English gardening style was spreading to the Continent and gained expression in France in such gardens as the Marquis de Laborde's at Chateau de Méréville (Essonne) from the 1780s. Washington likely knew little of this expansion of English gardening ideas, but it is still worth noting that his gardens at Mount Vernon were part of an international movement. The French, like the Germans in that period, tended to prefer those English gardens that included a liberal sprinkling of outbuildings, follies, caves, tombs, and so forth about the grounds, even in avant-garde cases.

This abundance of the man-made along with the natural is fraught with tension, however, and some resolved the issue by leaning away from artificialities. A second major trend of the eighteenth century was the style of gardening that Lance-lot "Capability" Brown practiced from about 1740 until his death in 1783. It was based on idealizing Nature, relying even less on enhancements of artifice. His style was, according to Walpole's classification, part of the first group mentioned, as he combined in his gardens both Nature and man-made material objects. However, there were some main differences, and we would do well to consider him in a school of his own, as did some contemporaries.[20] Claiming the authority of nature itself, his goal was to establish the equivalent of the beauties of Nature along the lines of idealization achieved by the ancient artist Zeuxis, who chose the best around him to imitate; Brown selected and improved on what he regarded as the finest aspects of the natural world. He was not content to integrate his system with the old, and by further eliminating the signs of Man he was more of a revolutionary even than Kent and his followers.

In its final effect, Brown's style was soft, flowing, and green, with broad lawns and delicate clumps of trees. Brown worked more from plans than from views, and he was regarded as having been somewhat distanced from the idea that a garden is pictorial, but there are certainly links between his forms and ideal landscape painting. Brown's style, which was widely imitated, can be seen in some surviving gardens maintained today in accordance with his original

FIGURE 5.7. Gardens at Petworth, West Sussex, 1750s. Lancelot Brown's manipulation of Nature is indicated in this reconstruction of his intentions, with groves of trees, as well as grouped and single trees spaced across a field. For his part, Washington left careful instructions to his managers to arrange trees singly and in groupings and to play them off against the smooth, uniform surface of grassy fields. Photo: Author.

intentions, including extensive parts of the garden at Blenheim (see Figure 5.1) and sections at Stowe, such as the Elysian Fields. Most impressive are the great parklands at Petworth (Figure 5.7), with rolling hills, groves, and two serpentine lakes carefully crafted by Brown. Going from a garden by Brown to one by Kent or Chambers, one is keenly aware of the relative artifice of these earlier designers. Some, in criticizing Brown for destroying older trees and noble gardens of the past, unfairly accused him of constructing "common fields," and others were surprised at the extent to which he attempted to disguise the hand of the master designer.

A third major category of English gardening—landscape crafted under Asian influence—is to some extent an outgrowth of the first category, Nature mingled with a heavy dose of "Art," and included spontaneous and cursive garden design elements. The English manner was generally not imitative of other traditions. However, a few writers and practitioners looked for inspiration at what they believed to be Chinese models. Much of the admiration of the Chinese style—built on delicate, irregular rock formations, curving ponds and tightly winding pathways, a delicate scale of plantings, and an apparently insouciant placement of trees and shrubbery—was fostered by William Chambers in two books

and in his practice. Chambers, who, like Kent, did not reject art and artifice, incorporated curious Chinese style buildings, and he was happy to imagine an English gardening rooted in Chinese natural taste.[21] His lofty pagoda in the Asian manner in Kew Gardens still stands, and other such structures by him are lost. Chambers was reacting to Brown in designs for highly crafted Asian gardens adorned with little architectural structures, and he was proposing a system of gardening that intervened more forcibly in the landscape than did the less "artful" style of Brown. Some English gardens, such as Hugh Hamersley's garden at Woodside (Berkshire) came to include buildings and landscaping reminiscent of the Chinese style (Figure 5.8). In the American context, William Paca of Annapolis built a small footbridge adorned with Chinese fretwork and turned at an angle as one sees in little bridges in chinoiserie and japanning (Figure 5.9). Even Thomas Jefferson borrowed from the Asian style in the Chinese railings at Monticello.[22] Awareness of the Chinese manner perhaps fortified a tendency in England toward cursive lines and spontaneity in gardening, but specific borrowings never became particularly widespread in Anglo-American landscape design.

A fourth manner of English eighteenth-century garden-

FIGURE 5.8. Thomas Robins, *Chinese Pavilion in an English Garden* (*The Garden at Woodside*), 1750s, watercolor and gouache on paper. This view of Hugh Hamersley's garden shows the integration of Asian motifs in English gardening in the later eighteenth century. Private collection. Photo: The Bridgeman Library / Alinari.

ing, corresponding again to a trend noted early on by Walpole himself, was the ornamental farm. It was frequently described by English writers, beginning with Stephen Switzer, with the French phrase, *ferme ornée*. If the point of landscape gardening was to relate it to beauty or the picturesque, to evoke feelings, achieve variety, or any of the (often overlapping) goals of gardening theory, farmland and farm buildings could achieve the same result as a landscape garden. The theoretical model for this goes back to Joseph Addison, who stated how pretty it would be if one gardened merely by putting a path through one's agricultural fields.[23] The practical application of the ornamental farm is credited to Phillip Southcote, who built a farm that was consciously prettified through design and the placement of suggestive objects and inscriptions. William Shenstone designed his farm Leasowes, outside of Birmingham, England, in a manner so plain that even the frontier gardener Thomas Jefferson remarked during his visit in 1786 that "this is not even an ornamented farm." In 1793, artist George Parkyns published several possible designs for ornamented farms, in which the practical aspects of the places are beautified and integrated into the larger landscape and the residence.[24] The ornamented farm often remained an idea rather than an actuality, and few were consciously built in England, but the notion endured through the end of the century. Most famous were Marie Antoinette's ornamental farm buildings at Versailles where she "played" as dairymaid, the conceit ultimately relying on the English idea of the garden as ornamental farm. To be sure, farming and gardening share a purpose and process, involving growth from the earth, and in an aesthetic age it was expected that owners of farmlands would want to present them in a beautiful way. The transition from admiring beautiful farms to establishing picturesque farms was an easy one.

Some critics and designers thought that earlier styles, such as Capability Brown's and the ornamental farm idea, were too bland and insufficiently natural, and later in eighteenth-century England a fifth approach to gardening arose based on "curious" particulars and irregularities. Some sought to bring piquant interest through rough or irregular natural elements. This trend in British theory and practice, the fifth one identified here, embraced irregularity and a greater sense of a wild place. Early on in the intellectual develop-

FIGURE 5.9. Chinese footbridge (reconstructed), garden of the William Paca House, Annapolis, Maryland, c. 1770. Paca put in a little footbridge over the curving canal near his summerhouse. The form of the bridge and its off-axis angle in the garden were inspired by Chinese landscape artistry. Photo: Author.

ment of this school of thought, Walpole described a "kind of alpine scene, composed almost wholly of pines and firs, a few birch, and such trees as assimilate with a savage and mountainous country . . . all is great and foreign and rude: the walks seem not designed, but cut through the wood of pines."[25]

The word "picturesque" was broadly regarded as relating to pictures or modeled on practices of painters, but Price and Gilpin defined it in another way. The new notion, first published by Price in 1794, put "picturesque" somewhere between the beauty and the sublime of Edmund Burke, that is, neither perfectly pleasing and lovely nor terrifying. Gilpin was particularly keen in representing English scenery replete with rocky outcroppings, irregular tree branches, and other curious natural effects. There was some difference between the theorists, for "unlike Gilpin, who sought the picturesque in natural scenes throughout Great Britain, Price was concerned with the picturesque in the form of the estate garden."[26] For Price, an outcropping of rock, an overgrown corner of a wood, a thorny patch, a wooden bridge a bit too

precariously perched, or a stream tumbling over some jagged rocks added an element of the "curious," as well as fear and beauty. Proponents of this new movement especially embraced pine trees because of their jagged branches and sharp needles, and on account of their melancholy associations and their prevalence in wild settings in the Alps, Scandinavia, and North America. Widely read and influential garden theorist Thomas Whately went so far as to suggest that the sublime could be created in a garden with a steep cliff, but in general curious irregularities were enough.[27] Brown's gardening style was regarded as beautiful in the Burkean sense but blandly lacking in incident. As for the ongoing interest of English gardeners in "Art," within the picturesque school of thought and practice some wanted to keep artifice and architecture at a minimum, while others were willing to admit structures, fountains, bridges, and so forth, which they thought added piquancy and spurred emotions.

The sixth tradition, the continuation of the older geometric styles, needs little description here. Not every garden owner wanted to tear up past efforts, and they maintained the established gardens. A few designers continued the conservative styles of before. One idea that makes this traditionalism more explicable is Walpole's idea that keeping part of the garden in traditional form gives variety and interest to one's landscape gardening. He noted in particular that "the total banishment of all particular neatness immediately about a house . . . is a defect."[28] Even the somewhat radical naturalist Whately noted that small gardens work well in geometric form, and he saw the value in some kinds of ordered nature.[29] In British colonies and America, innovations came about even more slowly, and it is hardly surprising that geometrically arranged walkways, squared flower beds, and symmetrical layouts continued longer than in Britain itself.

To be sure, George Washington was living in the middle of a great evolutionary process of the Anglo-American garden. He also formed his gardens against the backdrop of the changing political circumstances in America and his own place within American politics and society. Having never traveled to England and not having extensive exposure to English writings about the aesthetics of gardening, he came up with his own interpretation, influenced by some of the major movements sketched above.

An American Place: George Washington Crafts His Gardens

Washington's gardens were carefully conceived to work with the "genius of the place" (Alexander Pope, "Epistle IV to Richard Boyle, Earl of Burlington," line 57), in this case the splendid site on the Potomac, and they expressed Washington's artistic style and moral values. In comparison with the first British school, which produced natural landscapes peppered with temples, statues, follies, and obelisks, the inclusion of objects and eye-catchers is almost completely absent at Mount Vernon. Instead of the Doric temples and hermit houses seen in England, Washington's buildings at the Mansion House Farm consisted of smokehouses, necessaries, stables, and other practical and largely unornamented buildings.[30] Washington could easily have built a summerhouse, scenic little bridge, gazebo, or pavilion, but he did not. As for statuary, Washington chose not to acquire and place sculpture on the grounds, even in the walled gardens. In the colonial period in America, there were fine sculptures at Robert Carter III's Nomini Hall and at William Byrd's Westover. At Cliveden, home of the Chew family in Germantown, Pennsylvania, some original statuary from the colonial period is still present. By 1772, the William Paca garden in Annapolis had a summerhouse, footbridge, and some formal parterres. So, Washington's garden was unusual in its avoidance of man-made objects, and his placement of a modest sundial on the ground and a dove of peace weathervane atop the cupola is as far as he went in this direction. When manager Whitting wrote to President Washington in Philadelphia in 1792 that it might look good to place an obelisk at the end of a vista, as he had seen on other American estates, Washington greeted his suggestion with silence and took no further action.[31] Washington's abjuring of crafted three-dimensional art at Mount Vernon must have been a conscious effort to exclude fancy objects associated in the Anglo-American world with high-style pleasure gardens.

If Washington were thinking of any particular English model for his gardening in the bowling green, east lawn, and deer park, it was probably the work of Capability Brown. Apart from larger design issues, when Washington used details they tended to be soft and cursive, such as willow trees, honeysuckle tendrils, and locust groves. Washington was closest to Brown in how he developed the lawns and adjoining wildernesses and shrubberies, especially in the east lawn and the wooded areas and grassy hills that descended the hill from it. Brown's stylistic effects were soft, curving, green, and struck contemporaries as a bit too common or ordinary. Brown regarded his gardening as art, but art as expressed in the ancient idea that "Ars est celare artem." The art is to hide the art, to make a beautiful landscape look like it might have occurred on its own. Obviously, symmetrical aspects of the bowling green and the geometries of the walled gardens at Mount Vernon were unlike Brown's art, but the more natural sections were remarkably in harmony with the details and overall lines of his designs.

In the spirit of Brown's gardening style, Washington was so committed to the idea of the "green" farm that he sought to create live fences across the estate (formed of dense natural growth rather than timber), and he also wanted to disguise or at least reduce the brick appearance of the ha-ha walls. These were already invisible from "uphill," and Washington planted ivy on the ha-ha walls at the north end of the lawn and along the ha-ha walls on either side of the bowling green gate. He also wanted ivy to grow around the icehouse on the edge of the east lawn; this was largely below ground level, and what was above ground level would have been hidden via the sloping hill, the ha-ha wall, and the ivy that Washington ordered planted.[32] Washington wanted to increase, as much as possible, a view of green grass, ivy, flowering trees, and distant crops and pastures, and these ivy plantings helped him to achieve it. Washington's "hand" in his gardening art was, like Brown's, soft, green, cursive, and it brought out the beauties of nature.

Contemporaries noticed the connection to Brown's style; visiting English lieutenant John Enys observed that "[Capability] Brown was he alive and here would certainly say this spot had great Capabilities but he could never call it good soil."[33] Brown's gentle, rounded style succeeded best with moist weather, and the warmer climate of Virginia and the upland setting of Mount Vernon made for a contrast with his verdant gardens in England. Still, the gardens at Mount Vernon inspired thoughts of Capability Brown in this English visitor. Similarly, architect and Englishman Benjamin Henry Latrobe described Washington's gardens in 1796 in exactly the kind of language used to characterize Capability Brown. In the east lawn and the view from the portico, Latrobe noted that "towards the East Nature has lavished magnificence, nor has Art interfered but to exhibit her to advantage."[34] This expressed well the understanding that Washington, like Brown, brought forth the beauty of nature so that observers would be unaware of the extent to which the hand of the gardener had shaped it, bringing out its best and most beautiful features.

Washington not only shared Brown's point of view of improving and cleaning up Nature but also found in true, raw Nature a pleasing appearance when it resembled man's improvement of the natural landscape. In April 1791, Washington noted of land in Delaware, "the appearances of it are agreeable, resembling a lawn well covered with evergreens and a good verdure below from a broom or course grass which having sprung since the burning of the woods had a neat & handsome look especially as there were parts entirely open and others with ponds of water which contributed not a little to the beauty of the Scene."[35] In visiting the property of Governor Johnson in Maryland on 26 September 1784, he noted that "these glades have a pritty appearance, resembling cultivated Lands & improved Meadows at a distance; with woods here and there interspersed . . . The growth of them, is a grass not much unlike what is called fancy grass, without the variegated colours of it; much intermixed in places with fern and other weeds, as also with alder & other Shrubs."[36] In clearly Brownian sentiment, Washington thought the glades pretty because they looked like grassy, open land that has been improved, and the grass was pleasing because it recalled a kind used in landscape gardening for lawns.

It would seem that young Nelly Custis, George's step-granddaughter and Martha's granddaughter, and resident at Mount Vernon, accepted this attitude, and she placed Nature itself ahead of art and crafted beauty. In 1797 she wrote to her friend Elizabeth Bordley Gibson, "When I look at this noble river, & all the beautifull prospects around—I pity all those who are in Cities, for surely a country life, is the most rational & the most happy of any—& all the refinements of art & luxury are nothing in comparison to the Beauties of Nature." Similarly, she wrote on 3 February 1799, soon before her wedding and departure from Mount Vernon, "I pity those who can prefer the Dissipations of a City life, & artificial beauties to the simplicity[,] cheerfulness & content of a Country residence, & to the contemplation of the innumerable Beauties of Nature."[37] The parklands at Mount Vernon were calculated to appeal to this taste, to make the landscape embody as much as possible the "beauties of Nature." Nelly, through conversations with George Washington and through living at Mount Vernon, had imbibed the attitude that natural beauty, without the refinements of "art & luxury," was supreme. In his own way, Washington out-Browned Capability himself and his grounds were even more natural and green. Brown incorporated many artistic man-made elements into his gardens, including stone bridges, a "Gothic Church" at Croome Court (Worcestershire), a Gothic bathhouse at Corsham Court (Wiltshire), and even a Gothic shelter for deer (Scampston, Yorkshire). Brown's highly natural, rambling grounds at Petworth include his "ruins" of a medieval tower, his gazebo in the form of an Ionic rotunda, and a Doric temple nestled in the green landscape.[38] He retained many earlier buildings in his works,

FIGURE 5.10. Aerial view of the central buildings and gardens at Mount Vernon, mid-twentieth-century. The practical buildings, such as the Wash House and Salt House, helped to form two pretty streets as if in a country village, with matching white colors, consistent brickwork in the English bond, and uniform reddish roof tiles. Courtesy of the Mount Vernon Ladies' Association.

such as the medieval ruins at Sanbeck, the great bridge at Blenheim, and the Temple of Concord and Victory at Stowe that overlooks his Grecian vale. Washington's landscape gardening was highly progressive in America, and in some ways he eliminated the unnatural even more thoroughly than did many of the most natural landscape gardeners in eighteenth-century England.

Like the natural style of English landscape gardening, the notion of the ornamental farm was highly significant for Washington and played a role in his gardening and the layout of the estate. In addition to integrating ideas from the most natural landscape gardeners such as Capability Brown, he sought to make the Mansion House Farm, in particular, into an ornamental farm. Mansion House Farm was not a farming enterprise in the sense of Dogue Run Farm or River Farm. Washington declared that Mansion House Farm was to have its major crop farming aspects phased out by 1798, and it included distinct pleasure grounds and a large residence (Figure 5.10). Still, that it was farmed to some extent and was the organizational center of a five-farm enterprise was obvious to any visitor, and Washington wanted to prettify the agricultural elements there.

David Humphreys observed that the Mansion House Farm looked like a rustic village. Washington had set in a scenic row the outbuildings, unified by white paint, English bond brick, red roofs, spacing, and scale. He produced a seamless integration of classicizing mansion house, "rustic village," kitchen gardens, pleasure gardens, and distant woods. Washington consciously sent the visitors from the west gates in front of a field and then through roads with a view of the working farm. This route let the visitors take in the orchard on the sloping hill on the right. The service buildings, beginning with the stable, did indeed give the appearance of a little village.[39]

As for the lands themselves, words reinforced deeds, and in Washington's letters, especially after the Revolution, we can see him proclaiming the ornamental farm effect at Mount Vernon or directing farm managers to prettify his farmlands there. For example, he wrote to the Marquise de Lafayette that if she comes to Mount Vernon she will see Washington's "small Villa," where he is surrounded by "implements of Husbandry and little Lambkins," all of which "will diversify the Scene" (itself a literary and theatrical word). He wrote elsewhere that he "delighted" in seeing sheep and that farms ruined by weeds were not beautiful, meaning that he saw beauty in neat, well-kept agricultural fields.[40]

Young Washington noted that he was struck by the beauty of the farms in Barbados, and this aesthetic interest intensified in the last decade of his life. He clearly had heard of the English ornamental farm, for President Washington's letters were filled with advice to farm managers for prettifying his farm, and he often used the words "ornamental" and "ornament," especially beginning in the 1790s. In a long memorandum about trimming trees, meant for William Pearce before James Anderson took over management at Mount Vernon, Washington wrote on 5 November 1796 of fields of Corn to the west of the bowling green and mansion house:

[Those trees] on the right hand going from the house (on the left hand, if I recollect rightly, they are sufficiently thin already for the purpose of ornament, which is my first object) may be a

good deal thinned by taking them up, invariably, by the Roots. Where the trees stand very thick, leave circular clumps (of from 30 to 50 yards across) without trimming the Trees. But all single trees should be trimmed to one regular height, and as high as can be reached by a Chissel on a long staff; that the Corn may be less shaded in its growth. In leaving the clumps, if it can be done consistent with the thick growth of the Trees, pay attention to the look of them, in going to, or returning from the house.[41]

These instructions show Washington's brilliant landscape design and his artistry and make clear that his main concern was making the farmlands beautiful with "ornament." The clumps were to be irregular and untrimmed but the single trees left isolated and brought to uniform size. Pearce was to make sure the clumps looked good to visitors going from the house and heading toward it. Washington overlooked no detail but also (perforce, because of his absence) left decisions in the hands of his managers.

Similarly, in a letter to Whitting, Washington directed the planting of ornamental trees:

Plant fresh clumps as soon as the trees can be removed; in the Buck Wheat Lot; the two clover lots; &ca; & of the best, & most ornamental trees—quick in their growth. These clumps are not to be placed with regularity as they respect one another—nor the trees in each, individually. Nor are the clumps to cover (individually) half the ground those did which were planted out last fall, Winter, & Spring. In a word, the trees are to be so close together in each Clump as for the tops, in a little while, to appear as if they proceeded from one trunk. they can always be thinned if found too thick. Those clumps wch are already planted (if alive) may be thickened in the manner I have described, and with the same kind of trees; provided they do not stand in too formal a point of view, one to the other.[42]

Along these same lines, Washington wrote abroad to Edward Newenham:

The manner in which you employ your time at Bell champ (in rasing nurseries of fruit, forest trees, and shrubs) must not only contributes to your health & amusement, but it is certainly among the most rational avocations of life for what can be more pleasing, than to see the work of ones own hands, fos-

FIGURE 5.11. Modern "live fence" near the Vineyard Enclosure at Mount Vernon. Washington was insistent on the production of live fences on his estate, both to save wood and for their sylvan appearance. Thorns, honey locust, and other trees and shrubs pressed together would keep pests out of fields. The theory worked better than the practice, and he ended up relying on traditional wooden fences, like the one seen here supplementing the natural planting. Photo: Author.

tered by care and attention, rising to maturity in a beautiful display of those advantages and ornaments which by the Combination of Nature and taste of the projector in the disposal of them is always regaling to the eye at the sametime in their seasons they are a grateful to the palate.[43]

In writing to a British recipient, he emphasized the "amusements" of rural life and the ornamental potential of farming.

He wanted a pretty farm, and his fields of crops and grasses had to be attractive. This was an attitude that Washington held since his youth. As early as 1751, he praised the "fields of cane, corn, fruit-trees, &c. in a delightful green" in Barbados. While "farming" as president, he wrote to Anthony Whitting in 1792: "If that meadow should ever be thoroughly reclaimed, and in good grass, a walk along the edge of it would be an agreeable thing."[44] Rather than maximize income from land, he preferred to have it aesthetically pleasing above all, and he instructed Pearce to engage in "clearing the ground; beautifying it with trees; and laying it

to grass." Similarly, he wrote to Pearce on 27 July 1794, complaining of unkempt common fields, saying "to have any part of the inclosure in grass, and part in rushes, alders and other Shrubs, is not only an eye sore, but is a real disadvantage; as they are continually encroaching on the mowing ground."[45] For Washington, a well-run farm was exemplified by tidy and planned growth, which was both useful and beautiful.

The live fences at Mount Vernon, including those at the Mansion House Farm, were integrated with the other aesthetic features of the estate and were in sympathy with Washington's broader emphasis on ornamental farming (Figure 5.11). In harmony with the ornamental farm concept and the natural gardening movement, live fences—formed of bushes, small trees, thorns, and other plants rather than fence wood—were a green solution that would have been economical and appropriate for the verdant, natural style of gardening Washington sought to practice. Live fences, known and used in

England, were fitting for the woodsy effect that Washington wanted to achieve on his American country retreat. Something of a quixotic idea, the live fences never worked as a barrier against small animals as Washington hoped, but we can appreciate his attempt to achieve in his ornamental farm an improved form of Nature, and his beautiful elimination of wooden fencing in favor of clustered natural specimens. Washington linked live fences to ornamental farming in a letter to Whitting and pointed out that these would spare trees elsewhere on his lands: "Let me therefore in the strongest terms possible, call your attention to this business, as one, than which nothing is nearer, both to my interest and wishes; first, because it is indispensably necessary to save timber & labour; and secondly, because it is ornamental to the Farm, & reputable to the Farmer. If you want Honey locust seed, or any thing else from hence to enable you to effect these I will send them."[46]

Ideas about the beauty of agriculture and the ornamental farm had infiltrated his thoughts so thoroughly that it is likely that English discussions on this topic fed his mind. Through conversation he likely learned about English thought, and we also have letters to him that touch on this subject. This exchange worked two ways: George William Fairfax wrote a glowing report of his own farm and villa in England near Bath, in language and imagery he must have felt that Washington would appreciate. Fairfax shared with Washington a love of earth and pretty farms: "A [House in the Country] . . . is situated, in a plesant Vale, in a beautiful hilly Country, and surrounded by dairy-Farms, so that We have abundance of sweat Meadows to look upon, wherever we turn . . . which altogether cons[t]itutes as perfect an Arcadia as ever Poet's fancy formed, here we enjoy sweat Air, much composure, and time for contemplation . . . our Garden produces the sweetest Vegitables I ever tasted, and the flowers and Shrubs employ me, and delight my old Woman."[47] For his part, Washington continued to praise the beauties of the farm and the healthy moral qualities of actions as farmer, as he wrote to agricultural reformer Arthur Young: "The more

I am acquainted with agricultural affairs the better I am pleased with them. Insomuch that I can no where find so great satisfaction, as in those innocent & useful pursuits. In indulging these feelings, I am led to reflect how much more delightful to an undebauched mind is the task of making improvements on the earth; than all the vain glory which can be acquired from ravaging it."[48]

In looking at the rough picturesque, the fifth approach or tradition listed above, it would seem at first that Washington would be removed from the avant-garde ideas of Price, Knight, and Gilpin. Their theories came rather later in the century, and he did not share their language of irregularity and roughness, nor favor rocky outcroppings or jagged irregularities. Still, while Washington's approach to gardening differed from the English theories of the rough picturesque, he gardened in some ways that happened to correspond to their suggestions. The English theorists of the curious picturesque favored pine trees, and Washington had long integrated these into his farm, whether in his wildernesses or in the Pine Grove near the Hell Hole swampy area further downhill from the Old Tomb and Vineyard Enclosure. Washington planted a grove as early as April 1760, when he planted "20 Pine Trees" at the head of the Cherry Walk and more on April 18. The Pine Grove, useful for beauty and for the erosion-fighting qualities of the tree, was a garden form that Washington made throughout his life.[49] In England, the pine brought forth feelings of melancholy, as they did in the romantic paintings of Caspar David Friedrich in Germany. Even if this association was not prevalent in America, the pine tree's texture and shape evokes something sharp and wild.

Washington incorporated woods into the scheme and wanted the main vista of all to the west to be of forest land. The English built what they called American gardens, just as they built Chinese gardens. The English idea of an American garden was that it was somewhat wild and made of scraggly American trees and shrubs, such as pines. These gardens were kept somewhat like wildernesses, with little sign of "civilization." It is hard to imagine that Washington was making an American garden in the European sense, which was a niche garden among many choices for English gardeners. However, just as Benjamin Franklin wore a raccoon cap in Paris and Thomas Jefferson modestly called himself a farmer, there was a fashion at the time of sporting an American identity. In a well-visited and symbolic place like Mount Vernon, Washington had to achieve a certain attitude: practical, natural, and without frippery, in line with what he stated was his republican lifestyle. Without setting out to imitate an English idea of an American garden, he achieved a real American garden. Thomas Jefferson famously stated that Americans had an easier task than Europeans in creating a noble garden: "We have only to cut out the superabundant plants."[50] His remark, meant partly in jest, expressed the real feeling that a garden could be formed from the American wilderness itself. George Washington's former neighbor Bryan Fairfax wrote on 22 August 1798 that land near Dover, England, reminded him of Mount Vernon and Virginia: "I found it a very pleasant Country to pass thro'— fine Roads & scarce any Hills—Trees tho common in Hedges hardly to be seen in woods. I passed one place of a few Acres that put me in mind of Mt Vernon it was a Wilderness, but the Trees were rather thicker, and it always pleased me to see any thing that put me in mind of Virginia."[51] Consider the distant woods seen in the west vista, the light woodlands in the former deer park (called by Vaughan a "hanging wood"), the woods and groves passed on the entrance to the Mansion House Farm near the first vista point, and the many views of woods seen from the portico and east lawn, some as far away as the Maryland side of the river. Washington clearly used woods to enhance how people experienced his gardens and set his estate in a rough and irregular American context that both proclaimed its setting in the New World and corresponded to the taste in England for a picturesque landscape.

A final category of English gardening is symmetrical and geometric arrangements. Washington clearly retained this aspect of traditional English gardening in the walled gardens, the symmetry of the bowling green paths, the poplar trees planted in corresponding pairs on either side of the "courtyard," and the paired mounds planted with willow trees near the bowling green gate. We can surmise that the four smaller and two large ovals were, in some way still unknown, set in echoic balance on the bowling green. Latrobe disliked the balanced walkways around the bowling green ("a wide but extremely formal serpentine walk"), his outlook reflecting the latest British tastes.[52] Jefferson's serpentine walkways at Monticello were irregular and more in accord with English taste of the last decades of the eighteenth century, and his ovals beds were placed rather irregularly about the lawn (Figure 5.12). In another departure from natural gardening practice, Washington was happy to incorporate more geometric aspects of gardening by using "flower knots," which again brought Latrobe's censure. Washington was no ideologue in gardening, and he chose those currents, past and present, from English gardening that suited his tastes and intentions. The overall result at Mount Vernon was that of an ornamental farm that included highly natural areas as well as formal, rigid ones. Above all, it was an American garden, where restraint was appropriate and the luxury of fancy, man-made objects was out of place.

The oft-stated observation that Washington relied on English gardening as a point of departure is true but must be greatly qualified. Of the six schools of thought traced here, he rejected two: gardens laden with man-made art objects, and the Chinese garden. If some of his landscape gardening resembled the rough picturesque manner of late eighteenth-century England, it was only because Washington embraced pines and rambling woods in crafting his American setting. As for the other three schools, he accepted some tenets of each. Washington clearly relied on the gardening manner championed by Capability Brown but only for some sections of his estate, which was also devoted to geometrical gardening and, most extensively, to ornamental farming. He

FIGURE 5.12. Thomas Jefferson, garden at Monticello, view of serpentine walk. Jefferson returned from his years in France and travels in England in the 1780s with ideas for landscape gardening based on curving lines and sweeping prospects. Photo: Author.

knew the English traditions but took what he wanted to create his own work of art.

Sources for Mount Vernon's Gardens

No extensive American landscape gardens existed before or during the Revolutionary War. Washington returned from the great conflict and almost immediately laid out a radical and thorough revision of the grounds at Mount Vernon. His gardens were American and fit his new role as moral leader of a republican nation, but he drew from English ideas, as Americans did in all cultural expressions. We can see from his letters that he was well aware of the language used and concepts widespread in English gardening theory and practice. Some of the terms linking his gardens to English thought were not his own, such as "hanging wood," used by Londoner Samuel Vaughan and not a widespread term in British gardening in any case. Most of Washington's lan-

guage, though, was straightforward and coterminous with English gardening.

While Washington borrowed many general gardening ideas from the English, such as that of the ornamental farm, his use of specific concepts or words clearly indicates his knowledge of contemporary English gardening and aesthetics. These included Hogarthian ideas about serpentine beauty; water meadows; shrubberies, groves, wildernesses, and labyrinths; the clumping or single spacing of trees; ha-ha walls; and the deer park.

Washington drew up a remarkable memorandum and sketch for the building of the east ha-ha wall, which was built in 1798. His proposal bears the unmistakable mark of his awareness of William Hogarth's theory of beauty. Washington wrote, illustrating his drawing (Figure 5.13), that he did not want necessarily to follow the contours of the hill, and he wanted the hill to be built up in places, all "to prevent

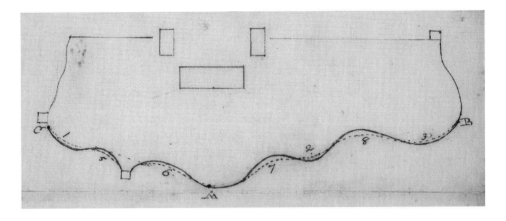

FIGURE 5.13. George Washington, drawing for the placement of the ha-ha wall around the east lawn at Mount Vernon, undated. Washington accompanied the drawing with a memorandum instructing his managers to make the wall neither too straight nor too curving. Courtesy of the Mount Vernon Ladies' Association (RM-770, MS-5082).

its being too serpentine or crooked." Washington insisted that it not be built in a zigzag of short, straight lines, as he instructed the "whole of it is [to be] serpentine." He reiterated in the memorandum, "It is not my wish to have it very serpentine nor would I have it quite strait if I could—a little curving and meaning would be my choice."[53] This not only indicates what is clear from the design, an embracing of the gentle curve, but also indicates a likely direct knowledge of the arguments of William Hogarth concerning the "line of beauty." Hogarth had advised in the *Analysis of Beauty* (1753) that an important contribution to beauty comes from the variety and grace produced by the serpentine line, and he argued that straight lines failed to provide the variety necessary for beauty and visual interest. On the one hand, "regularity and sameness, according to our doctrine, is want of elegance and true taste."[54] On the other hand, artists should also avoid excessiveness. Hogarth cautioned that it was thus essential that a line be neither too serpentine nor too curved. He applied this concept to the serpentine line in the abstract, as well as to aspects of the human body, the cabriole leg on furniture, and other visual forms (cf. Figure 5.14). Hogarth was influenced by garden theory, and in turn English garden designers quickly embraced his published principles. The notion of the perfectly curved line served as fundamental support to the natural gardening movement in the English world.[55] Hogarth's principle was thus well established and widely known, and whether Washington learned of it through conversation or from perusing Hogarth's book, he was clearly aware of this important idea in English aesthetic thought.

Just down the hill from the beautifully serpentine brick wall on the east lawn, Washington wanted to construct another garden element derived from the English: a water meadow. Such a meadow is not merely wet or flooded from time to time by nature, nor is it a flowing stream. As Mark Everard has defined it, it is "a man-made irrigation system operated at the discretion of the farmer . . . The high degree of management differentiates them from grazing marshes and from flood meadows and other naturally-flooded areas."[56] Washington, writing in frustration from Philadelphia, wanted his estate manager Anthony Whitting to expedite the experiment of diverting water from the spring near the Old Tomb, bringing it across the hill in front of the mansion house, and then having it spill down the hill in a water meadow that would been both scenic and functional in aiding the growth of plantings between the upper part of the hill and the Potomac. He wrote to Whitting on 18 November 1792:

> You have entirely mistaken my idea respecting the conducting of the Water from the *present* Spring . . . Instead of carrying it to the Wharf, my intention was to carry the whole, as high up the side of the Hill as the level of it would admit when the whole should be united at, or below the Spring (according as the level would allow) until it was brought as far, & right opposite to,

the River front of the Mansion House . . . I wanted to see how high up the side of that hill I could carry the water, and what advantage I might hereafter turn it to . . . There will be some difficulty, I am sensible, in taking it over the sunken place East of the Spring House; but a trough would remove it: after which, the water would go on a level, as in the case of Sideland Meadows to the place I have in view.[57]

Washington affirmed his intention in another letter to Whitting the next month: "In short, I want the water carried on its level to the front of the Mansion house, as it is done in Watered Meadows; that I may, if I should hereafter want to water any, or all of that ground, or to make a pond on the level, directly in front, along the Visto that was opened in a line between the two doors, that so much of the work may be done to my hands."[58] This would have formed a beautiful stream of dispersed water meandering down the slope of the hill (Figure 5.15).

Water meadows, although they have all but disappeared from the present-day British landscape, were well suited to the climate and terrain of England, with its rolling terrain, abundant rain, and long-standing custom of labor-intensive farming. Although the scheme never came to pass, probably because the water would not cooperate with Washington's plan, it shows that he was eager to experiment with an English concept applied to the improvement of the landscape.

Washington used phrases that correspond to English usage, but his application of English ideas was particular to his own aesthetic desires and understanding. He wrote often of his shrubberies, which flanked the bowling green; these seem mostly to have been similar to English shrubberies and included shrubs, bushes, and smaller trees, especially flowering or "clever" ones. On 2 March 1785 he noted the "fringe trees" to be planted in the shrubberies, including black haws, berried thorn trees, and other berry bushes and locust trees.[59] So, the shrubberies were to be of bushes and smaller to mid-size trees, especially curious or interesting ones with flowers and berries. In Washington's interpretation of shrubberies, though, he insisted on a clean separation of plants within

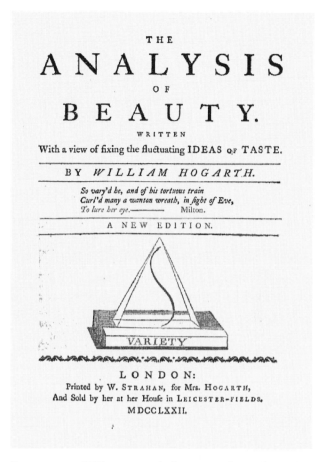

FIGURE 5.14. William Hogarth, frontispiece from *The Analysis of Beauty* (London, 1753 [1772 ed.]). Washington knew of the Englishman's ideas concerning one aspect of beauty, namely, that it would ideally embrace lines that curve neither too little (dull) nor too much (excessive and graceless). In the pyramid, Hogarth illustrates a line that is just right. Photo: Andrew Taylor.

the area. He introduced an element of symmetry: on 22 February 1785, Washington "removed from the Woods and old fields, several young Trees of the Sassafras, Dogwood, & red bud to the Shrubbery on the No. side [of] the grass plat," and he noted the planting of mock orange and lilacs in similar areas. He tried to balance one side with the other, for on 23 February he "planted trees on the South Shrubbery similar to those of yesterday, in the South Shrubbery except the Lilacs for which I thought the ground too wet."[60] The shrubberies

FIGURE 5.15. View across the hill between the east lawn and the Potomac River. Washington wanted to bring a spring across this hill and then direct the water downward, creating a scenic water meadow. These were widespread in England at the time. The effect would have been visible from the east lawn because this area formed part of the open vista Washington had created earlier from the mansion to the river. The spring does not seem to have cooperated, and Washington's correspondence about this with his estate manager ended abruptly. Photo: Author.

were to form, in the larger mass, a balance on either side of the bowling green, and even individual trees were to complement trees on the other side, one of the many aspects of symmetry in the bowling green and pleasure garden before his house.

As for groves and wildernesses, again Washington conformed to English ideas. A grove is a group of trees, either of one kind or of mixed types. He wrote in August 1776 that he wanted the caretakers to plant "groves of Trees at each end of the dwelling house," to be planted "without any order or regularity," and "to consist that at the North end, of locusts altogether. & that at the South, of all the clever kind of Trees (especially flowering ones) that can be got."[61] From the beginning of the period after the expansion of the mansion house, he understood the flexibility of groves in the English sense. The word "wilderness" also appears in his writings; he wanted, for example, to plant wildernesses on the sides of the serpentine walkways leading ultimately to the entrance on the west façade, with a mixture of shrubs, trees, and other plantings, and different colors for variety, as one would see

in a true wild forest. The English themselves often had a confusion of groves and wildernesses, and Alexander Pope spoke of his "wilderness grove," indicating that the terms were used somewhat interchangeably. Washington liked to clear undergrowth, as he did in the grove near the entrance gates, and in January 1785 "Began to grub & clear the under growth in my Pine Grove on the margin of Hell hole."[62] On the entrance road from the present west gates there were groves of trees, and the underbrush there was also cleared and the trees trimmed. Still, Washington thought of a grove as easily turned into a wilderness, and his categories were flexible. In his diaries, he showed some doubt about whether he had a "shrubbery or grove at the South end of the House."[63] We saw earlier that Washington did not know which end of the house, the north or the south, to make a grove and which a wilderness; he would decide, he thought, after the war ended.

One of Washington's clearly English practices was his spacing of trees into clumps or single trees. In such details, his delicacy and greatness as a landscape gardener were apparent. On 14 October 1792, Washington took a break from the drudgeries of the presidency to send a directive to Whitting, revealing his skillful hand as a landscape artist:

> To plant fresh clumps as soon as the trees can be removed; in the Buck Wheat Lot; the two clover lots; &ca; & of the best, & most ornamental trees—quick in their growth. These clumps are not to be placed with regularity as they respect one another—nor the trees in each, individually. Nor are the clumps to cover (individually) half the ground those did which were planted out last fall, Winter, & Spring. In a word, the trees are to be so close together in each Clump as for the tops, in a little while, to appear as if they proceeded from one trunk. they can always be thinned if found too thick. Those clumps wch are already planted (if alive) may be thickened in the manner I have described, and with the same kind of trees; provided they do not stand in too formal a point of view, one to the other.[64]

Another area was to be "grubbed" (dug up and cleared) "except such clumps or single trees, as one would wish to leave for Ornament." Elsewhere, on 11 November 1792, Washington wrote to Whitting:

> I shall again express my wish, and, as the raising of corn at the Mansion-House is given up, will also add my anxiety, to have all the ground (except single trees and clumps here and there) cleared, and well cleared, as mentioned in a former letter, between the old clover lot and the sunken ground quite from the wharf to Richard's house and the gate; but, previously, do what has been desired from the cross fence by the spring, to the wharf. In clearing the whole of this ground, let all the ivy and flowering trees and shrubs remain on it, over and above the clumps, and other single trees where they may be thought requisite, for ornament. The present growing pines within that enclosure might be thinned, and brought more into form. When this is done, and all the low land from the river up to the gate laid down in grass, it will add much to the appearance of the place, and be a real benefit and convenience, as it will yield an abundance of grass.[65]

As Washington wrote to Whitting in 9 December 1792: "The Clumps, as marked by the Gardener are very well designed but if there had been *more* trees in them, they wd not have been the worse for it."[66] At any rate, Washington clearly understood the English practice of clumping trees together or setting them out singly as the most pleasing way to create a landscape. Washington later wrote that as a general rule trees ought to be planted singly or in clumps.[67] This approach generally follows English sources but was shaped in its particulars by Washington's experience and application of the ideas, with the help of managers on site.

A salient part of the natural views at Mount Vernon resulted from the continuity of the lawns as abetted by the use of brick ha-ha walls, supposed so-called because one says "ha ha" or "aha aha" in surprise while falling unexpectedly off the edge. These walls stand at the end of an excavation on a hillside and were usually built of brick. Although the French had long used trenches and walls in their gardens, the English claimed that these sunken fences were "invented" by their own Charles Bridgeman (1690–1738), whom Horace Walpole noted as a key figure in the early development of natural landscape gardening in England. Bridgeman retained geometries and clipped bushes in his designs but also, according to Walpole, introduced groves and wilderness aspects to English gardens. In his *On Modern Gardening,* Walpole noted, "though he still adhered much to straight walks with high clipped hedges, they were only his great lines; the rest he diversified by wilderness, and with loose groves of oak, though still within surrounding hedges."[68]

Perhaps to our surprise, Walpole gives the ha-ha walls the key place in the history of modern English landscape gardening.

> I call a sunk fence the leading step [in the new, natural style], for these reasons: No sooner was this simple enchantment made, than levelling, mowing and rolling, followed. The contiguous ground of the park without the sunk fence was to be harmonised with the lawn within; and the garden in its turn was to be set free from its prim regularity, that it might assort with the wilder country without. The sunk fence ascertained the specific garden; but that it might not draw too obvious a line of distinction between the neat and the rude, the contiguous outlying parts came to be included in a kind of general design: and when nature was taken into the plan, under improvements, every step that was made, pointed out new beauties and inspired new ideas.[69]

So, the park, the lawn, and the garden could blend seamlessly into another, and the unity of the English garden became more easily achieved.

Echoing Walpole's assessment, garden historian Ralph Dutton called the ha-ha wall an "epoch-making invention" and claimed that "the invention of the ha-ha sealed the fate of the formal garden" because the "whole of the park adjacent to the house became a background for the garden."[70] Indeed, ha-ha walls were a signature of English gardening, and one can hardly imagine landscape gardening without them, as they unify the view and keep a sense of continuous rolling landscape even as they protect sections of an estate from animals. At Mount Vernon, they served the purpose of keeping out farm animals (pigs, sheep, and cows) as well as allowing a sweeping and uninterrupted view across the grass from the portico, east lawn, or bowling green.

It is worth noting that ha-ha walls in England were not always level with the upper ground, and they sometimes rose a few inches or even more from the level of the earth. This is how they sometimes appear in period prints and paintings. Practical reasons of upkeep and drainage made it sometimes more desirable to have the walls raised a bit from the ground. But in his application of this English idea, Washington seemed to have wanted to keep his level with the ground above. Estate manager Lund Washington reported to General Washington on 12 November 1775 that it was too cold "to Turf the Ha Has," meaning that he planned to put dirt over the top edge, which would have thus been completely covered from view.[71] A rare witness in this regard was Sally Foster Otis, who in 1801 commented that "the wall is of brick which encloses it but sunk so that in appearance tis an open lawn."[72] The tops of the brick ha-ha walls were essentially at ground level; her visit was in January, and if it looked like continuous lawn then, the effect would have been even greater during seasons when the grass helped to conceal the transition further.

For about six years, Washington kept a deer park on the slope of the hill between the east lawn and the river. Deer parks in Britain date back to the Middle Ages and were widespread on country estates for centuries, and a number of such parks existed on American estates before Washington. Washington visited in 1773 Lord Stirling's famous deer park in Basking Ridge, New Jersey, and deer parks at George Mason's Gunston Hall and elsewhere served as local examples. There was a deer park established at the Governor's Palace in Williamsburg by 1727.[73] Washington noted in August 1785 that he was beginning the fencing around the deer paddock near the river, and his letters and diaries record his efforts to continue the fencing and secure deer for the park, where the trees were said to be "thickly planted."[74]

In building a deer park, Washington was following a long-standing pattern of the Anglo-American elite. At that date, however, his type of deer park was more characteristic of earlier generations in England. The tendency in England by the later eighteenth century was to remove the fencing and have the deer roam wild and at will across the entire estate, even approaching the mansions themselves, a phenomenon captured in countless British prints and paintings. Washington's deer park was a fenced-in paddock, where the deer were contained and tightly controlled. (The deer were not to be fed or approached by people lest they become too tame and not "wild" enough; cf. Plate 15.) At any rate, the deer park should not be overestimated in Washington's gardening. He started it late in life, and it was only in place for about six years. He abandoned the idea when the deer repeatedly broke through the fencing or swam away past the water fence, and he chose not to restock it after 1792.[75] It could have been part of the larger design to turn the east view into a magnificent picture, but the deer park was hardly visible from the house or portico or even much of the east lawn and thus must have had only a minimal visible effect for many visitors. The actual deer park fence was about sixty feet further east, down the hill from the present brick wall, which is a restoration of one built in 1798 after the deer park was abandoned (cf. Fig. 4.20).

For reasons of practicality, changing tastes, and economy,

he made a more natural and open area of the sloping hill and riverside and took a more modern approach to the deer, as well. Consistent with English practice in the later eighteenth century, he let them roam freely over the whole estate and form part of the diversity of scenery. Unmolested and unhunted, they were visible to family and visitors, even if their appearances were more fleeting. When William Pearce reported to the president that the deer were damaging the plantings, Washington replied, "I am at a loss therefore in determining whether to give up the Shrubs or the Deer! Is there no way of freightening them from these haunts?"[76] He was willing, even if he lost some plants, to refrain from having the deer shot to eliminate their troublesome behavior. The deer continued to run freely, and they were fed in winter in hopes that they would leave the plants alone. On 29 January 1797, Washington wrote to manager Anderson that "if feeding the Deer will not divert them from their mischievous tricks, they must, after I come home, be killed, unless the fear of hounds would keep them at a distance."[77] He made every effort to keep the deer and allow them to remain part of the visual experience of the diversified scene of his mansion house estate.

We have looked at a number of English gardening ideas and noted where Washington differed from English practice, and we might wonder whether any particular written sources stimulated his ideas and his practice. He did own a number of gardening books. One of them, Thomas Mawe and John Abercrombie, *Every Man his Own Gardener* (1769), contained practical advice and has little information about layout or other broader aesthetic concerns.[78] Washington owned Batty Langley's *New Principles of Gardening* (first published 1727), and many have claimed that it served as a significant source for Washington's beautification of the landscape at Mount Vernon.[79] Some general ideas might at first seem to indicate the influence of Langley. For example, he called for an end to the stiff style of regimented gardening, and some of his specific advice, such as placing groves at the ends of a house, corresponds with actions taken by

Washington. He asked that groves be planted "promiscuously" and naturally, a direction consistent with Washington's approach and even his language.[80] Langley's favoring of the "rural manner" would seem to be behind the larger layout of the open parklands at Mount Vernon.

It is difficult, however, to establish that Washington actually used the book to derive either the broad principles or the details of arranging his garden at Mount Vernon. Langley's book was rather out of date in the English context by the time Washington owned it, and it was still indebted to earlier, formal, Continental ideas of gardening. Langley praised natural gardens and encouraged curving lines and mixed plantings grouped together, but that was all rather standard fare, and Washington could have easily learned of the English trends elsewhere. He had owned Langley's book for decades before he set out to alter his estate after the Revolutionary War, and he hardly needed Langley's text to learn what he must have heard during many conversations with others who knew well the character of modern English landscape gardening.

There were certainly major differences between Washington and Langley's approaches to gardening. While Langley calls for groves, serpentine lines, and undulating, open lawns, he also mentions the inclusion in gardens of grottoes, ruins, haystacks, aviaries, cabinets, statues, and amphitheaters.[81] Washington never tried to develop with his abundantly available water any of the canals, basins, or fountains that Langley recommends. Langley asks for the liberal use of statuary on the grounds, directing "That the grand Front of a Building lie open upon an elegant Lawn or Plain or Grass, adorn'd with beautiful Statues," or "that the Intersections of Walks be adorn'd with Statues." Washington had no statuary at all outside on his property.[82] The vision painted in Langley's verses is thus alien to Mount Vernon:

Statues of various Shapes may be dispos'd
About the Tube; sometimes it is inclos'd
by dubious Scylla, or with Sea-Calves grac'd,
Or by a Brazen Triton 'tis embrac'd.

A Triton thus at Luxembourg presides,
And from the Dophin which he proudly rides,
Spouts out the Streams . . . [83]

In prose, he calls for a host of classical figures—including Mars, Mercury, Flora, Diana, Bacchus, and many others—to occupy the dry land of a garden. Washington crafted a more natural garden, and he eschewed the mixture of Nature and Art as on the estates of Stowe, Stourhead, and numerous other English gardens in the generation before Capability Brown. The ornamental farm at Mount Vernon, adorned also with green pleasure parklands, fundamentally differed from Langley's vision of an ornate English estate devoted to fine arts and contrived walkways and parterres.

Langley's book provided a number of specific designs for gardens. Most of his illustrated views, which included very formal views in the manner of the Baroque gardens at Versailles, quickly became strikingly outmoded in English terms. He also illustrated grandiose views of ruins, fountains, and trees in straight alignment (Figure 5.16); these were not characteristic of Washington's gardening at Mount Vernon. Washington might have been tempted to draw from Langley's numerous figures for serpentine walks (cf. Figure 5.17), but these designs are contrived and improbable, and the tight curls of their lines never became fashionable in England, let alone America. The grand-scale designs by Langley for a house and extensive garden (see Figure 5.16) recommend a level of geometry and rigidity that Washington avoided, apparently adopting his gardening ideas from his own experience in his American garden. That Langley still asked for "grand Avenues" and represented trees in old-fashioned allées is telling, and Washington chose instead by the 1780s to develop winding, circuitous paths in his pleasure gardens.[84]

On the whole, Langley's book was largely devoted to particular aspects of gardening, including how to plant, the hardiness of different flora, appropriate soils, and so forth. There is a long section on kitchen gardening, with an almost

FIGURE 5.16. Batty Langley, "Shady walks with Temples of Trellis work after the grand manner at Versailes" and "An Avenue in Perspective with the ruins of an ancient Building after the Roman manner." Washington owned Langley's book early on, but many of its designs were old-fashioned by Washington's time, even by American standards. *New Principles of Gardening* (1727/1728), plate 2. Photo: Andrew Taylor.

dictionary- or encyclopedia-like listing of herbs and other comestibles. Washington must have found this kind of particular, practical information useful, and it is the kind of information that appears in his own notes, writings, and letters, but he never referred to Langley by name in letters to friends or his estate managers. Even in smaller-scale matters, Washington deviates from Langley. The latter said honeysuckle is a lover of liberty and should be left to roam freely up trees and allowed to delight in the shade. Washington

FIGURE 5.17. Batty Langley, designs for serpentine paths and a fountain. Washington's serpentine paths have little in common with Langley's. Some other ideas in Langley's book might have been useful for Washington, such as the Englishman's remarks about groves. *New Principles of Gardening* (1727/1728), plate 5. Photo: Andrew Taylor.

had his honeysuckles adhere to his square columns in the arcades of the arms connected to his dependencies.[85] One could look throughout Langley's treatise and discover that Washington went his own way, using native soils and plants and what he learned from others in America to come up with his gardening solutions.

More promising than Langley as a source for George Washington's garden was Philip Miller's best-selling *Gardeners Dictionary,* of which Washington owned the abridged 1763 edition.[86] Washington cited Miller in two 1785 letters, saying in one that Miller "seems to understand the culture of Trees equal to any other writer I have met with," and writing in the other about Miller's nomenclature for the Magnolia tree.[87] Those are the extent of his mentions of Miller, however, and Washington gives no broader evidence that Miller influenced his gardening style in general. For his part, manager George Augustine Washington cited Miller's book to Washington regarding magnolia trees.[88]

Miller's book is mostly a list of different species, with re-marks on qualities of the plants, conditions for growing them, and so forth, and we know Washington used Miller's book for finding information about individual species of plants and trees. Miller also throws light on broader issues in some of his entries, and Washington's general ideas seem more in accord with Miller than Langley. Washington's understanding of groves, wildernesses, and shrubberies, for example, conforms with the dictionary definitions of Miller. Under "Groves," Miller says:

> Groves are the greatest ornaments to a garden; nor can a garden of any extent be complete which has not one or more of these . . . in planting of these Groves, it is much the best Way to dispose all the Trees irregularly, which will given them a greater Magnificence, and also form a Shade sooner, than when the Trees are planted in Lines . . . Most of the Groves which have been planted either in England, or those celebrated Gardens in Frances, are only a few regular Lines of Trees; many of which are Avenues to the Habitation, or lead to some Building, or other Object: but these do not appear so grand, as those which have been made in Woods, where the Trees have grown accidentally, and at irregular Distances.[89]

He goes on to note that "most of the planted Groves have generally a Gravel-walk, made in a strait Line between them; which greatly offends the Sight of Persons who have true Taste: therefore whenever a Gravel-walk is absolutely necessary to be carried through the Groves, it will be much better to twist it about, according as the Trees naturally stand, than to attempt Regularity."[90] Although he had winding, gravel paths, Washington did not always follow Miller, and the trees along his serpentine paths in the bowling green are less spontaneous than the irregular arrangement that Miller suggested. We saw in chapter 2 that Washington rather pointedly paid little attention to Miller's design for a greenhouse, except in practical matters such as using flues under the floor, shutters, and the plastering of inside walls. The wings in Miller might have inspired Washington's design, although his are used as slave quarters, which is not the use Miller suggested. As with Langley, much of Miller's discussion is rather

Figure 5.18. William Watts and G. Barret, "Trentham in Staffordshire, the Seat of Earl Gower." Washington owned Watts's book, and it may have influenced his final gardening plans, especially in his ideas, only partially executed, for integrating the banks of the Potomac into the rest of the parklands at Mount Vernon. William Watts, *Seats of the Nobility and Gentry* (1779–1786), plate 31. Photo: Andrew Taylor.

general, and Washington still had to apply broad ideas to his particular setting. He thus might have read the following and learned little: "Groves are not only treat ornaments to Gardens, but are also the greatest Relief against the violent Heats of the Sun, affording Shade to walk under, in the hottest Part of the Day, when the other Parts of the Garden are useless; so that every Garden is defective which has not Shade."[91] Washington had to find his own way, despite the general advice and stimulation provided by Miller's dictionary. Washington followed the "genius of the place," to use Pope's expression, and did not need or want to follow any writer too closely.

Washington received his copy of *The Seats of the Nobility and Gentry* (1779–1786) by William Watts in 1796, too late for it to be greatly influential on his broader plans, but it could have informed some of his last schemes, and his acquisition of the book certainly indicates his interest in the subject.[92] He must have read this with great interest, comparing his estate with a wide range of English seats. The book may well have had a strong influence on his last gardening

schemes, which involved linking the house visually to the river via walkways to the east and across grassy lawns to the southeast. A number of plates in Watts's tome illustrate the then-current English vogue for arranging an easy sweep from the mansion to the water, which was treated as a potential area for leisurely foot traffic. If Washington saw the plates for Trentham Hall (Figure 5.18), Chatsworth, or any number of the English seats, he could have seen that the inaccessibility of the Potomac from the house was not pleasant or in fashion, which could explain his last actions as a gardener. He wanted a gravel walk and fishpond near the river and increased footpaths to it, and he planned to remove the Old Tomb and have the grass sweep pleasantly and dramatically from the south side of the mansion house to the banks of the Potomac. On the whole, this volume must have been of great interest to Washington and confirmed his general arrangement of house, lawn, groves, and so forth.

Washington took some ideas from books and bookplates, but conversation and observation were his chief ways of gathering information, and he reacted pragmatically to his own situation. He also wrote letters to English correspondents, such as Arthur Young, mostly asking about agricultural technique but also receiving information related to his gardening and introduction to his estate of grasses, plants, and trees. Washington's social circumstances differed from those of the British, and his mansion house afforded a river prospect largely without parallel in England. In the next chapter, we see how Washington's life experiences intersected with gardening, views, and landscape art at Mount Vernon.

CHAPTER SIX

Prospects, Pictures, and the Picturesque

[Mount Vernon stands] in a situation more magnificent than I can paint to a European imagination.

GEORGE GRIEVE, 1780s

The situation of the house & the view from the back of it the most magnificent I ever beheld.

MARY BAGOT, 1816

GEORGE WASHINGTON spent much of his life measuring views as a surveyor and relying on them in military planning. We can regard a "view" as a general term for something seen, and it could include any sight in the gardens. In the context of the time, the words "vista" and "prospect"—both subsumed under the larger concept of the view— were part of the vocabulary and expected experience in a garden. A prospect was a distant, usually broad, view, especially as seen from an elevated location. A vista (sometimes spelled "visto" in the Anglo-American world) was a narrow view, usually cut through trees trimmed to create a tunnel-like opening. A landscape was an outdoor scene, the word having only recently sprung from its more exclusive use as referring to a painting of nature.

Vistas derived from Renaissance perspective and Baroque spatial play. Long a part of gardening in Italy and France, the vista was becoming by the late eighteenth century a bit old fashioned, and more spontaneous and natural-looking narrow views through trees were coming into favor in England. In the Continental European tradition, the vista was highly defined by trees and often had as a focal point a man-made object, such as a fountain, obelisk, statue, or building. English vistas, the forerunners of Washington's "vistos," were usually less artificial than those seen across the Channel.

FIGURE 6.1. View of a Seaside Villa, fresco, first century AD, Castellamare di Stabia, Italy. It was well known in the eighteenth century that ancient Roman villas often had long porticoes with garden or water views. Photo: Scala / Art Resource, NY.

As for the prospect, there were different trends in the English school of gardening and landscape art in the eighteenth century, but it was agreed that the grand prospect was highly desirable. British readers could read in ancient texts of the Roman penchant for placing seaside villas and country seats on hillsides so that they might enjoy good prospects, and in antiquity there was a school of art that captured such views in panel and mural painting (Figure 6.1).[1] While medieval peoples certainly must have enjoyed views, it was not until Francesco Petrarca's description of his ascent of Mount Ventoux in France in 1336 (*Epistolae familiares,* IV, 1), that one recorded the experience of a view enjoyed for its own sake.[2] It was not long before Italian Renaissance artists set out to capture the beauties of the distant view, including the aerial perspective, expanse of space, and visual domination of the countryside below. The profound beauty of the view became established in Renaissance culture and was among the elements of the rediscovery of Nature and of antiquity that was handed down to English culture. A sweeping prospect from an English country house or gazebo was deemed important, for it was such a view that set into play the picturesque variety of color, texture, and form produced by the garden designer's naturalistic shaping of the land-

scape. The desire to experience a prospect was exploited by writers and artists as well as landscape gardeners, and the social event of the private outing to visit and picnic at a notable viewing point on a hill or mountain formed an integral part of Georgian culture.

The word "landscape" originally meant a painting, not a natural setting, but the senses came to merge in the eighteenth century. Although gardeners did not generally imitate landscapes by specific artists, it was thought that a good (real) garden landscape should utilize pictorial ideals, and gardeners consciously borrowed ideas of variety, spatial devices and distancing (pushing back and creating space with objects placed in the foreground), framing with trees, offering prospects, and using water to advantage. Despite their differences, all schools of eighteenth-century British gardening had some relationship to the landscape painter's art. The title of this book uses landscape in a dual sense, to refer to nature and to pictures, as Washington was concerned with both.

Vistas, prospects, landscapes—all of these concepts were widespread in American discussion of gardening and art, and Washington was hardly alone in his creation of a visual world invested in these ideas. The love of a good prospect, for example, was embedded in the names chosen for a number of colonial country estates, some of which exaggerate the elevations on which they sat. The names of Belvoir, the home of the "beautiful view" of the Fairfaxes, Mount Airy (Virginia) of the Tayloes, Mount Pleasant of Captain MacPherson in Philadelphia, and Mount Airy (Maryland) of the Calverts call attention to the hillside settings of the mansion houses that enjoyed fine distant views.[3] Thomas Jefferson read in Book Two of his translation of Andrea Palladio's *Quattro Libri dell'Architettura* (1570) that a country house is best placed on a "little mountain" ("monticello" in the original text). Whether or not he named his estate directly after this particular passage, by using an Italian word he was evoking the Renaissance tradition of creating a country villa with a pleasant prospect on a little hill that provides healthy breezes as well as fine views.[4] While he was acting in a larger American context, George Washington was not surpassed by anyone in American in his shaping of the landscape and his development of various kinds of views.

Vistas and Prospects at Mount Vernon

It was not enough, as General Nathanael Greene reported on 13 September 1783, that Mount Vernon sat on "one of the most beautiful situations in the world."[5] In carefully building his gardens, Washington planned and maintained several particular vistas from and near the mansion house, and he helped improve the prospect across the river by trimming trees and framing the view.

The specific idea of the vista, "a long, narrow view as between trees" (*OED*), only appeared in Washington's known correspondence in 1785, when he was fifty-three, and it was only at that time that he set out to make them at his estate. He did so most likely in response to information that he had gathered during or immediately after the war. The vista was not a widespread or established idea in the colonies, although it was far from unknown. But even the sophisticated John Custis, father-in-law of Martha, only first heard the word "visto" in 1717, the term having been used by Governor Spotswood.[6]

In addition to broader prospects, Washington was keenly interested in creating narrower vistas on his estate. These consisted of the main vista on the western approach to the house, which we discussed in chapter 3; another narrower vista planned on the west side of the house radiating off to the right (northwest) as one looks from the house and bowling green; a vista from the mansion house and east lawn down the hill to the water; several vistas through a large pine grove planted in low-lying ground near the Potomac southeast of the mansion house; and a view or broad kind of vista planned (but not fully executed) from the south side of the house and the windows of Washington study, passing across the present south lawn and intended to go all the way to the Potomac.

Given the length of the main, west vista, its form shifted somewhat over time as various groves and the bowling green area were developed. The exact time of its first establishment and its initial appearance are unknown. Washington did confirm the vista's existence in 1787: "The plan [sent by Samuel Vaughan] describes with accuracy the houses, walks, shrubs beries &ca except in the front of the Lawn—west of the Ct yard. There the plan differs from the original—in the former, you have closed the prospect with trees along the walk to the gate—whereas in the latter the trees terminate with two mounds of earth one on each side on which grow Weeping Willows leaving an open and full view of the distant woods—the mounds are at 60 yards apart. I mention this because it is the only departure from the origl."[7]

The width of the vista in the bowling green would later have been determined by the six oval beds that were incorporated into the area. There were two large beds and four smaller ones; each had trees of a size that would both immediately and gradually block the main vista. It is likely that the beds were pushed off to the side of the lawn, ran east to west lengthwise, and ran parallel or in harmony with the curving lines of the serpentine paths. Given Washington's penchant for symmetry, it is likely that one large oval balanced another across the lawn and that the four smaller ones were also broken down into two paired groups that echoed each other. As for the vista itself, the trees in the oval beds must have further framed the vista and perhaps pinched it in, at least in the bowling green itself. An effect of the oval would have been to turn the vista into an even more tunnel-like experience when one walked in the "courtyard" between the mansion front and the bowling green gate.

Farther from the house, the width and nature of the vista also changed over time. In 1792, Washington was having workers make it one hundred feet wide, assuming that in the relevant document the "White Gate" was the entrance gate in the view's path. The vista, as yet only forty feet wide at that point, was to be lined with evergreens and "some Other trees." Anthony Whitting wrote to Washington:

> I have Grubbd the Visto through to the White Gate Only yet forty feet wide as there is now a better Oppertunity of Staking it properly. I Could wish if You Sir have no Objection to plant Ever Greens & some Other trees in a Line with the Outsides that is at fifty feet each side from the Centre as at present the trees are so thin no regular line will be seen, from this appearance now to be seen it will look very well when 100 feet wide, and I think will be improved by trees planted as above. A farther improvement might be made by continuing the Visto as far as a prospect can be Obtaind. that may be to the extremity of the hill leading to Muddy hole Branch any farther attempt I believe would be fruitless this however would be then better seen if the fall there should be so Great as not to admit of the tops of the trees being seen it might bring to View some of the Grounds over by Pools, if not there might be a Large Clump of Ever Greens planted on each side and Something like an Obelisk fixd in the Centre where it terminates. this I have seen done when no farther prospect could be Obtaind and it has lookd very well[.][8]

Washington's managers followed instructions but perforce (in the president's absence) had to make decisions along the way. Washington, however, never accepted Whitting's suggestion that an obelisk would look good at a far endpoint to the vista, and we hear no more of that in any correspondence or description of the estate.

Many visitors commented on the house's extraordinary first vista when exiting the woods and the public road two-thirds of a mile away, near the present west gates and Bushrod's porters' lodges (see Figure 4.2 and Plate 10). Robert Hunter Jr. noted on 16 November 1785, "His seat breaks out beautifully upon you when you little expect, being situated upon a most elegant rising ground on the banks of the Potomac." Roger Griswold wrote to his sister Fanny on 1 December 1800, "As you approach the house from the Country, its appearance strikes you very forcibly—the gardens, out houses (which are very numerous) and pleasure ground are laid out with great tast[e], and I do not recollect ever to have seen a situation more pleasing." The presence and success of this vista is confirmed by nearly every early account. Sally Foster Otis noted in January 1801, after being lost in the mass of wood, "at half past two surmounted all perils by land & by water and had the satisfaction to see on a beautiful emminence the Mansion of the great Washington and here description fails me, I can only tell you tis all that we, in our most romantic moments have imagined of grandeur[,] taste and beauty."[9] The first vista was an important visual beginning for a long approach to the mansion house, set on the "beautiful emminence" of the hillside.

Near the time the main west vista was being improved, Washington urged his managers to create yet another vista on the west side, beginning at the house and running west but slightly veering to the right compared to the main vista (Figure 6.2). Even in the heat of the Revolutionary War, Washington planned a vista (apparently not created) toward the northwest of the house; he asked manager Lund Washington on 3 April 1779, "have you opened the Visto to Muddy hole?" During the presidency, he pursued the idea of a vista in about this same place ("towards muddy hole branch"). In 1792 and 1793, Washington, absent from the estate, worked via letter with his manager on the spot in staking out the vista direction but wrote several times from Philadelphia trying to spur progress on the project. This vista was not the same as the main vista, already established

Proposed new vista

FIGURE 6.2. Aerial view, Mount Vernon, showing the proposed vista that Washington planned c. 1792–1793 to the right of the main vista. He wrote letters from Philadelphia to his estate manager at home to try to create this vista, but the project did not bear fruit; perhaps the terrain would not support the vista that Washington wanted. Image: Author, with the assistance of Kay Fukui.

by 1792, and he called it the "second vista." as opposed to the first vista toward the present west gates. He wrote to Whitting on 14 October: "The second Visto which I mentioned to you is but a secondary object, and yet I am anxious to know over what ground it will pass; but this may be done by a line of stakes in an avenue not more than Six feet wide."[10] Washington wrote in frustration on 2 December 1792: "Before I left home, I desired you to mark out another Visto on the West front of the Mansion house, merely to see over what ground it would go, that I might thereby be enabled to decide, whether to open it or not; but as you have mentioned nothing of it in any of your letters, I suppose it is not yet done." He was more emphatic in a letter to his manager two weeks later: "I would have you open the second Visto 20 feet wide, as far as muddy hole branch, and let me know whether the hill on the other side of it is high or low; and whether it will require much work to open it to the full width 'till you pass it; for as to opening it beyond the hill I

conceive it to be as unnecessary, as it was in the first Visto, after you descend into the flat beyond it."[11]

That this vista was intended to be useful for viewing the house from afar is clear from Washington's note to Whitting in January 1793: "My object in clearing the grounds *out side* of the pasture, along the Road from the Gum Spring, was, that you might see the Mansion house as soon as you should enter the little old field beyond it."[12] Two months later, Washington asked about progress on the project and how it looked from the mansion house: "Have you got the second Visto so much opened as to be able to form any opinion of the view, & how it will appear from the House?" Washington was very concerned with how it would appear from the house, and he wanted reassurance that some progress was underway. Despite the many inquiries and direction, when Whitting responded on 20 March 1793, little had been done: "We shall fix the Gates at the different farms as soon as the weather will permit but the Ground must be dry or they will never be fast—I have not Opened the Second Visto so as to se[e] what Ground it will run over but could do it in a very few Days."[13] The matter was resolved via now-lost correspondence or after Washington returned for a visit from Philadelphia. Probably because the terrain was not right for it, the vista was never fully established beyond staking it out and initial grubbing (clearing). Had the plan succeeded, another visual point of interest would have existed while looking to and from the house, and something of a goose-foot (*patte d'oie*) effect would have been established in conjunction with the wider main vista running straight out from the house toward the west gates. While a goose-foot arrangement of paths or vistas radiating from a single point was widespread and long known in gardening (multiple vistas through trees appeared, for example, in Batty Langley's *New Principles of Gardening,* Plate 1), Washington's immediate point of inspiration was likely the famous radiating avenues of Pierre L'Enfant's plan for the District of Columbia. Washington knew of those plans by the summer of 1791, and he was among those officials to approve the dy-

FIGURE 6.3. Mount Vernon, view from the east lawn toward the Potomac. For a while, Washington kept a deer park in the area between the east lawn and river. After 1792, he abandoned the deer park and had a vista cut through the wooded area. Photo: Author.

namic arrangement of streets and sightlines in the new capital city.

Washington established another important vista at Mount Vernon from the house through the old deer park and to the river (Figure 6.3). Once the deer park idea was abandoned in 1792 and the animals left to roam on their own, Washington decided to cut through the somewhat thickly planted "hanging wood" between the east lawn and the Potomac. The vista, as discussed in letters of November and December 1792, would have emanated from a central spot between two doors, presumably the central door on the east and the door to the south. The hillside water meadow that we discussed in chapter 5 would have run down the ground of this vista; Washington wrote on 20 January 1793 of "the Ditch which was intended to conduct the Water from the Springs under the Hill to the Visto in front of the Mansion house." This vista

would have been particularly scenic, encompassing a view from the house to river and vice versa, as well as including the innovative water meadow, made from the spring to the south, that Washington wanted brought across the hill so that it could trickle according to the terrain down to the river.[14]

This whole area of the vista, including land that was being given up from the enclosed (and thus somewhat old-fashioned) deer park, would have been a dynamic, open, and modern work of landscape gardening. Washington himself set out the vista by laying out stakes while he was there, and on 18 November 1792 he wrote to his estate manager to see whether the work had been done:

You have entirely mistaken my idea respecting the conducting of the Water from the *present* Spring, and those I desired might be opened (to see what a body of it I could collect). Instead of carrying it to the Wharf, my intention was to carry the whole, as high up the side of the Hill as the level of it would admit when the whole should be united at, or below the Spring (according as the level would allow) until it was brought as far, & right opposite to, the River front of the Mansion House (that is to the Vista in a line with the two doors which I had opened whilst I was at home, by stakes which I suppose may be standing there yet).[15]

He insisted to Whitting on 2 December 1792: "I want the water carried on its level to the front of the Mansion house, as it is done in Watered Meadows; that I may, if I should hereafter want to water any, or all of that ground, or to make a pond on the level, directly in front, along the Visto that was opened in a line between the two doors, that so much of the work may be done to my hands."[16] While the water meadow never came about, the vista was cut and is maintained in approximate form today, constituting an important part of the experience of the river view from the portico and east lawn.

Another vista, or rather a series of them, was formed through pine forests near the edge of Hell Hole, an area south and west of the house and so called because of the swampy ground there. (Today it includes the educational Pioneer Farm.) Just as he staked out the vista to the river, Washington was present to oversee the formation of these vistas in 1785: "Laid out a walk for the wilderness, intended on the No. of the Serpentine road on the right. Began to open Vistos throw the Pine grove on the Banks of H. Hole. Visited my Plantations at the Ferry, Muddy hole, & Dogue run."[17] These vistas (Washington used the plural) through the Pine Grove must have been intended for viewing by someone on foot and were not necessarily visible from nor emanated from the mansion house. These seem to have been smaller vistas cutting swaths through the pine grove to allow the passage of persons as well as views, and they perhaps facilitated hunting or access for the harvesting of trees. These vistas were, of course, less accessible to the average viewer than the entrance vista and are not mentioned in visitors' accounts. At any rate, Washington's diary entry makes one

wonder how many other smaller vistas he may have opened on his estate while he was there and not recording his directions and actions in correspondence with managers.

We will not look at every view or open sight at Mount Vernon, but one in particular is worth mentioning here because it nearly had the character of a vista—the planned view from the side of the house, the portico, and the windows of Washington's study down the south lawn to the river. This view was not a vista per se and was hardly remarked upon at the time, but it was clearly created over time and offered a long view for Washington in his frequently used study. He kept the south grove back from the plane of the house in the 1780s, so he already had some view of the lawn. In a letter to Whitting in January 1793, Washington stated that he wanted the grass to grow "quite from the River bank" to various points uphill toward the Vineyard Enclosure and the wharf.[18] As a nephew of Washington's reported after his uncle's death, Washington specifically planned to have the lawn continue past the Old Tomb, which needed to be removed because of the moisture and damage from tree roots. This plan made sense in the context of the other vistas, which tended to radiate from a central point (the mansion house).[19] He did take the lawn far down the hill, but the Old Tomb and its surrounding trees were a great obstacle to Washington's gardening scheme, and he never effected its removal. This terrain was a rare place on the broad hillside where the eye could travel across the surface of the ground and reach the river, as all other views from the house and portico could see the river only after a drop-off (Figures 6.4 and 6.5). The continuous and grassy lawn to the Potomac would have added a new element to the views at Mount Vernon and pleased the eye with a long view that continued not just to the river's edge but well beyond to a scenic and majestic sweep south of the Potomac River.

The view from the study windows was just one of the excellent views from the house itself. The other main view from the house was the view of the grove of locust trees and other greenery from the window of the Large Dining Room.

FIGURE 6.4. Mount Vernon, view from portico down the south lawn. The ha-ha wall helped created the effect of a continuous lawn. At the end of his life, Washington planned to create a long, dramatic view from his study window and portico past the Old Tomb and toward the water's edge. Photo: Author.

The window surround and the view itself form a curious mixture of stylized nature and natural nature; the acanthus, bell-flowers, and swags, carried in a linear fashion expressive of the Adamesque style, present Nature in its controlled, artistic form, while the view through the window is of an irregularly planted group of trees (Plate 4). The striking contrast of order and irregularity represents basic eighteenth-century ideas about Nature and Art. Other fine views were framed by the doors of the central passage out toward the river and toward the west vista, while a variety of good views were available from the Lafayette Bedroom upstairs, from the Little Parlor, and from other windows. Poet John Searson, surely not alone among visitors, climbed the stairs and viewed the landscape all around from the cupola. Still, the chief view of them all was the prospect of the lawn, woods, river, and Maryland shore as seen from the portico and east lawn, a prospect that was the capstone of the entire aesthetic experience at Mount Vernon.

The Prospect from the Portico and East Lawn

The stunning view from the east side of the mansion house was the highlight of the visual experience at Mount Vernon, as often noted by visitors through the decades (Plates 18 and 19; cf. Figure 6.4). A study of extant features, early views, and descriptions allows us to recreate the sequential views from the portico, from the irregular planting of trees on the north grove to the open lawn and colorful south grove. The result demonstrates Washington's skill as a landscape artist work-

FIGURE 6.5. View up the south lawn toward the mansion house at Mount Vernon. There was a view down this hill toward the Old Tomb, which at the end of his life Washington had planned to remove and replace with an open lawn. The south grove near the house shielded the residents from a view of the dung repository (*left, center*). Photo: Author.

ing successfully with the natural and man-made elements to create views replete with pictorial variety, framing, and spatial distancing.

Searson, who visited in May 1799, gives us a sense of the sweep of the panorama from the portico and indicated how contemporaries read the view from side to side: "The prospect from it must e're please the mind, / When elegant Potowmack here we find. / From right to left, from left to right we see, / Th' beauteous Potowmack, that arm of the sea."[20] The locust grove, with some other plantings, was quite visible on the left, as Washington had kept it forward from the plane of the house. Further to the right, one looked across a descending lawn, past the north ha-ha wall that preserved the continuously green view and toward a field used for pasture or crops. A watercolor by Benjamin Henry Latrobe suggests that one had a generous view of River Farm; that same stretch of land is today obscured by a thick growth of mature trees (Figure 6.6).

In the same direction (looking northeast from the portico), planted close to the brow of the hill, Washington

planted or let stand a swamp chestnut oak that, remarkably, still stands today (Plate 18). This tree, planted no later than 1771, served to push back the space, forming the kind of *repoussoir* device used by painters as well as garden designers of the time.[21] Also pushing back space and adding variety to the view were a pair of isolated trees on the right of the view out from portico; these, too, were planted toward the brow of the hill, just below the brick ha-ha wall on the east. They appear quite clearly in the most reliable of the early views, including those by Edward Savage (Plate 14) and Latrobe (Figure 6.7). Similar trees appear in perhaps less reliable views by George Parkyns (Figure 6.8; 1797), after William Birch (see Figure 4.18), and Francis Jukes (Figure 6.9). Artists liked to represent pairs of trees, and we might suspect that there was some license involved, but there are too many early views for us not to conclude that major trees stood on the hill, perhaps shown most accurately in the views by Latrobe. Given the size of the trees in views of the 1790s, it is clear that they date from plantings of the 1780s or possibly even earlier. A white oak tree, probably dating to the eighteenth century, presently stands obscured by a great Cedar of Lebanon; that oak may well have been one of the pair frequently seen in the early views.[22] Certain works of art in Washington's own collection, including his overmantel of c. 1755–1757, employ trees to push back pictorial space, and it is likely that in his landscape gardening Washington was consciously inspired by period works of art (Plate 20).

Far below any trees that stood near the top of the hill was what Samuel Vaughan called a "hanging wood," formed of trees planted further below and allowed to grow only so high. Washington trimmed these trees to preserve the view of the Potomac from the portico and lawn, but he also kept them present to set up a bottom to the visual composition, a kind of green frame for his "landskip" with river. The term "hanging wood" was not widespread in England, and Washington never used it, but he clearly desired this effect, and he died in December 1799 soon after exposure to the cold while marking some trees in this area for pruning.

FIGURE 6.6. Benjamin Henry Latrobe, *View to the north from the lawn of Mount Vernon, 17 July 1796*, pencil, pen and ink, and watercolor on paper, 7″ × 10.25″. This view shows the prospect as more open than today. Trees seem to push back space on the brow of the hill, while others below were trimmed and formed what Samuel Vaughan called a "hanging wood," framing the view on the lower edge of the viewing field. Courtesy of The Maryland Historical Society (1960.108.1.2.10).

The presence of a necessary (an "outhouse" in the modern sense) on the brow of the hill on the east lawn obstructed the fine view from the house and porch. Marked clearly on the Vaughan plans (see Figures 4.3 and 4.4), Washington asked for it to be removed as part of his post-presidency garden improvements. He wrote to William Pearce that this necessary was "not only useless where it is, but . . . an eyesore" as well, and he wanted it cleaned up in anticipation of having company soon "of the most respectable sort."[23] It might seem remarkable that this necessary remained standing as long as it did. After returning from the Revolutionary War, Washington only lived at Mount Vernon for a few years before moving to New York and Philadelphia. He undertook many garden improvements at that time, but the sheer number of them were overwhelming, and the inertia of leaving the outhouse there won out. During the presidency, he was away nearly all of the time and apparently did not worry about it. His decisive removal of it in 1796 formed part of his final improvements of the area, along with the ha-ha wall of 1798 and the gate leading to the former deer park area. The necessary's removal must have been a great

relief and an immediate improvement to the view. It could take some time for Washington to give up practical advantages for aesthetic ones—Dennis Pogue has shown that an open refuse pit in the area of the present south grove stood until the 1770s.[24]

Among the finest of the views at Mount Vernon, often overlooked, is the calculated view from the porch to the south (see Figures 6.4 and 6.7). With the trees pushed back in this south grove, the lawn sweeping downward, and Washington's conscious attempt to keep an open, grassy, and continuous (aided by the ha-ha walls) view, the vista forms a kind of picture, framed by the portico itself. Louis Mignot, with, with his pictorial eye, captured this framed view, making it a picture within a picture (Figure 6.10).[25] The "picture" toward the south grove formed a fine conclusion to the sweep from left to right for a viewer standing on the portico of the mansion house.

Washington the gardener and landscape designer had the advantage of having a house on a spectacular promontory rising 127 feet above a wide, curving river. Such a site was rare in England, and visitors compared his estate to Conti-

FIGURE 6.7. Benjamin Henry Latrobe, *View of Mount Vernon looking towards the South West,* 1796, pencil, pen and ink, and watercolor on paper, 7″ × 10.25″. One of the two trees near the top of the hill is perhaps a white oak tree still extant. Courtesy of The Maryland Historical Society (1960.108.1.2.11).

nental European examples, such as the Czartorysky estate in Cracow, Poland. More than one viewer called attention to the especially fine natural view. Through the use of trees and the portico columns to create a *repoussoir* effect and the disappearance of the close bank of the river (caused by the sharp angle of the hill and the blockage by the hanging wood), Washington increased the visual power of the already fine site. Vaughan was correct in calling this a perspective view, as it did not happen by chance: "From the House to Maryland is a perspective view. The lawn in view from the House is about 100 paces; from thence is a descent down to the River, about 400 paces adorning with a hanging wood with shady walks."[26] The success of the spatial devices—the open lawn, trees and pillars, and hanging wood, the breadth of the river—is indicated in part by the early overestimates of the distance of the height of the mansion above sea level. The portico floor is actually 127 feet above the water level, but early estimates range much higher than this, often 200 feet.[27] One writer, Francis Glass, penning his description in Latin in 1835, put the height as "pedibus ducentis mare superat," two hundred feet over water.[28] The *Hartford Adver-tiser* in 1823 said the elevation over sea level was "several hundred feet." George Washington was interested enough in the question to have made an exact measurement himself, noting the height to a fraction of an inch, in a payment book for the "cost of things bot. In Phila. by Mrs. Washington" in October 1783, the verso of the accounting sheet reads: "Hight of Mt. Vernon above the river by measurement of Genl. Washington 124 feet 10 ½ inches."[29]

The height of the promontory seemed great to early viewers, as did the width of the river. The spacing devices established by Washington increased the apparent distance to the river from the house and the apparent width of the river to the Maryland shore. Gen. James Taylor, visiting in 1805, stated—after noting more or less accurately that the tomb stood about sixty yards from the house—that "the house stands on a lofty bluff of the Potomac, and it must be from 3 to 400 yards to the water." This was a very great overestimation, as the water is 125 yards to the near point and about 186 yards straight ahead from the portico.[30] As for the width of the river, although the shoreline has changed somewhat, it is essentially the same today, about three-quarters

FIGURE 6.8. George Parkyns (attributed to), *View of Mount Vernon from the Northeast,* c. 1797, watercolor, dimensions unknown. This watercolor by the English artist was photographed in the 1920s but is now not locatable. It is a rare eighteenth-century view of the portico and east lawn. Courtesy of the Mount Vernon Ladies' Association.

FIGURE 6.9. Francis Jukes, *Mount Vernon in Virginia, dated 31 March 1800,* aquatint, measured in frame: image height 14.5″ × 18.5″ (width does not include margins). Jukes's view, less reliably accurate than some other early images, stands as a picturesque response to Washington's creation of house and gardens. Courtesy of the Mount Vernon Ladies' Association (Print-4160).

FIGURE 6.10. Louis Rémy Mignot, *View of the Southeast from the Piazza of Mount Vernon,* c. 1858–1859, oil on canvas, 35.5″ × 47.37″. Several early artists captured this view through the south end of the portico, reflecting the fine "picture" that Washington had created using the porch as a frame for the composition. Courtesy of the Mount Vernon Ladies' Association (M-3108/A).

of a mile across, but some viewers put this width at two miles. Typical is the account of William Loughton Smith of Charleston, South Carolina, who visited on 12 April 1791:

> The road [is] mostly through fine woods, and little of the river is seen; and much like the road from Middletown place on Ashley river down to the ferry. The house at Mount Vernon is most magnificently situated; I hardly remember to have been so struck with a prospect. It stands on a small plain near the river, which is 200 feet below; the view extends up and down the river a considerable distance, the river is about two miles wide, and the opposite shore is beautiful, as is the country along the river; there is a verdant lawn between the house and the river, and a rapid descent, wooded, down to the river. From the grand portico which fronts the river, the assemblage of objects is grand beyond description, embracing the magnificence of the river with the vessels sailing about; the verdant fields, woods, and parks."[31]

German visitor Friedrich Wilhelm Hoeninghaus called it "one of the most splendid sights I have ever had. We were more than 200 feet above the surface of the Potomac River which is here two miles wide, and saw this magnificent river

and its romantic shores for at least twenty miles."[32] He had been led to the portico by Washington himself, after a breakfast in the small parlor where they were viewing the "sea battles." Echoing others who saw the mansion as set at a great height above sea level, Searson wrote, "This pleasing seat hath its prospects so high, / That one would think 'twas for astronomy." The Marquis de Lafayette commented on "so charming a prospect" from the mansion house, and he wrote to his wife that it seemed that the Potomac was created to make Mount Vernon beautiful. In 1801, Sally Foster Otis remarked, "On the front of the House is a gradual declivity to the Potowmac & where the scene is indiscribably grand & beautiful."[33] These effects are still present today.

We tend to think of the view (and photograph it) in the green seasons, but the winter view also had an effect on Washington's contemporaries. The soft green of the summer gave way to a different aesthetic sensibility in snowy and icy weather. Under the influence of the vogue for the "gothic" (that is, strange and horrifying) and the widely sought-after "sublime," Nelly Parke Custis, still resident at Mount Vernon, described the winter view across the river: "We have had some Winter weather, the Trees, grass, houses &c all covered with ice. The appearance is beautiful, & the river looks so wide & desolate—the Maryland shore so bleak & sublimely horrifying that I am quite delighted—& in better trim than ever to enjoy the beauties of *Ossians Poems* & the *Mysteries of Udolpho*. I am sadly afraid my poor pericranium will be rather the worse for my Country residence this Winter—what with the *Blues* in rainy weather—& the *extacies* from seeing all nature dressed in *snow* & *ice*."[34]

There are many more trees at Mansion House Farm than in Washington's period, and there was not then a vast forest of pure, green woods on the Maryland shore. Washington created natural, green surroundings for himself but also integrated agricultural aspects all around. The view across the Potomac was farmed in his time, and there were docks and small buildings visible on the opposite bank. Like the verdant, curving parkway leading up to the area of Mount Vernon, the view across the Potomac, preserved for all time now from development, is a Colonial Revival creation, shaped by a modern vision of the past that arose in the Romantic period and was reinforced by the anti-industrial movement. Manasseh Cutler noted in 1802 that the view from the portico largely showed "an extended woods," with only a few houses or farms in view, but others emphasized the checkerboard of farms visible across the Potomac.[35] Vaughan noted that "Maryland on the opposite side of the River, is variegated & in high cultivation." His plans show houses across the Potomac and activity on the bank. Claude Blanchard, writing in 1782 before the land was further developed, noted that the "opposite shore needs rather more houses and villages." His opinion indicates that there was no prejudice then against the development of farms and built structures.[36] Today, a Maryland shore devoted partly to farming would bring the view back to how it was in Washington's period and accord with his desire to make the ornamental farm part of the visual beauty of Mount Vernon.

Views in George Washington's Life

George Washington shared in the American taste for the perspective in landscape, whether called prospect, vistas, or simply viewing of particulars. Like many children of his social class, George Washington received an early education in measuring and surveying land.[37] He spent several years as surveyor, and while he was not the only well-born American of his generation to get experience at surveying, he was rare in later taking up a substantial landscape gardening project that, over the course of decades, shaped hundreds, even thousands, of acres of topography. He kept surveying his own lands until the end of his life, and his notes on the subject suggest the development of his particular aesthetic point of view.[38]

"A natural skill for mensuration, growing out of his mathematical knowledge and his habit of ascertaining the measures and distances of objects which interested him, the size of trees, the depth and extent of ponds and rivers, the height of mountains and the air-line distance of his favorite summits . . . led him continually into new and secluded grounds, and helped his studies of Nature."[39] Thus did Ralph Waldo Emerson characterize Henry David Thoreau, who is closely identified today with the American landscape. Similarly, Washington's work as a surveyor during his later teen years, a time of intense intellectual and mental development, gave him a peculiarly sensitive ability to assess and analyze a view. In order to create the accurate line of demarcation, he had to develop a special set of skills and an appreciation for the nuances of nature. He needed to establish straight lines of sight. A naturally open vista, for example, would have facilitated his work and given him pleasure. Where such a vista was not possible to find, he tended to work when the leaves were bare or thin, especially at certain times in the spring and fall. Around the trees, and under them, the ground swelled, and young Washington noted these spots in his notebooks as markers: a "hollow glade" here, a "steep hill" there.[40] Just as significantly, these trees

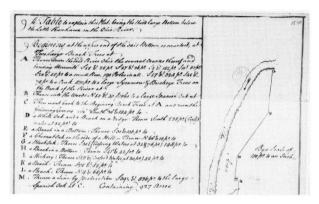

FIGURE 6.11. George Washington, survey of lands along the Ohio River, pen and ink on paper. With the identification and measurements based on the location of sycamore, Spanish oak, white oak, and beech trees, as noted in the accompanying text, Washington was training his eye for landscape gardening and landscape painting. He had used trees for such measurements since his teenage years as a surveyor. George Washington Papers, 1741–1799, Series 4: General Correspondence, 1697–1799, Lands for Veterans, Virginia Ordinance of December 15, 1769, May 1771, Surveys and Four Plats, Library of Congress.

were not merely anonymous objects in his way but useful tools of his trade, as certain individual trees marked lines of ownership. He would leave hatchet marks on various trees, which he had to identify and document: "a hickory on a knowl" or a Spanish oak on top of a hill. Sometimes these individual marker trees stand in giant scale on his survey drawings. Thus, surveying gave him experience of individual elements of a landscape, of prospects and sight lines, of trees and their types, and of sensitivity to natural borders (streams and rivers) (see Figure 6.11).[41]

Eighteenth-century writers noted a connection between surveying and gardening. Batty Langley opened his *New Principles of Gardening* (one of the garden books owned by Washington) by noting the usefulness for a gardener of measuring tools: "In Consideration of the great Use as Geometry is of to Gardeners, in furnishing them with excellent Rules for their sure and speedy Execution of Surveys, Measures, Levels, Drawings, Working, &c. therefore I have first laid down all the most useful Principles thereof, and in a

very concise and familiar Manner." Washington had this experience with "sure and speedy Execution of Surveys," as well as the other measuring and drawing skills needed to work with a landscape.[42]

Washington's work as a surveyor complemented his early appreciation of natural beauty. When he was sixteen years old, on Sunday, 13 March 1748, he described the beauty of the trees and the overall "richness" of the land he was surveying for Lord Fairfax in the frontier of Virginia near the Shenandoah River: "Rode to his Lordships Quarter about 4 Miles higher up the River we went through most beautiful Groves of Sugar Trees & spent the best part of the Day in admiring the Trees & richness of the Land."[43] The notion of the "richness of the land" expressed here was an aesthetic reaction but also an observation of the future economic possibilities of the land for farming.

Young Washington's interest in prospects is clear from the diary entries he made in Barbados, where he went following his several years of work as a surveyor.[44] Some of these early entries are still untranscribed, as the document sheets are fragmentary. When nineteen-year-old George traveled to Barbados with his brother Lawrence, who was ill with tuberculosis, he had a couple of months to observe and enjoy the island's architecture and landscape. On 5 November 1751, he wrote: "In the cool of the evening we rode out accompanied by Mr. Carter to seek lodgings in the country, as the Doctor advised, and were perfectly enraptured with the beautiful prospects, which every side presented to our view,—the fields of cane, corn, fruit-trees, &c. in a delightful green."[45] This last phrase includes a rare, specific reference by Washington to the aesthetic quality of a color in nature. Similarly, he rejoiced that "there is seen regular risings in this Island one [?] above another so that scarcely any part is deprived of a beautiful Prospect both of Sea & Land and what is contrary to the observation in other Countrys is that each rising is better than the other belo[w]." It seems that Washington finds the view to get better the higher one goes.[46]

The Washington brothers used their social connections

to get access to the aristocratic houses of Barbados, and George took the opportunity to note their prospects. The home they rented, at a price he thought rather high, possessed an excellent view of land and sea: "Came Capt[ai]n Crofton with his proposals which tho extravagantly dear my brother was oblig'd to give[.] L. 15 per month is his charge exclusive of Liquor & was [illegible] which we find. In the evening we summoned some of our things up and . . . its very pleasantly situated pretty [lacuna] the Sea and about . . . from town[.] the prospect is extensive by land and pleasant by Sea as we command the prospect of Carlyle Bay . . . the shipping in such manner that none can go in or out without being open to our view."[47] The pleasant quality underscores the aesthetic effect, while, this language of "commanding" a view of the bay and the idea that no ship can pass without being open to their inspection indicates the feeling of power that a prospect conveyed beyond mere aesthetic consideration.

This pleasure of commanding a view would, of course, over time be reinforced by Washington's unusually extensive military experience. The wartime need to discover sight lines for firing, to employ natural vistas and open fields, to use dense brush as cover, and to interact with the natural environment in other ways informed his landscape gardening in peacetime. Even his later preference for spending time out of doors was necessarily shaped by his military experiences. He spent a remarkable number of years of his life in the field and in the countryside. He lived on the frontier in the French and Indian War, and during the American Revolution he was encamped nearly all of the time outside of cities, usually in rural farm areas, including Morristown, White Plains, Valley Forge, Newburgh, and Wethersfield. His eye was constantly trained in woods and farmlands, and he learned to gauge distance and measure during his exposure to both rough nature and improved agricultural land.

Washington was a great user and collector of telescopes, necessary for obvious reasons in the military field, and how telescopes shape one's habits of seeing are of interest in a consideration of his aesthetics. A telescope forms a kind of vista in the sense that it provides a narrow view into the distance. Telescopes work well in open ground, collapse distances, bring things in and out of focus, and empower a viewer. They are linked to surveying tools and scoping of distances, and they must have sharpened Washington's sense of vision and reinforced the pleasure he felt in seeing the "grubbing" of vistas, the clearing of fields, and the trimming of trees that would allow distant views. In addition to Latrobe's notable watercolor showing the use of the telescope from the portico (Figure 6.12), there is a jovial and picturesque letter from the Marquis de Chastellux, writing from Paris, imagining his visit to Mount Vernon:

> What satisfaction should it be for me, if I was walking upon your bowlingreen, to look upon the Potomack, and endeavour with the help of a Telescope to distinguish, whether the aproaching vessel wears the american, the french or the brittish colours; to say: *'tis a brittish* [illegible] *who comes and fetch tabacco*; then continue quietly our walk and go towards the grove to observe the growth of your trees, even of your vineyard, that a french man can, I dare say, examine without jealousy; for, my dear general, you can sow and reap laurels, but grapes and wine are not within the compass of your powers.[48]

All of Washington's active time out of doors shaped his eye for views, terrain, and natural growth. He brought about in his farming an intersection of landscape gardening, forest maintenance, and ornamental farming. Even in his passion for fox-hunting, he had to consider topography, direction of movement, and seasonal changes in growth, as well as foliage and trees types. David Humphreys, Washington's official biographer, mentioned the role of both surveying and fox hunting in shaping Washington's character and military mind, and we can add to this his general proclivity for views, measurement, and understanding topography. As Humphreys noted: "[H]unting and surveying—the first gave him activity & boldness—the second the means of improving the *Coup d'oeil* in judging of military positions & measuring by the eye the distance between different places." This *"coup*

FIGURE 6.12. Benjamin Henry Latrobe, *President Washington and His Family on the Portico of Mount Vernon*, 1796, pen and ink and watercolor on paper, 18″ × 25″ (approx.). Latrobe captured the two trees that stand on the brow of the hill, the dense locust grove on the right, and the fine view south as the Potomac flows toward the sea. Courtesy of Louise and Brad Mentzer.

d'oeil" and instinct for space was indeed useful in gardening, architectural design, and judging paintings, especially landscape pictures.[49]

Washington loved a view from an elevation. On 19 August 1769, he wrote: "Rid with Mrs. Washington & others to the Cacapehon Mountain—to see the prospect from thence. Mr. Barclay, Mr. Thruston & Mr. Power dined with us."[50] Five days later he went there with others, including members of the Fairfax family: "Rid to Cacapeon with Lord Fairfax, the 2 Colo. Fairfaxs, Mr. Kimble Mrs. Washington & Patcy Custis."[51] Overlooking the upper reaches of the Potomac and near Berkeley Springs, the view from Mount Cacapon

remained famous for years. Washington had surveyed the area, and he continued his economic interest there through landholding and interest in the canalization of the Potomac. The time he dedicated to a day's viewing of a particularly striking "prospect" demonstrates that it was an important source of entertainment and delight to Washington and his fellows. In another diary entry, Washington mentioned the beautiful prospect from Wallingford, Connecticut, and the "pretty view" on the banks of the Susquehanna.[52] He also liked the view in Charleston, South Carolina, with the "Gardens & green trees which are interspersed adding much to the beauty of the prospect."[53]

Sometimes he gave a moral or allegorical slant to his mentions of viewing. He wrote to Henry Knox soon after his retirement, describing his own weariness: "I feel now, however, as I conceive a wearied Traveller must do, who, after treading many a painful step, with a heavy burden on his Shoulders, is eased of the latter, having reached the Goal to which all the former were directed—& from his House top is looking back, & tracing with a grateful eye the Meanders by which he escaped the quicksands and Mires which lay in his way, and into which none but the All-powerful guide, & great disposer of human Events could have prevented his falling."[54]

It was not only in the company of Tidewater aristocrats that Washington discussed views and architecture. In a remarkable episode seldom mentioned in the literature on him, Washington spoke to a Native American in November 1770 in the environs of present-day Pittsburgh. Washington was inspecting lands in the area:

> Here it was for the 2d. time that the Indian with me spoke of a fine piece of Land and beautiful place for a House & in order to give me a more lively Idea of it, chalk out the situation upon his Deerskin. It lyes upon Bull Creek, at least 30 Miles from the Mouth, but no more than 5 from the Mouth of Muddy Creek, in an ESE direction. The spot he recommends for a House lyes very high commanding a prospect of a great deal of level Land below on the Creek—the Ground about it very rich & a fine spring in the middle of it about which many Buffaloes use & have made great Roads. Bull Creek according to his Acct. Runs parallel with the long reach in the Ohio—not above 6 or 7 Miles from it, having fine bottoms which widen as it extends into the Country & towards the head of it is large bodies of level rich Land.[55]

This telling incident, itself forming a kind of picturesque moment—an American Indian sketching out for George Washington with chalk on his deerskin a house site with a prospect of rich lands and creek—indicates the level of interest, both aesthetic and financial, that Washington took in such matters, and his search for a fine home site surrounded by rich lands and abundant, clean water. This conversation

was the second on the same subject between Washington and "the Indian" in question. If Washington was discussing a prospect and home site with a Native American in the woods of Pennsylvania, we can only imagine how extensive his conversations must have been with American elites on the subject of architecture, gardening, and the siting of buildings in the natural environment.

Washington himself "saw" the prospect of the gardens and river from the mansion house differently than we do. For example, he commented on the high, healthy country in which the mansion house at Mount Vernon was constructed. Like his contemporaries, he associated high ground with distance from the festering waters and poor air around docks and low-lying swampy land, which were believed to cause diseases (hence the word "malaria" for bad air). Although unaware that mosquitoes were the actual cause of some fevers, they did have the correct instinct that height and a good distance from the water were more salutary.

Aside from the potential health benefits of its site, Mount Vernon was thought by some to possess the greatest view in the world. But the view, artistic as it was, also overlooked the core of Washington's economic interests. One could see (unlike today) far views of his active farm properties, including a glimpse of River Farm. The river itself was traversed by a ferry that Washington ran for a profit, taking passengers across to the Maryland side. Apart from ferries, commercial river traffic was a frequent part of landscape description in the eighteenth century, and certainly Washington was aware of more than the scenic aspects of river shipping. Just as at the age of nineteen he had enjoyed watching trade shipping in Barbados, he took pleasure in the economics of shipping on the Potomac as seen from his porch and estate grounds.[56]

Washington ran a vigorous herring and shad fishing industry from the river, and the haul formed part of the varied economic output of his estate. He lived on "one of the finest rivers in the world—a river well stocked with various kinds of fish at all seasons of the year, and in the spring with shad, herrings, bass, carp, sturgeon, etc., in abundance. The bor-

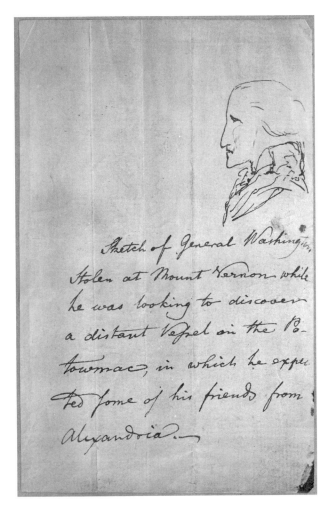

FIGURE 6.13. Benjamin Henry Latrobe, *Sketch of General Washington Stolen at Mount Vernon while he was looking to discover a distant Vessel in the Potowmac, in which he expected some of his friends from Alexandria*, 1796, pen and ink on paper. This remarkable drawing captured a rare candid moment, as Washington gazed from the portico toward the Potomac. The drawing is lost, and the image here is from a photostat of the original sheet. Courtesy of The Maryland Historical Society (MS 523).

which made all imports expensive. The fishing industry was an external business, and he made money from the millions of herrings he traded for other goods and "sold to the country people, who salt it for provisions"; fish also provided a way for Washington to feed his "Negroes."[58] He himself liked to fish for sport and did so frequently, even during the Revolutionary War.

Another part of the economics of the river was its great commercial potential. Imagining the possibilities beyond the original constraints of the natural river itself, Washington, along with other investors in the Potowmack [Potomac] Company (of which Washington was president and a founding member in 1785), had the longtime dream of combining stretches of the river, locks, and canals to create a navigable waterway. The passage was to connect the Atlantic coastline to the interior of America and form what the Mississippi River and the Erie Canal became—major pathways to the agricultural heartland of the growing nation in Ohio and beyond. If we could look at the Potomac with Washington's eyes, we would see and sense the economic well-being of his estate and the growing wealth of the nation as a whole. A striking drawing by Latrobe candidly captures Washington's countenance as he takes in the view toward the river and scours the scene for the expected arrival of a boat (Figure 6.13). Washington had a number of practical reasons, beyond aesthetic appreciation of the prospect, to gaze at the river from the vantage point of his mansion house.

Pictures and the Picturesque at Mount Vernon

In creating his gardens, Washington was acting under broader Anglo-American concepts of the picturesque, using specific devices employed by painters. For example, we have seen that he established *repoussoir* devices, with trees in the middle and foreground to push back space and create a distancing effect, thus mimicking the painter's work. He was clearly shaping his landscape on the east lawn, the bowling green, and the serpentine walks in a pictorial manner.

Other pictorial aspects of Washington's landscape expe-

ders of the estate are washed by more than ten miles of tidewater; several valuable fisheries appertain to it; the whole shore, in fact, is one entire fishery."[57] In his eyes, the river had the abundance of Flemish still-life. In it he saw an economic boon, as he was trying to diversify and achieve self-sufficiency in the context of the colonial mercantile system, rience relate to melancholy and the morbid picturesque. Across the Atlantic, a thirst for contrived melancholy was so strong that fake ruins were built in England as garden follies, and ruins often appear in European landscape painting of the time. British planners sometimes incorporated real ruins into landscape gardens, as Capability Brown did in including the medieval ruins of Roche Abbey in his work at Sandbeck (Yorkshire).[59] Washington had no need or desire to build false ruins on his grounds, as the ruins of the mansion house at nearby Belvoir, estate of the Fairfax family, could be seen from Mansion House Farm. Unoccupied after George William and Sally Fairfax left it in 1773 to return to England, the house burned in 1783. After the war, Washington brought visitors to these ruins, and in his letters he movingly described the melancholy and "romantic" sentiments evoked by the crumbling architecture and by his warm recollection of the family that had fled. Samuel Powel, who visited in 1787, noted: "Rode with the general & the Ladies to view a Seat of Col. Fairfax, Seven Miles distant, beautifully situated on the Patowmack. The House which was of brick is burnt, & the Walls only standing."[60] Washington himself noted the outing in his diary: "Rid with him & Mrs. Powell to see the Ruins of Belvoir."[61]

The nearby remains of the burnt-out mansion house of his friends provided a convenient picturesque site for a highly charged viewing experience, one that reverberated with the Anglo-American penchant for emotional effects in painting, poetry, and other arts. A genteel outing to Belvoir was an opportunity to reflect on the events of the Revolution and to see a mansion house parallel to Washington's own in ruins. William Loughton Smith visited in 1791: "From the portico is a view on the same side of the river of Colonel Fairfax's Seat; the house was burnt some years ago, but the woods about the ruins have a romantic appearance." Smith felt the romantic associations of the entirety, including the ruins themselves and the intermingling of Nature in the form of woods with the burnt-out family seat.[62] George Washington wrote to the former resident of Belvoir, his friend

George William Fairfax, on 27 February 1785 that he had visited the ruins of the mansion: "I was obliged to fly from them; & came home with painful sensations, & sorrowing for the contrast." To Sally Fairfax, Washington, reflecting on their past friendship and flirtations, wrote, "It is a matter of sore regret, when I cast my eyes towards Belvoir, which I often do, to reflect [that] the former Inhabitants of it, with whom we lived in such harmony & friendship, no longer reside there; and that the ruins can only be viewed as the memento of former pleasures."[63]

Belvoir was not part of the Mount Vernon grounds, but its ruins, whether visited up close or seen from a distance, were capable of evoking reflections on destruction and the passing of glory, similar to those eighteenth-century travelers reported when visiting the ruins of ancient Rome. Pictorial representations of such ruins were not unknown in the colonies and the early national period. Roman ruins (after Panini) appear in the wallpaper at the Jeremiah Lee Mansion in Marblehead, Massachusetts, and ruins were known from prints as well. For example, in the *Maryland Gazette* on 1 April 1762, there was a lottery for a house on the Potomac, that of Joseph Watson, a merchant in Alexandria, "A considerable Collection of Perspective Views of the most magnificent public and private Edifices, Bridges, Monuments, and Ruins, in *Rome, Venice, France, England,* and *China.*"[64] Belvoir provided contemporaries with a recent and domestic specimen of passing glory, much closer than those of classical civilization.

Another melancholy element of the viewing experience at Mount Vernon was the New Tomb, placed at the foot of the Vineyard Enclosure not far from the mansion house, as Washington instructed in his will of 1799. (It was not built until several decades later.) Practical considerations, including moisture in the ground, poor topography, and the overbearing presence of trees, caused Washington to pick a new spot for the tomb. He chose to place it in the foot of an orchard, and it became part of a circuit walk of the estate. Close to the house, it was a conspicuous and frequent destination, especially in the Romantic nineteenth century. The condition of the Old Tomb during the first decades of the century provoked visitors to complain about its state of decay and the disrespect shown the father of his country, buried in an overgrown, crumbling structure that resembled a humble icehouse.

Washington's presentation of Nature and views hardly stopped with his development of the actual views from the portico and elsewhere. We look in chapter 7 at Washington as art collector, but we should note here the landscapes and seascapes that he placed throughout the house, including a number of fine oil paintings in the Large Dining Room and Claudian prints in the central passage. The collecting and display of such art marked a change of the iconographic emphasis in the house toward images of nature and the land, and it differed from the smattering of portraits and prints on various subjects typically found in early American homes of those of Washington's social status.

Washington started his collection of landscapes quite early. In 1757, fifteen years before he ever sat for a portrait, and decades before such pictures became common in American homes, he ordered a "Neat Landskip, after Claud Lorrain" from England (Plate 20).[65] The oil on canvas, painted in 1755–1757 and likely by an English artist, has never left Mount Vernon, except for conservation. The work is abraded and might have been cut down somewhat on the right, either by the agent or by Washington, to fit the particular spot. It was sold to Washington as being after Claude Lorrain, but it cannot be considered to be even a poor copy after him, as certain aspects of the composition, such as the width of the tree trunk on the right and the flat, simple triple tree trunks on the left, are not characteristic of Claude. Still, although there is no known composition like this by Claude, the early designation accurately assesses his influence on the anonymous artist, who depicts a distant prospect of water with varied trees and figures in the foreground and a coulisse of trees on either side. The variety and contrived spatial jump are notable, and works of this kind, indeed probably

this particular painting, can be seen as models for the shaping of the landscape view from the portico of Mount Vernon, from which one could see a Claudian *repoussoir* device of trees located on the brow of the hill. As for a specific attribution for the picture, a number of English painters in the eighteenth century, including John Griffier, George Lambert, and John Wooton, imitated the golden skies, leafy coulisses, and idyllic mood of Claude's paintings.[66] The work is perhaps closest in style to the work of George Smith of Chichester, a highly influential and successful English artist of the time who specialized in such idealized landscapes. Washington's picture is by only an imitator of Smith, as certain flat or cursory passages in the overmantel at Mount Vernon set it apart from Smith's work. Apart from questions of quality and authorship, it is remarkable that as early as 1757 Washington chose a landscape as an artistic centerpiece of his home, and he worked with an English agent to get the finest "neat" work that he could.

Among the more striking of these landscapes at Mount Vernon is the pair of oil paintings by English painter George Beck (1796) representing the Great Falls of the Potomac and the confluence of the Potomac and the Shenandoah at Harper's Ferry (Plates 21 and 22). These scenes continue for the visitor to Mount Vernon the striking experience of viewing the Potomac, the wider prospect of which was available from the portico or even through the open door of the Large Dining Room. Beck's paintings also resonated with Washington because they relate to his economic interests in developing the Potomac as a great inland water route to America's heartland.

Washington took an interest in the American landscape as subject matter for paintings, and he played a role in determining the iconography of Beck's pictures. In a notice that is posthumous to Washington but rather believable, Joseph May recorded that in May 1800 he visited Mount Vernon and Mrs. Washington told him that one of these two paintings "was the View of the Great Falls of the Potomac, painted as Mrs. Washington told me, under the direction of her husband, by Beck, an English artist."[67] May eventually bought the painting in question. May did not report on the origins of the second picture, but we can assume that Washington suggested it or approved of Beck's choice. Washington described the *Falls of the Potomac* in 1797 as of that river "at the F[ederal] City." Beck's representation is quite accurate and corresponds remarkably well to the Great Falls even as they appear today. This is a part of the river that Washington knew well and that the artist could visit easily from the new capital. (In 1796, Washington inquired of one visitor whether he "had visited the Great Falls of the Potomac, and being answered in the negative, observed to me, that I ought not to leave that part of the country without visiting them." Washington encouraged Americans to move away from portraits, which he never embraced as fully, toward landscapes.[68]) Washington knew the falls from his interest in navigating the Potomac, and his detailed knowledge is indicated in his diary entry for 3 August 1785: "we proceeded to examine the falls; and beginning at the head of them went through the whole by water, and continued from the foot of them to the Great fall." He follows this notice with observations on the depth and nature of the river and falls. Earlier, Washington wrote to Richard Washington in England (27 September 1763) that "We have few things here [in America] striking to European Travellers (except an abundant Woods)."[69] This thought would reverberate throughout the eighteenth and nineteenth centuries—that Europe had its castles and Roman temples and vast cities, while America's best visual assets were its natural surroundings. When Washington had a chance to encourage artists to capture such images, he did so, and bid them look to the wildest and most striking sights.

Washington called the other Beck picture, not specified by Mrs. Washington as having been recommended by her husband, "a View of the Passage of the Poto'k through the blew Mountain at the Confluence of that River with the Shan'h [Shenandoah]." J. Hall Pleasants noted, "As the Potomac, after its junction with the Shenandoah, breaks

through the Blue Ridge at Harper's Ferry and is bordered on both sides by steep mountains, this . . . title appears inapplicable."[70] Allowing for some artistic license, however, this early title seems appropriate for the painting, and the artist has attempted to convey some sense of hills, especially on the right side of the picture.[71]

The style of these pictures is, in the context of 1790s America, remarkably rugged and "romantic," showing darkening skies, turgid streams, hard rocks, and dramatic trees and roots. They correspond to the grand subjects that Washington suggested in another context and idealize American scenery through a heroic rendering. No people or evidence of human activity appears in either work, and they are completely about the American wilderness and the grand scale of the American continent. They represent a bridge between the emotive landscapes of eighteenth-century England and the romantic, site-specific landscapes of Thomas Cole and others. Thomas Jefferson also fostered knowledge of American scenes, especially the most unusual or dramatic ones, such as the spectacular Natural Bridge, in which he took a particular interest.

The other major oil paintings in the Large Dining Room were by William Winstanley (1775–1806), an English landscape and portrait painter.[72] In the 1790s, he garnered the admiration of a number of collectors and government officials, such as Alexander Hamilton. While the four paintings by Winstanley at Mount Vernon seem less linked with Washington's landscape project and land interests, they are relevant nonetheless. Two of the sizeable oil-on-canvas paintings represent, or were thought at the time to represent, idealized views of the Hudson (or North) River (payment to Winstanley on 6 April 1793 in the Household Accounts book, 30 guineas). They are, at best, idealized representations of the Hudson, capturing the spirit if not the detail of the upper stretches of that scenic river. The pair hung in the executive mansion in Philadelphia before being moved to Mount Vernon and are now known as *Morning* and *Evening* (Plates 23 and 24).[73] Alexander Hamilton said, "there are two

FIGURE 6.14. William Winstanley, *Meeting of the Waters: Potomac and Shenandoah at Harper's Ferry,* c. 1793–1795, oil on canvas, 35″ × 49.25″. This is the kind of dramatic, grand view of American scenery that Washington suggested to Englishman Winstanley, although the provenance of this painting is uncertain. Courtesy of the Munson-Williams-Proctor Arts Institute, Museum of Art, Utica, New York (63.94).

views of situations on Hudson's River painted by Mr. Winstanley in the drawing room of Mrs. Washington, which have great intrinsic merit—and considered with reference to his opportunities, as related, announce a very supreme genius in the branch of painting, worthy of encouragement."[74] Although *Morning* and *Evening* were not painted in response to Washington's suggestion, he had recommended to Winstanley that he paint scenes of a grand nature. Washington wrote to the Commissioners for the District of Columbia on 5 September 1793: "Mr Winstanley, a celebrated Landskip Painter, is disposed to take a view of the Federal City, or of the grounds in the vicinity of it. As you will be there about the time he may arrive, I take the liberty of giving him this letter of introduction to you. His designs are more extensive—and I have suggested the Great & little Falls; the passage of the River Potomac through the Blew Mountains—the Natural bridge; &ca as grand objects."[75]

Washington added two more pictures by Winstanley in April 1794 to the collection in Philadelphia (Household Accounts, 1793–1797, "two large paintings."). The painting of the Genesee Falls once at Mount Vernon found its way to the Smithsonian Collection and is now on loan to Mount Vernon. While there is no evidence that Washington saw the Falls himself, they were first known to non-native populations around 1750 and became a destination for hardy travelers in the eighteenth century. Aaron Burr visited in 1795, and Louis-Philippe also traveled to the area. A painting now in Utica (Munson-Williams-Proctor Arts Institute), the *Meeting of the Waters Potomac and Shenandoah at Harper's Ferry* (Figure 6.14), may well have been a fourth painting by Winstanley at Mount Vernon.[76] It is possible that these two paintings, along with *Morning* and *Evening,* made up the "4 [large Gilt frame Pictures] representing water Courses" as mentioned in the inventory of the New Room.[77] There is, however, no documented provenance showing a connection between Washington and *Meeting of the Waters.* As for the *Morning* and *Evening,* Washington had a deep interest in the Hudson River and had spent several years toward the end of the war in its vicinity or headquartered on its banks. After coming to peace terms with England, he immediately took a fishing trip to the Adirondacks, traveling up the Hudson Valley and enjoying the natural scenery along the way.

Painted in a soft, idealizing style, Winstanley's compositions altogether are less jagged and challengingly picturesque than Beck's. James Thomas Flexner has argued that Washington's acquisition of the two Winstanley paintings of more dramatic scenery was consequent to the president's suggestion that the painter look for "grand objects" of this kind among American waterways. If so, we find Washington as a patron and an active agent in pushing painting in the new republic in a romantic and emotionally charged direction. Washington toyed with the idea of keeping the Winstanleys in the president's house in Philadelphia, but his successor, John Adams, did not choose to buy them. Washington easily could have sold them in Philadelphia, as others were clamoring for the paintings and prints in his collection, disappointed that he was selling only furniture and other objects.[78] The paintings made an apt addition to the mansion house at Mount Vernon, and they helped turn the Large Dining Room into an innovative display of the American landscape in art. Winstanley's style, with a clever use of *repoussoir* trees and soft, golden light, conveys a sensibility similar to Washington's own undulating and verdant style as a landscape designer, and the views, on a smaller scale, recall the prospects overlooking the Potomac as seen from the porch and east lawn. In discussing the painting in Utica, Edward Nygren has recognized in Winstanley an expositor of the "beautiful," as expounded by Edmund Burke. This painting style, similar to that of Claude Lorrain and as found in prints at Mount Vernon, corresponded to Washington's own "beautiful" and cursive style of landscape gardening.[79]

Not the least of the landscape paintings in the Large Dining Room is *Moonlight on Rocky Coast* (Plate 32), which was observed hanging there by Joshua Brookes and listed in the inventories of George and Martha. It replaced the *Battle of Minden*, which Samuel Vaughan had sent as a gift to be hung over the mantelpiece.[80] The *Battle of Minden* was relegated to the downstairs bedroom, and *Moonlight on Rocky Coast* (provenance unknown) put in its place after the presidency.[81] None of the early letters, inventories, or visitor reports mention an attribution, and the authorship of the painting was likely not a significant matter for Washington. This work is close in style to the work of Abraham Pether, who specialized in moonlit scenes and earned the name "Moonlight Pether." He was active by 1773 and would have been near the peak of his reputation when Washington was collecting.[82] The particular style of the painting, especially the odd squiggles of the reflections on the water and the schematic treatment of the rocks on the upper left, rule out Pether himself as the artist, although the painting is clearly in his mode and forms part of the romantic nocturne tradition so powerful in England and embraced by painter Joseph Wright of Derby. The figures have the appearance of the "banditti" types made famous by Salvator Rosa in the seventeenth century and taken up by some romantic landscape artists. If this scene is the seaside rock arch known as Durdle Door, Dorset, England, near the Isle of Wight, it would be an English equivalent of the Virginia Natural Bridge or similar wonders of nature. At any rate, the picture was a good picture for Washington's New Room, befitting his taste for dramatic paintings. The canvas worked well because it was a water and landscape scene and because it had a romantic nocturnal appearance lacking in the room's other oil paintings.

While president, Washington purchased a number of prints, and a remarkable number of them relate to landscape.[83] Many of the works are straightforward natural scenes (e.g., *Morning and Evening, Moonlight* (Figure 6.15), and *Storm with Lightning*. Many of these prints include views of water, as is consistent with nonportrait oil paintings that Washington had collected over the years, such as the prints of the "Whale fisheries" and "Views of the Po." Classical subjects set in bucolic nature form another leitmotif of the collection, and Washington listed "Cupid's Pastime," "Nymphs,"

FIGURE 6.15. Engraved by Richard Brookshaw, after Hendrik Kobell, *Moonlight,* 1783, stipple engraving, approx. 15″ × 24″. According to the inventory taken after Washington's death, this print was hanging, along with other water views and classicizing scenes of nature, somewhere "from the foot of the Stair case to the Second floor." The print is in the Romantic taste and corresponds to the painting of moonlight displayed over the mantelpiece of the New Room. Courtesy of the Mount Vernon Ladies' Association (M-93/B).

FIGURE 6.16. After Claude Lorrain, *The Dancing Shepherds,* c. 1784, stipple engraving, 19.5″ × 23.75″. In the central passage and stairwell, Washington placed several prints copied after or inspired by works of the French painter Claude Lorrain. The soft, idealizing style of the classical landscapes accorded well with Washington's own landscape gardening as seen from the house and portico on the east side of the mansion house. Courtesy of the Mount Vernon Ladies' Association (W-966).

"Diana and Nymphs," "Venus attired," "Judgment of Paris," and others of that type. Washington grouped these pictures with themes of prospects and water on the east, river side of the house, echoing the actual view from the portico and east lawn. The central passage formed a particularly spectacular landscape experience. Out the front door was the vista to the west of the distant woods. From the east door, framed as if a picture, was the view of the lawn, treetops, and broad river, and on the walls of the central passage Washington grouped some of his finest prints, many of them ideal landscapes in the manner of Claude Lorrain (Figure 6.16), being literally after his paintings or made in his spirit. Even the later graining of the paneling and doors in the central passage (which replaced earlier paint) gives a natural aspect to the room, linking it to the woodsy landscape (Plate 7).

Along with the paintings and prints, there were porcelain landscapes on display. If the "5 China flower pots" that were listed in the inventory as being in the "front [West] Parlor" indeed included a 9 × 14 inch hexagonal pot and similar examples (Figure 6.17), the room was graced with the pots' broad, stylized landscapes that showed built structures and garden walls from which the represented figures would have had fine views of water and mountains.[84] While this study places limited emphasis on gifts that Washington received, the retention and placement of those gifts tell us something about his eye and sensibilities about art. In 1786, Samuel Vaughan sent to Washington porcelain vases to adorn a mantel he'd sent the previous year (Figure 6.18 and Plate 32). (Martha called them "Fine Old China jars" when she left them in her will to grandson George Washington Parke Custis.)[85] The vases, decorated by Irishman Jefferyes Hammett O'Neale, include fierce animals in landscape on one side and pure landscape views on the other, with the usual *repoussoir* trees, views of water, and rocks. These came to Washington early enough that they might have influenced his gardening. At any rate, they were appropriate to the Large Dining Room and expanded the theme of landscape art there. These "fine old jars" formed just one part of

FIGURE 6.17. Flowerpot, Jingdezhen, China, c. 1760–1790, porcelain, 9.25″ × 14″. Several vases and flowerpots at Mount Vernon represented landscapes, supplementing the large collection of two-dimensional landscape imagery displayed in the mansion house. Courtesy of the Mount Vernon Ladies' Association (W-2329).

the landscape iconography of the house. We will see in chapter 7 how Washington's collection of such landscape art fit into the larger scheme of his acquisitions and display at Mount Vernon.

For many years, visitors could not help but respond to Mount Vernon pictorially, both in language and in visual art. As early as 1783, Nathanael Greene noted that "Mount Vernon [has] one of the most beautiful situations in the world. The house has more dignity than convenience in it. Nature never formed a finer landscape than may be seen at this seat. The Potomac River in full view, with several little bays and creeks. The plain and the hills, joined to the features on the waters, forms a most beautiful scene." There is also a long, striking description from David Humphrey's "Life of General Washington," quoted by Jedidiah Morse and published by him in 1789, that gives a verbal picture of the landscape. One sections reads: "A small Park on the margin of the river, where the English fallow-deer & the American wild-deer are seen through the thickets, alternately with the vessels as they are sailing along, adds a romantic & pic-

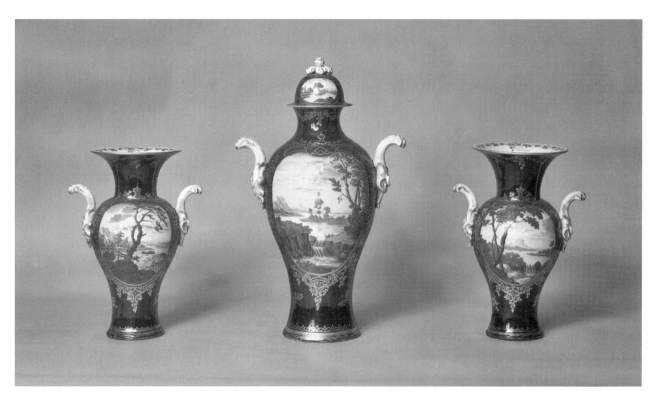

FIGURE 6.18. Garniture set, 1768–1770, porcelain, enamel, and gilding, 12.75″ (height of smaller vases) and 18.75″ (height of central vase). The three jars in the garniture set—made by Jefferyes Hammett O'Neale in Worcester, England, and given to Washington by Samuel Vaughan—were usually placed over the fireplace in the Large Dining Room, but Martha Washington's will implied that they were sometimes displayed elsewhere in the house. One side of the set represented pure landscapes (shown here), making them good additions to the public rooms of the house and to the other landscape art in the Large Dining Room. (See also Figure 7.20 for the other side of the vases.) Courtesy of the Mount Vernon Ladies' Association (W-972, W-2260).

FIGURE 6.19. Isaac Weld, *View of Mount Vernon the Seat of General Washington,* 1799, stipple engraving. A fantastic and artistic response, Weld's view reflected the idyllic and rural quality of the estate. From *Travels through the States of North America* (1799). Photo: Mina Rees Library at the City University of New York Graduate Center.

turesque appearance." William Talbot, visiting on 18 October 1793, described the location of the house on the "Banks of the Patowmack" as "a most romantic and rural situation."[86]

It is noteworthy that artists were rarely inspired by anything other than the parklike aspects of the estate or the house itself. The smaller, walled gardens appear in no early views at all, despite their extent and the fascination the exotic citrus and other trees there held for visitors. Early views from the water are also rare, though many at the time saw the estate from the river. Nearly all views were toward the house and showed some section of the garden, and they mostly included the east lawn, the most parklike area of the estate.

The pair of paintings by Edward Savage, never owned by Washington, are notable for their complete depiction of the house on both sides and for showing Washington walking in the garden. The view of the west front is extraordinary in that it shows the bowling green in use by the president and his family. It also shows the serpentine roads in use and gives a sense of the layered plantings, combining trees and lower shrubs. The casual poses and apparent purposelessness of the strollers bespeak the leisurely use of the estate.

Another extraordinary picture attributed to Savage is the distant view of the east front, in which he was inspired to show the effect of the rustic village, the distant prospect, the mansion house itself, the dominance of the portico in the view, the little lambkins, the freshly planted wooded groves and sloping deer park, and the east lawn protected by the ha-ha wall. Englishman George Parkyns captured the picturesque quality of the house, river, and bowling green as seen from the west, offering a rare (if fantastical) eighteenth-century look at the bowling green area (see Figure 4.10).[87] Isaac Weld also offered a response and an interpretation of the house and east lawn (Figure 6.19), though an editor's note in 1799 acknowledged that Weld's view was not taken from the spot. Still, like other early published views, Weld's helped to feed the public imagination and its appetite for images of the great man's house.[88]

Benjamin Henry Latrobe was perhaps the most sophisticated artistic thinker to pass through the estate during Washington's lifetime, and he made a number of views from the portico and lawn, illuminating what Washington had accomplished. Washington had created a living picture at Mount Vernon, and artists needed to do little more than capture the features that stood before them.

CHAPTER SEVEN

Washington as Artist, Critic, Patron, and Collector

To encourage Literature and the Arts, is a duty which every good Citizen owes to his country.

GEORGE WASHINGTON to Daniel Boinod and Alexander Gaillard, 18 February 1784

THERE WERE MANY FACETS to George Washington's interest in the visual arts, beyond landscape gardening and architectural design. These include his authorship of two-dimensional works of art, opinions about art and artists, efforts—assisted by Martha Washington—as collector and patron, and the thoughtful display of art at Mount Vernon.

Artist

Washington was an artist in his creative work as architect and landscape gardener. His years as a surveyor involved the gauging of landscape, the application of draftsmanship, and other design considerations. It was during his early surveying years that Washington became acquainted with the tools, literally and figuratively, that he would later employ in beautifying his estate's gardens and architecture. Beyond working in those expansive and monumental media, Washington produced a number of drawings of aesthetic interest. Much of his two-dimensional art was both marginalia and juvenilia, yet it offers some insight into his lifelong attitudes toward measurement and the visuality of landscape.

Drawings bordered the pages of his schoolbooks and the surveys he made in his youth. In these he sometimes evinced a delight in the cursive lines of handwriting, the fine art of which was taught to genteel schoolboys of the time. Some of these constituted Rococo flourishes on capital letters, while others were playful intertwining doodles (Figure 7.1). His bold, cursive writing style indicates his confidence and bravura as a person. In such script, it is as if he were

FIGURE 7.1. George Washington, "Geometrical Problems," 1745, pen and ink on paper. Washington delighted in penning bold flourishes on his capital letters. George Washington Papers, 1741–1799, Series 1a: George Washington, School Book Copy Book: Volume 1, 1745, Library of Congress.

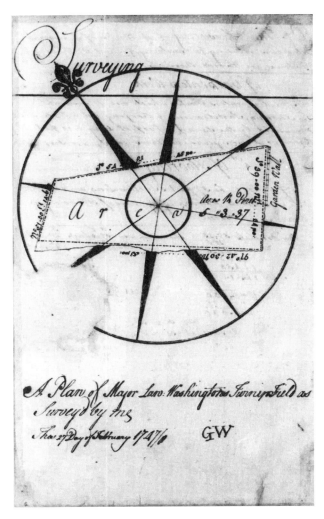

FIGURE 7.2. George Washington, "Surveying: A Plan of Major Lawrence Washingtons Turnip Field as Survey'd by me," 27 February 1747, pen and ink on paper. Washington usually made his compass indications with extra artistic touches, seen here in the fleur-de-lis and the changes from thick to thin lines for the directional indicators. George Washington Papers, 1741–1799, Series 1a: George Washington, School Book Copy Book: Volume 2, 1745, Library of Congress.

freeing his hand from the rigidity of the geometry of the surveys and school exercises, a propensity that later showed itself when he broke away from formal gardening and moved in the direction of more spontaneous and natural shapes.[1] The elaborate handwriting as seen in his schoolboy exercises continued throughout his adult life. In the professional surveys, his calligraphic writing lent an official and clerkish air, appropriate given that records of property lines actually did serve in support of legal claims.

Young Washington seemed to delight in the art of drawing. This can be seen in an early survey of a turnip field belonging to his half-brother Lawrence, made 27 February 1747 ("A Plan of Major Law. Washington's Turnip Field as Survey'd by me . . . GW"; Figure 7.2).[2] In addition to showing the surveyed field, young George designed an impressive, elaborate compass, sporting a fleur-de-lis pointing north and concentric circles and directional indicators rendered in bold, crisp lines.

One should not make too much of Washington's youthful doodles or school assignments. Still, some schoolboy designs from his middle teenage years seem to have anticipated his mature aesthetic. The black and white checkering he added as a border to a school exercise on "Memorial Verses"

FIGURE 7.3. George Washington, "Memorial Verses," 1745, pen and ink on paper. Washington took the trouble to make clear and attractive borders with black and white checker patterns. George Washington Papers, 1741–1799, Series 1a: George Washington, School Book Copy Book: Volume 1, 1745, Library of Congress.

FIGURE 7.5. George Washington, "Geometrical Definitions," 1745, pen and ink on paper. The worksheet for the schoolboy includes his fine shading of a cube and sphere. George Washington Papers, 1741–1799, Series 1a: George Washington, School Book Copy Book: Volume 1, 1745, Library of Congress.

FIGURE 7.4. George Washington, drawing for repairing frost damage on the portico tiles at Mount Vernon, after 1787, pen and ink on paper, 9″ × 7.5″. Washington had initially planned a black and white pattern. Courtesy of the Mount Vernon Ladies' Association (W-498).

(Figure 7.3) is not unlike the black and white pattern he later planned for his portico paving (see Figure 3.11). Another school geometry exercise bears a striking resemblance to his own (undated) drawing of the portico paving made in preparation for repairing damage from moisture and freezing (Figure 7.4).[3] Young Washington sometimes divided his surveys into sixteen or thirty-two sections, following the divi-

sions of the compass points; when he came to place posts in his oval turnaround, he set out thirty-two, and later he developed a centralized, sixteen-sided barn at Dogue Run Farm (see Figure 2.23). One of his school exercises involved gauging the volume of "square pillars" and "round pillars," looking forward to his later construction of square columns on his portico. Washington drew geometric shapes as part of his school assignments, and in one instance he did some fine shading on a cube and a sphere, training his eye for pictorial three-dimensionality and architectural geometry (Figure 7.5).[4] As was true for other Tidewater elites, such school exercises in geometry, gauging, and surveying helped to prepare one for overseeing the art of building and shaping an estate.

The early drawings, many done in the context of his work as a surveyor, include small specimens of landscape artistry, again foretelling some of his later visual interests. Washington represented water with some artistic sense, imbuing it with a sense of surface and movement. In his "Plan of Alexandria, now Belhaven" of 1748 (Figure 7.6), the sixteen-year-old surveyor took the trouble to stipple the water with dots to indicate shallow depth near the banks, and he tended to apply thinner dots spaced more closely nearer to the shore to give a sense of the greater action of

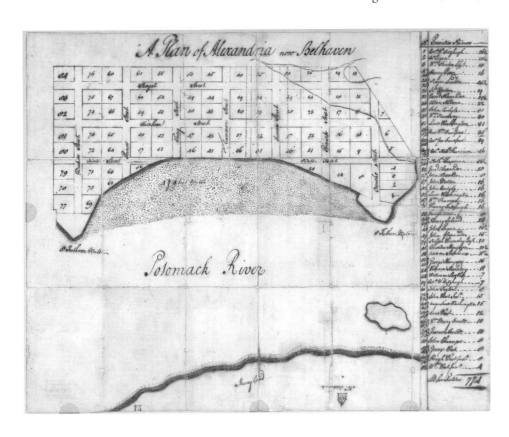

FIGURE 7.6. George Washington, "A Plan of Alexandria now Belhaven," 1748, pen and ink on paper, 12.5″ × 15.75″. Washington nicely stippled the water, characteristic of little naturalist touches on his early maps and surveys. George Washington Papers, Geography and Map Division, Library of Congress.

the water away from the banks.[5] Along the shore itself, tight lines indicate the transition from water to land. Together with the beautiful script, the orderly list of families on the right, and a harmonious spacing of the elements, the page has a charm and beauty despite its limited format. In the related map, "Platt of Alexandria" from 1749, some marshland is suggested via a broad stippling style (Figure 7.7). The stippling in all of these juvenilia is compatible with period stylistic conventions used by both amateur and professional mapmakers.

Many of the trees in young Washington's surveys are stiffly drawn, though adequate to the purpose, but one sees calligraphic and cursive qualities in the "slooping white Oak" drawn on a survey of 5 November 1762 (Figure 7.8). Washington also produced larger-scale landscape scenes. Among his finer early drawings is the view of the Mount Vernon estate, drawn as a schoolboy for his half-brother

Lawrence (Figure 7.9).[6] The inscription "Mount Vernon Hills" is above a nicely stylized rendering of wavy hills, with shadowing, an abstract ridge line, and descending marks to represent shadows in little valleys. The drawing shows George Washington's lack of training as an artist but suggests his curiosity about the appearance and rendering of Nature. He could little have known at this point that he would inherit those very hills and make their natural adornment through landscape gardening one of his chief efforts. Another attractive early drawing represents the Cacapon River, the stylized, low mountains cleverly shown as overlapping and defined by vigorous shading. The mountains are abstract and geometric but not without charm and visual energy.

Washington's modest efforts in landscape drawing continued past his youth. In 1766, at the age of thirty-four, Washington was still interested in putting some artistic touches

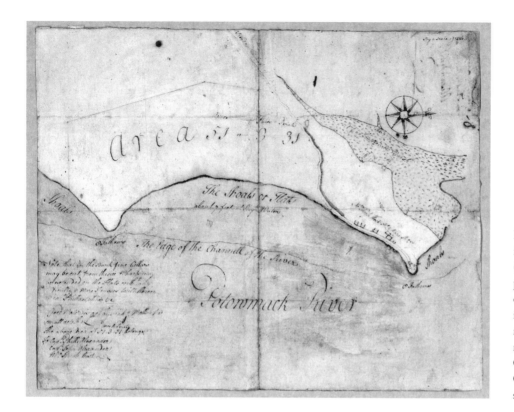

FIGURE 7.7. George Washington, "Platt of Alexandria" (detail), 1749, pen and ink on paper, 14.2" × 17.3". Among other artistic touches, Washington impressionistically marked the wetlands and the marshy banks of a stream. George Washington Papers, Geography and Map Division, Library of Congress.

FIGURE 7.8. George Washington "Slooping White Oak," survey of 5 November 1762, pen and ink on paper. Surveying his own lands, Washington drew this vignette of a drooping oak tree. Courtesy of the Mount Vernon Ladies' Association (MS 4966, RM-737).

on his maps. In a 1766 view of the farm at Little Hunting Creek, Washington depicted a forest, with an appealing spacing of the trees, interspersed with stippled marking and abstract bushes or shrubbery (Figure 7.10).[7] The trees nearly all cast a shadow below, giving a sense of space. Most interesting are the squiggled lines representing agricultural fields; the marks, reminiscent of folk art, are turned in a lively way and set out on the sheet with a good sense of line and dynamism. The banks of the rivers are lined with a subtle green

color. In a design from 1754, Washington drew an extensive hilly landscape with a prominent inscription, "Aligany Mountains," stretching across the middle of the sheet. He took evident delight in making the shading atop the peaks and in the abstract wavy pattern of lines of the mountains (Figure 7.11). The drawing clearly indicates both the artist's lack of training and an amateur's love of form, the lines conveying a decorative effect.[8] Even the rivers, which are evidently drawn with a mind to showing accurately their shape and apparent extent, somehow participate in the same brittle style as the mountains, an effect amplified by the reverberating lines that define the river banks.

Washington's designs sometimes included the representations of material objects and the decorative arts. In making a small drawing of a compass, chain, and scale, he took the time to represent the shadowing and metallic texture on the compass (Figure 7.12). Later, Washington used the American Indian phrase "brighten the Chain" to Henry Knox and

Plate 17. View at Mount Vernon from the entrance oval to the south arm of the colonnade. By eliminating the back wall, Washington opened up views through the square columns of his covered ways north and south of the house. He ordered that each column support a honeysuckle plant that would display its leaves and flowers on the spandrels above. Photo: Author.

PLATE 18. Prospect of the Potomac from the portico at Mount Vernon, looking toward the northeast. Washington kept trees near the top of the hill to increase the sense of spatial depth. The remarkable swamp chestnut oak tree seen prominently here was planted no later than 1771 and still forms part of the prospect. Photo: Author.

PLATE 19. Prospect of the Potomac and Maryland shore, looking from the east lawn, Mount Vernon. The view of the river from the portico and east lawn was the climax of the garden experience at Mount Vernon; Polish visitor Niemcewicz called this "the finest view in the world." Trees below growing nearer to the river level were trimmed regularly and formed a green border to the base of the composition. Photo: Author.

PLATE 20. English School, *Landscape* (overmantel), c. 1755–1757, oil on canvas, 22.5″ × 36″. Washington ordered this "Neat Landskip, after Claud Lorrain" from England in 1757. Landscape painting at that time was not unknown in the American colonies, but it was hardly widespread. Except for removal for conservation, the picture has never left its spot in the West Parlor. Courtesy of the Mount Vernon Ladies' Association (W-356).

PLATE 21. George Beck, *The Great Falls of the Potomac River,* 1796, oil on canvas, 39" × 50". Washington engaged Beck to represent dramatic natural scenes of the American landscape. After hanging in an upstairs drawing room of the president's mansion in Philadelphia, this work and the companion piece (see Plate 22) adorned the Large Dining Room at Mount Vernon. Like the central passage and the Little Parlor, the Large Dining Room held several views of landscape with water, echoing the real view to the east of the mansion house. Courtesy of the Mount Vernon Ladies' Association (W-2).

PLATE 22. George Beck, *Passage of the Potomac through the Blue Mountains at the Confluence with the Shenandoah,* 1796, oil on canvas, 39" × 49.5". Martha Washington vouched that her husband suggested to the artist the exact subject of this painting. Washington seems to have had a patriotic sense for American landscape and a taste for dramatic scenery in art. Courtesy of the Mount Vernon Ladies' Association (W-3).

PLATE 23. William Winstanley, *Morning,* 1793, oil on canvas, 36.25" × 49.2" Washington collected this pair of pictures by English painter Winstanley. Often generically called *Morning* and *Evening* (Plate 24), the works were early on called views of the North River (i.e., Hudson River) and possibly represent idealized views of the upper Hudson Valley. Courtesy of the Mount Vernon Ladies' Association (W-1179).

PLATE 24. William Winstanley, *Evening,* 1793, oil on canvas, 36.4″ × 49.2″. Courtesy of the Mount Vernon Ladies' Association (W-1180).

PLATE 25. Cupola and weathervane, mansion house, Mount Vernon. The weathervane was produced by Joseph Rakestraw of Philadelphia (reproduction shown here; original weather-vane MVLA), 1787, copper, iron, lead, gilt, paint (ornament); wrought iron (rod and directionals); gilded copper (ball). The bird, undoubtedly intended to be a dove, carries an olive branch as one did after the biblical Flood, making the weathervane a highly visible marker of the calm and peace brought to America following the successful Revolution. Photo: Author.

PLATE 26. Little Parlor, mansion house, Mount Vernon. In the last few years of his life Washington turned a small bedroom into this parlor. Its decoration includes dramatic scenes of ships at sea. Courtesy of the Mount Vernon Ladies' Association.

PLATE 27. Saucer and covered cup (part of the "States China"), Chinese, c. 1795, porcelain, saucer 6″ in diameter, cup 5″ in height. The inscription "Decus et Tutamen ab Illo" means "Glory (or Honor) and Defense by Him," referring to George Washington. The dinner service was a gift from a Dutchman to Martha Washington, and honored her and her husband. Courtesy of the Mount Vernon Ladies' Association (W-1497/A–C).

PLATE 28. Argand lamp, English or French, c. 1790, silver plate, 6″ × 9″. Especially in the period after the Revolutionary War, Washington consistently preferred unostentatious and "elegant" decorative arts. Courtesy of the Mount Vernon Ladies' Association (W-1545).

PLATE 29. Jean-Antoine Houdon, *George Washington,* 1785, clay, 22", signed and dated "Houd-on F[ecit]. 1785." Of all the known portraits, Houdon's bust probably best records Washington's appearance. Courtesy of the Mount Vernon Ladies' Association (W-369).

PLATE 30. Charles Willson Peale, *George Washington as a Colonel in the Virginia Regiment*, 1772, oil on canvas, 50.5″ × 41.5″. Washington is not known to have sat for a portrait before this one. It celebrates his leadership success in the French and Indian War. Courtesy of the Washington-Custis-Lee Collection, Washington and Lee University, Lexington, Virginia, U1897.1.1.

PLATE 31. Anonymous, probably Italian, *Virgin Mary,* eighteenth century, pastel on paper, 19.5" × 24", frame probably original. This small pastel hung prominently in the Large Dining Room. Representing an unusual subject for Protestant America, it helped give Washington's Large Dining Room the character of a sophisticated art gallery. Courtesy of the Mount Vernon Ladies' Association.

PLATE 32. View of the south wall of the Large Dining Room, mansion house, Mount Vernon. This view shows *Moonlight on Rocky Coast* (anonymous, in the manner of Abraham Pether) and the marble chimneypiece, attributed to Henry Cheere, assisted by William Collins, c. 1745, 67.75″ × 82.5″; installed at Mount Vernon in 1785 (W-940). When Englishman Samuel Vaughan sent the chimneypiece, Washington expressed concern, partly in jest but concealing a truth, that a large, marble piece such as this would not accord with his "republican stile of living" and thus might reflect poorly on him. Courtesy of the Mount Vernon Ladies' Association.

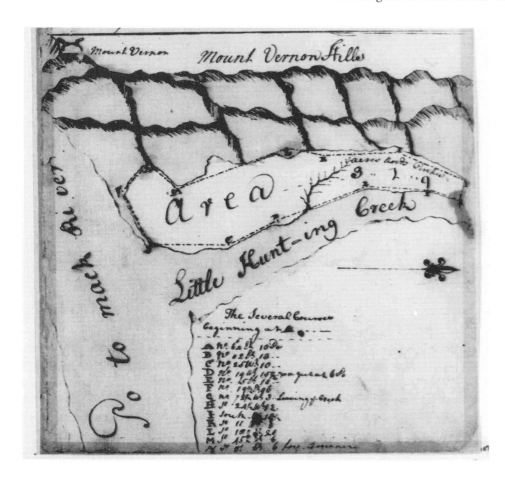

FIGURE 7.9. George Washington, drawing of the Mount Vernon estate, 1745, pen and ink on paper. Young Washington took some pleasure in shading the hills near Mount Vernon. George Washington Papers, 1741–1799, Series 1a: George Washington, School Book Copy Book: Volume 2, 1745, Library of Congress.

others; in this drawing he did so literally, taking the trouble to delineate the chain with careful precision.[9] The scale is also meticulously drawn, showing the intricate graining of the wood. The presentation on the page is well spaced and harmonious, and Washington added a directional fleur-de-lis.

The mature Washington, in addition to buying furniture, at least once tried his hand in its design. There was a joinery at Jefferson's Monticello, but no such extensive production occurred at Mount Vernon, which relied on makers offsite for all but the most rudimentary wooden furniture. But in the late summer of 1788, Washington contributed some design ideas for a chair to be made by a craftsman near Philadelphia; that chair was then to serve as a model for a set that Washington would commission from craftsmen closer to home. Philadelphian Elizabeth Powel communicated Wash-

ington's intentions and ideas (and hers) to the maker in Trenton. Washington suggested that the chair have a circle on the back to receive a cushion, an idea that the maker hesitated for practical reasons to carry out. Samuel Powel wrote to Washington:

At present I fear it will not fully accord with your Ideas, as he said that a Circle in the Back to have received a Cushion, would weaken the chair; & it did not appear practicable to prevail on him to deviate from his accustomed Mode of working with any Prospect of Success. The chair, such as it is, is the neatest I have seen of his making; &, should you be desirous of having a Sett of them, may be made for less than Two dollars each. The tedious Time that you have waited for this Trifle, will not, I hope, deter you from honoring us with any little Commission that you may wish to have executed here; as it will ever give us real pleasure to be, in any way, serviceable to you.[10]

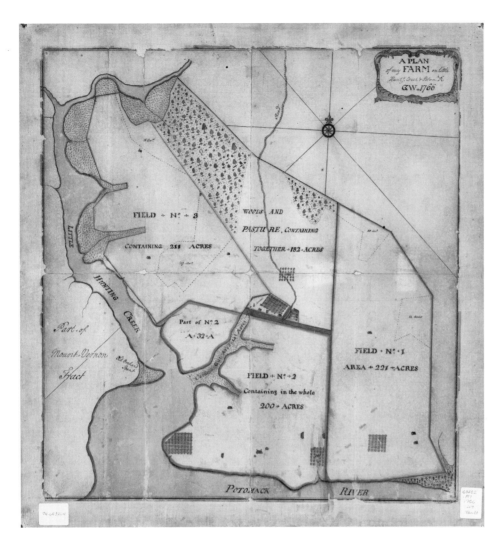

FIGURE 7.10. George Washington, "A Plan of my Farm at Little Hunting Creek," 1766, pen and ink and watercolor on linen mounted on cardboard, 18.1″ × 17.3″. Washington added naturalistic touches (trees, marshland, water) to enliven the plan. The frame around the inscription on the upper right was influenced by bookplate designs that Washington knew. George Washington Papers, Maps of North America, 1750–1789, Geography and Map Division, Library of Congress.

Washington received the model chair, thanked the Powels, and stated his intention to make further improvements, particularly in the upholstery: "I think it handsome & neat; and with some additions which I will take the liberty sometime hence of proposing (such as can readily be inserted) they may be made to suit the colour and furniture of the room for which they are intended as a well as a chair of quadruple their cost."[11] In this exchange, Washington proposed an important design element, even though he did not understand the structural requirements for chairs, and he later planned to unify them coloristically with the rest of the room. He favored the perfect shape of the circle and wanted it to dominate the chair backs. This design suited his taste for simplicity, was within his capabilities as a draftsman, and would have helped create a neat and plain work of art.

Washington designed other useful objects, some merely practical and some also of aesthetic interest. One was what Niemcewicz called a "plow of his own [Washington's] invention."[12] When Washington needed four iron firebacks for the mansion house in 1787, he determined what size they needed to be to fit the fireplaces well ("that the castings may be proportioned thereto") and conveyed the specifications

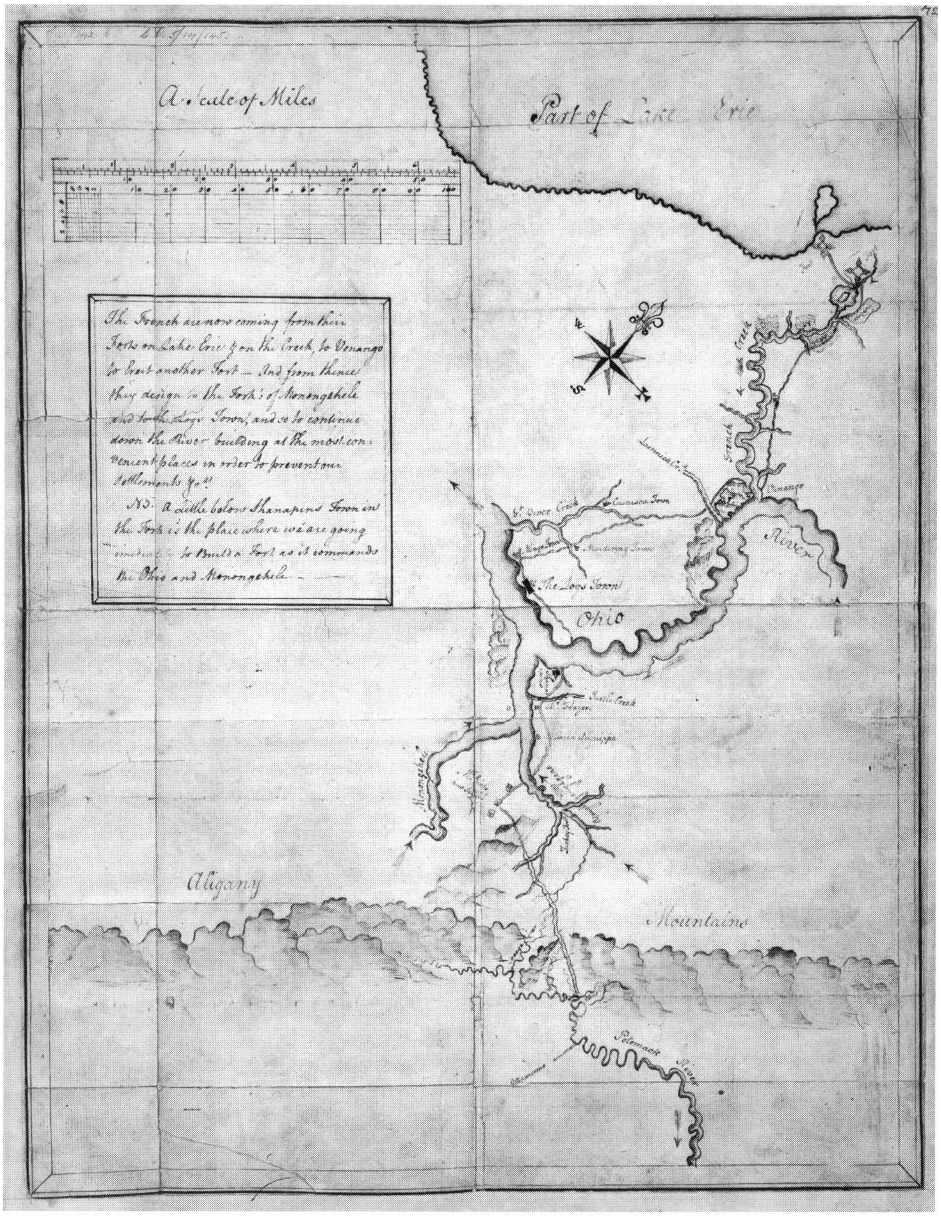

FIGURE 7.11. George Washington, map of the region including the Ohio River Valley and the "Aligany Mountains," 1754, pen and ink on paper, 14.8″ × 18.8″. Washington included here a dramatic view of the Allegheny Mountains. The young colonel produced this map of the land and river systems from Lake Erie to the Potomac, providing the information for his superiors, including Gov. Robert Dinwiddie. Courtesy of the National Archives, Kew, Richmond, UK (MPG/118).

to the maker, who followed the general's instructions and added the crest and cipher of the Washington family.[13] In a similar commission, Washington sent to agent Clement Biddle in Philadelphia a sketch and instructions for a stove that he wanted for a garret bedchamber: "I am in want of an *open stove* for a room that has no fire place in it . . . Enclosed I have endeavoured to describe in a parallel sketch my idea of the Kind and size I want." It is likely that Washington expected Biddle to buy a stove already made, and this sketch was not necessarily a design for new piece, but the transaction shows Washington's careful attention to detail in shaping his physical surroundings.[14] In a less practical example of Washing-

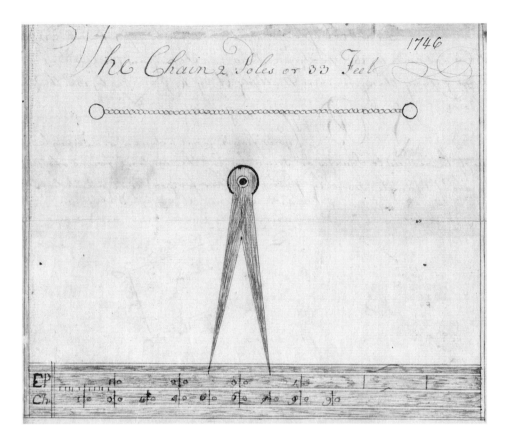

FIGURE 7.12. George Washington, *The Chains and Poles or 33 Feet,* 1746, pen and ink on paper, 6.5″ × 7.5″. Young Washington made this drawing of some of the tools he used in his work as surveyor. This sheet is among the papers collected by historian Jared Sparks (d. 1866). Courtesy of the Division of Rare and Manuscript Collections, Cornell University Library, Ithaca, NY (4600 Bd. Ms. 548++, folder 1).

ton's design, an inscription in a 1766 map is framed with delicate flourishes of leaves and other effects, including gadrooning, a widespread ornamental motif in Rococo furniture and silver (see Figure 7.10). This design likely was modeled on either a bookplate that Washington had in front of him or one that he remembered.

Washington as Art Critic

The painter John Singleton Copley complained that in the American colonies "the people generally regard it [painting] no more than any other usefull trade, as they sometimes term it, like that of a Carpenter[,] tailor[,] or shew maker, not as one of the most noble Arts in the World. Which is not a little Mortifiing to me."[15] From the 1770s to the 1790s, some Americans, such as William Hamilton of Philadelphia, traveled in Europe and collected and displayed fine art at home. Even Thomas Jefferson, urbane and well traveled, had by European standards only an average eye for fine art, and he collected some inexpensive works in Europe, including copies of masterworks, to adorn the walls of Monticello. Concerning painting and statuary in America, Jefferson wrote, "Too expensive for the state of wealth among us. It would be useless therefore and preposterous for us to endeavor to make ourselves connoisseurs in those arts. They are worth seeing, but not studying."[16] On the whole, the fine and decorative arts, including painting, did not garner as much critical attention in America as they would in the nineteenth century and later. Perhaps we should not expect George Washington to have developed an advanced critical language for the fine arts. Still, Washington has been underestimated as a connoisseur, and he actually had a well-developed sense of style, of iconography, and of the role of a sitter, and he was engaged at every level with style and subject matter and was aware of the cultural importance of art.

There is evidence from his letters and diaries that Washington had a fairly good connoisseurial eye for paintings and prints. He carried on an intelligent exchange in March 1785 with historian William Gordon about some silhouette portraits, which Washington deemed "imperfect"; he preferred the work of contemporary artist Pierre Eugène du Simitière. Washington gave or loaned the profiles he had to Gordon, while also noting Martha's reluctance to spare them:

> I found a difficulty in complying with your request respecting the profiles—the latter is not in my power to do now, satisfactorily. Some imperfect miniature cuts I send you under cover with this letter—they were designed for me by Miss D'Hart of Elizabethtown—& given to Mrs Washington; who in sparing them, only wishes they may answer your purpose. For her I can get none cut yet. If Mr Du'Simitere is living, & at Philada, it is possible he may have miniature engravings of most, if not all the military characters you want, & in their proper dresses: he drew many good likenesses from the life, and got them engraved at Paris for sale; among these I have seen Genl Gates, Baron de Steuben, &c.—as also that of your humble serv[an]t.[17]

Washington's knowledge of and interest in styles of portrait painting went well beyond the characteristic emphasis in the period on accuracy of likeness. For example, in January 1784, he gave to a European patron a sensitive description of the style of American painter Joseph Wright, who had already taken Washington's likeness. Washington arranged for Wright to make a replica of an earlier work, and the new version was sent abroad. In one of his first letters after his return to Mount Vernon at the end of the Revolutionary War, Washington wrote that he had

> employed a Gentleman to perform the work, who is thought on a former occasion to have taken a better likeness of me, than any other painter has done: his forté seems to be in giving the distinguishing characteristics with more boldness than delicacy—And altho' he commonly marks the features very strongly, yet I cannot flatter you, that you will find the touches of his pencil extremely soft, or that the portrait will in any re-

FIGURE 7.13. Joseph Wright, *George Washington*, c. 1783, oil on canvas, 14″ × 12″. Washington arranged to have a similar portrait (now lost) sent to the Graf zu Solms und Tecklenberg. The German count wanted to hang Washington's portrait in his library in Königstein, Germany. Washington offered the count a good, critical analysis of Wright's style. Courtesy of the Philadelphia History Museum at the Atwater Kent, The Historical Society of Pennsylvania Collection.

spect equal your expectations. Such as it may be (& for your sake, I would wish the execution was as perfect as possible) it will be forwarded from Philada, to the order of the Count de Bruhl, as soon as it is finished.[18]

The portrait was intended to hang in the German palace of Friedrich-Christoph, Graf zu Solms und Tecklenberg.[19] Although this particular portrait cannot be located today, related paintings of Washington by Wright do survive, and the painter's style is much as Washington described it, as the portraitist did mark the features strongly, and the facial features are prominently rendered (Figure 7.13). The painter's

Figure 7.14. Edward Savage, *Constellation and L'Insurgent—the Chace,* 1799, aquatint. Savage sent this and another experimental aquatint to Washington, who responded critically to the new medium. Savage must have made few of these, as known impressions have always been rare. From Charles Hart, *Edward Savage: Painter and Engraver* (1905), between pp. 12 and 13.

work is marked by open brushwork and is indeed carried out with boldness rather than delicacy. Washington mentions in the letter that he had discussed with others Wright's ability to convey verisimilitude, thus revealing that his ideas on painting were a topic of conversation. As he often did when addressing members of the upper class in Europe, Washington wrote this analysis in his loftier style, using the word "forté" and giving a sensitive description of the painted surface.[20]

Washington evinced another subtle and insightful aesthetic response following his reception of a pair of seascape prints from Edward Savage (Figure 7.14). Savage wrote to Washington six months before the ex-president's death that he had introduced into his oeuvre what was for him a new method of working: aqua fortis (aquatint, or eau-forte), a form of etching that offers subtler tonal effects than traditional etching:

> Sir: The print I promist to Send Mrs Washington was ready Last March I have Been So unlucky as to Miss Every oppertunity Since; till the present one; it is Shipt on board the Schooner Tryal Capt. Hand Master, Not being acquainted

with any one in Alexandra I Directed the Cas to the Care of the Customhouse.

> This Last winter I Discovered the Method of Engraving with Acquafortis, in order to proove my Experement I Executed two prints which is my first Specimen in that Stile of Engraving, one is the Chace the other the action of the Constellation with the L'Insurgent, I have put two of those prints into the Case for you to See that Method of working on Copper. I intend as Soone as time will permit, to Execute a Set of Large prints of the Most Striking and Beautifull Views in America, in that Stile of Engraving, as it is Best Calculated for Landskips: and a very Expeditious Method of working.

> I hope Yourself and Mrs Washington will Excuse the Delay of the print it woud have been Sent Last Summer if the Sickness Had not Dreven me out of the City before I had time to print any in Colours. I am Sir your Much Oblidg'd Humble Sert. Edward Savage.[21]

Washington responded to Savage:

> Sir, Your letter of the 17th instant and the Print (which is exceedingly handsome, and well set) have come safe; and receives, as it highly deserves, the thanks of Mrs Washington; to whom you have had the kindness, and politeness to present it.

> I thank you also for the prints of the Chase, & action between the Constellation and the L'Insurgent; exhibiting a specimen of the art of Engraving by means of Aquafortis. The invention is curious, and if the sample of it which you have sent is the first essay, it will, no doubt, prove a valuable discovery, as, like all other discoveries[,] it will undergo improvements.

> Mrs Washington is thankful for your kind remembrance of her, and joins in every good wish for you & yours, with Sir— Your Most Obedt & very Hble Servant Go: Washington.

> P.S. Whenever you have fixed upon your Landscapes, for Engraving by means of Aquafortis, and have executed them, be so good as to inform me thereof.[22]

Washington, looking carefully at the stylistic effect of the aqua fortis technique, found the novel technique "curious" (not the kindest word) and noted condescendingly that it would undoubtedly "undergo improvements" in the future. This last comment was likely a polite way of saying that he was not smitten but was intrigued and would like to see the technique advanced and applied to landscapes, as Savage

promised. Aquatint can produce a soft, tonal effect and offers more expressive possibilities than the more linear engraving or even traditional etching. Washington recognized
in the two prints harsh tonal contrasts, as in the sharp differences between light and shadow on the sails of the ships
and the waves. He did have the perspicacity to see that—
perhaps better than the marine representation of the chase
and battle between the "L'Insurgent" and the "Constellation"—aqua fortis would work well in representations of
landscape, where well-applied chiaroscuro and a broader
rather than a linear technique might help to achieve a lumi-
nous and painterly landscape effect through aerial perspective and tonal distinctions. Washington thought that Savage could do better.

Artists writing to Washington understood that he would
exercise his aesthetic judgment upon viewing their works.
When Edward Savage sent some prints of the famous *Washington Family* (visible in Plate 5) on 3 June 1798, he anticipated Washington's possible negative reaction to their dark
tonality. After reassuring Washington that the engravings
sent were among the first and best impressions available,
Savage wrote: "Agreeable to Col. Biddies order I Delivered
four of the best impressions of your Family Print[.] they are
Chose [*sic*] out of the first that was printed, perhaps you may
think that one two [*sic*] Dark, but they will Change Lighter
after hanging two or three months."[23] Similarly, in 1787
Charles Willson Peale sent Washington a print of portraits
of prominent Americans, making excuses for the crudeness
of the style. Peale commented, conventionally, on the lifelikeness that would please Washington but apologized, "as
this Print is much coarser than the others will be."[24] For his
part, James Manley, producer of the portrait that we now
call the "Manley Medal," wrote to Washington in February
1790 and sent to George and Martha an "Impression on
Lead, taken from the Die." Manley, who did not actually cut
the dies himself, apologized for the level of "releif [*sic*], or
sharpness." He promised that the final version would be better and asked Washington for suggestions for changes (Fig-

FIGURE 7.15. "Manley medal" (profile portrait of George Washington), 1790, bronze, 2″ (diameter). James Manley sent an earlier
impression of this medal to Washington, with apologies for the
quality. Courtesy of the Mount Vernon Ladies' Association (M-
3057/A).

ure 7.15).[25] These three artists expected that Washington was
carefully studying and judging the style of the works.

Washington had intelligent exchanges with other collectors on the subject of art. Samuel Powel's wife Elizabeth
wrote in December 1798 to Washington: "I have the Pleasure to send the Book of Prints that you were so obliging as
to accept from your Friend. I have also taken the liberty to
add a few that I admire on a presumption that the Mind capable of tracing with Pleasure the military Progress of the
Hero whose Battles they delineate will also have the associate Taste and admire fine representations of the Work of
God in the human Form."[26] This is a sophisticated statement, declaring that a fine moral mind also prefers a fine
style. The letter indicates that Mrs. Powel was acquainted
with neoplatonically inflected thought (art as the "Work of
God in the human Form") and also contemporary argu-

ments concerning the association of tastes, in particular the relationship of moral sense (she mentions "the military Progress of the Hero") with aesthetic perception of "fine representations." Her remarks recall ideas concerning association as discussed by Francis Hutcheson, David Hume, and other English writers. Washington did not respond to Mrs. Powel at this intellectual level, but her letter indicates his participation in a new, higher level of art criticism and commentary that was developing in the United States.

Washington himself addressed the question of the mind behind the understanding and enjoyment of art. He asked the Marquis de Lafayette to help spread the word about John Trumbull's prints illustrating "the most important Events of the Revolution in this Country." Washington declared that "his pieces, so far as they are executed, meet the warm applause of all who have seen them. The greatness of the design and [the] masterly execution of the Work equally interest the man of a capacious mind and the approving eye of the Connoisseur."[27] Washington discussed the perception and understanding of works of art by calling attention to two traits of the viewer characteristically desired in eighteenth-century aesthetics: the eye, that looks for such things as details of execution, "masterly design," and lifelikeness, and the capacious mind of the viewer, whose intelligence helps him or her sense higher ideas beyond what is merely visible. The notion of the capacious mind is central to the aesthetics of Joseph Addison and David Hume and informs the famous *Lectures* of Joshua Reynolds, who stressed that moral improvement and reason abet a deeper appreciation of art. Washington was aware that while art provides sensory pleasure, its reception also relies on the imagination and moral qualities of the viewer. In his letter to Lafayette, he was imagining the mind of the viewer stirred by the moral events of the American Revolution, including his own participation as illustrated by Trumbull. Writing to a European and an aristocrat, Washington again communicated to an elite foreign recipient at a high intellectual level and in his better literary form.

Washington had a good eye for art, but he employed a limited vocabulary, in line with his American contemporaries. In a 1785 letter to William Paca of Annapolis, Washington referred to Robert Pine's paintings as offering "many pleasing & forcible specimens of genius."[28] He employed the word "handsome" quite often, as when he characterized some prints sent by John Trumbull as "very handsome" and "much admired by others." He called a three-part garniture set sent to him in November 1786 "handsome."[29] One phrase that he used in discussing art was "plain and neat" (or "neat and plain"). This was a widely used phrase in eighteenth-century America, and Virginia in particular, and described something well made and without excessive ornament. Washington used the words "neat" or "plain" when discussing or ordering furniture or other objects. In June 1764, Washington ordered from middleman James Gildart "Two Elbow—& Ten common sitting Chairs for an Entertaining Room—to be large neat and fashionable, and not to exceed 25/ apiece."[30] Washington consistently preferred objects that were of high quality, simple, and unadorned (Figure 7.16). He wrote to Gouverneur Morris in Paris on 28 November 1788 that he wanted an unostentatious French watch: "I wish to have a gold watch procured for my own use (not a small trifling, nor finical ornamented one) but a watch *well* executed in point of Workmanship; and about the size & kind of that which was procured by Mr Jefferson for Mr Madison."[31]

An early, secondhand anecdote illustrates Washington's known preference for the plain and neat. At a military banquet in September 1783, silver goblets were used for the toasts. Having been told that the goblets had been made by a man who had since become a Quaker preacher, Washington is said to have quipped that he wished the craftsman "had been a Quaker preacher before he had made the cups."[32] The remark (if accurately recorded) shows his persistent taste for neat and plain and also his awareness of the Quaker manner in the decorative and other arts, a style that tended toward solid and "honest" construction and spare use of ornament.

FIGURE 7.16. Pocket watch, 1793–1794, gold, base metals, and porcelain, 2″ (width). Washington, especially later in life, preferred his personal objects to be without finicky ornament, as with this pocket watch made in London by James McCabe and James Richards. Courtesy of the Mount Vernon Ladies' Association (W-446).

Washington liked when artists received broad esteem. He often chose to hold back his own opinion and convey instead the opinions of knowledgeable viewers, or he expressed his approval along with that of others; this modesty was both real and calculated. We have seen that he suggested that Trumbull's pieces "meet the warm applause of all who have seen them." Of Pine's paintings of Washington's family members, the general said, "The pictures arrived shortly after in good order, & meet the approbation of Mrs Washington & myself." After sitting for Pine and seeing his work, Washington expressed to George William Fairfax not his own opinion of the results but the view that "Mr Pine's reception in this Country had been favourable; and indicative of a plentiful harvest in the line of his profession. Consequent of your good report of this Gentleman, I furnished him with letters to many of the first characters in Philadelphia & Annapolis."[33]

Typical of his time, he used lifelikeness in portraiture as another measure of artistic achievement. On 3 October 1789, Washington wrote in his diary: "sat about two o'clock for Madame de Brienne [Bréhan] to complete a Miniature profile of me which she had begun from Memory and which she had made exceedingly like the Original."[34] He told Lafayette later that John Trumbull "spared no pains in obtaining from the life the likenesses of the characters . . . who bore a conspicuous part in our Revolution." On 28 May 1779, he wrote to Nicholas Rogers of a portrait miniature of Martha that "difficult as it is to strike a likeness on so small a scale, it is the opinion of many that you have not failed in the present attempt."[35] Washington in this remark combined his esteem for verisimilitude with his usual comfort in believing that the highest esteem for an artist's work "is the opinion of many."

In assessing a range of arts—from prints to decorative arts to architecture—Washington frequently used the word "elegant," which for him was high praise indeed. The word's meaning at the time was more or less in line with Noah Webster's definition in the *American Dictionary* (1828): "Pleasing to good taste. Neat; pure; rich in expressions; correct in arrangement, as language." Washington used Argand lamps made in the new neoclassical style in the presidential mansion in Philadelphia and later at Mount Vernon (Plate

28). In addition to appreciating their practical benefits (they "consume their own smoke, do no injury to furniture, give more light, and are cheaper than candles"), he told Morris that they were "very elegant—much admired—and do great justice to your taste."[36] Two proof prints that Charles Buxton sent to Washington from New Jersey in April 1799 were "elegantly executed," and Washington modestly noted that if he had not been included in the image, he would say more about the "fruitfulness of the Design."[37] The word "elegant" was widely used at the time, and correspondents used it in letters to Washington. In sending him the firebacks for Mount Vernon, Charles Pettit wrote from Philadelphia that they were less "elegant" in style than he would have wished "but they are nevertheless far from bad."[38]

Washington never openly stated a preference for any of the art-historical styles that were available for viewing in his life time, such as those we know as Baroque, Rococo, Gothic or Gothic Revival, or Neoclassical. American patrons of the time rarely referred to such stylistic designations, but some expressed a dislike of the "Chinese" style (the Asian-influenced form of the Rococo), while the ancient foundation of the classical style was well known and discussed. For his part, when a style was in fashion, Washington accepted it and wanted "elegant" specimens, if they were what he considered to be plain and neat, made with good workmanship. Again and again, Washington asked for objects of beauty that were fashionable or in the current taste. Acquiring something that was out of fashion was an embarrassment for Washington, especially while he was a colonial subject. Washington was aware of the kind of prejudice that English writer Samuel Johnson expressed when he stated that Americans were "a race of convicts, and ought to be thankful for any thing we allow them short of hanging." English dealers, Washington thought, exported shoddy, overpriced decorative goods to what they considered their colonial inferiors.[39] He complained to agent Robert Cary in London in 1760:

> It is needless for me to particularise the sorts, quality, or taste I woud choose to have them in unless it is observd; and you may believe me when I tell you that instead of getting things good and fashionable in their several kind we often have Articles sent Us that coud only have been usd by our Forefathers in the days of yore—'Tis a custom, I have some Reason to believe, with many Shop keepers, and Tradesmen in London when they know Goods are bespoke for Exportation to palm sometimes old, and sometimes very slight and indifferent Goods upon Us taking care at the sametime to advance 10, 15 or perhaps 20 prCt upon them.[40]

As he had complained of his insulting treatment within the military hierarchy in the context of British and colonial relations in the 1750s, the retired colonel seethed in anger that the British dumped old-fashioned and poorly made goods on the Americans. We see here Washington's concern even early on with "fashion," and we also get a glimpse into a cause of the American Revolution.

As T. H. Breen has noted, anglicized provincials insisted on receiving the "latest" English goods and were "remarkably attuned to even subtle changes in metropolitan fashion." Washington kept this desire for fashionableness, hardly unique, as he became a world figure, and throughout his life he asked that items sent to him be currently in fashion. When looking for some tableware, he wrote to his nephew Bushrod and asked "whether French plate is fashionable and much used in genteel houses in France and England."[41] George ordered a watch for Martha in November 1785, requesting "a handsome & fashionable gold watch, with a fashionable chain or string, such as are worn at present by Ladies in genteel life." Washington also wrote to Gouverneur Morris, then residing in London, and asked him to acquire "mirrors for a table, with neat & fashionable but not expensive ornaments for them; such as will do credit to your taste."[42] That these would serve as a mark of fashion and restraint as they hung in the presidential mansion in New York was a political matter as well as one of pure "taste," and Washington had to make sure that the presidential mansion set a high international standard that would help earn respect for the new republic.

We can imagine, given his taste for simplicity and functionality, that a sparer neoclassical look answered his needs for "plain and neat." Indeed, the whole neoclassical movement fulfilled a long-standing desire for virtuously restrained ornament, the display of which allowed one to convey an admiration of antiquity. When neoclassicism arose, it spread quickly and widely across the western world. George Washington was a man of his times in his easy acceptance of neoclassicism, which came to be the current taste, overtaking the Rococo, and he expressed approval at the neoclassical Argand lamps and the plain and neat stucco decoration in the Large Dining Room. It is unfortunate that he made no known comments on the extensive set of neoclassical chairs by John Aitken placed in the Large Dining Room (Figure 7.17) or any of the other Federal period furniture that entered his collection in Philadelphia or at Mount Vernon.[43]

In addition to his critical observations about art, we have a few remarks by Washington concerning artists themselves. Washington harbored some qualms about artists and their craft. Many came from humble backgrounds, and tension between artists/intellectuals and elite patrons is longstanding and widespread in history. Washington complained about artists' persistent desire for financial gain, and he singled out those who made money from the portraits they made of him, objecting that while he volunteered his time so that his image might become known, the artists profited financially. Calling portraitists, disparagingly, "these kind of people," he wrote to social equal Henry Lee on 3 July 1792:

> I am so heartily tired of the attendance which from one cause or another has been given [to] these kind of people, that it is now more than two years since I have resolved to sit no more for any of them and have adhered to it, except in instances where it has been requested by public bodies, or for a particular purpose (not of the Painters) and could not, without offence be refused.
>
> I have been led to make this resolution for another reason besides the irksomeness of sitting, and the time I loose by it— which is, that these productions have in my estimation, been made use of as a sort of tax on individuals by being engraved (and that badly) and hawked about or advertised for Sale.[44]

Washington disliked the "irksome" act of enduring the making of his portrait, and in particular he did not like the

FIGURE 7.17. Side chair, c. 1797, mahogany, 37.45″ (height) × 20.6″ (width) × 18.75″ (depth). Washington readily accepted the neoclassical style, and he ordered two dozen of these chairs and two sideboards from John Aitken of Philadelphia. Courtesy of the Mount Vernon Ladies' Association (W-2820).

process of sitting for a life mask.[45] Artists who annoyed Washington included the painter Gilbert Stuart, who once overslept for a sitting; rather than scolding the painter, the president vented his anger to the artist's servant. He was less patient with sculptor Joseph Wright, who dropped the life mask that he had painstakingly made of Washington. Washington then disappointed, and likely offended, the artist by refusing to sit through the ordeal again. On another occasion, he reported to Robert Morris that Wright "is said to be a little lazy."[46]

Washington had excellent relations with Charles Willson Peale, for whom the colonel first sat in 1772.[47] The men exchanged cordial letters and played horseshoes together at Mount Vernon. On 2 January 1774, Washington wrote in his diary: "Mr. Benjs. Dulany[,] Mr. Peale and Mr. Cox came here to Dinner, & stayd all Night." The next day, "Mr. Dulany & Mr. Cox went away after Breakfast as also did Mr. Custis to Maryland. Mr. Peale stayed."[48] Washington and Peale had much in common. They shared the experience of fighting in the Revolutionary War. Peale eventually bought a farm and for a time, like Washington, set out to live a retired agricultural life. Both were interested in unusual animals; Washington sent rare Chinese golden pheasants to Peale to be mounted in the exhibition rooms in Philadelphia. Washington visited Peale's museum "room" there in 1787, and Peale invited the president to "an Exhibition" including stuffed animals. After the visit, Peale wrote Washington that he had since added "a pair of Panthers, Male & female of full groath—most Terrifick Animals," a touch of the taste for the "gothic" shared between the two men.[49]

Washington liked artists, such as Peale, who possessed what he considered upstanding moral character. It was a sentiment shared by the contemporary elite in America. Thomas Jefferson played up to Washington's desires in this regard, telling the president of Jean-Antoine Houdon's fame in Europe and reassuring him that Houdon was of fine character, that is, "disinterested, generous, candid, & panting after glory: in every circumstance meriting your good opinion." Washington asserted to Lafayette that John Trumbull possessed merit "as a man and as an artist."[50] As with his attitudes toward other types of people, Washington seems to have had little interest in artists "born under Saturn"—those who displayed oddities or unsocial behavior.

Patron and Collector

Washington had his own particular purposes for the gathering and display of art objects, and the works at Mount Vernon carried a message that was appropriate to Washington himself, his life's achievements, and the site on the hilltop above the Potomac. Washington had a larger and broader art collection than most leading citizens in America at the end of the eighteenth century, and he far surpassed many of them. Even by 1799, the year of his death, extensive art collections with a wide range of subjects—portraits, landscapes, religious art, and curiosities—were rare in America, and the master of Mount Vernon was among the most important and thoughtful collectors of his generation in the new nation. Most Americans—lacking the funds, the desire to collect, access to galleries and dealers, and the social pressure to acquire fine two-dimensional art—had little art in their homes. Even among leading citizens it was common to find, beyond the usual fine furniture and other decorative arts (porcelain, silver tableware, mirrors, and so forth), mostly portraits and relatively few other kinds of artwork. Such was the case with nearly all of the Founding Fathers; John Adams famously stated that knowledge of painting, sculpture, and other fine arts was a subject for later generations of Americans to study and enjoy.[51] Of the Founding Fathers who bought and collected art during Washington's lifetime, only Jefferson rivaled him in the sphere of the fine arts. And unlike Jefferson, John Adams, Benjamin Franklin, John Jay, and Silas Deane, Washington never saw the private art collections of Europe or had the chance to purchase art while abroad. Other leading citizens in taste centers such as Philadelphia, New York, and Boston and Tidewater elites, such as George Mason of Gunston Hall, bought and displayed very fine furniture and other objects, but their display of two-dimensional art was dominated by portraiture.[52] Some collectors, including the Chews at Cliveden in Philadelphia and William Byrd of Westover, surpassed Washington in collecting garden sculpture, but Washington likely restrained himself in this sphere to keep his grounds unornamented.

In eighteenth-century America, George Washington was hardly alone in having a fine and varied art collection, even in the narrow circle of Tidewater elites. The Governor's Palace inventory of Lord Botetourt made in October 1770 indicates that he possessed many fine and decorative arts objects, including religious paintings associated with Roman Catholic traditions.[53] Thomas Jefferson owned a substantial art collection by 1790, much of it amassed in France during his time as minister. Jefferson's collection was notable for the number of oil paintings and the sophisticated variety of subject matter, including religious paintings.[54] The father-in-law of Martha Washington, John Custis, displayed a large collection of paintings and prints on diverse subjects in his house (Custis Square) in Williamsburg.[55] Washington corresponded with and visited William Hamilton of Philadelphia, whose fine houses, gardens, and art collection were widely admired. Hamilton, who was preceded in the family's efforts by his uncle James Hamilton (d. 1783), amassed a fine collection of marble figures, reliefs, oil paintings, and bronzes that was "distinct from most of their contemporaries" in its quality and extent.[56]

Over time, Washington attempted to gather fine art in a range of subject matter, in line with what was known to be characteristic of European collecting, although his collection was on a much smaller scale. George Washington was more than just another wealthy art collector, though, and his patronage and display were increasingly shaped by his unique social position and status as a national and world figure. He developed a predilection for collecting landscapes, which tied in with elaborate landscape gardening and the American setting. His systematic collection and display of art was propelled by his desire to raise the standard of the arts in America and to have his own walls stand up to the scrutiny of the many visitors, including Europeans, who would pass through his home.

Before he became the leader of a nation, Washington was a retired colonel and a well-to-do Chesapeake region farmer. His collecting before the Revolutionary War was fair but not extraordinary. The mansion house at that time did shelter a few portraits, including those by John Wollaston brought to the marriage by Martha, and Washington ordered from England some minor mantel and table ornaments and even

a few pieces of sculpture. Characteristically, his attempts at collecting were not haphazard. After expanding the mansion house and retiring in the late 1750s, he set out to collect sculpture appropriate for the home of a military man. In September 1759, Washington ordered from Robert Cary, his agent in London, six busts of military men and also a pair of "wild beasts" to fit into the "broken pediments" over doors on the ground floor of the house.[57] They were to be "Copper. Enamel. or Glazed." Except for the wild beasts, Cary could not obtain sculptures of the figures that Washington specified, namely, Alexander the Great, Julius Caesar, Charles of Sweden, the King of Prussia, Prince Eugene (of Savoy), the Duke of Marlborough (John Churchill), and "two furious Wild Beasts of any kind, not to exceed 18 inches in length & 12 in higth [sic] but as near that size as may be[,] drawn as if approaching each other & eager to engage, at the distance of about 4 feet, to be the same Colour as those above."[58] The personal care that Washington took concerning the iconography, interactions, and color harmony is remarkable, making this an impressive commission of a meaningful and extensive iconographic program. So that Cary could visualize the intended locations in the mansion for the busts of the Duke of Marlborough and Prince Eugene of Savoy, Washington sketched out for him the form of the pediments in question.[59]

The busts that Washington wanted were unavailable on the ready-made market in London. Cary, working with local dealers, offered to supply Washington instead with statues of "Homer, Virgil, Horace, Cicero, Plato, Aristotle, Seneca, Galens, Vestall Virgin[,] Faustina[,] Chaucer, Spencer, Johnson, Shakespear[e], Beaumont[,] Fletcher, Milton, Prior, Pope, Congreve, Swift, Addison, Dryden, Locke, Newton." These apparently did not meet Washington's needs, and from the initial request Cary ended up sending him only the lions ("Two Lyons after the Antique Lyon's in Italy finisht Neat & Brozd with Copper"). Washington did receive other smaller pieces, including "A Groupe of Aeneas carrying his Father out of Troy with 4 Statues viz.—his Father Anchises, his wife Creusa, himself and his Son Ascanius, neatly finisht and bronzd with Copper," plus a "Bacchus & Flora, finisht Neat, & bronzd wt. Copper," and ornamented Vases with "Faces & Festoons of Grapes & Vine Leaves." The London supplier of the statuettes, somewhat condescendingly, offered Washington a suggestion for how to group the figures on a mantelpiece.[60]

Although he did not obtain busts in this early period, Washington clearly knew of the tradition, born in the Renaissance, of adorning a room with "uomini famosi" or series of great men. Much later he returned to the theme, partly using gifts, and placed busts of himself, admiral John Paul Jones, and French finance minister Jacques Necker in his private study, along with a painted portrait of his half-brother Lawrence Washington. The bronzed terracotta lions ordered in 1759 ended up over doors in the central passage; the copies still visible there today are inconspicuous (Figure 7.18). Fierce lions, redolent of the masculine and warlike, were more appropriate to Washington in 1759 than after the Revolutionary War, when he developed a more peaceable iconography at Mount Vernon. Over time, he did hang gifts representing battle scenes, but these formed a minor part of the iconography of his house and were largely pushed off to the side. An oil painting on canvas representing *The Battle of Minden,* a gift from Vaughan, ended up in a bedroom, largely out of view of visitors. Washington came to prefer to display portraits, landscapes, and seascapes, mixed with sundry religious art, mythological imagery, and genre scenes.

As he developed his collection of paintings, prints, and sculpture, and decorative art, Washington was sensitive to all details of his aesthetic surroundings. Early on, Washington paid little heed to particulars of color. In 1757, he sent only general orders for wallpaper to Richard Washington in England, asking for "Paper differing in their Colours," for various rooms and "paper of a good kind & colour for a Dining Room." Over time his choices became more sophisticated. For the Large Dining Room, Washington wanted

Philadelphia merchant Clement Biddle to send him a "small slipe of the plain blew & green paper—with a sample of the paupier-Maché & gilded borders." In June 1784, Washington left Biddle specific instructions to get "70 yds of gilded Border for papered rooms (of the kind you shewed me when I was in Phildelpa)—That which is most light and Airy I should prefer—I do not [know] whether it is usual to fasten it on with Brads or Glew."[61] Washington also asked a social equal, William Hamilton of Philadelphia, for his opinion about paving, and he thus took a similar approach to getting information about fine wall coverings in Philadelphia. As for the trim in the New Room in 1787 (Figure 7.19), he wrote from Philadelphia to manager George Augustine Washington that "the Wood part of the New room may be painted of any tolerably fashionable colour—so as to serve present purposes; and this might be a buff. 'Tis more than probable it will receive a *finishing* colour hereafter. The buff should be of the lightest kind, inclining to white." In addition, he knowingly recommended that small brushes be used for painting the detailed moldings.[62]

Washington's sensitive eye for coloristic and tonal harmonies is further revealed in a letter from George Augustine Washington, in which the manager of Mount Vernon told Washington that smoke from the fireplace in the Large Dining Room was making the color of the room "a gloomy one, but supose on acc[oun]t of the firniture you would have it of the same."[63] He meant either that the president wanted the walls to remain as they had been so they would still match the color of the upholstery and curtains or (less likely) that Washington would not mind the green walls turning brown from the smoke, as that would make them harmonize with the mahogany chairs, table, and mirrors. In either case, this exchange shows that George Augustine was aware of Washington's desire for visual harmonies.

Washington's interest in details of interior decoration continued to the end. He asked Tobias Lear to acquire a new carpet for the West Parlor. Since the furniture was uphol-

FIGURE 7.18. View of the central passage, Mount Vernon, looking east. We see here above the door the two terracotta lions from c. 1755–1757. The lions survive from the early years of Washington's collecting, when he hoped to have wild beasts and busts of famous men adorning the overdoors in his house. Courtesy of the Mount Vernon Ladies' Association.

FIGURE 7.19. Stucco and wallpaper trim in the Large Dining Room. Washington left the particulars of the stucco designs to his craftsmen, but he himself arranged for the colors of the room and the gilded trim on the wallpaper. Courtesy of the Mount Vernon Ladies' Association.

stered in blue, he thought that the "the ground or principal flowers in it ought to be blue also" and that the carpet should have a suitable border (of unstated appearance).[64] Sometimes Washington simply wanted a general color, as when he ordered curtains to be dyed green (no shade specified), but other times he had a more specific idea of what he wanted, as when Lear—writing to Clement Biddle but probably reflecting Washington's wishes—ordered for the presidential mansion in Philadelphia a carpet with a "Pea-Green ground with white or light flowers or spots."[65] Washington conveyed his specific ideas for acquiring some pieces, writing to Biddle that he was "in want of Glass (for a Particular pur-

pose)" and asking for a quantity to be sent in the "Inclosed Pattern," either referring to a drawing he was providing or an actual specimen to be copied.[66]

Washington was particularly concerned about getting the right frames for his two-dimensional works of art. Making no references to the framed prints themselves, he wrote in May 1786 to engraver Joseph Brown of England, maker of portraits of Washington and Gen. Nathanael Greene, that "the frames of these pictures are quite equal to my wishes, & you will please to accept my best acknowledgments of it; & assurances that an apology for their being inferior to those sent to Congress, was altogether unnecessary." In 1795, he wanted Trumbull to supply handsome frames like one he had sent earlier. When Washington bought a number of prints in Philadelphia during the presidency, he personally ordered the frames and took careful measurements of each one in a handwritten inventory.[67]

By looking at his ordering of carriages or "chariots," we gain a further sense of Washington's eye and insight into his role as patron. While in Philadelphia, Washington wrote to Samuel Powel in July 1787 that he was following the progress of the painting of his coach: "Having seen some of his work and . . . induced thereto by the further consideration of seeing every day as I pass his workshop the progress he makes."[68] Earlier, Washington had taken care when ordering a chariot from abroad to leave explicit instructions for the color and form. Washington wrote to London agent Robert Cary on 6 June 1768:

> My old Chariot havg run its race, & gone through as many stages as I coud conveniently make it travel, is now renderd incapable of any further Service; The intent of this Letter therefore is to desire you will bespeak me a New one, time enough to come out with the Goods (I shall hereafter write for) by Captn Johnstoun, or some other Ship.
>
> As these are kind of Articles, that last with care a gt number of years, I woud willingly have the Chariot you may now send me made in the newest taste, handsome, genteel, & light; yet not slight & consequently unserviceable. To be made of the best Seasond Wood, & by a celebrated Workman. The last Importation which I have seen, besides the customary Steel springs have others that play in a Brass barrel, & contribute at one & the sametime to the ease & Ornament of the Carriage; One of these kind therefore woud be my choice; & Green being a colour little apt, as I apprehend, to fade, & grateful to the Eye, I would give it the preference unless any other colour more in vogue & equally lasting is entitled to precedency in that case I woud be governd by fashion. A light gilding on the mouldings (that is round the Pannels) & any other Ornaments that may not have a heavy & tawdry look (together with my arms agreeable to the Impression here sent) might be added, by way of decoration. A lining of a handsome, lively col[ore]d leather of good quality, I shd also prefer; such as green, blew, or &ca as may best suit the colr of the outside. let the box that slips under Seat, be as large as it conveniently can be made (for the benefit of Stoage upon a journey) and to have a Pole (not Shafts) for the Wheel Horses to draw by—together with a handsome sett of Harness for four middle sized Horses orderd in such a manner as to suit either two Postilions (without a box) or a box & one Postilion—The Box being made to fix on, and take of occasionally, with a hammel Cloth &ca suitable to the lining. On the Harness let my Crest be engravd.[69]

Although Washington said that he might be "governd by fashion" in the choice of color, he had a good idea of what he wanted, and the details of the message speak for themselves, including his notion that green was "grateful to the Eye," which has repercussions for his collection of landscape art and his gardening at Mount Vernon. He had a sensitive eye to want a light gilding that would help the overall appearance avoid a "heavy & tawdry" look. Along these same lines, in 1790, when Washington was having "repairs and alterations" made to his old coach, he offered the craftsmen several suggestions concerning the painting, silvering, and plated moldings that might be added to unify the appearance of the whole.[70]

One commission in the realm of clothing will throw some light on Washington's sense of decorum and beauty, two elements ideally present in all of his art commissions. In 1799, he was concerned about the new uniform being made for him as head of the American army, which he was prepared to lead in case of war with France. Washington wrote to Secretary of War James McAlpin on the subject; McAlpin and others would advise on the design, but Washington had his say: "Let your blue cloth be of the best & softest French or Spanish; and the finest you can procure, of a deep colour. And the Buff of the very best sort, fine, & not inclining to Yellow or Orange, like what I have been accustomed to wear. The buttons are to be plain, flat, and of the best double gilt . . . The waistcoat should be straight breasted, that is without lapels. And the Cuffs of the Coat neither large, nor tight; observing a just medium between the two."[71] He wanted a coat that would be just right, of deep color, fine fabric, and a kind of Golden Mean of fit between bulky and tight.

FIGURE 7.20. Garniture set, 1768–1770, porcelain, enamel, and gilding, 12.75″ (height of smaller vases) and 18.75″ (height of central vase). This side of the set (also pictured in Figure 6.18) shows animals in landscapes. Courtesy of the Mount Vernon Ladies' Association (W-972, W-2260).

It is harder to judge Washington's taste from objects he received as gifts, but his acceptance, use, and placement of them are telling. Samuel Vaughan sent a three-part garniture set to Washington in November 1786 (Figure 7.20, cf. Figure 6.18); the donor intended the trio to go on the marble mantelpiece he had sent earlier for the Large Dining Room.[72] Vaughan knew Washington's goal of establishing his reputation as the new Cincinnatus, that is, as the citizen-hero giving up power and retiring to his agricultural estate. The chimneypiece shows agrarian scenes appropriate for Washington and Mount Vernon. The vases also include iconography well chosen for Washington, including landscapes on one side and animals in nature on the other. (Washington had long before asked for imagery of "wild beasts" when he wrote to London agent Robert Cary in the 1750s.) Although

somewhat ornate, these vases, decorated by the Irish painter Jefferyes Hammett O'Neale for the Worcester factory in 1768–1770, are in a vigorous, classicizing shape.[73] Washington's choice to place them on the mantel was astute, as they work well with the landscape themes of the Large Dining Room, and they echo the rich classicism of the marble mantelpiece and its reliefs (see Figure 7.20 and Plate 32). Washington responded to Vaughan with his usual minimal critical language, and he promised to accede to the donor's suggestion for their location at Mount Vernon: "The picture of a battle in Germany, & the Jarrs came very safe. The first is fine: the latter is also fine and exceedingly handsome— they shall occupy the place you have named for them."[74] Washington, who seems from this quote to have liked the jars better, eventually relegated the oil painting of the *Battle of Minden* (a British victory in the Seven Years War) to the downstairs bedroom, a private and "old" room in the mansion house (with paneling perhaps from the time of Lawrence). Washington likely did not favor the picture's martial and anti-French iconography for so central a spot in the house as the overmantel in the New Room, and he replaced it with *Moonlight on Rocky Coast* (Plate 32), which extended the range of his landscape theme with a painting that is a nocturne and a rocky, romantic seascape.

After the Revolutionary War, and even more after being president, Washington was aware of his place in history and of the precedents he was setting. In the arts, he was keenly aware of the historical importance of patronage by leaders. He wrote in 1788, reflecting the widespread admiration in Anglo-American society for the first Roman emperor: "Augustus was the professed and munificent rewarder of poetical merit—nor did he lose the return of having his atcheivments [*sic*] immortalised in song. The Augustan age is proverbial for intellectual refinement and elegance in composition; in it the harvest of laurels and bays was wonderfully mingled together." Washington noted elsewhere in a letter to the Marquis de Lafayette that under Louis XIV in France and Queen Anne in England the literary arts flourished.[75] After 1784, Washington felt a special mission as a patron of the arts, and his collecting reflected that sense of responsibility, which is shown in his gathering of diverse and fine art objects, his patriotic fostering of American landscape imagery, and his preference for art that was elegant and restrained. He expended his time and money as a collector and patron, although—like Jefferson and others of his generation—he feared that other Americans would not be able to acquire fine art. He wrote in 1795 to the Italian sculptor Giuseppe Ceracchi that Americans "cannot spare money for the purposes of there gratif[icatio]ns and ornimental figures as in the wealthy countries of Europe."[76]

Whether the objects came in as purchases or gifts, Washington was interested in the subject matter of works he collected, and he thoughtfully placed them in the mansion house in effective and meaningful ways. Because of the lack of full inventories, we are uncertain about the display of art objects at the presidential mansions in New York and Philadelphia. We have seen that he hung the prominent landscapes by Winstanley and Beck at the executive mansion in Philadelphia. A chief purpose of the houses was to entertain guests at frequent receptions, and some of these guests left accounts commenting on the display of certain pieces, including the ceramics, pyramids, and the silver plateau from France. Many of these pieces were suitable for a presidential mansion but less so for a private residence, and other pieces were not needed for his house in Virginia, including much of the furniture, some of which he tried (unsuccessfully) to sell to the incoming president, John Adams. The extravagant table pieces ("Images[,] flowers (artificial)[,] &ca.") used in Philadelphia were perhaps inappropriate for Mount Vernon, and in 1797 Washington ordered sold "a Platteau in nine pieces" and other figures. Those pieces that remained unsold went to Mount Vernon with Washington.[77] A marble sculpture of Washington by Ceracchi was on loan at the mansion in Philadelphia, but Washington made it clear to Ceracchi that he would not purchase it. (It is now at the Metropolitan Museum of Art in New York.)

As a result, undoubtedly, of his new position as world leader and role model for America, Washington's fine painting and print collection grew considerably from 1784 to 1799. His personal role was decisive. He wrote to Mary White Morris of the "Pictures" in the two largest rooms of the executive mansion in Philadelphia, "all of which were fancy pieces of my own chusing."[78] He was fond of the works of his "own chusing," and these he took to Mount Vernon after the presidency. The public apparently was disappointed that he did not sell them, as he did some decorative arts. He wrote to Biddle on 29 January 1798: "If the Plateaux are not sold, nor a probability of getting nearly what they cost—say currency for Sterling—I request that they may be carefully packed up and sent to me, together with the two smallest of the large groups of Porcelain, and the twelve single images (Arts & Sciences) with which my Table, on Public days, was ornamented. The large group (Apollo instructing the Shepherds) and the two Vases, may be sold for whatever they will fetch."[79] In short, when Washington left Philadelphia for Mount Vernon in 1797, he took two-dimensional objects with him, kept much furniture and chinaware, but he sold or attempted to sell some works less suited for what he was fancying to the world was his "small Villa" or "rural cottage."

A list of prints Washington purchased in Philadelphia during his presidency shows the scrupulous care he took in his collection.[80] The titles or subject matter are expressed in Washington's own way on a handwritten list that throws light on his understanding of the art in question. He took careful note of the "Prints purchased and at what prices," recording with a clear hand the inventory number and cost. He then made a separate list of the "size of the impression" and another list of each design area's dimensions ("size within the impression"). Overall, his emphasis was on subject matter and not attribution. He made few remarks about authorship, never noting, for example, Claude Lorrain by name, although he did record the names of "Hobima" (Meindert Hobbema), (Thomas) Gainsborough, and "[George] Smith of Chichester." Washington listed a range of works, nearly all landscapes or subjects in landscape settings, in addition to a few battle scenes. He made special note of which works were colored in. A remarkable number of these prints relate to landscape, in whole or in part. Many are straightforward natural scenes (e.g., *Morning and Evening, Moonlight* (see Figure 6.15), and *Storm with Lightning*). Some show views of water, as is consistent with nonportrait oil paintings that he had collected over the years, such as the prints of the "Whale fisheries" and "Views of the Po." Classical subjects set in bucolic nature form another leitmotif, and Washington listed "Cupid's Pastime," "Nymphs," "Diana and Nymphs," "Venus attired," "Judgment of Paris," and others of that type. Many of these prints survive or are identifi-

able and substitutes have been found, and they are presently displayed at the mansion house in a manner consistent with their original positions and manner of hanging.

For eighteenth-century America, the gathering of landscape art at Washington's mansion house at Mount Vernon—including paintings and prints—was highly unusual and foretold the rise of that genre in the Romantic period and the nationalizing sentiments expressed in the Hudson River School and beyond. Works of art with water and land views combined occupied a substantial part of his collection and tied it to the views from the house and grounds of the estate. Portraiture was widely in vogue in early America, and a taste for landscape art was growing only slowly in the later eighteenth century. Washington was in the avant-garde in this area of American collecting. By the end of his life, Washington had on display nineteen landscapes or seascapes in the three spaces of the mansion nearest the river view: the Large Dining Room, the central passage, and the Little Parlor, the last of which has two windows with exposure to the river. These nineteen works did not include scenes in the public rooms with water views; one such work, hanging in the Small Dining Room, was the portrait of Lafayette at the Battle of Yorktown, with a view in the middle ground of the "riviere de Chesapeake."[81]

The inventory made after George Washington's death and accounts by period visitors indicate that he cleverly carried out a pervasive and thoughtful grouping of works of art in differently themed rooms. The Little Parlor was the latest to join the ranks of the public rooms. Until 1797 it had served as a bedroom, but Washington turned it into a genteel space of leisure and entertainment, furnished with a spinet and Windsor chairs (Plate 26). The room near the portico had a river view, and after 1797 it contained sea battle scenes and stormy or romantic seascapes (Figures 7.21 and 7.22), each reinforcing the emotional effect of the other. There were two storms at sea, one sea fight, one "distressed situation" of the fighting ship Quebec, and two prints of whale fisheries. The seascapes corresponded well with the

FIGURE 7.21. Engraved by Fittler and Lerpinière, after Richard Paton, *The Distressed Situation of the Quebec and the Surveillante a French Ship of War,* 1780, aquatint, 19.5″ × 26.35″. Washington's iconographic theme for the Little Parlor included this work, called in the estate inventory "the distressed situation of the Quesbec &c." Courtesy of the Mount Vernon Ladies' Association (M93/T).

FIGURE 7.22. Engraved by Robert Dodd, *The North West or Davis's Streights Whale Fishery,* 1789, aquatint, 16″ × 25.75″. Whale fishing alongside the icebergs of the north Atlantic was an exotic, difficult, and fairly new activity at this time. Along with other dramatic sea scenes, this work was placed in the Little Parlor (listed in the estate inventory as "the whale fishery at Davies Streights"). Courtesy of the Mount Vernon Ladies' Association (M93/Q).

FIGURE 7.23. Robert Edge Pine, *Fanny Bassett*, 1785, oil on canvas, 24.75″ × 19.5″. Family portraits were hung in the West Parlor and greeted visitors as they entered the home through the west door. A niece of Martha, Fanny Bassett married George Augustine Washington, who served for a time as trusted estate manager. Courtesy of the Mount Vernon Ladies' Association (W-1488).

view of the Potomac offered outside the window, and they contrasted with the calm landscape imagery in the adjoining New Room and central passage. The Little Parlor contained sundry other pictures, some identified in the wills, others unknown. The "wrought" work (probably needle work) representing the "likeness of a deer" (paired with a "chicken in a basket") was, like the water views, appropriate insofar as it stood in the room that overlooked the defunct deer park. The sensible and suggestive grouping of works in the Little Parlor was not unnoticed at the time. German visitor Friedrich Wilhelm Hoeninghaus noticed the sea battles in the

little parlor, where he breakfasted with Washington in 1798, calling the room a "Seeschlachten dekoriertes Zimmer nach dem Potomac hin," a "room toward the Potomac decorated with sea battles." Similarly, Niemcewicz described the Little Parlor as "decorated with beautiful engravings representing storms and seascapes."[82]

The front (west) parlor, the first to be seen by most visitors, was graced with numerous family portraits. Although they had no children together, the Washingtons sheltered in their household and under their guardianship a number of children, including grandchildren and others (such as the son of the Marquis de Lafayette). Their images, along with those of George and Martha, graced the West Parlor's walls, and the room conveyed to visitors the family aspect of the home. These works included portraits by Robert Pine, such as the one of Fanny Bassett, Martha's niece who lived in the mansion during the presidency (Figure 7.23).[83] Also in the room was a now unidentifiable portrait of Thomas Law, husband of Martha's grandchild Betsey Parke Custis, and a pair of pastels (c. 1795) by James Sharples of George and Martha (visible in Plate 6).[84] Instead of the heroic imagery and public figures that dominated the wall of the Small Dining Room across the hall, the West Parlor's iconography was intimate and familial.

Hung in the West Parlor was the earliest known portrait of Washington, the 1772 painting by Charles Willson Peale showing him in his colonel's uniform of the Virginia Regiment of the British military; the work includes a prospect on the left side and a verdant backdrop and a stream in the background (Plate 30). Washington himself recorded little about the work, noting in his diary only that he posed for Peale in his uniform one day and that at another sitting "Mr. Peale finished my face."[85] Depicting Washington as a leader in backwoods military action, the portrait was made long after his military career with the Virginia Regiment. The background resonates with his earlier work as a surveyor, as well as his interests as an estate owner. Thus, the portrait neatly brings together the activities of Washington's youth up to those to 1772, when he was intent on beautify-ing the natural surroundings about his mansion house. Judg-ing from what we know of Peale's working methods and from Washington's character, there is every reason to think that the colonel himself had a role in choosing not only the uniform but also the verdant landscape, water element, and vista in the background.

The nearby central passage of the mansion house was dominated by prints, mostly ideal landscapes in the Clau-dian mode, including those with mythological themes, but as in the other rooms, especially the dining rooms, there was a political element here. The hallway included two objects related to the history of liberty in France—a drawing of the Bastille made after revolutionaries reduced it to ruins and a key to the Bastille (Figure 7.24). The key was kept in a wooden and glass box, where a copy resides today. (The original is in the museum gallery at Mount Vernon.) Which door or doors this key opened will always be impossible to confirm. The key was a gift from that champion of liberty, the Marquis de Lafayette, but French royalist Chateaubri-and, visiting the president in Philadelphia, disapproved of the exhibition of this "toy" and the mob that brought down the prison.[86] Washington displayed it prominently at Mount Vernon to suggest the influence of the American Revolution on the spread of liberty in Europe. At first, Americans "looked at the key with indifference, as if wondering why it had been sent," as Louis Otto, French chargé d'affaires, noted on 4 August 1790, but it was often mentioned in ac-counts by visitors as a highlight of the collection.[87] In dis-playing the key, Washington was acting in the tradition of the *Kunst- und Wunderkammern,* chambers of art and "mar-vels," which first flourished in the sixteenth century. Jeffer-son was to create such a chamber on a grander scale in his entrance hall at Monticello, where he hung Native Ameri-can decorations, animal oddities, and assorted prints. Washington kept in the private space of his study "some In-dian presents," but the key to the Bastille was the most prominent and meaningful "curiosity" at Mount Vernon.

This successful exhibition of politically charged material worked as an inspiration throughout the nineteenth cen-tury and still does today. In Washington's time, a carved stone model of the Bastille was kept on the portico (and much used and greatly damaged over time), taking the ico-nography of liberty from the central passage to the linked portico space.

Down a side hallway from the central passage was George Washington's study, which held his books and a writing desk and served as his retreat from guests and family alike (Plate 8). Few visitors had a chance to see Washington's study, al-though he took the trouble to create a small but thoughtful grouping of portraits of famous men and other virile imag-ery. He put a bust of John Paul Jones, given to Washington by Jones himself, in his study, placing it "opposite to my own [bust] . . . on a similar bracket," an honor that embarrassed Jones. Washington adorned the room with representations of other famous men, including Jacques Necker, a French finance minister to Louis XVI of some fame at the time. Ad-miral and Count d'Estaing (Charles-Hector Théodat, Comte d'Estaing) sent that bust, carved by Louis Simon Boizot, to Washington.[88] In addition to the Houdon bust of Washing-ton, the study also contained Joseph Wright's highly classi-cized plaster profile, which harnesses Washington's aloof-ness and makes it palatable through its timeless style (Figure 7.25). Not least in significance in the room was the portrait of Lawrence Washington, George's beloved half-brother and early builder at Mount Vernon (Figure 7.26). The inventory after Washington's death also indicates that the room con-tained a "hunting piece." (That work is today not identi-fied.) The chamber included Revolutionary, historical prints by John Trumbull, in which Washington figures promi-nently. Perhaps he thought these were too self-centered for inclusion in the public parts of the house. The room was used for study, writing, and as an office, and while overseers or others might have conducted business there, the room was largely off-limits to outside visitors. A few distinguished guests, such as Philadelphia mayor Samuel Powel, gained en-

FIGURE 7.24. View of the central passage at Mount Vernon. Washington grouped together the key to the Bastille and a drawing of it in ruins. The stone model of the Bastille kept on the portico further echoed the theme. Courtesy of the Mount Vernon Ladies' Association.

trance to the "very handsome" chamber during Washington's lifetime. Despite the small number of visitors, Washington was interested in having a fine surface to the room, and he had the chamber walls grain painted in 1786.[89] In addition to the exhibited art, he kept prints there in a portfolio and twenty-three prints in storage on the third floor.

From a short passage near the study, one can glimpse the Small Dining Room. This room, one of the four original downstairs rooms from Lawrence's time, ended up with a fairly unified collection of heroic images, consistent with its position as a public room. The iconography was in large part political and inspirational, with historical and religious prints.

FIGURE 7.25. Joseph Wright, *Profile Portrait of George Washington,* 1783–1785, plaster, 16.75″ × 13.75″. This fine and highly classicizing relief portrait seems to have hung in George Washington's study by 1799 (inventory: "1 Profile in plaister"). Courtesy of the Mount Vernon Ladies' Association (W-2261).

FIGURE 7.26. Anonymous, *Lawrence Washington,* c. 1743, oil on canvas, 30.5″ × 25″. Washington placed this portrait in his study along with other masculine images, including a hunting scene and busts of great men. Courtesy of the Mount Vernon Ladies' Association (W-126).

The room contained portraits of Benjamin Franklin, Gen. Anthony Wayne, the American scientist David Rittenhouse, Gen. Nathanael Greene, and the Marquis de Lafayette "on conclusion of the late war."[90] Also there was Robert Pine's *America,* an engraving including images of a number of American patriots (gift from George William Fairfax), and *Death of General Wolfe* and *William Penn's Treaty with the Indians* (both after Benjamin West). An engraving after Copley's *Death of the Earl of Chatham* was a gift from Copley to Washington (Figure 7.27). The room included two prints with scenes of Alfred the Great undertaking grand and moral acts, including *Alfred visiting his Noblemen* and Alfred "dividing his loaf with the Pilgrim." Washington included his

own image in the room but only in the familial context of the notable group portrait in Savage's stipple engraving *The Washington Family* ("the Washington family of Mount Vernon"), one of the four that he received from the artist in 1798 (see Plate 5).

The Small Dining Room was dominated by prints, while the Large Dining Room was the architectural and fine arts showcase of the house and featured Washington's best paintings. It was among the finest rooms created in eighteenth-century America. Despite the rather modest floor covering of matting, visitors were impressed by the architecture, including the large proportions, the high ceiling, the Palladian (Venetian) window, the stucco work, and the fine decorative

FIGURE 7.27. Engraved by Francesco Bartolozzi, after John Singleton Copley, *The Death of the Earl of Chatham*, 1791, engraving, 25.75″ × 32.5″. Washington displayed this work in his Small Dining Room (inventory: "death of the late Earl of Chatham"), part of the heroic or moralizing images he placed there. Photo: Courtesy of the Mount Vernon Ladies' Association (Print-5228/A).

arts, including the marble fireplace surround.[91] In 1796, Washington asked that his new Windsor chairs go into the room, but after the presidency he installed there instead the fine and up-to-date side chairs and the pair of Sheraton sideboards (see Plate 4) that John Aitken in Philadelphia had made for him while he was president.[92] In addition to housing the landscape works we have seen by William Winstanley and George Beck, and the anonymous *Moonlight on Rocky Coast,* the Large Dining Room was the main art gallery in the house, replete with a number of prints that supplemented the large landscapes, the scale of which were best accommodated by the thirty-two-foot long room. Some of the works have an intriguing subject matter. Washington must have been happy to include in this public space a kind of antiwar work, the *Dead Soldier* by Joseph Wright of Derby, two prints of which were given to him and which he hung in the Large Dining Room. The scene is pathetic, with the dead soldier being mourned by his newly widowed wife and infant child (Figure 7.28). A print of Louis XVI was a

rare monarchical image in a republican house, no doubt chosen because he supported the American cause (Figure 7.29).

Religious works were present in the house, some explicit, like the print *Descent from the Cross,* others of moral/religious themes, such as *A Parson* in the Washingtons' bedroom.[93] In the Large Dining Room hung two pastels of half-length figures of the Virgin Mary and Saint John the Baptist (Plate 31). (The two works later fell into private hands; the *Virgin* has returned to Mount Vernon, and the painting of the Baptist remains in a private collection.)[94] These delicate pastel works, displayed in a prominent place in the room that serves as the main art gallery, are unusual for the house in that they are religious in theme, Continental European (probably Italian, mid-eighteenth century), and ornately framed. The Madonna image is sentimental in content and feathery in execution, characteristic of pastels. The Virgin Mary, in particular, is a rather unusual subject for any Protestant collection in the early United States. Overall, the pair might seem more appropriate for a Rococo Venetian palace

FIGURE 7.28. Engraved by James Heath, after Joseph Wright of Derby, *The Dead Soldier,* 1797, aquatint, proof print, 20″ × 25″. Courtesy of the Mount Vernon Ladies' Association (Print-5227).

than a "republican" house in America, especially in a room so carefully designed around landscape oils and prints of war and famous men.

A few considerations may help explain Washington's prominent placement of the pair. Although they are recognizable today as middling copies or as only competent religious images from mid-eighteenth-century Italy, they would have been deemed fine pictures in the Anglo-American context of the late eighteenth century. Even the best English collections at this time contained a large number of mediocre copies after Italian and French pictures. The two pastels help to turn the Large Dining Room into an international picture gallery, and they would have been considered luxury items in late eighteenth-century Virginia. As for the iconography, religious art was hardly unprecedented for the colonies or young nation. The Governor's Palace in Williamsburg contained three large pictures of Roman Catholic subjects, according to the Botetourt inventory of 1770, and Hudson Valley Dutch and some ethnic German homes in

America contained religious pictures.[95] We do not know whether Washington bought the *Virgin Mary* and *Saint John the Baptist* or received them as gifts. Such small-scale religious works as this were often intended for private devotion in smaller chambers or other private spaces, but he did not put them in a bedroom or hallway upstairs. Just as Washington perhaps kept an old-fashioned, clipped part of his upper garden so that foreign (Continental) visitors would feel at home, these pictures could have served a similar purpose. They show the breadth and the (literal) catholicity of his taste, and made his picture gallery more universal and familiar to potential visitors, especially French, Italian, or other Catholic viewers. A final possible reason for their presence and exhibition at Mount Vernon is that Saint John the Baptist was a kind of patron saint of the Freemasons. Washington belonged to that group and accepted an invitation to a Masonic dinner in Alexandria for St. John the Baptist's Day on 24 June 1784. Knowing how the pair of pictures entered Washington's collection would throw light on their

FIGURE 7.29. Engraved by Charles-Clément Bervic, after An-toine-Francois Callet, *Louis Seize,* c. 1790, engraving (with original frame), 28.25″ × 21.5″. Louis XVI helped the American revolution-ary cause, and Washington had his portrait adorn the walls of the Large Dining Room. Courtesy of the Mount Vernon Ladies' As-sociation (W-767A–B).

purpose and meaning for him, but Washington must have liked the subject matter of Saint John.

The less-seen second floor contained a smattering of two-dimensional works on various subjects. Some bedrooms contained prints that Washington bought in Philadelphia as president, including works after Claude Lorrain and Hob-bema. A work perhaps too erotic for the downstairs formal rooms, *Nymphs Bathing* (Christian Wilhelm Ernst Diet-rich) was placed in "the first room on the second floor," that

is, the first bedroom to the left after the stairs (Figure 7.30). Washington could have hidden the work in a portfolio, but the style accorded well with the neoclassical style and with the idyllic subject matter elsewhere in the residence. Still, the work was fairly daring for an American home of the 1790s, embodying subject matter of little gravitas, and Washington did not choose it for a well-trafficked space downstairs. A large-scale oil painting of the Marquis de La-fayette was placed in a second floor bedroom because there was already a portrait of him downstairs. In 1785, Washing-ton received a portrait of Lafayette and his family and hung it in the West Parlor, fulfilling the general's promise to hang the work in "the best place in my House."[96]

The upstairs bedrooms were the place to hang secondary works of art, but some works in Washington's collection were not displayed at all, likely for ideological reasons. For example, Washington rejected, although in polite fashion, a gift of a portrait of Louis XV, saying that he could not place it in a conspicuous place where the whole world could ad-mire it.[97] He himself went to war against Louis XV, and it is hardly surprising that he would not accept his portrait. On the other hand, Washington did not hesitate to hang a full-length, beautifully framed portrait of Louis XVI in the Large Dining Room, no doubt because this monarch helped the American cause during the Revolution (see Figure 7.29). He kept other items in his collection in cabinets. There were, for example, five prints of Alexander the Great (by Pieter Stevens van Gunst, after Charles Le Brun) by long dead artists. (This was unusual for Mount Vernon; even works after Claude and Hobbema were "modern" produc-tions.)[98] The subject matter did not suit George Washing-ton of the 1790s; Alexander the Great—conqueror and im-perial ruler of a distant civilization—fit poorly with the other iconographic emphases at Mount Vernon. Similarly, in a posthumous act of deaccessioning, Washington—again perhaps for political reasons—directed in his last will the return to the Earl of Buchan of Scotland a small box the earl had given him in 1793. The box was made from the oak that

FIGURE 7.30. Christian Wilhelm Ernst Dietrich, *Nymphs Bathing*, c. 1765–1774, stipple engraving, 26.5″ × 33″. Perhaps thinking the work too frivolous or erotic for the public rooms downstairs, Washington hung this in a bedroom on the second floor. Courtesy of Yale University Art Gallery, New Haven. Gift of de Lancey Kountze, B.A. 1899 (1939.59).

sheltered Scottish patriot William Wallace, making it a highly charged political piece that, unlike the key to the Bastille, Washington chose not to display in his mansion house.[99]

Some early visitors praised the collection in general, and a few noted the groupings of works of art in rooms by themes. Several commented on the portraits in the West Parlor that served as an introduction to the family. For his part, Joshua Brookes, a young Englishman, noted in 1799—conflating the hall with the Little Parlor—that "the passage or [central] hall was hung round with many trophies of American valor by sea and land, besides several beautiful views and landscapes." The Little Parlor contained "several views," while the Large Dining Room housed a "number of fine paintings by known artists, and two in a particularly bold style (this was the pinacoteca)."[100] Sally Foster Otis had just the kind of reaction that Washington would have wanted: at Mount Vernon, she wrote, there is "a large Hall [New Room] hung with the most elegant painting from all parts of Europe (I

presume presents)—himself & favorite horse not the least interesting."[101] It is noteworthy that Otis already minimized Washington's reputation as a collector, as she assumed (wrongly) that the works were all gifts and not a combination of gifts, purchases, and commissions. For his part, poet John Searson, who visited in May 1799, stated with admiration: "The rooms adorned with pictures very fine, / That ev'n a prince might there with pleasure dine."[102]

Not every part of the collection was inside the house. Two objects that graced his house and grounds and were visible to all were the sundial (Plate 10) and the weathervane (Plate 25). The sundial was more than an eye-catcher in the center of a lawn: it symbolized the essence of his estate as the center of a working farm. Many visitors noted Washington's punctuality.[103] He kept to a strict schedule in making his rounds on his farms, writing letters, and turning in for the night. Eating began within five minutes of the appointed mealtime, whether all guests were seated or not. In his diary entries on the hunt, Washington usually marked the time needed to catch a fox or pursue one when discovered. Punctuality was a famous trait among Virginia planters, and tutor Philip Vickers Fithian described the regularity of Robert Carter III and his family at Nomini Hall.[104] Jefferson did Washington better with the size and complexity of his clock and calendar at Monticello, but that impressive machine appeared in the entrance hall amid other objects and gadgets. Washington's sundial is simple in form, modest in size, and helped set a sober mood to the farm and house.

Even more fraught with meaning was the "bird" (surely a dove) of peace weathervane. The iconographic significance of this is so obvious as to be almost heavy-handed, but it did stand as an appropriate crowning element on the home of the new Cincinnatus. This feature took a purely natural form—a bird with a vegetal element—rather than a statue of Pax or some other allegorical figure; it thus constituted a kind of landscape art. Without access to the mass-manufacturers of weathervanes who would later flourish in America, Washington had his designed by architect and contractor Joseph Rakestraw of Philadelphia, and the style is effective but unrefined. Washington took great care to get a proper weathervane for his house, and he provided a drawing of the cupola for the craftsman. He gave manager George Augustine Washington a drawing and exact instructions on 12 August 1787 for coloring parts of the weathervane and for applying white paint to the unfinished cupola, although it is uncertain whether Washington or Rakestraw had initially determined the colors for the weathervane. The general wrote: "The spire (if it is not the case already) must have that of black; the bill of the bird is to be black. And the olive branch in the mouth of it, must be green."[105] The purpose of the bird was visual and iconographic, and Washington did not care whether it spun with the wind or not: "I should like to have a bird (in place of the Vain) with an olive branch in its Mouth—The bird need not be large (for I do not expect that it will traverse with the wind & therefore may receive the real shape of a bird, with spread wings)—the point of the spire not to appear above the bird—If this, that is the bird thus described, is in the execution, likely to meet any difficulty, or to be attended with much expence, I should wish to be informed thereof previous to the undertaking of it." Washington gave George Augustine a drawing and detailed suggestions on how to integrate the weathervane onto the octagonal structure atop the house.[106]

Modern technical investigation has revealed no remaining trace of the original surface colors, but the document records Washington's desire for black on the dove's bill and green leaves. In two paintings of the mansion house attributed to Edward Savage (cf. Plates 14 and 15), the dove appears gilded. Savage was originally trained as a goldsmith, was surely aware that it was not uncommon for weathervanes to be gilded, and had himself visited Mount Vernon. Still, it is most likely that Savage, who omitted the black and green in the two pictures, was harmonizing the weathervane with the golden sky in the picture, not representing its actual appearance. It is hard to imagine that Washington, who wanted to convey a sense that his little "Cottage" was the rustic villa of a retired soldier and farmer, would have gilded such a prominent feature. His instructions mention no gilding, no early observer mentioned gilding, and a recent technical investigation revealed no indication of original gilding.[107] Washington did have the ends of the four lightning rods on the house tipped in gold, but this was done for practical reasons of conducting electricity. Washington called for gilding when it was subdued, as when he ordered books to be bound in calf and gilt, or in a public setting away from his estate, as when he and George William Fairfax donated gold for gilding inscriptions and carvings in the new Pohick Church in 1773–1774.[108] He had gold trim on his English-made carriage in 1768–1769, one of the fancy and luxurious purchases he was making in those years, but over time he wanted to project a moderate image, and gilding his weathervane would hardly have fostered that.[109]

In addition to considering the works that Washington displayed, we might conclude with a look at two minor works on paper that formed part of his visual world: his ex libris bookplate, ordered in 1771 (Figure 7.31), and the watermark that he commissioned and used after 1792 (Figure 7.32).[110] In the design of the bookplate, Washington surely chose the elements, asking for the name in an escutcheon and providing the family motto, "Exitus acta probat," which has been variously translated; it means, roughly, that the outcome demonstrates the value of an action. Washington's motto is more prominent than in similar plates by the family in the English line, as in the plate used by Richard Washington around 1750, and George may well have suggested that the words be emphasized. He might also have recommended the presence or abundance of the foliage, which is not called for by the coat of arms and adds a touch of the natural, corresponding, in Rococo fashion, to the asymmetrical design of the shield and the plate on the bottom. "Exitus acta probat" had long been the motto of the Washington family, and he truly embraced the idea behind the motto: "With me, it has always been a maxim, rather to let my designs appear from my works than by my expressions," meaning his verbal expressions. The drawing of the actual design was likely beyond his skills and was undoubtedly left to the artist; the result rather conventionally falls in line with the Rococo taste as seen in contemporary bookplates, but Washington could have advised on a number of the elements finally chosen in the design (presumably 1771).[111]

Washington's watermark, designed in 1792, bears his name in a circle; a figure of Liberty, seated on a plow, holding a liberty cap; and a dove of peace and an olive branch. The figure derived from various English designs showing Britannia in a similar pose. The American transformation forms a brilliant conceit, combining the symbols of peace (olive branch, freedom, and agrarian output) with a patriotic allegorical figure and topping them with the same bird (probably a griffin) that appears in Washington's coat of arms. Washington may well have personally designed this watermark, which is hardly high style and was easily within his power as a draftsman. An early anecdote records that in 1790 President

FIGURE 7.31. Washington's engraved bookplate, ex libris. Washington ordered hundreds of these bookplates from England with his family motto, "Exitus Acta Probat." Washington may have asked that the shield receive its abundance of floral adornment. Courtesy of the Mount Vernon Ladies' Association.

Washington took an interest in papermaking and tried his hand at making a sheet at Hendrick Onderdonk's paper mill on Long Island.[112] If Washington did not draw this watermark out himself, he must have suggested the elements and approved the design. Even for this small, nearly undetectable commission, Washington took great care with visual images associated with him.

Martha Washington's Eye

No study of George Washington as collector and patron can overlook Martha Washington's role. Her contribution to the

FIGURE 7.32. Liberty watermark (adapted here as a drawing), found on Washington paper used after 1792. The modest artistic level exercised here was well within Washington's own design powers, and he himself may have sketched out a prototype for this watermark, which represents Liberty seated on a plow with an olive branch and liberty cap. The iconographic scheme was tailored to Washington's international reputation as a peaceful, freedom-loving farmer. Courtesy of the Mount Vernon Ladies' Association.

development of the collection and the interiors at Mount Vernon is not perfectly clear, although enough evidence survives to show that it was significant.

Martha Dandridge was descended from an English family that included prominent painters. The most successful among them was her uncle Bartholomew Dandridge (1691–c. 1754), a portraitist of some note and a student of Sir Godfrey Kneller. The National Portrait Gallery in London pos-

sesses a portrait by Dandridge of William Kent, whose revolution in naturalistic gardening would later reverberate at Mount Vernon.[113]

Martha certainly came to her marriage to George in 1759 steeped in an awareness of art and its potential for beauty and prestige within a domestic setting. Although she apparently retained few objects from the estate of her first husband, Daniel Parke Custis (d. July 1757), Daniel's father John (d. 1749) had acquired a substantial collection that was displayed in his home in Williamsburg, where Daniel and Martha visited. The house, called Custis Square, contained a remarkable number of paintings, glass prints, maps, and so forth, including "12 Caesars" and "5 prints of Alexander battles."[114] At the time of his death, George Washington had in his study "5 prints of Alexanders Battles," and these are perhaps the ones (or similar to those) that belonged to Daniel and to his father, John Custis, before him.[115] Several family portraits from the time of her first marriage remained with Martha and were displayed at Mount Vernon, namely, the John Wollaston portrait of Martha and another of the children Jacky and Patsy. She also received some fruit and flower pieces from Custis Square House from her father-in-law: "An Account of sundrys taken and used by Mrs. Custis out of the Inventories" under "James City . . . a set fruit peices 5 / a set of flower peices 5 / ___; 10." George Washington copied this lists of objects in 1761 during the settlement of that estate, showing his legal interest if not his aesthetic appreciation.[116]

Partly because they shared ideas with each other, and partly because they lived in the same time, place, and social class, Martha used the same critical language as George. In 1780, Martha thanked Arthur Lee for an "elegant piece of china" and asked Charles Willson Peale to take miniature portraits of family members that he had made in 1776 and turn them into a pin, doing so in "neat and plain" fashion.[117] Just as George Washington and their contemporaries praised verisimilitude in portraiture, Martha wrote to granddaughter Nelly that "the only value of a picture is the likeness it bears to the person it is taken for." Martha was keenly interested in portraits, but her letters do not indicate an awareness of the artistic possibilities of portraiture beyond verisimilitude. She was a tough critic. She complained to John Pintard on 31 July 1801 that she did "not think [Gilbert] Stuart's celebrated painting a true resemblance," and Pintard reported that "there are several medallions and miniatures of the President in the house, none which please Mrs. Washington." Martha's appreciation of decorative art comes across in her characterization of the Vaughan ceramics over the mantelpiece as "fine old china jars that usually stand on the Chimney Piece in the New room." That her opinions mattered is indicated by a letter to George Washington from Savage, who sent four of the best impressions of the family print to George, with apologies that they would seem dark until bleached a bit by sunlight. Savage must have had a sense of Martha's taste, as he added that "As Soone as I have one printed in Colours I Shall take the Liberty to Send it to Mrs Washington for her Acceptance, I think She will Like it better than a plain print."[118]

Martha, like George, wanted art or fine objects to be in current taste; at times Martha also specified that she wanted to acquire works that would find favor among the genteel and better sorts of society. Considering whether to send some head adornment to her niece and friend Fanny Bassett Washington, she wrote from Philadelphia that "all the genteel people say Crape cushing is not proper to send to you." Writing again to Fanny in 1789, Martha said of a certain jewelry piece that the "chain is of Mr Lears choosing and such as Mrs Adams the vice Presidents Lady and those in the polite circle wares."[119] Without having traveled in Europe or lived in an urban taste center in America, she and George had to learn what, in all of the arts, was current among the better, polite sorts of people in society.

Martha destroyed her correspondence with George, and only a handful of letters survive between them, none touching on the arts. Had the full correspondence survived, we would certainly have a better sense of Martha's role in developing the collection at Mount Vernon. Even from the surviving documentation, however, we can discern that Martha took an active interest in the collection and helped determine its scope and the placement of objects within the house. In acknowledging a bust from Joseph Wright, Washington said nothing about the work except to offer thanks but noted of Martha that "she prays [the commission] may give you no uneasiness or hurry; your convenience in the execution will be most agreeable to her wishes."[120] When in March 1785 historian William Gordon requested profile miniatures from Washington for use in his publication on the recent war, the general sent some "designed for me by Miss D'Hart of Elizabethtown—& given to Mrs Washington; who in sparing them, only wishes they may answer your purpose." (Sarah De Hart had made the miniatures in 1783.)[121] Edward Savage made two mezzotints, one a portrait of George Washington "first Sketch'd in black Velvet." On 6 October 1793 Savage sent an impression of each, hoping to meet the approbation of both the president "and Mrs Washington, as it is the first I Ever published in that method of Engraving." He added, "Please to present my Most Respectfull Compliments to Mrs Washington."[122] Clearly, others regarded Mrs. Washington as a significant force in assessing art and forming the household art collection.

Many people also sent Martha gifts. John Trumbull sent her a small version of the full-length portrait of George Washington at Verplanck; the artist cheerfully signed his note to her "con amore."[123] On another occasion, Martha expressed flattering sentiments to Trumbull for a print he sent to her of the general. Tobias Lear wrote to George Washington on 4 February 1794, mentioning that he was sending via ship a gold chain for Martha and "a profile of the Earl of Buchan [David Erskine], by Tassie, which Lady Buchan committed to my charge with a note for Mrs. Washington." George William Fairfax sent to Mount Vernon two prints as gifts, one for George Washington and another for Martha.[124] Martha also received "a Glass Case with Wax or Grotto Work, presented by Mr Francis to Mrs Washington and by him left with Mrs Clinton to forward." The maker sent instructions for repairing the delicate item ("a very Ginger Bread piece of work") in case any damage occurred during shipping. The work arrived safely, and Martha expressed her appreciation.[125]

Andreas Everardus van Braam Houckgeest, an agent for the Dutch East India Company, sent Martha a set of china in 1796. The pieces included an inscription referring to George and a list of the fifteen states in the union at that time; hence, the name "States China" was used to describe this unique set (Plate 27). The inscription, "Decus et Tutamen ab Illo," has been variously translated. "Ab" in Latin can mean "from" but often forms the ablative of personal agent and would here signify "by," expressing George Washington's agency as patriot. The inscription likely means "Glory ["decus" = glory, honor, or virtue] and defense by him."[126] The "ab illo" or "by him" honored Martha's husband for having achieved honor or glory and as being the defender of the new nation, whose states are listed and joined by a protective serpent wrapped around the perimeter. Martha willed this set to her grandson George Washington Parke Custis, and the inscription, while honoring George Washington, refers to him in the third person and affirms the set as Martha's.

Documentation for commissions from Martha is rare, since George wrote the requests and paid the bills. Many of these orders likely reflected her wishes, though, as was undoubtedly the case with smaller decorative arts, luxury goods such as fine cloth, and jewelry. One commission for large-scale furniture is known to have been hers: she ordered bedroom furniture and accompanying textiles that were used initially at the presidential mansion in Philadelphia and then later moved to Mount Vernon. She left her grandson several fine items, including "the new bed stead which I caused to be made in Philadelphia together with the bed, mattrass, boulsters and pillows and white dimity Curtains belonging thereto" (cf. Figure 1.2).[127] In December 1775, Lund Washington reported to George that William Bernard Sears "has a picture frame to make which Mrs Wash-

ington directd him about." Earlier in the month, Lund noted the remarkable information that Mrs. Washington had given orders for the building of a chimney in a dependency building; Lund reported defensively that it was "rather larger than it should be, it was done by Mrs Washingtons Derection."[128]

A chance exchange throws considerable light on Martha's role in determining the material and aesthetic appearance of the mansion house. Preparing for his return to Mount Vernon in 1797, the president directed Tobias Lear to acquire new carpeting for the West Parlor and added that "Mrs. Washington requests that you would add the Bellows and the Vessels (Iron & Tin) in which the ashes are carried out." She was clearly sitting near her husband when he was writing, and he consulted her on the order. Even more tellingly, two days later the president wrote to Lear again and stated "that if Wilton Carpeting was not much dearer than Scotch I should prefer it. Mrs. Washington says there is a kind different from both much in use (Russia) if not dearer or but little more so than the former I would have it got."[129]

Mrs. Washington was in charge of running the households at Mount Vernon and elsewhere, and while George was active in arranging his art and furniture, Martha surely was, too. While the arrangements and decorative decisions for the first presidential mansion in New York fell to owner and recent resident Mrs. Osgood, assisted by Lady Kitty Duer, Washington noted in his diary on 13 February 1790 that in the second presidential residence in New York he "walked in the forenoon to the House to which I am about to remove—Gave directions for the arrangement of the furniture &ca. and had some of it put up."[130] (He meant "furniture" in the larger sense, including curtains and mirrors, as well as seating, table, and case pieces). But in November 1775, with George away at war, Lund Washington noted that Martha determined the decoration scheme of the owners' bedroom, asking for it to be plain and receive "no ornaments," as were being applied to the stucco-adorned public rooms downstairs. Over time she likely determined the iconography of the room; unlike the manly subject matter in the study below, we can sense a feminine and motherly theme in the couple's bedchamber, which contained a number of small-scale round works on moral, literary subjects, including the *Countess of Huntington* and *A Parson,* as well as small portraits of grandchildren.[131]

Many decisions concerning the collection were matters internal to the household and were resolved by private discussions, and we will never know how great a role Martha played at Mount Vernon, especially in determining the acquisition and display of art in the more public rooms. With the man of the house writing the letters and making the payments, the surviving correspondence might imply that he had a greater role than he actually did. The extent of Martha's contribution, likely strong, is obscured by our ignorance of their conversational exchanges and nearly all letters sent between them. The pattern of gifts and commissions, inflected by the gender roles of the couple and expectations of the time, would suggest that Martha took a larger part in choosing the decorative arts and portraiture, and somewhat less of a part in selecting oil painting or larger sculptural pieces. When Niemcewicz visited in 1798, it was Martha, not George, who "showed me a small collection of medals struck during the Revolution." Elizabeth Powel probably summarized it well when she wrote to Martha praising the operations of the Mount Vernon estate, declaring that it is a place "where the good Order of the Master's Mind, seconded by your excellent abilities, pervades every Thing around you."[132] Mrs. Powel stated it aptly: George Washington held the leading role, while Martha, contributing her "excellent abilities," also helped to shape the practical, moral, and aesthetic character of the Mount Vernon estate.

Washington as Sitter

Washington always had an uneasy relationship with portraiture; he sat only later in life, usually under duress, and often complained about the process. Ironically, he ended up, following his rise as national figure, as a major focus of early American portraiture.[133] As far as we know, Washington did not sit for a portrait until he reached the age of forty (Plate 30). That first sitting, for Charles Willson Peale in 1772, was perhaps at Martha's request. Peale took Washington's pose in military clothing one day and captured Washington's "face" on another day.[134] Except for other painted portraits of him by Peale made during the war, it was not until after the Revolutionary War ended that the general (now past fifty) sat for other artists for anything more than a lead pencil profile by Pierre Eugène du Simitière and a silhouette by Miss Sarah De Hart of New Jersey. Friends and associates understood that he did not like to sit and sympathized. Francis Hopkinson, hoping to get his cooperation to sit for Robert Pine, wrote to Washington in 1785, "I know you have already suffer'd much Persecution under the Painter's Pencil—& verily believe that you would rather fight a Battle, on a just Occasion, than sit for a Picture. because there is Life and Vigour in *Fortitude,* & *Patience* is but a dull Virtue."[135]

For a person of his wealth, social standing, and fame, Washington had a limited history of sitting, indicating a genuine personal resistance on his part. Many of the portraits made from 1783 on he permitted only under pressure from political bodies and from social organizations, and he finally declared that he would sit no more unless his refusal would give offense. For example, although he had declined to sit for him earlier, Washington sat for William Joseph Williams for a Masonic portrait on 18 September 1794, out of desire not to offend the Freemasons. On another occasion, Washington instructed Tobias Lear to turn down a request for the president to sit for an artist commissioned by the Tammany Society in New York, pleading a lack of time.[136] Still, Washington recognized the political value of portraiture, he knew that the public wanted his image, and he strategically allowed portraitists access when he deemed it useful.

Whether from personal sentiments or the outward modesty and nonchalance characteristic of his social class, Washington at least once suggested that portraiture was vanity.

FIGURE 7.33. *George Washington, Esquire,* mezzotint, 12.5″ × 9.84″. This print was ascribed to the fictitious artist "Alexander Campbell" and produced by C. Shepherd (London, 1775). Shepherd issued two portraits of Washington. The general was undoubtedly referring to this fiercer one when he commented facetiously on the representation of his fearful visage. From William Loring Andrews, *An Essay on the Portraiture of the American Revolutionary War* (New York, 1896), opposite p. 33.

He wrote to the Marquis de Lafayette on 25 September 1778 that he let go a chance to have Peale make his portrait at Valley Forge, "but I really had not so good an opinion of my own worth, as to suppose that such a compliment would not have been considered as a great instance of my Vanity, than a mean[s] of your gratification." Washington often spoke of portraiture with humor. Of a print (Figure 7.33) made by an anonymous hand (but ascribed to a fictitious Alexander Campbell of Williamsburg), he wrote to Joseph Reed: "Mrs Washington desires I will thank you for the Picture sent her. Mr Campbell whom I never saw (to my knowledge) has made a very formidable figure of the Commander in Chief giving him a sufficient portion of Terror in his Countenance."[137] In 1796, he sent to Mrs. Walter Stewart an engrav-ing designed by Madame de Bréhan, who captured his likeness in other media as well (cf. Figure 7.34): "Not for the representation or the value, but because it is the production of a fair Lady, the President takes the liberty of presenting the enclosed with his best regards, to Mrs. Stewart, praying her acceptance of it."[138] Washington pleaded that it was not the likeness of himself that mattered but that the picture was the production of a "fair lady," not unlike the recipient.

After getting some practice, Washington reported that he had become accustomed to sitting. He joked to Pennsylvania judge Francis Hopkinson:

In for a penny, in for a pound, is an old adage. I am so hack-neyed to the touches of the Painters pencil, that I am *now* alto-gether at their beck, and sit like patience on a Monument whilst they are delineating the lines of my face. It is a proof among many others, of what habit & custom can effect. At first I was as impatient at the request, and as restive under the operation, as a Colt is of the Saddle—The next time, I submitted very reluctantly, but with less flouncing. Now, no dray moves more readily to the Thill, than I do to the Painters Chair. It may easily be conceived therefore that I yielded a ready obedience to your request, and to the views of Mr [Robert] Pine.[139]

By "dray" he meant dray horse, and the thill was the rod or shaft that connected the draft horse to the wagon. He was not used to being commanded, at least not since his early military training, and the experience also struck him as an imposition and as unnatural. He also joked, quoting from Shakespeare's *Twelfth Night,* that he had to "sit like patience on a Monument," thus imagining himself as an allegory of Patience, seated in a public monument and made of stone or bronze. Similarly, he joked to David Humphreys that he gave in to "the pressing calls of the Great Ones" in agreeing to sit for Mr. Houdon.[140] Washington apologized on another occasion to Robert Morris for involving him with dealings over a portrait, writing to him "I am sorry to give you trouble about trifles."[141] In 1792, Washington complained to Henry Lee about the "irksomeness of sitting, and the time I loose by it."[142] All of these protests were part of a consistent pattern of avoiding sitting at all, making light of the process, and mocking himself for being obedient enough to sit for such a trifling and vain undertaking.

Despite his personal feelings about the discomfort or the vanity of sitting, Washington was keenly aware of the power of images, and he wanted to shape the result. In March 1777, during some of the darker days of the war, he wrote to Samuel Washington: "The request you make with respect to my Picture, I should have no difficulty in complying with, if it were practicable to gratify you, but, at present, two insurmountable obstacles offer themselves—the want of a Painter—and, if a Painter could be brought hither, the want of time to Sit. If ever you get a Picture of mine, taken from the life, it must be when I am remov'd from the busy Scenes of a Camp, & ought to be at a time when the Mind is not bent down

FIGURE 7.34. The Marchioness of Bréhan (Marquise Jean-François-René-Almaire de Bréhan), *George Washington,* 1789, watercolor on ivory, 2.625″ × 2.125″. Washington sat for Madame de Bréhan, who made profile images of him in different media, and he praised her style. Courtesy of Yale University Art Gallery, New Haven, Mabel Brady Garvan Collection (1947.220).

with care."[143] Knowing the importance of projecting an inspiring image to the nation, Washington wanted the artist to capture a confident face.

His duties as a sitter included having his face covered in wet plaster by the sculptor Houdon (Figure 7.35 and Plate 29). Nelly Parke Custis as a child saw him during the making of the life mask and later reminisced about having seen him "as I supposed, dead, & laid out on a large table coverd with a sheet. I was passing the white servants hall & saw as I

FIGURE 7.35. Jean-Antoine Houdon, life mask of George Washington, 1785 (October), plaster, 12.5″ (height). Washington was fascinated by the plaster medium and technique of Houdon. Courtesy of the Pierpont Morgan Library, New York. Gift of J. P. Morgan Jr., 1924 (AZ151).

thought the corpse of one I considered my Father, I went in, & found the General extended on his back on a large table, a sheet over him, except his face, on which Houdon was engaged in putting on plaster to form the cast. Quills were in the Nostrills. I was very much alarmed until I was told that it was a bust, a likeness of the General, & would not injure him."[144]

Washington is famously stiff in many of his portraits, and this mien was not completely a fabrication by artists. Martha's grandson George Washington Parke Custis described

George Washington in real life as appearing absent and absorbed in thought even when among family. Silas Deane of Connecticut described Washington as hard in countenance.[145] Elkanah Watson pointed out the "cautious reserve" in his bearing, and others noted his chilly demeanor. Washington was, according to Sen. William Maclay of Pennsylvania, a "cold formal Man." William Thornton exchanged warm letters with Washington but said of the president that "in his address he is cold, reserved, and even phlegmatic, though without the least appearance of haughtiness or ill-nature." For his part, Benjamin Henry Latrobe sensed a "reserve but no hauteur in his manner," and although Washington joked with others at times he also showed a slight air of "moroseness."[146] French officers who met him toward the end of the Revolutionary War called him gracious and kind, and capable of a gentle smile, but also characterized him variously as "distant," "overcome with sadness," "grave and serious," and "infinitely cold, prudent, and reserved."[147] Although Washington laughed and cried, and became angry and joyous, as other mortals did, contemporaries found that, especially when he was still and not speaking, his visage was naturally reserved, chilly, passive, and grave. More than one portraitist captured this stiffness that was inherent to his personality.

Washington was not unaware of his role in shaping his image, and he did not want to convey too stoical a mood. He expressed his fear that he was too sullen when Charles Willson Peale painted his image in spring 1772: "Inclination having yielded to Importunity, I am now, contrary to all expectation under the hands of Mr Peale; but in so grave—so sullen a Mood—and now and then under the influence of Morpheus, when some critical strokes are making, that I fancy the skill of this Gentleman's Pencil, will be put to it, in describing to the World what manner of Man I am."[148] This passage, which includes witty and learned reference to Morpheus, Roman god of sleep and dreams, again shows Washington's reluctance to sit. He wanted to come across as larger than life, "describing to the World what manner of Man I am," and most later portraitists and their public wanted the same. Washington realized the power of portraits in conveying a public message. He was amused when his attempts at projecting gravitas were upset by events. In January 1785, while making a plaster life cast of the general, Joseph Wright captured a momentary smile George could not suppress when Martha entered the room and screamed at seeing him covered.[149]

It is remarkable that Washington sat for the renowned Jean-Antoine Houdon yet left no known reaction to the images. Thomas Jefferson had arranged for Houdon to take Washington's likeness. He apologized to Washington for sending Houdon over unasked, but he was arguably the greatest sculptor in the world, working on an image of the King of France at that moment. The public would appreciate having Washington's image captured by so great an artist.[150] Houdon worked at length on Washington, taking a cast of his face and making a bust from life (see Figure 7.35 and Plate 29). Washington wrote little in his diary and letters about the artist's style, yet he was fascinated by the process itself, and he took copious notes. In October 1785, Washington wrote:

> Observed the process for preparing the Plaister of Paris, & mixing of it—according to Mr. Houdon. The Oven being made hotter than it is usually heated for Bread, the Plaister which had been previously broken into lumps—that which was hard, to about the size of a pullets egg; and that which was soft, and could be broken with the hands, larger; was put in about Noon, and remained until Night; when, upon examination, it was further continued until the Morning without any renewal of the heat in the Oven, which was close stopped. Having been sufficiently calcined by this operation, it was pulverized (in an Iron Mortar) & sifted for use through a fine lawn sieve, & kept from wet.
>
> When used, it is put into a Bason, or other Vessel with water; sifted through the fingers, 'till the Water is made as thick as Loblolly or very thick cream. As soon as the plaister is thus put into the Water, it is beat with an Iron spoon (almost flat) until it is well Mixed, and must be immediately applied to the purpose for which it is intended with a Brush, or whatever else best answers.[151]

FIGURE 7.36. Jean-Antoine Houdon, *George Washington,* 1785–1792, marble, 79″ (height). Washington offered his opinion on the clothing that should be represented here. He preferred that Houdon show him in contemporary garb, not the clothing of antiquity. State Capitol, Richmond, Collection of the Commonwealth of Virginia. Photo courtesy of the Library of Virginia.

This passage indicates Washington's practical, American turn of mind, and there is a charm in his analogies with foodstuffs. He seems to have wanted to record this technique for future use by his own craftsmen, perhaps for making molded plaster reliefs.

In considering Washington's role as a sitter, we should recall that in everyday life he was noted for judging men's qualities and abilities by their outside appearance. As early biographer Humphreys wrote, "It is presumed that in his long & extensive intercourse with mankind, he paid a considerable attention to physiognomy in selecting persons for particular places; for in speaking of their various qualities he seldom failed (if they were not intimately known to him) to make some observations upon their exterior appearance."[152] Washington, prone to judging men by their appearance, was careful to cultivate his own, and that included his face and body as a sitter for portraits. He must have looked for character when he studied the portraits of others, just as he did when looking at real people.

Such matters came into consideration when Thomas Jefferson raised the question of whether Washington ought to be shown in modern or classical clothing in the full-length portrait Houdon made for the State of Virginia (Figure 7.36). Washington approved of using modern garb, having heard from others that "This taste ... has been introduced in painting by West I understand is received with applause & prevails extensively."[153] Washington referred to the "servile adherence to the garb of antiquity" and wrote to Jefferson:

In answer to your obliging enquiries respecting the dress, attitude &ca which I would wish to have given to the Statue in question—I have only to observe that not having a sufficient knowledge in the art of sculpture to oppose my judgment to the taste of Connoisseiurs [sic], I do not desire to dictate in the matter—on the contrary I shall be perfectly satisfied with whatever may be judged decent and proper. I should even scarcely have ventured to suggest that perhaps a servile adherence to the garb of antiquity might not be altogether so expedient as some little deviation in favor of the modern custom, if I had not learnt from Colo. Humphreys that this was a circumstance hinted in conversation by Mr West to Houdon. This taste, which has been introduced in painting by West, I understand is received with applause & prevails extensively.[154]

Surely, Washington, even if fancied by others as the new Cincinnatus, could live comfortably in his own time, and clothing himself in a toga would only undermine his image. Jefferson agreed with Washington and passed along the approval of "West, Copeley, Trumbul & Brown in London, after which it would be ridiculous to add ... my own. I think a modern in an antique dress as *just* an object of ridicule as an Hercules or Marius with a periwig & chapeau bras."[155] For his part, the natural leader Washington was loath to submit to a "servile adherence," even to the precedents of antiquity. Comparing Horatio Greenough's famous sculpture of Washington in a classicized, semi-nude state with Edward Savage's equally noted *The Washington Family,* the hero comes across better in his own period costume than in the artificial dress of antiquity.[156] In his own time, Washington was adept at controlling the presentation of his likeness to the public.

CHAPTER EIGHT

Under His Vine and Fig Tree

Biblical and Classical Perfection at Mount Vernon

At length my Dear Marquis I am become a private citizen on the banks of the Potomac, & under the shadow of my own Vine & my own Fig tree, free from the bustle of a camp & the busy scenes of public life.

GEORGE WASHINGTON to the Marquis de Lafayette, 1 February 1784

GEORGE WASHINGTON was fond of framing his actions in a broad moral and historical context. In his writings, he described many aspects of his life in the context of classical thought and biblical scripture, and he arranged some of his material surroundings in a way that would reinforce the message. Paul Boller has argued that Washington was something of a Unitarian, while others see him as more of a Deist, like Thomas Jefferson and others of the time. Mary Thompson has argued recently that Washington was an upstanding Anglican/Episcopalian but certainly not an "enthusiast," to use a period word.

Talk of religion rarely enters his letters and diaries. He clearly knew the Bible and quoted directly or indirectly from it on many occasions.[1] He never mentioned Jesus Christ in his known writings, and only once signed his name to a document, written by an aide, in which Christ's name was used,—a message to American Indians meant to shape their behavior and beliefs.[2] To his brother-in-law Burwell Bassett, Washington joked: "I was favoured with your Epistle wrote on a certain 25th of July when you ought to have been at Church, praying as becomes every good Christian Man who has as much to answer for as you have—strange it is that you will be so blind to truth that the enlightening sounds of the Gospel cannot reach your Ear, nor no Examples awaken you to a sense of Goodness—could you but behold with what religious zeal I hye me to Church on every Lords day, it would do your heart good, and fill it I hope with equal fervency." The letter is ironic in that Washington attended church service about once a month, on average.[3]

George Washington believed in a God, however, an "All-wise Providence" or benign "Supreme Architect" who acted as a force for good, and he commented repeatedly about the role that such a divine Being played in supporting the American Revolution. He wrote to the clergy of Newport in 1790: "I am inexpressibly happy that by the smiles of divine Providence, my weak but honest endeavors to serve my country have hitherto been crowned with so much success, and apparently given such satisfaction to those in whose cause they were exerted."[4] He saw the world as a structure under a benevolent, watchful eye. He did pray, although it is a matter of debate how fully he expected prayer to shape the unfolding of earthly events, as he often wrote to those with ill or dying relatives that they should accept the plan of Providence as it happens. He told David Humphreys that outcomes are known "only to the great Ruler of events; and confiding in his wisdom & goodness, we may safely trust the issue to him, without perplexing ourselves to seek for that which is beyond the human ken, only taking care to perform the parts assigned us, in a way that reason & our consciences approve of." Thus he called for a kind of acceptance of the plan of Providence, and he bid others to act virtuously in the theater of the world and trust God's judgment. Washington's religious ideas were Deistic, tinged with elements of Stoicism and an Enlightenment reliance on reason, but, as Thompson noted, "he was raised within the tolerant, liberal wing of the Anglican Church, as it developed in Virginia in the late seventeenth and early eighteenth centuries" and "he remained a member of the Church until his death."[5]

He believed that God was watching over him and America, and he saw the world, his own leadership, and his estate at Mount Vernon in benign biblical terms. His crafting of biblical, or specifically Solomonic or Masonic, connections to himself and Mount Vernon corresponds to what we know of his relationship to sacred texts and to religious practice of his day. Washington quoted or referred to Genesis, the letters of St. Paul, Ezekiel, the Sermon on the Mount, and other passages in the Bible for advice or guidance on contemporary matters, and it is hardly surprising that he would, through his words and the display of objects at Mount Vernon, evoke biblical history and ideas.

George Washington's Retirements at Mount Vernon

George Washington and his contemporaries recognized that Mount Vernon, in addition to being a productive farm, served as the site of Washington's well-deserved retirement, his blissful rest from action on the world's stage (Figure 8.1). His recusals from the world after the Revolutionary War and presidency were widely regarded as philosophic retreats and as among his greatest achievements, and Washington himself helped to shape the public perception of his retirement to the shady paths and "rural cottage" at Mount Vernon. No moral theme was more consistent in Washington's life, and he expressed his intentions and desires most fully in letters to those in or near his social class (Marquis de Lafayette, Thomas Jefferson, John Trumbull, and others). He hoped Mount Vernon would be his refuge from the cares of warfare, politics, and public scrutiny, and he framed his presence there evoking classical and biblical ideals and using pictorial language.

George Washington's retirements to Mount Vernon sprang from a long tradition in Western thought—the practice of rural retreat. The ideal of philosophical retirement arose under social conditions particular to antiquity. The wealthy aristocrat sought to leave Rome, stay at his landed estate, and live an ideal life of culture and thought. In times of political turmoil, when one's confidence in shaping the affairs of state was shattered and people faced an uncertain, violent, and capricious state of things, the ideal of agricolan retirement was especially appealing. Among the ancients, it was perhaps Cicero who most famously led the ideal country life. He owned a number of landed estates, filled his villas

FIGURE 8.1. Mansion house at Mount Vernon, east façade, seen from the Potomac. Washington's much-publicized retirements unfolded in a diversified scene of mansion, groves, lawns, and pebbled walks. Photo: Author.

with artworks, and developed farmlands and pleasure gardens. Despite Cicero's frequent engagement with politics (an activity that cost him his life), he returned again and again to his beloved estates to write, think, and relax. Similarly, Horace, in his *Sermones,* described the blessing of time away from the woes and cares of the city and engagement with business, politics, and urban crowds.

The classical ideal of rural retirement, enthusiastically embraced in European Renaissance culture, was especially well suited for adoption by the upper classes in England. While the French nobility stayed close to the court in Versailles or Paris, English aristocrats—given the political events of the sixteenth and seventeenth centuries—spread out across the nation on country estates and lived more independently of the royal court. The English elites associated country life with freedom from political ties and the urban problems of dirt, crime, and crowding. Alexander Pope wrote in *The First Satire of the Book of Horace* of a country retreat where politics and war have no place: "Know, all the distant Din that World can keep, / Rolls o'er my Grotto and but soothes my Sleep. / There my Retreat, the best Companions grace, / Chiefs out of War, and Statesmen out of Place."[6] A garden fostered the classical ideals of philosophic contemplation and calm of mind, as well as carried biblical connotations. Maynard Mack has noted that in the seventeenth and eighteenth centuries, English writers never had the first garden, the Garden of Eden, far from their minds in thinking about their gardening. Joseph Addison mentions the ancient notion of tranquility: "A Garden was the Habitation of our First Parents before the Fall. It is naturally apt to fill the Mind with Calmness and Tranquillity, and to lay all its turbulent Passions to rest." In his 1799 poem "Mount Vernon," John Searson refers to Adam and Eve, saying "a garden was the first habitation of our parents."[7] In short, social considerations as well as classical and biblical precedent encouraged the development of the English landscape garden as a site of escape and moral improvement.

The glorification of the country estate as a place of retreat became deeply embedded in the English mentality, and George Washington imbided this ideal from an early age. Elite American colonists sang the praises of country life, just as English writers did. Virginian Landon Carter named his farm Sabine Hall, after Horace's country home, showing the influence of antiquity on the Tidewater colonial landholding elite. To gain a sense of day-to-day reality into what rural retirement entailed, it is useful to look at the diary of Philip Vickers Fithian, a young man from New Jersey who served as the tutor to the children of Robert Carter III at Nomini Hall. He offered a lengthy description of life at a Virginia estate of the stature and quality of Mount Vernon.[8] Apart from his own feelings, Fithian recorded the Carter family, including the lady of the house, as engaging in country walks, perusing the gardens, enjoying the vistas, and studying with delight the growth of crops and ornamental plants.

The character of retirement in America was different from that in England. In the mother country, the landed nobility had larger incomes, and management of agricultural land was more fully left to overseers, while the owners enjoyed truer retirement from mundane activities. The English notion of rural amusements, carried out on estates arrayed with pleasure buildings, fountains, grottoes, and ornamental bridges, differed from life in the business-oriented world of a productive Tidewater plantation. The wealthiest landowners in England did not, like George Washington, direct the activities of overseers and workers every day in the fields, riding for hours as they did so, and the pleasure grounds on English estates were much larger than those in America. When the American elite spoke of withdrawal to the country, they meant a retirement from politics, war, urban life, and non-agrarian commercial trade but not from the duties of running a farm. Country life in the New World was different from that of the city legislator, ship captain, or urban businessman, and the idea of rural retirement had real meaning for Americans, even if the escape was limited by European standards.

The aristocratic European ideal, derived from ancient classical writers, was toward self-improvement through literature, art, and the calming effect of withdrawal from the world. Washington was more like those English landed gentry—far more numerous than the more idle British aristocrats—who contributed to the economic leadership of their farms. Like Thomas Jefferson, who called himself a farmer and also extolled the goodness of agrarian life, Washington was an agricultural businessman. Still, his engaged kind of retirement fulfilled, in an active way, the traditional Western desire for the benefits of removal from public life or urban residence. Insofar as Washington's retirement was to be understood as involving leisure and private enjoyments, the groves of screening trees and protective ha-ha walls were essential for Washington's purposes, as they kept the livestock away from the porch and east lawn, and created a noble pleasure zone. For their part, the farm lands were also a place of retreat for Washington, as they were aesthetically pleasing, under his control, and removed from many problems of the world at large.

The trope of retirement had become embedded in Washington's mind at an early age. The young Washington wrote to a certain "Robin" around 1749 or 1750 concerning the fairer sex: "thats only adding Fuel to fire it makes me the more uneasy for by often and unavoidably being in Company with her revives my former Passion for your Low Land Beauty whereas was I to live more retired from yound [*sic*] Women I might in some measure eliviate my sorrows by burying that chast and troublesome Passion in the grave of oblivion or etarnall forgetfulness."[9] The youth was already striking the theme of the grave as respite from care, as he would later. Washington later transferred this idea of retirement from giving up amorous passion to laying down arms and returning to his mansion house and farms.

Mount Vernon was Washington's place of retreat from public life, and he retired there in 1758, 1783, and 1797, each time following a period of military or political service. David Humphreys, in a passage of his biography that Washington, looking at the manuscript, viewed but did not correct, wrote, "The success of this campaign [against the French and Indians] having restored tranquility on the frontiers of the Middle States and the health of Washington having become extremely debilitated by an inveterate pulmonary complaint, in 1759 he resigned his military appointment."[10] Even apart from medical considerations, others recognized that he deserved to return to his private affairs. John Kirkpatrick, Washington's secretary, praised his services in July 1758 and truly hoped that they may "produce their due reward for the toils that accompany them—A Glorious & peacefull retirement to the pleasures of Private Life."[11] The pattern was set for one of the themes of American culture of the 1780s and 1790s: public support for Washington's retirements to Mount Vernon.

Washington's departure from the military during the French and Indian War in late 1758 gained him little praise, criticism, or attention at the time, and formed no part of his heroic legend. The greatest moments of withdrawal from the world and to Mount Vernon were his retirement from the military after the Revolutionary War and his stepping aside after two terms of the presidency. For contemporaries, the greatest of the retirements was his relinquishing of power in December 1783, an act that earned him the reputation as being a new Cincinnatus; the scene of his resigning his sword to Congress in Annapolis is among the four great canvasses by John Trumbull that adorns the central rotunda of the Capitol building (Figure 8.2). Later on, Henry ("Light Horse Harry") Lee penned the famous lines, "First in war, first in peace, first in the hearts of his countrymen," adding the lines, quoted less often, that Washington was also "first in the little scenes of domestic peace." Understandably, in the minds of the public, private virtue took second place to Washington's public contributions. Few had seen such a relinquishing of power, and Washington's retirement from military command was widely hailed and formed a capstone to his life at that point.

By December 1783, Washington was back at Mount Vernon. He had anticipated a peaceable retirement there as early as November 1776, when he expressed to his brother John Augustine Washington a wish to be "fixed among you in the peaceable enjoym[en]t of my own vine, & fig Tree."[12] After the great war, in an extraordinary series of letters, Washington described in richly pictorial and horticultural imagery his return to country life. He wrote to Jonathan Trumbull Jr. of Connecticut, his secretary during the last two years of the war, on 5 January 1784: "Be so good as to present my most cordial respects to the Governor and let him know that it is my wish the mutual friendship & esteem which have been planted & fostered in the tumult of public life, may not wither and die in the serenity of retirement: tell him we should rather amuse our evening hours of life, in cultivating the tender plants & bringing them to perfection before they are transplanted to a happier clime."[13] This passage began the long series of postwar letters in which Washington almost literally pictured his retirement, using imagery of nature and evoking the aesthetic beauty of his life at Mount Vernon. For him, the vision of retirement was a pastoral, and he eventually brought together a self-presentation that united these letters, his gardening at Mount Vernon, and the landscape art in the collection at the mansion house.

Washington soon developed a consistent, pictorial manner of representing an idyllic retirement. The letters, filled with garden imagery, coincided with his major efforts to

FIGURE 8.2. John Trumbull, *The Resignation of George Washington's Commission, Annapolis, December 23, 1783*, 1824–1828, oil on canvas, 20″ × 30″. In this picture, a smaller version of the painting he made for the central Rotunda of the U.S. Capitol, Trumbull captured one of the great moments of American history: Washington resigning as commander of the armed forces. Trumbull Collection (1832.8). Photo: Yale University Art Gallery / Art Resource, NY.

construct the lawns, groves, walks, wildernesses, and shrubberies of the pleasure grounds of his estate on the Potomac. They formulated an essential vision of his retirement, expressed in his best literary fashion. Washington composed his most thoughtful and stylish letters to Europeans, perhaps hoping for or anticipating publication of them abroad. He wrote to the Marquis de Chastellux on 1 February 1784:

> I am at length become a private citizen of America, on the banks of the Potowmac; where under my own Vine & my own Fig tree—free from the bustle of camp & the intrigues of a Court, I shall view the busy world, "in the calm lights of mild philosophy"—& with that serenity of mind which the Soldier in his pursuit of glory, & the Statesman of fame, have not time to enjoy. I am not only retired from all public employments; but I am retiring within myself & shall tread the private walks of life with heartfelt satisfaction.[14]

He cited the biblical "vine and fig-tree," as he did in nearly all other such declarations of retirement, setting the scene in a garden-like site. With horticultural language, he pointedly noted that he was on the banks of Potomac and that he was engaged in his pursuit of philosophical calm in viewing

("view the busy world") and in walking ("the private walks of life with heartfelt satisfaction"). The quote "in the calm lights of mild philosophy" comes from Joseph Addison's *Cato* (1710), one of Washington's favorite plays.[15] He was painting a moral picture, as it were, and his laying out walks, viewing prospects and vistas, and gardening his site on the river—all part of his shaping of his estate—suddenly take on an explicitly moral quality through their association with the picturesque description conveyed in this letter. For his part, Chastellux responded in kind and offered Washington still more vivid imagery of this type. The marquis wrote on 6 March that "perhaps when this letter reaches you, it may find you sitting under the shade of those trees you have planted, surveying with delight the magnificent view of [the] patomack."[16]

Chastellux and Washington were speaking the same language and sharing the same sense of retirement as a becalming, distant vision from a garden. In a similar exchange with a European, when writer and editor Jean Luzac wrote to Washington from Leiden and sent a gift of a book, Washington responded with landscape imagery and moral sentiments. "I have steered by Bark amid the intricacies of variegated public employment, to a haven of rest with an approving conscience . . . In times of turbulence, when the passions are afloat, calm reason is swallowed up in the extremes to wch measures are attempted to be carried; but when those subside and the empire of it is resumed, the man who acts from principle—who pursues the paths of truth, moderation & justice, will regain his influence."[17] He paints a river landscape, evoking the banks of the Potomac, that reminds us of the landscape paintings in his collection.

Among Washington's finest letters of retirement were those crafted for the Marquis de Lafayette and his wife. On 1 February 1784, Washington wrote to his friend and fellow revolutionary officer:

> At length my Dear Marquis I am become a private citizen on the banks of the Potomac, & under the shadow of my own Vine & my own Fig tree, free from the bustle of a camp & the busy scenes of public life, I am solacing myself with those tranquil enjoyments, of which the Soldier who is ever in pursuit of fame—the Statesman whose watchful days & sleepless Nights are spent in devising schemes to promote the welfare of his own—perhaps the ruin of other countries, as if this Globe was insufficient for us all—& the Courtier who is always watching the countenance of his Prince, in hopes of catching a gracious smile, can have very little conception. I am not only retired from all public employments, but I am retireing within myself; & shall be able to view the solitary walk, & tread the paths of private life with heartfelt satisfaction—Envious of none, I am determined to be pleased with all. & this my dear friend, being the order for my march, I will move gently down the stream of life, until I sleep with my Fathers.[18]

This rich passage throws light on Washington's eye and pictorial sense. The letter is clearly written as if it would be passed along to others (the marquis hardly needed to be told that Washington was retiring along the banks of the Potomac), and the style is high flown for Washington, even within the letter itself (not quoted here), which is more mundane in other parts. He painted the garden imagery of the vine and fig tree (both of which really did shade him at Mount Vernon), the solitary walk, and the banks of the river. We also have another pictorial image in his notion of the "scenes" of public life. He asks us to imagine the activity of public life as scenes, evoking a theatrical or pictorial model. The bustle of an army camp, too, becomes vivid here, as does the life of the sycophantic courtier. The last sentence makes the clever transition from military life to retirement: his marching orders are now to live a life of calm, and until his death he will continue to "move gently down the stream of life." The presence of the Potomac in real life reinforces this imagery; at Mount Vernon he indeed had shade trees, paths to tread, and a gently moving river, and he had stepped away from military and public duties. Later in the letter he called the mansion house a "Cottage" and noted that he had been holed up in frost and snow during Christmas time, a cozy image. Washington had already referred to his mansion house as a "humble Cottage" to Lafayette in another letter, anticipating the marquis visiting in peacetime when the olive branch has been extended across the American land.[19] Washington and Lafayette spent much time together during the war and could share ideas of liberty, and this letter of February 1784 expressed shared values as well as values specific to Lafayette and his Continental context. In particular, the reference to the courtier looking to the countenance of the prince reflects Old World experiences. Washington combined his sense of a moral retirement with broader international ideals of liberty, all painted in words as if he were making a "neat landscape."

Once he had developed this letter announcing his retirement, he added idyllic imagery to his moral pastoral. To Rochambeau (also on 1 February 1784), he wrote: "The tranquil walks of domestic life are now unfolding to my view; & promise a rich harvest of pleasing contemplation," suggesting that he was viewing a walk, not merely treading it, and we are asked to imagine the walks unfolding to his view.[20] This letter to General Rochambeau created a conscious and effective construction of moral nature painting: walks, views, treading, harvest . . . all are conducive to contemplation and tranquility.

Perhaps the finest, as well as the most charming, of Washington's letters on his retirement and rural location was his missive and invitation in 1784 to Adrienne, Marquise de Lafayette, whom he would never meet. This is among his most florid prose on any topic, and he painted an extraordinary visual and moral image of his life at Mount Vernon:

> From the clangor of arms & the bustle of a camp—freed from the cares of public employment, & the responsibility of Office—I am now enjoying domestic ease under the shadow of my own Vine, & my own Fig tree; & in a small Villa, with the implements of Husbandry & Lambkins around me, I expect to glide gently down the stream of life, 'till I am emtombed [*sic*] in the dreary mansions of my Fathers . . . You have youth . . . and *must* have a curiosity to see the Country, young, rude & uncultivated as it is; for the liberties of which your husband has fought, bled, & acquired much glory—Where every body admires, every body loves him—Come then, let me entreat it, & call my Cottage your home; for your own doors do not open to you with more readiness, than mine wou'd. You will see the plain manner in which we live; & meet the rustic civility, & you shall taste the simplicity of rural life—It will diversify the Scene & may give you a higher relish for the gaieties of the Court, when you return to Versailles.[21]

Washington has magnificently succeeded here in painting a new and fuller kind of picture, a pastoral, to be sure, but one set in a *ferme ornée,* an ornamental farm. Again there is a vine and fig tree, but instead of solitary walks and views of his own path, he is on a pretty farm, with little lambs and farming tools all around him. Here the stream is evoked again, and now appears the gothic image of the "dreary mansions of my Fathers," referring to the family tomb.

The marquise will experience the simple virtues of rural life, and the pretty elements will "diversify the scene" of her life. Again, the word "scene" explicitly evokes a pictorial or theatrical image and the phrase "diversify the scene" is borrowed from the language of English pastoral poetry and connoisseurship. Just as Marie Antoinette diversified her scene with the Hameau at Versailles, Washington thought his country estate would do the same for the marquise, al-

though in his case the scene is a serious working farm and the virtues of the country life are real. Indeed, Washington elsewhere described his passion for gardening, and when he asked for a variety of trees of different form and color, he pronounced again that these will amuse him and help to "diversify the scene."[22] He had learned this vividly visual phrase as part of the language of natural landscape gardening, and he applied it to the visual effects of natural growth as well as to the moral aspects of the picturesque rustic farm setting, far from the frivolities of high society, that he painted for the marquise. His letter to Adrienne was meant to appeal to her gender in its soft picture of little lambs and a diverse countryside. This letter sidesteps consideration of the magnificent "Colonnade" and the fine decoration of the West Parlor and Small Dining Room, favoring the image of the country "cottage." Similarly, he wrote to Chastellux of "this Cottage," and he wrote to La Luzerne from this "cottage of retirement."[23] So here in his description to the Marquise de Lafayette was a complete package: garden, cottage, lambs, farm tools, river, family tomb, all set in a picturesque farm that would offer the marquise a delightful and morally uplifting break from the gaieties of French court life.

In his letters to Europeans, Washington passed himself off as little more than a humble farmer. As he attempted to shape public perception of his residence at Mount Vernon and retirement from the military, Washington used agricultural imagery. Even the stucco work in the New Room was adorned with "implements of husbandry." His very name "George," coming from the Greek ("geo," earth, and "ergon," work, alluding to working the earth), means "farmer," and he played up this aspect of his life, as did Thomas Jefferson, who described himself as a farmer. In the Anglo-American world, the ideas of Virgil's *Georgics,* which glorified farming life, were well known. It is not necessary to know whether Washington was immersed in this poetry; the ideal of the beautiful life on an active farm was ennobled in classical and modern poetry, and educated eighteenth-century people were accustomed to comparing painting and poetry. Washington's account of his little lambkins and implements of husbandry, and similar letters, form his own kind of *Georgic*, and his writing is certainly colored by his and his readers' awareness of the tradition of pastoral poetry.

Washington's social equals had their own opinions on the general's retirement, and some doubted it was good for the country or possible for Washington to achieve. After the war, Gouverneur Morris told Washington that he doubted the general would truly gain tranquility from his retirement, and Washington acknowledged to Ben Franklin that "retirement from the public walks of life has not been so productive of the leisure & ease as might have been expected."[24] Elizabeth Powel told Washington that he was needed for the second presidency and that he would be letting down society by retiring. Most of the public, though, happily shared in the ideal of Washington's "philosophic" retirement. Scotswoman Henrietta Liston noted the pleasure that Washington felt when he spoke of retirement.[25] English writer Catharine Sawbridge Macaulay Graham assured Washington that she recognized on 30 October 1789 that, "y[ou]r philosophic turn of mind would have lead you to the completion of human happiness in a private station."[26] Rochambeau knew from afar that Washington was flourishing in his "glorious and Philosophical retreat" and "with Sobriety and philosophy you live under a pur skie and in good air." Nelly Parke Custis shared her adoptive father's vision of a rural retreat, writing to her friend Elizabeth Bordley Gibson that "I am at present quietly seated in this still retreat, free from noise & bustle . . . I am not at all surprised that you wish for retirement, I would not exchange mine, for all the pomp & Vanity of this wicked world."[27]

Washington described his retirement in painterly terms; for their part, contemporaries who wrote to him about his retirement helped to define it for him and also often used garden or farming imagery, contrasting it with the former public life of their Cincinnatus. Humphreys described Washington's house and grounds, noting "such are the philosophic shades, to which the late Commander in Chief of the American armies has retired, from the tumultuous scenes of a busy world."[28] John Searson's 1799 poem "Mount Vernon" is replete with moral reflections on the gardens of the estate: "Rural shades, and groves, e'er attract the mind, / And lead the thoughts, to the things that's divine," and "Tis natural to fill the mind with peace, / And ev'ry ruder passion here should cease." Similarly, he wrote in the verses "Thoughts on Mount Vernon" (1796) that Washington "Tir'd with the tumults of the noisy life, / He now retires to live from ev'ry strife."[29] In the eighteenth-century language of rural retirement, the picture was important, and the phrase "philosophic shades" embodies what Washington wanted to convey with his scene painting; it was either a tumultuous battle scene (another widespread subject matter in seventeenth and eighteenth-century painting) or a verdant landscape of philosophical calm. Pierre-Étienne Du Ponceau, writing in 1837, recalled that when he visited Mount Vernon in 1780 he already had a sense that the mansion house was in line with the idea of a Cincinnatus, and he thought of the times of the Roman Republic when a citizen might have taken up the temporary reins of power. Nathanael Greene, visiting Mount Vernon the same year, thought that it would be a sacrifice to leave such a place for the life of politics or the military.[30] The Chevalier de la Luzerne noted that "I have the pleasure to see him a simple citizen, enjoying in the repose of his retirement the glory which he so justly acquired. He dresses in a gray coat like a Virginia farmer" and bore "no traces of his former greatness."[31] Washington encouraged people to associate the Cincinnatus legend with him, and William Strickland wrote to Washington that his reputation "seemed capable of increase by retirement alone."[32] Only departure from the world's stage could add to Washington's reputation.

The reaction to Washington's retirement was not only verbal. The famous painting attributed to Savage showing Washington and family on the bowling green conveys the idyllic image of his time at Mount Vernon as understood by the broader public and as fostered by Washington himself

(Plate 14). Alexander Lawson's 1799 engraving and etching after John James Barralet (Figure 8.3) celebrated Washington's resignation from the presidency in 1797 and gave a sense of the shared public vision of his retreat from politics and triumphant return to Mount Vernon. The work is filled with allegorical and other details reflecting an actual entertainment held in Philadelphia in 1797 to mark this great event. Of particular note for us was "a beautiful landscape, representing Mount Vernon, in front of which were seen oxen harnessed to the plough."[33] Washington's great acts of resignation always ended at Mount Vernon, which became a national symbol for his reward and a reminder of the power he relinquished.

Mount Vernon and Ideals of Classical Antiquity

Washington's hope to create an ideal realm at Mount Vernon reflected the eighteenth-century understanding of perfection, which itself reflected notions drawn from classical antiquity as well as biblical accounts. We should not underestimate the extent of the intellectual roots of Washington's ideas about philosophical retirement. He was clearly aware of and was using ideas embedded deep in the history of Western thought, situating his own retirement in relationship to a long classical tradition and with awareness of Old Testament ideals and considerations. We have seen that Washington accepted and magnified the public's recognition of him as the new Cincinnatus. His broad, moral worldview—largely shared by others of his time, place, and social class—was rooted in classical antiquity. It is not surprising that many of the ideas and precepts Washington held can be found in *Seneca's Morals,* which he owned as early as 1749.[34] One modern author wrote of Washington that "the ancient civilizations on which the culture of a gentleman was supposed to be grounded meant nothing to him . . . He hardly ever looked to the past: Precedents were not to be followed but made."[35] On the contrary, Washington knew and admired historical ethical models; he echoed those ideas explicitly in his writings and in his daily life as,

FIGURE 8.3. Engraved by Alexander Lawson, after John James Barralet, *Washington Resigning the Presidency,* 1799, engraving, 7.5″ x 4.5″. This image captured the sense, shared across the country and abroad, that the Mount Vernon estate was the well-deserved reward for the hero's retirement from power and public duties. Courtesy of the Mount Vernon Ladies' Association (SC-116).

for example, in his desire to dress plainly and avoid superfluous luxuries.

Washington's writings were sprinkled with references to classical culture. To South Carolinian Charles Pinckney, Washington wrote of being caught "between the rocks of Sylla and charibdas [Charybdis]." He evoked the image of the godlike mortal of Greco-Roman culture when he dictated a letter to Catherine Littlefield Greene Miller, expressing his hope that the girl might "find a god like man" in marriage.[36] He joked to James McHenry about Lawrence Lewis's upcoming marriage to Nelly Parke Custis, reporting on 16 February 1799 that the young man was "to relinquish the field of Mars for the Sports of Venus." Under the watchful eye of the public during his presidency, Washington complained to nephew Bushrod that "the eyes of Argus are upon me."[37] Several times over the years Washington joked about the "shades" at Mount Vernon, playing on the double meaning of the gardens' shadows and the classical notion of the shades in the underworld.[38]

Washington was hardly a classical scholar, but he certainly had more than a passing knowledge of classical culture and mores. He owned a copy of *The Lyric Works of Horace, Translated into English Verse,* and he admired modern works on antique themes, such as Joseph Addison's play *Cato.* When American Francis Hopkinson sent Washington a "Book of Songs" in 1788, Washington wrote the following witty response, revealing his familiarity with the reputation of music and poetry in antiquity:

> We are told of the amazing powers of musick in ancient times; but the stories of its effects are so surprising that we are not obliged to believe them, unless they had been founded upon better authority than Poetic assertion—for the Poets of old (whatever they may do in these days) were strangely addicted to the marvellous; and if I before *doubted* the truth of their relations with respect to the power of musick, I am now fully convinced of their falsity—because I would not, for the honor of my Country, allow that we are left by the Ancients at an *immeasurable* distance in everything; and if they could sooth the ferocity of wild beasts—could draw the trees & the stones after them—and could even charm the powers of Hell by their musick, I am sure that your productions would have had at least virtue enough in them (without the aid of voice or instrument) to soften the Ice of the Delaware & Potomack.[39]

Washington's description of landscape, especially of the one he shaped at Mount Vernon, was tinged by ideas from antiquity, and he described the next life in classical landscape terms. He wrote to Robert Morris that he would glide down the stream of life "till I shall arrive at the world of Sperits [*sic*]." He referred to Elysium, the part of the underworld reserved by the gods for heroes and the virtuous, when writing to Henry Knox on 25 February 1787: "to see this Country happy whilst I am gliding down the stream of life in tranquil retirement is so much the wish of my Soul, that nothing on this side Elysium can be placed in competition with it."[40]

Some of his ideas about the estate and about retirement rely on specific ancient philosophical ideas. In his letter to the Marquis de Lafayette on 1 February 1784, he wrote that he not only was retiring but was retiring "within himself." Washington most likely derived this idea from a passage in *Seneca's Morals.* This book was clearly a major source for Washington's ethical thought, and it reechoed throughout the actions of his life, from the Stoic desire for simplicity of dress and manners, to acceptance of death, to suppression of emotions in the face of Fate. In the notion of retirement from the bustle of the world, Washington paraphrased Seneca's Epistle XV, which reads: "Let every man retire into himself . . . We should, therefore, fly the world, withdraw into ourselves, and in some sort avoid even ourselves too."[41] This idea was also expressed by Marcus Aurelius in his *Meditations* (VII, 28): "Retire into yourself. The nature of the rational principle that rules us is to be content with itself when it does what is just, and so secures tranquility."[42] The admonition of Seneca and Marcus Aurelius is that one can be content with one's own reason and just actions, without a need to seek outside gratifications and pleasures. Washington was drawing from a noble Stoic tradition in saying that his retirement would be self-sufficient and lead to inner peace. In his final retirement, he liked to tell others that he planned to travel no further than twenty-five miles from his estate. On the estate itself, he intended to seek an individual peace; his retiring into himself, away even from others on the estate, was a learned reference to the classical past. His house and gardens would be the site of that retirement where he could rely on his own reason, good actions, and good will, and he would be happy with all, "envious of none."

There are other Stoic ideas found in Washington's retirement letters, the most pervasive being his easy acceptance of death, which was a widespread theme of Stoic philosophy. Again, these beliefs were born out in his landscape gardening, which included the placing of his tomb on his ornamental farm. He used the phrase "dreary mansions of my fathers," which is redolent of the "mansions of the dead" spoken of by Homer and later classical writers. His retirement, Washington declared, would sweep naturally into his death, and he accepts the course of Fate. The Potomac was to be like the River Styx, and the metaphorical barque of his journey would enable his voyage to the classical underworld. He had no apparent fear of death and saw it as the ultimate form of retirement to be achieved at Mount Vernon, where he wanted to be buried. Also Stoic in spirit, and carrying pictorial or natural associations, was Washington's quoting of the phrase "in the calm lights of mild philosophy," which he borrowed from his favorite play, *Cato*. Addison's drama is all about duty and virtue, and Washington drew this phrase from a passage that used the word "lights" and is thus pictorially evocative. Washington cheerfully attacked the opposite of Stoicism, Epicureanism or the embracing of pleasure, in a letter to Annis Boudinot Stockton, when he wrote of the "Muse of Morven" and that he would be "strongly disposed to dispute your Epicurean position."[43]

On the whole, Washington embraced Stoic thought, and Mount Vernon was meant to become for him a site of calm, withdrawal, reflection, and tranquil death. Washington was no hardened Stoic, however, and recognized the need to allay common suffering, one tool being art. He wrote to European correspondents Nicholas Simon van Winter and Lucretia Wilhelmina van Winter, on 8 January 1788: "The Muses have always been revered in every age, & in all Countries where letters & civilization have made any progress. As they tend to alleviate the misfortunes, and soften the sorrows of life, they will ever be respected by the humane & virtuous."[44]

Biblical Allusions

Washington framed his retirement and other aspects of his life in biblical as well as classical terms. Part of the landscape picture he (verbally) painted of his retirement includes a persistent use of the phrase "under my vine and fig tree." The phrase, which appears in a number of passages of the Bible, is used most famously (and most relevantly for Washington) in Micah 4:4, where we also find allusions to peace after war and idyllic references to mountains, houses, paths, farms, and gardens:

> Come let us go to the mountain of the Lord, to the house of the God of Jacob; that he may teach us his ways, and we may walk in his paths. For out of Zion shall go forth the law, and the word of the Lord from Jerusalem. He shall judge between many peoples, and shall decide for strong nations afar off; and they shall beat their swords into plowshares, and their spears into pruning hooks, nation shall not lift up sword against nation, neither shall they learn war any more; but they shall sit every man under his vine and under his fig tree, and none shall make them afraid; for the mouth of the Lord of hosts has spoken.

Washington used the phrase "none to molest or make him afraid" along with the vine and fig tree allusion in a letter to English historian Catharine Sawbridge Macaulay Graham in July 1791.[45]

He was conscious of the scrutiny with which his life and words would be regarded, and he must have used the phrase with great awareness of its biblical resonance and application to his life and situation. The phrase appears many times in the Bible beyond Micah. In 1 Kings 4:1–34, particularly, it evokes a picture of not only rural bliss but abundance, peace, divinely blessed existence, and wisdom such as Solomon's:

> So king Solomon was king over all Israel . . . Judah and Israel were many, as the sand which is by the sea in multitude, eating and drinking, and making merry. And Solomon reigned over all kingdoms from the river unto the land of the Philistines, and

unto the border of Egypt: they brought presents, and served Solomon all the days of his life. And Solomon's provision for one day was thirty measures of fine flour and threescore measures of meal, ten fat oxen, and twenty oxen out of the pastures, and an hundred sheep, beside harts, and roebucks, and fallow-deer, and fatted fowl. For he had dominion over all the region on this side of the river, from Tiphsah even to Azzah, over all the kinds of this side of the river: and he had peace on all sides round about him. And Judah and Israel dwelt safely, every man under his vine and under his fig tree, from Dan even to Beersheba, all the days of Solomon. And Solomon had forty thousand stalls of horses for his chariots, and twelve thousand horsemen. And those officers provided victual for king Solomon, and for all that came unto king Solomon's table, every man in his month: they lacked nothing. Barley also and straw for the horses and dromedaries brought they unto the place where the officers were, every man according to his charge. And God gave Solomon wisdom and understanding exceeding much, and largeness of heart, even as the sand that is on the sea shore. And Solomon's wisdom excelled the wisdom of all the children of the east country, and all the wisdom of Egypt. For he was wiser than all men . . . and his fame was in all nations round about . . . And he spake of trees, from the cedar tree that is in Lebanon even unto the hyssop that springeth out of the wall: he spake also of beasts, and of fowl, and of creeping things, and of fishes. And there came of all people to hear the wisdom of Solomon, from all kings of the earth, which had heard of his wisdom.

Excepting perhaps the dromedaries, this description comes close to the ideal realm of Mount Vernon and the public image that George Washington desired. He can be thought of as Solomonic in his wise leadership, and the passage likely evoked for him the peace he brought to the land and the plenty on his side of the river. Like Solomon's kingdom, Mount Vernon was a place of agricultural abundance, providing wheat flour, meal, and other crops, and inhabited by sheep, oxen, deer, fat fowl, and horses. Washington was wise, and he himself spake of trees, beasts, and fish. Many people could and did come to his estate to talk to him. Above all, Mount Vernon, and America in general, was after his leadership a land of peace and plenty. Washington's allusion to the

Solomonic "vine and fig tree" would have suggested to any contemporary reader acquainted with this memorable passage that Washington had established on "this side of the [Potomac] river" a verdant, abundant place of peace and God-sent good fortune.

Washington was retiring to an estate that he thought of in terms rooted in historical places, from the country villas of classical antiquity to English estates of the previous two hundred years. But in letters to others, he most often referred to the Old Testament, especially in his allusion to the vine and fig trees of biblical gardens and to his dwelling in a land of peace under the watchful eye of Providence. Echoing the passage in Kings, Washington wrote to Rochambeau on 10 August 1790: "Heaven smiles upon us with favorable seasons and abundant crops."[46] As in Micah, Washington (and America) had turned from war to peace, and none could make the nation afraid. When Washington addressed the Jews of Newport, Rhode Island, he used the phrase "vine and fig tree" and reassured them of their religious freedom.[47] In the context of Mount Vernon, the phrase took on a vivid landscape metaphor, and he integrated it into descriptions of the paths, river setting, and shady trees of the estate, which he positioned through his writings as a divinely blessed garden and abundant farm. In the passage from Micah, the "swords into plowshares" line reminds one of the peace after the war; "strong nations afar off" (such as England) will come to peaceful terms with others. It might be too much to equate Mount Vernon with the mountain of the Lord, but that we "walk in his pathways" is relevant, and Washington often referred to walking in his calm retirement through the shady paths. Finally, if he positioned Mount Vernon as a biblical paradise, it would not have escaped many visitors who knew his insistence on using the phrase "under my vine and fig tree" that he, like Solomon, was the architect of his house.[48]

The Freemasons regarded Solomon as a seminal architect, and it is worth pondering yet another possible factor behind Washington's architectural and artistic thinking: the influence of Freemasonry and allied biblical ideas. Washington joined the Masons after his time as a young surveyor, entering into the Fredericksburg Lodge (no. 4) and attending meetings as early as 1752. At the age of twenty-one, he became a Master Mason. He later was a member of the Alexandria Lodge (Lodge no. 39, which became no. 22 in 1792).[49] Over the years, Washington was invited to meetings and received gifts of Masonic aprons. He sat, reluctantly, for a Masonic portrait painted in 1794 by William Williams, and although not at his request or following any specifications in his final will, the Masons staged Washington's funeral in December 1799. Washington stated to a Mason in a letter of 25 September 1798 that he did not then preside over any Masonic lodge, "nor have I been in one more than once or twice, within the last thirty years."[50] That he joined early in life can be explained as the actions of a young man who wanted to join an organization that would lead to his societal advancement, and it is telling that he was little involved with the Masons later in life. One would have to conclude that he knew and respected Masonic beliefs, traditions, and rites, but he was not deeply committed to the group. Still, it is plausible that he might have worked some Masonic notions into his building. Washington referred to God as the Supreme Architect of the universe, following the designation used by the Freemasons, and the Masons identified their group with the craft of architecture. They especially looked at Old Testament architecture, in particular that of King Solomon, believing architecture to bear on the very meaning and purpose of their organization.

Washington lived at a time when Masonic influence was present for a broad public, and it would be surprising if Freemasonry left no mark on Washington's mind and architectural designs. Freemasonry reached its zenith of influence in England and America during the eighteenth-century Enlightenment, as the view of a benign, rational God and an orderly universe found broad favor. Recent literature has recognized Freemasonry as standing at the heart of some of the most prominent architecture of eighteenth-century

Britain. The important Chiswick House (1726–1729) designed by Richard Boyle (with interiors by William Kent) has recently been identified as containing a number of Masonic elements. At John Wood the Elder's Circus at Bath (1754–1768), there is Masonic significance in the sculptural reliefs of the Doric frieze and Masonic symbolism in the plan itself, and Wood also used Masonic and, more generally, Solomonic and biblical symbolism elsewhere in his work.[51] It would seem difficult to place Washington's architecture in that particular orbit. Still, Washington was enough of a Mason for us to imagine a connection between his mansion house and that group's ideas, especially since their building was based on the broadly shared biblical tradition.

Among the pervasive aspects of the mansion house at Mount Vernon are the use of numerical ratios, especially those involving the number three, as in the footprint of the house (3:1, width to depth) and the width of the pediment in relation to the width of the house as a whole (1:3). Other noteworthy features of the house are its prominent porch and the twin colonnades. Both proportionality and a substantial porch appear in the House of Solomon and the Temple of Solomon as described in various places in the Old Testament, especially the Book of Kings and Chronicles 2. The temple of Solomon and the house of Solomon, like Noah's Ark (another construction that inspired Freemason building), were built on numerical ratios. One number, in particular, is intriguing for us, and that is for the Temple of Solomon as told in Chronicles 2, which give, differing from the numbers appearing in Kings, a proportion of three to one (sixty cubits by twenty cubits), like Mount Vernon's approximate ninety-six by thirty-two feet. Building on these biblical proportions, the Freemasons favored the numbers three and nine. Such numbers, floating around in Washington's head, must have had an effect, even if he was not constructing an explicitly Masonic or even Solomonic building.

The issue of the columns is intriguing. In the Solomonic tradition, 1 Kings 7:1–7 states that Solomon's own house had long porches outside and in courtyards:

But Solomon was building his own house thirteen years, and he finished all his house. He built also the house of the forest of Lebanon; the length thereof was an hundred cubits, and the breadth thereof fifty cubits, and the height thereof thirty cubits, upon four rows of cedar pillars, with cedar beams upon the pillars. And it was covered with cedar above upon the beams, that lay on forty five pillars, fifteen in a row. And there were windows in three rows, and light was against light in three ranks. And all the doors and posts were square, with the windows: and light was against light in three ranks. And he made a porch of pillars; the length thereof was fifty cubits, and the breadth thereof thirty cubits: and the porch was before them: and the other pillars and the thick beam were before them.

Solomon's house was of costly stone and fine wood (cedar of Lebanon), and Mount Vernon's rusticated surface, added in the 1750s and retained for the expansion of the house in the 1770s, gives an appearance of stone. (A "mason" is a stone carver.) Chronicles also notes a porch that runs completely along the short side of the twenty-cubit-breadth building. Even if it is not related directly, Proverbs 9:1 says that Wisdom had built a house with "seven pillars"; since wisdom is associated with Solomon, this seems to be another connection to wise rule and pillared porches. The translation of the word as "pillars" and not "columns" might suggest to an eighteenth-century reader square columns or thick piers rather than rounded columns, and the biblical "porch of pillars" could be echoed in the portico and the posts of the "covered ways" at Mount Vernon. The association of columns with Masons well preceded Washington, and some American Masonic imagery, including nineteenth-century works focused on Washington himself, illustrated columns and colonnades; these could be part of the same Masonic influence and ideology that helped to shape the form of the portico of the mansion house at Mount Vernon.[52]

Harmonious proportions, columns, porches, and other features mentioned below, such as checkerboard paving, are found widely in Georgian architecture, and a symbolic interpretation for Mount Vernon is, to be sure, conjectural. The possibilities remain, however, and for other details of

FIGURE 8.4. *Vide, Aude, Tace.* George Washington was a Mason and must have been well acquainted with the group's ideas and visual symbols. Frontispiece of *Jachin and Boaz; or, an Authentic Key to the Door of Free-Masonry, Both Antient and Modern* (London, 1776). Photo: Andrew Taylor.

the architectural articulation one could also, again tentatively, propose a biblical meaning. The Temple of Solomon was supported by arches, and the arch on the typical Masonic apron reflects that motif. Washington placed three barrel vaults under his "porch of pillars" (a barrel vault is essentially a series of arches connected), and, again, the number three was possibly Solomonic or Masonic in intent. Checkerboard (mosaic) flooring was a frequent motif in Masonic art (Figure 8.4), referring to the "vicissitudes of life, or the chequered existence, and also the Trials of a candidate." As we have seen, Washington had planned a checkered floor for his "porch of pillars."[53] Also intriguing in this context is the faux, "mahoganized" paneling in the central passage (now restored throughout the central passage and doors, upstairs and down). This finish might remind one of 1 Kings 6:14–20, where Solomon lines the House of the Lord with cedar. Nor is it implausible to interpret the honeysuckles attached to the pillars of the covered ways at Mount Vernon as a nod to the integration of flora with columns in the Solomonic/Masonic tradition.

These suggestive and symbolic connections to the Bible continue in Washington's display of objects and artworks. John the Baptist, one of two saints exhibited in the mansion, was the celebrated patron saint of the Masons. It is perhaps no coincidence that nearly every three-dimensional art object on the central axis of the ground floor of the house is connected to biblical passages, perhaps filtered in Washington's mind through contemporary Masonic imagery. The lions in the central passage could be given a Solomonic interpretation related to the lions on the king's throne (Chronicles 9:19). Lions were long used as a symbol of the Virgin Mary, who herself was the *Sedes sapientiae,* or Throne of Wisdom. At Mount Vernon, such symbols would refer not only to Solomonic architecture and Freemasonry but also to Washington's wise leadership in a land of peace and abundance that flourished under God's watchful eye. The display of the key to the Bastille in the central passage has been regarded as a purely political symbol (see Figure 7.24); however, the key is a symbol of Masonic achievement. It appears in Masonic imagery and on prints and aprons of the time (see Figure 8.4). The donor of the Bastille key, the Marquis de Lafayette, became a Mason, and his gift to Washington might have been intended as symbolic on more than one level. Especially in the context of other items of Masonic, Solomonic, or biblical character in the house, the key has potentially charged meaning.

The dove of peace and the olive branch are, obviously, taken from Genesis and the story of Noah. As during the peace of Israel and Judah under the wise rule of Solomon, the recession of the flood waters brought calm and new hope, and the dove is a sign that troubles are over and life is returning to normal after the turbulent storm. This imagery conformed to the Cincinnatus legend of a return to peace, as well as being redolent of the Old Testament visions of peace evoked in Washington's letters. In addition, the dove and the ark were typical Masonic iconography, appearing on paintings, prints, and aprons.[54] Apart from any specific connection to the Masons, the use of the dove was a clear proclamation of Washington's linking of his estate to Old Testament ideals of peace and divine will. The very presence and action of the dove evokes other associations: of the mansion house with the ark itself; the Potomac with the flood waters; the hilltop site with Mount Ararat; and the nearby agricultural land with the farms and vineyards that flourished after the flood, easily associated with the late war against the English. The dove and olive branch adumbrate specifics of the biblical narrative, while serving more surely as markers of postwar peace and the blessing of benign Providence.

Sundials also appear in the Old Testament, mentioned in Isaiah and Kings, near the Solomonic narrative. "In those days Hezekiah became sick and was at the point of death. And Isaiah the prophet the son of Amoz came to him, and said to him, 'Thus says the Lord: Set your house in order; for you shall die, you shall not recover.' But God responded to Hezekiah's prayer and added years to his life; the sign to him would be 'Behold, I will make the shadow cast by the declining sun on the dial of Ahaz turn back ten steps'" (Isaiah 38:1). The story is told also in 2 Kings 20:1–11: "And this shall be a sign unto thee from the LORD, that the LORD will do this thing that he hath spoken; Behold, I will bring again the shadow of the degrees, which is gone down in the sun dial of Ahaz, ten degrees backward. So the sun returned ten degrees, by which degrees it was gone down." The shadow on a sundial will be set back to show God's good will; it is a tool for God to communicate to man divine forgiveness. The story as told in Isaiah includes the famous admonition to set one's house in order, and the sundial's precision and usefulness are appropriate for Washington. Sundials were hardly rare on early American estates, but they often appeared in more secluded parts of gardens and in walled areas.[55] Hezekiah, son of King Ahaz of Judah, had a sundial from his father in his palace courtyard. The sundial at Mount Vernon was prominent in its isolation on the grassy plat on the west side of the house, which Washington and his contemporaries referred to as a "courtyard." In the mid-1780s, in the context of deliverance from the hand of enemies and the defense of a nation, Washington may well have been moved by the biblical account of the sundial. He was very careful in his planning, restricting the iconography of his estate and choosing objects that created the visual image that echoed his literary description of the estate as a land of biblical bliss and peace.[56]

In short, we can imagine Washington inserting Solomonic proportions into his house before the Revolutionary War and then after its conclusion building a biblical iconographic program. He seems to have gone about this quite systematically in his choice and arrangement of material objects and in the writing of his biblical and Solomonic letters, which he sent across the country and across the Atlantic. He framed his life and his estate in biblical terms and made it clear that Mount Vernon was the epicenter of a new peaceable land of plenty and goodwill.

The Morality of Mount Vernon's Gardens

The gardens at Mount Vernon formed part of the moral presentation of George Washington to society. We have seen in a number of ways how this played out. For example, through Washington's hospitality, the walled and open gardens served as places of enjoyment for a broad number of visitors, the morality not being in the pleasure seized but in the pleasures and kindness offered. Above all, the gardens served as the main site of his philosophical retirement, and they were the locus of his search for calm retreat from the bustle of the world. Batty Langley, whose book Washington owned, quoted Rapin "that we the

City now no more respect, or the vain Honours of the Court affect; But to cool Streams and aged Groves retire."[57]

Tranquility was a moral state beloved by philosophers of antiquity, and Washington addressed the specific question of tranquility in a 1786 letter to George Fairfax, his former neighbor at Belvoir who was then dwelling in England:

> Though envy is not among the ingredients which compose my constitution, yet the picture you have drawn of your present habitation & mode of living, is enough to create strong desires in me to be a participator of the tranquillity and rural amusements you have described. I am gliding into the latter as fast as I can, being determined to make the remainder of my life easy let the world, or the concerns of it, go as they may; & I am not a little obliged to you, my good Sir, for the assurance of contributing to this by procuring me a Buck & Doe of the best English Deer; but if you have not already encountered this trouble I would now wish to relieve you from it, as Mr Ogle of Maryland has been so obliging as to present me Six fawns from his Park of English Deer at Bell-Air.[58]

Washington used the phrase "rural amusements," wider spread in word and action in England than in America, but linked it to the more philosophical "tranquility" and made it a cultural achievement than mere fun in the countryside.

We have also touched on another moral aspect of Washington's gardening; namely, his integration of the farming components of the estate with the house and pleasure grounds called attention to his life as a productive contributor to American weal. Around the Mansion House Farm proper, there were outbuildings, livestock, the Vineyard Enclosure, kitchen gardens, fields of corn and other crops. Even an ornamental farm is a farm, and Washington's reputation as an agricultural leader and innovator rested on the public perception of his farming activities. The whole country wished, as Thomas Paine wrote (28 April 1784), that Washington, the leader of the "late Army," would retire "to private Life on the principles of Cincinatus." It was a broadly felt wish and expectation in America and abroad that General Washington would return to his farm, tend his lands, and live the life of the country gentleman.[59]

One question we have not broached is Washington's understanding of the political morality of the gardens at Mount Vernon. It is a much discussed feature of both period and modern literature that, in the English context, the natural, serpentine, green gardening that overthrew the formal style of Continental European gardening was a marker of political and personal freedom. Eighteenth-century British theorists spread the idea that the natural, spontaneous garden was opposed to the regimented gardening style of France and other Continental European countries, where authoritarian rule and religious persecution prevailed. Horace Walpole conveyed to readers the political dimension of garden design. As Stephen Bending noted, "For Walpole, the history of stylistic change is an emblem of English liberty, gained by Whig politics and stylistic and political history running in parallel."[60] The curving paths and seemingly spontaneous grounds of English gardens symbolized traditional English liberty and in particular the Whiggish politics that dominated in the early eighteenth century.[61] There was some feeling that Toryism, royalism, and traditional and well-ordered gardens were ideologically linked, as were Whiggism, liberty, parliamentary power, and "free," natural gardens.

Washington never explicitly mentions the political meaning of his garden in his writings, but he could not have been unaware of the origins of the English style in Whig ideology and its opposition to Continental, royal absolutism. His frequent references to his plain, republican style of living and to the solace provided by the modest house and grounds at Mount Vernon show his thoughtful consideration of the moral meaning of his aesthetic choices. He certainly knew of the English arguments concerning their gardens, as they were by the 1780s well worn themes in society on both sides of the Atlantic. What is impressive is the extent, as we have seen, to which he out-Englished the English, and even out-naturalled Capability Brown, in his emphasis on the natural in his park, the ornamental farm, and the views of elements such as rivers and raw woodlands. That was his own political

and moral statement, and his patriotic embrace of the American landscape, the American farm, and the productive place of agriculture was appropriate for a retired hero in the mold of Cincinnatus. He made a moral statement, putting his lands in the context of American values and mores by excluding the European pomp and luxury of statuary, bridges, and urns in favor of the fruits of the earth, honeysuckle, orchards, groves, live fences, grassy lawns, and views of woods and broad, untamed water. His development of the grounds in the 1780s must at some level have been motivated by his awareness of the connection between freedom in politics and freedom of design and movement in gardens.[62]

He received a letter in March 1798 from none other than Uvedale Price, whose writings on the picturesque in gardening formed an important contribution to English landscape gardening in the generation after Capability Brown. His letter to Washington accompanied his gift of his *Essay on the Picturesque* and is worth quoting extensively:

> The subject of the work which I have taken the liberty of sending to you, may possibly have engaged but little of your attention, occupied as you have been with affairs of the highest importance; yet still, whatever relates to the pleasures which arise from visible objects, & from all their various characters, combinations, & effects, cannot be foreign to a cultivated mind. The best title which this work can claim to your notice is, that it opposes a kind of systematic despotism in gardening; by which term, taken in an extended sense, I mean all that is done for the purpose of improving the outward appearance of natural objects. In this country, nearly for these last forty years, there has been a close resemblance between the prevailing system in politics, & that in gardening: whatever has a strongly marked character either in our minds, or our places, was to be new-modelled according to those prevailing systems, & reduced to the tamest uniformity. It has been your noble task, (the noblest that man can perform) to free a whole empire from so degrading a system in politics: the humble task in which I have been engaged, I trust is not totally without it's use; for whatever teaches men to think for themselves, & points out more liberal & enlarged principles even in the slightest matters, may assist in strengthening the general habit of the mind.

Mr West, whose eminent talents in the highest line of painting reflect so much honour both on his native, & on his adopted country, has frequently talked to me with enthusiasm of the picturesque character of american scenery, as infinitely beyond any thing that we are here acquainted with: perhaps therefore the discussion of a character, which, though mixed with all that is sublime & beautiful, is so peculiarly displaid in that scenery, may not be uninteresting to you, & may prove no unworthy relaxation of your mind, now that it is free from the immediate care of watching over the country which your exertions had preserved. May you long enjoy the exalted pleasure of contemplating the great work in which you bore so distinguished a part, & the inestimable benefits which it has diffused among your grateful fellow citizens.[63]

Price does not introduce the older argument that natural gardening is anti-monarchical; he is more modern and casts the blame (indirectly) on Capability Brown. For Price, the uniformly Brownian style in gardening needs to be rebelled against and a liberty of thought effected in the sphere of garden design. Price suggests that the "picturesque character of american scenery" is both sublime and beautiful. Even a rougher American scenery, with irregular cliffs and thorny growth, is visually attractive, and Washington would have embraced this view. (We know that he suggested grand and sublime American scenes to painters.) Even though he disagrees with Walpole's theory and Brownian practice, Price makes the link between gardens and belief. He even dares compare himself to Washington: the general gave men political liberty, while Price gave them freedom of thought in the area of landscape. We know of no response by Washington to this letter, but he must have read it with great interest.

For Washington, gardening was a healthy, rational, and fruitful activity, moral in that it is the right endeavor for a rational person and gives pleasure visually and through the food produced. He wrote abroad to Edward Newenham on 20 April 1787:

The manner in which you employ your time at Bell champ (in rasing nurseries of fruit, forest trees, and shrubs) must not only contributes [sic] to your health & amusement, but it is certainly among the most rational avocations of life for what can be more pleasing, than to see the work of ones own hands, fostered by care and attention, rising to maturity in a beautiful display of those advantages and ornaments which by the Combination of Nature and taste of the projector in the disposal of them is always regaling to the eye at the sametime in their seasons they are a grateful to the palate.[64]

Washington recognized the practical and aesthetic benefits of gardening and farming, and saw them as highly rational activities.

Washington lived in an allegorical age. We have already seen how he found or created biblical corollaries at Mount Vernon, with the vine and fig trees, Noah's ark, the shady walks, and so forth. We also can recognize other gardening metaphors and allegories in Washington's correspondence. In 1784, Rev. Jonathan Boucher wrote to Washington concerning contemporary controversies; he remarked that many of the speculations of recent times "resemble your Persimmons before the Frost: They are fair to the Eye & specious; but really disgusting & dangerous."[65] Some of the gardening metaphors Washington made were unconsciously moral but still telling. In the darkest days of 1776, he wrote to Lund Washington, asking that a room under construction be centralized and masterly in presentation. He asked Lund to plant either "good & well set Holly" or "young & strait bodied Pines"; as for other plantings, Lund should "let them be tall & strait." It was as if these plants were symbolic of youths under military training and were to be strong and upright.[66]

On a less martial note, Washington used a garden metaphor in a letter to George William Fairfax, long departed from Virginia: "As the path, after being closed by a long, arduous, and painful contest, is to use an Indian Methaphor, now opened and made smooth." He was capable of seeing the pathways of his estate in a meaningful and moral fashion, just as the shade from the trees symbolized leisure and calm, and the river symbolized the landing of his "barque" in a safe place.[67] To Jonathan Trumbull Jr., the general wrote to pass along to his father, Governor Trumbull, that he hoped the "mutual friendship & esteem which have been planted in difficult times might not wither and die in the

FIGURE 8.5. Thomas Whateley (design) and H. Sinclair (coloring), *The Two Hundred Acres Purchased by the Ladies' Association*, 1859, lithograph, 15.25″ × 24″. Washington insisted on being buried on his estate, a choice consistent with the practice of other Tidewater aristocrats. The selection of a burial spot on his private estate underscored to the public his modesty and his desire to avoid aggrandizement. The place he chose for the New Tomb was integrated on the estate with orchards and nursery beds and is visible on the left side of this lithograph. Courtesy of the Mount Vernon Ladies' Association (EV-4442).

serenity of retirement," and that they should amuse their "evening hours of life, in cultivating the tender plants & bringing them to perfection."[68] Washington had a full understanding of the moral and allegorical meaning of his actual gardens, of the words he used to describe his gardens, and of the horticultural and landscape imagery that he integrated into his letters. Farming and the encouraging of natural growth gave him a sense of well-being.

Washington compared the shades of retirement to the shades of the classical underworld, and it is appropriate to discuss his tomb in the context of his rural retirement and his establishment of a biblically inflected iconographic pro-

gram for Mount Vernon. He intended that his ultimate retirement, burial itself, would take place on his estate. The endearing scenes of his private life were, in a fashion, to continue in the tomb, which he instructed in his will was to be for his wife and other family members who might choose to be buried there. The executors were to oversee the construction of a new tomb, to be built of brick, down the hill from the porch and lawn and on the edge of an orchard in the area he called the Vineyard Enclosure (Figure 8.5). The tomb, finally built in the 1830s, is well integrated into the agricultural heart of the estate, accessible along something like a circuit walk. Washington could have chosen a site in a more classically idyllic location, such as in the wooded areas, off the open fields on the north, or (less bucolically) closer to the service roads lined with outbuildings.[69] The new tomb's location is entered from a kind of rural pathway and derives a romantic air from its placement in an area of the estate that combined the purposes and appearance of nursery and orchard. The romantic rural cemetery developed first in the Netherlands in the seventeenth century and flourished most famously in the Anglo-American world in the nineteenth century. Washington's siting of the New Tomb on his farm stood in the midst of that development and his final rest there formed a capstone to his moral retirement and refuge at Mount Vernon.

Epilogue

Mount Vernon, the mecca of every American.

MRS. JOHN PARKER (née Anne Sargent) of Boston, 18 May 1831

Let one spot in this grand country of ours be saved from change.

ANN PAMELA CUNNINGHAM, founder of The Mount Vernon Ladies' Association, June 1874

THE PUBLIC RESPONDED early on to Washington's masterful integration of architecture and landscape at Mount Vernon, and the estate and its illustrious occupant attracted a range of visitors in the eighteenth century. By the nineteenth century, a new level of interest arose in the face of social changes in America. Mount Vernon, with its picturesque setting, came to represent for some the best days of a genteel and semifeudal South and the gracious lifestyle that many imagined flourished on such an estate. For others, a visit was a pleasant excursion from the city and a chance to celebrate the Father of the Country. Tourists arrived by the boatload, and artists supplied a ready public with ideal images of the great man's house and gardens. Ann Pamela Cunningham, a founder and first regent of the Mount Vernon Ladies' Association, spoke for many when she asked that progress be excluded from the estate. America was witnessing steady industrialization and urbanization, and Mount Vernon, with its gracious lawns, winding paths, and welcoming portico, seemed the perfect antidote. An awareness of the deteriorating condition of Washington's house brought urgency to the whole project of protecting America's past in the face of the rapid changes occurring in nineteenth-century America, and the saving of Mount Vernon in the 1850s through the efforts of the Mount Vernon Ladies' Association was an important moment in the historic preservation movement (Figure E.1).

FIGURE E.I. Anonymous, *View of the East Front of the Mansion House at Mount Vernon, Seen from the Southeast,* c. 1858, photograph. Courtesy of the Mount Vernon Ladies' Association (CT-7043).

Americans did not only passively view the estate. Artists altered the scenery in their works, as they had from the beginning, and endowed it with extra idyllic qualities. The grounds remained a point of imitation for some developing their own picturesque gardens in the romantic period. In the twentieth century, the architecture of Mount Vernon was particularly influential. It is a marvel to consider the extensive heritage of Mount Vernon's porch, echoed in the lofty porticoes of many American banks, restaurants, country clubs, college buildings, and even gas stations, not to mention residences in Virginia and well beyond. Washington himself, in changing times—from a civil war to two world wars, from industrial progress to economic depression—

seemed to offer a stable historical presence. He was a man and leader who could be admired by any citizen of any political persuasion, northern or southern, native born or immigrant.

In addition to their associations with Washington, the open arcades and the portico at Mount Vernon have come to convey a sense of freedom and Americanness. The much-imitated porch creates a space that is horizontal and open. The portico is about accessibility, movement, and dignified leisure, and is about landscape as much as architecture. Developing a similar idea, Thomas Jefferson turned the wings connecting his mansion house at Monticello to the dependencies into open, unroofed platforms, providing wide, distant views and offering a sense of liberation. Washington's portico also offered dynamic views and permitted free movement; people can enter and leave the space with ease. At once high style in form and vernacular in its accessibility, it formed a link between aristocratic Europe and the more democratic New World. The same liberated feeling arises when one walks the rambling paths and country lanes of the estate. Not surprisingly, when Washington came to consider Pierre L'Enfant's design for the District of Columbia, the president, with his usual expansive mentality, approved the plan's broad scale and dynamic lines of vision.

In his integration of house and landscape, Washington succeeded in creating a place that is deeply American. We know an American house and landscape when we see them, and there is a line of descent from a place like Mount Vernon to Philip Johnson's Glass House in New Canaan, Connecticut, both homes designed with sobriety and calming proportionality and sited in nature to take advantage of prospects of the surrounding land. Similarly, at Fallingwater (the Kaufmann House) in Pennsylvania, Frank Lloyd Wright achieved results similar to those at Mount Vernon. Wright used covered and uncovered terraces, expansive windows, and projecting planes to produce an interpenetration of outdoors and indoors, and he embedded the house in nature to offer the residents and visitors multiple prospects of water and trees. Fallingwater presides over a natural landscape, like Mount Vernon, without a fountain, obelisk, or outdoor sculpture to interfere with the greenery and vivid presence of water. (When Washington spoke in 1770 with a Native American about a site for a house and its prospects, he did so on land not far from Fallingwater, south of present-day Pittsburgh.) Mount Vernon is about the land and man's easy relationship to it; it is a home deeply embedded in woods, gardens, and unpretentious fields and farmlands.

The exhibition of landscape continued inside the house. As an art collector, Washington was unusual in early America for his preference for landscape painting and prints. It is difficult to gauge historical causality, but surely the presence of such art in the presidential mansion in Philadelphia, as well as in the much-visited home on the banks of the Potomac, had some effect on American viewers, collectors, and artists. Washington managed to presage the range of taste that would flourish in the nineteenth century, as he collected landscape works characterized by rough, dramatic expression as well as the softer manner of the classical idyll. Washington deeply and fundamentally recognized that America was about the land, and he embraced this in his landscape gardening, art collecting, farming, and even in his economic investments in real estate and the canalization of the Potomac.

Beyond his embrace of American landscape scenery in both art and life, Washington employed what we would now call "green" and sustainable farming solutions, such as the use of live fences and fertilization from manure heaps and necessaries. Today we recognize other democratic and American aspects of Washington's life and his creations at Mount Vernon: his productivity and economy, his pragmatism in experimenting with seeds and soils, his sense that God was watching over the American nation, and his biblical conception of living in peace under his own vine and fig tree. That he wanted to return to Mount Vernon to retire "into himself" is rooted in the ideals of classical antiquity, but the idea resonates for us as similar to the thoughts of Emerson and, above all, to the experiences of Thoreau, that champion of living in harmony with Nature. Washington created a haven for himself and his family, but in the end Mount Vernon remains accessible to a broader populace and will always form part of the American landscape.

Abbreviations

Diaries   *The Diaries of George Washington.* 6 vols. Ed. Donald Jackson and Dorothy Twohig. Charlottesville: University Press of Virginia, 1976–1979.

Humphreys   *David Humphreys' "Life of General Washington," with George Washington's Remarks.* Ed. Rosemarie Zagarri. Athens: University of Georgia Press, 1991.

MVLA   Mount Vernon Ladies' Association

MVLAAR   *The Mount Vernon Ladies' Association of the Union Annual Report.* After 1996 called *The Annual Report of the Mount Vernon Ladies' Association of the Union.*

Papers   *The Papers of George Washington.* Ed. W. W. Abbot, Dorothy Twohig, Philander Chase, Beverly Runge, and Frederick Schmidt. Charlottesville: University Press of Virginia/University of Virginia Press, 1983–. Available online at http://gwpapers.virginia.edu.

Writings   *The Writings of George Washington from the Original Manuscript Sources, 1745–1799.* Ed. John Fitzpatrick. 30 vols. Washington, DC: U.S. Government Printing Office, 1931–1944.

Chapter 1. George Washington

Epigraph. Humphreys, 35.

1. The rules were translated c. 1640 by Francis Hawkins from a set of precepts gathered by French Jesuits at the end of the sixteenth century. For Washington's *Rules of Civility,* see the text and editorial commentary in *George Washington's Rules of Civility, and Decent Behaviour in Company and Conversation,* ed. Charles Moore (Boston and New York: Printed for Houghton Mifflin Co. by the Riverside Press, 1926). See Richard Brookhiser, *Founding Father: Rediscovering George Washington* (New York: Free Press, 1996), 127–129; and *Papers,* Colonial Series, 1:3, editor's note.

2. George Washington to James Anderson, 21 Dec. 1797, *Papers,* Retirement Series, 1:525–526. For Washington's motto, see also "Ancestral Origins and Emblems," *MVLAAR,* 1963, 23. The motto was adapted by the Washington family from Ovid's *Heroides* (2-55, line 85; cf. Loeb Classical Library edition, ed. G. Showerman [London: W. Heinemann; New York, Macmillan, 1914], 26).

3. Quoted from Howard Rice Jr., review of Henriette de Beaufort, *Gijsbert Karel van Hogendorp* (Rotterdam: A. Donker, 1948), in *William and Mary Quarterly,* 3rd ser., 7, no. 3 (July 1950): 489.

4. "The Host of Mount Vernon, A Contemporary Describes George Washington," 1798, cited from the copy in the MVLA Library.

5. Quoted from Gilbert Chinard, ed., *George Washington as the French Knew Him: A Collection of Texts* (Princeton: Princeton University Press, 1940), 75 (12 Sept. 1779).

6. George Washington to Lund Washington, 30 Sept. 1776, *Papers,* Revolutionary Series, 6:442.

7. See Marguerite Castillon du Perron, *Louis-Philippe et la Révolution Française,* 2 vols. (Paris: Librairie Académique Perrin, 2:152) ("Je n'ai jamais écrit une lettre ni même un mot qui n'auraient pu être publiés").

8. Christy Anderson, "Masculine and Unaffected: Inigo Jones and the Classical Ideal," *Art Journal* 56, no. 2 (1997): 50.

9. John Onians, *Bearers of Meaning: The Classical Orders in Antiquity, the Middle Ages, and the Renaissance* (Princeton: Princeton University Press, 1988), 33–40, 271–273. For the related Doric order, Onians noted—in an observation relevant also for the history of Anglo-American architecture—that for Renaissance architect Filarete "the quality of Doric matches that of a gentleman; so his house should be Doric" (167).

10. Henry Peacham, *The Compleat Gentleman* (London: Printed for Francis Constable, 1634), 221.

11. Thomas Jefferson, *Notes on the State of Virginia,* ed. William Peden (Chapel Hill: University of North Carolina Press, pub-

lished for the Institute of Early American History and Culture at Williamsburg, VA, 1982), 153.

12. *The Journal of Nicholas Cresswell, 1774–1777* (New York: Dial, 1924), 255.

13. See James Whitehead, ed., "Notes and Documents: The Autobiography of Peter Stephen Du Ponceau, II," *Pennsylvania Magazine of History and Biography,* 63, no. 3 (July 1939): 313. For Du Ponceau's account, see also Chinard, *George Washington as the French Knew Him,* 18. Evelyn Acomb, "The Journal of Baron von Closen," *William and Mary Quarterly,* 3rd ser., 10, no. 2 (Apr. 1953): 226–231.

14. See William Blount's letter to his brother, John Gray Blount, in Archibald Henderson, *Washington's Southern Tour, 1791* (Boston and New York: Houghton Mifflin, 1923), 6. Charles Varlo, quoted in William Spohn Baker, *Washington after the Revolution, MDCCLXXXIV–MDCCXCIX* (Philadelphia: J. B. Lippincott, 1898), 18.

15. See William Baker, "Washington after the Revolution, 1784–1799," *Pennsylvania Magazine of History and Biography* 18 (1894): 394 (12 Apr. 1784). The assessment of Dutch soldier Francis Adrian van der Kemp is cited here from the editor's note, *Diaries,* 5:369–370. Washington recorded that "Mr. Vender Kemp" came to dinner at Mount Vernon on 29 July 1788.

16. *Extracts of the Journals of Rev. Dr. Coke's Five Visits to America* (London: Printed by G. Paramore, and sold by G. Whitfield, 1793), 45; see also *The Journals of Dr. Thomas Coke,* ed. John Vickers (Nashville, TN: Kingswood Press / Abingdon Books, 2005), 63.

17. J. P. Brissot de Warville, *New Travels in the United State of America, Performed in 1788,* trans. from the French (London: Printed for J. S. Jordan, 1792), 428; French edition, Brissot de Warville, *Nouveau voyage dans les États-Unis de L'Amérique septentrionale, fait en 1788,* 2 vols. (Paris: Chez Buisson, 1791), 2:266. Benjamin Henry Latrobe, *The Virginia Journals of Benjamin Henry Latrobe, 1795–1798,* vol. 1, *1795–1797,* ed. Edward Carter (New Haven: Yale University Press, 1977), 1:164: "Every thing else is extremely good and neat, but by no means above what would be expected in a plain English Country Gentleman's house of £500 or £600 a Year."

18. Humphreys, 56.

19. *Correspondence of Andrew Jackson,* ed. John Bassett, 7 vols. (Washington, DC: Carnegie Institution of Washington, 1926–35), 2:219.

20. Washington to the Marquis de Lafayette, 30 Sept. 1779, *Writings,* 16:370; and Harlow Unger, *The Unexpected George Washington: His Private Life* (Hoboken, NJ: John Wiley and Sons, 2006), 129–130. Washington to Edward Newenham, 10 June 1784, *Papers,* Confederation Series, 1:439.

21. Quoted from Rice, review of *Gijsbert Karel van Hogendorp,* 489.

22. Washington to James Duane, 10 Apr. 1785, *Papers,* Confederation Series, 2:486; Washington to Annis Boudinot Stockton, 31 Aug. 1788, *Papers,* Confederation Series, 6:497.

23. Washington to Thomas Gibson, 10 July 1773, *Papers,* Colonial Series, 9:270. According to the editor's note, this order to the tailor was sent along with a letter of the same date to Robert Cary in London.

24. George Washington to Bushrod Washington, 15 Jan. 1783, *Writings,* 26:40.

25. Washington to James McHenry, 27 July 1798, *Papers,* Retirement Series, 2:458.

26. Washington to Lt. Col. Nicholas Rogers, 28 May 1779, *Writings,* 15:175.

27. See Washington's letter and editor's note, *Writings,* 15:175.

28. See editor's note and citation in *Diaries,* 5:455–456.

29. Gouverneur Morris to Washington, 12 Apr. 1790, *Papers,* Presidential Series, 5:329.

30. Gouverneur Morris to Washington, 24 Jan. 1790, *Papers,* Presidential Series, 5:48–49. See also "Handsome and Useful Coolers," *MVLAAR,* 1972, 12–18.

31. Washington to Gouverneur Morris, 13 Oct. 1789, *Papers,* Presidential Series, 4:178.

32. Entry for 6 Apr. 1785, *Diaries,* 4:114, and editor's note there. Washington described Vidler as an "Undertaker" rather than an "architect." This was likely Washington's first real glimpse of the contents of the boxes, and any earlier remarks about the chimneypiece were based on the number of boxes and only a presumption of its appearance.

33. Washington to jobseeker John Armstrong, 20 Mar. 1770, *Papers,* Colonial Series, 8:321.

34. Tobias Lear to Washington, 7 Nov. 1790, *Papers,* Presidential Series, 6:636; Washington to Lear, 14 Nov. 1790, *Papers,* Presidential Series, 6:654 (see note that the phrase "rich and elegant" appears only in the letter book copy of the missive, not in the autograph letter received by Lear).

35. George Washington to Bushrod Washington, 15 Jan. 1783, *Writings,* 26:40. The rules are cited here from *George Washington's Rules of Civility and Decent Behavior in Company and Conversation* (Boston: Applewood Books, 1988).

36. Peacham, *The Compleat Gentleman,* 54.

37. For the costly acquisition of fine and decorative art for Mount Vernon after their marriage being in competition with the Fairfaxes and reflecting "George's, rather than Martha's requirements and taste," see Helen Bryan, *Martha Washington: First Lady of Liberty* (New York: John Wiley and Sons, 2002), 138. Bryan

also argues that Martha's tastes while married to George were "notably restrained" compared to the extravagant orders she placed while the wife of Daniel Parke Custis (136). Lund Washington to George Washington, 24 Nov. 1775, *Papers,* Revolutionary Series, 2:421–422. Claude Blanchard, *The Journal of Claude Blanchard,* ed. William Duane and Thomas Balch (Albany, NY: J. Munsell, 1876), 67. See also Robert Dalzell Jr. and Lee Baldwin Dalzell, *George Washington's Mount Vernon: At Home in Revolutionary America* (New York: Oxford University Press, 1998), 106.

38. George Washington to Catharine Sawbridge Macaulay Graham, 9 Jan. 1790, *Papers,* Presidential Series, 4:554.

39. Philip Vickers Fithian, *Journal and Letters of Philip Vickers Fithian, 1773–1774: A Plantation Tutor of the Old Dominion,* ed. with an intro. by Hunter Dickinson Farish (Williamsburg, VA: Colonial Williamsburg, 1957), 61.

40. Washington to William Pearce, 23 Nov. 1794, *Writings,* 34:42. For his reference to "Virginia Hospitality," see the invitation in the letter from George Washington to Richard Washington, 10 Aug. 1760, *Papers,* Colonial Series, 6:453.

41. For Trumbull's notice, see "Minutes of Occurrences respecting the Seige [*sic*] and Capture of York in Virginia, extracted from the Journal of Colonel Jonathan Trumbull, Secretary to the General, 1781," in *Proceedings of the Massachusetts Historical Society* 14 (1875–1876): 333.

42. Kevin Sweeney called attention to the nonbookish aspects of Tidewater colonial mansions in his "High-Style Vernacular: Lifestyles of the Colonial Elite," in *Of Consuming Interests: The Style of Life in the Eighteenth Century,* ed. Cary Carson, Ronald Hoffman, and Peter Albert, 1–58 (Charlottesville: University Press of Virginia, published for the United States Capitol Historical Society, 1999). He noted that "despite its monumental character, the large veranda or piazza probably had its origin in vernacular building traditions" (39–40).

43. Dalzell and Dalzell, *George Washington's Mount Vernon,* 98.

44. See *The Selected Papers of Charles Willson Peale and His Family,* vol. 2, part 2, *Charles Willson Peale: The Artist as Museum Keeper, 1791–1810,* ed. Lillian Miller (New Haven: Yale University Press, published for the National Portrait Gallery, Smithsonian Institution, 1983), 695, 29 May–21 June 1804.

Chapter 2. The Mansion House at Mount Vernon and Other Architectural Designs

Epigraph. Humphreys, 40.

1. For the lease to George, see E.M.C., "The Mount Vernon Lease," *MVLAAR,* 1985, 16–21. George Washington called the five farms of his estate "Mount Vernon," but he never referred to the mansion house itself as "Mount Vernon." He called the farm sur-rounding the house "Mansion House Farm" or (especially earlier) "Home House Farm."

For information on the development of the estate at Mount Vernon, see Morley Williams, "Washington's Changes at Mount Vernon Plantation," *Landscape Architecture* 28, no. 2 (1938): 63–73; Charles Wall, "Notes on the Early History of Mount Vernon," *William and Mary Quarterly,* 3rd ser., 2 (1945): 173–190; Dennis Pogue, "Mount Vernon: Transformation of an Eighteenth-Century Plantation System," in *Historical Archaeology of the Chesapeake,* ed. Paul Shackel and Barbara Little (Washington, DC: Smithsonian Institution Press, 1994), 104–106.

2. There have been a number of fine biographies of George Washington. For some useful discussions of his life and career before the Revolutionary War, see vols. 1–3 of Douglas Southall Freeman, *George Washington: A Biography,* 7 vols. (New York: Scribner, 1948–1957); Marcus Cunliffe, *George Washington: Man and Monument* (New York: New American Library, 1982), 3–75; Harrison Clark, *All Cloudless Glory: The Life of George Washington, From Youth to Yorktown,* 2 vols. (Washington, DC: Regnery, 1995–1996), 1:11–172; Willard Sterne Randall, *George Washington: A Life* (New York: Henry Holt, 1997), 1–196; Joseph Ellis, *His Excellency: George Washington* (New York: Alfred Knopf, 2004), 3–72; Harlow Unger, *The Unexpected George Washington: His Private Life* (Hoboken, NJ: John Wiley and Sons, 2006), 9–86. See also James Flexner, *Washington: The Indispensable Man* (Boston: Little, Brown, 1974); Richard Ketchum, *The World of George Washington* (New York: Harmony Books, 1974); Edmund Morgan, *The Genius of George Washington* (New York: Norton, 1980); Gary Wills, *Cincinnatus: George Washington and the Enlightenment* (New York: Doubleday, 1984); John Ferling, *The First of Men: A Life of George Washington* (Knoxville: University of Tennessee, 1988); Paul Longmore, *The Invention of George Washington* (Berkeley: University of California Press, 1988); Richard Brookhiser, *Founding Father: Rediscovering George Washington* (New York: Free Press, 1996); Albert Marrin, *George Washington and the Founding of a Nation* (New York: Dutton, 2001); Robert Jones, *George Washington: Ordinary Man, Extraordinary Leader* (New York: Fordham University Press, 2002); Henry Wiencek, *An Imperfect God: George Washington, His Slaves, and the Creation of America* (New York: Farrar, Straus and Giroux, 2003); James Burns and Susan Dunn, *George Washington* (New York: Times Books, Henry Holt and Co., 2004); Don Higginbotham, *George Washington: Uniting a Nation* (Lanham, MD: Rowman and Littlefield, 2002); Peter Henriques, *Realistic Visionary: A Portrait of George Washington* (Charlottesville: University of Virginia Press, 2006); and Ron Chernow, *Washington: A Life* (New York: Penguin, 2010).

3. For Belvoir, see Edward Russell, "Belvoir Manor," *Historical*

Society of Fairfax County, Virginia 9 (1964–1965): 8–12; James River Institute for Archaeology, Inc., Williamsburg, Va., "Draft Report. Signage. A.S. Army Garrison Fort Belvoir. Site 44FX4, Belvoir Manor, Fort Belvoir, Virginia," 15 July 1994, especially the sections "Mansion," "Courtyard," and "Ha-Ha" (on file, MVLA Library); and James Kornwolf, with the assistance of Georgiana Kornwolf, *Architecture and Town Planning in Colonial North America,* 3 vols. (Baltimore: Johns Hopkins University Press, 2002), 2:661. Thomas Waterman, *The Mansions of Virginia, 1706–1776* (Chapel Hill: University of North Carolina Press, 1945; New York: Bonanza Books, 1945), 330–334; HABS documentation can be found at: www.loc.gov/pictures/item/VA0402/?sid=76512440d b9ob08fbe653fcd8857890e (accessed June 2010).

4. The mansion house at Belvoir burned in 1783. In 1774, Washington bought over forty lots at auction from the departed Fairfaxes, including a mahogany chest of drawers and sideboard, looking glasses, and andirons. For the Belvoir auction, see Unger, *The Unexpected George Washington,* 94; and Randall, *George Washington: A Life,* 257. See also Christine Meadows, "The Belvoir Sale," *MVLAAR,* 1991, 35–38, with reference to Mount Vernon's manuscript "Sales of Furniture at Belvoir 15th Aug. 1774" and the *Inventory of House Furniture bought by Colo George Washington, at Colo Fairfax's Sale at Belvoir* in the Huntington Library, San Marino, CA.

5. For the architecture of the mansion house at Mount Vernon, see Hugh Morrison, *Early American Architecture, from the First Colonial Settlements to the National Period* (New York: Oxford University Press, 1952; 3rd printing 1966; New York: Dover, 1987); Walter Macomber, "Mount Vernon's 'Architect,'" *The Historical Society of Fairfax County, Virginia* 10 (1969): 1–10; Matthew Mosca, "The House and Its Restoration," *Antiques* 135 (Feb. 1989): 462–473; Scott Owen, "George Washington's Mount Vernon as British Palladian Architecture," master's thesis, School of Architecture, University of Virginia, 1991; Robert Dalzell Jr. and Lee Baldwin Dalzell, *George Washington's Mount Vernon: At Home in Revolutionary America* (New York: Oxford University Press, 1998); Allan Greenberg, *George Washington, Architect* (London: Andreas Papadakis, 1999); Robert F. Dalzell Jr., "Constructing Independence: Monticello, Mount Vernon, and the Men Who Built Them," in "Thomas Jefferson, 1743–1993: An Anniversary Collection," special issue, *Eighteenth-Century Studies* 26, no. 4 (Summer 1993): 543–580; John Waite, *Mount Vernon: Historic Structure Report,* 3 vols., Feb. 1993, Mesick-Cohen-Waite Architects, Albany, NY (on file, MVLA Library); Allan Greenberg, "Architecture: The Mansion House of Mount Vernon," in Wendell Garrett, ed., *George Washington's Mount Vernon* (New York: Monacelli Press, 1998), 46–63. Robert Dalzell Jr., "George Washington, Mount Vernon, and the Pattern Books," in *American Architects and Their Books to*

1848, ed. Kenneth Hafertepe and James O'Gorman (Amherst: University of Massachusetts Press, 2001), 35–58, esp. 36–38; Kornwolf, *Architecture and Town Planning,* 2:679–685; Tom Killian, "Reflections on Mount Vernon: A Declaration of Architecture," *Material Culture* 37, no. 2 (Fall 2005): 60–64; and Justin Gunther, "Mount Vernon and Pattern Books," *Palladiana: Journal of the Center for Palladian Studies in America* 3, no. 2 (Spring 2009): 2–5. See also the data and photographs in the Historic American Buildings survey at www.loc.gov/pictures/item/VA0436/?sid=0e2fcf0 69ed4d3baa57f64f14b8adcab (accessed June 2010).

6. In considering the larger question of who was the architect of the house at Mount Vernon, Thomas Waterman questioned Washington's authorship and attributed the design instead to John Ariss (1725–1799), to whom Waterman also ascribed a number of Tidewater Georgian homes (*The Mansions of Virginia, 1706–1776,* 244–248, 271–298, and 406–408). Waterman also thought that, in designing Mount Vernon, Ariss used bookplates he found in William Adam's *Vitruvius Scoticus.* However, Adam's book was published only posthumously in 1812 and could not have been a source for eighteenth-century Virginians. Ariss's own oeuvre is uncertain, and the attribution of other houses to him remains conjectural. Ariss, who had traveled in England, took out an advertisement in the *Maryland Gazette* on 22 May 1751, offering his skills as a designer of buildings in the style of James Gibbs, and it is not implausible to attribute a building like Washington's to Ariss either on the basis of style or chronology. Despite this possibility, there is no evidence that anyone besides Washington designed the broad lines of the house. While Walter Macomber and others have affirmed Washington's authorship, his role and his seriousness as an architect are sometimes doubted. Although not accepting Waterman's attribution to Ariss, Margaret Brown Klapthor and Howard Morrison wrote that "Washington, perhaps fancying himself something of an architect, dabbled in designs for renovations of the mansion house" (*George Washington: A Figure Upon the Stage,* exhibition catalogue, National Museum of American History [Washington, DC: Smithsonian Institution Press, 1982], 137). In a recent essay, Robert Dalzell Jr., while still attributing the design to Washington, asked whether William Buckland could also be considered as having designed the alterations of 1773–1774 ("George Washington, Mount Vernon, and the Pattern Books," 36–38). Waterman's attribution is frequently mentioned even if not necessarily accepted; see, e.g., Kornwolf, *Architecture and Town Planning,* 2:674. Washington later rented land to Ariss; see their correspondence on 5 and 8 Aug. 1784, *Papers,* Confederation Series, 2:24, 28. For the architecture of Mount Airy, see Morrison, *Early American Architecture,* 353–355; and William Pierson, *American Buildings and Their Architects,* vol. 1, *The Colonial and Neoclassical Styles*

(Oxford: Oxford University Press, 1970), 115–117. See Macomber, "Mount Vernon's 'Architect,'" 1–10, esp. 1–5 for the attribution of the mansion house to Washington. Washington's authorship is also recognized in "The Right Wing of my Dwelling," *MVLAAR,* 1970, 20.

7. George William Fairfax to Washington, 25 July 1758, *Papers,* Colonial Series, 5:328–329.

8. George William Fairfax to Washington, 5 Aug. 1758, *Papers,* Colonial Series, 5:371–372.

9. John Patterson to Washington, 13 Aug. 1758, *Papers,* Colonial Series, 5:390–391.

10. Washington to Robert Cary, 6 Oct. 1773, *Papers,* Colonial Series, 9:343; Washington to Bryan Fairfax, 4 July 1774, *Papers,* Colonial Series, 10:109; Washington to Sarah (Sally) Cary Fairfax, 16 May 1798, *Papers,* Retirement Series, 2:272. A telling verbal indication of Washington's leading role as building designer at Mount Vernon is contained in a letter from South Carolina legislator Jacob Read, who wrote to Washington from Annapolis on 29 June 1784. Read sent an architect, Edward Vidler, to visit Mount Vernon and deliver a letter to the owner. He implied that Washington might need help with improving his efforts, saying that Vidler's "Visit to Virginia is to inform himself from his own Observation of the best place in which he Can settle and exercise his trade . . . and [he] Will be particularly happy if he Can assist in perfecting any of your plans for improving or beautifying Mount Vernon." Vidler finally visited in Apr. 1785, when the building and decoration were all but complete; he is not known to have done any work (Read to Washington, 29 June 1784, *Papers,* Confederation Series, 1:471). See Washington entry for 6 Apr. 1785, *Diaries,* 4:114.

11. George Washington Parke Custis, *Recollections and Private Memoirs of Washington* (Washington, DC: Printed by W. H. Moore, 1859), 11, 65.

12. Robert Hunter Jr., *Quebec to Carolina in 1785–1786: Being the Travel Diary and Observations of Robert Hunter, Jr., A Young Merchant of London,* ed. Louis Wright and Marion Tinling (San Marino, CA: Huntington Library, 1943), 191–198, esp. 195; also Jean Lee, ed., *Experiencing Mount Vernon: Eyewitness Accounts, 1784–1865* (Charlottesville: University of Virginia Press, 2006), 31.

13. Shippen's comments are cited in Robert Lancaster, *Historic Virginia Homes and Churches* (Philadelphia and London: J. B. Lippincott, 1915), 362. The baron's remarks, recorded by Du Ponceau in Sept. of 1837, appear in translation in James Whitehead, ed., "Notes and Documents: The Autobiography of Peter Stephen Du Ponceau," in *Pennsylvania Magazine of History and Biography* 63, no. 3 (July 1939): 312–313. For Du Ponceau's account, see also Gilbert Chinard, ed., *George Washington as the French Knew Him: A Collection of Texts* (Princeton: Princeton University Press, 1940; New York: Greenwood Press, 1969), 18.

14. Quoted from Lee, *Experiencing Mount Vernon,* 99; see also Thomas P. Cope, *Philadelphia Merchant: The Diary of Thomas P. Cope, 1800–1851,* ed. and with an introduction and appendices by Eliza Cope Harrison (South Bend, IN: Gateway Editions, 1978), 113. For William Russell Birch's publication, first issued in 1808, see Birch, *The Country Seats of the United States,* ed. Emily Cooperman, Penn Studies in Landscape Architecture (Philadelphia: University of Pennsylvania Press, 2009), 54. Cooperman observes that about five years before the publication date Birch made a drawing of Mount Vernon that served as the basis for his view (18).

15. *Correspondence of Andrew Jackson,* ed. John Bassett, 7 vols. (Washington, DC: Carnegie Institution of Washington, 1926–1935), 2:219. Letter X, Sept. 1818, John Duncan, *Travels through Part of the United States and Canada in 1818 and 1819,* 2 vols. in 1 (Glasgow, University Press; London, Hurst, Robinson, and Company, 1823), 1:290–291.

16. Charles Ruggles to Sarah Ruggles, 28 Apr. 1822, manuscript A-833 in the MVLA Library, transcribed in Lee, *Experiencing Mount Vernon,* 117.

17. Benson Lossing, *Mount Vernon and Its Associations* (New York: W. A. Townsend, 1859), cited here from Lossing's revised edition, *The Home of Washington, or Mount Vernon and Its Associations, Historical, Biographical, and Pictorial* (New York: Virtue and Yorston, 1870), 151.

18. John Harris and Robert Hradsky, *A Passion for Building: The Amateur Architect in England 1650–1850* (London: Sir John Soane's Museum, 2007), 5, and passim.

19. Barbara Burlison Mooney, *Prodigy Houses of Virginia: Architecture and the Native Elite* (Charlottesville: University of Virginia Press, 2008), esp. 149–224.

20. The drawing is 6.5 inches (height) by 8.12 inches (width), pen and brown ink on paper, W-1369a, MVLA, acc. no. A-286. George Washington to James Anderson, 11 June 1798, *Papers,* Retirement Series, 2:321.

21. Washington's drawing of the west facade elevation and basement floor plan of Mount Vernon were first published in Justin Winsor, *Narrative and Critical History of America,* 8 vols. (Boston and New York: Houghton, Mifflin and Co., 1884–1889), 7:224–225. For both drawings, see Dennis Pogue, "New Light on the Mansion Basement," *MVLAAR* 1994, 17–23. See also, with reference to the elevation drawing only, Klapthor and Morrison, *George Washington,* 137. For the drawing of the basement level, see Charles Wall, "Notes on the Early History of Mount Vernon," *William and Mary Quarterly,* 3rd ser., 2, no. 2 (Apr. 1945): 173–190; William Macomber, "The Pantry Restoration," *MVLAAR,* 1962, 15.

22. Mooney, *Prodigy Houses of Virginia,* 221–222, and Kevin Sweeney, "High-Style Vernacular: Lifestyles of the Colonial Elite," in *Of Consuming Interests: The Style of Life in the Eighteenth Cen-*

tury, ed. Cary Carson, Ronald Hoffman, and Peter Albert (Charlottesville: University Press of Virginia, for the United States Capitol Historical Society, 1994), 11.

23. George Washington to Lund Washington, 30 Sept. 1776, *Papers,* Revolutionary Series, 6:442.

24. Washington to John Rawlins, 29 Aug. 1785, *Papers,* Confederation Series, 3:207. For this commission and Washington's dealings with his workmen, see also Worth Bailey, "General Washington's New Room," *Journal of the Society of Architectural Historians* 10, no. 2 (May 1951): 16–18.

25. Washington to John Rawlins, 30 Nov. 1785, *Papers,* Confederation Series, 3:421–422.

26. Washington to Tench Tilghman, 30 Nov. 1785, *Papers,* Confederation Series, 3:424; for final approval of the project and the letters of agreement with Rawlins, see Tilghman to Washington, 22 Feb. and 1 Mar. 1786, *Papers,* Confederation Series, 3:571, 576, and notes on 576–577. Before the commission with Rawlins, Washington did not know whether the stucco would be painted or left the color of the mixture, and he asked Vaughan for advice. Washington had borrowed Benjamin Higgins's *Experiments and Observations Made with the View of Improving the Art of Composing and Applying Calcareous Cements* (1780) from Vaughan, but this recipe book for mixing cement and for stucco formulae contains no illustrations useful for Washington, who wrote that Rawlins would be the one to "think of a design." When Washington told Vaughan that he had from Higgins "extracted such parts as I mean to carry into practice," he must have meant general information about stucco and not particular design solutions, which were clearly left to Rawlins; see Washington to Vaughan, 14 Jan. 1784, *Papers,* Confederation Series, 1:45.

27. Tilghman to Washington, 16 Jan. 1786, *Papers,* Confederation Series, 3:507.

28. Although the decoration at Mount Vernon is often compared to the work of Robert Adam, such as the stucco decorations in Osterley Park and Sion House, the ornament at Mount Vernon is relatively spare and linear.

29. For Thorpe (or Tharpe), see Washington to Edward Newenham, 10 June 1786, *Papers,* Confederation Series, 4:106; and Washington to Johnzee Sellman, 25 Sept. 1787, *Papers,* Confederation Series, 5:340–341.

30. Washington to Vaughan, 14 Jan. 1784, *Papers,* Confederation Series, 1:45.

31. See Washington to Clement Biddle, 17 Jan. 1784, *Papers,* Confederation Series, 1:49–50, and for the glass panes in the room, see George Washington to George Augustine Washington, 1 July 1787, *Papers,* Confederation Series, 5:243.

32. William Pain, *The Practical Builder, or, Workman's General Assistant: Shewing the Most Approved and Easy Methods for Drawing and Working the Whole or Separate Part of Any Building* (London: Printed for I. Taylor, 1774). Fielding Lewis to Washington, 23 Apr. 1775, *Papers,* Colonial Series, 10:343. The name of the plaster/stucco worker who worked at Mount Vernon and Kenmore is unknown. For the room, see also Melissa Naulin, "A Dramatic Transformation," *MVLAAR,* 2001, 15–25.

33. Thomas Jefferson, *Notes on the State of Virginia,* ed. William Peden (Chapel Hill: University of North Carolina Press, published for the Institute of Early American History and Culture at Williamsburg, Virginia, 1982), 153.

34. Abraham Swan, *The British Architect: or, The Builder's Treasury of Stair-Cases* (London: Printed for the author, 1745). For fireplace surrounds, see Dalzell and Dalzell, *George Washington's Mount Vernon,* 104–105, and 114; and Greenberg, *George Washington, Architect,* 66–71.

35. George Washington to Bushrod Washington, 15 Jan. 1784, *Papers,* Confederation Series, 1:48–49. For coloring of the Small Dining Room, see the report by Susan Buck, *Mount Vernon, Virginia. Small Dining Room Paint Analysis,* 25 July 2002, on file at the MVLA Library. The verdigris-based green paint is the second generation of pigment on the walls.

36. Washington to Samuel Vaughan, 5 Feb. 1785, *Papers,* Confederation Series, 2:326. The attribution to Henry Cheere and William Collins (the three panels with rustic scenes) was proposed by Phillip Dunthorn in "The Chimney Piece in the Banquet Room at Mount Vernon," 1971 (privately produced), on file at the MVLA Library (NA 7210.D86). Dunthorn compared the work to several others by Cheere, including a similar fireplace surround in the Morning Room of the Saltram House, Plympton (Plymouth), England.

37. Powel said of the chimneypiece "it would have been handsomer without the columns"; see Powel's account in Lee, *Experiencing Mount Vernon,* 51. For Latrobe's remark, see Benjamin Henry Latrobe, *The Virginia Journals of Benjamin Henry Latrobe, 1795–1798,* vol. 1, *1795–1797,* ed. Edward Carter (New Haven: Yale University Press, 1977), 163.

38. Francis Price, *The British Carpenter: Or, a Treatise on Carpentry,* 5th ed. (London: Printed by H. Baldwin, 1765), 57.

39. Waite, *Mount Vernon: Historic Structure Report,* 1:121–129. Owen, "George Washington's Mount Vernon as British Palladian Architecture," 42–48, discussed the Tuscan order at Mount Vernon and the British bookplate sources. For the larger question of British sources, see Bennie Brown, "The Ownership of Architectural Books in Colonial Virginia," in *American Architects and Their*

Books to 1848, ed. Kenneth Hafertepe and James O'Gorman (Amherst: University of Massachusetts, Press, 2001), 17–33.

40. Washington to James Hoban and Stephen Hallet, 1 July 1793, *Papers,* Presidential Series, 13:168.

41. For information on the Greenhouse, see Oehrlein and Associates, *Final Report. Condition Assessment: Greenhouse and Slave Quarters, Mount Vernon, Virginia,* prepared for the MVLA, 31 July 1992, by Oehrlein and Associates, Architects, Washington, DC, on file at the MVLA Library. The report includes useful information on the modern reconstruction of the Greenhouse (1950–1952). See also Macomber, "Mount Vernon's 'Architect,'" 7–10; Walter Macomber, "The Rebuilding of the Greenhouse-Quarters," *MVLAAR,* 1952, 19–26; E. John Long, "Mount Vernon's New-Old Greenhouse," *Nature Magazine* (Oct. 1953), 405–408; Klapthor and Morrison, *George Washington,* 158; Dennis Pogue, "Slave Life at Mount Vernon," *Archaeology* 43, no. 6 (1990): 26; and Dennis Pogue, "A Glassy Penthouse of Ignoble Form," *Early American Life* 40, no. 1 (Feb. 2009): 38–45. The Greenhouse and attached Quarters burned in Dec. of 1835, so the insurance view and print by G. and F. Hill of 1859 are not reliable. For the 1803 insurance drawings, see "A Recently Discovered Plan of Mount Vernon," *MVLAAR,* 1952, 42–43. The 1805 drawing is illustrated in "Greenhouse-Quarters Reconstruction," *MVLAAR,* 1951, 38. The drawings that accompany Washington's memorandum (W-1369b, MVLA Library) are discussed in Winsor, *Narrative and Critical History,* 7:225 ("Plan for Greenhouse Quarters").

42. Weekly Reports, for 27 Jan. 1787 to 28 Apr. 1787 (on file, MVLA Library).

43. For the keystone, see Oehrlein and Associates, *Final Report… Greenhouse and Slave Quarters,* 4. Reference to the "Ox eye" appears in Washington to Anthony Whitting, 21 Apr. 1793, *Papers,* Presidential Series, 12:465.

44. Washington to Tench Tilghman, 11 Aug. 1784, *Papers,* Confederation Series, 2:30–31. Pogue, "A Glassy Penthouse," 38–45, traced the origins and spread of the greenhouse in eighteenth-century America and called attention to the greenhouses of Drayton, Lloyd, and Carroll.

45. Tench Tilghman to Washington, 18 Aug. 1784, *Papers,* Confederation Series, 2:42.

46. Tilghman to Washington, 18 Aug. 1784, *Papers,* Confederation Series, 2:42–43.

47. Tilghman to Washington, 18 Aug. 1784, *Papers,* Confederation Series, 2:42–44.

48. The undated memorandum by Washington is at the MVLA Library (W-799).

49. The drawings that accompany the memorandum are at the MVLA Library (W-799), pen and ink on paper, 6.5″ (height) × 8.1″ (width).

50. Washington to Tench Tilghman, 11 Aug. 1784, *Papers,* Confederation Series, 2:30.

51. George Augustine Washington to George Washington, 15 Apr. 1792, *Papers,* Presidential Series, 10:270.

52. For information on the Carroll greenhouse, see Pogue, "A Glassy Penthouse," 40–43.

53. Washington was absent from Mount Vernon for long periods from 1787 until 1797, but ice was placed in the icehouse regularly; see, e.g., Washington to William Pearce, 19 Jan. 1794, *Papers,* Presidential Series, 15:84, and Washington to William Pearce, 18 Jan. 1795, *Writings,* 34:96, and Washington's memorandum to his manager, 5 Nov. 1796, *Writings,* 35:265.

54. Washington to Robert Morris, 2 June 1784, *Papers,* Confederation Series, 1:421; and Robert Morris to Washington, 15 June 1784, *Papers,* Confederation Series, 1:451–452.

55. Morley Jeffers Williams, Director of Research and Restoration, reported on 14 May 1937 (*Minutes of the Council of the Mount Vernon Ladies' Association,* 42): "We know from the evidence of the few views we have that the door was on the south side. We also have fairly good evidence in the soil to substantiate the belief that the door was on the south side; so, briefly, I believe that it was three feet lower than at present, sodded over, and could not be seen from this side, and the door went through the south side, through the Ha-Ha wall to the south lot." Further, he noted "that the doorway was known to have been adorned with a pediment" (116–117). Thus, the icehouse could not be seen from the portico side because of the ha-ha wall, the grade of the hill, and because the icehouse was largely sunken into the ground. Morley contended that Washington filled the icehouse for one winter only. Everything now visible above ground was reconstructed in the 1930s; see "Restorations," *MVLAAR,* 1939, 29–32 and "Construction, Research, and Restoration," in *Council Minutes of the Mount Vernon Ladies' Association,* vol. 9 (June 1939), 99–102.

56. For the civic-minded promotion of buildings in the city, see Washington to Alexander White, 12 Sept. 1798, *Papers,* Retirement Series, 2:605. For a reconstruction of the houses by Faith Jones, and for discussion of the architecture, see Deering Davis, Stephen Dorsey, and Ralph Hall, *Georgetown Houses of the Federal Period, Washington, D.C., 1780–1830* (New York: Bonanza Books, Architectural Book Pub. Co., 1944), 110–117; see also Dalzell and Dalzell, *George Washington's Mount Vernon,* 74–76. For Thornton's role, see Gordon Brown, *Incidental Architect: William Thornton and the Cultural Life of Early Washington, D.C., 1794–1828* (Athens: Ohio University Press, published for the U.S. Capitol

Historical Society, 2009), 23–24: "[Washington] turned to Thornton to help him in overseeing the construction, if not the design, of a double building not far north of the nearly completed north wing of the Capitol. For much of 1798 and 1799, then, Thornton supervised the work of builder George Blagden, making suggestions and changes as necessary."

57. Washington to William Thornton, 1 Oct. 1799, *Papers,* Retirement Series, 4:334: "Sanding, is designed to answer two purposes—durability, & representation of Stone; for the latter purpose, and in my opinion a desirable one; it is the last operation, by dashing, as long as any will stick, the Sand upon a coat of thick paint. This is the mode I pursued with the painting at this place, & wish to have pursued at my houses in the City. To this, I must add, that as it is rare to meet with Sand perfectly white, & clean; all my Houses have been Sanded with the softest free stone, pounded and sifted; and it is my wish to have those in the City done in the same way."

58. Washington to William Thornton, 30 Jan. 1799, *Papers,* Retirement Series, 3:347.

59. Washington to Alexander White, 12 Sept. 1798, *Papers,* Retirement Series, 2:605.

60. Washington to Thornton, 20 Dec. 1798, *Papers,* Retirement Series, 3:274–275.

61. Washington to Thornton, 30 Dec. 1798, *Papers,* Retirement Series, 3:300.

62. The proposal for the project stated that "if the frontispiece is done in Stone add 150 Doll[ars];" and the contract (5 Nov. 1798) with the builder George Blagdin affirmed that "the said George Washington will pay to the said George Blagdin one hundred and fifty Dollars on Condition of his making the Frontispiece of the front Doors of Stone instead of Wood"; see *Papers,* Retirement Series, 3:149, 150.

63. Washington to Thomas Waggener, 21 July 1756, *Papers,* Colonial Series, 3:278–279, and Washington to Robert Stewart, 22 July 1756, *Papers,* Colonial Series, 3:282–283. The editor notes that

two of these plans seem to be those that GW designed for the forts that Waggener and Peter Hog were to construct in a chain along the frontier. If so, it was copies of these that GW enclosed in this letter to Waggener and in his second letter to Peter Hog of this date. The first of the two plans for the frontier forts is a plat of the fort, and the plat is keyed to a table giving the various dimensions of the fort. GW stipulates that the lines of the exterior square of the fort should be 132′ and those of the interior square, 100′. The curtains were to be 60′ long, and the wall was to be 15′ high. The bastions at the corners were to have 19¼′ flanks, 30′ faces, and be 20½′ wide at the mouth. (279)

For the background to these projects, see William Ansel, *Frontier Forts Along the Potomac and Its Tributaries* (Parsons, WV: McClain, 1984), esp. 62–68, 121–126.

64. William Fairfax to Washington, 10 July 1756, *Papers,* Colonial Series, 3:247.

65. See Washington to Thomas Waggener, 21 July 1756, *Papers,* Colonial Series, 3:279, note 1.

66. Washington to Waggener, 21 July 1756, *Papers,* Colonial Series, 3:278–279; Washington to Robert Stewart, 22 July 1756, *Papers,* Colonial Series, 3:282.

67. William Fairfax to Washington, 10 July 1756, *Papers,* Colonial Series, 3:247.

68. George Washington to Lund Washington, 8 Jan. 1782, *Writings,* 37:556–557; see Carrie Schoemig, *Historic Structure Report, Mount Vernon Estate and Gardens: The Mansion Stable,* Summer 2003 (on file, MVLA Library). "The Barn Restoration," *MVLAAR,* 1938, 25–26. The dormers were rebuilt in their original places on the roof; see Walter Macomber's report of Oct. 29, 1949, *Architect for Restoration's Report of Restoration, Construction, Research, and Incidental Projects for the year ended Sept. 30, 1949* (on file, MVLA Library).

69. The windows would be "one on each side of the Pedement, dividing the space equally between the latter, & the ends of the house" (18 Aug. 1793), and, as Washington noted to Pearce, the "back dormant windows could be completed on the range with those already in, and of the same size, and appearance"; see Washington to Howell Lewis, 18 Aug. 1793, *Papers,* Presidential Series, 13:488; and Washington to William Pearce, 5 July 1795, *Writings,* 34:230. See also Washington to William Pearce, 23 Dec. 1793, *Papers,* Presidential Series, 14:606. "Dormant" was in frequent use as a variant on "dormer."

70. A similar pediment appears on the eighteenth-century stable at the Tayloes' Mount Airy (Warsaw, Virginia), and the overall division of the elevation and the rhythm of the doors and windows there bear similarities to the north elevation of the stable at Mount Vernon. As Carrie Schoemig pointed out, brick stables were rare in eighteenth-century Virginia, and brick would have been considered a prestigious material for such a building; see Schoemig, *Historic Structure Report . . . The Mansion Stable,* 26. The dormers were rebuilt on their original locations; see Macomber, "Architect for Restoration's Report . . . 1949."

71. Lund Washington to George Washington, 15 Oct., 5 Nov. 1775, *Papers,* Revolutionary Series, 2:173, 307.

72. The drawing for the house near the gristmill at Dogue Run is in The George Washington Papers at the Library of Congress, 1741–1799, Series 4, General Correspondence, 1697–1799, George Washington, 1798, House for Miller: Plan and Specifications. It

was not unusual for Chesapeake plantation owners of the colonial period to serve as their own contractors or "undertakers" and to order materials for their building projects; see Mooney, *Prodigy Houses of Virginia,* 149–165.

73. The sixteen-sided barn of Dogue Run Farm was reconstructed in 1996 at the present-day Pioneer Farm at Mount Vernon.

74. When Washington built a large brick barn in 1788 at Union Farm, he adapted a design sent to him by English agriculturalist Arthur Young; the appearance of that barn is unknown, although a drawing by Washington for the adjacent stables survives. Also lost is a brick barn, sixty by thirty feet, at River Farm; Washington designed it in 1795 in sketches that would give the local builders "my ideas so fully." He gave Pearce a list of bricks needed for each section, totaling exactly 139,980 bricks. For that barn, as for the sixteen-sided barn at Dogue Run, there is no evidence that he relied on or altered any previous models. For Washington's improving Young's plan for the brick barn at Union Farm, see Jacques-Pierre Brissot de Warville, *New Travels in the United State of America, Performed in 1788,* trans. from the French (London: Printed for J. S. Jordan, 1792; New York: Augustus Kelley, Publishers, 1970), 428. The French edition is Brissot de Warville, *Nouveau voyage dans les États-Unis de l'Amérique Septentrionale, fait en 1788,* 2 vols. (Paris: Chez Buisson, 1791), 2: 266. For general information about the brick barn, which was finished in 1789, see the editor's discussion in *Papers,* Presidential Series, 1:45; for the naming of Union Farm in 1793, the name replacing the earlier "United Plantations" or "Ferry and French's," see editor's note in *Papers,* Presidential Series, 1:213. For the barn at River Farm, see Washington to William Pearce, 10 and 24 May 1795, *Writings,* 34:193–195, 203–204.

75. For payments to carpenters and craftsmen, see various dates for 1770–1771 in *Papers,* Colonial Series, 8: 290, 291, 322–323, 363–364, 424–425, 512. For the early record of the house before it was demolished, see Deering Davis, Stephen Dorsey, and Ralph Cole Hall, *Alexandria Houses 1750–1830* (New York: Bonanza Books and Architectural Book Pub. Co., 1946), 68–69.

76. Entry for 28 Sept. and 4 Oct. 1769, *Diaries,* 2:182, 186. See also the illustration of the early drawing in *Diaries* 3:47.

77. Washington to William Pearce, 27 Apr. 1794, *Papers,* Presidential Series, 15:662.

78. For improvements to the house, see Washington to William Pearce, 16 Feb., 6 Apr. 1794, *Papers,* Presidential Series, 15:238–239 and 524, and Washington to William Pearce, 8 June 1794, *Writings,* 33:400. Fanny Bassett Washington to George Washington, 22 Nov. 1793, *Papers,* Presidential Series, 14:416; and George Washington to Fanny Bassett Washington, 15 Dec. 1793, *Papers,* Presidential Series, 14:525.

79. For the house at Bath, see Washington's entry for 6 Sept. 1784, *Diaries,* 4:10–11. See also Unger, *The Unexpected George Washington,* 161.

80. Washington's entry for 6 Sept. 1784, *Diaries,* 4:10.

81. The list of proportions of the outbuildings at Mount Vernon is not in Washington's hand; see 13 Mar. 1799, *Papers,* Retirement Series, 3:418.

82. The structure, originally built as a sick house, was used as a gardener's house beginning in 1793. The documents begin with the letter from Lund Washington to George Washington, 12 Nov. 1775, *Papers,* Revolutionary Series, 2:356. For a discussion of the timeline and building details in John Waite, *The Gardeners' House at Mount Vernon: An Evaluation of Historic Building Fabric,* Mesick-Cohen-Waite Architects, Albany, New York, prepared for The Mount Vernon Ladies' Association of the Union, Mount Vernon, Virginia, Jan. 1992, on file, MVLA Library.

83. Lund Washington to George Washington, 29 Sept. 1775, *Papers,* Revolutionary Series, 2:65.

84. Washington to William Thornton, 30 Dec. 1798, *Papers,* Retirement Series, 3:300–301.

85. Bryan Fairfax to George Washington, 29 Mar. 1778, *Papers,* Revolutionary Series, 14:350.

86. George Washington to Lund Washington, 30 Sept. 1776, *Papers,* Revolutionary Series, 6:442.

87. Entry for 21 Oct. 1789, *Diaries,* 5:470–471.

88. For his references to Portsmouth, New Hampshire, see 3 Nov. 1789, *Diaries,* 5:490. For Wilmington, Delaware, see 24 Apr. 1791, *Diaries,* 6:119. Similarly, some houses in Maryland were "good mostly of Stone" (1 July 1791, *Diaries,* 6:167), and on the road from Reading to Lebanon in Pennsylvania, the barns were "large & fine; and for the most part of Stone" (13 Oct. 1794, *Diaries,* 6:190).

89. Entry for 4 June 1791, *Diaries,* 6:158. Over the years of the presidency, he wrote little about the architecture of the presidential mansions, either the first one on Cherry Street in New York, the second on Broadway, or the mansion in Philadelphia. Martha Washington called the first presidential house in New York "a very good one" and "handsomely furnished," and George took the trouble to improve the Philadelphia mansion with up-to-date bay windows, but it is striking, given his interest in architecture and in shaping his surroundings, that he had nothing of substance to say about the presidential houses. See Martha Washington to Fanny Bassett Washington, 8 June 1789, in Joseph Fields, ed., *"Worthy Partner": The Papers of Martha Washington* (Westport, CT: Greenwood, 1994), 215.

90. See George Washington to the Commissioners for the District of Columbia, 31 Jan. 1793, *Papers,* Presidential Series, 12:71 and 249. Using similar language, Tobias Lear wrote to Washington on 3 Nov. 1793, calling the public buildings in the federal city

chaste, magnificent, and beautiful; see *Papers,* Presidential Series, 14:326.

91. See Jefferson, *Notes on the State of Virginia,* 153.

92. Concerning Jacky's "elegant buildings," see Washington to Robert Cary and Company, 10 Nov. 1773, *Papers,* Colonial Series, 9:375. For the District of Columbia buildings "are not costly, but elegantly plain," see George Washington to John Avery, 25 Sept. 1799, *Papers,* Retirement Series, 4:323. George Washington to John Francis, 25 Aug. 1799, *Papers,* Retirement Series, 4:270.

93. For a list of books in Washington's library, see William Lane, "The Inventory of Washington's Books," in Appleton Griffin, *A Catalogue of the Washington Collection in the Boston Athenaeum* (Boston: The Boston Athenaeum, 1897), 479–566; Eugene Prussing, *The Estate of George Washington, Deceased* (Boston: Little, Brown, and Co., 1927), 418–433. Prussing noted that the appraisers' "report was not filed in court until August 20, 1810, yet they acted promptly [after GW's death], for the references to Mrs. Washington and the conditions at Mount Vernon show it to have been made in 1800" (86). The list of items at Mount Vernon after Washington's death also appears in Worthington Chauncey Ford, *Inventory of the Contents of Mount Vernon, 1810* (Cambridge, MA: The University Press, 1909).

94. For this trip, see entries for May and June 1773, *Diaries,* 3:178–187. For Washington's dinner with William Paca, see 23 July 1774, *Diaries,* 3:263. Washington likely saw Edward Lloyd's spectacular three-story house, built in the latest style, in Annapolis on 8 Oct. 1772 (*Diaries,* 3:137). He dined with Governor Penn on 17 May 1773 and John Cadwalader in Philadelphia on 20 May 1773, and on 24 May was at Lord Stirling's in Basking Ridge (*Diaries,* 3:180 and 181). Washington and his family dined with several members of the Calvert family at Mount Vernon on 24 July 1773, and on 30 and 31 July he visited them at their estate (Mount Airy) in Maryland (see *Diaries,* 3:194).

95. For the expansion of the mansion house in 1757–1759, see Dalzell and Dalzell, *George Washington's Mount Vernon,* 40–67; Greenberg, *George Washington, Architect,* 6–9, 10–34, and passim; and Robert Dalzell Jr., "George Washington, Mount Vernon, and the Pattern Books," 39–42. For reconstructions of the house under Lawrence and Washington's expansion in 1757, also see "Cousin Lund," *MVLAAR,* 1965, 11–16.

96. For the reconstruction of the main dependencies and outbuildings in existence from the 1750s until 1775, see Waite, *Mount Vernon: Historic Structure Report,* 1:14–24.

97. Colen Campbell, *Vitruvius Britannicus or The British Architect,* 3 vols. (London: Printed and sold by Colen Campbell et. al., 1715–1725), 2:36.

98. For the circuit plan in England, see Giles Worsley, *Classical Architecture in Britain: The Heroic Age* (New Haven: Yale University Press, 1994), 234–235.

99. For the flourishing of the five-part villa plan in England in the 1750s and after, see Worsley, *Classical Architecture in Britain,* 228–230. After 1748, the villa plan replaced the great house as the more widespread plan for country houses in Britain.

100. Waterman, *The Mansions of Virginia, 1706–1776,* 105–339, and Mooney, *Prodigy Houses of Virginia,* 140–148.

101. Rudolf Wittkower, *Palladio and English Palladianism* (London: Thames and Hudson, 1974); Robert Tavernor, *Palladio and Palladianism* (New York: Thames and Hudson, 1991); and Worsley, *Classical Architecture in Britain,* 105–173.

102. Washington wanted Lund to put quoins on the new kitchen and the servants' hall in imitation of those on the New Church (Pohick Church); see George Washington to Lund Washington, 20 Aug. 1775, *Papers,* Revolutionary Series, 1:337.

103. Campbell, *Vitruvius Britannicus,* vol. 3 (1725), plates 29 and 30.

104. The roofs of the dependencies, gardener's house, and manager's house, are recorded as green in the c. 1791 views attributed to Edward Savage (see Plates 14 and 15) and were subsequently painted to harmonize with the reddish roof of the mansion house.

105. Greenberg, *George Washington, Architect,* 19–29.

106. Abraham Swan, *The British Architect: or, The Builders Treasury of Stair-Cases* (London: Printed for the author, 1745), engravings by Edward Rooker. (A later edition was printed for Robert Sayer, London, 1765.)

107. The actual measurement is close to ninety-four by thirty-two feet, but some visitors, including Isaac Weld and Samuel Vaughan, stated this as ninety-six feet, probably reflecting the figure given to them by Washington. Washington himself recorded the measurement of ninety-six by thirty-two feet for the house, writing out the measurements as provided by the county assessor's, namely, "Dwelling House 96 feet by 32, of Wood"; see "List of Houses at Mount Vernon," 13 Mar. 1799, *Papers,* Retirement Series, 3:417–418. David Humphreys gives the width of the portico as ninety-six feet. Samuel Vaughan, visiting from 11 to 17 Aug. 1787, said that the house was ninety-six by thirty-two feet; see Edward Williams, ed., "Samuel Vaughan's Journal," *Western Pennsylvania Historical Magazine* 44, no. 3 (1961): 273; see also "The Vaughan Plan," *MVLAAR,* 1976, 9. Isaac Weld, *Travels through the States of North America, and the provinces of Upper and Lower Canada, during the years 1795, 1796, and 1797,* 2 vols. (London: Printed for John Stockdale, 1799), 1:92. Friedrich Wilhelm Hoeninghaus visited on 18 Mar. 1798; *see Reise eines Krefelders nach Nordamerika, 1797–1798: Tagebuchaufzeichnungen und Briefe,* ed. Wolfhart Langer (Krefeld, Germany: privately printed, 1973), 33–34. Hoeninghaus

recorded the width as 196 feet, which was either a misprint or his mistake. He likely meant the German foot, which differed in length according to region but was close to the English foot. See also Humphreys, 40.

108. Washington, writing to Rumney for finer stone to replace the "hard stone of the Country" already laid down, gave the measurement of the floor of the "Gallery," not counting the border, as 92′ 7.5″, by 12′ 9.25″ (22 June 1785, *Papers,* Confederation Series, 3:72).

109. Washington to Robert Hooe, 27 Nov. 1786, *Papers,* Confederation Series, 4:400 ("The plank I want is to floor a room 24 by 32 feet"). The New Room actually measures 30′ 6″ by 22′ 9″ by 16′ 6″. For the proportionality of the room, see Owen, "George Washington's Mount Vernon as British Palladian Architecture," 10–11. For Washington's note to Rawlins, see note 24 above.

110. For the rustication of buildings in early America, see Kevin Sweeney, "High-Style Vernacular: Lifestyles of the Colonial Elites," 16. The paint surface—sand and white pigment that is brushed over pine boards that are beveled to look like finely cut stone—is itself a rather fragile technique, and the coating already had to be replaced by Washington in the last years of his life. Today, it is repainted periodically.

111. Jefferson, writing in 1781, lamented that "the unhappy prejudice prevails that houses of brick or stone are less wholesome than those of wood" (*Notes on the State of Virginia,* 153).

112. For the presence of rustication on the Mount Vernon of 1757–1759, see Charles Wall, "Restoration Repainting," MVLA Library (Mount Vernon Reference Notebook 10, "Building Materials"); see also Dalzell and Dalzell, *George Washington's Mount Vernon,* 250, note 12. A letter of 5 Nov. 1796, referring to new construction in the national capital, indicates Washington's keen personal interest in the fineness of the sand used for a faux surface and the application for best imitating stone; see his memorandum to his estate manager (*Writings* 35:263–264). See also *MVLAAR,* 1938, 19.

113. For the rustication at the Merchent House in Dumfries, see Pasteur and Galt Apothecary Shop Architectural Report, Block 17 Building 32 Lot 56, originally entitled, "Architectural Report Pasteur-Galt Apothecary Shop and Outbuildings (Reconstructed) Block 17, Building 32 Colonial Lot 56," A. Lawrence Kocher, 1953, Colonial Williamsburg Foundation Library Research Report Series—1375, Colonial Williamsburg Foundation Library, Williamsburg, Virginia, 1990, 11, electronic version available online.

114. For Mount Pleasant, see Morrison, *Early American Architecture,* 526–528, and Kornwolf, *Architecture and Town Planning in Colonial North America,* 2:1232–1234. For Nomini Hall, "built with Brick, but the bricks have been covered with strong lime Mor-

tar," see Philip Vickers Fithian, *Journal and Letters of Philip Vickers Fithian, 1773–1774: A Plantation Tutor of the Old Dominion,* ed. with an intro. by Hunter Dickinson Farish (Williamsburg, VA: Colonial Williamsburg, 1957), 80.

115. For the soft brick exterior of Pohick Church, protected by being "painted with white Lead and Oyle," see 8 July 1771, *Diaries,* 3:39, note 8. Washington often worshiped there and served for decades as a vestryman.

116. For Powel, see Lee, *Experiencing Mount Vernon,* 48. Martha Babcock Amory, *The Domestic and Artistic Life of John Singleton Copley* (New York: Kennedy Galleries, and Da Capo Press, 1969), 160: letter from young Copley to Rev. Richard Bellward, vice-chancellor of the University of Cambridge, 1795, trans. from Latin by William Heath Bennet and published in *Select Biographical Sketches* (London: George Routledge and Sons, 1867), 186. For Brookes, see R. W. G. Vail, ed., "A Dinner at Mount Vernon: From the Unpublished Journal of Joshua Brookes (1773–1859)," *New-York Historical Society Quarterly* 31, no. 2 (Apr. 1947): 77. Latrobe, *Virginia Journals,* 1:163. Alexander Graydon to sister Rachel Graydon, 1814, in the Alexander Graydon Collection, Historical Society of Dauphin County, Pennsylvania; cited here from the copy in the MVLA Library.

117. It was decided by 14 Nov. 1796 that the west front's first floor interior blinds would be changed to exterior ones and matching outside shutters added to the second floor; see Washington to William Pearce, 14 Nov. 1796, *Writings,* 35:279–280. See also Washington to Pearce, 7 Feb. 1796, *Writings,* 34:450, and 5 June 1796, *Writings,* 35:80, in which Washington noted he had earlier dictated the way the shutters should look.

118. Alexander Graydon to Rachel Graydon, 1814.

119. The racking (pattern of missing bricks) still exists on the ruins of the main house at Rosewell, indicating where the arms would have connected.

120. See Susan Stiles Dowell, *Great Houses of Maryland* (Centreville, MD: Tidewater Publishers, 1988), 48–85. For the recent discovery of the colonnades and walls at Drayton Hall, see George McDaniel and Carter Hudgins, "Mystery at Drayton Hall," *Antiques* 177, no. 4 (Summer 2010): 148–151.

121. William Rasmussen, "Sabine Hall, a Classical Villa in Virginia," *Journal of the Society of Architectural Historians* 39, no. 4 (Dec. 1980): 294–295. Entry for 27 Mar. 1760, *Diaries,* 1:258.

122. A payment made the week of 7 Apr. 1792 was for "small fluted rails between the Pilasters of the Archway between the Mansion House kitchen and Servants hall"; see Weekly Reports, 7 Apr. 1792, MVLA Library. Wind blew down the south colonnade, and it was completely restored in 1874. An 1853 photo shows both arcades looking the same. All columns in the north colonnade were

replaced in 1951, but most of the original framing still exists, so the intercolumniations are original. Stonemason Henry Young paved the covered ways in brick in 1781 (see note 12 in *Papers,* Colonial Series, 10:106).

123. Richard Parkinson, *A Tour in North America in 1798, 1799, and 1800* (London: Printed for J. Harding and J. Murray, 1805), 55. The same quote is in Parkinson's text published as *The Experienced Farmer's Tour in America* (London: Printed for John Stockdale, 1805), 55.

124. Edward C. Carter II, John C. Van Horne, and Charles Brownell, eds., *Latrobe's View of America, 1795–1820: Selections from the Watercolors and Sketches,* Papers of Benjamin Henry Latrobe, ser. 3, The Sketchbooks and Miscellaneous Drawings (New Haven: Yale University Press, 1985), 92; and Latrobe, *Virginia Journals,* 1:163.

125. For William Blount's letter to his brother John Gray Blount, see Archibald Henderson, *Washington's Southern Tour, 1791* (Boston and New York: Houghton Mifflin, 1923), 6. For the baron's remark, see Chinard, *George Washington as the French Knew Him,* 18; the notice was recorded by Pierre-Étienne Du Ponceau, aide-de-camp to Baron von Steuben, on 9 Sept. 1837, referring back to Steuben's visit in Nov. 1780. See Whitehead, "Notes and Documents," 313; and Dalzell and Dalzell, *George Washington's Mount Vernon,* 5.

126. George Washington Greene, *The Life of Nathanael Greene, Major-General in the Army of the Revolution,* 3 vols. (New York: G. P. Putnam and Son [vol. 1] and Hurd and Houghton [vols. 2 and 3], 1867–1871), 3:507–510; Charles Akers, *Abigail Adams: An American Woman* (Glenview, IL: Scott, Foresman / Little, Brown Higher Education, 1980), 173–174; see also Abigail Adams to her sister, Mary Smith Cranch (Mrs. Richard Cranch), 21 December 1800, cited from the copy in the MVLA Library (original letter privately owned). Charles Varlo, quoted in William Spohn Baker, *Washington after the Revolution, MDCCLXXXIV–MDCCXCIX* (Philadelphia: J. B. Lippincott, 1898), 18.

127. Humphreys, 40.

128. Jefferson, *Notes on the State of Virginia,* 153; Weld, *Travels through the States of North America,* 95; Duncan, *Travels,* 1:290–291.

129. Letter from Elijah Fletcher to unknown "Sir," 1 Oct. 1810; see Martha von Briesen, ed., *The Letters of Elijah Fletcher* (Charlottesville: University Press of Virginia, 1965), 18.

130. For Sally Foster Otis's letter, see "A Visit to Mount Vernon—1801," *MVLAAR,* 1961, 35. William Parker Cutler and Julia Perkins Cutler, eds., *Life, Journals, and Correspondence of Rev. Manasseh Cutler, LL. D.,* 2 vols. (Cincinnati, OH: Robert Clarke and Co., 1888; Athens: Ohio University Press, 1987), 2:57.

131. Margaret Bailey Tinkcom, "Caviar along the Potomac: Sir Augustus John Foster's 'Notes on the United States,' 1804–1812," *William and Mary Quarterly,* 3rd ser., 8, no. 1 (Jan. 1951): 90; Duncan, *Travels,* 1:291.

132. Whitehead, "Notes and Documents," 313.

Chapter 3. George Washington's Portico

Epigraph. *Diary of Col. Winthrop Sargent* (Wormsloe, GA: privately printed, 1851), quoted in "Diary of Col. Winthrop Sargent, Adjutant General of the United States' Army, during the Campaign of MDCCXCI," *Ohio Archaeological and Historical Publications* 33 (1924): 274.

1. English speakers first called porticoes "piazzas" in the seventeenth century. They also used "portico," with its ancient Roman and Italian Renaissance precedents, and its verbal diminutive, "porch," which can also signify a portico. A colonnade usually referred to a large or finer portico, especially a long one where the row of columns made an effect. "Gallery," which Washington sometimes used for the portico at Mount Vernon, could also refer in early usage to an interior space. The Hindi word "veranda" was only just coming into use in the eighteenth century and was not applied to Washington's porch. For these various terms, see Carl Lounsbury, *An Illustrated Glossary of Early Southern Architecture and Landscape* (New York: Oxford University Press, 1994), esp. 87–88, 154, 285–286; and Therese O'Malley, with contributions by Elizabeth Kryder-Reid and Anne Helmreich, *Keywords in American Landscape Design* (Washington, DC: National Gallery of Art, the Center for Advanced Study of the Visual Arts, in association with Yale University Press, 2010), 484–500.

Nearly all visible aspects of the portico have been replaced since Washington's time. The columns and capitals together have been replaced fully two times (late nineteenth century and again in the early twentieth century), and the capitals were later replaced a third time (mid-twentieth century). The paving tiles, too, have all been replaced, some more than once, in campaigns from the late nineteenth century to the early and middle twentieth century, although the present paving approximates the color and texture of the original Whitehaven flagstone.

2. Washington to John Rumney Jr., 22 June 1785, *Papers,* Confederation Series, 3:72. Washington specified the size of the paving "within the margins" as 92′ 7.5″ by 12′ 9.5″. As Greenberg has suggested, the form of the square columns was perhaps derived from the same plate by Batty Langley that served as a model for the Venetian window in the New Room (*George Washington, Architect* [London: Andreas Papadakis Publisher, 1999], 45).

3. Washington noted William Hamilton's previous mention of the variegated paving that he had installed; see Washington to Hamilton, 15 Jan. 1784, *Papers,* Confederation Series, 1:47–48. For

the most recent full replacement of the tiles, using Whitehaven flagstone similar to the originals, see "Report of the Regent, 1966–1967," *MVLAAR*, 1967, 6.

4. Washington to John Rumney Jr., 5 June 1786, *Papers*, Confederation Series, 4:96. See Greenberg, *George Washington, Architect*, 34–46. Washington's rough estimate of the size of the porch floor ("100 feet by 12 or 14") is in Washington to William Hamilton, 6 Apr. 1784, *Papers*, Confederation Series, 1:267. Later (22 June 1785), Washington offered a precise area for the gallery floor. He requested a price estimate for black and white tiles a foot square and gave the dimensions as 92′ 9″ by 12′ 8″ "within the border or margin, which surrounds it" (*Papers*, Confederation Series, 3:72). See also Washington to John Rumney Jr., 3 July 1784, *Papers*, Confederation Series, 1:483, and a summary of their correspondence in an editor's note on p. 484, note 1. For the installation of the new tiles, see 22 May 1786, *Diaries*, 4:334: "Began to take up the pavement of the Piaza."

5. For archaeology of these underground vaults, see John Waite, *Mount Vernon: Historic Structure Report*, 3 vols., Feb. 1993, Mesick-Cohen-Waite Architects, Albany, NY (on file, MVLA Library), 2:283–289. The piazza, erected in the later 1770s, must have been planned from the beginning, as its paved surface was to be instrumental in shielding the vaults from rainwater. The mansion house at Mount Vernon and one of these underground, vaulted chambers were featured dramatically in the film *National Treasure: Book of Secrets*, directed by Jon Turteltaub, Walt Disney Studios, 2007.

6. Wine was stored there; similarly, in 1798 Washington ordered that in his townhouses in the District of Columbia "a part of the Cellars should be vaulted, for the benefit of Wine" (Washington to William Thornton, 28 Oct. 1798, *Papers*, Retirement Series, 3:153).

7. For information on the portico at Mount Vernon and on Washington as architect, see Thomas Waterman, *The Mansions of Virginia, 1706–1776* (Chapel Hill: University of North Carolina Press, 1946), 268–298; Hugh Morrison, *Early American Architecture: From the First Colonial Settlements to the National Period* (New York: Oxford University Press, 1952; New York: Dover, 1987), 355–367; Scott Campbell Owen, "George Washington's Mount Vernon as British Palladian Architecture," master's thesis, University of Virginia, School of Architecture, 1991; Allan Greenberg, "Architecture: The Mansion House of Mount Vernon," in *George Washington's Mount Vernon*, ed. Wendell Garrett (New York: Monacelli Press, 1998), 46–63; Robert F. Dalzell Jr. and Lee Baldwin Dalzell, *George Washington's Mount Vernon: At Home in Revolutionary America* (New York: Oxford University Press, 1998), 100–124; Greenberg, *George Washington, Architect*, esp. 34–46; Michael Dolan, *The American Porch: An Informal History of an Informal Place* (Guilford, CT: Lyons Press, 2002), passim; Robert F.

Dalzell Jr. and Lee Baldwin Dalzell, "Interpreting George Washington's Mount Vernon," in *George Washington Reconsidered*, ed. Don Higginbotham (Charlottesville: University Press of Virginia, 2001), 104–106; James Kornwolf, with the assistance of Georgiana Kornwolf, *Architecture and Town Planning in Colonial North America*, 3 vols. (Baltimore: Johns Hopkins University Press, 2002), 2:679–685. Young Washington visited Greenway Court (near Winchester, Virginia), the rural seat of Lord Fairfax, in 1748 (16 Mar. 1748, *Diaries*, 1:10). This house, as pointed out by Allan Greenberg (*George Washington, Architect*, 43–44), is shown with a piazza in a nineteenth-century view; however, the structure is no longer standing, and we cannot be sure of the mid-eighteenth century state and appearance of the house.

There is no conclusive evidence that Washington saw any paradigms for such a portico in Barbados when he traveled there with his half-brother Lawrence at the age of nineteen. For Washington's visit and the architecture there, see Richard Goddard, *George Washington's Visit to Barbados, 1751* (Wildey, St. Michael: Cole's Printery, 1997), 6–18, 109–111, 194. Much damage was done by a hurricane in 1780, obscuring our knowledge of architecture there at the time of Washington's visit. For layout of Richard Crofton's house, Bush Hill, where Washington stayed, see Goddard, *George Washington's Visit*, 3, 194. For the influence of the West Indies on the development of the American porch, see John Crowley, "Inventing Comfort: The Piazza," in *American Material Culture: The Shape of the Field*, ed. Ann Smart Martin and J. Ritchie Garrison (Knoxville: University of Tennessee, 1997), 285–293.

8. Dalzell and Dalzell, "Interpreting George Washington's Mount Vernon," 105. For literature on the development of the porch in early America, see Jay Edwards, "The Complex Origins of the American Domestic Piazza-Veranda-Gallery," *Material Culture* 21, no. 2 (Summer 1989): 2–58; Jay Edwards, "Cultural Syncretism in the Louisiana Creole Cottage," *Louisiana Folklore Miscellany* 4, no. 1 (1980): 9–40; Jessie Poesch, "A British Officer and His 'New York' Cottage: An American Vernacular Brought to England," *American Art Journal* 20, no. 4 (1988): 74–97; W. Barksdale Maynard, *Architecture in the United States, 1800–1850* (New Haven: Yale University Press, 2002), 167–218; Dolan, *The American Porch*; Crowley, "Inventing Comfort," 277–315; and Joseph Manca, "On the Origins of the American Porch: Architectural Persistence in Hudson Valley Dutch Settlements," *Winterthur Portfolio: A Journal of American Material Culture* 40, nos. 2–3 (Summer–Autumn 2005): 91–132.

9. Paula Henderson, "The Loggia in Tudor and Early Stuart England: The Adaptation and Function of Classical Form," in *Albion's Classicism: The Visual Arts in Britain, 1550–1660*, ed. Lucy Gent (New Haven: Yale University Press, 1995), 111.

10. For Horton Court, see Paula Henderson, *The Tudor House and Garden: Architecture and Landscape in the Sixteenth and Early Seventeenth Centuries* (New Haven: Yale University Press, 2005), 154–155; and Henderson, "The Loggia in Tudor and Early Stuart England," 109–145.

11. Leon Battista Alberti, *On the Art of Building in Ten Books* [*De re aedificatoria*], trans. Joseph Rykwert, Neil Leach, and Robert Tavernor (Cambridge, MA: MIT Press, 1988), 300.

12. For Holland House, Cranborne Manor, and Camden House, see Nicholas Cooper, *Houses of the Gentry, 1480–1680* (New Haven: Yale University Press, 1999), 131–136.

13. For Old Hall, Nether Hambleton, and Houghton Conquest, see Henderson, "The Loggia in Tudor and Early Stuart England," 109–132, and Cooper, *Houses of the Gentry,* 190–193.

14. For Kirby Hall and Hatfield House, see Cooper, *Houses of the Gentry,* 88–89, and Henderson, "The Loggia in Tudor and Early Stuart England," 109–132.

15. For information on Green Spring, see Kornwolf, *Architecture and Town Planning in Colonial North America,* 2:555–557; Henry Chandlee Forman, *The Architecture of the Old South: The Medieval Style, 1585–1850* (Cambridge, MA: Harvard University Press, 1948), 43, 46; Louis Caywood, *Green Spring Plantation: Archaeological Report,* Prepared for Virginia 350th Anniversary Commission and Jamestown-Williamsburg-Yorktown-Celebration Commission (on file at the Rockefeller Library, Williamsburg), 12 and 17; for the gallery or arcade, the foundation was built at a later time than the house "according to the mortar used, a white oyster shell mixture." Virginia Barrett Price, "The Making, Remaking, and Unmaking of Green Spring between 1643 and 1803," master's thesis, University of Virginia, School of Architecture, 2000, and her "Constructing to Command: Rivalries between Green Spring and the Governor's Palace, 1677–1722," *Virginia Magazine of History and Biography,* 113, no. 1 (2005): 2–45; see also M. Kent Brinkley, *The Green Spring Plantation Greenhouse/Orangery and the Probable Evolution of the Domestic Area Landscape,* Research Report, Colonial Williamsburg Foundation for Colonial National Historical Park, National Park Service, United States Department of the Interior, 31 Dec. 2003 (Rockefeller Library, Williamsburg, VA). Especially useful for information on the social context of Green Spring is Cary Carson, "Plantation Housing: Seventeenth Century," chap. 6 in *The Chesapeake House: The Practice of Architectural Investigation by Colonial Williamsburg,* ed. Carl Lounsbury and Cary Carson (forthcoming, Chapel Hill: University of North Carolina Press). Cary Carson kindly shared with me a draft of the manuscript. Unknown to Washington because of its destruction by fire in 1729, Virginian Robert Carter I's Corotoman (begun in 1720), sported a two-story porch; see Barbara Burlison Mooney,

Prodigy Houses of Virginia: Architecture and the Native Elite (Charlottesville: University of Virginia Press, 2008), 153–154, 300.

16. See Edward C. Carter II, John C. Van Horne, and Charles Brownell, eds., *Latrobe's View of America, 1795–1820: Selections from the Watercolors and Sketches,* Papers of Benjamin Henry Latrobe, series 3, The Sketchbooks and Miscellaneous Drawings (New Haven: Yale University Press, 1985), 100–102. Washington's letter to Richard Corbin dates to Feb.–Mar. 1754; see *Papers,* Revolutionary Series, 1:70–71.

17. Carson, "Plantation Housing: Seventeenth Century," 3.

18. Carson, " Plantation Housing: Seventeenth Century," 4.

19. For Bond Castle, see Forman, *Architecture of the Old South,* 135–138. For the early State Houses in Maryland, see Kornwolf, *Architecture and Town Planning in Colonial North America,* 2:716–717, 729–730. For Malvern Hill, see Forman, *Architecture of the Old South,* 70–72, 84; and Kornwolf, *Architecture and Town Planning in Colonial North America,* 2:565–566.

20. William Fairfax to Robert Fairfax, 14 July 1735, Correspondence of the Fairfax family, Additional Manuscripts, 30306, fol. 144, British Museum, London. (There is a handwritten reference, with citation, to this letter in the Rockefeller Library, Colonial Williamsburg, in manuscript archives under "portico.")

21. Lounsbury, *Illustrated Glossary,* 286.

22. Maude Woodfin, ed., *Another Secret Diary of William Byrd of Westover, 1739–1741* (Richmond, VA: Dietz Press, 1942); the references to his gallery begin only on 20 Dec. 1740 (p. 121).

23. Woodfin, *Another Secret Diary of William Byrd,* 133.

24. Pliny the Younger wrote of his own portico and garden: "My villa, though situated at the foot of the mountain, commands as wide a prospect as the summit affords . . . The exposure of the main part of the house is full south; thus it seems to invite the sun, from midday in summer (but something earlier in winter), into a wide and proportionally long portico, containing many divisions, one of which is an atrium, built after the manner of the ancients. In front of the portico is a terrace divided into a great number of geometrical figures, and bounded with a box hedge." See Pliny the Younger's *Letter to Domitius Apollinaris,* Book V, no. 6. For this quote, and for Pliny and English landscape gardening, see Isabel Wakelin Urban Chase, *Horace Walpole: Gardenist* (Princeton: Princeton University Press, 1943), 6–8, 46–47.

25. Greenberg, *George Washington, Architect,* 43–44.

26. With its appearance engraved by 1720, knowledge was spread by printed image and word-of-mouth of this extraordinary, monumental *all'antica* facade. For Blenheim Palace, see Kerry Downes, *Hawksmoor* (London: Thames and Hudson, 1969); and David Green, *Blenheim Palace* (Oxford: Alden Press, 1982).

27. For the architecture at Stowe, see Christopher Hussey, *En-*

glish Gardens and Landscapes, 1700–1750 (New York: Funk and Wagnall's, 1967), 89–113; and Michael McCarthy, "The Rebuilding of Stowe House, 1770–1777," *Huntington Library Quarterly* 36, no. 3 (May 1973): 267–298.

28. Balconies and various kinds of verandas, especially two-story, exterior loggias, and small vernacular porches were widespread in the Caribbean and South America by 1750; see Edward Crain, *Historic Architecture in the Caribbean Islands* (Gainesville: University Press of Florida, 1994).

29. George Milligen Johnston, *A Short Description of the Province of South-Carolina, with an Account of the Air, Weather, and Diseases at Charles-Town* (London: Printed for J. Hinton, 1770), 141 (reprinted in Chapman Milling, ed., *Colonial South Carolina: Two Contemporary Descriptions by James Glen and George Milligen-Johnston* [Columbia: University of South Carolina Press, 1951]). For these South Carolina piazzas, see Lounsbury, *Illustrated Glossary*, 269, and idem for the notice of 1748 (*South Carolina Gazette*). For a South Carolina parsonage with a piazza by 1739, see Lounsbury, *Illustrated Glossary*, 269.

30. For Bartram's observation, see John Bartram, *Diary of a Journey through the Carolinas, Georgia, and Florida, from July 1, 1765 to Apr. 10, 1766,* annotated by Francis Harper, *Transactions of the American Philosophical Society,* new ser., 33, no. 1 (Dec. 1942): 30. See William Bartram, "Travels in Georgia and Florida, 1773–74. A Report to Dr. John Fothergill," annotated by Francis Harper, *Transactions of the American Philosophical Society,* new ser., 33, no. 2 (Nov. 1943): 134. For colonial domestic architecture in Charleston, see also Kornwolf, *Architecture and Town Planning in Colonial North America,* 2:867–891; and Gene Waddell, *Charleston Architecture, 1670–1860,* 2 vols. (Charleston, SC: Wyrick and Co., 2003), 1:36–78, esp. "The Charleston Piazza," 68–70.

31. *Virginia Gazette* (Purdie and Dixon), 15 Aug. 1766, no. 795, 3. Looking at another Virginia building, Allan Greenberg, in *George Washington, Architect,* 43–44, usefully called attention to the long one-story portico at Lord Fairfax's wooden house, Greenway Court, in the Shenandoah Valley. This house was indeed known to Washington, but the image has a romantic flavor and the appearance of the porch in the eighteenth century is uncertain. See also note 7, above.

32. First published in 1800, cited here from Mason L. Weems, *A History of the Life and Death, Virtues and Exploits of General George Washington* (Philadelphia and London: J. B. Lippincott Company, 1918), 75.

33. Isaac Weld, *Travels through the States of North America, and the Provinces of Upper and Lower Canada, during the Years 1795, 1796, and 1797,* 2 vols., 4th ed. (London: printed for John Stockdale, 1807), 1:156.

34. Entry for 6 Sept. 1784, *Diaries,* 4:10.

35. For information on Holly Hill, see Donna Ware, *Anne Arundel's Legacy: The Historic Properties of Anne Arundel County* (Annapolis, MD: Anne Arundel County, Office of Planning, and Zoning, 1990), 34–36; see also Cary Carson, Norman Barka, William Kelso, Garry Wheeler Stone, and Dell Upton, "Impermanent Architecture in the Southern American Colonies," *Winterthur Portfolio: A Journal of American Material Culture* 16, nos. 2/3 (Summer–Autumn 1981), 176–178; and Mills Lane, *Architecture of the Old South: Maryland* (New York: Abbeville, 1991), 15–17.

36. See 3 Mar. 1764, *The Diary of Colonel Landon Carter of Sabine Hall, 1752–1778,* 2 vols., ed. Jack P. Greene (Charlottesville: University Press of Virginia, 1965), 1:259: "Colo. Tayloe's stone cutter Ralph finis[hed] 16 Capitols for my Piazzas and went away home at night. He came to work Feb. 3 and has been here 25 days, that is 4 weeks and 1 day[,] So that Jammy is to work as many days for Colo. Tayloe. Colo. Tayloe's stone Cutter worked 2 days more." See also Carter's diary entry for 4 May 1764 (*Diary,* 1:267). See also Waterman, *Mansions of Virginia,* 130–136; Kornwolf, *Architecture and Town Planning in Colonial North America,* 2:661–664; and William Rasmussen, "Sabine Hall, a Classical Villa in Virginia," *Journal of the Society of Architectural Historians* 39, no. 4 (Dec. 1980): 286–296.

37. For Godolphin, see Cooper, *Houses of the Gentry,* 225–226. For the reconstruction of Tudor Hall, see Henry Chandlee Forman, *Early Manor and Plantation Houses of Maryland,* 2nd ed., rev. (1934; repr., Baltimore: Bodine and Assoc., 1982), 50.

38. A letter of 1767 records the building of a "Portico or Colonade to be Joined to the Front of a House and project Eight feet from it, An Arch at Both Ends, for a Passage through it." See Michael Trostel, *Mount Clare, being an Account of the Seat Built by Charles Carroll, Barrister, Upon his Lands at Patapsco* (Baltimore: National Society of the Colonial Dames of America in the State of Maryland, 1981); and Lounsbury, *Illustrated Glossary,* 88.

39. According to the journal of family tutor Philip Vickers Fithian, "There is a beautiful Jutt, on the South side, eighteen feet long, & eight Feet deep from the wall which is supported by three tall pillars." On the north side stood "a large Portico in the middle," and this was "the most beautiful of all." (No substantial trace of Nomini Hall remains today.) Philip Vickers Fithian, *Journal and Letters of Philip Vickers Fithian, 1773–1774: A Plantation Tutor of the Old Dominion,* ed. with an intro. by Hunter Dickinson Farish (Williamsburg, VA: Colonial Williamsburg, 1957), 80.

40. For Monticello, see Waterman, *Mansions of Virginia,* 382–394; Morrison, *Early American Architecture,* 373–376; and Kornwolf, *Architecture and Town Planning in Colonial North America,* 2:690–693; and William Howard Adams, *Jefferson's Monticello* (New York: Abbeville, 1983), 40–85. For Whitehall, see Charles

Scarlett Jr., "Governor Horatio Sharpe's Whitehall," *Maryland Historical Magazine* 46, no. 1 (Mar. 1951): 8–26; and Lane, *Architecture of the Old South: Maryland,* 48–53. For Shirley and Brandon, see Waterman, *Mansions of Virginia,* 173–178, 346–358, 367–373; Morrison, *Early American Architecture,* 370–372; and Kornwolf, *Architecture and Town Planning in Colonial North America,* 2:664–667, 687–689. Washington visited Strawberry Hill, home of Richard Sprigg, on 29 Sept. 1773 (*Diaries,* 3:205–206). The house, designed by William Buckland and overlooking the water in Annapolis, appears in a watercolor of c. 1797 with a long portico. For Strawberry Hill, see Rosamond Randall Beirne and John Henry Scarff, *William Buckland, 1734–1774: Architect of Virginia and Maryland* (Baltimore: Maryland Historical Society, 1958, *Studies in Maryland History,* no. 4; Lorton, VA: Board of Regents, Gunston Hall, 1970), 76. See also "The Calvert-Stier Correspondence: Letters from America to the Low Countries, 1797–1828, ed. William Hoyt, Jr.," *Maryland Historical Magazine* 38, no. 2 (June 1943): 127, note 5.

41. Entry for 23 Mar. 1769, *Diaries,* 2:135. For the attribution to Ariss, see Waterman, *Mansions of Virginia,* 268–298, esp. 247, 271, 406–408. I discuss the questionable evidence of Waterman and the attribution to Washington rather than Ariss in chap. 2. For Ariss and Mount Airy, see Waterman, *Mansions of Virginia,* 243–248, 253–261; Morrison, *Early American Architecture,* 353–355; William Pierson, *American Buildings and Their Architects,* vol. 1, *The Colonial and Neoclassical Styles* (Oxford: Oxford University Press, 1970), 115–117; and Kornwolf, *Architecture and Town Planning in Colonial North America,* 2:668–670.

42. See the entries for May 1773 in *Diaries,* 3:178–181, and p. 185 for his return trip to Philadelphia on June 1–2. For remarks on the early portico (c. 1770) at The Woodlands, the first of its kind in Philadelphia, see the historic structure report by James Jacobs, "Addendum to The Woodlands," Historic American Building Survey (HABS no. PA-1125), 1, 25, 27–29, 75, at www.cr.nps.gov/hdp/samples/HABS/woodlands/WoodlandsText.pdf (accessed Oct. 2010). See also James Jacobs, "William Hamilton and the Woodlands: A Construction of Refinement in Philadelphia," *Pennsylvania Magazine of History and Biography* 130, no. 2 (Apr. 2006): 181–209. Dalzell and Dalzell (*George Washington's Mount Vernon,* 69–83) rightly called attention to the importance of this trip for Washington in the formation of his architectural taste. Porch building was becoming diffuse at this time in Philadelphia; the Carpenter's Company there published a price list in 1786 for "Porches, with posts of pine or oak scantling, the heads turn'd," and "ditto, with the posts cap'd" and "red cedar posts, the heads turn'd" and "cap'd," noting that "those porches are not to have wooden floors at the foregoing prices; and if done different from those described, value accordingly." See Charles Peterson, ed., *The Rules of Work of the*

Carpenter's Company of the City and County of Philadelphia, 1786 (Princeton, NJ: Pyne Press, 1971; facsimile reprint of *Articles of the Carpenters Company of Philadelphia* [Philadelphia: Printed by Hall and Sellers, 1786]), 35.

43. For the architecture of Drayton Hall, see Kornwolf, *Architecture and Town Planning in Colonial North America,* 2:917–921. Lansdowne, built for John Penn circa 1773 (contemporaneously with the final expansion of the mansion house at Mount Vernon), appears in William Birch, *The Country Seats of the United States* (1808), ed. Emily Cooperman (Philadelphia: University of Pennsylvania Press, 2009), 50–51.

44. For Gunston Hall, see Waterman, *Mansions of Virginia,* 223–230; and Kornwolf, *Architecture and Town Planning in Colonial North America,* 2: 670–673. See also Terry Dunn, ed., *The Recollections of John Mason: George Mason's Son Remembers His Father and Life at Gunston Hall* (Marshall, VA: EPM Publishers, 2004), 73–74. Unlike Washington, Mason also built a portico on the land entrance to his mansion house.

45. For the Pinckney mansion and its British, Palladian context, see Giles Worsley, *Classical Architecture in Britain: The Heroic Age* (New Haven: Yale University Press, 1994), 173. For the Shirley Place mansion, see Morrison, *Early American Architecture,* 484–485; and Kornwolf, *Architecture and Town Planning in Colonial North America,* 2:1100–1102.

46. See Greene, *The Diary of Colonel Landon Carter,* 2:706. For Hamilton's letter to Washington, mentioning the "variegated floor" for his green house and "open portico in the front of my House on the Schuylkill," see 20 Feb. 1784, *Papers,* Confederation Series, 1:135–136. In addition to the fine paving for the portico, the brick and stone-border paving on the west front was changed to all stone (Mount Vernon, archaeology department archives, and on file at the library there; undated memo: "The Brick pavements at the West door, are, between the tiles 5 f. 3 I. By 9 f. 6 I.—The tiles are 12 I. Square—and a stone margin around them of 6 in: on the outer edge & 9 I. On the inner next the house.") Thus, there was a paving, now gone or covered, of brick and tile, between the front door on the west and the side doors on the front. The colonnades were paved in brick in 1774, but Washington later made provision for ordering extra Whitehaven stone to repave the colonnades. On 25 Aug. 1793, Washington wrote to manager Howell Lewis that he had thoughts of replacing the stone on the west platforms with Italian marble (*Papers,* Presidential Series, 13:544–545).

47. Various entries for May 1773, *Diaries,* 3:179–181.

48. For porches among the early Dutch, see Manca, "On the Origins of the American Porch," 91–132. For further literature on the building forms of the Dutch in America, see Helen Wilkinson Reynolds, *Dutch Houses in the Hudson Valley before 1776* (New

York: Payson and Clarke, 1929; New York: Dover, 1965); Rosalie Bailey, *Pre-Revolutionary Dutch Houses and Families in Northern New Jersey and Southern New York* (New York: William Morrow, 1936; New York: Dover, 1968); Morrison, *Early American Architecture,* 119–133; Henry Glassie, *Pattern in the Material Folk Culture of the Eastern United States* (Philadelphia: University of Pennsylvania Press, 1969), 145–153; Clifford Zink, "Dutch Framed Houses in New York and New Jersey," *Winterthur Portfolio* 22, no. 4 (1987): 265–294; Kornwolf, *Architecture and Town Planning in Colonial North America,* 1:379–422; Harrison Meeske, *The Hudson Valley Dutch and Their Houses* (Fleischmanns, NY: Purple Mountain Press, 2001); Roderic Blackburn, *Dutch Colonial Homes in America* (New York: Rizzoli, 2002); and John Stevens, *Dutch Vernacular Architecture in North America, 1640–1830* (West Hurley, NY: Society for the Preservation of Hudson Valley Vernacular Architecture, 2005).

Consistent with the arguments here, Kevin Sweeney characterized Mount Vernon as a "large, academically enhanced vernacular dwelling," not so beholden to pattern books, and he noted that any academic forms there were adapted to "local priorities" ("High-Style Vernacular: Lifestyles of the Colonial Elites," in *Of Consuming Interests: The Style of Life in the Eighteenth Century,* ed. Cary Carson, Ronald Hoffman, and Peter Albert [Charlottesville: University Press of Virginia, 1994], 39–40).

49. James Thacher, *A Military Journal during the American Revolutionary War, from 1775 to 1783* (Boston: Cottons and Barnard, 1823; 2nd ed., rev. and corr., 1827), 154. Aquackanock included what is now Clifton and parts of Passaic. Washington also met Dutch populations outside the New York area. He noted in his diary that he worked with and visited the house of Henry van Meter of New York colony in matters related to his surveying work (*Diaries,* 1:15, 19). Washington also had a good deal of contact with Germans in America, many of whom shared a heritage with the Old World populations of the Netherlands by residing there before emigration to America, or by exchanging ideas after settlement in the New World. In 1748 and 1755, Washington went to Frederickstown, a town chiefly "Dutch" (German, in this case) with about two hundred houses. In Mar. 1748 he "took a Review of the town," the earliest record we have of Washington looking at architecture (16 Mar. 1748, *Diaries,* 1:11, and 6 May 1755, *Papers,* Colonial Series, 1:266).

50. For information on the Jonathan Hasbrouck House (Washington's headquarters), see Neil Larson, *The Jonathan Hasbrouck House* (New Paltz, NY: Hasbrouck Family Association, 2000); and Manca, "On the Origins of the American Porch," 118–119. See also Walter Anthony, *Washington's Headquarters, Newburgh, New York: A History of Its Construction and Its Various Occupants* (New-

burgh, NY: Historical Society of Newburgh Bay and the Highlands, 1928), 9–67. Anthony believed that the section of the house with the porch was added in 1750; Larson dated the portico to no later than 1750 and possibly as early as the mid-1720s (p. 8). The historic structure report is on file both at the Newburgh Public Library and the curatorial offices of the Hasbrouck House; see John Waite, "A Compilation of Reports on Washington's Headquarters, the Hasbrouck House, Newburgh, Orange County. II—Existing Conditions Report on Washington's Headquarters (Hasbrouck House)." The report indicates that the shingles, roofing boards, porch posts, floor, steps, and benches date from restoration efforts in 1914 and 1952, while the roof rafters, which are notched into the plate of the house frame, are original and date from the earliest period, placed by Waite at 1750. For the Terwilliger House, see Manca, "On the Origins of the American Porch," 119–121, and Crawford and Stearns and Neil Larson and Associates, *Historic Structure Report for the Evert Terwilliger House, Gardiner, Ulster County, New York,* 2004, on file at the Huguenot Historical Society, Library and Archives, New Paltz, NY. For the Guyon-Lake-Tysen House, see Edward C. Delevan Jr., "The Guyon House," *Proceedings of the Staten Island Association of Arts and Sciences* 6, part 2 (Feb. 1916): 113–139; and William McMillen, "Guyon-Lake-Tysen House," *Historian* 29, no. 1 (Jan.–Mar. 1968): 38–39; and "Guyon-Lake-Tysen House, Historic Structure Fact Sheet," IV, p. 4, prepared by Elsa Gilbertson and William McMillen, June 1983, on file at the library of the Staten Island Historical Society. A painting of Andrew Mille's homestead on Staten Island, made by English painter John Bradley c. 1832–1847 (presently at the museum in Historic Richmond Town, on loan from the Staten Island Institute of Arts and Sciences, The Staten Island Museum), shows a gambrel roofline and portico very similar to that of the Guyon-Lake-Tysen House.

51. Anne [MacVicar] Grant, *Memoirs of an American Lady: With Sketches of Manners and Scenes in America as they Existed Previous to the Revolution,* 2 parts (New York: Dodd, Mead, and Company, 1903), part 1, pp. 166–168. The Schuyler house was subjected to alterations and fires over the years and finally burned to the ground in 1962. For Grant's description of the home, see part 1, pp. 165–166. For the history of the house and an illustration of the earliest photograph, see Reynolds, *Dutch Houses,* 94–96, 150.

52. *The Revolutionary War Memoir and Selected Correspondence of Philip Van Cortlandt,* vol. 1 of the *Van Cortlandt Family Papers,* ed. Jacob Judd (Tarrytown, NY: Sleepy Hollow Restorations, 1976), 31. Philip Van Cortlandt wrote, "Shortly after the Decease of his Grand Father the Honorable Philip Van Cortlandt he was born and his Father and Mother removed to their Manor of Cortlandt and possessed the House and lot at Croton, the House hav-

ing been built." See also *Architectural Record of the Restoration of Van Cortlandt Manor at Croton-on-Hudson,* prepared by the Architect's Office of Colonial Williamsburg, 1 May 1959 (on file at the library of Historic Hudson Valley, Sleepy Hollow, NY), 27–28, 159. For Pierre's addition to the manor house and estate in midcentury, see Antoinette Downing, *The Van Cortlandt Manor Research Report,* Dec. 1953, 2 vols., 1:xii–xiv, and the *Interpretative Paper,* 49 (both kept on file at the library of Historic Hudson Valley, Sleepy Hollow, NY). The period of 1748–1750 was the time of the chief building of the economic estate, an effort that continued into the next decade and beyond, and the porch likely dates to c. 1749. For the stylistic influence of the West Indies on the Van Cortlandt house, see Roger Kennedy, *Architecture, Men, Women and Money in America, 1600–1860* (New York: Random House, 1985), 62; see also Manca, "On the Origins of the American Porch," 124–126.

53. The house was demolished in the 1980s and had already lost its porch, but it is documented extensively in the Historic American Buildings Survey. Notice of the sale is found in *New-York Weekly Journal* 306 (22 Oct. 1739): 4. (I am grateful to Neil Larson for calling this document to my attention.) For the HABS survey, which also includes photographs of the house, search "John Haskell House New Windsor" at http://memory.loc.gov/ammem/index .html (accessed Apr. 2010).

54. *Letters and Papers of John Singleton Copley and Henry Pelham* (New York: Kennedy Graphics, 1970 [unabridged republication of *Proceedings of the Massachusetts Historical Society,* Boston, 1914, vol. 71]), 136–137; see p. 162 for Pelham's reply of 24 Sept. 1771. See also Jules Prown, *John Singleton Copley in America, 1738–1774* (Cambridge, MA: Harvard University Press, 1966), 79–82. There are useful discussions of Copley's letter in John Crowley, "Inventing Comfort," 293–299, and Jessie Poesch, "A British Officer and His 'New York' Cottage: An American Vernacular Brought to England," *American Art Journal* 20, no. 4 (1988): 77–79. Copley's drawing of "piazzas" for his house is in the London Public Record Office, London, pencil on paper, 1771, illustrated in Poesch, "A British Officer," 84, and *Letters and Papers of John Singleton Copley and Henry Pelham,* opp. p. 136.

55. See Bartram, *Diary of a Journey,* 52 for the description of St. Augustine. Washington's trips to French forts on the frontier are noted in *Diaries,* 1:123, 148–149 (13 Dec. 1753) and *Diaries,* 2:280–284 (17–31 Oct. 1770). Period descriptions of the French frontier forts appear in William Hunter, *Forts on the Pennsylvania Frontier, 1753–1758* (Harrisburg: Pennsylvania Historical and Museum Commission, 1960), 61–167; esp. useful is the detailed description of Fort Duquesne (97–136).

56. See Sophia Hinshalwood, "The Dutch Culture Area of the Mid-Hudson Valley," Ph.D. diss., Rutgers University, 1981, p. 58,

for the Dutch cultural influence on groups such as Huguenots in the Hudson Valley.

For further history of the Bevier-Elting House, there is an account and an historic structure report in the federal government's Historic American Buildings Survey; search under "Bevier-Elting" at http://memory.loc.gov/ammem/collections. The account includes a report of May 26 1934 by Myron Teller, who noted (p. 3 of the "Data Pages") that "it would seem that the lean-to porch roof was built on the north side when the middle portion of the building was added [before 1750, following his dating] and was for the protection of the two outside entrance doors, No. 1 and No. 6, as well as affording a space for temporary storage when supplies were delivered."

For the French contribution to the porch in North America and Old World precedents, see Edwards, "Complex Origins," 11, 37–43, and "Cultural Syncretism," 16–19. See also Nellis Crouse, *French Pioneers in the West Indies, 1624–1664* (New York: Columbia University Press, 1940), 211–212.

57. J. Hector St. John de Crèvecoeur, *Letters from an American Farmer,* first published in London, 1782, ed. Susan Manning (Oxford: Oxford University Press, 1997), 36.

58. According to Carl Lounsbury, the piazza that burned in 1747 has in modern times been incorrectly reconstructed as having piers three rows deep; see Lounsbury, *Capitol Architectural Report, Block & Building 11, lot 00,* 1989, Colonial Williamsburg Foundation Library Research Report Series—1137, in the Colonial Williamsburg Foundation Library. For a history of the Capitol, see Marcus Whiffen, *The Public Buildings of Williamsburg, Colonial Capital of Virginia: An Architectural History,* Williamsburg Architectural Studies 1 (Williamsburg, VA: Colonial Williamsburg, 1958), 34–52.

59. Carl Lounsbury has shown how these kinds of arcaded porticoes were derived from English town halls and other public buildings of the seventeenth and eighteenth centuries. See 7 Nov. 1768, *Diaries,* 2:108, for Washington's staying at the inn near the courthouse. For courthouses in colonial Virginia, see Carl Lounsbury, *The Courthouses of Early Virginia: An Architectural History* (Charlottesville: University of Virginia Press, 2005); esp. 43–44 for the King William County Courthouse. Also useful for courthouses in colonial Virginia is Kornwolf, *Architecture and Town Planning in Colonial North America,* 2:626–630.

60. For his reference to the "piazza" at Mount Vernon, see, e.g., *Diaries,* 4:335, 336, notes made at the time of the laying of pavement in May 1786. For his reference to the portico as a "gallery" and "colonnade," see, e.g., Washington's letters to John Rumney Jr. in England in *Papers,* Confederation Series, 1:483 (3 July 1784), 3:72 (22 June 1785), and 4:96 (5 June 1786), and a letter to William

Hamilton of Philadelphia, 15 Jan. 1784, *Papers,* Confederation Series, 1:48.

Washington intended to build a modest dwelling house 36 by 24 feet at Bath (then also called Warm Springs), Virginia, with a "gallery of 7 feet on each side of the House, the whole fronts . . . the stair case to go up in the Gallery—galleries above also." See 6 Sept. 1784, *Diaries,* 4:10.

For use of the word "colonnade" in the colonial South, see Lounsbury, *Illustrated Glossary,* 87–88.

61. Lund Washington to George Washington, 31 Jan. 1776, *Papers,* Revolutionary Series, 3:232. Lounsbury, *Illustrated Glossary,* 327. Washington referred to the "open shed" in Alexandria sheltering his tobacco on 25 Jan. 1760, *Diaries,* 1:228.

62. Hunter's observation can be found in Robert Hunter Jr., *Quebec to Carolina in 1785–1786: Being the Travel Diary and Observations of Robert Hunter, Jr., a Young Merchant of London,* ed. Louis B. Wright and Marion Tinling (San Marino, CA: Huntington Library, 1943), 196; see also Jean Lee, ed., *Experiencing Mount Vernon: Eyewitness Accounts, 1784–1865* (Charlottesville: University of Virginia Press, 2006), 33.

63. For the porch at Todd's Black Horse Tavern, see Alexander Hamilton, *Gentleman's Progress: The Itinerarium of Dr. Alexander Hamilton, 1744,* ed. Carl Bridenbaugh (Pittsburgh: University of Pittsburgh Press, 1992), 79. For the City Tavern in Philadelphia, see *Diaries,* 3:274–275 (with illustrations).

For contemporary evidence of the prevalence of tavern/inn porches in eighteenth-century America, see Marquis de Chastellux, *Travels in North America in the Years 1780, 1781 and 1782,* trans. and intro. by Howard Rice, 2 vols. (Chapel Hill: University of North Carolina Press, 1963), 2:592–593; the translator of the Marquis de Chastellux's travel diary, the Englishman George Grieve, noted in 1787 that in America "every tavern or inn is provided with a covered portico for the convenience of its guests, and this evidently from the necessity of the case [to keep out bad weather]" (2:592–593); for information on this 1787 translation, see 1:48, note 12.

The importance of taverns in fostering the development of the porch in early America is argued for by W. Barksdale Maynard, *Architecture in the United States, 1800–1850* (New Haven: Yale University Press, 2002), 187–197. Maynard also noted the presence of porches in early American spas.

64. Catherine Schlesinger, *Christiana Campbell's Tavern Architectural Report, Block 7, Building 45, Lot 21,* 1977, Colonial Williamsburg Foundation Library Research Report Series, 1102, on file, Colonial Williamsburg Foundation Library, p. 5.

For the Raleigh Tavern's portico, see, e.g., *Virginia Gazette* (Purdie and Dixon), no. 1138, 20 May 1773. For Wetherburn's Tavern

in Williamsburg, see *Wetherburn's Tavern Historical Report, Block 9 Building 31,* originally entitled "Wetherburn's Tavern Interpretation," J. Douglas Smith, 1968, Colonial Williamsburg Foundation Library Research Report Series, 1638, on file, Rockefeller Library, Williamsburg, electronic version available online. For the Charlton Coffeehouse, see *Charlton House Historical Report, Block 9 Building 30 Lot 22,* originally entitled "Charlton House," Mary E. McWilliams, 1943, Colonial Williamsburg Foundation Library Research Report Series, 1161, on file, Rockefeller Library, Williamsburg, electronic version available online. The Rising Sun Tavern is discussed in Thomas Boswell, "The Rising Sun Tavern— An Original Porch Reconstruction," guest ed. Catherine A. Von Briechinridge, *Discovery* (Fall 1978), 4–5. For the portico of the inn at the King William County Courthouse and his visit there, see the note in *Diaries,* 2:108, referencing the description of the portico in *Virginia Gazette* (Dixon and Hunter), no. 1395, 26 Dec. 1777, p. 1. See also Lounsbury, *The Courthouses of Early Virginia,* 43–44.

65. William Chambers's essay "Of the Art of Laying Out Gardens Among the Chinese" appears in the volume *Designs of Chinese Buildings, Furniture, Dresses, Machines and Utensils* (London, 1757); see also William Chambers, *Dissertation on Oriental Gardening* (Dublin: Printed for W. Wilson, 1773).

66. For Asian wallpaper now at Winterthur (acquired by Henry Francis du Pont in 1928), information about Chinese wallpaper in the eighteenth century, and further bibliography, see Diana Rowan, "Reading the Wallpaper of the Chinese Parlor at the Winterthur Museum," *Antiques* 161 (Mar. 2002): 116–125; and Jay Cantor, *Winterthur: Expanded and Updated* (New York: Harry Abrams, 1997), 47, 88, 186.

Washington's *famille rose* tea service from the 1750s is discussed in Carol Borchert Cadou, *The George Washington Collection: Fine and Decorative Arts at Mount Vernon* (Manchester, VT: Hudson Hills Press, for the MVLA, 2006), 44–45. See also Susan Detweiler, "The Ceramics," *Antiques* 135 (Feb. 1989): 498, and *George Washington's Chinaware* (New York: Harry N. Abrams, 1982), 24. For the garniture set (MVLA, 2004.04.01), see Cadou, *George Washington Collection,* 194–195.

67. A Chinese glass painting showing an open portico is *An Oriental Beauty,* enamel on silvered glass, c. 1760, now in the Marble Hill House in Richmond, England.

68. See David B. Warren, Michael K. Brown, Emily Ballew Neff, and Elizabeth Ann Coleman, *American Decorative Arts and Paintings in the Bayou Bend Collection* (Princeton, NJ: Princeton University Press, 1998), 44–46.

69. Edward Kimber, *Itinerant Observations in America,* ed. Kevin J. Hayes (Newark: University of Delaware Press; London:

Associated University Presses, 1998), 34. This description is echoed by a letter from Samuel Fayrweather (25 May 1748), which gives the dimensions of the piazza, including its impressive height: "The first Story, is 10 feet being pannelld Work, its Second Story is eight feet, being wheather boarded, it has a hip Roof with Dormant Window. It has a Piazza all around of 10 feet Broad, Near 20 feet high." See "Collections of the Georgia Historical Society, Other Documents and Notes: A Description of Whitefield's Bethesda: Samuel Fayrweather to Thomas Prince and Thomas Foxcroft," ed. Lilla Mills Hawes, *Georgia Historical Quarterly* 45 (1961): 364–365. See a similar description in John Bartram, *Diary of a Journey,* 29 (25 Sept. 1765).

70. See *The Journal of William Stephens, 1741–1743,* 2 vols., ed. E. Merton Coulter (Athens: University of Georgia Press, 1958–1959), 1:87.

71. See *Letters and Papers of John Singleton Copley and Henry Pelham,* 136–137.

72. Edward C. Carter II, John C. Van Horne, and Lee W. Formwalt, eds., *The Journals of Benjamin Henry Latrobe, 1799–1820, from Philadelphia to New Orleans* (New Haven: Yale University Press, 1980), 266 (22 Mar. 1819).

73. Elizabeth Cometti, ed., *The American Journals of Lt. John Enys* (Syracuse, NY: Syracuse University Press, 1976), 246. For Augustus John Foster, see *Jeffersonian America: Notes on the United States of America Collected in the Years 1805–6–7 and 11–12 by Sir Augustus John Foster, Bart.,* ed. with an intro. by Richard Beale Davis (San Marino, CA: Huntington Library, 1954), 115.

74. Julian Ursyn Niemcewicz, *Under Their Vine and Fig Tree: Travels through America in 1797–1799, 1805, with Some Further Account of Life in New Jersey,* trans. and ed. Metchie J. E. Budka (Elizabeth, NJ: Grassmann, 1965), 96.

75. *Papers,* 30 Nov. 1785, Confederation Series, 3:422.

For uses of the central passage in eighteenth-century Tidewater architecture, see Mark R. Wenger, "The Central Passage in Virginia: Evolution of an Eighteenth-Century Living Space," *Perspectives in Vernacular Architecture* 2 (1986): 137–149. Cary Carson has underscored the growing degree of architectural ornamentation in the passage during the eighteenth century ("The Consumer Revolution in Colonial America: Why Demand?," in Carson, Hoffman, and Albert, *Of Consuming Interests,* 625); Kevin Sweeney has discussed the leisure uses of the passage during the time ("High-Style Vernacular," 19–21). See also Dell Upton, "Vernacular Domestic Architecture in Eighteenth-Century Virginia," *Winterthur Portfolio: A Journal of American Material Culture* 17 (1982): 103–104, with consideration of the passage and the demise of the old porch space.

76. Dunn, *The Recollections of John Mason,* 69.

77. See Niemcewicz, *Under Their Vine and Fig Tree,* 97–102.

78. *Memoir of Thomas Handasyd Perkins,* ed. Thomas Cary (Boston: Little, Brown and Co., 1856), 199. Thomas Pym (sometimes given as Pim) Cope mentioned the caged parrots on the porch in 1802; see Lee, *Experiencing Mount Vernon,* 100. See also Patricia Brady, *Martha Washington: An American Life* (New York: Penguin, 2005), 226.

79. Albert Beveridge, *The Life of John Marshall,* 4 vols. (Boston and New York: Houghton Mifflin, 1916), 2:374–379.

80. Hooker was on his way home from Columbia, South Carolina, where he had been tutoring at Columbia College in 1808; see "Diary of Edward Hooker, 1805–1808," in *The Annual Report of the American Historical Association for the Year 1896, in Two Volumes* (Washington, DC: Government Printing Office, 1897), 1: 920 (entry for 8 December 1808); original document is in the Edward Hooker Papers, South Caroliniana Library, University of South Carolina. George Washington Parke Custis, *Recollections and Private Memoirs of Washington* (Washington, DC: Printed by W. H. Moore, 1859), 9; Sally Foster Otis (Mrs. Harrison Gray Otis) to Mrs. Charles Apthorp, 13 Jan. 1801, cited from copy, MVLA Library; the original document is part of the Harrison Gray Otis Papers at the Massachusetts Historical Society; see also a shorter, edited transcription in Alexander Campbell, "Mrs. Harrison Gray Otis at Mount Vernon, 1801," *Antiques* 108 (July 1975): 42–44.

81. Philadelphia craftsmen Robert and Gilbert Gaw made thirty Windsor chairs for Washington in 1796; see "The Gaw Windsors," *MVLAAR,* 1971, 27–29. For the Windsor chairs at Mount Vernon, see "Chairs for Common Sitting," *MVLAAR,* 1962, 19–21. By 1799, ten Windsor chairs, with yellow upholstery on the seats, stood also in the adjacent Little Parlor (see "Chairs for Common Sitting," 20–21). Niemcewicz, *Under Their Vine and Fig Tree,* 95–108 (June 1798); and Benjamin Henry Latrobe, *The Virginia Journals of Benjamin Henry Latrobe, 1795–1798,* vol. 1, *1795–1797,* ed. Edward Carter (New Haven: Yale University Press, 1977), plate 20.

82. For early English banqueting houses, see Paula Henderson, "Tudor and Early Stuart Banqueting Houses," *Antiques* 169 (June 2006), 76–85; Henderson, *The Tudor House and Garden,* 213–214.

83. Crowley, "Inventing Comfort," 306–315. Crowley noted that "garden pavilions and summerhouses were virtually piazzas without houses attached to them" (312).

According to Robert Beverley, summerhouses were already present in the colony by 1705 (*The History and Present State of Virginia,* ed. with an intro. by Louis B. Wright [Chapel Hill: University of North Carolina Press, 1947], 299). Did George Washington have a summerhouse? The English visitor Samuel Vaughan listed and drew a "summerhouse" on the map of the estate that he sent to George Washington; this appears at the west end of the lower wall garden (see Figure 4.4). Still, there is no other evidence for this, and Vaughan himself had not earlier noted the presence of a summerhouse in the journal map he made during his actual visit (see Figure 4.3).

The summerhouse at the edge of the east lawn and the sloping hill was built by Bushrod Washington and documented as early as 1815. It occupied the spot over Washington's brick icehouse. On this same place, a summerhouse/gazebo appears in the view of Mount Vernon in Isaac Weld's book of 1798, but Weld's view is replete with fanciful elements (see Figure 6.19). A curious piece of literary information, cited by Benson Lossing, comes in the form of a letter supposedly written by Martha to a "kinswoman in New Kent," mentioning that George Washington had "dreamed that he and I were sitting in the summer-house" at Mount Vernon (Benson Lossing, *Mary and Martha, the Mother and the Wife of George Washington* [New York: Harper and Brothers, 1886], 324–326). The existence of this letter, which Benson stated he had seen at Arlington House and was dated 18 Sept. 1799, is not substantiated; nor is its style consistent with Martha Washington's. On the whole, given the lack of physical, documentary, or visual evidence, we can conclude that there was no summerhouse at Mount Vernon. However, there could well have been a "mount" over the icehouse at the edge of the east lawn, forming a spot for viewing.

After giving a review of the evidence, the presence of a summerhouse on the grounds during the time of George Washington is denied in John Rhodehamel's "Memorandum to the Director," written 9 Dec. 1980 (on file, MVLA Library).

84. Humphreys, 40. Offered as an unsigned article in "American Advices," in *Osborne's New Hampshire Spy* (Portsmouth) 10, no. 3 (19 Apr. 1791): 10, and in Jedidiah Morse, *The Universal American Geography,* 2 vols. (Boston: Isaiah Thomas and Ebenezer Andrews, 1793), 1:549. For Latrobe's notice, see Carter, Van Horne, and Brownell, *Latrobe's View of America,* 92; and Edward C. Carter II, John C. Van Horne, and Lee W. Formwalt, eds., *The Journals of Benjamin Henry Latrobe, 1799–1820: From Philadelphia to New Orleans,* 3 vols. (New Haven: Yale University Press, 1980), 1:163.

85. *The Selected Papers of Charles Willson Peale and His Family,* vol. 2, part 2, *Charles Willson Peale: The Artist as Museum Keeper, 1791–1810,* ed. Lillian Miller (New Haven: Yale University Press, 1983), 695–696 (29 May–21 June 1804); entry for 23 Apr. 1791, "Journal of William Loughton Smith, 1790–1791," *Massachusetts Historical Society Proceedings* 51 (Oct. 1917–June 1918): 63. See Cometti, *The American Journals of Lt. John Enys,* 246.

Chapter 4. Washington as Gardener

Epigraph. William Blount, North Carolinian political leader who was appointed territorial governor by George Washington in 1790, the year he visited Mount Vernon; see Blount's letter to his brother, John Gray Blount, in Archibald Henderson, *Washington's Southern Tour, 1791* (Boston and New York: Houghton Mifflin, 1923), 6.

1. For the pruning of trees near the river before his death, see Tobias Lear's account of the events of 12 Dec. 1799 in *Papers,* Retirement Series, 4:547: "he [Washington] however went out in the afternoon into the ground between the House and the River to mark some trees which were to be cut down in the improvement of that spot." For the cause of Washington's death, see the online article by White McKenzie Wallenborn, "George Washington's Terminal Illness: A Modern Medical Analysis of the Last Illness and Death of George Washington," in *Papers,* Articles, 1999, at http://gwPapers.virginia.edu/articles/wallenborn.html (accessed Apr. 2010).

2. For a good overview of the development of the land and buildings on the estate, see Dennis Pogue, "Mount Vernon: Transformation of an Eighteenth-Century Plantation System," in *Historical Archaeology of the Chesapeake,* ed. Paul Shackel and Barbara Little (Washington: Smithsonian Institution Press, 1994), 101–114, esp. 104–106. Also useful is Morley Williams, "Washington's Changes at Mount Vernon Plantation," *Landscape Architecture* 28, no. 2 (1938): 63–73; Thomas Beaman Jr., "The Archaeology of Morley Jeffers Williams and the Restoration of Historic Landscapes at Stratford Hall, Mount Vernon, and Tryon Palace," *North Carolina Historical Review* 79, no. 3 (July 2002): 347–372, esp. 358–362. A recent, thorough treatment of different aspects of the grounds appears in John Milner Associates, Inc., *Mount Vernon Estate and Gardens: Cultural Landscape Study,* 2 vols., prepared for the MVLA, Mount Vernon, Virginia, by John Milner Associates, Inc., Charlottesville, Virginia, in association with Rivanna Archeological Consulting, Charlottesville, Virginia, Nov. 2004 (manuscript available at the MVLA Library).

3. For some studies of George Washington as gardener, see Robert Fisher, *The Mount Vernon Gardens* (MVLA, 1960); Elizabeth Kellam de Forest, *The Gardens and Grounds at Mount Vernon: How George Washington Planned and Planted Them* (MVLA, 1982); Deborah Nevins, "The Gardens," *Antiques* 135 (Feb. 1989): 524–531; Peter Martin, *The Pleasure Gardens of Virginia, from Jamestown to Jefferson* (Princeton: Princeton University Press, 1991), 134–144; Rudy Favretti, "Landscape: George Washington's Ordered Beauty," in *George Washington's Mount Vernon,* ed. Wendell Garrett (New York: Monacelli Press, 1998), 108–122; Mac Griswold, *Washington's Gardens at Mount Vernon: Landscape of the Inner Man* (Boston: Houghton Mifflin Company, 1999); and Andrea Wulf, *Founding Gardeners: The Revolutionary Generation, Nature, and the Shaping of the American Nation* (New York: Alfred A. Knopf, 2011), 13–34. There is little evidence for Washington's gardening at

any of his other residences or properties; for actions taken in the garden of the presidential mansion in Philadelphia, see Tobias Lear to George Washington, 1 Apr. 1791, *Papers,* Presidential Series, 8:38. Lear noted that a gardener, acting on his own initiative or on the orders of Washington or someone else, had trimmed trees, put borders in order, planted grass plats, established or improved walks, and fixed a broken garden urn. For Mount Vernon's gardens in a larger regional context, see Barbara Sarudy, *Gardens and Gardening in the Chesapeake, 1700–1805* (Baltimore: Johns Hopkins University Press, 1998).

4. Humphreys, 39–40. The text is based on the manuscript unpublished by Humphreys. In a final version, Humphreys would surely have edited the redundant passages in the text in the section that includes the phrases "While the cultivation declivities" and "While to blended verdure." Humphreys's description appeared, without attribution, in various editions of Jedidiah Morse's *The American Geography; or, A View of the Present Situation of the United States of America,* Elizabethtown [NJ]: Printed by Shepard Kollock for the author, 1789), 381, and in an unattributed article in "American Advices," in *Osborne's New Hampshire Spy* (Portsmouth), 10, no. 3 (19 Apr. 1791): 10. The passage in *The American Geography* is different enough from Humphreys's actual text that it is worth recording here, especially as it is what would have been read by Washington's contemporaries, who never saw Humphreys's unpublished life of George Washington. Morse presented the popular 1793 edition of *The American Geography* to Washington, and it remained in his library at Mount Vernon (see Jedidiah Morse to George Washington, 25 June 1793, *Papers,* Presidential Series, 13:148–149). The passage below is quoted here from Morse's *The American Universal Geography,* 2 vols. (Boston: Isaiah Thomas and Ebenezer Andrews, 1793), 1:549:

> Mount Vernon, the celebrated seat of General Washington, on the Virginia bank of the river Patomak, where it is nearly two miles wide, and is about 280 miles from the sea. It is 9 miles from Alexandria, and 4 above the beautiful seat of Col. Fairfax, called Bellevoir. The area of the mount is 200 feet above the surface of the river, and after furnishing a lawn of five acres in front, and about the same in rear of the buildings, falls off abruptly on the two quarters. On the north end it subsides gradually into extensive pasture grounds; while on the south it slopes more steeply, in a shorter distance, and terminates with the coach-houses, stables, vineyards and nurseries. On either wing is a thick grove of different flowering forest trees. Parallel with them, on the land side, are two spacious gardens, into which one is led by the two serpentine gravel walks, planted with weeping willows and shady shrubs. The mansion house

> itself (though much embellished by, is not yet perfectly satisfactory to the chaste taste of the present possessor) appears venerable and convenient. The superb banqueting room has been finished since he returned from the army. A lofty portico, ninety six feet in length, supported by eight pillars, has a pleasing effect when viewed from the water; and the tout ensemble the whole assemblage of the green house, school house, offices and servants hall, when seen from the land side, bear a resemblance to a small rural village, especially as the lands on that side are laid out somewhat in the form of English gardens, in meadows and grass grounds, ornamented with little copses, circular clumps and little trees. A small park on the margin of the river, where the English fallow deer, and the American fallow deer, and the American wild deer, are seen through the thickets, alternately with the vessels as they are sailing along, add a romantic and picturesque appearance to the whole scenery. On the opposite side of a small creek to the northward, an extensive plain exhibits corn fields and cattle grazing affords in summer a luxuriant landscape to the eye; while the blended verdure of woodlands and cultivated declivities on the Maryland shore, variegates the prospect in a charming manner. Such are the philosophic shades to which the late commander in chief of the American armies retired from the tumultuous scenes of a busy world.

5. Martha Babcock Amory, *The Domestic and Artistic Life of John Singleton Copley* (New York: Kennedy Galleries, Inc. and Da Capo Press, 1969), 160; the letter was from J. S. Copley Jr. to Rev. Richard Bellward, Vice-Chancellor of the University of Cambridge, 1796, earlier translated from Latin by William Heath Bennet and published in "Select Biographical Sketches," London, 1867. Julian Ursyn Niemcewicz, *Under Their Vine and Fig Tree: Travels through America in 1797–1799, 1805, with Some Further Account of Life in New Jersey,* trans. and ed. Metchie J. E. Budka (Elizabeth, NJ: Grassmann, 1965), 95.

6. See Sally Foster Otis (Mrs. Harrison Gray Otis) to Mrs. Charles Apthorp [13 Jan. 1801], cited from "A Visit to Mount Vernon—1801," *MVLAAR,* 1961, 34. See also the edited transcription in Alexander Campbell, "Mrs. Harrison Gray Otis at Mount Vernon, 1801," *Antiques* 108 (July 1975): 42–44; and copy of the letter, MVLA Library.

7. Washington to Samuel Vaughan, 12 Nov. 1787, *Papers,* Confederation Series, 5:432–433.

8. William Parker Cutler and Julia Perkins Cutler, eds., *Life, Journals, and Correspondence of Rev. Manasseh Cutler, LL. D.,* 2 vols. (Cincinnati, OH: Robert Clarke and Co., 1888; Athens: Ohio University Press, 1987), 2:55. See "Diary of Edward Hooker, 1805–

1808," in *The Annual Report of the American Historical Association for the Year 1896, in Two Volumes* (Washington, DC: Government Printing Office, 1897), 1:919 (entry for 8 December 1808). The little houses, built of dried, pressed clay mixed with sand, were rebuilt in brick in 1875–1876 and were restored in the 1930s. See Milner, *Cultural Landscape Study,* 1:2-74-2-76.

9. Milner, *Cultural Landscape Study,* vol. 2, Appendix B, p. 3, and Dennis Pogue, "Approaching Mount Vernon," 20 Sept. 2002 (on file, MVLA Library), 4, have suggested that the White Gates referred to in early accounts were at the site of the present west gates. Other gates on the estate included the bowling green gates, a gate into the ha-ha wall from the east lawn, and gates to the upper and lower gardens. These have all been rebuilt following designs typical for the period; for gates on the estate, see Milner, *Cultural Landscape Study,* vol. 2, Appendix B, p. 4. The White Gates, bowling green gates, and smaller garden gates were painted white. For documentation of the gates and gatekeeper's lodges, see Bushrod Washington to Robert Harper, 19 Mar. 1812, manuscript A-409, MVLA Library. Bushrod described the material of the lodges as "earthwork mixed with sand" and the size of each as "12 or 14 ft. square and ten high." For the architecture of the gatekeeper's lodges, see Benson Lossing, *The Home of Washington, or Mount Vernon and Its Associations, Historical, Biographical, and Pictorial* (New York: Virtue and Yorston, 1870), 210; and Charles Brownell, Calder Loth, and William Rasmussen, *The Making of Virginia Architecture* (Richmond: Virginia Museum of Fine Arts; distributed by Charlottesville: University Press of Virginia, 1992), 302–303; and Pogue, "Approaching Mount Vernon," 12 and 18.

10. Washington to Samuel Vaughan, 12 Nov. 1787, *Papers,* Confederation Series, 5:433.

11. Cope's account appears in Jean Lee, ed., *Experiencing Mount Vernon: Eyewitness Accounts, 1784–1865* (Charlottesville: University of Virginia Press, 2006), 97.

12. For the approach to Gunston Hall, see Kornwolf, *Architecture and Town Planning in Colonial North America,* 2:672–673; Thomas Waterman, *The Mansions of Virginia, 1706–1776* (Chapel Hill: University of North Carolina Press, 1946), 223–230; Terry Dunn, ed., *The Recollections of John Mason: George Mason's Son Remembers his Father and Life at Gunston Hall* (Marshall, VA: EPM Publications, 2004), 74–75. HABS documentation is found at: http://lcweb2.loc.gov/cgi-bin/query/D?hh:2:./temp/~pp_iklI:: (accessed Apr. 2010).

13. Samuel Powel's description of 1787 appears in Lee, *Experiencing Mount Vernon,* 48. The clearing of woods on the estate was an ongoing concern with Washington (see, e.g., Washington to William Pearce, 11 Jan. 1795: "to clear up...the woods between the Alexandria road and the pasture fence," *Writings,* 34:83). See Ed-

ward G. Williams, ed., "Samuel Vaughan's Journal," *Western Pennsylvania Historical Magazine* 44, no. 3 (1961): 273. For the related plan sent later to Washington, see "The Vaughan Plan," *MVLAAR,* 1976, 8–11. Benjamin Henry Latrobe, *The Virginia Journals of Benjamin Henry Latrobe, 1795–1798,* vol. 1, *1795–1797,* ed. Edward Carter (New Haven: Yale University Press, 1977), 1:163.

14. Merchant John Pintard's diary entry of 31 July 1801, manuscript collection of The New York Historical Society, cited from the copy at the MVLA Library, 1.

15. Allan Greenberg, *George Washington, Architect* (London: Andreas Papadakis Publisher, 1999), 11–15; Pogue, "Approaching Mount Vernon," 8–9. See also the alternatives discussed in Milner, *Cultural Landscape Study,* vol. 2, Map 2-2, "Period Plan, circa 1799." Washington himself drew out a straight approach from the gate to the bowling green in his famous Five Farm map of 1793 (cf. Figure 4.1), but this was surely a shorthand indication and not meant to reflect the actual route, as we know the road curved to some extent. Frenchman Brissot de Warville remarked only that "after having passed over two hills, you discover a country house"; see J. P. Brissot de Warville, *New Travels in the United States of America, Performed in 1788,* trans. from the French (London: Printed for J. S. Jordan, 1792), 428; French edition, Brissot de Warville, *Nouveau voyage dans les États-Unis de L'Amérique septentrionale, fait en 1788,* 2 vols. (Paris: Chez Buisson, 1791), 2:264. See also Powel, in Lee, *Experiencing Mount Vernon,* 48.

16. For Latrobe's "Sketch from memory, showing the effect of Mount Vernon on approaching this place from the West on the road from Colchester," see Latrobe, *Virginia Journals,* 1:163.

17. For the planting of buckwheat, timothy, or orchard grass in the field, see Washington to Anthony Whitting, 4 July 1792, *Papers,* Presidential Series, 10:517–518. For rye, corn, oats, orchard grass, and clover in the field in front of the white gates, see Washington to James Anderson, 18 June 1797, *Papers,* Retirement Series, 1:191; in that same letter, Washington wrote that "there will be little or no cultivation at the Mansion house after the year 1798" (1:192).

18. Pogue, "Approaching Mount Vernon," 8–9. If the west gates by Bushrod were preceded on that very spot by earlier gates put there by George Washington, those earlier gates were also out of alignment with a straight line from the mansion house. But they may well have been established before the prospect from the house was planned after the Revolutionary War, and thus the misalignment not planned from the beginning.

19. Lee, *Experiencing Mount Vernon,* 48.

20. Brissot de Warville, *New Travels,* 428 (and Brissot de Warville, *Nouveau voyage,* 2:264–265).

21. Washington to William Pearce, 23 Nov. 1794, *Writings,* 34:41.

22. Latrobe, *Virginia Journals,* 163.

23. For Brookes and his visit, see R. W. G. Vail, ed., "A Dinner at Mount Vernon: From the Unpublished Journal of Joshua Brookes (1773–1859)," *New-York Historical Society Quarterly* 31, no. 2 (Apr. 1947): 76–77. According to a note in Isaac Weld, *Travels through the States of North America and the Provinces of Upper and Lower Canada, during the Years 1795, 1796, and 1797* (London: Printed for John Stockdale, 1799), 53, the slave cabins were among the first buildings seen at Mount Vernon, perhaps implying in that case an entrance to the left or north route around the bowling green and upper garden.

24. For the paintings by Edward Savage and their attribution, see Carol Borchert Cadou, *The George Washington Collection: Fine and Decorative Arts at Mount Vernon* (Manchester, VT: Hudson Hills Press, for the MVLA, 2006), 206–207. See "Rare Early Views," *MVLAAR,* 1964, 14–17. A pair of similar paintings are in the State Department (purchased at Christie's, New York, exhibition catalogue of 18 Jan. 1997, p. 148); although they derive from the pair at Mount Vernon and fine particulars of animals and humans appear, they show less detail for the buildings and greenery. A fireboard painting, in a folk style, records the same composition as Savage's view of the west front (American [anonymous], 1792 or after, *A View of Mount Vernon,* oil on canvas, 23″ × 35.12″, gift of Edgar William and Bernice Chrysler Garbisch, 1953.5.89, National Gallery of Art, Washington, DC). Savage himself listed two paintings of this description, probably the pair now at Mount Vernon, in his catalogue of 1802; he said the east view had been taken on the spot (*A West View of Mount Vernon,* no. 136, and *A North-East View of Mount Vernon,* no. 123, Columbian Gallery, New York City).

25. Washington to William Pearce, 5 June 1796, *Writings,* 35:79–80. For the bowling green gate and its reconstructions in the nineteenth and twentieth centuries, see Milner, *Cultural Landscape Study,* vol. 2, Appendix B, p. 4.

26. Nelly Custis to her friend Elizabeth Bordley Gibson, 29 Apr. 1823, transcribed in Patricia Brady, ed., *George Washington's Beautiful Nelly: The Letters of Eleanor Parke Custis Lewis to Elizabeth Bordley Gibson, 1794–1851* (Columbia: University of South Carolina Press, 1991), 134. Washington Irving wrote that Washington "treated his negroes with kindness"; see his *Life of George Washington* (1855–1859), 5 vols. in 3, vols. 19–21 of *Complete Works of Washington Irving,* ed. Allen Guttmann and James A. Sappenfield (Boston: Twayne, 1982), 1:177. For an overview of Washington as slaveholder, see the essays in Philip Schwartz, ed., *Slavery at the Home of George Washington* (Mount Vernon, VA: MVLA, 2001); and see Fritz Hirschfeld, *George Washington and Slavery: A Documentary Portrayal* (Columbia: University of Missouri Press, 1997).

27. Washington took steps to remove the "old Quarter" (brick slave family house) close to the mansion house, helping to keep the slaves further away from the owner's residence (memorandum, George Washington to George Augustine Washington, June 1791, *Writings,* 31:307–308, note 4, and *Papers,* Presidential Series, 8:301, editor's note 1). The structure was adjacent to the brick Greenhouse and slave quarters, and located between them and the mansion house (visible in Plate 15). The placement away from the house of the common "negro houses" is evidenced by William Loughton's Smith's account of 23 Apr. 1791; see "Journal of William Loughton Smith, 1790–1791," *Massachusetts Historical Society Proceedings* 51 (Oct. 1917–June 1918): 64.

28. Entry for 23 Apr. 1791, "Journal of William Loughton Smith," 64.

29. For the forbidding of slave children playing near the mansion house, see Washington's directive to William Pearce, 23 Dec. 1793, *Papers,* Presidential Series, 14:609–610.

30. Manasseh Cutler, 2 June 1802, Cutler and Cutler, *Life,* 2:57.

31. James Taylor, "Narrative of General James Taylor of Newport, Kentucky," 1805, cited from copy at the MVLA Library (from document at the Cincinnati Historical Society Library). Cf., among other documents, Washington's entry for 6 Feb. 1786, *Diaries,* 4:272: "Planting pines in the wilderness on the left of the lawn and spading the ground there to day."

32. The 1805 insurance drawing is illustrated in "Greenhouse-Quarters Reconstruction," *MVLAAR,* 1951, 38.

33. For Brookes, see "A Dinner at Mount Vernon—1799," 77.

34. See Cadou, *George Washington Collection,* 208–209.

35. Washington called it a "Circle" in an undated manuscript with measurements of the estate, first published in "Washington Document in Rare Collection," *Evening Sun,* 30 Apr. 1912. Washington called it an "oval" in his diary entry of 10 Mar. 1785, *Diaries,* 4:100, and noted that the posts were turned by "Mr. Ellis [William Allison]" at "the Snuff Mill on Pohick [Creek]." See the memorandum from George Washington to George Augustine Washington, cited from *Writings,* 31:307, note 4; the post wood was probably rotting, Washington wrote that "New Posts for the circle before the door must be thought of, but of what kind is not absolutely resolved on at present" (cited also in Washington to Tobias Lear, 26 June 1791, *Papers,* Presidential Series, 8:302, note 1). George Washington to William Pearce, 29 Nov. 1795, *Writings,* 34:378. See the undated manuscript (1930s?), "Location of Posts as Determined from Excavation," MVLA, listed as produced by the "Office of Research and Restoration," photostat available at the MVLA Library; according to that report, eighteen post holes were located, the spacing indicating that there were thirty-two posts.

36. Taylor, "Narrative." Esther White, Director of Archaeology at Mount Vernon, confirmed to me that the oval drive was originally cobblestoned (written communication, Mar. 2010). The manuscript with Washington's measurements is on file in the archaeology department at Mount Vernon.

37. For an overview of the works of Robert Adam, see Geoffrey Beard, *The Work of Robert Adam* (Edinburgh: J. Bartholomew, 1978); and David King, *The Complete Works of Robert and James Adam* (Oxford: Jordan Hill / Boston: Butterworth Architecture, 1991).

38. For the insurance view of 1803, see "A Recently Discovered Plan of Mount Vernon," *MVLAAR,* 1952, 42–43.

39. Marquis de Chastellux to George Washington, 12 Dec. 1785, *Papers,* Confederation Series, 3:451. Hunter's observation of the "most delightful bowling green before the house" dates to 17 Nov. 1785; see Robert Hunter Jr., *Quebec to Carolina in 1785–1786: Being the Travel Diary and Observations of Robert Hunter, Jr., a Young Merchant of London,* ed. Louis Wright and Marion Tinling (San Marino, CA: Huntington Library: 1943), 195, and Lee, *Experiencing Mount Vernon,* 31.

40. Information conveyed to me by Esther White, Director of Archaeology at Mount Vernon, interview, June 2009; at that time, an ongoing excavation revealed the gravel in a section of the original serpentine walk near the upper garden gate.

41. Washington to Henry Knox, 28 Feb. 1785, *Papers,* Confederation Series, 2:400.

42. Henry Knox to Washington, 24 Mar. 1785, *Papers,* Confederation Series, 2:459.

43. See, e.g., entries for various dates in 1786 in *Diaries,* 4:79, 94, 294; "roads" in *Diaries,* 4:78, 95, 104, 294.

44. John Searson, *Mount Vernon, A Poem: Being the Seat of His Excellency George Washington, in the State of Virginia* (Philadelphia: Printed for the author by Folwell, 1800), 11. For the account of Amariah Frost (entry of 26 June 1797), see Hamilton Staples, ed., *A Day at Mount Vernon in 1797: A Paper Read Before the American Antiquarian Society at Their Semi-Annual Meeting in Boston, Apr. 30, 1879* (Worcester, MA: Press of Charles Hamilton, 1879), 11. Frost built in the District of Columbia, and his structure shared a common wall with George Washington's townhouses (see William Thornton to Washington, 25 Oct. 1798, *Papers,* Retirement Series, 3:141, note 5).

45. Taylor, "Narrative."

46. Entry for 6 Oct. 1785, *Diaries,* 4:202, "levelled & smoothed of it, with English grass Seeds."

47. Louis-Philippe d'Orléans, *Journal de mon voyage d'Amerique,* ed. Suzanne d'Huart (Paris: Flammarion, 1976), 53–55. Niemcewicz, *Under Their Vine and Fig Tree,* 95, called the grass "a green carpet of the most beautiful velvet."

48. Washington to Clement Biddle, 3 Nov. 1784, *Papers,* Confederation Series, 2:114.

49. Washington to Clement Biddle, 3 Nov. 1784, *Papers,* Confederation Series, 2:114; Richard Parkinson, *A Tour in America in 1798, 1799, and 1800* (London: Printed for J. Harding and J. Murray, 1805), 52 (also published by Parkinson as *The Experienced Farmer's Tour in America* [London: J. Stockdale, 1805, 52]).

50. Taylor, "Narrative," 65 ff.; John Duncan, *Travels through Part of the United States and Canada in 1818 and 1819,* 2 vols. in 1 (Glasgow: University Press, 1823), 1:290.

51. Washington described the distance from mound to mound as sixty yards in a letter to Samuel Vaughan, 12 Nov. 1787, *Papers,* Confederation Series, 5:432–433.

52. For trees cited as having been in the shrubberies, see Milner, *Cultural Landscape Study,* 1:2–23, citing a list compiled by Benson Lossing; see Milner, *Cultural Landscape Study,* 2:5–22 for a summary of Washington-period trees now extant on the estate (as of Nov. 2004). That list is now superseded by the research in the Oxford Dendrochronology Laboratory, Interim Report 2006/34, D. W. H. Miles and M. J. Worthington, "The Tree-Ring Dating of Trees from the Mount Vernon Estate and Gardens, Fairfax County, Virginia," prepared for J. Dean Norton, Director of Horticulture, MVLA, Oct. 2006, Table 1. Entry for 9 Feb. 1785, *Diaries,* 4:86–87. Niemcewicz, *Under Their Vine and Fig Tree,* 98. See also 9 Feb. 1785, *Diaries,* 4:87 (moved apricot and peach trees "which stand in the borders of the grass plats").

53. Sally Foster Otis (Mrs. Harrison Gray Otis) to Mrs. Charles Apthorp [13 Jan. 1801], cited from the copy in the MVLA Library; and "A Visit to Mount Vernon—1801," 35; and Campbell, "Mrs. Harrison Gray Otis at Mount Vernon, 1801," 44. For the planting of pines on the estate, see 18 Mar. 1785, *Diaries,* 4:104.

54. George Washington to George Augustine Washington, 8 July 1787, *Papers,* Confederation Series, 5:251.

55. George Washington to George Augustine Washington, 8 and 24 July 1787, *Papers,* Confederation Series, 5:251, 269–270.

56. Entry for 31 Mar. 1785, *Diaries,* 4:111; Niemcewicz, *Under Their Vine and Fig Tree,* 98.

57. George Washington to John Christian Ehlers, 7 Nov. 1792, *Papers,* Presidential Series, 11:353–355.

58. George Augustine Washington to George Washington, 8 Apr. 1792, *Papers,* Presidential Series, 10:231. See also George Augustine Washington to George Washington, 15 Apr. 1792, *Papers,* Presidential Series, 10:272.

59. Taylor, "Narrative"; and Frost, in Staples, *A Day at Mount*

Vernon in 1797, 11; George Washington to George Augustine Washington, 27 May 1787, *Papers,* Confederation Series, 5:198–199 ("endeavor to keep the willow in the Serpentine walks upright by means of the Stakes").

60. Latrobe, *Virginia Journals,* 1:165. For William Blount's account, see Henderson, *Washington's Southern Tour, 1791,* 6.

61. See 13 and 14 Oct. 1793, in *Diary of Col. Winthrop Sargent* (Wormsloe, GA: Privately printed, 1851); referenced here from "Diary of Col. Winthrop Sargent, Adjutant General of the United States' Army, during the Campaign of MDCCXCI," *Ohio Archaeological and Historical Publications* 33 (1924): 274. The original manuscript is in the Ohio Historical Society, Ohio State Museum (Columbus). The presence of the dove of peace weathervane (1787) and the Family Quarters for Slaves (ordered to be demolished in 1791) helps to set dates for the pictures. Indeed, Savage visited Mount Vernon in the early summer of 1791 and had left America for Europe in July or August of that year, so the painting, and certainly the record of the architectural elements in the painting, likely predate that time.

62. For the Savage paintings at Mount Vernon, see Cadou, *George Washington Collection,* 206–207.

63. This kind of lancet form, like some other Gothic shapes, was incorporated into decorative arts in the same period and is found also in the book cabinets in Washington's study in the mansion house (visible in Plate 8). The lamp (tinned sheet iron, brass, paint, and glass, W-15, MVLA), made by John Drinkwater of London, was ordered in 1760 and appears in Robert Cary's invoice of 31 Mar. 1761 ("1 Best Japand Lanthorn with a Glass Shade with Brass").

64. Entries for 16–19 Feb. 1785, *Diaries,* 4:91–93.

65. For example, at Osterley Park, an old walled garden, perhaps out of character with the surrounding natural landscape gardening by Capability Brown, stood by the mansion house throughout the eighteenth century. For walled gardens in England, see Diana Saville, *Walled Gardens: Their Planting and Design* (London: Batsford, 1982).

66. For the archaeology of the pathways in the walled gardens, see Harold Abbott, "Report of the Landscape Architect," in *Minutes of the Council of the Mount Vernon Ladies' Association of the Union,* 1935, 38–42.

67. Letter dated 18 Mar. 1797; see Brady, *George Washington's Beautiful Nelly,* 32.

68. Niemcewicz, *Under Their Vine and Fig Tree,* 97.

69. Washington to Arthur Young, 4 Dec. 1788, *Papers,* Presidential Series, 1:159–160.

70. Entry for 16 Apr. 1785, *Diaries,* 4:121. For Sally Foster Otis's account, see Sally Foster Otis (Mrs. Harrison Gray Otis) to Mrs.

Charles Apthorp [13 Jan. 1801], cited from the copy in the MVLA Library; and "A Visit to Mount Vernon—1801," 36; and Campbell, "Mrs. Harrison Gray Otis at Mount Vernon, 1801," 44.

71. See the "List of Plants from John Bartram's Nursery," Mar. 1792, *Papers,* Presidential Series, 10:175–182.

72. For the restoration of the lower garden according to Colonial Revival tastes, see de Forest, *The Gardens and Grounds at Mount Vernon,* 71–77. Mount Vernon archaeologist Esther White conveyed to me the conjectural placement of the well in the lower garden and other aspects of the restoration that adhere to twentieth-century ideas (interview, June 2009).

73. Weld, *Travels through the States of North America,* 53 (Dec. 1795).

74. Taylor, "Narrative"; Latrobe, *Virginia Journals,* 1:165; Williams, "Samuel Vaughan's Journal," 273.

75. Taylor, "Narrative."

76. De Forest, *The Gardens and Grounds at Mount Vernon,* 34; Batty Langley, *New Principles of Gardening* (London: Printed for A. Bettesworth, et al., 1728 [published in Dec. of 1727 and dedicated to the king, but date on title page is 1728]), Section XXIII, p. 186. See George Washington's directive to John Christian Ehlers, 7 Nov. 1792, *Papers,* Presidential Series, 11:354: "The other parts of all of them [oval beds] to receive the Shrubs—putting the tallest, always, nearest the middle, letting them decline more into dwarfs towards the outer parts. This was my intention when they were planted in the Ovals."

77. Entry for 10 June 1787, *Diaries,* 5:166–167: "Breakfasted by agreement at Mr. Powell's, and in Company with him rid to see the Botanical garden of Mr. Bartram; which, tho' Stored with many curious plts. Shrubs & trees, many of which are exotics was not laid off with much taste, nor was it large." Latrobe, *Virginia Journals,* 1:165.

78. De Forest, *The Gardens and Grounds at Mount Vernon,* 48–51, has stressed that flowers must have been more numerous and varied at Mount Vernon than the thin documentation indicates. For Washington's reaction to William Prince's gardens in Flushing, Long Island, on 10 Oct. 1789, see his entry for that day, *Diaries,* 5:458.

79. Latrobe, *Virginia Journals,* 1:165.

80. For the early "Flour knots" near the mansion house, see Lund Washington to George Washington, 30 Dec. 1775, *Papers,* Revolutionary Series, 2:621.

81. Washington had recently hired from Europe "a Gardner, who professes a knowledge in the culture of rare plants and care of a Green-House," referring to Ehlers; see Washington to Margaret Tilghman Carroll, 16 Sept. 1789, *Papers,* Presidential Series, 4:43. Another German gardener who might have contributed to the de-

sign of the formal garden was indentured servant John [Johann] Gottlieb Richler (see Washington to Frances Bassett Washington, 28–29 July 1793, *Papers,* Presidential Series, 13:298, note 8). For this other "Dutch gardener," see also Washington to Howell Lewis, 25 Aug. 1793, *Papers,* Presidential Series, 13:544, 546, note 16). For the gardener's residence during this time, see John Waite, *The Gardener's House at Mount Vernon: An Evaluation of Historic Building Fabric,* Jan. 1992, Mesick-Cohen-Waite Architects, Albany, New York.

82. For Latta's identification, see Robert F. Dalzell Jr. and Lee Baldwin Dalzell, *George Washington's Mount Vernon: At Home in Revolutionary America* (New York: Oxford University Press, 1998), 286, and *Papers of George Washington,* Diaries, 6:355, identified as Rev. James Latta (1732–1801), Presbyterian minister from Lancaster County, Pennsylvania, or one of his sons (the latter identification preferred by the Dalzells). For Latta's visit, see also "A Visit to Mount Vernon in 1799," *MVLAAR,* 1937, 42–43.

83. For Walpole's sanctioning of old-fashioned gardens, see *The Works of Horatio Walpole, Earl of Orford,* 5 vols. (London: Printed for G. G. and J. Robinson, and J. Edwards, 1798), 2:539–540. Walpole had written the essay in question, "On Modern Gardening," by 1770.

84. "The Journal of Baron von Closen," *William and Mary Quarterly,* 3rd ser., 10, no. 2 (Apr. 1953): 229 (17 July 1782). Searson, "Mount Vernon, A Poem," 11; see also John Searson to George Washington, 18 Apr. 1799, *Papers,* Retirement Series, 3:485–486. (Searson visited Mount Vernon on 15 May 1799.)

85. Taylor, "Narrative."

86. Lossing, *The Home of Washington,* 158. For Osgood's account of 28 June 1839, see "MT Vernon in 1839 by a Native of this Country," *MVLAAR,* 1952, 59 (manuscript owned by the MVLA). Frost in Staples, *A Day at Mount Vernon in 1797,* 8, noted the fruit in the garden.

87. Elijah Fletcher to unknown "Sir," 1 Oct. 1810, Elijah Fletcher, *Letters,* ed. Martha von Briesen (Charlottesville: University Press of Virginia, 1965), 18.

88. Alexander Graydon to Rachel Graydon, 1814, cited from the copy in the MVLA Library. For early reference to the exotics from the West Indies, see Lossing, *The Home of Washington,* 158.

89. For the list of exotics, see Thomas Law to Washington, 9 Apr. 1799, *Papers,* Retirement Series, 3:472, note 4.

90. Latta, "A Visit to Mount Vernon in 1799," 42–43.

91. Frost, in Staples, *A Day at Mount Vernon in 1797,* 8.

92. It is worth noting that Washington did not know them by the name "French honeysuckle," while his professional gardener knew that term. For the planting of these at the columns of the covered ways, see the entry for 31 Mar. 1785, *Diaries,* 4:111; and for

green paint on the boards see George Washington to George Augustine Washington, 29 July 1787, *Papers,* Confederation Series, 5:276–277. For Washington's order to Robert Cary in London for "Beverley's history of Virginia," see "Invoice to Robert Cary & Co.," 20 June 1768, *Papers,* Colonial Series, 8:102.

93. Robert Beverley, *The History and Present State of Virginia* (1705), ed. with an intro. by Louis Wright (Chapel Hill: University of North Carolina Press, 1947, published for the Institute of Early American History and Culture, Williamsburg, Virginia), 299. For references to honeysuckle in books owned by Washington, see Langley, *New Principles of Gardening,* 173, 183, and Philip Miller, *The Abridgement of the Gardeners Dictionary* (London: Printed for the author, 1763), under "Periclymenum."

94. For the icehouse and Bushrod's summerhouse, see Milner, *Cultural Landscape Study,* 1:2-76, 2-95, 3-30. The summerhouse appeared in a number of nineteenth-century views before it was demolished (cf. Figures 3.17 and 8.5).

95. George Washington to Lund Washington, 19 Aug. 1776, *Papers,* Revolutionary Series, 6:85.

96. Entry for 8 Apr. 1786, *Diaries,* 4:306. See also 7 Mar. 1785, *Diaries,* 4:99.

97. For the plantings in the south grove, see George Washington to Lund Washington, 19 Aug. 1776, *Papers,* Revolutionary Series, 6:85.

98. George Washington to Lund Washington, 25 Dec. 1782, *Writings* 25:472.

99. Entry for 27 May 1715, in *The Journal of John Fontaine: An Irish Huguenot Son in Spain and Virginia, 1710–1719,* ed. with an intro. by Edward Porter Alexander (Williamsburg, VA: The Colonial Williamsburg Foundation, distributed by Charlottesville: University Press of Virginia, 1972), 80–81.

100. Morley J. Williams, "Report on Research and Restoration of Deer Park Wall," 30 Nov. 1934, on file, MVLA Library.

101. For his order of the removal of the necessary, see Washington to William Pearce, 29 May 1796, *Writings,* 35:72 ("the old necessary on the brow of the Hill . . . is not only useless where it is, but is an eyesore"). Milner, *Cultural Landscape Study,* 1:2-29; Brookes, "A Dinner at Mount Vernon," 78.

102. See the Boston newspaper *J. Russell's Gazette,* 30 Jan. 1800, p. 3, column 1. The editor stated that the letter was written by a Philadelphia gentleman on 20 Jan. 1800 (about a month after Washington's death).

103. For this account, see James K. Paulding, in his *Life of Washington,* 2 vols. (New York: Harper and Brothers, 1835), 2:195.

104. See Williams, "Samuel Vaughan's Journal," 273. Taylor, "Narrative," Cutler and Cutler, *Life,* 2:58 (2 Jan. 1802).

105. See, e.g., Washington to Anthony Whitting, 28 Oct. and

18 Nov. 1792, *Papers,* Presidential Series, 11:276, 403. See chap. 5 for more about the proposal to divert the spring and create a water meadow.

106. According to Taylor, "Narrative," the hill was "graded in waves along the summit of the bank."

107. Washington to James Anderson, memorandum, 1 Nov. 1798, *Papers,* Retirement Series, 2:167.

108. In an undated memorandum (probably 1798 or later, and no earlier than 1784), Washington calculated the "fall from the level of the pavement of the Piazza to the top of the Brick Wall in front of the House," his measurements including distances all the way to the river bank (see George Washington Papers, Library of Congress, 1741–1799, Series 4, General Correspondence, 1697–1799, image 987). Those figures are not useful in gauging details of the shaping of the earth on the east lawn in Washington's last years. For another sheet drawing by Washington of the east lawn, ha-ha wall, and top of the hill near former deer park, see Figure 5.13 (MVLA, RM-770, MS-5082).

109. Copley, in Amory, *The Domestic and Artistic Life of John Singleton Copley,* 160.

110. Abigail Adams to her sister, Mary Smith Cranch (Mrs. Richard Cranch), 21 December 1800, cited from the copy in the MVLA Library (original letter privately owned).

111. See Cutler and Cutler, *Life,* 2:58.

112. Letter by Roger Griswold, to Fanny Griswold, 1 Dec. 1800, cited from copy, MVLA Library, original document part of the Roger Griswold Papers, Yale University Library, Manuscripts and Archives; and William Blount's account in Henderson, *Washington's Southern Tour, 1791,* 6.

113. Niemcewicz, *Under Their Vine and Fig Tree,* 98.

114. Latrobe, *Virginia Journals,* 1:165.

115. Weld, *Travels through the States of North America,* 53. Joseph Hadfield, visited Mount Vernon in 1785 and saw Washington again in 1787; see Joseph Hadfield, *An Englishman in America, 1785: Being the Diary of Joseph Hadfield,* ed. Douglas Robertson (Toronto: The Hunter-Rose Co., 1933), 13.

Chapter 5. Mount Vernon and British Gardening

Epigraph. John Enys, *The American Journals of Lt. John Enys,* ed. Elizabeth Cometti (Syracuse, NY: Syracuse University Press, 1976), 245.

1. See 10–11 Mar. 1775, *Diaries,* 3:319.

2. References to the Cherry Walk appear in Washington's diary entries only from 5 Apr. 1760 to 30 Mar. 1765; see *Diaries,* 1:263 and 337. For the Circular Banks, see George Washington to Lund Washington, 10–17 Dec. 1776, *Papers,* Revolutionary Series, 7:289. The earlier, more formal aspects of the gardens from this period

are discussed in John Milner Associates, Inc., *Mount Vernon Estate and Gardens: Cultural Landscape Study,* 2 vols., prepared for the MVLA, Mount Vernon, Virginia, by John Milner Associates, Inc., Charlottesville, Virginia, in association with Rivanna Archeological Consulting, Charlottesville, Virginia, Nov. 2004 (manuscript available at the MVLA Library), 1:2-14, 2-15.

3. Julian Ursyn Niemcewicz, *Under Their Vine and Fig Tree: Travels through America in 1797–1799, 1805, with Some Further Account of Life in New Jersey,* trans. and ed. Metchie J. E. Budka (Elizabeth, NJ: Grassmann, 1965), 98. Humphreys, 39, and 35 for Washington's curiosity.

4. For English gardening of the eighteenth century, see, e.g., Charles Quest-Ritson, *The English Garden: A Social History* (Boston: David R. Godine, 2003); John Dixon Hunt, *The Picturesque Garden in Europe* (London: Thames and Hudson, 2002); David Jacques, *Georgian Gardens: The Reign of Nature* (Portland: Timber Press, 1984).

5. *The Works of Horatio Walpole, Earl of Orford,* 5 vols. (London: Printed for G. G. and J. Robinson, and J. Edward, 1798), 2:543. For the complex text and publication history of Walpole's "On Modern Gardening" (printed in 1771; first published in 1780), see Isabel Wakelin Urban Chase, *Horace Walpole: Gardenist* (Princeton: Princeton University Press, 1943), xix–xxv.

6. Chase, *Horace Walpole,* 46–47, and *The Works of Horatio Walpole,* 2:522–523. Yu Liu argues that Pliny's text was misused by eighteenth-century English writers in "Castell's Pliny: Rewriting the Past for the Present," *Eighteenth-Century Studies* 43, no. 2 (Winter 2010): 243–257.

7. William Gilpin, *Three Essays: On Picturesque Beauty; On Picturesque Travel; and On Sketching Landscape; to which is added a Poem, On Landscape Painting* (London: Printed for R. Blamire, 1792); Uvedale Price, *An Essay on the Picturesque, as Compared with the Sublime and the Beautiful; and on the Use of Studying Pictures, for the Purpose of Improving Real Landscape* (London: Printed for J. Robson, 1794). For the picturesque in English painting and gardening, see also Ann Bermingham, *Landscape and Ideology: The English Rustic Tradition, 1740–1860* (Berkeley and Los Angeles: University of California Press, 1986), 57–85; Bermingham stresses throughout that "the picturesque was a refuge from the agricultural revolution [in England]."

8. Quoted from William Brogden, "The Ferme Ornée and Changing Attitudes to Agricultural Improvement," in *British and American Gardens in the Eighteenth Century: Eighteen Illustrated Essays on Garden History,* ed. Robert Maccubbin and Peter Martin (Williamsburg, VA: Colonial Williamsburg, 1984), 41–42.

9. See Hunt, *The Picturesque Garden in Europe,* 52–53. In other art forms, the English often turned to the Low Countries for cul-

tural models, yet the Dutch Baroque painters, with their devotion to minute truth and haphazard naturalism, were less imitated by English landscapists.

10. Letter XXXI, Tobias Smollett, *Travels through France and Italy,* 2 vols. (Dublin: Printed for J. Hoey et. al., 1766), 2:111–112; John Dixon Hunt, *Garden and Grove: The Italian Renaissance Garden in the English Imagination, 1600–1750* (London: Dent, 1986), 98.

11. Humphreys, 35.

12. See Peter Martin, *The Pleasure Gardens of Virginia: Jamestown to Jefferson* (Princeton: Princeton University Press, 1991); see also Martin's "'Long and Assiduous Endeavors': Gardening in Early Eighteenth-Century Virginia," in Maccubbin and Martin, *British and American Gardens in the Eighteenth Century,* 107–116.

13. For a description of the gardens of Robert Carter III at Nomini Hall, see Philip Vickers Fithian, *Journal and Letters of Philip Vickers Fithian, 1773–1774: A Plantation Tutor of the Old Dominion,* ed. with an intro. by Hunter Dickinson Farish (Williamsburg, VA: Colonial Williamsburg, 1957), 78–81 and 116. For Belvoir, see chap. 2, note 3.

14. For Jefferson as garden designer, see William Howard Adams, *Jefferson's Monticello* (New York: Abbeville, 1983), 146–189. Abbott Lowell Cummings, "Eighteenth-Century New England Garden Design: The Pictorial Evidence," in Maccubbin and Martin, *British and American Gardens in the Eighteenth Century,* 130.

15. For William Kent's contributions to landscape gardening, see Margaret Jourdain, *The Work of William Kent: Artist, Painter, Designer and Landscape Gardener* (London: Country Life, 1948); and John Dixon Hunt, *William Kent, Landscape Garden Designer* (London: A. Zwemmer, 1987). For English landscape gardening of Kent's generation, see Christopher Hussey, *English Gardens and Landscapes, 1700–1725* (New York: Funk and Wagnalls, 1967), esp. 40–48. Walpole, "On Modern Gardening," 536 and 539. Kent even "planted" some dead trees in a garden for variety and natural effect, although Walpole claims that adverse opinion caused him to remove these.

16. Cf. Roger White, *Chiswick House and Gardens* (London: English Heritage, 2001), 19–30. For Jefferson and gardening, see note 19.

17. For the garden at Stourhead, see Hussey, *English Gardens and Landscapes,* 158–164; see 12–28 for gardens, architecture, and picturesque connection to Gaspard. See also Malcolm Kelsall, "The Iconography of Stourhead," *Journal of the Warburg and Courtauld Institutes* 46 (1983): 133–143; Oliver Garnett, *Stourhead Landscape Garden, Wiltshire* (Swindon, UK: National Trust, 2000); and Kenneth Woodbridge, *The Stourhead Landscape* (London: National Trust: 2002).

18. For Stowe, see Hussey, *English Gardens and Landscapes,* 89–113; and *Stowe Landscape Gardens: A Comprehensive Guide* (Swindon, UK: National Trust, 1997).

19. For Thomas Jefferson's gardening, see Edwin Betts and Hazlehurst Perkins, *Thomas Jefferson's Flower Garden at Monticello* (Charlottesville: University Press of Virginia, 1971); William Adams, *The Eye of Thomas Jefferson* (Washington, DC: National Gallery of Art, 1976), 314–351; William Howard Adams, *Jefferson's Monticello* (New York: Abbeville, 1983), 146–189; Robert Baron, *The Garden and Farm Books of Thomas Jefferson* (Golden, CO: Fulcrum, 1987); Peter Hatch, *The Fruit and Fruit Trees of Monticello* (Charlottesville: University Press of Virginia, 1998); and H. Peter Loewer, *Jefferson's Garden* (Mechanicsburg, PA: Stackpole, 2004).

20. For the gardening of Lancelot Brown, see Edward Hyams, *Capability Brown and Humphry Repton* (New York: Scribner, 1971); Dorothy Stroud, *Capability Brown* (London: Faber, 1975); Roger Turner, *Capability Brown and the Eighteenth Century English Landscape* (London: Weidenfeld and Nicolson, 1985); Thomas Hinde, *Capability Brown: The Story of a Master Gardener* (London: Hutchinson, 1986).

21. For Chambers and Asian inspiration, see William Chambers's essay "Of the Art of Laying Out Gardens Among the Chinese," which appears in the volume *Designs of Chinese Buildings, Furniture, Dresses, Machines and Utensils* (London: 1757), and William Chambers, *Dissertation on Oriental Gardening* (Dublin: Printed for W. Wilson, 1773). The French, who liked to denigrate the English, sometimes called the whole century's style "le jardin Anglais-Chinois" to suggest that the British style was merely derivative.

22. For the William Paca House, see Susan Stiles Dowell, *Great Houses of Maryland* (Centreville, MD: Tidewater Publishers, 1988), 49–55. For Chinese railing at Monticello, see Adams, *Jefferson's Monticello,* 180–185.

23. For a selection of Addison's thoughts on gardening, see John Dixon Hunt and Peter Willis, eds., *The Genius of the Place: The English Landscape Garden, 1620–1820* (Cambridge, MA: MIT Press, 1988), 138–147. See also Brogden, "The Ferme Ornée."

24. Christopher Gallagher, "The Leasowes: A History of the Landscape," *Garden History* 24, no. 2 (Winter 1996): 201–220.

25. Walpole, "On Modern Gardening," 541.

26. Gilpin, *Three Essays*; Richard Payne Knight, *An Analytical Inquiry into the Principles of Taste* (London, 1805), soon followed, and went into several editions that the author revised and expanded. Uvedale Price, *An Essay on the Picturesque* (London: printed for J. Robson, 1796); Bermingham, *Landscape and Ideology,* 66; Thomas Whately, *Observations on Modern Gardening* (Dublin: Printed for James Williams, 1770).

27. Whately, *Observations on Modern Gardening,* 85, men-

tioned, e.g., a "house placed at the edge of a precipice" as providing visual interest and exciting the imagination.

28. Walpole, "On Modern Gardening," 539–540.

29. Whately, *Observations on Modern Gardening*, 115.

30. Niemcewicz wrote that the house "is surrounded by a ditch in brick with very pretty little turrets at the corners; these are nothing but outhouses" (*Under Their Vine and Fig Tree,* 95).

31. Anthony Whitting to Washington, 15–16 Jan. 1792, *Papers,* Presidential Series, 9:436–437.

32. Washington to Anthony Whitting, 14 Oct. 1792, *Papers,* Presidential Series, 11:224.

33. Enys, *The American Journals,* 245.

34. For Latrobe's remark, see Benjamin Henry Latrobe, *The Virginia Journals of Benjamin Henry Latrobe, 1795–1798,* vol. 1, *1795–1797,* ed. Edward Carter (New Haven: Yale University Press, 1977), 1:165.

35. Entry for 24 Apr. 1791, *Diaries,* 6:119.

36. Entry for 26 Sept. 1784, *Diaries,* 4:45.

37. Patricia Brady, ed., *George Washington's Beautiful Nelly: The Letters of Eleanor Parke Custis Lewis to Elizabeth Bordley Gibson, 1794–1851* (Columbia: University of South Carolina Press, 1991), 31, 60.

38. Thomas Rowell, "The Park, Pleasure Ground and Estate," in *Petworth House* (Swindon, UK: National Trust, 1997), 49–55.

39. Cf. Robert Hunter Jr., *Quebec to Carolina in 1785–1786: Being the Travel Diary and Observations of Robert Hunter, Jr., a Young Merchant of London,* ed. Louis Wright and Marion Tinling (San Marino, CA: Huntington Library, 1943), 196; and Jean Lee, ed., *Experiencing Mount Vernon: Eyewitness Accounts, 1784–1865* (Charlottesville: University of Virginia Press, 2006), 33–34.

40. Washington to Adrienne, the Marquise de Lafayette, 4 Apr. 1784, *Papers,* Confederation Series, 1:258.

41. Washington, memorandum, 5 Nov. 1796, *Writings,* 35:259–260.

42. Washington to Anthony Whitting, 14 Oct. 1792, *Papers,* Presidential Series, 11:223.

43. Washington to Edward Newenham, 20 Apr. 1787, *Papers,* Confederation Series, 5:152.

44. Entry for 5 Nov. 1751, *Diaries,* 1:73; Washington to Anthony Whitting, 11 Nov. 1792, *Papers,* Presidential Series, 11:374.

45. Washington to William Pearce, 22 Feb. 1794, *Papers,* Presidential Series, 15:258; Washington to Pearce, 27 July 1794, *Writings,* 33:445.

46. Washington to Anthony Whitting, 14 Oct. 1792, *Papers,* Presidential Series, 11:225. Similarly, Washington emphasized to William Pearce in 1795 that he needed live fences "in lieu of dead ones, which, if continued upon the extensive scale my farms require, must exhaust all my timber" (22 Nov. 1795, *Writings,* 34:370).

Washington instructed Pearce to plant English thorn, honey locust, and cedar for this purpose (34:371). Washington asked Whitting to get ten or twelve thousand "English thorn" bushes and asked him to keep thinking about ways to achieve natural hedging (20 Jan. 1793, *Papers,* Presidential Series, 12:33).

47. For the shared appreciation of farming and Nature, see George William Fairfax to Washington, 23 June 1785, *Papers,* Confederation Series, 3:76.

48. Washington to Arthur Young, 4 Dec. 1788, *Papers,* Presidential Series, 1:156.

49. For Washington's references to pines, see entry for 18 Apr. 1760, *Diaries,* 1:269: "Planted other Pine Trees in the Fencd place at the Cornr. of the Garden." There were numerous later references to pines, including *Diaries,* 4:103 (15 Mar. 1785).

50. *The Papers of Thomas Jefferson,* ed. Julian P. Boyd (Princeton, NJ: Princeton University Press, 1950–), 13:269.

51. Bryan Fairfax to Washington, 22 Aug. 1798, *Papers,* Retirement Series, 2:549.

52. Latrobe, *Virginia Journals,* 1:165.

53. MVLA, RM-770, MS.-5082.

54. William Hogarth, *The Analysis of Beauty. Written with a View of Fixing the Fluctuating Ideas of Taste* (London: Printed by J. Reeves for the Author, 1753), 63.

55. Hogarth, *The Analysis of Beauty,* esp. 48–67, "Of Composition with the Waving-Line" and "Of Compositions with the Serpentine-Line."

56. Mark Everard, *Water Meadows: "Living Treasures in the English Landscape"* (Sŵn y Nant, UK: Forrest, 2005), 9.

57. Washington to Anthony Whitting, 18 Nov. 1792, *Papers,* Presidential Series, 11:403.

58. Washington to Anthony Whitting, 2 Dec. 1792, *Papers,* Presidential Series, 11:462.

59. Entry for 2 Mar. 1785, *Diaries,* 4:97. There is a useful analysis of Washington's use of the term "shrubbery" and of the other terms he borrowed from English gardeners, in Therese O'Malley, with contributions by Elizabeth Kryder-Reid and Anne Helmreich, *Keywords in American Landscape Design* (New Haven: Yale University Press, 2010), 330–331 ("grove"), 574–576 ("shrubbery"), 669–674 ("wilderness").

60. Entries for 22 and 23 Feb. 1784, *Diaries,* 4:94.

61. George Washington to Lund Washington, 19 Aug. 1776, *Papers,* Revolutionary Series, 6:84.

62. For Pope, see Maynard Mack, *The Garden and the City: Retirement and Politics in the Later Poetry of Pope, 1731–1743* (Toronto: University of Toronto Press, 1969), 240. Entry for 20 Jan. 1785, *Diaries,* 4:79.

63. Entry for 6 Apr. 1786, *Diaries,* 4:304.

64. Washington to Anthony Whitting, 14 Oct. 1792, *Papers,* Presidential Series, 11:223.

65. Washington to Anthony Whitting, 4 and 11 Nov. 1792, *Papers,* Presidential Series, 11:332, 370.

66. Washington to Anthony Whitting, 9 Dec. 1792, *Papers,* Presidential Series, 11:489.

67. Washington to William Pearce, 25 Jan. 1795, *Writings,* 34:102.

68. Walpole, "On Modern Gardening," 535.

69. Walpole, "On Modern Gardening," 535–536.

70. Ralph Dutton, *The English Garden* (London: B. T. Batsford, 1937), 76.

71. Lund Washington to George Washington, 12 Nov. 1775, *Papers,* Revolutionary Series, 2:356.

72. Sally Foster Otis, in "A Visit to Mount Vernon—1801," *MVLAAR,* 1961, 35.

73. Carl Lounsbury, *An Illustrated Glossary of Early Southern Architecture and Landscape* (New York: Oxford University Press, 1994), 110.

74. See entry and editor's note for 18 Aug. 1785, *Diaries,* 4:184.

75. For the setting up of the deer park at Mount Vernon, see entry for 24 Aug. 1785, *Diaries,* 4:186: "Measured round the ground which I intend to inclose for a Paddock, and find it to be ab[ou]t. 1600 yards," and for 31 Mar. 1786, *Diaries,* 4:302: "Got my Paddock fence quite inclosed except along the Margin of the Rivr."

76. Washington to William Pearce, 28 Dec. 1794, *Writings,* 34:74.

77. Washington to James Anderson, 29 Jan. 1797, *Writings,* 35:378.

78. Thomas Mawe and John Abercrombie, *Every Man His Own Gardener* (London: Printed for W. Griffin, 1769).

79. First edition was Batty Langley, *New Principles of Gardening* (London: Printed for A. Bettesworth et al., 1728 [published in Dec. of 1727 and dedicated to the king, but date on title page is 1728]). For arguments in favor of Langley's influence on George Washington, see Morley Williams, "Washington's Changes at Mount Vernon Plantation," *Landscape Architecture* 28, no. 2 (1938): 69–70; John Rhodehamel, "Langley's Book of Gardening," *MVLAAR,* 1984, 26–29; Mac Griswold, *Washington's Gardens at Mount Vernon: Landscape of the Inner Man* (Boston and New York: Houghton Mifflin, 1999), 35, 48; and Milner, *Cultural Landscape Study,* 1:2–22.

80. Langley, *New Principles of Gardening,* 186, 202.

81. Langley, *New Principles of Gardening,* 195.

82. Langley, *New Principles of Gardening,* 195, 197.

83. Langley, *New Principles of Gardening,* 197.

84. Langley, *New Principles of Gardening,* cf. 12, 16.

85. Langley, *New Principles of Gardening,* 173.

86. Philip Miller, *The Abridgement of the Gardeners Dictionary* (London: Printed for the author, 1763).

87. Washington to George Clinton, 20 Apr. 1785, *Papers,* Con-federation Series, 2:511; George Washington to George Augustine Washington, 6 Jan. 1785, *Papers,* Confederation Series, 2:258. For Washington's copy of Miller's book, see *Papers,* Confederation Series, 2:512, editor's note 5. See also Barbara McMillan, "The Gardener's Gardener," *MVLAAR,* 1987, 28–34.Washington probably was referring to Miller's book also when he wrote to Tobias Lear that he should not forget "the dictionary at Mrs. Law's" (31 Mar. 1799, *Papers,* Retirement Series, 3:453).

88. George Augustine Washington to George Washington, 25 Feb. 1785, *Papers,* Confederation Series, 2:384.

89. Miller, *The Abridgement of the Gardeners Dictionary,* s.v. "Groves."

90. Miller, *The Abridgement of the Gardeners Dictionary,* s.v. "Groves."

91. Miller, *The Abridgement of the Gardeners Dictionary,* s.v. "Groves."

92. William Watts, *The Seats of the Nobility and Gentry* (Chelsea: W. Watts, 1779).

Chapter 6. Prospects, Pictures, and the Picturesque

Epigraph. George Grieve, early translator of the Marquis de Chastellux's travel account (see *Travels in North America in the Years 1780, 1781 and 1782 by the Marquis de Chastellux,* 2 vols., rev. translation, intro., and notes by Howard Rice [Chapel Hill: University of North Carolina Press, 1963], 2:597). Bagot was the "wife of Charles Bagot, the first British diplomatist posted to the United States after the War of 1812"; see David Hosford, "Exile in Yankeeland: The Journal of Mary Bagot, 1816–1819," *Records of the Columbia Historical Society, Washington D.C.* 51 (1984): 38.

1. For an awareness of Pliny's villas and their gardens, see *The Works of Horatio Walpole, Earl of Orford,* 5 vols. (London: Printed for G. G. and J. Robinson, and J. Edward, 1798), 2:521–523.

2. For Petrarch's ascent and the larger theme of Renaissance landscape, see Ernst Gombrich, "The Renaissance Theory of Art and the Rise of Landscape," in *Norm and Form: Studies in the Art of the Renaissance* (London: Phaidon, 1966), 107–121.

3. See also Philip Vickers Fithian, *Journal and Letters of Philip Vickers Fithian, 1773–1774: A Plantation Tutor of the Old Dominion,* ed. with an intro. by Hunter Dickinson Farish (Williamsburg, VA: Colonial Williamsburg, 1957), 178.

4. For the siting of Monticello, see Jack McLaughlin, *Jefferson and Monticello: A Biography of a Builder* (New York: Henry Holt, 1988), 33–36.

5. George Washington Greene, *The Life of Nathanael Greene, Major-General in the Army of the Revolution,* 3 vols. (New York: G. P. Putnam and Son [vol. 1] and Hurd and Houghton [vols. 2 and 3], 1867–1871), 3:508.

6. Peter Martin, *The Pleasure Gardens of Virginia: From James-town to Jefferson* (Charlottesville: University Press of Virginia, 1991), 38, recording an exchange from 1717.

7. George Washington to Samuel Vaughan, 12 Nov. 1787, *Papers,* Confederation Series, 5:432–433.

8. Anthony Whitting to George Washington, 15–16 Jan. 1792, *Papers,* Presidential Series, 9:436–437.

9. Diary entry for 16 Nov. 1785, Robert Hunter Jr., *Quebec to Carolina in 1785–1786: Being the Travel Diary and Observations of Robert Hunter, Jr., a Young Merchant of London,* ed. Louise Wright and Marion Tinling (San Marino, CA: Huntington Library, 1943), 191; Jean Lee, ed., *Experiencing Mount Vernon: Eyewitness Accounts, 1784–1865* (Charlottesville: University of Virginia Press, 2006), 27; Roger Griswold to Fanny Griswold, 1 Dec. 1800, cited from copy in the MVLA Library; original document part of the Roger Griswold Papers, Yale University Library, Manuscripts and Archives; Sally Foster Otis (Mrs. Harrison Gray Otis) to Mrs. Charles Apthorp [13 Jan. 1801], cited from the copy in the MVLA Library (document part of the Harrison Gray Otis Papers at the Massachusetts Historical Society); and "A Visit to Mount Vernon-1801," *MVLAAR,* 1961, 35; see also the edited transcription in Alexander Campbell, "Mrs. Harrison Gray Otis at Mount Vernon, 1801," *Antiques* 108 (July 1975): 42–44.

10. George Washington to Lund Washington, 3 Apr. 1779, *Papers,* Revolutionary Series, 19:735; Washington to Anthony Whitting, 14 Oct. 1792, *Papers,* Presidential Series, 11:227.

11. Washington to Anthony Whitting, 2 Dec. 1792, *Papers,* Presidential Series, 11:462–463; Washington to Whitting, 16 Dec. 1792, *Papers,* Presidential Series, 11:522–523.

12. Washington to Anthony Whitting, 13–14 Jan. 1793, *Papers,* Presidential Series, 11:627.

13. Washington to Anthony Whitting, 3 Mar. 1793, *Papers,* Presidential Series 12:258–259; Whitting to Washington, 20 Mar. 1793, *Papers,* Presidential Series, 12:352.

14. Washington to Anthony Whitting, 20 Jan. 1793, *Papers,* Presidential Series, 12:34.

15. Washington to Anthony Whitting, 18 Nov. 1792, *Papers,* Presidential Series, 11:403.

16. Washington to Anthony Whitting, 2 Dec. 1792, *Papers,* Presidential Series, 11:462.

17. Entry for 15 Mar. 1785, *Diaries,* 4:103.

18. Washington to Anthony Whitting, 20 Jan. 1793, *Papers,* Presidential Series, 12:35.

19. James K. Paulding, in his *A Life of Washington,* 2 vols. (New York: Harper and Brothers, 1835), 2:195–196.

20. John Searson, *Mount Vernon, a Poem: Being the Seat of His Excellency George Washington, in the State of Virginia* (Philadelphia: Printed for the author by Folwell, 1800), 9.

21. D. W. H. Miles and M. J. Worthington, "The Tree-Ring Dating of Trees from the Mount Vernon Estate and Gardens, Fairfax County, Virginia," Oxford Dendrochronology Laboratory, Interim Report 2006/34, prepared for J. Dean Norton, Director of Horticulture, Mount Vernon Ladies' Association of the Union, Oct. 2006, Table 1: swamp chestnut oak, no later than 1771, poplar trees, no later than 1796, eastern hemlock, 1778–1805 (probably eighteenth century), and white oak tree on the brow of the hill near the icehouse, no later than 1783.

22. Miles and Worthington, "Tree-Ring Dating," Table 1. I am also grateful to Dennis Pogue of Mount Vernon for sending me his summary of the 2006 dendrochronology study of the early trees on the estate.

23. Washington to William Pearce, 29 May 1796, *Writings,* 35:72.

24. Dennis Pogue, "Digging for Trash Beneath George Washington's 'Vine and Fig Tree,'" *MVLAAR,* 1991, 29–34.

25. Cf. views by Alexander Jackson Davis, watercolor, pencil, and ink on paper, Houghton Library, Harvard University; see also "Early Views of Mount Vernon," *MVLAAR,* 1955, 33–34.

26. Edward G. Williams, ed., "Samuel Vaughan's Journal," *Western Pennsylvania Historical Magazine* 44, no. 3 (Sept. 1961): 273. For the related plan sent later to Washington, see "The Vaughan Plan," *MVLAAR,* 1976, 8–11.

27. Entry for 23 Apr. 1791, "Journal of William Loughton Smith, 1790–1791," *Massachusetts Historical Society Proceedings* 51 (Oct. 1917–June 1918), 63–64; Friedrich Wilhelm Hoeninghaus, *Reise eines Krefelders nach Nordamerika 1797–1798: Tagebuchaufzeichnungen und Briefe,* ed. Wolfhart Langer (Krefeld: privately printed, 1973), 33–34. (Hoeninghaus was using regional German feet, which differed slightly from the English foot.)

28. Francis Glass, *A Life of George Washington in Latin Prose,* 8 vols., ed. J. N. Reynolds (New York: Harper and Brothers, 1835), 133.

29. Notice in *Hartford Advertiser,* 14 Jan. 1823, called the bank from the river to the house "several hundred feet in height." The manuscript, in George Washington's hand, giving the height from the river is "Cost of things bo[ugh]t. In Phila[delphia]. by Mrs. Washington" in Oct. 1783 (W-667, MVLA).

30. James Taylor, "Narrative of General James Taylor of Newport, Kentucky," cited from the copy in the MVLA Library (original from document in the Cincinnati Historical Society Library).

31. Entry for 23 Apr. 1791, "Journal of William Loughton Smith, 1790–1791," 63.

32. Hoeninghaus, *Reise eines Krefelders nach Nordamerika 1797–1798,* 33–34.

33. Searson, *Mount Vernon,* 20; Marquis de Lafayette to George Washington, 10 Aug. 1784, *Papers,* Confederation Series, 2:28 ("In a few days I'll Be at Mount vernon, and I do already feel delighted with so charming a prospect"); Sally Foster Otis (Mrs. Harrison Gray Otis) to Mrs. Charles Apthorp [13 Jan. 1801]; and "A Visit to Mount Vernon-1801," 36; see also the edited transcription in Campbell, "Mrs. Harrison Gray Otis at Mount Vernon, 1801," 42–44.

34. Patricia Brady, ed., *George Washington's Beautiful Nelly: The Letters of Eleanor Parke Custis Lewis to Elizabeth Bordley Gibson, 1794–1851* (Columbia: University of South Carolina Press, 1991), 43.

35. William Parker Cutler and Julia Perkins Cutler, eds., *Life, Journals, and Correspondence of Rev. Manasseh Cutler, LL. D.,* 2 vols. (Cincinnati, OH: Robert Clarke and Co., 1888; Athens: Ohio University Press, 1987), 2:57.

36. "The Vaughan Plan," 9; Claude Blanchard, *The Journal of Claude Blanchard,* ed. Thomas Balch (Albany: J. Munsell, 1876), 167.

37. For this topic, see Carter Laughlin, "George Washington, Surveyor," *MVLAAR,* 1997, 9–13. For a discussion of Washington's school exercises, see editor's discussion in *Papers,* Colonial Series, 1:1–4.

38. For young Washington's work as a surveyor, see editor's discussion in *Papers,* Colonial Series, 1:8–19.

39. Ralph Waldo Emerson, "Thorea," in *Selected Essays,* ed. Larzer Ziff (Harmondsworth, UK: Penguin, 1982), 395.

40. 19 Oct. 1750 and 23 Apr. 1750, *Papers,* Colonial Series, 1:13, 24.

41. See illustrations and comments on the early surveys in *Papers,* Colonial Series, 1:15, 21.

42. Batty Langley, *New Principles of Gardening* (London: Printed for A. Bettesworth et al., 1728 [published in Dec. of 1727 and dedicated to the king, but date on title page appears as 1728]), 1.

43. Entry for 13 Mar. 1748, *Diaries,* 1:7.

44. See chap. 3, note 7.

45. Entry for 5 Nov. 1751, *Diaries,* 1:73.

46. Entry probably for 22 Dec. 1751 (sheet damaged), *Diaries,* 1:87.

47. Entry for 8 Nov. 1751, *Diaries,* 1:76–77.

48. Marquis de Chastellux to George Washington, 12 Dec. 1785, *Papers,* Confederation Series, 3:451–452.

49. Humphreys, 7.

50. Entry for 19 Aug. 1769, *Diaries,* 2:176.

51. Entry for 24 Aug. 1769, *Diaries,* 2:177.

52. See 19 Oct. 1789, *Diaries,* 5:467, and 2 July 1791, *Diaries,* 6:169.

53. Barbados fragment undated, c. Nov. 1751–Apr. 1752, *Diaries,* 1:70–77. For the gardens in Charleston, see 7 May 1791, *Diaries,* 6:132.

54. Washington to Henry Knox, 20 Feb., 1784, *Papers,* Confederation Series, 1:138.

55. Entry for 16 Nov. 1770, *Diaries,* 2:315.

56. Entry for 8 Nov. 1751, *Diaries,* 1:77.

57. See Benson Lossing, *The Home of Washington, or Mount Vernon and Its Associations, Historical, Biographical, and Pictorial* (New York: Virtue and Yorston, 1870), 67–68.

58. For the fisheries at Mount Vernon, see entry for 23 Apr. 1791, "Journal of William Loughton Smith, 1790–1791," 64; and Julian Ursyn Niemcewicz, *Under Their Vine and Fig Tree: Travels through America in 1797–1799, 1805, with Some Further Account of Life in New Jersey,* trans. and ed. Metchie J. E. Budka (Elizabeth, NJ: Grassmann, 1965), 106. See also James Wharton, "Washington's Fisheries at Mount Vernon," *Commonwealth* (Aug. 1952), 11–13, 44.

59. Thomas Hinde, *Capability Brown: The Story of a Master Gardener* (London: Hutchinson, 1986), 125–127.

60. Powel, in Lee, *Experiencing Mount Vernon,* 53.

61. Entry for 9 Oct. 1787, *Diaries,* 5:249.

62. "Journal of William Loughton Smith, 1790–1791," 64.

63. Washington to George William Fairfax, 27 Feb. 1785, *Papers,* Confederation Series, 2:388; Washington to Sarah Cary Fairfax, 16 May 1798, *Papers,* Retirement Series, 2:273.

64. From Joseph Watson, a merchant in Alexandria, "A considerable Collection of Perspective Views of the most magnificent public and private Edifices, Bridges, Monuments, and Ruins, in *Rome, Venice, France, England,* and *China,*" Jan. 1763, *Papers,* Colonial Series, 7:179, editor's note.

65. W-356, MVLA, 22.5″ × 37″. For the invoice to Richard Washington, see 15 Apr. 1757, *Papers,* Colonial Series, 4:134: "A Neat Landskip 3 feet by 21 ½ Inches—1 Inch Margin for a Chim[ne]y." For a description of the work in Washington's hand, see *Papers,* Colonial Series, 4:358, note 4: "Landskip by 3 feet by 21 ½ Inchs. One Inch Margin."

66. For eighteenth-century English paintings inspired by Claude Lorrain, see Elizabeth Manwaring, *Italian Landscape in Eighteenth Century England* (New York: Oxford University Press, 1925), 72–73.

67. For Beck's work, see Edna Whitley, "George Beck: An Eighteenth Century Painter," *Register of the Kentucky Historical Society* 67, no. 1 (Jan. 1969): 20–36.

68. For Washington's remark of 1796, see *Memoir of Thomas Handasyd Perkins,* ed. Thomas Cary (Boston: Little, Brown, and Co., 1856), 200–201. See J. Hall Pleasants, *Four Late Eighteenth Century Anglo-American Landscape Painters* (Worcester, MA: American Antiquarian Society, 1943; repr. from the *Proceedings of the American Antiquarian Society* 52 [Oct. 1942]), 24, for Washington's title, found "in a list in Washington's handwriting [now Pennsylvania Historical Society] of furnishings in the Executive Mansion in Philadelphia at the close of his second term, 1797."

69. George Washington to Richard Washington, 27 Sept. 1763, *Papers,* Colonial Series, 7:257.

70. For Washington's title, see Pleasants, *Four Late Eighteenth Century Anglo-American Landscape Painters,* 24.

71. The inventory made after Washington's death is not helpful in this regard, as it gives only generic titles: "2 large Gilt frame Pictures representing falls of Rivers" and "4 do. Representing water Courses." See Eugene Prussing, *The Estate of George Washington, Deceased* (Boston: Little, Brown, and Co., 1927), 410.

72. For Winstanley's career in America, see William Dunlap, *A History of the Rise and Progress of the Arts of Design in the United States,* 3 vols., ed. Frank Bayley and Charles Goodspeed (New York: G. P. Scott, 1834; Boston: C. E. Goodspeed and Co., 1918), 1:164, 235–237.

73. The pair by Winstanley were identified early on as scenes of the North (Hudson) River. See "Two Pictures Owned by Washington," *MVLAAR,* 1941, 32; and Pleasants, *Four Late Eighteenth Century Anglo-American Landscape Painters,* 24.

74. Cf. "Two Pictures Owned by Washington," *MVLAAR,* 1941, 32.

75. George Washington to Commissioners for the District of Columbia, 5 Sept. 1793, *Papers,* Presidential Series, 14:27.

76. Paul D. Schweizer, ed., assisted by Sarah Clark-Langager and John R. Sawyer, *Masterworks of American Art from the Munson-Williams-Proctor Institute* (New York: H. N. Abrams, 1989), 23, note 3; see also "Two Pictures Owned by Washington," 32–33.

77. Prussing, *The Estate of George Washington,* 410; cf. Schweizer, *Masterworks,* 23, note 3.

78. Tobias Lear to George Washington, 15 Mar. 1797, *Papers,* Retirement Series, 1:37.

79. Schweizer, *Masterworks,* 23.

80. See R. W. G. Vail, ed., "A Dinner at Mount Vernon: From the Unpublished Journal of Joshua Brookes (1773–1859)," *New-York Historical Society Quarterly* 31, no. 2 (Apr. 1947): 78.

81. *Moonlight on Rocky Coast,* anonymous, probably English, 31″ × 43.5″, oil on canvas, currently exhibited at Mount Vernon, on loan from the Smithsonian Institution (control number 55300022, ascribed to George Beck; see Art Inventories Catalog in http://siris-artinventories.si.edu).

82. Letter from P. L. Sulley (UK) to Mount Vernon curators, 15 Jan. 1996 (on file, MVLA Library), suggesting Abraham Pether as author and the natural rock arch, Durdle Door, as the possible subject matter.

83. For Washington and his prints, see Robert Harley, "George Washington Lived Here, Some Early Prints of Mount Vernon, Part I," *Antiques* 47, no. 2 (Feb. 1945): 103–105; and R. T. H. Halsey, "Prints Washington Lived with at Mount Vernon," *Bulletin of the Metropolitan Museum of Art* 30, no. 3 (Mar. 1935): 63–65, for general information, and 64 for mention of Washington's list of prints acquired while president. For Washington's print collection and their placing, see also "A Bicentennial Homecoming," *MVLAAR,* 1974, 13–17; and Wendy Wick Reaves, "The Prints," *Antiques* 135 (Feb. 1989): 502–511. See also the exhibition catalogue, *Prints Collected by Washington* (MVLA, 1939).

84. For the flowerpot (Jingdezhen, China, c. 1760–1780, porcelain, 9.25″ × 14″ wide, W-2329, MVLA), see Carol Borchert Cadou, *The George Washington Collection: Fine and Decorative Arts at Mount Vernon* (Manchester, VT: Hudson Hills Press, for MVLA, 2006), 191.

85. Joseph Fields, ed., *"Worthy Partner": The Papers of Martha Washington* (Westport, CT: Greenwood, 1994), 407.

86. Greene, *Life of Nathanael Greene,* 3:508; Humphreys, 39–40; William Talbot to George Wallace, 18 October 1793, copy in the MVLA Library (original document privately owned).

87. G. [George] I. [Isham] Parkyns, *Sketches of Select American Scenery* (Philadelphia: Printed by John Ormrod, 1799), first page (pages not numbered). For the aquatint by Parkyns, see "Accessions, 1950–1951," *MVLAAR,* 1951, 20. His watercolor of the house as seen from the east has disappeared but was photographed in the 1920s (on file, MVLA Library).

88. Isaac Weld, *Travels through the States of North America and the Provinces of Upper and Lower Canada, during the Years 1795, 1796, and 1797* (London: J. Stockdale, 1799), his account on 92–94, the editor's note on vii.

Chapter 7. Washington as Artist, Critic, Patron, and Collector

Epigraph. George Washington to booksellers Daniel Boinod and Alexander Gaillard, 18 Feb. 1784, *Papers,* Confederation Series, 1:126.

1. George Washington, "Surveying," 1745, George Washington Papers at the Library of Congress, 1741–1799, Series 1a, George Washington, School Copy Book, vol. 1, 1745.

2. George Washington, "Surveying: A Plan of Major Lawrence Washingtons Turnip Field as Survey'd by me," 27 Feb. 1747, George Washington Papers at the Library of Congress, 1741–1799, Series 1a, George Washington, School Copy Book, vol., 1, 1745.

3. Washington's undated drawing for repairing the portico is pen and ink on paper, 9″ × 7.5″, after 1787, W-498, MVLA.

4. George Washington, "Geometrical Definitions," 1745, George Washington Papers at the Library of Congress, 1741–1799, Series 1a, George Washington, School Book Copy Book, vol. 1, 1745.

5. See also Figure 7.7 for young Washington's mapping of the area near Alexandria.

6. George Washington "Slooping White Oak," survey of 5 Nov. 1762, MVLA, MS 4966, RM-737.

7. For the plan, see also Lawrence Martin, *The George Washington Atlas* (Washington, DC: United States George Washington Bicentennial Commission, 1932).

8. See also Martin, *The George Washington Atlas,* plate 11.

9. Washington to Henry Knox, 20 Feb. 1784, *Papers,* Confederation Series, 1:138. The compass here resembles the upright compass often found in Masonic images, but there is no known Masonic context for this early drawing. For the symbolism of the compass in Masonic art, see James Curl, *The Art and Architecture of Freemasonry: An Introductory Study* (London: B. T. Batsford, 1991), 236, and for illustrations of the upright compass, see John Hamilton, *Material Culture of the American Freemasons* (Lexington, MA: Museum of our National Heritage / Hanover, NH: Distributed by the University Press of New England, 1994). See also Daniel Béresniak, *Symbols of Freemasonry* (New York: Assouline, 2000), 50–59.

10. Samuel Powel to Washington, 9 Aug. 1788, *Papers,* Confederation Series, 6:435.

11. Washington to Powel, 15 Sept. 1788, *Papers,* Confederation Series, 6:515. For the chairs, see also Clement Biddle to Washington, 2 Oct. 1788, *Papers,* Presidential Series, 1:28, and editor's note 2.

12. Julian Ursyn Niemcewicz, *Under Their Vine and Fig Tree: Travels through America in 1797–1799, 1805, with Some Further Account of Life in New Jersey,* trans. and ed. Metchie J. E. Budka (Elizabeth, NJ: Grassmann, 1965), 101, with Niemcewicz's sketch of the plow illustrated on 102.

13. Washington had to make something of an aesthetic decision concerning the height; the firebacks, he noted, "do not go all the way up." Charles Pettit to Washington, 1 Nov. 1787, *Papers,* Confederation Series, 5:401; George Washington to George Augustine Washington, 3 June 1787, *Papers,* Confederation Series, 5:218.

14. For the letter concerning the stove, see Washington to Clement Biddle, 21 Aug. 1797, *Papers,* Retirement Series, 1:311–312; see the editor's note 3 on p. 312 for an explanation about the sketch, which is unpublished and remains in private hands:

The private owner of the letter from GW to Biddle of 15 Oct. 1797 also owns the sketch of an "open stove about 3 f. wide" with instructions, all in GW's hand. This is probably the memorandum that GW refers to here. With reference to the sketch, GW writes: "Iron hearth, to the back of the Stove
From 1 to 2 about 20 Inches—more or less
From 3 to 4 about 27   Do   Do   Do." He [Washington] then writes: "If there are no Stoves of the above form to be had, any other kind that is *open*, and can be fixed in the manner, and in such a place as is mentioned in the letter, will answer the purpose."

The owner of the drawing as of 1972 is given as Mr. Erskine B. Wood, Portland, Oregon (Retirement Series, 1:405).

15. Copley, letter to Benjamin West or Captain R. G. Bruce, c. 1767; see *Letters and Papers of John Singleton Copley and Henry Pelham, 1739–1776* (New York: Kennedy Graphics and Da Capo Press, 1970 ["unabridged republication of the first edition published in Boston in 1914 as Volume 71 of the *Collections of the Massachusetts Historical Society*"]), 65–66.

16. *The Papers of Thomas Jefferson,* ed. Julian P. Boyd (Princeton, NJ: Princeton University Press, 1950–), 13:269.

17. Washington to William Gordon, 8 Mar. 1785, *Papers,* Confederation Series, 2:411–412.

18. Washington to Friedrich-Christoph, Graf zu Solms und Tecklenberg, 3 Jan. 1784, *Papers,* Confederation Series, 1:8–9. For this work by Wright, see Monroe Fabian, *Joseph Wright: American Artist, 1756–1793* (Washington, DC: Smithsonian Institution Press, Published for the National Portrait Gallery, 1985), 100–101 (location listed as unknown), and 92–114 for other portraits of Washington by Wright. See also David Meschutt, "Life Portraits of George Washington," in *George Washington: American Symbol,* ed. Barbara J. Mitnick (Stony Brook, NY: Hudson Hills Press, 1999), 36.

19. For the commission and the placing of the portrait in the count's castle at Königstein, see editor's note 1, *Papers,* Confederation Series, 1:8–9, 32–33.

20. When referring to the portrait in a letter to Robert Morris, who was receiving the picture to forward to the count, Washington wrote, "I am sorry to give you trouble about trifles, but I know you will excuse it" (10 Jan. 1784, *Papers,* Confederation Series, 1:31).

21. Edward Savage to Washington, 17 June 1799, *Papers,* Retirement Series, 4:134.

22. Washington to Edward Savage, 30 June 1799, *Papers,* Retirement Series, 4:134–135, note 2.

23. Edward Savage to Washington, 3 June 1798, *Papers,* Retirement Series, 2:311–312.

24. Charles Willson Peale to Washington, 27 Feb. 1787, *Papers,* Confederation Series, 5:56. For Peale's work, see Wendy Wick, *George Washington, an American Icon: The Eighteenth-Century Graphic Portraits* (Washington, DC: Smithsonian Institution / Charlottesville: University of Virginia Press, 1982), 15–16.

25. James Manley to Washington, 13 Feb. 1790, *Papers,* Presidential Series, 5:110, note 2.

26. Elizabeth Willing Powel to George Washington, 3 Dec. 1798, *Papers,* Retirement Series, 3:242.

27. Washington to the Marquis de Lafayette, 21 Nov. 1791, *Papers,* Presidential Series, 9:217.

28. Washington to William Paca, letter of introduction for Robert Pine, 18 May 1785; see *Papers,* Confederation Series, 2:567, note 2.

29. Echoing this, in her will of June 1802, Martha Washington called the same vases "the Fine Old China jars which usually Stand on the Chimney piece in the New Room"; see Joseph Fields, ed., *"Worthy Partner": The Papers of Martha Washington* (Westport, CT: Greenwood, 1994), 407.

30. Washington to James Gildart, 5 June 1764, *Papers,* Colonial Series, 7:310–311.

31. Washington to Gouverneur Morris, 28 Nov. 1788, *Papers,* Presidential Series, 1:135.

32. For the testimony of David Howell of Rhode Island about that dinner of Sept. 1783, see Edmund Burnett, ed., *Letters of Members of the Continental Congress,* 8 vols. (Washington, DC: The Carnegie Institution of Washington, 1921–1936), 7:292; Douglas Southall Freeman, *George Washington: A Biography,* 7 vols. (New York: Scribner, 1948–1957), 5:453; and Harlow Unger, *The Unexpected George Washington: His Private Life* (Hoboken, NJ: John Wiley and Sons, 2006), 148, and 280, note 19.

33. Washington to Robert Pine, 26 Feb. 1786, *Papers,* Confederation Series, 3:573; Washington to George William Fairfax, 25 June 1786, *Papers,* Confederation Series, 4:126–127. For more on Pine's work for Washington, see "A Pretty Eminent Portrait Painter," *MVLAAR,* 1977, 10–15.

34. Entry for 3 Oct. 1789, *Diaries,* 5:451. For the watercolor by Bréhan and various later versions by her, see "A Washington Miniature," *MVLAAR,* 1968, 20–25.

35. Washington to the Marquis de Lafayette, 21 Nov. 1791, *Papers,* Presidential Series, 9: 217; Washington to Nicholas Rogers, 28 May 1779, *Writings,* 15:175.

36. These include Mount Vernon inv. nos. W-13, A-481, W-1545, W12, W-1411, and W-1871. Washington purchased silver-plated Argand lamps (6″ in height) to rest on table surfaces and Argand wall lamps; see text and illustrations in Carol Borchert Cadou, *The George Washington Collection: Fine and Decorative Arts at Mount Vernon* (Manchester, VT: Hudson Hills Press, for MVLA, 2006), 150–153. George Washington to Gouverneur Morris, 1 Mar., 15 Apr. 1790, *Papers,* Presidential Series, 5:193, 334. As for the set of Argand wall lamps, Washington referred to them as "oval Japan," referring to the mirrored surface in an uncustomary way for the time (see Cadou, *George Washington Collection,* 152, and 1797 list of public and private purchases for the executive residence). He used the word "Japan" in the broad sense of an object with an added surface, not in the restricted meaning of "japanned" to refer to the usual black and gilded surfaces made to imitate lacquered Asian boxes. For use of the word "elegant," see also Washington to John Trumbull, 31 Dec. 1795, *Writings,* 34:411–412.

37. Washington to Charles Buxton, 30 May 1799, *Papers,* Retirement Series, 4:27, note 3. Similarly, Washington characterized

an etching and a "proof Print" by Francis Philips (after Joseph Wright of Derby's *Dead Soldier*) sent to him in June 1798 as "two elegant Prints," and he offered thanks for the "Pictures" so "deservedly admired" (Washington to Henry Philips [brother of the print maker], 8 July 1798, *Papers,* Retirement Series, 2:354–355, note 2). Marble busts of Ariadne and Bacchus by Italian sculptor Giuseppe Ceracchi, who hoped to get a public commission from the U.S. Congress, were displayed in the presidential mansion in Philadelphia by Washington, who called them "very elegant" (Washington to Ceracchi, 10 May 1792, *Papers,* Presidential Series, 10:372). The message to Ceracchi was apparently formulated in collaboration with Thomas Jefferson (see editor's note to letter, 10:372; the date of the draft was 12 Mar. 1792).

38. Charles Pettit to George Washington, 1 Nov. 1787, *Papers,* Confederation Series, 5:401.

39. James Boswell, *Boswell's Life of Johnson,* 2 vols., ed. Chauncey Brewster Tinker (New York: Oxford University Press, 1933), 1:560.

40. Washington to Robert Cary and Co., 28 Sept. 1760, *Papers,* Colonial Series, 6:459–460.

41. T. H. Breen, "'Baubles of Britain'": Changing Lifestyles and Consumer Behavior in the Colonial Chesapeake," in *Of Consuming Interests: The Style of Life in the Eighteenth Century,* ed. Cary Carson, Ronald Hoffman, and Peter Albert (Charlottesville: University Press of Virginia, for the United States Capitol Historical Society, 1994), 459; George Washington to Bushrod Washington, 22 Sept. 1783, *Writings,* 27:160–161, discussed in Unger, *The Unexpected George Washington,* 148–149. (Tellingly, he asked that Bushrod make the inquiries discreetly on behalf of a "friend," without the nephew mentioning his famous uncle.)

42. Washington to Wakelin Welch, 28 Nov. 1785, *Papers,* Confederation Series, 3:417. For Morris's purchases for Washington, see also 7 Oct. 1789, *Diaries,* 5:455–456, editor's note.

43. See Cadou, *George Washington Collection,* 182–183. Washington bought twenty-four side chairs and two sideboards from Aitken in 1797. See also Marian Carson, "W. Furniture of Mount Vernon: I: The Banquet Hall," *American Collector* 16, no. 4 (May 1947): 6–17.

44. George Washington to Henry Lee, 3 July 1792, *Papers,* Presidential Series, 10:515–516.

45. Elkanah Watson, *Men and Times of the Revolution, or Memoirs of Elkanah Watson,* ed. Winslow Watson (New York: Dana and Co., 1856), 139. In January 1785 at Mount Vernon, Washington told Elkanah Watson the story of sitting for Wright.

46. See Monroe Fabian, *Joseph Wright: American Artist, 1756–1793,* 50, note 17; Margaret Bailey Tinkcom, "Caviar Along the Potomac: Sir Augustus John Foster's 'Notes on the United States,' 1804–1812," *William and Mary Quarterly,* 3rd ser., 8, no. 1 (Jan. 1951): 92–93. For Wright and the life mask, see also "The Genesis

of a Portrait," *MVLAAR,* 1967, 15. Washington to Robert Morris, 10 Jan. 1784, *Papers,* Confederation Series, 1:31.

47. For Washington and Peale, see 22 May 1772, *Diaries,* 3:109; entry in his day book for January 1774, see *Papers,* Colonial Series, 10:79, editor's note 20; entry for July 1787, *Diaries,* 5:242.

48. Entry for 2–3 Jan. 1774, *Diaries,* 3:225.

49. For the birds Peale wanted from Washington, see Peale's letter to him on 31 Dec. 1786, *Papers,* Confederation Series, 4:492. See also Peale to Washington, 27 Sept. 1787, and the editor's notes in *The Selected Papers of Charles Willson Peale and His Family,* vol. 1, *Charles Willson Peale, Artist in Revolutionary America, 1735–1791,* ed. Lillian Miller (New Haven, CT: Yale University Press, 1983), 473–474. For Peale's invitation to Washington to his "exhibition," see Peale to Washington, 6 Aug. 1787, *Papers,* Confederation Series, 5:283. In May 1787, Peale invited Washington to join some Society of the Cincinnati members in the gallery and "see my perspective Views with changeable effects"; see Peale to Washington, 16 May 1787, *Papers,* Confederation Series, 5:188.

50. For contemporary discussion of Houdon, see Thomas Jefferson to Washington, 10 July 1785, *Papers,* Confederation Series, 3:112; and David Humphreys to Washington, 17 July 1785, *Papers,* Confederation Series, 3:131. Washington to Lafayette, 21 Nov. 1791, *Papers,* Presidential Series, 9:217–218.

51. For John Adams and the fine arts, see David McCullogh, *John Adams* (New York: Simon and Schuster, 2001), 149–150, 236–237. For Adams, potentially tempted by the art galleries of Paris, "the conflict between the appeal of the arts and the sense that they were the product of a luxury-loving (and thus corrupt) foreign society played heavily on his mind" (236).

52. For a description of Gunston Hall, distinguished especially by the fine woodwork rather than a collection of two-dimensional objects, see Jeff Broadwater, *George Mason: Forgotten Founder* (Chapel Hill: University of North Carolina Press, 2006), 4–9.

53. For the inventory of 1770, see Graham Hood, *Inventories of Four Eighteenth-Century Houses in the Historic Area of Williamsburg* (Williamsburg, VA: Colonial Williamsburg Foundation, 1974), and *The Governor's Palace in Williamsburg: A Cultural Study* (Williamsburg, VA: Colonial Williamsburg Foundation / Chapel Hill: Distributed by University of North Carolina Press, 1991), 287–295.

54. Jefferson's art collection is discussed in Susan Stein, *The Worlds of Thomas Jefferson at Monticello* (New York: Abrams, 1993), 122–421, and his aesthetics and collecting more generally in William Adams, ed., *The Eye of Thomas Jefferson* (Washington, DC: National Gallery of Art, 1976).

55. For the collection of art at Custis Square in Williamsburg, see Fields, *"Worthy Partner,"* 94–96.

56. For William Hamilton, see James Jacobs, "William Hamilton and the Woodlands: A Construction of Refinement in Philadelphia," *Pennsylvania Magazine of History and Biography,* 130, no. 2 (Apr. 2006): 181–209, esp. 202–208.

57. Invoice to Robert Cary and Company, *Papers,* 20 Sept. 1759, Colonial Series, 6:355; Flexner, "George Washington as an Art Collector," *American Art Journal* 4, no. 1 (Spring 1972): 24–35.

58. Invoice to Robert Cary and Company, *Papers,* Colonial Series, 6:358, editor's note 77.

59. The little sketch, unpublished (MS 7799, Wellcome Library, London), is in the list of goods ordered from Cary in London in 1759; for mention of the manuscript but no illustration of the sketch, see "Enclosure. Invoice to Robert Cary and Company," 20 Sept. 1759, *Papers,* Colonial Series, 6:358, editor's note 77. A facsimile of the enclosure is at Mount Vernon (PS-675 and RM-240, MVLA).

60. Invoice from Robert Cary and Co., 15 Mar. 1760, *Papers,* Colonial Series, 6:399–400.

61. George Washington to Richard Washington, 15 Apr. 1757, *Papers,* Colonial Series, 4:133–134: let goods "be fashionable-neat-and good in their several kinds." Washington to Clement Biddle, 6 May, 30 June 1784, *Papers,* Confederation Series, 1:373, 474. For other indications of Washington's interest in wallpaper, see "A Mount Vernon Wallpaper," *MVLAAR,* 1960, 11–13.

62. Washington to William Hamilton, 17 Jan. 1784, *Papers,* Confederation Series, 1:49; George Washington to George Augustine Washington, 1 July, 15 July, 1787, *Papers,* Confederation Series, 5:243, 260.

63. George Augustine Washington to George Washington, 15 Apr. 1792, *Papers,* Presidential Series, 10:270.

64. Washington to Tobias Lear, 10 Mar., 12 Mar., 1797, *Papers,* Retirement Series, 1:27, 33.

65. Washington to Clement Biddle, 18 Aug. 1786, *Papers,* Confederation Series, 4:218. Tobias Lear to Clement Biddle, 10 Feb. 1790, *Papers,* Presidential Series, 5:72, note 2. For the presidential mansion in Philadelphia, "Washington had a tremendous capacity for detail and liked to arrange everything himself . . . even the color of curtains were dwelt on at length"; see Stephen Decatur Jr., *Private Affairs of George Washington* (Boston: Riverside Press, for Houghton Mifflin Co., 1933), 153, 206–207.

66. Washington to Clement Biddle, 18 May 1786, *Papers,* Confederation Series, 4:54.

67. Washington to John Trumbull, 31 Dec. 1795, *Writings,* 34:411–412; Washington to Joseph Brown, 30 May 1786, *Papers,* Confederation Series, 4:84.

68. Washington to Samuel Powel, 25 July 1787, *Papers,* Confederation Series, 5:274.

69. To Robert Cary and Company, 6 June 1768, *Papers,* Colo-

nial Series, 8:92–93, and Invoice from Robert Cary and Company, 28 Sept. 1768, *Papers,* Colonial Series, 8:135.

70. Washington to David and Francis Clark, 17 Sept. 1790, *Papers,* Presidential Series, 6:462.

71. Washington to James McAlpin, 27 Jan. 1799, *Papers,* Retirement Series, 3:341.

72. For the acknowledgment of the gift, see Washington to Samuel Vaughan, 18 Nov. 1786, *Papers,* Confederation Series, 4:384.

73. For the set, see "An English Admirer of Washington," *MVLAAR,* 1959, 15–20. Susan Detweiler, *George Washington's Chinaware* (New York: Harry N. Abrams, 1982), 97–102, and "The Ceramics," *Antiques* 135 (Feb. 1989): 496–501.

74. Washington to Samuel Vaughan, 18 Nov. 1786, *Papers,* Confederation Series, 4:384.

75. Washington to the Marquis de Lafayette, 28 May 1788, *Papers,* Confederation Series, 6:298.

76. Washington to Giuseppe Ceracchi, 9 Mar. 1795, *Writings,* 34:139.

77. Entry for 27 Aug. 1789, Kenneth R. Bowling and Helen E. Veit, eds., *The Diary of William Maclay and other Notes on Senate Debates,* vol. 9 of *Documentary History of the First Federal Congress of the United States of America, 4 Mar. 1789–3 Mar. 1791* (Baltimore: Johns Hopkins University Press, 1988), 136. For a good summary of the tableware and porcelain ornaments that Washington acquired during the presidency and sold or attempted to sell at the end of his second term, see Detweiler, *George Washington's Chinaware,* 103–158.

78. Washington to Mary White Morris, 1 May 1797, *Papers,* Retirement Series, 1:130. He presumably meant a mixture of paintings and prints, as in writing of the period one often did not make a distinction between the two.

79. Washington to Clement Biddle, 29 Jan. 1798, *Papers,* Retirement Series, 2:57.

80. George Washington, "Prints Purchased," February 1797, George Washington Papers at the Library of Congress, 1741–1799, Series 4, General Correspondence. 1697–1799. For Washington and his prints, see Robert Hartley, "George Washington Lived Here, Some Early Prints of Mount Vernon, Part I," *Antiques* 47, no. 2 (Feb. 1945): 103–105; and R. T. H. Halsey, "Prints Washington Lived with at Mount Vernon," *Bulletin of the Metropolitan Museum of Art* 30, no. 3 (Mar. 1935): 63–65, for general information, and 64 for mention of Washington's list of prints acquired while president. For Washington's print collection and its placement, see also "A Bicentennial Homecoming," *MVLAAR,* 1974, 13–17; and Wendy Wick Reaves, "The Prints," *Antiques* 135 (Feb. 1989): 502–511. See also the exhibition catalogue, *Prints Collected by Washington* (MVLA, 1939).

81. *Lafayette at the Battle of Yorktown,* MVLA, H-1367.

82. Entry for 18 Mar. 1798, Friedrich Wilhelm Hoeninghaus, *Reise eines Krefelders nach Nordamerika, 1797–1798: Tagebuchaufzeichnungen und Briefe,* ed. Wolfhart Langer (Krefeld, Germany: privately printed, 1973), 33; Niemcewicz, *Under Their Vine and Fig Tree,* 97.

83. Robert Pine, *Fanny Bassett,* 1785, oil on canvas, W-1488, MVLA.

84. The Law portrait is inv. no. W-2909, MVLA. For Sharples and his portraits of the Washington family, see Katharine McCook Knox, *The Sharples: Their Portraits of George Washington and His Contemporaries* (New York: Kennedy Graphics and Da Capo Press, 1972), esp. 13–17, 63–69. See also Robert Stewart, "Portraits of George and Martha Washington," *Antiques* 135 (Feb. 1989): 478–479. For the placement of portraits and other works in the room, see "A Bicentennial Homecoming," 13–17.

85. Entry for 22 May 1772, *Diaries,* 3:109: "Set for Mr. Peale to finish my Face. In the Afternoon Rid with him to my Mill."

86. For Chateaubriand's remark, see Gilbert Chinard, ed., *George Washington as the French Knew Him* (Princeton: Princeton University Press, 1940), 95. The French visitor noted that keys (plural) to the Bastille "were rather silly toys which were sent around at that time." For information about the key, see Christine Meadows, "Souvenir of the French Revolutions," *MVLAAR,* 1987, 26–36.

87. For Louis Otto's remark, see *The Writings of Thomas Paine,* ed. Mercure Conway, 4 vols., 1894–1899 (New York: G. P. Putnam's Sons, 1895), 3:v–vi.

88. For his instructions on how to place the bust, see George Washington to George Augustine Washington, 12 Aug. 1787, *Papers,* Confederation Series, 5:288. Washington to John Paul Jones, 2 Sept. 1787, *Papers,* Confederation Series, 5:308; Jones to Washington, 9 Sept. 1787, *Papers,* Confederation Series, 5:321. For the Necker bust (W-2548, MVLA), see "In the French Manner," *MVLAAR,* 1969, 26–29.

89. For the graining of the study in 1786, see "A Very Handsome Study," *MVLAAR,* 1980, 32–41.

90. See the estate items listed in Eugene Prussing, *The Estate of George Washington, Deceased* (Boston: Little, Brown, and Company, 1927), 412.

91. For the floor covering in the Large Dining Room and elsewhere in the principal rooms, see "Mount Vernon Floor Coverings: A Restoration Survey," *MVLAAR,* 1974, 21–26.

92. For the Windsor chairs ("let them be put in the New Room"), see Washington to William Pearce, 1 May 1796, *Writings,* 35:35. For Aitkens's sideboard and two dozen chairs in the neoclassic style, see Cadou, *George Washington Collection,* 182–183, and "The Mount Vernon Sideboards," *MVLAAR,* 1966, 27–33.

93. For the possible connection of this engraving with Freemasonry, see Mary Thompson, *"In the Hands of a Good Providence": Religion in the Life of George Washington* (Charlottesville: University of Virginia Press, 2008), 68.

94. For Washington's pastel of Mary, see Linda Ayres, "The Virgin Mary's Homecoming: Generous Descendant Contributes Period Pastel," *MVLAAR*, 2003, 22–25. Although the pair is not specifically mentioned in the early inventories, Mary Thompson thought they may have been at Custis Square in Williamsburg and then passed to John Custis's son Daniel and wife Martha. She noted that there is no bill of sale to George Washington or notice of gift for these paintings (memo from Mary Thompson to Gretchen Goodell, 13 Jan. 2004, 1, MLVA, in object file 2003.024.001); see also Ayres, "The Virgin Mary's Homecoming," 24. For the reception of religious art in England, where the pictures were "representative of a desire to glorify both the host's good taste and God's greatness," see Annabelle Church-Soulard, "From the Worship of God to the Worship of Beauty? The Reception of Italian Catholic Religious Paintings in the Private Chapels of English Country Houses, c. 1660–1768," *Journal for Eighteenth-Century Studies* 33, no. 2 (2010): 209–226.

95. See, e.g., Ruth Piwonka and Roderic H. Blackburn, *A Remnant in the Wilderness: New York Dutch Scripture History Painting of the Early Eighteenth Century* (Albany, NY: Albany Institute of History and Art, 1980), and *Remembrance of Patria: Dutch Arts and Culture in Colonial America, 1609–1776* (New York: Publishing Center for Cultural Resources, for the Albany Institute of History and Art, 1988), 209–255.

96. Washington to the Marquis de Lafayette, 25 July 1785, *Papers,* Confederation Series, 3:155. See Hunter in "An Account of a Visit made to Washington at Mount Vernon, by an English Gentleman, in 1785: From the Diary of John Hunter," *Pennsylvania Magazine of History and Biography* 17 (1893): 81; Robert Hunter Jr., *Quebec to Carolina in 1785–1786: Being the Travel Diary and Observations of Robert Hunter, Jr., a Young Merchant of London,* ed. Louis Wright and Marion Tinling (San Marino, CA: Huntington Library, 1943), 197; and Jean Lee, ed., *Experiencing Mount Vernon: Eyewitness Accounts, 1784–1865* (Charlottesville: University of Virginia Press, 2006), 34.

97. Washington to "Professeur de dessein" Pierre Francois Cozette, 19 June 1786, *Papers,* Confederation Series, 3:559, note 1:

Sir . . . I am highly oblig'd to you for the compliment which you pay me in desiring my acceptance of a portrait of Lewis the fifteenth, on horse back, which done by you & is at your disposal. I have not the least doubt Sir, but that the performance does honor to your abilities, & I join with you in wishing that it might be placed in some public & conspicuous situation, where the world could be gratified by seeing the picture of a good King, & where the merit of the performer meet with the applause which is due to it. Upon this principle Sir, (though I feel a grateful sense of the honor which you intended me) I must beg leave to decline the acceptance of it, as it could not here be placed in that conspicuous point of view which would do it justice.

98. Jan. 1759, "Inventory of the James City Estate," no. 163, "5 prints of Alexanders Battles," in Fields, *"Worthy Partner,"* 69; there is no firm evidence, however, to trace the provenance from Williamsburg to Mount Vernon, and the matter remains open. The prints are no. W-717 A-E, MVLA.

99. See Washington's will of 1799 in Prussing, *The Estate of George Washington,* 57, returning the box to the Earl of Buchan "with my grateful thanks for the distinguished honour of presenting it to me."

100. See R. W. G. Vail, ed., "A Dinner at Mount Vernon: From the Unpublished Journal of Joshua Brookes (1773–1859)," *New-York Historical Society Quarterly* 31, no. 2 (Apr. 1947): 78.

101. For Sally Foster Otis, see "A Visit to Mount Vernon—1801," *MVLAAR,* 1961, 35.

102. John Searson, *Mount Vernon, A Poem: Being the Seat of His Excellency George Washington, in the State of Virginia* (Philadelphia: Printed for the author by Folwell, 1800), 10.

103. For a discussion of the sundial, see chap. 8.

104. See, e.g., 16 Mar. 1768, *Diaries,* 2:45: "Started and catchd a fox in abt. three hours." For punctuality at Nomini Hall, see the letter from Philip Fithian to the Reverend Enoch Green, 2 Nov. 1773, in Philip Vickers Fithian, *Journal and Letters of Philip Vickers Fithian, 1773–1774: A Plantation Tutor of the Old Dominion,* ed. with an intro. by Hunter Dickinson Farish (Williamsburg, VA: Colonial Williamsburg, 1957), 21 ("a family remarkable for regularity, and oeconomy").

105. George Washington to George Augustine Washington, 3 June, 12 Aug., 1787, *Papers,* Confederation Series, 5:218, 287; Washington to Joseph Rakestraw, 20 July 1787, *Papers,* Confederation Series, 5:267.

106. George Washington to George Augustine Washington, 12 Aug. 1787, *Papers,* Confederation Series, 5:287; for Rakestraw (c. 1735–1794), s.v. Joseph Rakestraw in *Biographical Dictionary of Philadelphia Architects: 1700–1930,* ed. Sandra Tatman and Roger Moss (Boston: G. K. Hall, 1985), 641–642. Rakestraw was not a metalworker and was unlikely to have actually crafted the object himself. See also Marc Lefrancois, "The Crown Restored," *MVLAAR,* 1993, 15–20.

107. For the coloration of the weathervane, see Cadou, *George*

Washington Collection, 122. Technical investigation of the weather-vane was carried out at the Winterthur Museum in 1998 and revealed no traces of original surface paint or gilding (MVLA, object file).

108. Thompson, *"In the Hands of a Good Providence,"* 44, for gilding, and Washington to Clement Biddle, 3 Mar. 1798, *Papers,* Retirement Series, 2:115. For the Pohick Church, see the Invoice to Robert Cary and Co., 10 July 1773, *Papers,* Colonial Series, 9:273–276, including editor's note 5.

109. See note in the entry for 30 Oct. 1769, *Diaries,* 2:190, regarding an invoice of goods shipped to Washington in Sept. 1768.

110. Helen Comstock, "The George Washington Book-Plate," *Connoisseur* 94 (July 1934): 54–55; see also T. Pape, "The Washington Coat of Arms," *Connoisseur* 89, no. 366 (Feb. 1932): 100–107.

111. See entry and editor's note for 16 Dec. 1771, *Diaries,* 3:76. Washington ordered three to four hundred plates at that time. See also William Ivins Jr., "The Baillie Collection of Bookplates," *Bulletin of the Metropolitan Museum of Art* 15, no. 11 (Nov. 1920): 246–248. Comstock, "The George Washington Book-Plate," 54–55, disputed the contention of Moncure Conway (*Barons of the Potomack and the Rappahannock,* 1892) that George Washington altered the conventional shield of the Washingtons. See also "Ancestral Origins and Emblems," *MVLAAR,* 1963, 23–28. For the letter to Anderson, see Washington to James Anderson, 21 Dec. 1797, *Papers,* Retirement Series, 1:255–256.

112. For the substitution of Liberty for Britannia and other aspects of the iconography, see note in *The Last Will and Testament of George Washington and Schedule of His Property,* ed. John C. Fitzpatrick, 4th ed. (Mount Vernon: MVLA, 1972), ii. See also "Ancestral Origins and Emblems," 23–28. For the visit to the Onderdonk mill in Hempstead, Long Island, see 24 Apr. 1790, *Diaries,* 6:66; and Dard Hunter, *Papermaking: The History and Technique of an Ancient Craft* (New York: A. A. Knopf, 1947), 252–253.

113. See Fields, *"Worthy Partner,"* 427–429, for discussion of the English Dandridge line of painters. For a discussion of Martha's eye for fine art, jewelry, and fashion, see "Seed Pearls to Silk Gowns: The Personal Style of Martha Washington," in Cadou, *George Washington Collection,* 237–261.

114. See "The Appraisements of the Estate of Danl Parke Custis," 20 Oct. 1757, in *Papers,* Colonial Series, 6:220, 226.

115. Engraved by Pieter Stevens van Gunst after Charles Le Brun, late seventeenth century (inv. no. W-717); the possible origin from Martha's inheritance is discussed in an internal Mount Vernon report from historian Mary Thompson to curator Gretchen Goodell, 13 Jan. 2004 (object files, MVLA Library).

116. For the flower and fruit pieces, see Mary Stephenson, "Custis Square Historical Report, Block 4, Lot 1–8," Rockefeller Library, Williamsburg (electronic version available online) (origi-nally entitled "Custis Square"; Colonial Williamsburg Foundation Library Research Report Series, 1070): "These [pieces], doubtless, were sets of Furber and Catesby prints, which we know were owned by John Custis." For these works and other fine objects, see "Account of Sundrys taken and used by Mrs. Custis out of the Inventories [Oct. 1759]," in Fields, *"Worthy Partner,"* 109–112; see also 94–96, for the sale of the John Custis collection on 25 Oct. 1759, and 96 for the payment record to Wollaston for 3 pictures in 1757 ("Inventory of the Estate of Daniel Parke Custis"). Similar information on what Martha took away from her first marriage is in the list written up by George Washington, in "Settlement of the Daniel Parke Custis Estate," under "Account of the Items in the Estate Used by Martha Custis [1759]," in *Papers,* Colonial Series, 6:232–235.

117. Martha Washington to Arthur Lee, 15 Sept. 1780, in *"Worthy Partner,"* 184. For the making of the portraits, see "Peale's Custis Miniatures," *MVLAAR,* 1960, 20–22. For her directive to Peale, see Martha Washington to Charles Willson Peale, 26 Dec. 1780, *"Worthy Partner,"* 185; Peale painted the miniatures in 1776.

118. Martha Washington to Eleanor Parke Custis, 3 Jan. 1796, *"Worthy Partner,"* 289. John Pintard, diary entry, manuscript in the New-York Historical Society, cited here from the copy, p. 1, MVLA Library. For the "jars" and Martha's will, see Fields, *"Worthy Partner,"* 407. For the dark impressions, see Edward Savage to Washington, 3 June 1798, *Papers,* Retirement Series, 2:312.

119. Martha Washington to Fanny Bassett Washington, 8 June, 23 Oct. 1789, Fields, *"Worthy Partner,"* 215, 219.

120. Washington to Joseph Wright, 30 Jan. 1785, *Papers,* Confederation Series, 2:299.

121. See Washington to William Gordon, 8 Mar. 1785, *Papers,* Confederation Series, 2:412–413; and Gordon to Washington, 28 Mar. 1785, *Papers,* Confederation Series, 2:465–466. Gordon thought them imperfect (465) and called Washington's attention to the question of likeness in profiles and larger pictures.

122. Edward Savage to Washington, 6 Oct. 1793, *Papers,* Presidential Series, 14:174.

123. For Trumbull's 1790 gift to Martha Washington, see Hugh Howard, *The Painter's Chair: George Washington and the Making of American Art* (New York: Bloomsbury, 2009), 136. A larger version, commissioned for the mayor of New York, is now in the Winterthur Museum.

124. John Trumbull to Washington, 25 Apr. 1797, *Papers,* Retirement Series, 1:122; Tobias Lear to Washington, 4 Feb. 1794, *Papers,* Presidential Series, 15:178; George William Fairfax to Washington, 10 June 1784, *Papers,* Confederation Series, 3:91–92, note 3.

125. For the "Grotto Work," see George Clinton to Washington, 5 Mar. 1785, *Papers,* Confederation Series, 2:408. A wax work was listed in Martha's estate in 1802; see Fields *"Worthy Partner,"*

415. Washington thanked Clinton on Martha's behalf; see 20 Apr. 1785, *Papers,* Confederation Series, 2:511.

126. The set arrived in Philadelphia on 24 Apr. 1796 with the donor, Andreas Everardus van Braam Houckgeest (1739–1801), agent for the Dutch East India Company. For the translation as "A glory and a defense from it," see Jean Gordon Lee, *Philadelphians and the China Trade, 1784–1844* (Philadelphia: Philadelphia Museum of Art, 1984), catalogue no. 53. For the translation of "tutamen ab illo" as "defense from him" (the English king, George III), see Eleanor Gustafson, "Collectors' Notes," *Antiques* 166 (Oct. 2004): 38–40. See also Detweiler, *George Washington's Chinaware,* 151–158. The "States China" cup and saucer (W-1497, A-C, MVLA) and the commission as a whole are discussed in Cadou, *George Washington Collection,* 149.

127. The bed is recorded in Martha Washington's will of 1802; see *"Worthy Partner,"* 407; see also "George Washington Slept Here," *MVLAAR,* 1973, 9–14.

128. Lund Washington to George Washington, 3 Dec. 1775, *Papers,* Revolutionary Series, 2:477; and Lund Washington to George Washington, 17 Dec. 1775, *Papers,* Revolutionary Series, 2:571. For Martha's role in establishing female spaces at Mount Vernon, see Barbara Burlison Mooney, *Prodigy Houses of Virginia: Architecture and the Native Elite* (Charlottesville: University of Virginia Press, 2008), 236–239.

129. George Washington to Tobias Lear, 10, 12 Mar. 1797, *Papers,* Retirement Series, 1:27, 33.

130. Tobias Lear to Alexander Hamilton, 28 Nov. 1789, *Papers,* Presidential Series, 4:336. Entry for 13 Feb. 1790, *Diaries,* 6:31.

131. Lund Washington to George Washington, 24 Nov. 1775, *Papers,* Revolutionary Series, 2:421–422.

132. Niemcewicz, *Under Their Vine and Fig Tree,* 105; Elizabeth Willing Powel to Martha Washington, Nov. 1787, *"Worthy Partner,"* 198.

133. For George Washington's image and the public in early America, see Howard, *The Painter's Chair*; Mitnick, *George Washington*; Ellen Miles, *George and Martha Washington: Portraits from the Presidential Years* (Washington, DC: Smithsonian Institution, National Portrait Gallery / Charlottesville: University Press of Virginia, 1999); Barry Schwartz, *George Washington: The Making of an American Symbol* (New York: Free Press / London: Collier Macmillan, 1987); Wick, *George Washington;* Gustavus Eisen, *Portraits of Washington,* 3 vols. (New York: R. Hamilton and Associates, 1932).

134. Entries for 20–22 May 1772, *Diaries,* 3:108–109.

135. Francis Hopkinson to Washington, 19 Apr. 1785, *Papers,* Confederation Series, 2:508; Washington to Hopkinson, 16 May 1785, *Papers,* Confederation Series, 2:561.

136. See the request by the Masonic Lodge, No. 22, Alexandria, Virginia, to Washington, 29 Aug. 1793, *Papers,* Presidential Series, 13:575–576, and note 2. The Masons characterized Williams as "the most successful portrait painter that we have yet seen or heard of in America." See also Eisen, *Portraits of Washington,* 2:505–506.

137. Washington to the Marquis de Lafayette, 25 Sept. 1778, *Papers,* Revolutionary Series, 17:129; Howard, *The Painter's Chair,* 69–70; Washington to Col. Joseph Reed, 31 Jan. 1776, *Papers,* Revolutionary Series, 3:228–229. The editor's note 7 (3:229) explains the complex situation as follows:

On 9 Sept. 1775 a London publisher using the name C. Shepherd issued two mezzotints purporting to depict GW as commander in chief of the Continental army: a three-quarter-length portrait of a man in military uniform and a full-length picture of a uniformed figure on horseback. Reed sent Martha Washington a copy of one of these prints but which one is not certain. Both prints are inscribed: "Done from an original Drawn from the Life by Alexr Campbell of Williamsburgh in Virginia." No painter of that name has been identified. These obviously fictitious pictures are part of a series of very similar and equally inaccurate portraits of American and British leaders that were issued under the names of various publishers during the early years of the war. They proved to be very popular and were widely imitated.

See also Wick, *George Washington,* 18–22.

138. Washington to Mrs. Walter Stewart, 16 Mar. 1796, *Writings,* 34:500, note.

139. Washington to Francis Hopkinson, 16 May 1785, *Papers,* Confederation Series, 2:561–562.

140. Washington to David Humphreys, 30 Oct. 1785, *Papers,* Confederation Series, 3:328. For Houdon and Washington, see Anne Poulet, *Jean-Antoine Houdon: Sculptor of the Enlightenment* (Washington, DC: National Gallery of Art / Chicago: University of Chicago Press, 2003), 263–268; see also H. Arnason, *The Sculptures of Houdon* (New York: Oxford University Press, 1975), 72–78.

141. Washington to Robert Morris, 10 Jan. 1784, *Papers,* Confederation Series, 1:30–31:

The Count de Bruhl is informed by it that my Portrait (which I have begged the Count de Solms to accept) will be forwarded to his care by you, so soon as it is finished, & I request the favor of you to do it accordingly. Mr Wright is desir'd to hand it to you for this purpose. & as he is said to be a little lazy, you would oblige me by stimulating him to the completion. By promise, it was to have been done in five or six weeks from the time I left Philadelphia, near four of which are expired. I am sorry to give you trouble about trifles, but I know you will excuse it, in this instance.

142. Washington to Henry Lee, 3 July 1792, *Papers,* Presidential Series, 10:515.

143. Washington to Samuel Washington, 15 Mar. 1777, *Papers,* Revolutionary Series, 8:584.

144. Eleanor Parke Custis Lewis to George Washington Parke Custis, 3 Dec. 1849, MVLA, manuscript RM-185, Ms. 2571.

145. George Washington Parke Custis, *Recollections and Private Memoirs of Washington* (Washington, DC: Printed by W. H. Moore, 1859), 171; Unger, *The Unexpected George Washington,* 95, 165.

146. For Watson, see *Men and Times of the Revolution,* 243–244, and Unger, *The Unexpected George Washington,* 165. For Thornton's account, written on 2 Apr. 1792, see Decatur, *Private Affairs,* 268. Entry for 14 Jan. 1790, Bowling and Veit, *The Diary of William Maclay,* 182; Benjamin Henry Latrobe, *The Virginia Journals of Benjamin Henry Latrobe, 1795–1798,* vol. 1, *1795–1797,* ed. Edward Carter (New Haven: Yale University Press, 1977), 166, 172.

147. Chinard, *George Washington as the French Knew Him,* passim, esp. 13–95.

148. Washington to Jonathan Boucher, 21 May 1772, *Papers,* Colonial Series, 9:49.

149. See Watson, *Men and Times of the Revolution,* 139.

150. Thomas Jefferson to Washington, 10 Dec. 1784, *Papers,* Confederation Series, 2:177. See also Charles Seymour Jr., "Houdon's Washington at Mount Vernon Re-examined," *Gazette Des Beaux-Arts* 33, 6th ser. (Mar. 1948): 137–158. For the commission, see also "The Genesis of a Portrait," *MVLAAR,* 1967, 11–16; Cadou, *George Washington Collection,* 120–121; and Mary Thompson, "Houdon's Bust of Washington," *MVLAAR,* 1996, 10–16.

151. Entry for 10 Oct. 1785, *Diaries,* 4:204.

152. Humphreys, 57.

153. Thomas Jefferson to Washington, 4 Jan. 1786, *Papers,* Confederation Series, 3:490; Washington to Jefferson, 1 Aug. 1786, *Papers,* Confederation Series, 4:183–184.

154. Washington to Thomas Jefferson, 1 Aug. 1786, *Papers,* Confederation Series, 4:183–184.

155. Thomas Jefferson to Washington, 14–15 Aug. 1787, *Papers,* Confederation Series, 5:290.

156. For *The Washington Family* (1789–1796, oil on canvas, National Gallery of Art, Andrew W. Mellon Collection 1940.1.2), for which Savage made a number of preparatory paintings and, later, related stipple engravings, see Ellen Miles, with contributions by Patricia Burda, Cynthia J. Mills, and Leslie Kaye Reinhardt, *American Paintings of the Eighteenth Century* (Washington: National Gallery of Art / New York: Cambridge University Press, 1995), 146–158. See also Louisa Dresser, "Edward Savage, 1761–1817: Some Representative Examples of His Work as a Painter," *Art in America* 40, no. 4 (Autumn 1952): 202–204; and Howard, *The Painter's Chair,* 139. See also Joseph Manca, "A Theology of Architecture: Edward Savage's Portrait of George Washington and His Family," *Source: Notes in the History of Art* 31, no. 1 (Fall 2011): 29–36.

Chapter 8. Under His Vine and Fig Tree

Epigraph. Washington to the Marquis de Lafayette, 1 Feb. 1784, *Papers,* Confederation Series, 1:87–88.

1. Paul Boller Jr., *George Washington and Religion* (Dallas: Southern Methodist University, 1963). Boller quoted from Bishop William White's observation about Washington's guarding "against the discoursing of himself" (66), a diffidence that throws light on our difficulty in gauging nuances of his religious beliefs and views. Mary Thompson, *"In the Hands of a Good Providence": Religion in the Life of George Washington* (Charlottesville: University of Virginia Press, 2008); for Washington's quotes from the Bible, see 22–29. Washington used the word "surety-ship" in a letter to in-law Burgess Ball, "referring to the comments on suretyship made by Solomon in Proverbs [11:15]" (18 Jan. 1790, *Papers,* Presidential Series, 5:6, and 7, editor's note).

2. See Boller, *George Washington and Religion,* 68–69. George Washington's "Speech to the Delaware Chiefs," 12 May 1779, *Writings,* 15:55.

3. Washington to Burwell Bassett, 28 Aug. 1762, *Papers,* Colonial Series, 7:147. For Washington's record over time in attending church service on Sundays, see Thompson, *"In the Hands of a Good Providence,"* 50–74.

4. Washington to the Clergy of Newport, Rhode Island, 18 Aug. 1790, *Papers,* Presidential Series, 6:279.

5. Washington to David Humphreys, 23 March 1793, *Papers,* Presidential Series, 12:362.

6. Thompson, *"In the Hands of a Good Providence,"* 185–186; Maynard Mack, *The Garden and the City: Retirement and Politics in the Later Poetry of Pope, 1731–1743* (Toronto: University of Toronto Press, 1969), 241, and passim for the larger theme of rural retirement in England.

7. Mack, *The Garden and the City,* 24; John Searson, *Mount Vernon, A Poem: Being the Seat of His Excellency George Washington, in the State of Virginia* (Philadelphia: Printed for the author by Folwell, 1800), 15.

8. Philip Vickers Fithian, *Journal and Letters of Philip Vickers Fithian, 1773–1774: A Plantation Tutor of the Old Dominion,* ed. with intro. by Hunter Dickinson Farish (Williamsburg, VA: Colonial Williamsburg, 1957), passim.

9. Washington to an unidentified "Robin," c. 1749–1750, *Papers,* Colonial Series, 1:41.

10. Humphreys, 24, note 5. In a later retirement, Washington also mentioned physical ailments as a reason to avoid office in the

Society of the Cincinnati; his "indisposition" was caused by "Rheumatick complaints with which, at times, I am a good deal afflicted" (Washington to James Madison, 16 Dec. 1786, *Papers,* Confederation Series, 4:458).

11. John Kirkpatrick to Washington, 21 July 1758, *Papers,* Colonial Series, 5:315.

12. George Washington to John Augustine Washington, 6–9 Nov. 1776, *Papers,* Revolutionary Series, 7:105.

13. Washington to Jonathan Trumbull Jr., 5 Jan. 1784, *Papers,* Confederation Series, 1:12.

14. Washington to the Marquis de Chastellux, 1 Feb. 1784, *Papers,* Confederation Series, 1:86–87.

15. In Addison's *Cato,* the final lines of Act I, scene 1, are: "Thy steady temper, Portius, can look on guilt, rebellion, fraud, and Caesar in the calm lights of mild Philosophy." Washington mentioned the play in a letter to Sarah Cary Fairfax, 25 Sept. 1758, *Papers,* Colonial Series, 6:42. See also the discussion of *Cato* and Washington in Richard Brookhiser, *Founding Father: Rediscovering George Washington* (New York: Free Press, 1996), 123–127.

16. Marquis de Chastellux to Washington, 6 Mar. 1784, *Papers,* Confederation Series, 1:175.

17. Washington to Jean Luzac, 2 Dec. 1797, *Papers,* Retirement Series, 1:377–388.

18. Washington to the Marquis de Lafayette, 1 Feb. 1784, *Papers,* Confederation Series, 1:87–88.

19. Washington to the Marquis de Lafayette, 23 Mar. 1783, *Writings,* 26:251–255; and see Harlow Unger, *The Unexpected George Washington: His Private Life* (Hoboken, NJ: John Wiley and Sons, 2006), 143.

20. Washington to Rochambeau, 1 Feb. 1784, *Papers,* Confederation Series, 1:102.

21. Washington to Adrienne, the Marquise de Lafayette, 4 Apr. 1784, *Papers,* Confederation Series, 1:258.

22. Washington to William Grayson, 22 Jan. 1785, *Papers,* Confederation Series, 2:282: "Are there any young shoots which could be had of the Yew tree, or Hemlock (for I do not now recollect which of these it is) that grows on the margin of Quantico Creek? Plantations of this kind are now become my amusement & I should be glad to know where I could obtain a supply of such sorts of trees as would diversify the scene." Similarly, on 3 Apr. 1798, Washington wrote to John Henry: "If to relax, & diversify the scene a little, you should find it convenient & agreeable to yourself to extend your walks to the Potomac, I should be very happy in seeing you under my vine & fig tree" (*Papers,* Retirement Series, 2:220).

23. Washington to the Marquis de Chastellux, 1 Feb. 1784, *Papers,* Confederation Series, 1:86; Washington to La Luzerne, 5 Dec. 1784, *Papers,* Confederation Series, 2:173.

24. Washington to Benjamin Franklin, 26 Sept. 1785, *Papers,* Confederation Series, 3:275.

25. Elizabeth Willing Powel to Washington, 17 Nov. 1792, *Papers,* Presidential Series, 11:395–397. For the testimony of Liston, wife of the British minister, see Hugh Howard, *The Painter's Chair: George Washington and the Making of American Art* (New York: Bloomsbury, 2009), 194.

26. Catharine Sawbridge Macaulay Graham to George Washington, 30 Oct. 1789, *Papers,* Presidential Series, 4:257.

27. Rochambeau to George Washington, 12 May 1787, *Papers,* Confederation Series, 5:182–183; Patricia Brady, ed., *George Washington's Beautiful Nelly: The Letters of Eleanor Parke Custis Lewis to Elizabeth Bordley Gibson, 1794–1851* (Columbia, SC: University of South Carolina Press, 1991), 52. Nelly's wording is remarkably close to that of Washington thirteen years earlier, and one wonders how much her phrases were shaped by conversations with him.

28. Humphreys, 40.

29. Searson, *Mount Vernon, A Poem,* 15 and 24, and "Thoughts on Mount Vernon" in *Poems on Various Subjects and Different Occasions* (Philadelphia: Snowden and M'Corkle, 1797), 91.

30. James Whitehead, ed., "Notes and Documents: The Autobiography of Peter Stephen Du Ponceau," *Pennsylvania Magazine of History and Biography* 63, no. 3 (July 1939): 313; George Washington Greene, *The Life of Nathanael Greene, Major-General in the Army of the Revolution,* 3 vols. (New York: G. P. Putnam and Son [vol. 1] and Hurd and Houghton [vols. 2 and 3], 1867–71), 3:507–510.

31. For the chevalier's remark, see William Baker, "Washington after the Revolution, 1784–1799," *Pennsylvania Magazine of History and Biography* 18 (1894): 394 (12 Apr. 1784).

32. William Strickland to George Washington, 16 Dec. 1797, *Papers,* Retirement Series, 1:519. For George Washington's rural retirement as the new Cincinnatus, see also Andrea Wulf, *Founding Gardeners: The Revolutionary Generation, Nature, and the Shaping of the American Nation* (New York: Alfred A. Knopf, 2011), 13–34.

33. See Wendy Wick, *George Washington, an American Icon: The Eighteenth-Century Graphic Portraits* (Washington, DC: National Portrait Gallery, Smithsonian Institution / Charlottesville: The University Press of Virginia, 1982), 133–135.

34. Roger L'Estrange, *Seneca's Morals by Way of Abstract,* 15th ed. (London: Printed for S. Ballard et. al., 1746). See the list of Washington's books in William Lane, "The Inventory of Washington's Books," in Appleton Griffin, *A Catalogue of the Washington Collection in the Boston Athenaeum* (Boston: Boston Athenaeum, 1897), 488, no. 352; and Eugene Prussing, *The Estate of George Washington, Deceased* (Boston: Little, Brown, and Co., 1927), 427 ("Seneca's morals"). The volume of *Seneca's Morals* includes

George Washington's signature made at about the age of seventeen, and the book was thus likely acquired about 1749.

35. James Thomas Flexner, "George Washington as an Art Collector," *American Art Journal* 4, no. 1 (Spring 1972): 26.

36. Washington to Charles Cotesworth Pinckney, 24 Aug. 1795, *Writings*, 34:285. Martha Washington to Catherine Littlefield Greene Miller, 3 Mar. 1797, *"Worthy Partner,"* 297; see editor's note 4: "The diction of the letter is that of the President."

37. Washington to James McHenry, 16 Feb. 1799, *Papers*, Retirement Series, 3:384, and George Washington to Bushrod Washington, 27 July 1789, *Papers*, Presidential Series, 3:334.

38. Typical is a letter to Mrs. Powel, written in George Washington's hand and referring to his thoughts but signed by Martha Washington (17 Dec. 1797, *Papers*, Retirement Series, 1:520–521; see also *"Worthy Partner,"* 309–310): "neither his health, nor spirits, were ever in greater flow, notwithstanding, he adds, he is descending, & has almost reached, the bottom of the hill; or in other words, the shades below."

39. The book was sent to Washington in Dec. 1778. For his response, see Washington to Francis Hopkinson, 5 Feb. 1789, *Papers*, Presidential Series, 1:279.

40. Washington to Robert Morris, 5 May 1787, *Papers*, Confederation Series, 5:171. George Washington to Henry Knox, 25 Feb. 1787, *Papers*, Confederation Series, 5:52–53.

41. Roger L'Estrange, *Seneca's Morals*, acquired by George Washington by about 1749; Epistle XV, in *Seneca's Morals*, by Sir Roger L'Estrange (New York: A. L. Burt Company, 1900), 340: "Let every man retire into himself . . . We should, therefore, fly the world, withdraw into ourselves, and in some sort avoid even ourselves too."

42. Marcus Aurelius, *Meditations*, VII, 28. Marcus wrote in Greek "Ei auton suneilou," given in Latin translations as "In temet ipsum te contrahe."

43. Washington to Annis Boudinot Stockton, 31 Aug. 1788, *Papers*, Confederation Series, 6:496.

44. Washington to Nicholas Simon van Winter and Lucretia Wilhelmina van Winter, 8 Jan. 1788, *Papers*, Confederation Series, 6:19–20.

45. Washington to Catharine Sawbridge Macaulay Graham, 19 July 1791, *Papers*, Presidential Series, 8:358. For extended consideration of the phrase in Washington's correspondence, see Daniel Dreisbach, "The 'Vine and Fig Tree' in George Washington's Letters: Reflections on a Biblical Motif in the Literature of the American Founding Era," *Journal of Anglican and Episcopal History* 76, no. 3 (2007): 299–326. Dreisbach noted that the phrase, while appearing frequently with Washington, also appears in other early American sources (300–301).

46. Washington to Rochambeau, 10 Aug. 1790, *Papers*, Presidential Series, 6:232.

47. Washington to the Hebrew Congregation in Newport, Rhode Island, 18 Aug. 1790, *Papers*, Presidential Series, 6:286: "May the Children of the Stock of Abraham, who dwell in this land, continue to merit and enjoy the good will of the other Inhabitants; while every one shall sit in safety under his own vine and figtree, and there shall be none to make him afraid."

48. There is a large body of literature on Masons and their architecture. For some useful recent studies, see James Curl, *The Art and Architecture of Freemasonry: An Introductory Study* (London: B. T. Batsford, 1991); Laurence Gardner, *The Shadow of Solomon: The Lost Secret of the Freemasons Revealed* (London: HarperElement, 2005); and William Moore, *Masonic Temples: Freemasonry, Ritual Architecture, and Masculine Archetypes* (Knoxville: University of Tennessee Press, 2006).

49. George Washington to G. W. Snyder, 25 Sept. 1798, *Papers*, Retirement Series, 2:555, note 1: "The fact is, I preside over none [that is, lodges], nor have I been in one more than once or twice, within the last thirty years." For Freemasonry in early America, with references to George Washington, see J. Hugo Tatsch, *Freemasonry in the Thirteen Colonies* (New York: Macoy Publishing and Masonic Supply, 1929); Eugen Lennhoff, *The Freemasons: The History, Nature, Development and Secret of the Royal Art,* rev. ed. (London: Methuen, 1934; Plymouth, UK: Lewis Masonic, 1994), 167–176; and Christopher Hodapp, *Solomon's Builders: Freemasons, Founding Fathers and the Secrets of Washington, D.C.* (Berkeley, CA: Ulysses Press, 2007), esp. 25–31. For Freemasonry and the arts, see Robert Freke Gould, *The History of Freemasonry, Its Antiquities, Symbols, Constitutions, Customs, etc.,* 4 vols. (New York: John C. Yorston and Co., 1884–1889); and James Stevens Curl, *The Art and Architecture of Freemasonry: An Introductory Study* (London: B. T. Batsford, 1991).

50. For George Washington and Freemasonry, see Charles Callahan, *Washington: The Man and the Mason* (Washington, DC: National Capital Press, under the auspices of the Memorial Temple Committee of the George Washington Masonic National Memorial Association, 1913), esp. 265–327; Julius Sachse, *Washington's Masonic Correspondence* (Philadelphia: Press of the New Era, 1915); J. Hugo Tatsch, *The Facts about George Washington as a Freemason* (New York: Macoy and Masonic Supply, 1931); Allen Roberts, *George Washington: Master Mason* (Richmond, VA: Macoy Publishing and Masonic Supply Co., 1976), including a useful summary of Washington's Masonic activities or correspondence (187–190); Steven Bullock, *Revolutionary Brotherhood: Freemasonry and the Transformation of the American Social Order* (Chapel Hill: University of North Carolina Press, 1996); and Robert Hieronimus, with Laura Cortner, *Founding Fathers, Secret Societies: Freemasons, Illuminati, Rosicrucians, and the Decoding of the Great*

Seal (Rochester, VT: Destiny Books, 2006), 41–55. See also Richard Rutyna and Peter C. Stewart, *The History of Freemasonry in Virginia* (Lanham, MD: University Press of America, 1998); and Christine Meadows, "Masonic Associations," *MVLAAR,* 1995, 11–13. For Ramsay's funeral, see entry for 12 Feb. 1785, *Diaries,* 4:89.

51. For the Chiswick House and Masonic symbolism, see Jane Clark, "Lord Burlington is Here," in *Lord Burlington: Architecture, Art, and Life,* ed. Toby Barnard and Jane Clark (London: Hambleton, 1995), 251–310. For Masonic imagery in Wood's work, see Cathryn Spence, Amy Frost, and Timothy Mowl, *Obsession: John Wood and the Creation of Georgian Bath* (Bath, UK: The Building of Bath Museum, 2004), 64–71, 102–104.

52. Important studies of Masonic symbolism in early American art and architecture include Curl, *The Art and Architecture of Freemasonry* (see p. 245 for discussion of the number three). The 3:1 ratio of the footprint of the mansion house at Mount Vernon was mentioned by James Kornwolf, with the assistance of Georgiana Kornwolf, *Architecture and Town Planning in Colonial North America,* 3 vols. (Baltimore: Johns Hopkins University Press, 2002) 2:685.

53. Curl, *The Art and Architecture of Freemasonry,* 237, discusses the mosaic or checkerboard paving. See also the exhibition catalogue, *Masonic Symbols in American Decorative Arts,* preface and introduction by Clement Silvestro (Lexington, MA: Scottish Rite Masonic Museum of our National Heritage, 1976), 51, where such flooring is said to represent the floor of King Solomon's Temple and to be "symbolic of the good and evil in life." Such paving often appears in Masonic aprons and prints. For the Masonic apron in Washington's study at his death, see Prussing, *Estate of George Washington,* 417 ("one piece of Oil cloth cont[ainin]g orders of Masonry"). There is no evidence, as is often supposed, that the Marquis de Lafayette gave Washington a Masonic apron; for Washington and Lafayette as Masons, see the discussion in William Moore (with John Hamilton), "Washington as the Master of His Lodge: History and Symbolism of a Masonic Icon," in *George Washington: American Symbol,* ed. Barbara J. Mitnick (Stony Brook, NY: Hudson Hills Press, 1999), 79–80.

54. For the Masonic conception of Noah, the ark, and the dove, see Curl, *The Art and Architecture of Freemasonry,* 234, 241. See also *Masonic Symbols in American Decorative Arts,* 47 49, glossary under "ark" and "dove." Useful studies of Masonic iconography include Daniel Béresniak, *Symbols of Freemasonry* (New York: Assouline, 2000), and John Hamilton, *Material Culture of the American Freemasons* (Lexington, MA: Museum of our National Heritage / Hanover, NH: Distributed by the University Press of New England, 1994). Somewhat older but still useful studies include Charles Callahan, *George Washington: The Man and the Mason* (Washington, DC: National Capital Press, under the aus-

pices of the Memorial Temple Committee of the George Washington Masonic National Memorial Association, 1913), and Sachse, *Washington's Masonic Correspondence.*

55. There is some evidence that Belvoir had a sundial in the center of the formal garden court; see "Courtyard" in James River Institute for Archaeology, Inc., Williamsburg, VA, "Draft Report. Signage. A.S. Army Garrison Fort Belvoir, Site 44FX4, Belvoir Manor, Fort Belvoir, Virginia." report dated 15 July 1994, with entries for "Mansion," "Courtyard," "Ha-Ha".

56. Along these lines, and although it was a widespread motif in Georgian architecture, it is far from impossible that the prominent oval window over the central pediment on the west front might be interpreted as the eye of Divine Providence looking over the estate. The eye in the triangle or pyramid as a providential eye was well established by Washington's time and was adopted by the Freemasons, although it "was used as a Christian emblem of the ever-watchful Eye of God long before Freemasonry evolved." Not only does "oculus" mean eye in Latin; Washington called the oval oculus window in the Greenhouse an "Ox eye," indicating his association of the shape there with an eye (Washington to Anthony Whitting, 21 Apr. 1793, *Papers,* Presidential Series, 12:465). For the watchful "Eye of God" as a Christian emblem, see Gardner, *The Shadow of Solomon,* 306.

57. Batty Langley, *New Principles of Gardening* (London: Printed for A. Bettesworth et al., 1728 [published in Dec. of 1727 and dedicated to the king, but date on title page is 1728]), 207, quoting Rapin.

58. Washington to George William Fairfax, 25 June 1786, *Papers,* Confederation Series, 4:127.

59. Thomas Paine to Washington, 28 Apr. 1784, *Papers,* Confederation Series, 1:320.

60. Stephen Bending, "Horace Walpole and Eighteenth-Century Garden History," *Journal of the Warburg and Courtauld Institutes* 57 (1994): 222.

61. See John Dixon Hunt, *The Italian Renaissance Garden in the English Imagination: 1600–1750* (London: Dent, 1986), 176–177, for a discussion of classical imagery, classical architecture, and Whiggish sentiment in England.

62. In his study of Mount Vernon, Scott Owen stressed that the picturesque and the natural style of landscape gardening were not merely aesthetic issues but were linked to Whig ideology and freedom, while a more formal gardening was identified with the Tories and monarchy; see Owen, "George Washington's Mount Vernon as British Palladian Architecture," master's thesis, University of Virginia, School of Architecture, May 1991.

63. Uvedale Price to Washington, 31 Mar. 1798, *Papers,* Retirement Series, 2:165–166.

64. Washington to Edward Newenham, 20 Apr. 1787, *Papers,* Confederation Series, 5:152.

65. Jonathan Boucher to Washington, 25 May 1784, *Papers,* Confederation Series, 1:405.

66. Washington to Lund Washington, 10–17 Dec. 1776, *Papers,* Revolutionary Series, 7:289, 291–292.

67. Washington to George William Fairfax, 10 July 1783, *Writings,* 27:57.

68. Washington to Jonathan Trumbull Jr., 5 Jan. 1784, *Papers,* Confederation Series, 1:12.

69. Washington left no known instructions for the design of his own tomb, but he did specify in the will the site, material to be used (brick), and that it be a substantial size (large enough to hold himself and other family members). The Old Tomb was extremely simple and was in disrepair and decay from the moist ground, but there is no evidence that Washington envisioned or wanted a mausoleum as fine as the tomb built in the 1830s. For the will of George Washington, see Prussing, *Estate of George Washington,* 42–70; and "George Washington's Last Will and Testament," 9 July 1799, *Papers,* Retirement Series, 4:477–527. For his death and information about the Old Tomb, see Joseph Manca, "Moral and Moralizing Aspects of George Washington's Death and Funeral," *Constructions of Death, Mourning, and Memory Conference, Oct. 27–29, 2006: Proceedings,* ed. Lillian Zirpolo, WAPACC Text and Studies (Woodcliff Lake, NJ: The WAPACC Organization, 2006), 133–136; and Peter Henriques, *The Death of George Washington: He Died as He Lived,* foreword by Philander Chase (Mount Vernon, VA: MVLA, 2000). C. M. Harris, "Washington's Gamble, L'Enfant's Dream: Politics, Design, and the Founding of the National Capital," *William and Mary Quarterly,* 3rd ser., 56, no. 3 (July 1999): 527–564, argued that, apart from his will, Washington had privately assented to be buried under the dome of the new Capitol. See also *The Tomb of George Washington: Historic Structure Report,* Feb. 1993, Mesick-Cohen-Waite Architects, Albany, New York, prepared for the Mount Vernon Ladies' Association of the Union, Mount Vernon, Virginia, 3–5.

Epilogue

Epigraph. "A Trip to Mount Vernon, May, 1831," *MVLAAR,* 1964, 26; Ann Pamela Cunningham, "Farewell Address to the Council of the Mount Vernon Ladies' Association of June, 1874," reprinted in every issue of the *MVLAAR.* For the transformation of Mount Vernon into a shrine in the nineteenth century, see also Jean Lee, "Historical Memory, Sectional Strife, and the American Mecca," *Virginia Magazine of History and Biography* 109, no. 3 (June 2001): 255–300.